Perspectives on the Song of Songs
Perspektiven der Hoheliedauslegung

Beihefte zur Zeitschrift für die alttestamentliche Wissenschaft

Herausgegeben von
John Barton · Reinhard G. Kratz
Choon-Leong Seow · Markus Witte

Band 346

Walter de Gruyter · Berlin · New York

Perspectives on the Song of Songs
Perspektiven der Hoheliedauslegung

Herausgegeben von
Anselm C. Hagedorn

W DE G

Walter de Gruyter · Berlin · New York

∞ Printed on acid-free paper which falls within
the guidelines of the ANSI to ensure permanence and durability.

ISBN-13: 978-3-11-017632-2
ISBN-10: 3-11-017632-7

Bibliographic information published by Die Deutsche Bibliothek

Die Deutsche Bibliothek lists this publication in the Deutsche Nationalbibliografie; detailed bibliographic data is available in the Internet at <http://dnb.ddb.de>.

Printed in Germany

Cover Design: Christopher Schneider, Berlin

Hans-Peter Müller
in memoriam

Acknowledgements

Upon completion of a project it is a pleasure to express thanks to the many people involved.

First of all I would like to thank the contributors for their willingness to be part of the project – here, I am especially grateful to those colleagues who do not work in disciplines normally related to the Hebrew Bible to undertake the risk of being part of an essay collection dealing with the Bible.

Secondly, my sincere thanks to Prof. Dr. D. Otto Kaiser for enthusiastically embracing the project from the start, his many helpful ideas, his support and his initial acceptance of the volume into the series BZAW. Also many thanks to the new editorial board of BZAW, Prof. Dr. John Barton, Prof. Dr. Reinhard G. Kratz, Prof. Dr. Choon-Leong Seow and Prof. Dr. Markus Witte for their continued willingness to have the book included in their series as well as for several useful suggestions prior to publication.

The editorial staff at W. de Gruyter, Monika Müller and Dr. Albrecht Döhnert has been most helpful during the production of the volume. The co-operation has been wonderful – many thanks for that.

Finally, I thank Mr. Björn Corzilius (Berlin) and Ms. Teresa Nieser (Lyon) for copious proofreading and careful assistance during the preparation of the volume for publication. Needless to say, all remaining errors are the one of the editor.

Authors, editor, and publisher have undertaken every attempt to assert the rights of all other authors and publishers. We regret, however, that despite this effort we have not succeeded in clarifying the copyright situation for the following two figures: Figure 2 (p. 113): Fishing and fowling from the Dyn. XVIII tomb of Menena (TT 69), in: Alan H. GARDINER and N. M. DAVIES, *La peinture égyptienne ancienne*, vol. I, Paris: A. Guillot 1953 and Figure 5 (p. 116): Music and eroticism from the Dyn. XVIII tomb of Djeserkareseneb (TT 38), in: Alan H. GARDINER and N. M. DAVIES, *La peinture égyptienne ancienne*, vol. II, Paris: A. Guillot 1953.

At the same time, my sincere thanks to the Boston Museum of Fine Arts, the Oriental Institute of the University of Chicago, and the Egypt Exploration Society for granting permission to use their illustrations.

It was with great sadness that we learned of the untimely death of Professor Hans-Peter Müller, while this volume has been in preparation. The exegetical community in general and scholarship on the Song of Songs in particular has lost one of its most prolific members. As will be obvious from many essays in this volume we owe him a great deal in our interpretation of the Song of Songs. Despite this sombre moment, it is nevertheless a pleasure that Prof. Müller was able to contribute an article to this collection and that one of his last publications could be included here. I believe it is only fitting to dedicate this volume to his memory.

Anselm C. Hagedorn
Berlin, August 2005

Table of Contents

Acknowledgements vii
Contributors xi
List of Abbreviations xiii

ANSELM C. HAGEDORN
Introduction xvii

I. Biblical Perspectives

JOHN BARTON
On the Canonicity of Canticles 1
KATHARINE J. DELL
What is King Solomon doing in the Song of Songs? 8
F.W. DOBBS-ALLSOPP
Late Linguistic Features in the Song of Songs 27
J. CHERYL EXUM
The Poetic Genius of the Song of Songs 78
PETER FLINT
The Book of Canticles (Song of Songs) in the Dead Sea Scrolls 97

II. Comparative Perspectives

ANTONIO LOPRIENO
Searching for a common background: Egyptian love poetry and the Biblical Song of Songs 105
GERALD MOERS and HUBERTUS MÜNCH
Alles Liebe? Die kulturelle Semantik des Begriffs "Liebe" und die Konstruktion des liebenden Körpers im pharaonischen Ägypten 136
PASCAL VERNUS
Le *Cantique des Cantiques* et l'Egypte pharaonique. Etat de la question 150

KARL HECKER
'Kundbar werde mir Deine Sehnsucht'. Überlegungen zur akkadischen Liebeslyrik 163
JOAN B. BURTON
Themes of Female Desire and Self-Assertion in the Song of Songs and Hellenistic Poetry 180
ANSELM C. HAGEDORN
Jealousy and Desire at Night. *Fragmentum Grenfellianum* and Song of Songs 206
RICHARD HUNTER
'Sweet Talk' *Song of Songs* and the Traditions of Greek Poetry........ 228
HANS-PETER MÜLLER†
Zum Werden des Lyrischen. Am Beispiel des Hohenliedes und frühgriechischer Lyrik 245

III. Later Perspectives

ALISON SALVESEN
Pigs in the camps and the breasts of my lambs: Song of Songs in the Syriac Tradition 260
ELIZABETH A. CLARK
Origen, the Jews, and the Song of Songs. Allegory and Polemic in Christian Antiquity 274
ANETTE VOLFING
Middle High German Appropriations of the Song of Songs: Allegorical Interpretation and Narrative Extrapolation 294
ULRICH GAIER
Lieder der Liebe. Herders Hohelied-Interpretation 317
CONSTANZE M. GÜTHENKE
'Do not awaken love until it is ready' – George Seferis' *Asma Asmaton* and the translation of intimacy 338

Index 357

Contributors

JOHN BARTON, Oriel and Laing Professor of the Interpretation of Holy Scripture, University of Oxford (U.K.)

JOAN B. BURTON, Professor and Chair, Department of Classical Studies, Trinity University, San Antonio, Texas (U.S.A.)

ELIZABETH A. CLARK, John Carlisle Kilgo Professor of Religion, Duke University, Durham, North Carolina (U.S.A.)

KATHARINE J. DELL, Senior Lecturer in Old Testament Studies and Fellow in Theology, St. Catharine's College, University of Cambridge (U.K.)

F.W. DOBBS-ALLSOPP, Associate Professor of Old Testament, Princeton Theological Seminary, Princeton, New Jersey (U.S.A.)

J. CHERYL EXUM, Professor of Biblical Studies, University of Sheffield (U.K.)

PETER W. FLINT, Professor of Religious Studies and Canada Research Chair in Biblical Studies, Trinity Western University, Langley, British Columbia (Canada)

ULRICH GAIER, Emeritus Professor für Literaturwissenschaft, Universität Konstanz, Konstanz (Germany)

CONSTANZE GÜTHENKE, Assistant Professor of Classics and Hellenic Studies, Princeton University, Princeton, New Jersey (U.S.A.)

ANSELM C. HAGEDORN, Wissenschaftlicher Assistent Altes Testament, Humboldt-Universität zu Berlin (Germany)

KARL HECKER, Ordinarius für Altorientalistik Emeritus, Westfälische Wilhelms-Universität Münster (Germany)

RICHARD HUNTER, Regius Professor of Greek, University of Cambridge (U.K.)

ANTONIO LOPRIENO, Ordinarius für Ägyptologie, Universität Basel (Switzerland).

GERALD MOERS, Juniorprofessor der Ägyptologie, Georg-August-Universität Göttingen (Germany).

HANS-PETER MÜLLER†, Ordinarius für Altes Testament Emeritus, Westfälische Wilhelms-Universität Münster (Germany).

HANS HUBERTUS MÜNCH, DPhil candidate in Egyptology, The Oriental Institute, University of Oxford (U.K.).

ALISON E. SALVESEN, University Research Lecturer in Oriental Studies, University of Oxford and Fellow in Jewish Bible, Oxford Centre for Hebrew and Jewish Studies, Oxford (U.K.).

PASCAL VERNUS, Director of Studies, École pratique des hautes études IV, Sorbonne, Paris (France).

ANNETTE VOLFING, University Lecturer in Medieval German and Fellow of Oriel College, University of Oxford (U.K.).

List of Abbreviations

AB	Anchor Bible
ABD	Anchor Bible Dictionary
ABG	Archiv für Begriffsgeschichte
ABRL	Anchor Bible Reference Library
ÄAT	Ägypten und Altes Testament
ÄgAbh	Ägyptische Abhandlungen
ADAIK	Abhandlungen des Deutschen Archäologischen Instituts Kairo
AJPh	American Journal of Philology
AJSL	American Journal of Semitic Languages
AS	Acta Sumeriologica
ASJ	Acta Sumeriologica Japonica
ATD	Das Alte Testament Deutsch
AOAT	Alter Orient und Altes Testament
AOS	American Oriental Studies
ASORMS	American Schools of Oriental Research. Monograph Series
AZP	Allgemeine Zeitschrift für Philosophie
BAR	Biblical Archaeology Review
BASOR	Bulletin of the American Schools of Oriental Research
BBB	Bonner Biblische Beiträge
BdE	Bibliothèque d'Études
BEThL	Bibliotheca Ephemeridum Theologicarum Lovaniensium
BHTh	Beiträge zur Historischen Theologie
Bib	Biblica
BibInt	Biblical Interpretation
BibIntS	Biblical Interpretation Series
BiLiSe	Bible and Literature Series
BibOr	Biblica et Orientalia
BJRL	Bulletin of the John Rylands Library Manchester
BK	Biblischer Kommentar
BMMA	Bulletin of the Metropolitan Museum of Art
BSt (F)	Biblische Studien (Freiburg i. Br.)
BZ	Biblische Zeitschrift
BZAW	Beihefte zur Zeitschrift für die alttestamentliche Wissenschaft
CBQ	Catholic Biblical Quarterly
CdÉ	Chronique d'Égypte
ChH	Church History
ClAnt	Classical Antiquity
CR	Classical Review
CRRAI	Compte rendu de la Rencontre Assyriologique Internationale
CP	Classical Philology
CQ	Classical Quarterly
CSCO	Corpus Scriptorum Christianorum Orientalium
DE	Discussions in Egyptology

DJD	Discoveries in the Judean Desert
DSD	Dead Sea Discoveries
EI	Eretz Israel
EvTh	Evangelische Theologie
FOTL	The Forms of Old Testament Literature
GaR	Greece and Rome
GM	Giornale di metafisica
GOF	Göttinger Orientforschung
GRBS	Greek Roman and Byzantine Studies
HAR	Hebrew Annual Review
HAT	Handbuch zum Alten Testament
HÄB	Hildesheimer ägyptologische Beiträge
HSCP	Harvard Studies in Classical Philology
HSM	Harvard Semitic Museum
HSS	Harvard Semitic Studies
HThR	Harvard Theological Review
HUCA	Hebrew Union College Annual
IB	Introduction à la Bible
IEJ	Israel Exploration Journal
IOS	Israel Oriental Studies
JAAR	Journal of the American Academy of Religion
JANES	Journal of the Ancient Near Eastern Society
JAOS	Journal of the American Oriental Society
JARCE	Journal of the American Research Center in Egypt
JBL	Journal of Biblical Literature
JCS	Journal Cuneiform Studies
JEA	Journal of Egyptian Archaeology
JIES	Journal of Indo-European Studies
JJS	Journal of Jewish Studies
JNES	Journal of Near Eastern Studies
JQR	Jewish Quarterly Review
JSOT	Journal for the Study of the Old Testament
JSOTS	Journal for the Study of the Old Testament. Supplements
JSS	Journal of Semitic Studies
JThS	Journal of Theological Studies
KAT	Kommentar zum Alten Testament
KHAT	Kurzer Handkommentar zum Alten Testament
KHC	Kurzer Handcommentar zum Alten Testament
KP	Der Kleine Pauly
LAPO	Littératures anciennes du Proche-Orient
MAD	Material for the Assyrian Dictionary
MDAIK	Mitteilungen des Deutschen Archäologischen Instituts Kairo
MSP	Monumenta sacra et profana
NCeB	New Century Bible
NICOT	New International Commentary on the Old Testament
OBO	Orbis Biblicus et Orientalis
OLA	Orientalia Lovaniensia analecta
OLP	Oriental Library Publications
OLZ	Orientalische Literaturzeitung
OTL	Old Testament Library
OTWSA	Oud Testamentiese Werkgemeenschap in Suid-Afrika
Or	Orientalia

OrChr	Oriens Christianus
PCPS	Proceedings of the Cambridge Philological Society
PdÄ	Probleme der Ägyptologie
QUCC	Quaderni Urbinati di Cultura Classica
RA	Revue d'Assyriologie et d'Archéologie Orientale
RB	Revue Biblique
RBen	Revue bénédictine de critique, d'histoire et de littérature religieuses
RlA	Reallexikon der Assyriologie
RM	Rheinisches Museum für Philologie
RQ	Römische Quartalsschrift
SAK	Studien zur altägyptischen Kultur
SBLDS	Society of Biblical Literature. Dissertation Series
SBLMS	Society of Biblical Literature. Monograph Series
SBS	Stuttgarter Biblische Studien
SCO	Studi Classici er Orientali
ScrHier	Scripta Hierosolymitana
SHCANE	Studies in the History and Culture of the Ancient Near East
SIFC	Studi Italiani di Filologia Classica
SJOT	Scandinavian Journal of the Old Testament
SJT	Scottish Journal of Theology (SJTh)
STDJ	Studies in the Texts of the Desert of Judah
SQAW	Schriften und Quellen der Alten Welt
StSLL	Studies in Semitic Languages and Linguistics
SubBib	Subsidia Biblica
TRE	Theologische Realenzyklopädie
UCOP	University of Cambridge Oriental Publications
UF	Ugarit-Forschungen
VT	Vetus Testamentum
VT.S	Vetus Testamentum Supplements
WdO	Welt des Orients
ZA	Zeitschrift für Assyriologie
ZÄS	Zeitschrift für ägyptische Sprache und Altertumskunde
ZAH	Zeitschrift für Althebraistik
ZAW	Zeitschrift für die alttestamentliche Wissenschaft
ZBK	Züricher Bibelkommentar
ZDMG	Zeitschrift der Deutschen Morgenländischen Gesellschaft
ZDPV	Zeitschrift des Deutschen Palästinavereins
ZPE	Zeitschrift für Papyrologie und Epigraphik
ZThK	Zeitschrift für Theologie und Kirche

Introduction

Anselm C. Hagedorn

Hardly any Biblical book has stimulated such a plethora of interpretive approaches than the Song of Songs (Cant)[1] and in a way the essays assembled in this collection pay tribute to this diversity. The essays in this volume broadly fall into three categories: Biblical, comparative, and later (i.e. reception historical) perspectives. It was the main aim of the collection to offer a fresh look at this fascinating text by choosing a broad variety of approaches from different methodological angles. The essays are held together by the overarching theme of deciphering the rich texture of the Song of Songs and to explore its significance for ancient and modern readers.

JOHN BARTON takes a fresh look at the received opinion that there disputes about the canonicity of Cant in both, Judaism and Christianity around the turn of the era. By looking at the sources in question he is able to argue that the canonicity of Cant was ever doubtful, or that its canonicity depended on an allegorical reading of the text. Rather, Cant was already part of Scripture by the turn of the era, since all the debates could not have been arisen if the text was not already viewed as being scriptural. He argues that more books were candidates for admission into the canon than were finally accepted but this does not mean that the status of the books we now have was ever disputed.

In a way, PETER W. FLINT's contribution is also concerned with the status of the text – this time at Qumran. He provides a detailed overview of the manuscript evidence from the Dead Sea Scrolls and discusses several important questions such as the omission of several verses in 4QCant[a], arguing that this document may present a shorter edition of Cant as a whole.

KATHARINE J. DELL in her contribution investigates the possibility of a connection of the Song of Songs with the genre of wisdom literature. Starting point for her considerations is the attribution of Cant to Solomon as well as the statements from historical books such as 1Reg 4:32 and 1Reg 10:23. In a

1 A short overview of the studies published in the past ten years reveals that approaches range from an allegorical reading of the text (Kingsmill 2002), via 'classic' historical-critical (and comparative) studies to theological arguments for the sacramental character of marriage (Horine 2001) and questions of the interplay between erotic and spirituality (Carr 2003; Walsh 2000) and pornography (Boer 1999: 53-70).

careful analysis of the possible links between Proverbs and Cant, she is able to show that there have been close connections between those to documents of the Bible; nevertheless, Dell hesitates to classify Cant as 'wisdom literature' in any formal, form-critical sense.

The language of the Song of Songs is generally regarded as 'late',[2] but a detailed study of the features of the late biblical Hebrew of Cant has been missing so far. This gap is filled by the contribution by F.W. DOBBS-ALLSOPP, who undertakes the first detailed study of so called late linguistic features, by looking at orthography, grammar, syntax, and lexicon of Cant as well as discussing the issues of possible Aramaisms in the text, since it is one of the defining characteristics of late biblical Hebrew that we find a pronounced presence of Aramaic influence in various aspects of its grammar and syntax. Thus he is able to show that the language of Cant is unmistakably late biblical Hebrew.

Taking Cant 8:6-7, verses that would not appear be out of place in the book of Proverbs, as a starting point, J. CHERYL EXUM sets out investigate how Cant celebrates love within the poetic discourse of the document. She does not aim to pin down the 'message' of the poem to a single verse, but rather acknowledges that he medium is the message. "The message is the poem itself, the work of art, a literary creation by which the poet strives to make present, through language, what cannot be captured on the page, the lovers whose multiple identities enable them to stand for all lovers, and ultimately for love itself." Therefore, Exum can trace a twofold poetic genius of Cant, in which the poet shows us on the one hand how love can be strong as death and secondly how the poet explores the nature of love, looking at what it is like to be in love from both a woman's and a man's point of view.

Due to the relative uniqueness of Cant within the context of the Hebrew Bible, comparative material has been used frequently to interpret and to illuminate this biblical text.[3] Here, "Attention has been turned principally in two direction: to Mesopotamia on one hand and to Egypt on the other."[4] Furthermore, in recent years Greek (and even Latin) literature has again been used to illustrate several aspects of the Song of Songs.[5] Therefore, the second part of the collection is devoted to such comparison with extra-biblical material. Starting point is Egypt. In a richly illustrated contribution ANTONIO LOPRIENO searches for the possibility of a common background of Egyptian love poetry and the Song of Songs. He argues against any direct literary and textual influence of the Egyptian love songs on the Cant due to the disappearance of a written tradition of love poems after the end of the Bronze

2 Fox 1985: 186-190 and most recently Müller 2004: 1838.

3 See especially Fox 1985, Keel 1984, Keel 1992 and Nissinen 1998: 585-634.

4 Nissinen 1998: 585.

5 Cf. amongst others Garbini 1992, Hagedorn 2003: 337-352, Müller 1998: 569-584 and Eidelkind 2004: 219-230 for parallels from Tibullus and Propertius.

Age. Rather, the striking parallels and the continuity of form and contents can be explained by the origin if the genre within the common festive background in Israel and Egypt. "[T]he continuity in underlying performances, rooted in a dialectic between the sphere of periodic religious festivals and the context of episodic social events, proves to be much more stable than their impact on literary discourse." The question of discourse and more specifically the construction of loving bodies in Pharaonic Egypt is the topic of the investigation by HANS-HUBERTUS MÜNCH and GERALD MOERS. Using insights from the sociological study of pre-modern societies combined with he theoretical framework provided by the German sociologist N. Luhmann both authors argue that love is a social act determined by the structure of the society as well as by the individual's status within that particular society. The Egyptological contributions are completed with an essay by PASCAL VERNUS who takes the allusions to the Egyptian sphere within Cant as a starting point to investigate possible links to and influences of Egyptian culture within this biblical document.

From Egypt we move to Mesopotamia. KARL HECKER offers a convenient survey and classification of the scattered love poetry within the cuneiform corpus. He looks at the different settings (i.e. sacred marriage, divine union, human love) of the poetry and notes the often direct way of speaking (of gods and human beings) when expressing (sexual) desires.

The above mentioned renewed interest in Greek parallels to the Song of Songs has been the reason for including four essays that address this question. Two are written by Classicists and two by biblical scholars. JOAN B. BURTON, on the basis of her previous extensive study of Theocritus, investigates the modes of expression female desire and self-assertion in Hellenistic poetry and aims at a comparison of those expressions with the material found in Cant. She argues that Theocritus's urban mimes offer intriguing parallels to Cant in their way how women are portrayed as self-assertive, desiring subjects. She notes that the early Hellenistic age saw a general poetic engagement with changing gender roles, which seems to be tied to a change in social roles, due to increase mobility and the beginnings of erotic reciprocity and mutual passion combined with male helplessness and erotic passivity. The thematic parallels in Cant seem to point in a similar direction. ANSELM C. HAGEDORN takes up the question of expressing (female) feelings such as desire and jealousy by comparing Cant 3:1-5 and 5:2-8 with a longer erotic papyrus called *Fragmentum Grenfellianum*. Without postulating any literary influences he demonstrates that the female voice in Cant and the female voice in the papyrus seem to voice their feelings in a striking similar way. It becomes clear that poetry is utilized to create an anti-structure to the prevalent moral and societal system. RICHARD HUNTER, who remains sceptical as far as direct parallels are concerned, uses Homer, Iliad 22.122-130 as a starting point to emphasize that early Greek poetry cannot produce clear analogues for the apparent mutual love celebrated by man and woman in Cant. However, by looking at several well (such as Theocritus) and lesser known texts (such as the 'Cologne Epode') he is able to demonstrate that common to both traditions are not merely pastoral elements and imagery, but also a mimetic structure in which characters speak directly with each other. In the last essay deling with the Hebrew and Greek interface, HANS-PETER MÜLLER investigates why the human mind produces phenomena such as poetry. By applying insights from cognitive psychology and developmental biology to the Song of Songs and early Greek lyric he is able to show that certain human developments seem to strife for an integration of the human being into the surrounding nature as well as creating a certain counter-world which seems to resist the 'normal' physical reality.

Finally, the third part of the collection offers five 'later perspectives' ranging from antiquity to the 20th century.[6] ALISON SALVESEN explores the role of Cant in the Syriac tradition against the background of the Hebrew Bible in Syriac in general. She notes the different translation techniques and discusses reasons for deviation from the Hebrew *Vorlage*. In addition she explores the use of Cant in early Syrian commentaries on the Bible as well as the use of Cant in other Syriac literature, thus offering first detailed insights into a much under-studied subject. ELIZABETH A. CLARK's contribution looks at ways how Cant could be used by Origen in his debate with, polemic against, and utilization of Jewish thought in antiquity. Origen's interpretation of the Song of Songs emphasizes the Jewish-Gentile union in Christianity and the value of the Old Testament reveals both his faithfulness to Paul's vision as exemplified in Romans and his eagerness to claim the Jews' sacred books as a bulwark against Gnosticizing heresy. ANNETTE VOLFING's essay takes us into the Middle Ages. In a much welcomed bracketing out of Bernhard of Clairvaux's famous 86 sermons in favour of – at least to the exegete – lesser known sources such as Brun von Schönbeck's, *Das Hohe Lied* and the anonymous *Tochter Syon* material, she shows how medieval authors responded to the particular hermeneutical and narratological problems posed by the Song of Songs. The reason for those emerging problems were the fact that the standard method of interpretation of biblical texts (*vierfacher Schriftsinn*) could only be applied with much difficulty to Cant. This in turn led to the development of some new exegetical methods as well as resulting into independent myth-making, a process running counter to the accepted opposition between the Bible and human *fabulae*. ULRICH GAIER, devotes his attention to the interpretation of Cant as done by J.G. Herder. Rather than simply focussing on Herder's translation of the text he roots this enterprise in the larger intellectual-historical framework of Herder's own time as well as in the context of Herder's exegesis, poetry and theology.

6 A reception history of the Song of Songs is almost impossible to write, but see Astell 1990; Nieuviarts/Debergé 2002; Lerch 1957:257-277; Ohly 1957.

CONSTANZE GÜTHENKE's essay can probably be best described as reception within the reception of the Song of Songs. She explores the role and use of the language and topics of Cant in the transcription *'Asma Asmaton'* done by the Greek Nobel laureate G. Seferis. Seferis bases his transcription on the language and style of the Septuagint and his 'wrestling match' with the Greek language as well as with Cant in general makes the imagery and vocabulary of the text to a red thread that weaves through Seferis' work. The *Asma* is compatible with different aspects and interests of his work, and it answers the underlying parallel preoccupations of translation and different modes and models of erotic love that run alongside each other in his poetic work.

It is very much hoped that the essays in this collection will help to foster a better understanding of this fascinating text as well as open up new avenues of research.

Bibliography

ASTELL, A.W. (1990): The Song of Songs in the Middle ages, Ithaca/London.

BOER, R. (1999): Night sprinkle(s): Pornography and the Song of Songs, in: id. Knockin' on Heaven's Door. The Bible and Popular Culture, Biblical Limits, London, 53-70.

CARR, D.M. (2003): The Erotic Word. Sexuality, Spirituality, and the Bible, Oxford/New York.

EIDELKIND, Y. (2004): Cant 3:2-3, 5:6-7 and Parallels from Propertius and Tibullus, Babel und Bibel 1, 319-330.

FOX, M.V. (1985): The Song of Songs and the Ancient Egyptian Love Songs, Madison.

GARBINI, G. (1992): Cantico dei cantici, Biblica Testi e Studi 2, Brescia.

HAGEDORN, A.C. (2003): Of Foxes and Vineyards: Greek Perspectives on the Song of Songs, VT 53, 337-352.

HORINE, S.C. (2001): Interpretive Images in the Song of Songs. From Wedding Chariots to Bridal Chambers, Studies in the Humanities 55, New York/Frankfurt a.M.

KEEL, O. (1984): Dein Blicke sind Tauben. Zur Metaphorik des Hohen Liedes, SBS 114/115, Stuttgart.

– (1992): Das Hohelied, ZBK 18, 2nd ed. Zurich.

KINGSMILL, E. (2002): The Song of Songs and the eros of God: a study in biblical intertextuality, DPhil thesis, Oxford.

LERCH, D. (1957): Zur Geschichte der Auslegung des Hohenliedes, ZThK 54, 257-277.

MÜLLER, H.P. (1998): Eine Parallele zur Weingartenmetapher des Hohenliedes aus der frühgriechischen Lyrik, in: M. Dietrich/I. Kottsieper (Hgg.), "Und Moses schrieb dieses Lied auf." Studien zum Alten Testament und zum Alten Orient. Festschrift für Oswald Loretz zur Vollendung seines 70. Lebensjahres, AOAT 250, Münster, 569-584.

– (2004): Art. Hohes Lied, RGG^4, Tübingen, 1838-1840.

NIEUVIARTS, J./DEBERGÉ, P. eds. (2002): Les Nouvelles voies de l'exégèse: En lisant le Cantique des cantiques, XIXe congrès de l'Association catholique pour l'étude de la Bible (Toulouse, Septembre 2001), Lectio Divina 190, Paris.

NISSINEN, M. (1998): Love Lyrics of Nabû and Tašmetu. An Assyrian Song of Songs?, in: M. Dietrich/I. Kottsieper (Hgg.), "Und Moses schrieb dieses Lied auf." Studien zum Alten Testament und zum Alten Orient. Festschrift für Oswald Loretz zur Vollendung seines 70. Lebensjahres, AOAT 250, Münster, 585-634.

OHLY, F. (1957): Hohelied-Studien. Grundzüge einer Geschichte der Hoheliedauslegung des Abendlandes bis 1200, Schriften der wissenschaftlichen Gesellschaft an der Johann Wolfgang Goethe-Universität Frankfurt am Main. Geisteswissenschaftliche Reihe 1, Wiesbaden.
WALSH, C.E. (2000): Exquisite Desire. Religion, the Erotic, and Song of Songs, Minneapolis.

The Canonicity of the Song of Songs

John Barton

It is a received opinion that there were disputes about the canonicity of the Song of Songs in both Judaism and Christianity around the turn of the era. It is widely assumed that these disputes were caused by the erotic character of the Song, which made it hard for some to accept that it could stand as part of Holy Scripture. Canonicity was eventually secured for the book, so it is held, only by interpreting it allegorically as a celebration of the love of God for Israel (in Jewish circles) or for the Church (in Christian ones). The purpose of this paper is to argue that there is no evidence to support any of these beliefs. Here is a recent statement of the general consensus:

> Because of its frankness and unabashed celebration of sexual love, some of the early Rabbis and early church fathers were disturbed by this delightful little book, interpreting it in a variety of ways that played down its sexuality. Some early Jewish and Christian sages found the contents plainly unacceptable and attempted to block its acceptance into the canon of the Hebrew Bible. Certain Rabbis, however, recognized the Song of Songs as Scripture but sought to interpret its contents in terms of the relationship between God (the *lover* or *bridegroom*) and Israel (the *beloved* or *bride*). Many church fathers who also accepted this book as Scripture interpreted it as depicting the relationship between Christ and his church.[1]

It is hard to discuss supposed Christian opposition to the acceptance of the Song, since I am not aware of any evidence for it whatever. Some of the Fathers caution against the Song's being read by those new to the faith – thus Origen:

> Just as in childhood one is not affected by the passion of love, so also to those who are at the stage of infancy and childhood in their interior life it is not given to grasp the meaning of these sayings. They are those who are nourished in Christ by milk, not strong food, and who desire the milk that is reasonable and without guile. For in the words of the Song of Songs there is that food of which the Apostle says 'but solid food is for the mature, for those who have their faculties trained by practice to distinguish good from evil'.[2]

---

1 Abegg/Flint/Ulrich 1999: 611.

2 'Sicut puerilis aetas non movetur ad amorem passibilem, ita nec ad capienda quidem verba haec parvula et infantilis interioris hominis aetas admittitur, illorum scilicet qui lacte in Christo aluntur non cibo forti, et qui nunc primum rationabile et sine dolo lac concupiscent. in verbis enim Cantici Canticorum ille cibus est de quo dicit Apostolus:

Origen records that the same practice applied among Jews:

> For they say that with the Hebrews also care is taken to allow no one even to take this book in his hands who has not reached a full and mature age. And there is another practice too that we have received from them: that all the Scriptures should be delivered to boys by teachers and wise men, while at the same time the four passages they call *deuteroseis*, that is to say, the beginning of Genesis, in which the creation of the world is described; the first chapter of Ezekiel, which tells about the cherubim; the end of it, which contains the building of the Temple; and this book of the Song of Songs, should be reserved for study till the last.[3]

Similarly Jerome, in proposing a course of biblical study for beginners, suggests that they should begin by reading the wisdom books, then advance to the Gospels, followed by the apostolic writings, the prophets, and the Pentateuch, and only at the very last read the Song of Songs.[4]

But this makes sense only if the canonicity of the book is assumed; for Origen and Jerome, it is obvious that it has a high status, making it fit only for those advanced in the faith. None of the Fathers argues that the book is of doubtful status.

Of course it is true that the Fathers read the Song allegorically. But nowhere is there the smallest hint that this was a device to secure its acceptance as Scripture. On the contrary, allegorical reading in ancient times was practised precisely on books that had a high status. The assumption that it was highly serious texts that qualified for allegorical reading persisted down to the Enlightenment and even beyond. To interpret literally a text that had a high scriptural status would have struck many in the early and medieval Church as perverse. As Origen observes in *contra Celsum*, 'not even Celsus assets that only vulgar people have been converted by the gospel to follow the religion of Jesus; for he admits that among them are *some moderate, reasonable, and*

Perfectorum autem est solidus cibus et tales requirit auditores qui pro passibilitate sumendi exercitatos habeant sensus ad discretionem boni et mali', Origen, comm. in cantica canticorum prol. 1:4, referring to Heb. 5:14.

3 'Aiunt enim observari etiam apud Hebraeos quod, nisi quis ad aetatem perfectam maturamque pervenerit, libellum hunc nec in manibus quidem tenere permittatur. sed et illud ab iis accepimus custodiri, quoniamquidem moris est apud eos omnes scripturas a doctoribus et sapientibus tradi pueris, simul et eas quas deuterwseij appellant, ad ultimum quattuor ista reservari, id est principium Genesis, in quo mundi creatura describitur, et Ezechiel prophetae principia, in quibus de Cherubin refertur, et finem, in quo templi aedificatio continetur, et hunc Cantici Canticorum librum', ibid., 1:7. Cf. Jerome, comm. in Ezech., prologue: 'nam nisi quis apud eos aetatem sacerdotalis ministerii, id est tricesimum annum impleverit, nec principia Geneseos nec Canticum Canticorum nec huius voluminis exordium et finem legere permittitur, ut ad perfectam scientiam et mysticos intellectus plenum humanae naturae tempus accedat'. Note that the reason for reserving the reading of the Song to those of mature years is not its eroticism, but its esoteric character: like Gen 1, Ez 1, and Ez 40-48, it was thought to contain 'mysteries'.

4 Jerome, epistola 107:12; cited in von Harnack 1912: 127-8.

intelligent people who readily interpret allegorically'.[5] As M. HARAN writes of Jewish Scripture, 'It was probably regarded as most natural that God's message, bound in words and recorded in the Book, should hold a deeper significance that the mere literal drift arising from the text as it is'.[6] I do not believe there are any examples of a book whose canonicity was *secured* by interpreting it allegorically. Allegorical reading was a consequence, not a cause, of canonicity.

On the Jewish side, again, there is virtually no evidence of disputes about the Song's canonicity. The Qumran library, as Abegg, Flint, and Ulrich point out, contained a number of copies.[7] The sole passage that discusses matters relating to the status of the Song is the well-known Mishnah Yadaim 3:5:

> All holy scriptures (*kitbe-haqodesh*, 'writings of holiness') make the hands unclean. The Song of Songs and Ecclesiastes make the hands unclean. R. Judah said: The Song of Songs makes the hands unclean but there is a dispute concerning Ecclesiastes. R. Jose said: Ecclesiastes does not make the hands unclean but there is a dispute concerning the Song of Songs. R. Simeon said: Ecclesiastes is among the lenient decisions of the School of Shammai and among the stringent decisions of the School of Hillel. R. Simeon b. Azai said: I have heard a tradition from the seventy-two elders on the day that R. Eleazar b. Azariah was appointed head of the Academy, that the Song of Songs and Ecclesiastes make the hands unclean. R. Akiba said: God forbid that any man in Israel ever disputed concerning the Song of Songs, saying that it does not make the hands unclean, for the whole world is not worth the day on which the Song of Songs was given to Israel, for all the scriptures [or, all the Writings] are holy, but the Song of Songs is the holiest of the holy. If there was a dispute, it concerned Ecclesiastes. R. Johanan b. Joshua, the son of R. Akiba's father-in-law, said: According to what was said by Ben Azai, thus they disputed and thus they decided.

It is on this text that scholars once based the idea of the 'council of Jamnia (Yabneh)', which was supposed to have discussed the question of the scriptural canon in general, and to have ruled on its contents; but this 'council' is now generally agreed to have been a scholarly figment.[8] It remains possible, however, that the passage does reflect rabbinic disputes about the canonicity of the Song,[9] and it is to this that Abegg, Flint, and Ulrich are referring when they speak of 'some of the early Rabbis'. Nothing in the passage, we may note, suggests that the problem these rabbis had with the Song's status were connected with its eroticism: the content is not mentioned at all. The belief that it was this that caused a problem is a pure *decuit ergo factum* argument: this *must have been* the problem, even though there is not the slightest whisper about it anywhere in rabbinic literature. But that there was some dispute concerning the Song (and Qoheleth) is evident.

---

5 Origen, contra Celsum, 1:23. my italics.

6 Haran 1986: 19-48.

7 4QCant$^{a\text{-}c}$, and 6QCant.

8 For a recent discussion with bibliography see Lewis 2002: 146-61; also Cohen 1984: 27-53, and Maier 1990: 1-24.

9 See however the sceptical remarks in Lightstone 2002: 163-84, esp. 176-7.

What was the dispute about? Discussion has been dominated by the assumption that 'to make the hands unclean' is equivalent to 'to be canonical', an assumption which most scholars see no need even to justify. But it is far from evident that the two ideas are indeed equivalent.[10] 'Canonicity' is a concept to do with the authoritative status of books, their value and importance. 'Defiling the hands' belongs to the world of ritual practice. The non-equivalence can be seen clearly from the very next chapter of the Mishnah (m.Yadaim 4:5), where we read that biblical books do not defile the hands if they are in the wrong script, for example in proto-Hebraic rather than in square script (what the Mishnah calls 'Assyrian characters'), or if they are in Aramaic translation:

> The [Aramaic] version that is in Ezra and Daniel renders the hands unclean. If an [Aramaic] version [contained in the Scriptures] was written in Hebrew, or if [Scripture that is in] Hebrew was written in an Aramaic version, or in Hebrew script, it does not render the hands unclean. [The Holy Scriptures] render the hands unclean only if they are written in the Assyrian character, on leather, and in ink.

It can even make a difference where the book is. The 'scroll of the Temple Court', the supposedly normative scroll of the Torah (m.Moed Katan 3:4), is said in the Tosefta (t.Kelim 2:5, 8) to confer uncleanness only if removed from the Temple; within the Temple itself it did not make the hands unclean.

There are also later texts where the capacity of the book of Esther to cause uncleanness is said to have been disputed (Babylonian Talmud, Megillah 7a), and there was surely never any dispute about the canonicity of Esther, which has a whole tractate of the Mishnah devoted to it.

All this strongly suggests that the dispute was not about what we should call 'canonicity', but about the capacity of some other feature of the texts to cause uncleanness. This was presumably a physical characteristic, rather than a matter of content, since content would persist regardless of the physical form or location of the text in question. I have noted elsewhere,[11] and repeat the point here, that one feature shared by Ecclesiastes, the Song, and Esther is that all three lack the divine name YHWH. It is possible that this is why there was some dispute about whether scrolls containing these books conveyed uncleanness. If that were so, then the discussion in m. Yadaim would certainly not be about the canonicity of the books in question. It would, on the contrary, only be because of their admitted canonicity that the question of their physical ability to defile the hands arose at all. It is only the holy scriptures that defile in any case;[12] the question is, is that true even of those books that lack the divine name? Some authorities may have argued that it was not. That would not

10 Cf. Barr 1983: 50-1, and see my discussion in Barton 1997: 108-115.

11 Barton 1997: 116-7.

12 The idea that holy texts cause defilement is an odd one, and was regarded as odd by a number of rabbinic authorities. For a detailed discussion see Barton 1997: 109-112.

mean that they regarded these books, from the point of view of their content, as non-canonical; simply that they thought they did not need to be treated ritually with the same physical care as books in which the Name was present.

There might have been a theoretical problem about *non*-canonical books that *did* contain the Name, but in practice no such books existed among Jews in ancient times. Qumran practice, for example, was to substitute for the Name when it occurred in non-biblical texts. Christian books were a problem if they did contain the name: might one destroy such texts? The issue is discussed in some rabbinic texts, and it was certainly the opinion of some that such books might be destroyed 'with their names' (Shabbat 116a, t.Shabbat 13:5, t.Yadaim 2:13). But in general terms a book containing the Name would be a scriptural book.

It is important to emphasize, however, that my argument does not depend on this suggestion that it is was the lack of the Tetragrammaton that caused doubts about whether certain books defiled the hands. It is one possible explanation, but there may be others. Any plausible explanation must, though, take seriously the physical nature of the scrolls in question, and – I have argued – will not be connected with any doubts about the books' canonicity. That is the starting-point of the discussion: if the books were not scripture, the issue about defiling the hands would not arise anyway.

Apart from m.Yadaim 3:5, there i*s no other independent evidence at all* that the status of the Song of Songs was ever an issue for Jews, just as there is none that it was an issue for Christians. Whether the term 'canonical' is a good one to use may be disputed,[13] but if it is correct to refer to the Torah as 'canonical' around the turn of the era, then there is no reason to deny this description to the Song. No one tried to 'block' its acceptance into the Hebrew Bible, so far as we know. If they did, no record of the matter remains.

What of allegorical reading? The normal assumption nowadays is that this was a way of making acceptable a book that was in principle a problem for Jews and/or Christians. The difficulty here is that there is no evidence at all that any serious interpreters in antiquity ever read the Song 'literally' anyway. Even if it was composed as a set of erotic lyrics,[14] no ancient interpreter for whom we have any attestation ever read it so. Always it was read as an allegory of the love of God for Israel, or, in Christian texts, for the Church. It may be that this interpretation was forced on readers by the fact of the Song's scriptural status (as argued above, it can hardly have *caused* that status, since one would not bother to allegorize a text anyway unless it had scriptural

13 On this see Barton 1997, passim.

14 It has recently been argued that the Song was actually composed as an allegory in the first place: see Kingsmill 2003, a work to which I am indebted for some of the argumentation above. Even if this is not accepted, it is a striking fact that we do not possess a single ancient interpretation that chimes in with the modern reading of the Song as a set of erotic poems.

authority); but if so, we might expect some evidence for a preceding literal reading, and that is entirely lacking. Origen indeed, envisages that some people may *wrongly* read the text in a literalistic manner,[15] but there is never any suggestion that such a reading is natural or normal. This is contrary to what we as modern readers might expect, but it is simply a fact about the ancient interpretative tradition: the argument that people normally read the Song 'carnally', as Origen put it, and then needed to be talked into reading it spiritually, is another *decuit ergo factum* argument.

In short: there is no reason to think that the Song of Songs was ever of doubtful canonicity, or that its canonicity depended on its being read as an allegory. On the contrary, it was part of Scripture by the turn of the era. Any disputes there may have been concerned how a scroll containing it should be handled, and such a question would not have arisen in the first place if it had not been accepted as scriptural. No serious reader in ancient times ever read it as other than an allegory of the divine love.

Some readers may suspect that behind my argumentation there lies a 'conservative' desire to show that the canon of Scripture was 'closed' earlier than is sometimes allowed.[16] That is far from my intention. I do not believe that the canon was closed till well into the Christian era. But that means that *more* books were candidates for admission than were finally accepted, not that any of those we now have were doubted. I agree with the thesis first put forward by Sundberg,[17] that the canon remained open in both Judaism and Christianity – or fuzzy at the edges, as I would prefer to put it – till much later than conservative scholars allow. Many other books might well have been included in it. But there is nothing now in our canon that anyone seriously thought of *ex*cluding; and that is as true of the Song of Songs as of any other book of the Hebrew Bible.

---

15 Origen certainly argues that for 'carnal' minds there is a danger in reading the Song, and it is clear that by this he meant that they might read it 'literally', i.e. in an erotic sense. It is obvious to him, however, that such a reading is false; and his discussion in no way suggests that he thought the book lacking in authority or status – the fault lay with the 'carnal' reader.

16 As in a work such as Beckwith 1985.

17 Sundberg 1964.

Bibliography

ABEGG, M./FLINT, P.W./ULRICH, E.C. (1999): The Dead Sea Scrolls Bible: The Oldest Known Bible Translated for the First Time into English, San Francisco.

BARR, J. (1983): Holy Scripture: Canon, Authority, Criticism, Oxford/ Philadelphia.

BARTON, J. (1997): The Spirit and the Letter: Studies in the Biblical Canon, London (American edition Holy Writings, Sacred Text, Louisville 1997).

BECKWITH, R. (1985): The Old Testament Canon of the New Testament Church, Grand Rapids.

COHEN, S.J.D. (1984): The Significance of Yavneh, HUCA 55, 27-53.

HARAN, M. (1986): Midrashic and Literal Exegesis and the Critical Method in Biblical Research, in: S. Japhet (ed.), Studies in Bible, ScrHier 31, Jerusalem, 19-48.

KINGSMILL, E. (2003) The Song of Songs and the Eros of God: A Study of Biblical Intertextuality, DPhil. thesis, Oxford.

LEWIS, J.P. (2002): Jamnia Revisited, in: L.M. McDonald/J. A. Sanders (eds.), The Canon Debate, Peabody, 146-162.

LIGHTSTONE, J.N. (2002): The Rabbis' Bible: The Canon of the Hebrew Bible and the Early Rabbinic Guild, in: L.M. McDonald/J.A. Sanders (eds.), The Canon Debate, Peabody, 163-184

MAIER, G. (1990): Der Abschluß des jüdischen Kanons und das Lehrhaus von Jabne, in: G. Maier (ed.), Der Kanon der Bibel, Giessen, 1-24.

SUNDBERG, A.C. (1964): The Old Testament of the Early Church, Cambridge/MA.

VON HARNACK, A. (1912): Bible Reading in the Early Church, London/New York.

Does the Song of Songs have any connections to wisdom?

Katharine J. Dell

"Needless to say, the Canticle is not a wisdom book; it is a collection of love poems".[1] R.E. MURPHY in this opening comment on the Song of Songs in his introduction to the wisdom literature, *The Tree of Life*, appears here to settle the matter of the Song of Songs' relationship to wisdom in the negative. However, I would suggest that the issue is a little more complex than this statement implies. A few sentences later, Murphy qualifies it by asking the question, "as *edited*, [his italics] do these poems have a sapiential character on another level of understanding?"[2] Murphy is actually one of the few writers on wisdom who has included a section on the Song of Songs in his introductory textbook and he discusses it in a chapter entitled 'Wisdom's Echoes' in which claims of a wider range of literature to wisdom influence are aired. Is he right to see the Song of Songs as having gone through an editorial stage in which wisdom had an influence on the work? We will need to look at this suggestion. Moreover, what is the connection with Solomon who is mentioned in the opening verse of the Song just as he is mentioned in Proverbs and indicated in Ecclesiastes? These and other questions are raised when we start to look at the issue of the relationship of the Song to wisdom on which I suggest there is a debate to be had, hence the rationale for this paper.

When speaking of wisdom, it is helpful to distinguish between 'wisdom literature' which describes a certain corpus of closely defined books in the Bible, wisdom as a genre which might include evidence of wisdom influence in a predominantly non-wisdom text, and Wisdom, with a capital W, as referring to the female personification as found in Proverbs 1-9. Clearly, the Song is not to be characterized as wisdom literature in the same way as Proverbs or Ecclesiastes on a narrow, form-critical definition.[3] That which generally leads it to be considered, if at all, in this category is the attribution to Solomon in 1:1, "The Song of Songs, which is Solomon's". This attribution is arguably

1 Murphy 1990a: 106.

2 Murphy 1990a: 106.

3 I have argued elsewhere that on a narrow definition even the book of Job does not lie in the same main stream of wisdom literature as Proverbs and Ecclesiastes (cf. Dell 1991).

reinforced by the reference in 1Reg 4:32 to Solomon having composed 1005 songs and by rabbinic tradition which ascribes the Song to Solomon's youthful pen (Baba Bathra 15a). We will need to look at this attribution and its wider ramifications in more depth. Turning to classification of the Song in relation to the wisdom genre; even on a wider definition of the genre of wisdom, which might arguably include works influenced strongly by wisdom forms or ideas, the Song tends to stay off the list. The reason is because 'love songs' are a clearly defined genre in their own right and are paralleled by Egyptian love poetry.[4] With reference back to Solomon in 1Reg 4 again, it has been argued that 'songs' are part of the range of small wisdom genres. However, even then it would be a shared genre and whilst there may be interplay between the genres, they are still distinct. The agreed designation for the Song in modern times, despite all the varied suggestions of the past, is that of love songs.[5] However, a few scholars have gone so far as to classify the Song as wisdom in genre, at least at some stage in its literary development, and we need to look at the nuance of such suggestions. Finally, in relation to the female figure of Wisdom, we need to ask whether there are any connections between the Song and either her or her counterpart, the loose or foreign woman. One might regard the whole atmosphere of the Song as rather different from the more black and white, moralistic picture of the alternative paths of Wisdom and Folly. Yet, as we shall see, there are some interesting connections in the themes and imagery used. So, considering these three different definitions of wisdom provides a way of approaching the different facets of the possible wisdom connections to be found in the Song of Songs. I will therefore divide the paper into three parts corresponding to these three definitions.

4 For a full discussion of ancient Egyptian love poetry of a parallel nature to the Song see Fox, 1985. Interestingly, Fox argues that Egyptian love songs do not assume a married context. They never speak of the couple as already married and they often speak of obstacles in the path to love. The lovers sometimes travel some distance to be together and they appear unmarried as they express hope that they will spend their lives together eventually. Fox does not think either that the Song belongs to a wedding context or that the couple are already married, although he concedes that 3:7-11 may have been a wedding song before its inclusion in the Song and that parts of the Song may have been sung at weddings.

5 One very recent exception to this is to be found in the work of E. Kingsmill, *The Song of Songs and the eros of God: a study in biblical intertextuality* (DPhil thesis (Oxford), 2002) who argues that an allegorical interpretation is integral to an understanding of the genre of the Song.

1. Solomonic attribution and references to the king

The opening verse of the book is generally taken as a heading and ascription of the work to the Israelite king most famed for his wisdom, Solomon (1Reg 10:23). The phrase 'song of songs' is perhaps less a title than a superlative intended to set the Song apart from other songs. The attribution to Solomon can be taken in more ways than one. It could designate 'to Solomon' i.e. 'dedicated to', or 'by Solomon' i.e. 'from the mouth of Solomon', or 'concerning Solomon', 'in the style of Solomon', or 'belonging to Solomon'. It is generally thought that 'by Solomon' or 'belonging to' him is most appropriate, the latter of these has the advantage of not assigning authorship to him. One might ask why such a book would need Solomonic legitimization, if such an attribution could effectively achieve this purpose. Was this the only way for it to gain approval and ultimately acceptance into the canon? Or was the link made on the basis of traditions about Solomon's life, notably in relation to his numerous wives and concubines (1Reg 11:1-3; cf. Cant 6:8-9), to his interest in flora and fauna, (1Reg 4:32-3); to the references to exotic spices from abroad (1Reg 4:13-14) and to the images of wealth and luxury (1Reg 9-10), all of which, as we shall see, feature abundantly in the Song?

Or is there any historical basis for the attribution? It was common practice to attribute works to eminent figures from the past as we know from the attribution of the Psalms to David and the Law to Moses. We already have Solomonic attributions in Proverbs, and indication of authorship by Solomon in Ecclesiastes and the Wisdom of Solomon. A distant historical connection to Solomon certainly cannot be ruled out. It has been assumed that attributions of this sort automatically led to canonization of a work. This assumption clearly does not apply to the Wisdom of Solomon since it is found in the Apocrypha and not in the main canon, but it arguably follows in relation to Proverbs and Ecclesiastes.[6] There were questions raised about the Song's canonicity which were arguably quelled, in part at least, by this attribution, but which were also possibly stemmed by early allegorization of the work. We know that the Rabbis soon came to read the text in allegorical fashion to relate to the relationship between God and Israel.[7] We also know that the

6 I have argued in relation to Ecclesiastes, however, that attribution to Solomon, whilst important, was not the overriding factor leading to canonization and this point might be borne in mind here (cf. Dell 1994).

7 e.g. Mishnah Ta'anith 4:8 in which Cant 3:11 is mentioned as the day of Solomon's wedding and of his gladness of heart. The wedding is seen to represent the giving of the Law and the gladness represents the building of the temple.

Song was read as the Passover Scroll certainly from the 8th century AD.[8] Metaphorical references to Israel as 'lily', 'dove' and 'bride' in 2Esdras 5:24-7:26 may also directly reflect the language of the Song,[9] which may indicate a first century exegetical tradition for the Song and hence older roots for the allegorical interpretation. However, allegorization could have been the result of canonization rather than the cause. Solomonic attribution clearly weighed heavily with the early Rabbis. Rabbi Jonathan deduced that the Song was Solomon's first achievement. He wrote "When a man is young he composes songs; when he grows older he makes sententious remarks; and when he becomes an old man he speaks of the vanity of things" (Canticles Rabbah 1,1). An interesting reference, not often commented upon, is that in Sirach 47:12-22 when the author refers to songs in his description of Solomon (verse 17, "Your songs, proverbs, and parables, and the answers you gave astounded the nations").

The attribution issue is further complicated by references within the body of the Song to Solomon (in the third person and not explicitly as the speaker) of which there are five. The first is in 1:5 in the reference to Solomonic hangings, to which the woman likens her beauty. The second is in 3:7 which describes the 'litter of Solomon' guarded by sixty mighty men, the beginning of a passage that has been seen to describe Solomon's arrival for his wedding. Verse 9 speaks of Solomon's palanquin and verse 11 of Solomon's crown within the same context. Then, in 8:11-12 there is a reference to Solomon's vineyard, an indication of his great wealth. There are also the references to 'the king' who may or may not be Solomon and may even represent some kind of role-play by the lovers as I shall go on to discuss. However, it is interesting that in 3:9.11, the wedding song section, reference to Solomon is found in conjunction with that to 'the king', thereby suggesting a link between the two. Another reference to 'the king' is found in 1:4, "The king has brought me into his chambers." One might ask if this reference suggests a married situation in the Song (cf. references to 'my bride' in 4:8-12 and 5:1). Yet another reference to 'the king' is found in 1:12, 'the king was on his couch', which is found in the context of a discussion of perfume by the woman. In the next line the imagery of smell is continued with reference this time to 'my beloved' – we are led to ask whether this is one and the same person. In 7:5 the man is speaking about the woman's beauty and says "a king is held captive in the tresses", probably referring to the woman's hair as in the previous line. This could be figurative, but the king might speak of himself in

8 The earliest reference to this custom is in the post-Talmudic tractate Sopherim 14:16 (6th century AD) which indicates that the Song of Songs was read on the last two days of the festival of Passover.

9 Interestingly the same metaphors are used in Hosea and connected with Israel – Hos. 14:6 (lily); Hos. 7:11 and 11:11 (dove) and Hos. 4:13-14 'bride' (cf. Jer. 2:32).

those terms.[10] Continuing with the royal imagery there is also reference to a 'queenly' maiden in 7:1, which may be the king talking literally of his queen, but could again be seen as figurative. There are various references to riches which would fit the situation of a king, particularly one as wealthy as Solomon, for example in 1:13 in the reference to myrrh. Would an ordinary suitor have access to such treasures? That would surely be unlikely. In 1:10 the jewellery of the woman is described and if taken literally must indicate a situation of wealth and in verse 11 there is the promise of "ornaments of gold studded with silver" for her. In 3:6-11 the splendour of Solomon's litter is described and here it is clearly his wealth and power that is being emphasized. Again, we find rich perfumes such as myrrh and frankincense and the description of the palanquin as having "posts of silver, its back of gold, its seat of purple" is an indication of royal finery and wealth. If this passage describes a wedding ceremony as many scholars believe,[11] this would be a description of the royal entourage arriving for the special day.[12] This description can be compared with Psalm 45 (especially Ps 45:13-15 which describe rich wedding robes).

Another scholarly suggestion is that such royal references represent role playing by the lovers possibly following an ancient Near Eastern custom of ascribing royal personae to every bride and groom (as paralleled in modern times in some cultures) or simply reflecting an aspect of love which is enjoyment of 'make-believe' situations.[13] The Solomonic figure has also been seen in this light as a role played by one of the lovers[14] with the possible extra dimension that Solomon is seen as the quintessential Eastern monarch and hence as a poetic symbol for the splendour of the bridegroom.[15] The issue is also complicated by allusions to a shepherd figure. He has been seen as the rival to the king, and the one who eventually wins the woman.[16] The references to a 'herder of flocks' (1:7.8; 2:16 and 6:2.3) that indicate such a figure could in fact refer to a king in that ancient kings were commonly portrayed as shepherds responsible for their people (who are described as

---

10 More tenuous royal connections include 6:8-10, which mentions sixty queens, possibly a reference to Solomon's harem; 4:4 which likens the woman's neck to 'the tower of David', a reference possibly to Israel's king David and 2:4 which may indicate a royal banqueting house. I am grateful to my research student Yee Von Koh for drawing my attention to these references and for reading a draft of this paper.

11 E.g. Gordis 1974 sees this as referring not to a rustic wedding, but to one of great luxury and possessing national significance, i.e. that of Solomon.

12 "In a chariot beside my prince" in 6:12-13 may indicate the departure of the woman in 6:12.

13 See Murphy 1981 in the section on the Song of Songs (98-124).

14 See Bloch and Bloch 1995.

15 See Garrett 1993.

16 First suggested by J.S. Jacobi in 1771 in the context of the Song being a drama.

flocks). It is interesting that the two images of king and shepherd are never fused together which may suggest that they are not one and the same. However, the shepherd figure is not so fully explored as that of the king, and interpretations that see him as a third player in a drama are, in my opinion, somewhat forced.

This leads us on to the suggestion of seeing the Song of Songs as a drama with *dramatis personae* and chorus. Some scholars[17] have suggested that an actual historical situation in Solomon's life is being outplayed in the drama between Solomon and the Shulammite woman. This historical situation is Solomon's failed attempt to woo Abishag the Shunammite (1Reg 1:3-4). Even without an actual historical context there is the possibility of finding dramatic tension in the idea of king and shepherd vying for the woman, with the king losing out in 8:12 when Solomon's vineyards are seemingly rejected by the woman. Some scholars pursuing this line of interpretation have found two actors in the drama, some three. The consensus of opinion seems to be that to read drama into the piece is actually to force it unnaturally into a shape that it doesn't naturally have. So, in fact, although elements of plot can arguably be found, the Song is more generally agreed to be an episodic sequence of lyric poems rather than a drama.

So, this discussion leads us to ask: Is 'the king' figure to be identified with Solomon? Are we to see a Solomonic layer as an integral part of the Song or as a later stage in the development of the piece? Gordis (1974) argues that the royal wedding song in 3:6-11 is the oldest datable unit in the book which, he thinks, goes back to Solomon's reign. A further complication is that in 8:12 Solomon is the addressee rather than the speaker. Could this be another voice disputing Solomon's exclusive claim to love and evaluating love above the kind of wealth that Solomon enjoys? Could Solomon be being used as a foil here by one reflecting on the Solomonic situation, as seen also in the abstract musing on love in 8:6-7, rather as Qohelet appears to weigh up the Solomonic quest for meaning in life in the use of the royal testament form in Eccl 1:12-2:16? Childs (1979) argues, along these lines, that the Solomonic attribution in the Song performs a broader role than simply establishing authorship, it is, rather, an indication of later, wise voices that are added to the text at an editorial stage to establish and confirm the book's wisdom credentials. This leads us into our discussion in the next section of the possible editorial activity that may have been responsible for linking the love poems in the Song to wisdom genres. So we have seen that the Solomonic reference is quite probably more than just an attribution and may represent a deliberate attempt to associate this work, in a more integrated way, to wisdom's wisest patron, Solomon.

---

17 See Waterman 1948 for a historical approach.

2. *Editorial links with the wisdom genre*

The most widespread scholarly suggestion for linking the Song of Songs to the wisdom writers and hence the wisdom genre, is that the Song went through a stage of redaction that was connected with wisdom circles. Thus the sages, it is argued, placed their distinctive stamp on the material at a particular point in its development. The evidence for this is found in 8:6b-7 in arguably the only passage in the book that describes love in an abstract way in contrast to the specific context of the love of the man and woman that dominates the rest of the book. Audet (1955) distinguishes a pre-literary stage of the Song corresponding to the period in which its use for its original purpose as a betrothal song was widespread and a later literary stage, which he dates at the Exile. It is certainly possible that love songs performed at banquets and festivals would have been transmitted orally for a considerable length of time and important to distinguish this oral stage from that of being recorded in writing. Audet argued that at the later, writing down stage the Song became part of a wider wisdom collection and in the process of transformation into a literary text lost much of its distinctiveness.[18]

Cant 8:6b-7 is put into the mouth of the Shulammite woman, "for love is strong as death and passion fierce as the grave. Its flashes are flashes of fire, in a raging flame. Many waters cannot quench love, neither can floods drown it. If one offered for love all the wealth of his house, it would be utterly scorned." Tromp (1990)[19] argues that this passage was included in order to show the kind of love the whole song was really about, i.e. "an irresistible and quasi-fatal factor, a dynamic and vital force, a creative, divine power which unites a man and woman in an exclusive and lasting relationship".[20] This passage clearly puts the language of love onto a more cosmological level as it portrays personified forces of love over against chaos and death. Tromp sees love as a personified creative power in these lines (rather like Wisdom in Prov 8:22-31). Childs (1979) goes as far as to suggest that, in these verses, it is not human love that is celebrated but wisdom which represents 'sanctioned love', seen here as a vital part of human experience. Even if one might not wish to go as far as Tromp and Childs in identifying the love described in these verses with wisdom, clearly at the very least love is here made subject to abstract reflection in a way that the love of the individuals for each other is not. Sadgrove (1978) argues that this verse, closely similar in form to a proverbial saying, has the effect of both meditating on and universalizing all that has

18 Audet 1958 sees verse 1 as a later title for the book and verse 2 as the original title.

19 Tromp 1990 translates שַׁלְהֶבֶתְיָה 'in a raging flame' as 'flames of Yah' in reference to part of the divine name.

20 Tromp 1990: 94

gone before it in the Song. He writes "Indeed this is the only place in the Song where any attempt is made to probe the meaning of the love that is its theme; everywhere else it is simply described".[21] This is the stage at which an ethical point about the nature of love is therefore being introduced. He sees it as the climax of the Song in that it captures the meaning of the whole in a similar manner to the epilogue of Ecclesiastes (Qoh 12:13-14).

It is arguable, in my view, that the admonition spoken by the woman to the daughters of Jerusalem in Cant 2:7; 3:5 and 8:4, which in its repetition acts as a kind of refrain, can also be seen alongside 8:6b-7 as abstract reflection on the nature of love. Each time the woman says, "I adjure you, O daughters of Jerusalem, by the gazelles or the hinds of the field, that you stir not up nor awaken love until it please". She makes a type of oath perhaps somewhat surprisingly using animals as her witnesses, in which she urges the daughters to wait patiently for love rather than seek it hurriedly. This repeated refrain has, it seems to me, as much claim to be seen as abstract musing possibly from wisdom circles as 8:6b-7 and may, indeed, indicate that the wisdom editing was more pervasive than some have claimed.

Childs argues that later voices within a wisdom circle have added to the text (in 8:6b-7) and that this principle is established in the superscription to the book in the mention of Solomonic authorship. Thus he forges a link between the two main points of wisdom influence in the Song. Solomon is representative of Israel's wise and so the superscription sets the Song in the context of wisdom literature, as does the canon itself. In the light of this discussion he concludes that, "The Song is to be understood as wisdom literature".[22] Hence, in his view, other contexts of understanding are ruled out by the appropriation of the Song by wisdom circles of a later time than Solomon. This appropriation is for two reasons, first a thematic link in that love being so intrinsic to human experience is of interest to the sages (cf. Prov 15:17) and second a didactic link between later wisdom groups and their patron, Solomon. Childs sees the role of Solomon as having been extended into the Song itself, probably by later wisdom voices. He further suggests that the wise regarded the Song as a celebration of love within marriage. Childs argues that the kingly context was extended beyond that of Solomon to include the shepherd imagery that we have already noted. This broadened the reference away from the Solomonic situation, as did 8:6b-7 so that in its final canonical form the book could be appreciated more widely. It is interesting, in regard to the previous discussion about the possible connection between Solomon and the royal references, that Childs sees that connection as having been close in the Song's original context, linked indeed to the historical

21 Sadgrove 1978: 245.
22 Childs 1979: 574.

instance afforded by Solomon. Murphy (1990a) argues in a similar vein, as we noted at the start, for an edited stage that gives the poems a sapiential character on another level of interpretation. This does not mean that the book is entirely wisdom in character, but hints at the possibility that the work was read within the wisdom tradition that went back to Solomon and that it was handed down in such circles. It may well have relevant in the wisdom context of the training of young men in the ways of the world, notably here in the values of fidelity and mutuality in relation to love between the sexes (cf. Prov 5:15-20).

A few scholars have thought that the Song ultimately derived from wisdom circles,[23] being originally crafted by the wise in its entirety. However, there is little support for this idea in the light of the Song's character as a collection of love songs. The sophisticated nature of the poetry, coupled with imagery that implies a wealthy background, might suggest that the original composer of the poetry was associated with a group of intellectuals, as the sages of Israel would probably have been, but that observation does not confine it to the wisdom context since the genre used is quite different. Even if the Song is seen as primarily a literary creation rather than the product of oral culture, that wisdom circles were solely responsible for such a work cannot simply be assumed. Gerleman[24] has argued that if this is the case, both composition and transmission (and not just transmission as most have argued) could be assigned to the sages of Israel. However, even if this were the case, it would be wrong on grounds of genre to deny the book's nature as love poetry and simply assign it to wisdom literature.

A way of avoiding this problem of different genre classifications is to state that love songs as a genre are themselves to be incorporated within a broad definition of the genre of wisdom. Gordis (1974)[25] argues for this, taking wisdom to refer to skill of composition. For example, he points to the use of חָכְמָה to refer to the arts of poetry and song, especially for the composition of songs, e.g. women skilled in lamenting at funerals are called חֲכָמוֹת by Jeremiah (9:16). He argues that the terms wisdom and song were used interchangeably, as in reference to Solomon in 1Reg 4:32. Clearly there is overlap of interest between wisdom and the subject matter of the Song. Wisdom covers all aspects of human experience, including sexual love, and indeed there is the use of sexual imagery in Proverbs as we shall go on to explore. Yet there is a clear difference between the genres of song and usual wisdom genres such as didactic proverbs and I wonder whether the idea of

23 E.g. Würthwein 1969.
24 E.g. Gerleman 1965.
25 See Gordis 1974: 13-16.

incorporating one genre within another is not stretching definitions rather too much.

It seems then that the argument for a wisdom redaction or stage of literary transmission is quite convincing and yet it is hard to know at precisely what stage the wisdom editors would have made their mark. It arguably could have been quite early in the Song's development. This links up with issues of dating and of relationship with other material, the former of which I will discuss briefly in the conclusion, but the latter of which leads me into discussion of the relationship of this material to wisdom motifs in the mainstream wisdom books, notably in relation to the female figures in Proverbs 1-9.

3. *Relationship to wisdom motifs and female configurations in Proverbs*

We now turn to the question of relationship to Wisdom, the female personification in Proverbs 1-9, and indeed to the Loose Woman, and in this section I also want to include wider links with wisdom motifs where they are relevant.

a) Links with Woman Wisdom: The Song of Songs is most often characterized as being concerned with love, in this case between the sexes. Turning to Proverbs 8 we find similar language and imagery drawn from the experience of love with wisdom personified as a woman who calls young men to love her, as in verse 17, "I love those who love me, and those who seek me diligently find me." Like the Song, this verse from Proverbs emphasizes the reciprocal nature of love. This verse, which follows a couple of verses on kings and rulers, has led some commentators to suggest that it is love in a political context that is meant here (cf. Prov 8:21).[26] However, it may well have a broader reference as supported by the image of Wisdom inviting love in Prov 4:6 and open to an embrace in Prov 4:8. We also find imagery of human love in Prov 5:15-19, where the stress is on fidelity to one's wife. Her fidelity to her husband is assumed and indicated by the reference to her affection in v 19.[27] The stress is also on enjoyment of her beauty within the context of physical love, and in Proverbs it is important to remember it is only within the marital context that sexual love is condoned. In Proverbs, this pleasure in one's wife is one way for the husband of resisting other less-savoury temptations and, by contrast, in the Song there is no such moralizing, rather human love is celebrated for its own sake.

26 Lang 1975.

27 We might note the similar imagery of hinds and doves used in Prov 8:19 and in Cant 4:5.

There is some debate as to whether the Song describes married love or sex outside marriage. Murphy (1981) points out that the sole reference to marriage is in Cant 3:6 and so the rest of the poems are equally possible outside such a setting. Bloch and Bloch (1995) see the couple as unmarried, accusing pious exegetes of marrying them off. Many scholars have applied the wedding context to the whole Song and thus seen the pair as married. Childs (1979, 575) writes, "The Song is wisdom's reflection on the joyful and mysterious nature of love between a man and a woman within the institution of marriage." He is suggesting then that the wisdom writers have given the Song this context because of their own presupposition that such expressions of love are only right within the marital context.

Camp (1995) draws out aspects of the comparison between Wisdom and the Song of Songs which I shall discuss here. These are largely thematic. A motif strongly associated with Woman Wisdom is that of her pursuit – of seeking and finding her (as in Prov 8:17b). The man who finds Wisdom is deemed happy (Prov 3:13; along the same lines as finding a good wife in Prov 18:22; 31:10). This is echoed in the Song in 3:1-4; 5:2-8; 6:1-3 and 8:1-2 in the woman's quest for her lover.[28] Interestingly it is the young man in Proverbs who has to seek Wisdom in order to obtain 'favour from the Lord' (Prov 8:17.35-36; 2:1-5), and is rebuked for not doing so, whilst in the Song it is the woman who seeks her lover out (except in Cant 8:13). However, in Proverbs Woman Wisdom also plays a proactive role in seeking out those whom she wishes to follow her (Prov 8:1-4; 1:20-21). There is also in Proverbs 8:34 a corresponding motif of waiting. The young man waits at the doors of Wisdom's house[29] on a daily basis and in similar fashion in the Song the woman's lover stands behind the wall and gazes in at her window (Cant 2:9).

There is a stress on riches and material goods in relation to Wisdom in Prov 8. In verses 10-11 her instruction is better than silver, gold and jewels, and yet in verse 18 she offers riches and enduring wealth to those who follow her. Again she is greater than such treasures (verse 19), but then in verse 21 the endowment of wealth is closely linked to the call to love (cf. a similar tension in Prov 3:13-16). This of course reflects the world-view of the book of Proverbs that sees the acquisition of wealth as intimately linked to following the path of wisdom (Prov 10:20; 16:16; 20:15; 22:1; 25:11.12; cf. Prov 31). In the Song, the lover is described in metaphorical terms of precious metals and stones (Cant 5:11.14-15) conveying the beauty and value of the lover in the eyes of the woman, whilst the woman's finery is likened to Pharaoh's chariot

28 Camp (1995) notes that closely linked in the Song to this motif, indicated by vocabulary such as בקש and מצא, are the themes of presence, place and whereabouts (1:7-8; 2:8-9; 4:16-5:1; 8:5-6.13-14; cf. שחר and מצא in Prov 1:28; 8:17 and מצא in Prov 8:35-6).

29 Cf. Cant 8:2 in which the woman longs to take the man to her mother's house.

mares. The lover admires her adornment with jewels and promises her gold and silver ornaments (Cant 1:9-11). There is an element of this in the Wisdom imagery, although Wisdom's value is said to be greater than all these precious things. Should we see these metaphors of wealth in the Song as figurative, characterizing the intrinsic value of the referent rather than as materialistically motivated? The description of Wisdom worth in relation to precious stones in Job 28:15-19 would support the former position. However, only in Cant 8:6-7 is love explicitly valued over wealth.

Other smaller links are found for example in the imagery of Wisdom as a tree of life in Proverbs 3:18 which links up with the comparison in the Song of the woman to a palm tree which her lover is going to climb (Cant 7:7-8). Furthermore, all wisdom's paths are peace (שָׁלוֹם) in Prov 8:17 and in the Song the woman describes herself as 'one who brings peace' to her lover (Cant 8:10; cf. Prov 3:13, the one who finds wisdom also finds peace).[30] There is also the motif of Wisdom's power over life and death (Prov 8:36) which relates to the mention of death in Cant 8:6-7. In the Song, love is as strong as death, as is jealousy. Wisdom, on the other hand, offers life over death for those who follow her path. Jealousy would probably be seen as one of the vices that would lead down the road to death, but love, directed aright, is seen as life-giving. Camp writes in relation to Cant 8:7, "If the love between woman and man was in fact understood in Israel to have this power, then one can perhaps better comprehend the power of Wisdom the lover, who can defeat death with life for those who love her. The image of the lover has the capacity to draw together the experiences of daily life and the experiences of faith. The love of Wisdom for her lover is comparable to the mutual intimacy of the lovers in the Song of Songs ... But the power of love that is only hinted at at the end of the Song – its power over death – becomes personified Wisdom's special possession and gift in the sense that it is comparable only to the character and activity of Yahweh" (Camp 1995, 111).

Wisdom uses self-description in order to justify herself and motivate the object of her desire – the young men she wishes to follow in her path (Prov 8:6-21). Similarly in the Song, the woman uses self-description – this time of her physical beauty – both to justify herself and motivate her lover (Cant 1:5; 2:1-2; 8:10). It is interesting that in Proverbs 7:4 Wisdom is described as 'my sister'. We find this description also in the Song when in Cant 4:10 the woman

30 Camp (1995) notes also that wisdom's ways in Prov 3:17 are 'ways of pleasantness' (נעם) and in the Song (1:16) the beloved is described as pleasant (נָעִים) and pleasing (נעם) in 7:7, stately as a palm tree. Furthermore, Prov 3:18 speaks of 'laying hold' (מַחֲזִיקִים) of Wisdom as a tree of life, the same root חזק being used in Prov 4:13 to describe the young man's need to hold on to instruction and in 7:13 the loose woman's impudent approach to him.

is described as 'my sister, my bride!' and again in verse 12 and in 5:1.[31] It is an expression of intimacy from the man to the woman and likewise with Wisdom it is an expression of intimacy (although not coupled with 'bride' but with 'intimate friend').

The description of the diligent wife in Prov 31 has been widely seen to have close links with the portrayal of the figure of Wisdom (e.g. Prov 8:10-11; cf. Prov 31:10; and Prov 8:13; cf. Prov 31:30) and the values of Proverbs 5:15-19. It is interesting that in this description of the woman of worth, we again find reference to material goods in the context of the benefits of love for one's wife and of the marital relationship. She, like Wisdom, has to be 'found' (Prov 31:10); she is better than jewels (31:10) and her abilities lead her to accomplish wealth (31:21-2). One might also note the reference to coverings and clothing (31:22) that echo those of the loose woman in Prov 7:10; 16-17.

So the links between the portrayal of Woman Wisdom and the imagery of love and the language and actions of the lovers as used in the Song are quite extensive. It seems likely, however, that there was a certain caution exercised by the wise in Proverbs 1-9 in the use of love language because of the more defined moral framework of the work than we find in the Song. We will need to test this in reference to the portrayal of the loose woman.

b) Links with the Loose Woman: We now turn to the אִשָּׁה זָרָה, the loose, foreign, strange woman, often known as 'Woman Folly'. I will characterize her as the loose woman here, which seems to fit with the enticement aspect of love as revealed in the Song.

The key passage is Proverbs 7:5-27 in which physical allure and skill in lovemaking characterize the loose woman (cf. Prov 2:16-19; 5:3.20). The words of entrapment spoken by her in 7:14-20 echo a number of themes and motifs in the Song. We find the motif of seeking and finding and kissing her lover in both texts (Prov 7:10-15; cf. Cant 3:1-4; 5:6; 8:1b). The loose woman in Proverbs even lies in wait for her lover with the aim of entrapment. She has prepared her bed with expensive coverings and perfumed it with myrrh, aloes and cinnamon (vv. 16-17; cf. Cant 4:14; 5:5). She promises a night of love (v 18; cf. Cant 7:11-13) because her husband is out of town. It is therefore an invitation to adultery by one who is dressed as a harlot (vv. 10-11). The chief difference between this picture and that of the Song is the moral perception that this behaviour is wrong and is the path to death (vv. 21-7).

Grossberg (1994) has done an interesting study of Proverbs 7 in relation to the Song of Songs. He points to similarities such as between Proverbs 7:18, "Come, let us take [drink] our fill of love (דֹּדִים) till morning" and its echo in Cant 5:1b "Drink, deeply, O lovers (דּוֹדִים)!" We have already noted the use of spices in the two texts. Henna and saffron grew in ancient Israel, but myrrh,

31 This reminds us perhaps of the wife/sister motif in Num 12 and Ex 2 and 4.

cinnamon, and cane probably did not, while frankincense, aloes, and spikenard were imported from Arabia, India, Nepal and China (cf. Ps 45:8 in reference to the anointing of royalty). We find similar use of language in Prov 7:17 to refer to bed (מִשְׁכָּב) and couch (עֶרֶשׂ) in Cant 3:1 and 1:16 respectively. There are also differences between the texts, but they indicate shared imagery and themes, such as the fact that in Proverbs 7 the woman is the sole initiator of the action with the young man being largely passive. In the Song on the other hand the action is shared reciprocally between the man and the woman (as expressed in Cant 2:16; 6:3). Also the object of desire in Proverbs 7 is not one particular young man but anyone gullible enough to be lured into the loose woman's net which might be quite a number (Prov 7:26). In the Song of course the lovers only have eyes for each other (Cant 6:8-9). Another difference is in the use of animal imagery. In the Song we find a picture of harmony with nature and animals (Cant 4:1-2.5), but in Proverbs 7 we find the description of animals going to slaughter or caught in snares to describe the entrapment effected by the loose woman. The treatment of death is again different – in Proverbs, death is the end of such actions, whilst in the Song love conquers death (8:6-7). The handling of themes of family and house are different too in the two texts. In the Song the woman is closely knit to her family. There are repeated references to the woman's mother (1:6; 3:4.11; 6:9; 8:1.2.5), although interestingly not to her father who is conspicuous by his absence, even though there are brothers. In Proverbs 7, on the other hand, the woman is a social outsider and apparently has no family other than a husband who has gone away. There is mention of her house (v 29) which she is rarely in (v 11) but which leads to Sheol. This contrasts with the mention of the mother's house in the Song to which the woman is pleased to bring her lover (Cant 8:2). The instructions of Proverbs 1-9 suggest in general terms that the family context is important, as demonstrated by references to father, mother and 'my son'.

Again, interesting links are found between the portrayal of the loose woman and the Song of Songs, but the context into which the language is put is very different. Grossberg (1994) makes the point that the Song is a celebration of a joyful sexual relationship whilst Proverbs 7 adopts aspects of the genre in the service of an arresting wisdom lesson that warns against such a liaison. He argues that the teacher in Proverbs 7 deliberately exploits the love lyrics, subverting their charm by portraying the disastrous results of such activity. He writes of the two texts that they "echo one another, share images, and address similar issues of sexuality, albeit from differing perspectives".[32]

One might ask why the imagery of the Song seems to appear in fairly equal measure in both portrayals – that of Wisdom and of her counterpart, the loose woman. Camp (2000) suggests that there is a deliberate use of sexual

32 Grossberg 1994: 8.

language in reference to both figures in the contexts of both deceit and truth that blurs the distinction between the two. She writes, "Deceitful language is imaged as sexual in both process and content. "The lips of a strange woman drip honey and her speech is smoother than oil" (Prov 5:3). Her offer, of course, illicit sex. The contrast begins to blur, however, when the protection offered by Wisdom's truth is itself purveyed in erotic terms familiar from the Song of Songs and Egyptian love poetry".[33] Perhaps the sages were concerned with guarding the differentiation and so put the shared imagery into clear moral categories. The context of marriage as the right one for sexual relations certainly seems to dominate their concerns here.

c) Other areas of connection with wisdom motifs: I have mentioned the use of imagery from the natural world. This is also a feature of the wisdom literature in which comparisons are often drawn with nature and animals.[34] In the song we find nature imagery of vineyard and garden as well as animal imagery. Bloch and Bloch write of this: "The poem is set in early spring, with its intimations of ripening. The rains of the winter season have just ended, the vines are in blossom, the air is alive with scents and birdsong. Since the poem speaks through metaphor, this setting reveals something essential about the lovers, who live in harmony with the natural world. The images of spring reflect their youth, and the innocent freshness of their passion".[35] The use of animal imagery reflects veneration of animals for their power and beauty. The woman asks her man to be "like a gazelle, or a young stag upon rugged mountains" (Cant 2:17; cf. 8:14), with probable overtones of potency, and she asks her companions, the daughters of Jerusalem, swearing "by the gazelles, by the deer in the field" that they will not awaken love until the time is ripe (Cant 2:7). It is interesting that the swearing is by animals and not by God. Animal imagery is often used to depict the anatomy of the lovers, e.g. "your hair is like a flock of goats...your teeth are like a flock of shorn ewes that have come up from the washing" (Cant 4:1-2). This complements wisdom's use of imagery from the animal and natural world. The language of the song is poetic and looks at nature in a spirit of delight and celebration. Perhaps the closest parallel to this in the wisdom literature is in the description of animals in Job 38-40. There is detail about natural phenomena here on a greater scale than generally found in the wisdom literature. Murphy (1973)[36] has suggested that the Song might be read as an explication of Proverbs 30:19, which demonstrates the interest of the wise in natural phenomena and its mystery, itself part of a chapter that contains quite a large amount of nature imagery.

33 Camp 2000: 26.
34 See discussion in Dell 2000.
35 Bloch and Bloch 1995: 3.
36 Cf. Murphy's commentary on the Song of Songs (1990b).

This description however seems a little too limiting when looking, as we have done, at the range of echoes of wisdom texts in the Song.

Another area of linkage with wisdom is not with Proverbs, but with Ecclesiastes. Cant 2:7 (cf. 3:5; 8:4) talks of the time being ripe to awaken love and a parallel has been noted with the poem on the right time in Qoh 3:1.5b. The preacher sees love as a God-given consolation to make up for the dreariness of existence (Qoh 9:9). Landy (1983) explores the relationship of the Song and Ecclesiastes to wisdom and argues that they both relate in part ironically to that tradition. He says that both perform the same function of testing the worth of wisdom, power and pleasure (and they even use the same symbolic figure, that of Solomon who had all these things in large measure). He sees Ecclesiastes as negating the warmth and wonder of the Song in its evaluation of all as vanity. However love is exempt from this decree (9:9) and it is love that the Song celebrates and sees as greater than everything and strong as death. He writes, "The insidious irony that accompanies every reference to Solomon's realm does not apply to the love of the lovers".[37] He sees Wisdom as turned against itself in the Song which uses wisdom techniques of classifying experience and trying to understand the world but which subverts the genre by exposing its values. The Song turns wisdom's love of moderation into abandonment and "the submergence of consciousness in bliss".[38]

It looks then as if the relationship between Wisdom and Folly and the portrayal of love in the Song is a significant one. Von Rad when discussing Proverbs 8 wrote of a development in wisdom thought through the figure of wisdom in that it carries the dimension of the appeal of intellectual love, which went on to feature significantly in wisdom.[39] It may be that the sages took up images of love for use in this context as well as in the context of wisdom's moral alternative, the path of foolishness.

Conclusion

I wish to suggest then in this paper that the link of the Song of Songs with wisdom is somewhat closer than has generally been thought. Whilst I would hesitate to classify the Song as 'wisdom literature' in any formal, form-critical sense, one cannot ignore the interesting interaction with the wisdom genre and the link with wisdom's most famous figurehead – Solomon. Indeed, the Solomonic link seems to be more than just an attribution, in that the

37 Landy 1983: 29.
38 Landy 1983: 29.
39 von Rad1972: 166-168.

character of Solomon seems to pervade the Song in a more profound way than is often assumed. Wisdom's influence may be restricted to a more editorial level, along the lines that Childs (1979) has suggested. However I suggest that the process of linking up with various facets of wisdom could have happened earlier on at a pre-literary stage.[40] Links between Solomon and the king figure may have been forged during the oral stage, so that a wisdom context could be quite essential to the character of the Song rather than just an afterthought. Perhaps the echoes of the lovers in the Song in Proverbs 7 and 8 in the figures of Wisdom and the loose woman give us a clue as to when that process might have happened. It is arguable that during the period of the formation of Proverbs (and this depends on when one dates these poems in Prov 1-9) this descriptive language of love was known and informed the picture in Proverbs. This is perhaps more likely than the other way around, in that imagery that is used freely in the celebratory context of the Song seems to be put into a wider moral context in the proverbial material. The presentation of young men seeking wisdom and the portrayal of Wisdom herself as the object of the quest and her counterpart as the less favourable alternative gives a plausible context for the way the love imagery in the Song was in turn read and reused by the sages of Israel.

This decision partly depends on when one dates the Song, another uncertain exercise. The material, as with wisdom literature in general, has a timeless quality that makes it difficult to date. Despite linguistic forms (Aramaisms) that may indicate a later date of writing down, an older date for original elements of the Song has been suggested (cf. the reference to Tirzah, the early capital of Israel in 6:4 which suggests a date before 876 BC). However, older elements may only be arguable in relation to early oral tradition, a crucial stage in which these connections with Solomon and wisdom would have been formed. As Fox writes, "The Song may well have had a prehistory of centuries during which love songs were composed and transmitted, constantly mutating until they attained the form we know, in which form they were then written down"[41]. The Song is not necessarily a unity and is arguably a collection of songs from different periods, although the character portrayal remains consistent throughout the Song. The language generally indicates the post-exilic, possibly Hellenistic, period for the final product.

We know that allegorization was an early feature of reading the book, which might lead one to raise the question whether Israel ever read the Song as an allegory on the search for Wisdom, the woman in this context

40 As argued by Gerlemann 1965, and supported by the antiquity of Egyptian parallels in the love song genre.

41 Fox 1985: 190.

representing Wisdom and the man the seeker after her. Could the sages alternatively have adopted a metaphorical interpretation, which saw erotic yearning as a search for true wisdom? Interestingly, Don Isaac Abravanel, a medieval Jewish scholar writing in the mid sixteenth century, saw the characters of the Song not as God and Israel but as Solomon and the Bride who represented Wisdom. He therefore only regarded the Bride as an allegorical figure and saw Solomon as the Bridegroom speaking in his own person. His son, Leon Hebraus[42] noted that Wisdom is described in the wisdom literature as a beautiful woman and contrasted with folly. On that basis they both interpreted the woman in the Song as a typological symbol of Wisdom. It is possible that a similar interchange of ideas could have been occurring amongst the sages in the formation of the Proverbs texts themselves. These authorial and contextual processes are however lost in the mists of time and one can but conjecture on the interrelationship between texts in their formative stages. What I hope to have shown, at the very least, in this paper is that the question of possible connections between the Song of Songs and the wisdom genre is one that is worth asking and to which attention is usefully directed afresh.

Bibliography

AUDET, J-P. (1955): Le sens du Cantique des Cantiques, RB 62, 197-221.
– (1958): Love and marriage in the Old Testament, Scripture 10/11, 65-83.
BLOCH, A./BLOCH, C. (1995): The Song of Songs: A New Translation, Berkeley/Los Angeles/London.
CAMP, C. (1995): Wisdom and the Feminine in the book of Proverbs, Sheffield.
– (2000): Wise, Strange and Holy: The Strange Woman and the Making of the Bible, JSOTS 320, Sheffield.
CHILDS, B.S. (1979): Introduction to the Old Testament as Scripture, Philadelphia.
DELL, K.J. (1991): The Book of Job as Sceptical Literature, BZAW 197, Berlin/New York.
– (1994): Ecclesiastes as Wisdom: Consulting Early Interpreters, VT 44, 301-329.
– (2000): The use of animal imagery in the Psalms and Wisdom Literature of Ancient Israel, SJT 53, 275-291.
FOX, M.V. (1985): The Song of Songs and the Ancient Egyptian Love Songs, Wisconsin.
GARRETT, D.A. (1993): Proverbs, Ecclesiastes, Song of Songs, New American Commentary 14, Nashville.
GERLEMANN, G. (1965): Ruth. Das Hohelied, BK 18, 2nd ed. Neukirchen-Vluyn, 63-77.
GORDIS, R. (1974): The Song of Songs and Lamentations, New York.
GROSSBERG, D. (1994): Two kinds of sexual relationships in the Hebrew Bible, Hebrew Studies 35, 7-25.

42 Abravanel's views and those of his son are represented in the son's work - Leon Hebraus, *Dialogues d"amour* (the French translation attributed to Pontus de Tyard and published in Lyon, 1551 by Jean de Tournes), 1551. Republished by T.A. Perry, Chapel Hill: University of North Carolina Press, 1974.

LANDY, F. (1983): Paradoxes of Paradise: Identity and Difference in the Song of Songs, Bible and Literature Series 7, Sheffield.
LANG, B. (1975): Frau Weisheit, Düsseldorf.
MURPHY, R.E. (1973): Form-Critical Studies in the Song of Songs, Interpretation 27, 413-422.
– (1981): Wisdom Literature: Job, Proverbs, Ruth, Canticles, Ecclesiastes, and Esther, FOTL XIII, Grand Rapids.
– (1990a): The Tree of Life: An Exploration of Biblical Wisdom Literature, New York.
– (1990b): The Song of Songs, Hermeneia, Minneapolis.
SADGROVE, M. (1978): The Song of Songs as Wisdom Literature, Studia Biblica, Sheffield, 245-248.
TROMP, N. (1990): Wisdom and the Canticle: Ct. 8:6b-7b: Text, Character, Message and Import, in: M. Gilbert (ed.), La Sagesse de l'ancien Testament, BEThL 51, 2nd ed. Leuven.
VON RAD, G. (1972): Wisdom in Israel, London, [Translated by J.D. Martin from the German 1st ed. Weisheit in Israel, Neukirchen-Vluyn, 1970].
WATERMAN, L. (1948): The Song of Songs, University of Michigan.
WÜRTHWEIN, E. (1969): Das Hohelied, in: E. Würthwein/K. Galling/O. Plöger, Die Fünf Megilloth, HAT 18, Tübingen, 25-71.

Late Linguistic Features in the Song of Songs*

F. W. Dobbs-Allsopp

The central contention of the present essay is that the language of the Song of Songs (Cant) belongs to the phase of the Hebrew language known as late Biblical Hebrew (LBH).[1] That LBH is a distinguishable linguistic reality, well-defined both typologically and chronologically, is now widely accepted.[2] LBH may be recognized above all by its innovative elements, which, on the one hand, depart from the orthographic, grammatical, and syntactic norms of standard Biblical Hebrew (SBH), and, on the other hand, anticipate linguistic features that become more prominent in post-classical Hebrew – Qumran Hebrew (QH), Ben Sira, Mishnaic (or Rabbinic) Hebrew (MH).[3] The core of

* Many thanks to C.L. Seow and A. Hurvitz for reading through the manuscript in its entirety and for improving the argument significantly in places. Hurvitz reports that although he finds the arguments for the lateness of Cant's language "stronger and much more compelling" than ever, he is still unable himself "to tip the balance one way or the other," either to favor the northern or the late hypothesis (in a letter to the author, 30.8.2004). I also thank the editor of the present volume, A.C. Hagedorn, for his hard work on the manuscript of this essay in particular and for our many engaging conversations about Cant more generally.

1 The language of Cant has attracted a great deal of attention in the past, with many scholars recognizing its (potential) lateness (e.g., Graetz 1871: 40-91; Driver 1956: 448-49; Rudolph 1962: 110-12; Robert, Tournay, and Feuillet 1963: 22; Ginsberg 1969: 3-4; Givón 1977; Murphy 1990: 4-5), chief among them being M. Fox (1985: 186-90), whose basic conclusions are corroborated here.

2 The literature on LBH is now quite extensive. In addition to the still valuable insights by the nineteenth- and early twentieth-century scholars S.R. Driver (1956) and A. Kropat (1909), see the following representative examples of more recent contributions: Hurvitz 1972; 1973: 74-79; 1974: 24-56; 1982; 1997: 301-15; Givón 1974: 1-22; 1977: 181-254; Polzin 1976; Kutscher 1982; Rendsburg 1980: 65-80; Landes, 1982: *147-*70; Hill 1983: 77-89; Bergey 1984: 66-78; Gevirtz 1986: 25-29; Rooker 1990; Seow 1996: 643-66; Ehrensvärd 1997: 29-40; Dobbs-Allsopp 1998: 1-36; Eskhult 2000: 84-93.

3 The guidelines for determining what counts as a late feature are threefold: 1) the element appears exclusively or predominantly in biblical compositions of a securely established late date; 2) it contrasts with alternate forms and/or expressions known from SBH (and other early sources); and 3) it is prevalent and alive in late sources outside of the Bible. For details and elaboration, see Hurvitz 1973: 74-77; 1982: 7-10; 1995: 1-6; Polzin 1976: 1-25; Rooker 1990: 1-21, 55-64; Ehrensvärd 1997: 29-40; Dobbs-Allsopp 1998: 12-13. In most cases, especially where the feature under discussion has been treated previously, a feature's distribution in post-biblical sources is ascertained from the standard reference works. On those occasions, where previous discussions are judged to be deficient or

this essay falls into two main parts: one dedicated to identifying those features of Cant's orthography, grammar, syntax, and lexicon that are typologically late and another that takes up the issue of possible Aramaisms in Cant – one of the defining characteristics of LBH is the pronounced presence of Aramaic influence in various aspects of its grammar, syntax, and lexicon. A final brief section considers the possible existence of Persian and Greek loanwords in Cant as a means of fine-tuning our chronological evaluation of the language. I have tried to be thorough in my treatment of the relevant issues, though undoubtedly I will have missed something in the process. Still, the discussion as it currently stands is substantial and provides sufficient warrant for the thesis proffered, namely: that the language of Cant is unmistakably LBH.

1. Late Biblical Hebrew Features

1.1. Orthography

Orthography, like any other linguistic feature, is artifactual in nature and therefore susceptible to the processes of historical change and evolution. And these processes, in turn, are themselves susceptible to historical investigation, and, ultimately, to chronological mapping. Our current knowledge of Hebrew orthography remains very crude and we are still far from being able to accurately determine the date of composition based solely on the spelling practices reflected in specific texts – most troublesome, we still lack texts and manuscripts from the crucial period of ca. 600-300 B.C.E. and remain mostly ignorant of the basic motivations for the various spelling changes that can be observed, though scholars are generally more appreciative now of the variable spellings preserved in biblical manuscripts and aware that historical development *alone* cannot account for all of the variation in evidence.[4] Still, it is readily apparent that Hebrew spelling conventions did change over time, as shown early on by F.M. Cross and D.N. Freedman in their pioneering *Early Hebrew Orthography* (1952). And the basic trajectory of this change, as they argue – and as confirmed by all studies since, even those critical of Cross and Freedman more generally (see esp. Barr 1989: 199) – was for later texts to exhibit fuller spellings, i.e., more widespread use of *matres lectionis*.[5] Thus, we

where the identification of the late feature is original with me, I have made further recourse to the standard concordances and the original texts themselves. I use the term "Mishnaic Hebrew" (MH) according to custom, even though the source material is not always restricted to Tannaitic sources.

4 See esp. Andersen and Forbes 1986; Barr 1989.

5 That such a trajectory holds generally does not mean that in specific instances texts cannot deviate from the expected pattern. For example, the relative closeness of the orthography of the early Herodian manuscripts of Cant retrieved from Cave 4 at Qumran (4QCant[a-c]; see Tov 2000: 195-218) to that of MT, on the one hand, and the more conservative orthographies of 4QSam[b] from the third century B.C.E. and of Daniel

may at least make relative, if crude, chronological assessments of spelling practices in specific biblical compositions, and this is not an insignificant matter.

With respect to Cant, it may be observed (albeit very generally)[6] that the spelling conventions reflected in the received text (MT) are broadly consistent with that of later biblical compositions in general. In fact, more than sixty percent of the spellings in Cant are plene,[7] along with Esther, easily the highest percentage of plene spellings among biblical compositions. Consider, more specifically and as one example, the spelling *dwyd* (*dāwîd*) for "David" in 4:4. The spelling of the same name in SBH is normally (and very consistently) defective, *dwd*, while in LBH it is plene, *dwyd*.[8] The contrast becomes strikingly apparent when comparing the spellings in Samuel-Kings with those in Ezra, Nehemiah, and Chronicles.[9] Of the almost seven hundred times in which the name David occurs in Samuel-Kings, only on three occasions (1Reg 3:14; 11:4.36) does the plene spelling appear.[10] By contrast, in Ezra, Nehemiah, and Chronicles the name is always spelled plene – approximately 272 times! This trend continues into QH, where the plene spelling prevails, both in biblical and non-biblical texts.[11] Of the remaining eleven occurrences (minus our passage in Cant) of the spelling *dwyd* in the Hebrew Bible, seven are clearly late (Ezek 34:23, for which see Rooker 1990: 68-71; Zech 12:7, 8 [2x], 10, 12; 13:1) and one from a Psalm (122:5) that may be late.[12] The three occurrences from Hosea (3:5) and Amos (6:5; 9:11) are unexpected – Freedman (1983: 95) attributes these spellings to normalization toward the later orthography. Still,

---

from the second century B.C.E., on the other hand, are sufficient to show that the general chronological trajectory of Hebrew orthographic practices as broadly reflected in and discernable from the pre-exilic inscriptions, the biblical texts, and the DSS is not monolithic.

6 I have not undertaken the kind of detailed orthographic analysis called for by Barr (1989: 110-11, 212-15). Such an analysis can be expected to turn up other indisputably late spellings.

7 Andersen and Forbes 1986: 161.

8 Rooker 1990: 68-71.

9 Cf. Freedman 1983: 89-102; Andersen and Forbes 1986: 4-6; Barr 1989: 161.

10 Consonantal orthography of this kind is precisely what is expected in pre-exilic Hebrew, as judged by the epigraphic evidence, where the use of *matres lectionis*, though evident from the ninth through the sixth centuries (appearing first in final position and only later in word internal positions), is mostly sporadic and never systematic (for details see Cross and Freedman 1952; 1975: esp. 182; Zevit 1980). An indirect but contemporary witness to the consonantal (defective) spelling of David that prevails in SBH is provided now by the OA Tel Dan stele, where *bytdwd* "House of David" (l.9), is written defectively – and according to Lemaire (1994: 30-37) also in the ninth-century Mesha stele.

11 Kutscher 1974: 5, 79; Qimron 1986: 90; cf. Freedman 1983: 96-97; Rooker 1990: 69-70. Ben Sira, however, evidences only one example of the plene spelling of *dwyd* (49:4a); whereas the defective spelling (*dwd*) occurs seven times (45:25a ; 47:1b.2b.8c; 48:15f.22b; 51:12a).

12 For the possibility of dating Songs of Ascents (Pss 120-34) as a collection to the Persian period, see Knowles 2001.

that the use of the *mater* (i.e., the *yod*) in the spelling of the name David is a late orthographic feature is indisputable, and its presence in Cant is consistent with the plene character of Cant's spelling practices more generally, and both point to the language's relative lateness.

1.2. Grammar

a. *Independent pronouns*: The independent first person pronoun used exclusively throughout Cant is *ʾănî* "I" (1:5, 6; 2:1.5.16; 5:2.5.6.8; 6:3; 7:11; 8:10). Though this pronoun appears throughout BH, it dominates in LBH.[13] All of the books in which *ʾănî* is used exclusively (Haggai, Qohelet, Ezra, Esther) or almost exclusively (Malachi, Nehemiah, Chronicles, Daniel) are late.[14]

b. *Relative pronouns*: With the exception of 1:1 (*šîr haššîrîm ʾăšer lišlōmōh*), which has long been suspected of being an editorial addition,[15] *še-* is used exclusively as the relative particle in Cant (1:6 [3x].7.12; 2:7.17; 3:1.2.3.4 [4x].5.7.11; 4:1.2 [2x].6; 5:2.8.9; 6:5 [2x].6 [2x]; 8:4.8.12). Cant's thirty-two occurrences of *še-* is the second highest concentration of the particle in the Hebrew Bible, with only Qohelet tallying more instances (sixty-eight). Of the 136 occurrences of the particle in the Hebrew Bible, fully ninety-eight (not counting those in Cant) appear in passages that are probably exilic or postexilic.[16] It is this frequency and the exclusivity of usage that signify lateness.[17] Though perhaps a feature of northern Hebrew from early on,[18] there is simply no positive empirical evidence, biblical or otherwise, that prior to the exilic and postexilic periods *še-* was anything other than a rarely used dialectical variant of *ʾăšer*.[19] Even in the Gideon cycle, the (putative) northern source exhibiting the most concentrated use of *še-*, with three occurrences (Judg 6:17; 7:12; 8:26), *ʾăšer* overwhelmingly dominates as the relative particle of choice (with some forty-one occurrences). The hypothesis that *še-* formed

13 Fox 1985: 188; cf. Dobbs-Allsopp 1998: 14 and n. 67 with previous literature.

14 Cf. Kutscher 1982: 30; Seow 1996: 661.

15 E.g., Pope 1977: 295, Fox 1985: 9, Murphy 1990: 120. Presumably, the intention is to attribute authorship to Solomon, as in the Psalms (cf. Murphy 1990: 119), though this attribution need not be significantly later than the sequence itself – *ʾăšer* is also common in other post-classical Hebrew dialects, such as Ben Sira (e.g., 8.9; 10.9; 13.2; 18.32; 34.16) and QH (Qimron 1986: 82). Moreover, *ʾăšer* may well have been chosen more specifically for sonic considerations, i.e., the sequential chiming of *shins* and *reshes* that pervades the line with *ʾăšer* would be greatly diminished were *še-* used instead (**šîr haššîrîm šellišlōmōh*).

16 Seow 1996: 660-61.

17 Fox 1985: 188.

18 Jud 5:7 [2x]; cf. Seow 1996: 660-61.

19 *Contra* Pope 1977: 33; Rendsburg 2002: 103-4; also see the discussion of "mirage" forms in Kutscher 1982: 38-39.

part of the spoken vernacular in northern Israel[20] – as distinct from the literary language of the Bible – remains purely conjectural at this time.

c. *Prepositions*: In LBH,[21] QH,[22] and MH[23] the preposition *ʾēl* "to" becomes increasingly less common, as both *ʿal* and *lĕ-* encroach on its semantic domain, possibly as a result of Aramaic influence.[24] *ʾēl* is used properly in Cant on seven occasions (2:4; 3:4 [2x]; 4:6 [2x]; 6:11; 8:2). In addition there are several places where one might have anticipated the use of *ʾēl* but instead Cant has either *lĕ-* or *ʿal*, perhaps evidencing the decline of *ʾēl* so characteristic of post-classical Hebrew. The phrase *bwʾ* (Qal) *ʾēl* is ubiquitous in BH (also Lachish 3.obv.11, rev.3-4), but Cant has *yābōʾ dôdî lĕgannô* (4:16) and *bāʾtî lĕgannî* (5:1). This latter phrase (*bwʾ* [Qal] *l-*), in contrast, is much less common, occurring most prominently in LBH (e.g., Job 3:25; Esth 6:4; Ezra 2:68; Neh 13:7; 1Chr 24:19; 2Chr 29:17; 30:1; 31:16; cf. *DJD* ii 46.7) and in later dialects, such as QH.[25] In MH *bwʾ l-* becomes very common (as registered abundantly in the concordances). Note further that *ʾēl* alternates freely with *lĕ-* and *ʿal* in this idiom in the biblical DSS:

Ps 101:2 *tābôʾ ʾēlāy* = 11Q5 A,B,C i.2 *tbwʾ ly*
2Reg 8:1 *bāʾ ʾel-hāʾāreṣ* = 6Q4 xv.4 *bʾ ʿl hʾrṣ*
Ex 18:23 *ʿal-mĕqōmô yābōʾ* = 4Q22 xix.5 *ʾl mqw[mw ybwʾ]*
Is 59:20 *ûbāʾ lĕṣiyyôn* = 1QIsa^{a} *wbʾ ʾl ṣywn*

The preposition *lĕ-* is used another twenty-four times with the basic sense of "to" or in phrases that alternate elsewhere with *ʾēl* (1:7.9; 2:9 [4x].10.17 [4x]; 5:8; 6:2; 7:8.10.13.14; 8:11.12.14 [4x]).

The phrase *wĕʿālay tĕšûqātô* (7:11) may evidence the same kind of encroachment, though with *ʿal* instead of *lĕ-*. In Gen 3:16 and 4:7 *tĕšûqâ* is construed with *ʾēl*, giving rise to the suggestion to emend the text in Cant (see *BHS*). However, the emendation is hardly justified given the extension of the use of *ʿal* in LBH. In QH while *tšwqh* continues to be paired with *ʾl* (e.g., 1QM 13.12; 15.10; 4Q416f2 iv.3; 6Q18f2.4), it is also paired with *l-* (e.g., 1QS 11.22; 1QM 17.4).

d. *2/3fp > 2/3mp*: Already in LBH one sees the initial stages of erosion (leveling) of second and third person feminine plural forms in certain morphological categories. Though A. Hurvitz doubts that such gender

20 E.g., Kutscher 1982: 32. Though it should be noted that Kutscher's conjecture here does not keep him from also appreciating the late distribution of *še-* as well.
21 Rooker 1990: 127-31; Sáenz-Badillos 1995: 117.
22 Qimron 1986: 88.
23 Pérez Fernández 1999: 163.
24 See Rooker 1990: 129; Muraoka 2000: 204.
25 See Qimron 1986: 88.

inconsistencies are *always necessarily* chronologically significant in BH (1982: 168-69; admittedly, in regard to the suffixes, which Hurvitz is specifically commenting on, there are a significant number of places in SBH where masculine forms are used instead of the expected feminine forms, see GKC §135o), there is no doubt that the basic drift from LBH through QH and into MH is for the progressive leveling of the gender distinction in second and third person forms, with the attendant loss of the feminine forms. Cant itself evidences a number of cases where masculine plural forms are used instead of their expected feminine counterparts.

i. Pronouns: *hēm* and *hēmmâ* "them" (3mp) are used with feminine antecedents in 6:5 (*ʿênayik*) and 6:9 (*mĕlākôt*) – *hēnnâ* is not used.

ii. Suffixes: There are no occurrences of either the third or second person feminine plural suffixes (*-hen/-ken*) in Cant – though, except for those places where the "daughters of Jerusalem" are addressed, there is not much call for such forms in these poems. Still, in those cases where such forms are to be expected their masculine counterparts are used:

ʾetkem in the fourfold repetition of the phrase *hišbaʿtî ʾetkem bĕnôt yĕrûšālaim* (2:7; 3:5; 5:8; 8:4) where there is no question about the feminine plural antecedent.[26]

ʾăṭannĕpēm (5:3) in which the antecedent is the grammatically feminine *raglay*. The evidence for the progressive loss of third person feminine plural suffixes in LBH is quite compelling.[27]

More ambiguous are the 3mp suffixes in the twice-repeated simile in which the woman's teeth are compared to a flock of ewes (*šekkullām, bāhem*; 4:2; 6:6). While the metaphorical antecedent here would appear to be clear – the ewes, the nature of the grammatical concord in evidence is more confusing. The term for "flock," *ʿēder*, is grammatically masculine, the defining adjective (*qbṣ*) is feminine in 4:2 and masculine in 6:6, and the common plural *ʿālû* (perhaps construing *ʿēder* as a collective?) further confuses the issue. Still, on the positive side, *šakkūlâ* would appear to imply that the antecedent of *bāhem* is feminine.

iii. Imperfects (prefix conjugation): Already in LBH[28] the archaic second and third person feminine plural forms (*tiqṭōlnâ*) are in decline. At Qumran only three such forms are attested (according to Qimron 1986: 45). In MH the process continues (Pérez Fernández 1999: 106, 122). These forms are replaced by their masculine counterpart. Only one such form appears in Cant, *tiṭṭōpnâ* (3fp, 4:11), otherwise second person masculine plural imperfect forms are used

26 Cf. Bloch and Bloch 1995: 152.

27 See Kropat 1909: 61-62; Polzin 1976: 52-54; Rooker 1990: 78-81; Seow 1996: 662-63; Dobbs-Allsopp 1998: 20-21.

28 E.g., Jer 49:11; Jl 2:22; Esth 1:20; 2Chr 6:40; cf. JM §44d; §150a.c; Kutscher 1982: 41-42.

with feminine antecedents (all the "daughters of Jerusalem"): *ʾal-tirʾûnî* (1:6; 3:5.15), *ʾim-tāʿîrû wĕʾim-tĕʿôrĕrû* (2:7; 3:5), *ʾim-timṣĕʾû* (5:8), *mah-taggîdû* (5:8), and *mah-tāʿîrû ûmah-tĕʿôrĕrû* (8:4). Another possibility is *mah-teḥĕzû* in 7:1, but here the antecedent is not obvious.

iv. *wayyiqtols*: In 6:9, *wayyĕʾaššĕrûhā* "and they (mp) called her happy" and *wayhallûhā* "and they (mp) praised her" both have feminine antecedents, *bānôt* "daughters" with the former and *mĕlākôt ûpîlagšîm* "queens and concubines" with the latter. This is consistent with the trend observed with respect to the prefix conjugation above – historically the so-called *wayyiqtol* form is to be explained as a frozen form of the short prefix form, which (originally) grammaticalized perfectivity (see WOC §33.1.2).

v. Imperatives: Two feminine plural imperatives clearly appear in 3:11: *ṣĕʾeynâ ûrĕʾeynâ*. This raises the possibility that *sammĕkûnî* and *rappĕdûnî* in 2:5, which R. MURPHY (1990: 132) and Fox (1985: 109) construe as addressing the "daughters of Jerusalem" mentioned explicitly in 2:7, might evidence the very beginning of the erosion of the use of feminine plural imperatives that becomes typical of MH.[29]

In sum, the erosion of the gender distinction in second and third person plural morphs in Cant is consonant with the supposition of linguistic lateness, especially insofar as it has penetrated several different paradigms and in light of Cant's many other late linguistic features.

e. *Preference for plural forms of words*: LBH shows a tendency to pluralize nouns that are otherwise routinely used in the singular in SBH.[30] As R. POLZIN notes, this tendency is especially manifest in phrases involving the construct state where both the *nomen regens* and *nomen rectum* are pluralized, as with *qōrôt bāttênû* "beams of our houses" in Cant 1:17.[31] Similarly obvious is the use of the feminine plural *śiptôt* "lips" (4:3.11; 5:13) instead of the far more common dual form. The former occurs elsewhere in BH only in late texts.[32] It occurs as well in Ben Sira (*šptwty*, 51:22a), at Qumran (*spwt*, 1QM 5.12), and in MH.[33] In Aramaic, the feminine plural form turns up in Ahiqar (*TAD* C1.1.132) and later in Syriac (*sepwātāʾ*).

A final example in Cant of the late language's preference for the plural may be encountered in the threefold use of *mĕgādîm* (4:13.16; 7:14). With only a total of possibly twelve occurrences of the root *mgd* in BH, one can hardly speak of routine usage. Still, the distribution is tantalizing. The singular *meged* only occurs in Deuteronomy 33 (vv. 13.14 [2x].15.16), otherwise it appears in

29 Pérez Fernández 1999: 151.
30 Hurvitz 1972: 37-38; Polzin 1976: 42-43; Rendsburg 1980: 67; Rooker 1990: 75-77; Dobbs-Allsopp 1998: 14-16.
31 Fox 1985: 188; cf. Kutscher 1982: 82; Qimron 1986: 74-75; Pérez Fernández 1999: 70.
32 Is 59:3; Ps 45:3; 59:8; Qoh 10:12; cf. Seow 1997: 319.
33 E.g., *y.Ber.* 4b; *y.Sanh.* 25b; *m.Kelim* 4:4; cf. Segal 1927: 132.

the plural, either as *mĕgādîm*, as in Cant, or *migdānôt* (Gen 24:53; Ezra 1:6; 2Chr 21:3; 32:23). The presence of the Genesis passage makes Polzin hesitate to characterize the lexeme as late (1976: 141) – and indeed the limited attestation of the root is sufficient to warrant hesitation. But if the lexeme itself is not characteristically late, the preference for the pluralized form may well be. The lexeme is also only used in the plural in MH and in the Aramaic of the targums (Jastrow, I, 726).[34]

f. *Plurals of qvtl nouns in geminate roots*: The standard plural of the *qvtl* pattern with geminate roots in BH is *qvllîm* in the absolute and *qvllê* in the construct (cf. Fox 2003: 136, 147, 153). However, there are (roughly) several dozen exceptions in which the plural is formed on analogy with the strong root and provided with the typical infixed-*a* plural of *qvtl* nouns:

ʿam "people" => *ʿammîm* (1Reg 22:28, etc.), *ʿammê* (Deut 28:10, etc.)
ʿămāmeykā (Judg 5:14)
ʿămāmîm (Neh 9:22)
ʿamĕmê (Neh 9:24)
har "mountain" => *hārîm* (1Reg 19:11, etc.), *hārê* (Amos 3:9, etc.)
harărê (Num 23:7; Deut 33:15)
harĕrê (Hab 3:6; Ps 36:7; 50:10; 76:5; 87:1; 133:3; Cant 4:8 [the standard forms *hārîm* (2:8) and *hārê* (2:17; 8:14) appear as well])[35]
harăreyhā (Deut 8:9)
ḥēṣ "arrow" => *ḥiṣṣîm* (2Sam 22:15, etc.), *ḥiṣṣê* (Ezek 5:16, etc.)
ḥăṣāṣeykā (Ps 77:18)
ḥōq "statute" => *ḥuqqîm* (Deut 4:5, etc.), *ḥuqqê* (Ex 18:16, etc.)
ḥiqĕqê (Is 10:1)[36]
lēb "heart" => *libbôt* (Ps 7:10, etc.)
lĕbābôt (1Chr 28:9)[37]
ṣēl "shadow" => cf. Ug. *ẓlm*
ṣĕlālîm (Cant 2:17; 4:6)

---

34 And possibly at least once in QH (PAM43691 f53.1), but the text is broken (*mgdn*[*wt*]).

35 Apparently the reanalyzed form of the construct plural even starts to infiltrate the presuffixal form of the singular, *harĕrî* (Ps 30:8) and *harărām* (Gen 14:6; cf. BL §72t). *hărārî* in Jer 13:3, on the other hand, could be formed on analogy with the presuffixal forms of the *qatal* or *qital* patterns, though these patterns frequently form biforms with *qatl* nouns in Hebrew and other Semitic languages (see Fox 2003: 109).

36 Whether the form should be repointed as *ḥuqĕqê* (see 1QIsa[a] *ḥwqqy*), and if not how one should explain the form as written (cf. JM §96Ap; GKC §93bb; note also that in Semitic there is frequent alternation between *qitl* and *qutl* patterns, see Fox 2003: 108), is not entirely clear. Nonetheless, the understanding of the lexeme as denoting "statutes" is generally accepted (cf, NRSV; Wildberger 1991: 193).

37 The form is usually associated with the biform *lēbāb* (so *HALOT* 2, 516), however, again, this is not formally necessary (especially in light of *libĕbêhen* in Nah 2:8). Fox's explanation of *lēbāb* as a backformation from the reanalyzed -*a*- infixed plural *lĕbābôt*, as he notes, "a common analogy for noun patterns from geminate roots" (2003: 215-16; cf. 80, n. 43), is linguistically very plausible. Note that *lbb* is attested in both epigraphic Hebrew (*KAjr* 20:3), OA (*KAI* 223B.5; 224.15, 16), and Deir ʿAlla (ii.12, 14).

ṣilălê (Jer 6:4)[38]
tōk "oppression"
tĕkākîm (Prov 29:13)
ḥiqĕqê "searchings of" (so *NRSV*; Jud 5:15)[39]
Ar. *jillat* "dung" => cf. JA *gallayyā'*, *gallê* (Jastrow I, 243)
gelĕlê (Ezek 4:12, 15)[40]

Two observations may be made about these reanalyzed plurals. One, they clearly represent a secondary development in Hebrew.[41] That is, the normal form of the plural for *qvtl* nouns from geminate roots in BH (i.e., *qvllîm*/*qvllê*) is the older, original form. So in Akkadian case endings and the plural morphemes are added directly to the geminate base (*pass-*, *piss-*, *puss-*; cf *GAG* §§54l, 61e-i), and this remains the standard pattern in NWS more generally (e.g., there is no evidence for these reanalyzed plurals in Ugaritic), including Aramaic.[42] And two, while the reanalysis could have occurred at any point in

38 The form is extended further as the presuffixal form of the singular in Job 40:22 (*ṣilălô*; cf. BL §72t).

39 The precise sense intended here is unclear.

40 This form has influenced the shape of the presuffixal form in the singular, *gelălô* (Job 20:7; cf. BL §72t). The plural form *gĕlālîm* (Zeph 1:17) is usually associated with *gālāl* (1Reg 14:10; so *HALOT* I, 194), though this is not (formally) obvious nor necessary. One should note that there is mixture between *qatl* and *qatal* forms in Hebrew (Fox 2003: 109; and also in Arabic, as with *jalal*).

41 So rightly BL §72t.

42 The consonantal orthography in OA reveals the *qvtl* nouns from geminate roots were pluralized according to the common Semitic pattern, viz. *qvll* + plural morpheme: *mln* (*KAI* 224.2), *mly* (*KAI* 222B.8), and *mly'* (*KAI* 224.2) from **mlt'* "word"; *'my'* (*KAI* 224.10) from *'m* "people" (*KAI* 222B.5); *ḥṣy'* (*KAI* 222A.38) from **ḥṣ* "arrow" (if from ḥ-ṣ-ṣ and not the biform ḥ-ṣ-y); *ḥyn* (*KAI* 225.10) from *ḥy* "life" (*TAD* A2.5.9); and *ḥṭn* (*TAD* B4.1.2) from **ḥṭ* "wheat." The first evidence for the reanalyzed *a*-infixed plurals (so correctly Beyer 1984: 129; Leander §52b; cf. Segert §5.3.3.5) comes only with OffA: *dššy'* (*TAD* A4.7.11) and *dššn* (*TAD* B3.11.3) from *dš* "door" (*TAD* B3.10.13) as opposed to *dšyhm* (*TAD* A4.7.10); *kddn* (*TAD* D7.57.7) from *kd'* "pitcher" (*TAD* A4.2.13); *šqqn* "sacks" (*TAD* A4.7.15, 20), and *šṭṭn* (*TAD* A3.8.8, cf. Leander §52l). However, the common Semitic pattern persists in the period as well, and indeed is still dominant, e.g., *mlyn* (*TAD* A4.2.9), *mly'* (*TAD* A4.7.29), *ḥṭn* (*TAD* B4.1.2) and *kndn* (*TAD* C3.7 sr2: 8.; the nasalization is in substitution for gemination [Rosenthal 1995: 20-21], and thus likely does not represent the presence of the *a*-infix), *kpn* (*TAD* B2.6.16) (see Leander §52l-o). Muraoka and Porten (1998: 38-39) seem to think that these latter forms "indicate that the original [sic] short vowels between the two identical consonants had begun to be elided." Such an understanding cannot be ruled out. Unstressed short vowels in open syllables in Aramaic eventually reduce completely to zero (ca. 3rd c. at the earliest, cf. Kaufman 1984), and thus once an *a* is infixed it will eventually be reduced – so note writings like Syriac *'a(m)mîn* "peoples" with the *linea occultans* in which signs of both sound changes remain (the presence of the second *mem* indicative of the *a*-infix and the *linea occultans* evidencing the vowel reduction). Still, the OA and comparative evidence suggest that it is more likely that the spellings with a single consonant in OffA (but also likely in many cases in later dialects as well) reflect the earlier, original common Semitic pattern of forming plurals of *qvtl* nouns from geminate roots. The *a*-infixed plural becomes more numerous still in later dialects

the history of Hebrew (as the infixed-*a* in the plurals of *qvtl* nouns is a process that was generalized in NWS[43]), from the above examples it appears to have been operative during the earliest phases of the language, represented by the archaic poetry of Judges 5, Numbers 23, Deuteronomy 33, and Habakkuk 3, and during the latest phase, LBH (Jer 6:4; Ez 4:12, 15; Neh 9:22, 24; 1Chr 28:9; Prov 29:13; cf. Jer 13:3; Job 20:7; 40:22). These *a*-infixed plurals also appear frequently in the Psalms (36:7; 50:10; 76:5; 77:18; 87:1; 133:3; cf. 30:8), some of which are clearly late.[44] This pattern of reanalysis continues in MH as well.[45] Therefore, if *a*-infixing in plurals is not indisputably diagnostic of LBH, there is no denying that this form of reanalysis becomes (more) prominent in LBH and later dialects of Hebrew, though it never becomes standard. A general trend towards more prominence is to be observed diachronically in the Aramaic dialects as well.[46]

g. *Pual participle*: In MH the Pual binyan ceases to be productive, except with regard to the participle, which is used with an adjectival sense to describe a state or condition.[47] The Pual in MH is replaced by a reflexive stem, a common pattern of development seen throughout Semitic (e.g., in BH the Qal

---

(e.g., Beyer 1984: 129, 154), and in Syriac, as noted above, the infixed *a* is even eventually reduced to zero (Noldeke 2001: 61).

43 See Ginsberg 1970: 102; Huehnergard 1991: 284; Fox 2003: 215-16.

44 E.g., Ps 133:3, see Hurvitz 1972: 156-60.

45 Segal 1927: 126-28; Pérez Fernández 1999: 63.

46 G. Rendsburg (1990: 40-42) thinks that these "reduplicated plurals," as he calls them, are characteristic of "Israelian Hebrew," the northern dialect of Hebrew. On Rendsburg's analysis, both LBH and MH share many linguistic features in common with Israelian Hebrew (2002: 20-21), and therefore that we should find northernisms in late texts is to be expected. However, the major problem with Rendsburg's entire project is one of control. While no one disputes the reality of dialectic variation in ancient Hebrew – differences in the treatment of the diphthongs **aw* and **ay* and in the theophoric element used in personal names clearly distinguishes a northern and southern dialect in epigraphic Hebrew – there is no obvious non-circular means of controlling for the identification of specifically northern linguistic features beyond what can be established from epigraphic finds. That is, though Rendsburg has attempted to model his methodology after that of Hurvitz (and others) for distinguishing LBH, what he lacks is obvious strands of BH materials that are indisputably from the north (cf. Fox 1985: 189). Moreover, Rendsburg is not always as careful in his philological analysis as he might be (cf. Seow 1993: 334-37). Here, for example, he ascribes *a*-infixing as the standard "method of forming the plural" in Aramaic for these kinds of nouns. This is, as shown above (n. 42), patently incorrect, but it is incorrect even according to Rendsburg's putative source, Segert (§5.3.3). The significance of this lapse lies in how Rendsburg uses a putative isogloss with Aramaic to bolster his contention that *a*-infixing is a northern linguistic trait: "In short, we have isolated a grammatical feature which links Aramaic to IH, and we can use the presence of *harĕrê* in Ps 36:7 as another point in favor of our argument concerning this chapter's northern provenance" (1990: 42). The outstanding characteristic of the distribution of *a*-infixing in Aramaic is not its northern environs but its relative lateness, appearing only from the OffA period (and there only sporadically) on!

47 Segal 1927: 61-64; Pérez Fernández 1999: 95.

Passive is replaced by the Niphal; cf. Aramaic more generally). Of the six times that the Pual is used in Cant,[48] five involve participles:

> "What is this (*mî zōʾt*) ... perfumed (*mĕquṭṭeret*) with myrrh and frankincense" (3:6)
> "All of them (*kullām*) ... trained (*mĕlummĕdê*) for war" (3:8)
> "Cylinders of gold adorned (*mĕmullāʾîm*) with jewels" (5:14)
> "Ivory covered (*mĕʿullepet*) with sapphires" (5:14)
> "Columns of alabaster set (*mĕyussādîm*) in golden sockets" (5:15)

Each of these is clearly adjectival in nature. Moreover, the distribution of each of these forms is characteristically late: in BH *qṭr* is used in the Pual only here in Cant, while it occurs more frequently in MH in the Pual, but also only as a participle (Jastrow, II, 1352); though appearing early in the Pual in Hos 10:11 and Is 29:13; *lmd* also occurs in the late texts Jer 31:18 and 1Chr 25:7, and again is common as a participle in MH (Jastrow, I, 712); *mlʾ* in the Pual only occurs elsewhere in Thr 4:2; *ʿlp* appears only in BH in Cant with the precise meaning "to be covered," though it is possibly used meaning "to be faint" in Is 51:20 and perhaps in several other late texts; it appears only in the Pual in MH (Jastrow, II, 1085); aside from two occurrences in 1Reg (6:37; 7:10), *ysd* appears in the Pual in late texts (Ez 41:8; Hag 2:18; Zech 8:9; Ezra 3:6) and again the Pual participle occurs in MH (Jastrow, I, 582). In sum, while it cannot be contended that the five occurrences of the Pual participle in Cant are diagnostic of LBH – after all the decay of the Pual in the finite paradigms can be observed taking place already in BH,[49] where the participle accounts for more than forty percent of the attested forms in the Pual in BH (WOC §25.1b) – their form, characteristic adjectival usage, and the distribution of these specific roots in the Pual in BH and MH are consistent with the thesis that the language of these poems is later rather than earlier.

h. *Absence of paragogic* nun: The paragogic *nun* is already very much in decline in BH,[50] but this becomes very pronounced in LBH.[51] Lamentations, Qohelet,

---

48 The only non-participial use of the Pual occurs in 8:8 (*bayyôm šeyyĕdubbar-bāh*) lit. "on the day about which it (marriage) will be spoken with you." The idiom refers to part of the marriage custom. In 1Sam 25:39 David "speaks with Abigail (*wayyĕdibbēr baʾăbîgayil*) that he might take her himself for a wife." Syntactically, the passive construction in evidence in Cant is of the incomplete type involving the impersonal use of the third-person form without an expressed subject (cf. WOC §23.2.2e). Admittedly, the usage with *dbr* seems strained, perhaps indicative of the artificial nature of the usage of the Pual during this period (note the use of *še-* here, another late indicator). Otherwise, one would have to understand the construction as involving the promotion of the prepositional object (i.e., *bāh*) as the subject of the passive verb. The latter would involve an incongruity with respect to person (masculine verb form, feminine [promoted] subject, perhaps reflecting the loss of the feminine forms in LBH?).

49 Segal 1927: 63, n. 2; Hurvitz 1982: 27-30, 35-39.

50 Hoftijzer 1985: 2.

51 Hoftijzer 1985: 43-44; WOC §31.7.1a.

Esther, Daniel, Ezra, and Nehemiah do not attest a single instance of the paragogic *nun*, while Chronicles has only two examples (2Chr 6:26; 7:19), both likely influenced by Kings.[52] The picture in QH, Ben Sira (30:19; 45:20; 51:24), and MH is very similar to that of LBH, all evidence only a spare use of paragogic *nun*.[53] The paragogic *nun* is completely absent from Cant, very much in line with the other late books of the Bible and with the trend in post-classical Hebrew more generally.

1.3. Syntax

a. *Syntax of the pronoun:*

i. Possessive *šel-*: The possessive *šel-*, which develops into a fully independent particle in MH,[54] is attested only in the Bible in Cant: *karmî šellî* (1:6; 8:12). The particle appears in Ben Sira as well (e.g., 13:5; 30:28; cf. *šlnḥwšt* in TS 6.1 at Qumran). The particle has precursors in the BH syntagma *'ăšer lĕ* + pronominal suffix (e.g., Gen 23:9; Ex 38:30; Deut 8:13; 1Reg 1:33) and in Aramaic *zyl-/dyl-* .[55]

ii. Reduced use of *'et* with pronominal suffixes: As Polzin notes (1976: 28-31), LBH evidences a radically reduced use of the *nota accusativi* (*'et*) with pronominal suffixes, preferring, instead, forms in which the direct object suffixes are attached directly to the verb itself.[56] In Cant, there are approximately fifty-nine instances of the pronominal suffix attached to the verb, while *'et* takes a suffix on only four occasions (the particle itself is used seventeen times) – each involving the same phrase, *hišba'tî 'etkem* (2:7; 3:5; 5:8; 8:4). Moreover, it is likely that the use of *'etkem* in these latter instances is to be explained by the comparative rarity of second person plural object suffixes attached to verbs.[57] There are only 136 attestations of such suffixes in all of BH, and the vast majority of these are attached either to infinitives or to participles – there are only a handful of exceptions involving finite verb forms (e.g., Deut 32:38; Is 35:4; 38:11; 51:2; 66:13; Ps 34:12; 118:26; Job 16:5). In contrast, *'et* plus a second person plural suffix occurs some 299 times in BH.[58]

---

52 Cf. Peursen 2004: 100.

53 Qimron 1986: 45; Pérez Fernández 1999: 106, 127; Muraoka 2000: 198-99; Peursen 2004: 100-1.

54 Segal 1927: 43-44; Kutscher 1982: 124; Pérez Fernández 1999: 30-31.

55 Cf. Wagner 1966: 110. There is no reason to deny the likelihood of Aramaic as a contributing influence on the development of this particle in post-classical Hebrew (as does Givón 1974: 20), the existence of an obvious internal Hebrew pathway notwithstanding. The similar Aramaic construction would have only stimulated the Hebrew development, especially in a bilingual environment of the kind that would have prevailed during the Persian period (see Greenfield and Naveh 1984).

56 Cf. Rendsburg 1980: 66; Rooker 1990: 86-87: Seow 1996: 662; Dobbs-Allsopp 1998: 21.

57 Polzin 1976: 29.

58 As noted above, the gender mismatch involving *'etkem* in Cant may itself be an indicator of late usage.

iii. Pronominal copula: The pronominal copula appears in 6:8 (*šiššîm hēmmâ mĕlākôt*) and 6:9 (*'aḥat hî' yônāt'*).[59] While this syntagma was not unknown in SBH (e.g., Gen 42:6; 1Reg 18:39; 2Sam 7:28), Muraoka is probably correct in thinking that it is mostly a late development[60] – witness the five times that it occurs in Qohelet (1:17; 2:23; 3:13; 4:8; 5:18), its persistence into MH,[61] and its very common usage in Syriac (where indeed it is no longer restricted to third person pronouns). The discord with regard to gender in 6:8 is further suggestive of the lateness of this one example, at least (see above).

b. *Syntax of the noun*: In Cant, the genitive relationship is expressed mostly by the construct chain. However, in one instance Cant uses a circumlocution involving *šel-* that becomes very common in MH:[62] *miṭṭātô šellišlōmōh* "couch of Solomon" (3:7). Two observations may be offered here. One, the use of the proleptic suffix in the phrase is a typically late element.[63] And two, as M. PÉREZ FERNÁNDEZ notes (1999: 32), since there is no clear motivation for using the *šel* construction instead of the construct chain, the former may have been affected by Aramaic practice.[64]

c. *Syntax of the verb*:

i. Narrative and sequential discourse: In post-classical Hebrew, the system for realizing narrative (and narrative-like) discourse undergoes significant change, change that impinges most substantively on the usage of the *wayyiqtol* forms. The narrative form *par excellence* in SBH, the *wayyiqtol*, experiences a gradual decline in LBH and QH,[65] leading to its eventual disappearance in

59 Fox (1985: 153) does not think that *hî'* is a copula here. Instead, he construes it as the subject of the clause, as in the two parallel clauses. While there is no question about the grammatical analysis of the latter two parallel clauses, the first is ambiguous – perhaps intentionally so. Driver (1892: §200), JM (§154j), and Muraoka (1985: 67.76), for example, advocate the copular analysis. It may be that both analyses are relevant. Initially, the phrase may be construed as a nominal clause with a pronominal copula, especially as it comes so quickly on the heals of the pronominal copula in 6:8, and then reanalyzed retrospectively in light of the two following clauses.

60 Muraoka 1985: 69; cf. Fox 1985: 188.

61 Pérez Fernández 1999: 19.

62 See Segal 1927: 43-44; Kutscher 1982: 130; Pérez Fernández 1999: 71.

63 See Polzin 1976: 38-39; cf. Rooker 1990: 91-93; but note the cautionary comments by Hurvitz 1982:338-39, esp. in regard to cited examples from Numbers.

64 Cf. Wagner 1966: 110.

65 Givón 1977: esp. 225-26; Kutscher 1982: 45, 99; Smith 1991: esp. 31, 35-65; Sáenz-Badillos 1993: 120, 144; Eskhult 2000: 84. I make use of T. Givón's early and perceptive insights, while recognizing that his data sometimes needs adjusting from the perspective of a Semitist. For example, he does not distinguish between the imperfect and the *wayyiqtol* forms, which skews his data, and his general analysis of LBH phenomena requires some adjustment and supplementation in light of his dependence on poetic (Lam, Cant) and Wisdom (Qoh) works as his chief corpora of LBH, though he himself is not unmindful of this (see 1977: 223). Still, many of his insights deserve wider appreciation by biblicists and Semitists (Smith 1991 is an exception here). So, for example, he clearly shows the decline of the *wayyiqtol* (his "IMPERFECT" with "CONTINUITY function") as the principal narrative form in Lam, Qoh, and Cant (and the corresponding shift in the use of

MH[66] – though the form is still used robustly in Ben Sira.[67] The *wayyiqtol* appears only twice in Cant, both in 6:9 (*wayyĕʾaššĕrûhā, wayhallûhā*). Surely part of the explanation for this dearth of *wayyiqtol* forms must be attributed to Cant's lyric medium, a medium in which narrative generally does not factor prominently. Still, it is likely that the form's marked scarcity attests as well to the lateness of Cant's language.[68] Note, for example, that, if the LBH prose works (e.g., Chronicles, Nehemiah, Esther) still boast a healthy use of the *wayyiqtol* (though significantly reduced in comparison to comparable SBH prose compositions, see Eskhult 2000: 84, n. 2, and with other compensations, see Smith 1991: 28),[69] LBH lyric compositions exhibit the same marked lack of the *wayyiqtol* as witnessed in Cant: the sixth-century (for the date, see Dobbs-Allsopp 1998) Lamentations contains twenty-nine examples of the *wayyiqtol*;[70] the late Psalms (103, 117, 119, 124, 125, 133, 144) studied by Hurvitz (1972) have only twelve examples – ten of which are found in Psalm 119 and the other two in Psalm 144; and there is only one *wayyiqtol* in the Persian period "Song of Ascents" (Ps 120:1; on the date, see Knowles 2001). By contrast note that Book 1 of the Psalms contains sixty-two examples of the *wayyiqtol* form and the so-called "Elohistic psalter" (Pss 42-83) contains 113 examples.[71] Thus, Cant's lack of *wayyiqtols* is not accidental or inconsequential.

Given Cant's obvious lyricism and unique subject matter, however, it is often difficult to make fully transparent (and thus telling) comparisons in the area of syntax. One specific example, nevertheless, can be brought forward to spotlight the absence of the *wayyiqtol* in Cant.

the perfect and participle, which begin to shoulder more of the narrative/continuity function). Givón's insights here hold for the LBH prose works as well (see esp. the figures cited in Eskhult 2000: 84, n. 2).

66 Segal 1927: 72; Pérez Fernández 1999: 107.

67 Peursen 2004: 142-54.

68 So Givón 1977: 231; Fox 1985: 188.

69 In other words, the decline of the *wayyiqtol* in LBH is unmistakable if subtle. Both M. Smith (1991: 31) and Eskhult (2000: 84), for example, show very clearly that the *wayyiqtol* persists as the primary narrative form in LBH. But its percentage of use is down *and* other forms, e.g., perfect and participle, enjoy increased usage (cf. Givón 1977). Smith's (1991: 28) description of Esther illustrates well the emerging profile of LBH narrative prose. The *wayyiqtol* continues in Esther as the basic narrative form, though its percentage of use is down (cf. Givón 1977: 220; Eskhult 2000: 84, n. 2), and, as significant, it is supplemented by the use of freestanding perfects, unconverted perfects (to a lesser degree), and even participles, which are innovatively used for sequential narrative as well. So the decline of the *wayyiqtol*; is only one aspect of a larger system wide transformation.

70 Cf. Hillers 1992: 67-68.

71 A similar distributional trend may be noted for prophetic poetry: the pre-exilic First Isaiah has almost twice as many occurrences of the *wayyiqtol* (162x) as that found in Second and Third Isaiah combined (84x).

Direct address in Cant is introduced through a quotative frame on only one occasion (2:10), and its form is very telling:

> *ʿānâ dôdî wĕʾāmar lî* lit. "my beloved answered and said to me" (2:10)

The multi-verb quotative frame consisting of *ʿnh* and *ʾmr* is common in BH,[72] and in the great majority of cases (less than ten counter examples!) the *wayyiqtol* is used:

> *wyʿn yṣḥq wyʾmr lʿśw* (Gen 27:37)
> *wyʿn lbn wyʾmr ʾl-yʿqb* (Gen 31:43)
> *wyʿn blʿm wyʾmr ʾl-ʿbdy blq* (Num 22:18)
> *wtʿnw wtʾmrw ʾly* (Deut 1:41)
> *wyʿn dwd wyʾmr ʾl-ʾḥymlk* (1Sam 26:6)
> *wyʿn hmlk wyʾmr ʾl-ʾyš hʾlhym* (1Reg 13:6)
> *wyʿn ʿmws wyʾmr ʾl-ʾmṣyh* (Am 7:14)
> *wyʿn ʾywb wyʾmr* (Job 6:1; etc.)

The only divergences from this pattern come in prescriptive, future oriented contexts, in which the unconverted imperfect is used once (Is 14:10) and the converted perfect five times (Deut 21:7; 25:9; 26:5; 27:14, 15). This is quite striking. Never (as far as I can tell) is this particular multi-verb quotative frame used in sequential narrative in any form other than the *wayyiqtol*. This suggests that the form of the quotative frame appearing in Cant (freestanding perfects) owes something to the transformation of the verbal system that begins to take place in LBH.[73]

In fact, as a corollary to the decline of the *wayyiqtol* in LBH, scholars have observed a corresponding increase in the prominence of discourse featuring perfects (freestanding and unconverted) and participles.[74] Cant, of course, with only two *wayyiqtols*, shows a dramatic increase in the use of these latter forms.[75] But this usage is especially noticeable in the small narrative-like runs that pepper Cant's discourse. The perfect, as Givón's statistics suggest (1977: 232), dominates in this environment, carrying the mainline of the discourse forward, e.g., 1:9 (*niḥărû ... śāmūnî ... nāṭārtî*), 5:1 (*bāʾtî ... ʾārîtî ... ʾākaltî ... šātîtî*), and especially 5:2-8 (*pāšaṭtî ... rāḥaṣtî ... šālaḥ ... hāmû ... qamtî ... nāṭĕgû ... pātaḥtî ... ḥāmaq ʿābār ... yāṣĕʾâ ... biqqaštîhû ... mĕṣāʾtîhû ... qĕrāʾtîw ... ʿānānî ... mĕṣāʾūnî ... hikkûnî pĕṣāʿûnî nāśĕʾû*). The perfects in the quotative frame in 2:10 (*ʿānâ ... ʾāmar*), then, are of a piece with this larger pattern of usage in

72 Approximately 135 instances; for many details, see Miller 1996: 319-31.
73 Cf. Kutscher 1982: 45.
74 E.g., Givón 1977: 225-33, esp. 233; Kutscher, 1982: 45; Smith 1991: 28-30; Eskhult 2000: 86-87.
75 Givón 1977: 231-33.

Cant.[76] And indeed the frame itself introduces the male lover's brilliant (sequential) description of the onset of spring, also cast in perfects (*ʿābār* ... *ḥālap hālak* ... *nirʾû* ... *higîaʿ* ... *nišmaʿ* ... *ḥānĕṭâ* ... *nātĕnû*, 2:11-13). By contrast, note the little run of narrative at the beginning of Isaiah's "Song of the Vineyard" (a play on love songs of the kind found in Cant), which features the *wayyiqtol*: *wayʿazzĕqēhû* ... *waysiqqĕlēhû* ... *wayyiṭṭāʿēhû* ... *wayyiben* ... *wayqaw* ... *wayyaʿaś* (Is 5:2).[77] The contrast may be set in even starker relief by quoting in context:

Is 5:1b-2a	Cant 8:11
kerem hāyâ lîdîdî	*kerem hāyâ lišlōmōh*
bĕqeren ben-šāmen	*bĕbaʿal ḥāmôn*
wayʿazzĕqēhû waysiqqĕlēhû	*nātan ʾet-hakkerem lannōṭĕrîm*
wayyiṭṭāʿēhû śōrēq	*ʾîš yābîʾ bĕpiryô ʾelep kāsep*
My beloved had a vineyard	Solomon had a vineyard
on a very fertile hill.	in Baal-hamon.
He dug it and cleared it (of stones)	He gave the vineyard to keepers;
and planted it with choice vines.	each would bring in a thousand pieces of silver for his fruit.

Even though the sequential run in Cant 8:11 is not as long as one might like, the contrast with the Isaianic version is still evident, especially in the first line of the second couplet where the use of a *wayyiqtol* form in Isaiah (*wayʿazzĕqēhû*) contrasts with Cant's freestanding perfect (*nātan*).

Cant also exhibits evidence of a similar, innovative use of the predicative participle in sequential narrative runs.[78] The outstanding example is the female lover's vibrant description in 2:8-9 of her beloved as he bounds and

76 As noted above, there are no other examples of this particular multi-verb quotative frame in forms other than the *wayyiqtol* in LBH. In fact, the frame itself declines noticeably in LBH, occurring only seven times in all of Esther, Hebrew-Daniel, Ezra, Nehemiah, and Chronicles (Esth 5:7; 7:3; Ezra 10:2, 12; 1Chr 12:18; 2Chr 29:31; 34:15), though it is still abundantly attested at Qumran. But even at Qumran there is only one clear example in the non-biblical texts of the quotative frame with *wayyiqtols* (4QapocrMoses C f22 ii.3); otherwise it is realized with converted perfects – reflecting the prescriptive, future oriented nature of these texts' genre and style (cf. Smith 1991: 59). Note especially the following parallel with the usage in Deuteronomy: *wʿnw hlwym wʾmrw ʾl-kl-ʾyš yśrʾl* ... *ʾrwr* ... (Deut 27:14-15) ... *wʿnw wʾmrw ʾrwr* ... (1QS 2.3). However, other quotative frames persist in LBH and like Cant 2:10 they are not infrequently cast in the perfect. For example, there are a number of instances of *ʾmr* used in the perfect and by itself (or with *lēʾmōr*) to introduce direct or indirect (the latter becoming more frequent in LBH, see Eskhult 2000: 86, 90 and n. 31; compare 2Sam 24:18 with 1Chr 21:18 – the Chronicler transforms the passage in his source to an indirect quote and he does so by using the perfect of *ʾmr*) discourse in ways consistent with the emerging narrative use of the perfect in LBH (e.g., Qoh 10:2; Esth 1:10; Ezra 8:22; Neh 4:16; 1Chr 15:2; 23:25; 28:3; 2Chr 8:11; 24:22; 26:23; 35:21).

77 Cf. Bendavid 1967-71, vol I: 75.

78 Cf. Smith 1991: 28; Eskhult 2000: 88.

leaps gazelle-like up to her window and gazes in. The participle is used exclusively in these couplets seven times over: *bā'* ... *mĕdallēg* ... *mĕqappēṣ* ... *dômeh* ... *'ômēd* ... *mašgîaḥ* ... *mēṣîṣ*. The effect here is to accentuate through the use of the participles the dynamic and durative quality of the male lover's actions. Even his "standing" is imagined dynamically! More commonly, the poet uses the predicative participle to effect local bursts of dynamism (e.g., 2:5.16; 3:6; 5:2.8; 6:3; 7:10; 8:5). But either way more than half of the thirty-six participles in Cant are used sententially.[79]

M. SMITH notices that this broad pattern of verbal usage (i.e., increased verbal variety employing freestanding and unconverted perfects and participles as main verbs), while new with LBH in its application to narrative prose (and other sequential strings of discourse), is otherwise characteristic of direct discourse in SBH.[80] Intriguingly, Smith wonders whether the idiosyncratic use of verb forms in Qohelet may be due in part to "the character of the book as pseudonymous direct discourse".[81] If so, one might suggest something similar for Cant, though realized in a more dialogic mode. While it is not clear why LBH should take up and generalize the pattern of verbal usage typical of SBH direct discourse, the broad similarities between the two are indeed striking and it is hard to resist the idea that the speech of direct discourse provided at least one of the internal Hebrew pathways by which the LBH verbal system evolved.[82] However, accepting this does not necessarily require us to dismiss the likelihood of Aramaic influence as a contributing factor in the diachronic transformation of the post-classical Hebrew verbal system, especially, as Smith notes,[83] given the Hebrew-Aramaic bilingualism that likely prevailed during the Persian period in Palestine (cf. Greenfield and Naveh 1984). Scholars have long suspected Aramaic as playing an influential role in shaping the pattern of verbal usage that develops in later Hebrew.[84] Interestingly, the closest parallels, formally and temporally, to the quotative frame in 2:10 are in fact not Hebrew but Aramaic. Note the following examples taken from various Aramaic sources:

(a) Targum Neophyti
Gen 31:43: *w'n' lbn w'mr ly'qb*
Num 22:18: *w'n' bl'm w'mr l'bdwy dblq*
Deut 1:41: *w'nytwn w'mrtwn ly*

(b) Peshitta
Gen 27:37: *'n' 'ysḥq w'mr l'sw*

79 Givón 1977: 232.
80 Smith 1991: 21-23, 28; cf. Niccacci 1990.
81 Smith 1991: 30.
82 Cf. Smith 1991: 31-32.
83 Smith 1991: 31-32.
84 E.g., GKC §112pp; Kutscher 1982: 75, 81.

Deut 1:41: *wʿnytwn wʾmrtwn ly*
1Reg 13,6: *wʿnʾ mlkʾ wʾmr lnbyʾ dʾlhʾ*

(c) Ahiqar (*TAD* C1.1)
ʿnyt wʾmrt lnbwsm[skn] (45)
ʿnh ḥmrʾ wʾmr lʾryʾ (94)
ʿnh nmrʾ wʾmr lʿnzʾ (166)
[*ʿnt*] *ʿnzʾ wʾmrt lnmrʾ* (166-67)
ʿnw ʾmryʾ wʾmrw lh (169)

(d) Daniel
ʿnh mlkʾ wʾmr lkśdyʾ (2:5; cf. 3:16)
ʿnh wʿmr lʾrywk (2:15; cf. 3:24)
ʿnh dnyʾl wʾmr (2:20; 7:2; cf. 2:8; 3:28; 4:16, 27; 5:10; 6:13)
ʿnh mlkʾ wʾmr ldnyʾl (2:26; 5:13; 6:17, 21)
ʿnw wʾmryn lnbwkdnṣr (3:9)
ʿnh nbkdnṣr wʾmr lhwn (3:14)
ʿnh wʾmr lhdbrwhy (3:24)
ʿnh mlkʾ wʾmr lḥkymy bbl (5:7)

Although, as E.Y. KUTSCHER in particular notes, "it is not easy to distinguish those characteristics that might have been the product of inner Hebrew development rather than of Aramaic influence,"[85] in light of the above parallels neither is it easy in this instance to dismiss the possibility of Aramaic interference (however mediated) on the phrasing of the quotative frame in Cant 2:10. This is made all the more likely by the abundant number of other likely Aramaisms that are to be found in Cant (see below). My own hunch is that the two forces, one internal (Hebrew direct discourse) and one external (typical Aramaic verbal syntax), played contributing roles in the shaping of the kind of verbal usage that developed in post-classical Hebrew – though I doubt that this can be proved in detail.

ii. Infinitive construct with prefixed *lĕ-*: Aside from the problematic *bĕdabbĕrô* (5:6), Cant only knows the infinitive construct with a prefixed *lĕ-*: *liptōaḥ* (5:5), *lirʿôt* (6:2), *lilqōṭ* (6:2), *lirʾôt* (6:11 [2x]), and *lĕkabbôt* (8:7). The infinitive construct, especially as a verbal complement, in QH[86] and MH[87] invariably appears with a prefixed *lĕ-*, the bare infinitive construct of SBH having (mostly) died out. This is the pattern that prevails in Ben Sira as well, with only one counter-example being attested,[88] and early on Polzin observed a similar preference in Chronicles.[89] The pattern of usage in Cant, then, is

85 Kutscher 1982: 81.
86 Kutscher 1974: 41; Qimron 1986: 47; Muraoka 2000: 194.
87 Segal 1927: 165-66; Fernández 1999: 144.
88 Peursen 2004: 255-56.
89 Polzin 1976: 60-61; cf. Eskhult 2000: 90-91.

consistent with the developmental trend in post-classical Hebrew more generally.

iii. Infinitive absolute: The gradual but consistent demise of the infinitive absolute in post-classical Hebrew is no doubt part and parcel of the larger collapse of the earlier SBH complex system of narrative and consecutive forms (see above). The basic trajectory is that of the infinitive absolute becoming rarer in LBH, Ben Sira, and QH and ultimately disappearing in MH.[90] The use of the cognate infinitive with a finite verb is a case in point. The construction is very common in SBH, but does not appear at all in Qohelet, Ezra, or Daniel, and is very rare in Esther, Nehemiah, and Chronicles.[91] But that the decline was gradual and not unequivocally linear in nature is now suggested by the survival of the cognate infinitive construction in Ben Sira[92] and at Qumran.[93] Cant again would appear to fit nicely within a post-classical milieu, evidencing only a single instance of the infinitive absolute but in the cognate infinitive construction: *bôz yābûzû* (8:7).

d. *Word Order*: T. GIVÓN (1977) has mapped the basic drift from VS to SV word order in BH, finding that Cant, in its pronounced preference for SV word order (especially in main clauses), stands at the far end of the diachronic continuum. He further concludes that this VS-to-SV shift was driven above all by the reconfiguration of the LBH system of narrative tenses described above (Givón 1977: 240). As the perfect and participle became more prominent in narrative and sequential discourse their associated word orders were taken over as well, and these were dominantly SV in nature. In SBH narrative the perfect shows up in main clauses most prominently in topic shift and topic contrast constructions, where there is an overwhelming preference for SV syntax.[94] The participle promotes a similar word order preference, albeit for different reasons. SV syntax with the participle falls out as a consequence of the form's lack of subject indexing, which (usually) necessitates the appearance of an explicit subject in a clause's surface structure, and the fronting of subjects due to their high topicality.[95] The sum effect in both cases is the same: a strong tendency to promote SV word order.[96]

---

90 E.g., Segal 1927: 165-66; Kutscher 1974: 41; Polzin 1976: 43-44; Hurvitz 1982: 121-23; Pérez Fernández 1999: 144; Eskhult 2000: 29; Peursen 2004: 277-83.

91 See Segal 1927: 166; Polzin 1976: 43.

92 Smith 2000: 261; Peursen 2004: 279-80.

93 Qimron 1992: 358-59; Smith 2000: 263.

94 Givón 1977: 192.238.

95 Givón 1977: 240.

96 The only cautionary note to be raised is in regard to the difficulty of tracking word order in verse. It is not always possible to know in verse – especially given Cant's brevity – when a particular word order is a consequence of naturalness and when it has been manipulated for some poetic effect – or even when naturalness leads to effect (or vice versa). D.R. HILLERS, noting "divergences from normal prose order" in Lamentations (1992: 21), offers a similar caution. He observes that in such cases the divergences frequently will result from rhythmic and other poetic considerations. Therefore, any

e. *še-Clauses*: As C.L. SEOW points out with respect to the use of *še-* in Qohelet,[97] it is the particle's "wide and varied use" that identifies it as late. The same may be said about the use of *še-* in Cant. In particular, it functions both as a relative particle and, more innovatively,[98] as a clausal conjunction. The following may be offered to exemplify the more innovative uses of *še-* in Cant. In 1:6 *še-* introduces object clauses ("look not *that* [*še-*] I am dark,/*that* [*še-*] the sun has gazed....") where SBH employed *'ăšer* (Deut 1:31; 1Sam 18:15; Jer 29:32) or, much more commonly, *kî* (Gen 1:1, 4; 16:4; Deut 32:39; Judg 6:22; 2Reg 3:2).[99] The idiom is characteristic of LBH (e.g., Qoh 2:13; 3:18; 5:4),[100] occurs in Ben Sira,[101] and becomes commonplace in MH.[102] In 5:2 ("open to me ... for [*še-*] my head is wet with dew") and 6:5 ("turn away your eyes ... for [*še-*] they make me tremble") *še-* is used to introduce a causal (or explicative) clause. This use is otherwise rare in BH, where *kî* is the more common conjunction (cf. 1:2; 2:5, 11, 14; 8:6). It is attested in Qohelet (e.g., Qoh 2:17; 8:17; cf. Givón 1974: 13) and Ben Sira[103] and very common in MH.[104] Finally, note that several of the temporal conjunctions are compounded with *še-* in ways very reminiscent of MH: *ʿad-šehammelek bimsibbô* "*as long as* the king is on his couch" (1:12; cf. *ʿd 'šr* in Sir 13:7[105]) and *kimʿaṭ šeʿābartî ... ʿad šemmāṣā'tî* "I had scarcely passed ... before I found" (3:4).[106] In sum, not only is the use of *še-* in Cant frequent and near exclusive, but it is varied and innovative as well – all likely indicators of lateness.

1.4. Lexicon

Vocabulary and phrasing often betray a work's general time of composition. However, the presence in Cant of a great many rare and unique words[107] severely limits (as a practical matter) our ability to sift Cant's lexicon for chronological signifiers (though see below for a discussion of late Aramaic loanwords). Still, a number of words have been identified as possible late lexemes. The most plausible of these are considered briefly here.

detailed word order analysis of Cant will need to attend routinely to the poetics of the verse.

97 Seow 1996: 661.
98 Cf. Givón 1974: 1-22.
99 Cf. GKC §157; Fox 1985: 102.
100 Cf. Givón 1974: 14, 16; Polzin 1976: 128; Rooker 1990: 111-112.
101 Peursen 2004: 301-2
102 Segal 1927: 205; Pérez Fernández 1999: 51.
103 Peursen 2004: 380-81
104 Segal 1927: 227; Pérez Fernández 1999: 223.
105 Pérez Fernández 1999: 51.205-6; Peursen 2004: 327.
106 See Fox 1985: 188; Sáenz-Badillos 1993: 123-24.
107 Esp. Driver 1956: 448-9.

dbb (7:10): A *hapax legomenon* in BH, but appears otherwise only in MH.[108]

zāhāb ... hakkesep (1:11): The sequence *zhb wksp* is typical of LBH, while the reverse prevails in SBH.[109] The phrase is broken up across parallel lines in two instances in Cant: in 1:11 (*zāhāb // hakkesep*) the LBH order is followed (cf. Is 40:19; 46:6; 60:17),[110] while 3:10 (*kesep // zāhāb*) is structured according to the SBH order (cf. Is 13:17; Ez 7:19; Job 28:1; Prov 27:21). That the poet uses both orders suggests s/he is writing at a time when the later order (*zhb wksp*) was known.

ḥēk (2:3; 5:16; 7:10): Distributionally, *ḥēk* "palate, mouth" appears only in late texts in the Bible (Ez 3:26; Ps 119:103; 137:6; Job 6:30; 12:11; 20:13; 29:10; 31:30; 32:2; 34:3; Prov 5:3; 8:7; 24:13; Thr 4:4), with but one exception, the difficult Hos 8:1. Its exclusive use in prophetic, poetic and Wisdom writings – appearing in Ben Sira (6:5; 36:24; 49:1) and Ahiqar (*TAD* C1.1.163) as well! – suggests that the word is a part of the elevated diction that typifies these genres.[111] In later Hebrew dialects, *ḥēk* appears in Ben Sira, QH (1QH 5.31; 4QHa 13.31; 4Q429.f3.4), and MH (e.g., Cant. R. to 5:16; *Ketub.* 111b; *y. Sanh.* 30a; cf. Jastrow I, 455). The lexeme's attestation in the various cognate languages is late as well (e.g., no earlier than OffA (*ḥnk*) in Aramaic; for other possible etymons, see *HALOT*, 1, 313).

ketem pāz (5:11): Fox well describes the phrase as consisting of names for two kinds of gold "joined in a bound structure for poetic hyperbole" (1985: 147). The TgCant glosses the whole as *dhb ṭb*, its own way of rendering the hyperbole, "fine gold." *ketem* is a late lexeme (Is 13:12; Dan 10:5; Ps 45:10; Prov 25:12; Job 28:16.19; 31:24; Thr 4:1; cf. Dobbs-Allsopp 1998: 14).[112] Similarly, *pāz* appears prominently in late contexts (Is 13:12; Ps 19:11; 21:4; 119:27; Prov 8:19; Job 28:17; Thr 4:2; Sir 30:15; 35:6; also see *ketem ʾûpāz* in Dan 10:5).[113]

---

108 Fox 1985: 163; cf. Jastrow, I, 276.

109 Rooker 1990: 174-75; cf. Hurvitz 1969: 248-51.

110 The use of the definite article here is curious. With only one notable exception (*gěbîaʿ hakkesep* in Gen 44:2), the phrasing with the definite article (where *kesep* has its material connotation) appears only in late texts (Qoh 12:6; 1Chr 28:15, 16, 17). In particular, compare *kělê hakkesep* in 1Chr 28:14 with *kělê kesep* everywhere else (Gen 24:53; Ex 3:22; 11:2; 2Sam 8: 10; 1Reg 10:25; 2Reg 12:14; Ezra 1:6; 8:26; 1Chr 18: 10; 2Chr 9:24; 24:14). Perhaps the phrasing with the definite article reflects the influence of the Aramaic use of *kesep* in the determined state?

111 Thus, it is not likely that *ḥēk* replaces some earlier lexeme. Rather, it simply becomes (assuming the genuineness of Hos 8:1) a part of the high style in LBH.

112 On the possibility of seeing *ketem* as an Akkadian loanword (originally derived from Sumerian and likely transmitted through Egyptian), see Mankowski 2000: 76-77.

113 Whether or not the *hapax mûpāz* in 1Reg 10:18 is ultimately related to *pāz* is an open question (Cogan 2000: 318). The Chronicler renders *zāhāb mûpāz* as *zāhāb ṭāhôr* (2Chr 9:17; cf. LXX and Tg as well).

mēsab (1:12): Also with this sense in MH,[114] perhaps in place of *miškāb* (cf. *miškāb dōdîm*, Ez 23:17) or *miṭṭâ* (cf. Ez 23:41; Am 6:4), though it is difficult to find precise parallels.

ṣammâ (4:1, 3; 6:7): Outside of Cant, the term only appears in Is 47:2. The related (?) verbal root *ṣmṣm* appears in MH and JPA.

sammĕkûnî (2:5): The use of the Piel here may reflect the broader shift from Qal to Piel that occurs with some verbs in post-classical Hebrew,[115] though the Qal is still used in MH (e.g., *y. Qidd.* 61a; 64a; *y. Maʿaś.* 3a; *m. B. Bat.* 1:4; cf. Jastrow II, 1001).

ʿāsîs (8:2): A late lexeme, known outside of the Hebrew Bible only from MH and TA (Jastrow, II, 1097-98). In the Bible it is otherwise attested only in late prophetic texts (Is 49:26; Joel 1:5; 4:18; cf, Am 9:13).

qĕwuṣṣôt (5:2.11): Fox (1985: 187) suggests that *qĕwuṣṣôt* in 5:2 and 11 is a late counterpart of *maḥlĕpôt* in Jud 16:13 and 19. The two lexemes are too rare (only occurring in the passages cited) to establish this with certainty. Still, in favor of Fox's contention are the distribution of cognates or related lexemes in various of the Semitic languages – *mḫlpt* appears early in Ugaritic (*CTU* 1.19.II.33), while lexemes derived from the roots *qwṣ*/*qṣṣ* appear in later languages (MH: *qĕwûṣṣôt, qawwaṣ* "to curl," *qiwwēṣ* "one with curled hair" [Jastrow]; Syr *qawṣtāʾ*/*qûṣtāʾ*, pl. *qawṣātāʾ* "curl, ringlet"; Ar *quṣṣat* "bangs")[116] – and perhaps the consonantal articulation of the *waw*, which becomes more prevalent in MH (Segal 1927: 34).[117]

raʿyâ (1:9.15; 2:2.10.13; 4:1.7; 5:2; 6:4): The man's favorite pet name for his beloved (*raʿyâ*) is only used elsewhere at Qumran.[118]

rāṣûp (3:10): Possibly a late lexeme. As a verb it is only used here in BH. The related noun, *riṣpâ* "pavement," is clearly a late lexeme, appearing in late texts only (Ezek 40:17 [2x].18 [2x]; 42:3; Est 1:6; 2Chr 7:3) and in contrast with SBH lexemes (*qarqāʿ*, *marṣepet*[119]). There may be an early Akkadian reflex of this verb at Ugarit (Ugaritica 7 pl. RS 34.135:16), otherwise the cognate evidence (Aramaic and Arabic) is all late. The verb occurs in MH (e.g., *m. ʾOhal.*18:5; *m. Neg.* 11:9). Of particular interest is its use in Esth. R., where it is commenting on the use of *riṣpâ* in Esth 1:6: "his house was paved (*hyh bytw rṣwp*) with precious stones and jewels" (Jastrow, II, 1495).

---

114 Jastrow, II, 803; Fox 1985: 187.

115 Fox 1985: 108; Hurvitz 1982: 48-52; Rooker 1990: 153-55; Dobbs-Allsopp 1998: 19.

116 The BH term itself is derived from the root *qwṣ* in the *qutull* pattern (*qĕwuṣṣôt* < **quwuṣṣāt*; cf. Fox 2003: 281-86).

117 Driver (1956: 448) includes the word in hist list of Aramaisms in Cant.

118 Qimron 1986: 95.

119 See Hurvitz 1982: 135-38; cf. Polzin 1976: 150; Bergey 1983: 96; Rooker 1990: 162-63.

šēš (5:15): This is an Egyptian loanword[120] that appears to get borrowed into Semitic quite late, appearing in only late biblical texts (Esth 1:6; 1Chr 29:2 [*šayiš*]) and in Aramaic dialects from the Persian period (OffA *šyš*) and later (e.g., Palm *šyšʾ*; Syr *šîšāʾ*). *šayiš* also appears in MH (e.g., *m. Šeqal.* 6:4; *m. Tamid* 3:5; *m. Kelim* 22:1; cf. Jastrow, II,1569).

tîmărôt ʿāšān (3:6): The phrase occurs also in Jl 3:3 and may well be the LBH counterpart of SBH *ʿămûd ʿāšān* (Jud 20:40). However, the formal obscurity of *tîmărôt* complicates any analysis,[121] though the lexeme is taken up in MH (*Ber.* 43a; cf. Jastrow, II, 1679).

In sum, the evidence of late (non-Aramaic) linguistic features in Cant is considerable and manifest at every level of the language. Many of the items discussed are diagnostically late (e.g., *dwyd, ʾănî, še-, qōrôt bāttênû*, possessive *šel-*, decline of narrative *wayyiqtol, ḥēq, ketem pāz, šēš*, etc.), while many others are characteristically late.

2. *Aramaisms*

A final characteristic of LBH to be investigated with regard to the language of Cant is the potential presence of Aramaisms. Hurvitz opens his now seminal article on the "Chronological Significance of 'Aramaisms' in Biblical Hebrew" with the following statement:

> The critical point of contact between Hebrew and Aramaic is to be found, as is commonly recognized, after the Babylonian exile in the sixth century B.C. From the post-exilic period onwards, one can readily detect in Hebrew numerous new expressions and linguistic innovations, many of which are due to direct or indirect Aramaic influence. These neologisms produced fundamental changes in the structure of Biblical Hebrew.[122]

Indeed, so fundamental are the changes that these lexical and grammatical Aramaisms simply become part and parcel of all later dialects of Hebrew and their designation as "Aramaisms," therefore, except when in regard to certain diachronic interests such as ours, is something of a misnomer. Their presence is a defining feature of post-classical Hebrew,[123] much in the same way as French words become a substantial (and defining) part of the English lexicon

120 E.g. *šś* "alabaster"; Erman and Grapow, 4, 540; cf. *HALOT*, 1163; Gerleman 1962: 177.

121 The putative pattern on which this form is based, **qītalat*, is not reconstructible for PS (Fox 2003: 287) and there are no other obvious reflexes of this pattern in BH.

122 Hurwitz 1968: 234; also now see Hurvitz 2003: 24-37.

123 Cf. Greenfield and Naveh 1984: 120.

after the Norman conquest of England in 1066 C.E.[124] Indeed, the linguistic consequences of the Norman conquest for English and the Babylonia exile (and ensuing Persian period) for Hebrew are broadly analogous. Still, one thing that Hurvitz was quick to point out in his 1968 study was "that evidence of Aramaic influence alone cannot serve as a decisive proof for arguing a late date for a given text" (134). Cognizant that Aramaic influence on Hebrew is in evidence from very early on,[125] Hurvitz identified a number of "conditions" under which "a text containing Aramaisms" may be "considered late":[126]

- the Aramaisms are not isolated and are not attested in early sources (Aramaic or Hebrew)
- they contrast with appropriate SBH features – though in lieu of evidence for such contrasts, other suitable linguistic considerations for lateness may be adduced
- they remain vital in later Hebrew and/or Aramaic dialects
- they are accompanied by a profusion of other LBH features – "it is the heavy concentration of Aramaisms – *as well as other late elements* – that characterizes Late Biblical Hebrew and distinguishes it from the classical Biblical Hebrew as we know it from pre-exilic compositions (prosaic and poetic alike)" (emphasis added)

The basic intent of Hurvitz's essay, sometimes misconstrued, is to scrutinize methodology and to insist on rigor (themes that run throughout all of his writings) as means for securing the identification of genuinely late Aramaisms. This is made clear in the essay's concluding sentence, in which Hurvitz states (quite plainly) that, appropriately evaluated, "Aramaisms in Biblical Hebrew *may be utilized as a criterion for lateness*".[127]

A number of features of possible Aramaic derivation have already been encountered (e.g., decrease in use of *ʾēl, šel-* genitive construction, *ʿnh ... wʾmr* quotative frame). In what follows I consider in earnest the evidence for Aramaisms in Cant. This evidence is substantial, consists of elements at every level of the language (grammar, syntax, lexicon), and includes many diagnostically late features (i.e., they satisfy Hurvitz's several conditions of lateness), all of which, considered cumulatively and in concert with Cant's

124 In fact, more than sixty percent of the Old English lexicon was lost as a result of the large borrowing of French words into English following the Norman conquest (see Trask 1996: 20).

125 Cf. Kutscher 1982: 71. However, the precise nature of this inflkuence (if it exists) is extremely difficult to deetermine since the earliest ("Old") Aramaic inscriptions exhibit so few of the features usually considered diagnsotic of Aramaic (see Huehnergard 1995: esp. 268-272).

126 Hurwitz 1968: 238-39.

127 Hurwitz 1968: 240; emphasis added. If anything the importnace of Official Aramaic – the Aramaic of the Persian Empire – "as a watershed period in the history of the language" (Huehnergard 1995: 273 n30) is clearer today than in 1968 when Hurwitz's article was published. Most of the Aramaisms in the Bible are, in fact, late – that is, they are not generally traceable to a period earlier than Official Aramaic.

other many late linguistic features just discussed, provides compelling testimony to the lateness of Cant's language.

2.1. Grammar

lĕkî (K) (2:13): The last couplet in 2:13 forms an inclusio with the last couplet in 2:10, and thus the opening line in 2:13 might be expected to read *qûmî lāk raʿyātî* lit. "Arise (for yourself), my friend" as in 2:10 and as in Q of 2:13. LXX, reading *elthe* "come!", reflects the same *Vorlage* as that which underlies K (TgCant and Syr reflect the appropriate feminine forms in both verses; Vg does not reflect the preposition). K and LXX may be explained as scribal errors, anticipating the imperative *lĕkî* to come in the next line (cf. *BHQ*). Alternatively, both the Masoretes (Q) and the LXX translators may simply be trying to make sense out of the Hebrew text before them, Q correcting to the normal BH form and LXX construing as the feminine singular imperative from *hlk* "to go, come." Of the two variants, *lky* is clearly the *lectio difficilior* and would be preferred if acceptable sense could be made out of it. It may be the case that what we have here is an Aramaicized form of the suffix.[128] Such suffixes do appear elsewhere in BH (2Reg 4:2.3.7 [2x]; Jer 11:15; Ps 103:3.4.5; 116:7 [2x].19; 135:9; 137:6), mostly in late Psalms, where they have been understood as Aramaisms.[129] Indeed, this form of the suffix also appears in QH in the biblical and apocryphal texts.[130] As an illustration, Hurvitz cites the following passage from 1QIsa[a]:

MT: *lʾ yʾmr **lk** ʿwd ʿzwbh* (Is 62:4)
1QIsa[a]: *wlwʾ yʾmr **lky** ʿwd ʿzwbh*

And while neither the Hebrew of the DSS sectarian texts nor later MH use this form of the feminine singular suffix, the Aramaic form of the independent second person masculine singular pronoun (*ʾt*) does appear: at least once at Qumran[131] and frequently in MH.[132] This form appears as well in LBH (Job

128 Driver 1956: 448; cf. Gordis 1974: 22, n. 78.
129 So Wagner 1966: 130; Hurvitz 1972: 116-19. Rendsburg (1990: 83-84; 2002: 86-87) explains the occurrences of the suffix in 2Reg 4, Ps 116, and Cant 2:13 as evidencing the northern dialect of Hebrew. Leaving aside the Kings passage (which Rendsburg originally latches onto because it concerns Elisha, a northern prophet; see further his discussion in 2002: 86-95), the northern provenance of Cant is simply asserted (1990: 11; see below) and all of the features cited as evidence for the Israelian dialect of Psalm 116 are either attested in LBH (on the double plural, see Polzin 1976: 42) or are construable as Aramaisms – and note that neither *dbr* nor *yqr*, even if the proffered construals are correct, are attested earlier than OffA. At the very least, then, Rendsburg's contention that *-ky* is an Israelian linguistic feature stands or falls on the 2 Kings 4 passage.
130 Qimron 1986: 59. On the suffix in Qumran Aramaic, see Fassberg, 1996: 10-19.
131 According to Qimron 1986: 57.

1:10; Qoh 7:22; Neh 9:6). The Aramaic form of the third masculine singular suffix *-why* appears at least once in BH (*tagmûlôhî*, Ps 116:12) and appears as well in QH, and frequently in 1QIsa^{a}.[133]

min-lĕbānôn (4:15): Normally in BH (GKC §102b) the *nun* of the preposition *min* assimilates before a noun without a definite article. Non-assimilation of the *nun* appears in SBH but increases dramatically in LBH – some two-thirds of the instances listed in König (1895: 292) appear in late texts.[134] It is detectable in the Bar Kokbah letters (e.g., *mn yšwʿ*, *papMur* 42.1),[135] appears at least once in Ben Sira (*mn ʿpr* [36:10] vs. *mʿpr* [11:12]), and becomes more prevalent in QH.[136] Polzin correctly attributes the increased prevalence of this morphophonological development to Aramaic influence.[137] There is a tendency for the later Aramaic dialects, but not OA, to substitute nasalization for gemination.[138] Elsewhere in Cant the *nun* assimilates as expected (see esp., *millĕbānôn*, 4:8 [2x]).[139]

2.2. Syntax

Nota objecti l- (8:13): Polzin[140] admirably reviews the evidence for the use of *lĕ-* to mark the (definite) direct object in LBH and the origin of this syntactic feature in Aramaic.[141] The *nota objecti l-* appears at least twice in Cant: *lĕqôlēk hašmîʿînî* "cause me to hear your voice" (8:13[142]) and *šeʿiṭṭĕrâ-lô ʾimmô* "in which his mother crowned him" (3:11).[143] In SBH the Hiphil of *šmʿ* typically takes *ʾet* to mark one of the two objects that it governs (e.g., Deut 4:10; 30:12; 1Sam 9:27). Note in particular the following examples which provide a nice contrast with the use of *lĕ-* in Cant 8:13:

hišmîʿăkā ʾet-qōlô	"he made you hear his voice" (Deut 4:36)
wĕlōʾ-tašmîʿû ʾet-qôlĕkem	"do not let your voice be heard" (Josh 6:10)

132 Segal 1927: 40; Pérez Fernández 1999: 18. Segal specifically notes that *ʾt* is more frequent in later MH.

133 Qimron 1986: 61.

134 Cf. Polzin 1976: 66; Dobbs-Allsopp 1998: 29.

135 Assimilated forms also appear, e.g., *mmšmʿwn* (*papMur* 43.1).

136 Qimron 1985: 30-31.

137 1976: 66; cf. König 1895: 293.

138 Rosenthal 1995: 20-21; Muraoka and Porten 1998: 13-16; cf. Degen §20a; Segert §3.5.5.1-5; Hug 1993: 53.

139 However, the non-assimilation of the *nun* with *min* appears in seven separate instances in the three fragments making up 4QCant^{b} (containing parts of fifty-one lines), including two instances of *mn lbnwn* (2.ii.7 [2x]) for MT's *mlbnwn* (Cant 4:8 [2x]; see Tov 2000: 209).

140 Polzin 1976: 64-66; cf. Rooker 1990: 97-99.

141 Cf. Rosenthal 1995: 60; Folmer 1995: 340-71; Muraoka and Porten 1998: 261-63.

142 Cf. Fox 1985: 177.

143 Rudolph 1962: 111.140.

The SBH form is also attested in Cant: *hašmîʿînî ʾet-qôlēk* "cause me to hear your voice" (2:16). Similarly, the Piel of *ʿṭr* "to crown" takes an accusative direct object (e.g., *wĕkābôd wĕhādār tĕʿaṭṭĕrēhû* "with glory and honor you crowned him," Ps 8:6; see also Ps 65:12; 103:4), suggesting that *lô* in 3:11 is not to be construed prepositonally but accusatively (so *NRSV*). This use of the *nota objecti l-* emerges in earnest only beginning in OffA. In OA *wt* (*KAI* 214.28) and *ʾyt* (*KAI* 202B.5, 10; 222B.32; 223C.5; 224.11) are used.[144] The earliest likely attestation of the *nota objecti l-* comes on one of the Aramaic documents from Nineveh (*rhnw ʾšrḥm lšndlh bksp* "they gave PN_1 to PN_2 as pledge for silver," CIS ii 43.2-3; ca. 670 BCE; cf. Hug 1993: 18; Fales 1986: 158).[145] The *nota objecti l-* appears as well in Ben Sira (4:7) and MH.[146]

ʾăḥûzê ḥereb and *mĕlummĕdê milḥāmâ* (3:8): Commonly in Aramaic passive participles (*qtyl*) are used to denote perfect states that often have little or no notion of passivity associated with them, the so-called passive with active meaning.[147] This usage is characteristic of transitive verbs, especially those meaning "take, hold, carry" or the like,[148] and its penetration into post-classical Hebrew is usually attributed to Aramaic influence.[149] The expressions *ʾăḥûzê ḥereb* and *mĕlummĕdê milḥāmâ* in 3:8 are often cited as parade examples of this usage in LBH, as in JM (§50e) where they are glossed as "holding a sword, armed with a sword" and "well-versed in matters of war" respectively.[150] W.TH. VAN PEURSEN observes that Aramaic is the likely source for the former phrase in particular since its use "is difficult to explain in terms of an internal Hebrew development" (2004: 209, n. 42). The situation is more complicated, however. In Akkadian *aḫāzu* frequently has the extended meaning "to learn, understand" in the base stem (*CAD* A/1, 177-78). In fact, this sense appears to be very productive in Akkadian, common as a verbal adjective (e.g., *aḫiz ṭēmi u milki* "expert in understanding and counsel" – alongside *lamid šitūlit* "learned in deliberation," Böhl Leiden Coll 3 34:8), which would be equivalent to the usage being considered here, but predicated of finite forms as well (*aḫuz nēmeqi* ᵈ*Nabû* "I studied the wisdom of Nabû," Streck Asb. 4 i 31), and it is this sense that forms the basis from which is generated the meaning "to teach, educate, inform" in the causative stem (*šūḫuzu*). A similar usage of *aḫd* may be attested in Ugaritic as well (*aḫd ḥrṯ*

---

144 Segert §6.5.2.3.6; Kaufman 1992: 177; Folmer 1995: 365-66.

145 J. Fitzmyer (1995: 116-17) suggests seeing the *nota objecti l-* at Sefire (*lṭbt*[*ʾ*] *yʿbd*[*n*] "may they make good relations," *KAI* 222C.4-5), but this is disputed (see Degen 1969: 109; Garr 1985: 192).

146 Segal 1927: 168.

147 E.g., Nöldeke 2001: 220-21; Kutscher 1977: 75, 80-81; Muraoka and Porten 1998: 202.

148 Goldenberg 1998: 610; cf. Peursen 2004: 208-9.

149 So JM §50e; Kutscher 1977: 81, n. 50; Peursen 2004: 208, 209, n.42.

150 Cf. Hurvitz 1972: 119 n133; Fox 1985: 124.187.

"skilled in plowing," *CTU* 4.296.8; cf. Pope 1977: 434-35). In this light, then, it may well be the case that the passive participles in 3:8 conform to the more normative use of the passive participle in construct with its determining word (e.g., GKC §116k; JM §121o). That is, the extended sense of *ʾḥz* with the meaning "to learn" (as possibly in Qoh 2:3; or as here with the more specialized meaning of "practical learning, training"), as opposed to the root's base sense "to hold, seize, take," which is more prevalent in BH, may be legitimately passivized (cf. Greenfield 1964: 533, n. 5) – literally, "trained of sword." And certainly a straightforward rendering of *mĕlummĕdê milḥāmâ* as a passive is otherwise attested in BH: *mĕlummĕdê-šîr layhwh* "those who were trained in singing to Yahweh" (1Chr 25:7; cf. van Peursen 2004: 209 n44).[151] In the end, then, whether *ʾăḥûzê ḥereb* and *mĕlummĕdê milḥāmâ* in 3:8 evidence the late use of passive participles with active meaning is hard to tell.[152]

bĕʾaḥad ʿănāq (4:9): Gordis believes the word order here reflects Aramaic influence (1974: 87; cf. Fox 1985: 136), but this is unlikely. To be sure, in some later Aramaic dialects (e.g., JBA, Syriac) the indefinite *ḥad* may precede or follow the noun it governs,[153] but in BA and OffA (not attested in OA[154]) the normal word order is for *ḥad* to follow the noun,[155] just as in BH (WOC §13.8). The abnormal order (though see Dan 8:13; Hag 2:6) in this instance is perhaps better accounted for by the repetition and sequencing demands of staircase (or climatic) parallelism:[156]

libbabtīnî ʾăḥōtî kallâ
libbabtînî bĕʾaḥad mēʿênayik
bĕʾaḥad ʿănāq miṣṣawwĕrōnāyik

"You have captured my heart, my sister, my bride,
you have captured my heart with one of your eyes,
with a single strand of your necklace" (so Fox 1985: 132).

151 1Chr 9:22 offers a phrase very close to ours: *kullām habbĕrûrîm lĕšōʿărîm* "All of these, the ones who were chosen as gatekeepers" – though admittedly the text is late as well.

152 Perhaps a more compelling argument for lateness can be pressed in terms of the specific idiom reflected in *ʾăḥûzê ḥereb*, which is well-known in Syriac, *ʾaḥîday ḥarbāʾ* (cf. Driver 1956: 448; Robert, Tournay, and Feuillet 1963: 21). Note further the usage of *ʾḥyd* in the Peshitta of 1Chr 5:18, where it glosses the Hebrew *lĕmûdê milḥāmâ* (cf. Bloch and Bloch 1995: 163).

153 Muraoka 1987: 48; Sokoloff 2002: 431; cf. Nöldeke 2001: 185.

154 The only possible exception is *mn ḥd mlk* which appears in a badly broken passage from Sefire (*KAI* 222 B.30). The gammar of the phrase is likely indicated by the better attested construction with the plural *nomen rectum*, e.g., *mn ḥd bny* "any one of my sons" (*KAI* 224.10), suggesting that *mlk* here, if read correctly, may need to be understood as a collective (Degen §72; Fitzmyer 1995: 11; cf. 151).

155 Segert §§6.3.3.3; 6.4.2.1.2; Rosenthal 1995: 28; Muraoka and Porten 1998: 240.

156 See Greenstein 1974: 96-97.

The repetition of *bĕʾaḥad* in the second and third lines helps to secure (perceptually) the force of the parallelism that so typifies this particular trope. Semantically, the repetition of *ʾaḥad* stresses that only "one" eye and but a "single" strand of the woman's necklace is all it takes to capture the man's heart.[157]

2.3. Lexicon

ʾaggan (7:3): The ultimate origin of the term is unknown, though it appears to be non-Semitic.[158] The Hebrew term, spelled with a geminated middle radical (cf. Akk *agannu*), appears indebted to and likely derivative from Aramaic, which is spelled similarly (*ʾaggānāʾ*).[159] The early attestation of this lexeme in BH (Ex 24:6; Is 22:24; cf. Ug. *agn*) means that it is probably not diagnostically late.

ʾêkâ (1:7): In BH *ʾêkâ* is used either as an interrogative ("how?", Deut 12:30) or as an exclamatory ("alas!", Thr 1:1) particle. Only here (and *ʾêkōh* in 2Reg 6:13 – placed in the mouth of an Aramean!) is the particle to be construed as the interrogative "where?" The particle is common in later Aramaic dialects (JA *ʾykʾ*; JBA *hykʾ*; Syr *ʾaykāʾ*; cf. MH *hêkān* [*hê* = *ʾê*; *kān/kāʾn* = *kāh* (Aram.)]), and thus Wagner (1966: 23) and Driver (1956: 448) note the likelihood of Aramaic influence here on Cant. The lexeme is also reflected in later Akkadian dialects (esp, NB), *ēkâ, ēkâma, ēkânu* (*GAG* §118a).

bĕrôtîm (1:17): A widely recognized Aramaism.[160] The spelling with *t* betrays the influence of a post-OA dialect of Aramaic – only after the consonant mergers that become characteristic of Aramaic during the OffA period does PS **ṯ* > *t* (e.g., JBA *brātāʾ*; JPA *brwt*; Syr *brûtāʾ*). The BH lexeme is spelled *bĕrôš* (e.g., 2Sam 6:5; 1Reg 5:22; Hos 14:9) – reflecting the pattern of consonant mergers typical of BH, PS **ṯ* > *š* (cf. QH *brwš*, 1QHa 16:5; 4Q163 f8 10:3; 4Q522 f9ii:6; MH *bĕrôš* (alongside Aramaicized *bĕrôt*); Akk *burāšu*). Heb *bĕrôt/bĕrôš* is typically glossed as "cypress" (so NJV), presumably meaning the *Cupresus sempervirens* common to Israel.[161] However, M. Zohary believes that the Hebrew term is a "collective name" for at least three species of trees and that whenever it is coupled with "Lebanon" or "cedar" (*ʾezer*) it likely refers to *Abies cilicica*, the Cilician fir, which grows alongside the cedar in

157 See Fox 1985: 136. Incidentally, this example well illustrate something E. Greenstein observes in his discussion of climatic parallelism in Ugaritic, namely: that knowledge of literary forms and style can frequently be of great assistance in analyzing a language's (especially an extinct language!) syntax (1974: 99).

158 Perhaps Hittite *aganni* or its Hurrian ancestor [?], see Mankowski 2000: 22.

159 Cf. Mankowski 2000: 22.

160 Driver 1956: 448; Rudolph 1962: 110; Robert, Tournay, and Feuillet 1963: 21; Wagner 1966: 38; Fox 1985: 189; Murphy 1990: 4, n. 10; 132.

161 See Zohary 1982: 106; Jacob and Jacob 1992: 805.

Lebanon, or *Juniperus excelsa*, one of the conifers that grows in the same environment and is even called *brôtā'* by the local population.[162] The latter, Zohary says, is "surely identical with the *berothim* of Cant of Solomon" .[163]

ṭnp (5:3): The verb (*'ăṭannĕpēm*) only appears here in the Hebrew Bible. Wagner identifies it as an Aramaism (JPA, JBA, Syr, Mand; also very sporadically in later Akkadian dialects).[164] The basic sense appears to be "to foul, dirty," frequently with pronounced (religious) overtones of "defilement, pollution." Here, however, the primary sense is mundane, that of dirtying one's feet (on the dirt floor)[165] after having gotten into bed (cf. references to dirtying with *ṭnp* a garment in both JBA [*Šabb.* 48b(11)] and in MH [*t. Yoma* 5(4):5; cf. Jastrow I, 541]). And yet given the palpable eroticism of the immediate context – C. WALSH (2000: 113) even goes so far as to label 5:2-6 a "wet dream" – the likelihood that the verb is intended to allude more erotically seems good – lexemes from the root are commonly paired in Syriac with words derived from the root *zn'* (commonly glossed in English translations by terms such as "fornication" and "harlotry," though referring basically to extra-marital sex).[166]

kotlēnû (2:9): A *hapax legomenon* in BH. It is very common in the various Aramaic dialects (BA [Dan 5:5], Palm, JPA, JBA, CPA). There are no occurrences in OA or OffA, so it is not an early Aramaic lexeme. It appears in QH, where E. QIMRON (1986: 116; cf. 92) understands it as an Aramaic loanword. Wagner (1966: 142) is of the same opinion with regard to our lexeme in Cant.[167] It also appears in MH, where Fox (1985: 187) believes it begins to be used instead of *qîr*.

---

162 Zohary 1982: 106-7.

163 Zohary 1982: 107. The reference in *HALOT* (1, 155) and some of the commentaries (e.g., Keel 1994: 75) to *Juniperus phoenicea* would seem to be mistaken, even in light of the general nature of the Hebrew term, as the Phoenician juniper is a significantly different kind of tree and native to other parts of the country (cf. Zohary 1982: 117).

164 Wagner 1966: 60; cf. Kautzsch 1902: 34; Driver 1956: 448; Rudolph 1962: 111; Robert, Tournay, and Feuillet 1963: 21; Gordis 1974: 22, n. 78; Fox 1985: 189.

165 Recall that during antiquity most would have gone around bare footed or in sandals and thus foot washing was a commonplace (King and Stager 2001: 70-71). And even the ground floor in most common dwellings in most periods consisted of packed dirt. So that the basic idea in this verse is that the woman would have washed her feet in preparation for bed, and would dirty them again if she got up to answer the door.

166 Fox (1985: 145) is surely correct in stressing the delicacy and indirection of the sexual allusions in this passage. The possible play on the euphemistic use of *regel* as a designation for genitals (Ex 4:25; 2 Sam 11:11; Ruth 3:4, 7) as identified by M. Pope (1977: 515) is a good case in point. If such an allusion is being made it must hover very much in the background as the euphemism is always used of a man's genitals. Such a play would not be out of place, as the two lovers commonly speak possessively of one another (e.g., "I am my beloved's and my beloved is mine," 6:3; "let my beloved come to his garden," 4:16), but it is "delicate and indirect."

167 Cf. Kautzsch 1902: 45; Driver 1956: 448; Rudolph 1962: 133; Robert, Tournay, and Feuillet 1963: 21; Gordis 1974: 22, n. 78; Fox 1985: 189.

**mezeg* (7:3): A common Aramaic lexeme (e.g., JBA *mzîg*, Syr *mzāgā'*) designating wine that is mixed or diluted with water.[168] The root *mzg* becomes common in MH (e.g., *m. Nid.* 2:6, 7; cf. Jastrow I, 72-53) and contrasts with BH *mesek* in Ps 75:9 (cf. Ug. *msk*).

nṭr (1:6 [2x]; 8:11, 12): The root *nṭr* "to keep, watch" is an obvious Aramaism,[169] since in BH PS **ṯ* > *ṣ* (*nāṣar* < PS **nṯr*; cf. Arb. *nẓr*, Akk. *naṣāru*, Ph. *nṣr*, Ug. *nǵr*) and not *ṭ* as in the later Aramaic dialects (e.g., Syr *nṭar*). In OA the PS phonemic inventory remains in place (cf. Kaufman 1992), with PS **ṯ* written graphically with a *ṣ* (cf. *nṣr* in *KAI* 222 B 8; C 15, 17). The latest examples in which PS **ṯ* is realized as *ṣ* in Aramaic are found in the Nerab stela (*tnṣr*, *KAI* 225 12; ca. 700) and the Adon letter (*nṣr*, *KAI* 266 8; ca. 604-3; cf. Hug 1993: 13, 15, 51). V. HUG thinks that the shift **ṯ* > *ṭ* must have occurred at ca. 600 B.C.E. (1993: 51).[170] Therefore, the various forms of the root *nṭr* in Cant would likely not have been borrowed into BH much before the end of the seventh century or the beginning of the sixth century at the earliest. Of the other biblical passages cited by Wagner evidencing the root *nṭr* (Thr 3:12; Jer 32:2; Job 16:12; Neh 12:39), only one is possibly early (1Sam 20:20).[171]

swg (7:3) *sûgâ* (Qal Pass Part fs) is a *hapax legomenon* and a possible Aramaism.[172] The root does appear in Aramaic (e.g., Syr, JPA), but the overall sense of the metaphor in Cant (the woman's belly is likened to heaped wheat "fenced about with lilies") is somewhat obscure.

sĕmādar (2:13.15; 7:13): The word appears in Syr (*smādĕrā'*) and TA (*smādār*, TgIsa 18:5), Akk (*CAD* S, 107), where *samādiru* is likely an Aramaic loanword, and MH (Jastrow II, 998), and thus the lexeme is sometimes counted as an Aramaic loanword in Cant.[173] If so it is not a diagnostically

---

168 Kautzsch 1902: 40; Driver 1956: 448; Rudolph 1962: 111; Robert, Tournay, and Feuillet 1963: 21; Wagner 1966: 75-76; Fox 1985: 189.

169 Wagner 1966: 83-84; cf. Driver 1956: 448; Robert, Tournay, and Feuillet 1963: 21; Gordis 1974: 22, n. 78; Fox 1985: 189; Murphy 1990: 4, n. 10; Dobbs-Allsopp 1998: 27-28.

170 Segert (§3.2.7.5.4-5) cites a grave inscription from Sheikh Faḍl (*mṭ'*, 17.2) as the earliest example in which PS **ṯ* > *ṭ* (ca. 600). However, others date these inscriptions palaeographically to only the fifth century (e.g., Naveh 1970: 40-41).

171 1Sam 20:20 does not necessarily invalidate the conclusions just drawn about the projected time of borrowing for this root. Typically, diachronic change does not happen all at once, but occurs gradually over an extended period of time. 1 Sam 20:20 may reflect an early, sporadic example of the shift PS **ṯ* > *ṭ* (depending on when one dates the books of Samuel and its various sources).

172 Wagner 1966: 86; cf. Driver 1956: 448; Rudolph 1962: 111; Robert, Tournay, and Feuillet 1963: 21; Gordis 1974: 22, n. 78; Fox 1985: 189; Murphy 1990: 182

173 Driver 1956: 448; Wagner 1966:88; Gordis 1974: 22, n. 78; Fox 1985: 189.

late loan, as *smdr* appears on a late eighth-century Hebrew jar label from Hazor (*Hazr* 7).

sĕtāw (2:11): A distinct Aramaic loanword.[174] It contrasts with the standard BH term for "winter," *ḥōrep* (TgJ translates *teḥĕrāp* in Is 18:6 using *stw*ʾ), and manifests a number of phonological elements characteristic of Aramaic, including consonantal *waw* in word-final position, which is more common in Aramaic than Hebrew,[175] and the writing of etymological **sin* (*ś*) with *samek* (*s*), reflecting the merger of these two phonemes in Aramaic that starts after the OA period.[176] That the loan of *sĕtāw* into Cant must date no earlier than the Persian period is indicated, on the one hand, by the OA writing of the word as *štw*ʾ (*KAI* 216.18), and on the other hand, by the writing of the term in all other Aramaic dialects with a *samek* (*s*; e.g., TA *stw*ʾ, JBA *sytw*ʾ, Mand *sytw*ʾ, Syr *satwā*ʾ).

ʿešet šēn (5:14): Fox (1985: 148-49) has rightly understood the *hapax legomenon ʿešet* "work, artifact" as deriving ultimately from the Aramaic root *ʿšt* "to think, plan," attested in OA, OffA, BA and in the targums (Wagner [1966: 93] identifies the verbal use of *ʿšt* in Jon 1:6, *ʿaštût* in Job 12:5, and *ʿeštōnet* in Ps 146:4 as possible Aramaisms). The root is the Aramaic counterpart of BH *ḥšb* (the latter also appearing in some of the later Aramaic dialects instead of *ʿšt*, e.g., Syr, JPA, JBA). The Hebrew root has the extended meaning "to devise, invent" an art work (e.g., Ex 31:4; 2Chr 26:15), which ultimately gives rise to the nominal *ḥēšeb* "band, girdle" of the ephod in Exodus (28:27; 29:5; 39:20). The same general semantic development must be posited for MH *ʿešet* "wrought metal, bar" (Jastrow, II, 1128), of which *ʿešet šēn* in Cant and *ʿštwt zhb* in 3Q 15.ii.4 [cf. i.5] are surely precursors.[177]

rahîṭēnû (Q)[178] (1:17): There is no question that we have an Aramaic loanword here (*rhyṭy* "beam, rafter", Syn D A 10; Syr *rehṭā*ʾ "rafter"), as the root *rhṭ* "to run" is the Aramaic (e.g., Syr, JBA, JPA) equivalent of BH *rwṣ*.[179] MH exhibits both a nominal form, *rāhîṭ* "beam, rafter," and a denominative verbal form, *rhṭ* in the Hiphil with the meaning "to lay rafters" (Jastrow, II, 1454). The problematic *rĕhāṭîm* in Cant 7:6 is likely to be derived from the

174 Wagner 1966: 89; cf. Kautzsch 1902: 70; Driver 1956: 448; Rudolph 1962: 111; Robert, Tournay, and Feuillet 1963: 21; Gordis 1974: 22 n78; Fox 1985: 189; Murphy 1990: 139.

175 As indicated rather tellingly by Q, which construes the final *waw* as a pronominal suffix, viz. *sĕtāyw*; see also the explanation in *BHQ*.

176 Rosenthal 1995: 20; Muraoka and Porten 1998: 6. *Samek* and *śin* become increasingly confused in LBH, as well, likely under Aramaic influence.

177 See Cooper (1971:157-62) for the imagery of the plastic arts that informs this passage.

178 K reads *raḥîṭēnû* but no root with *ḥet* is known, and thus the reading in Q should be followed here (so Fox 1985: 161).

179 See Wagner 1966: 105-6.

same root as well (so Fox 1985: 161; cf. TgCant "who peeled the the rods at the watering-troughs [*brhṭy'*]"). However, given the relatively early attestation of *rahaṭ* "drinking trough" in BH (Gen 30:38, 41; Ex 2:16), one cannot be totally confident that the lexical reflexes of *rhṭ* in Cant are necessarily diagnostically late – though *rahîṭ* is attested otherwise only in later Hebrew.

še- "which, that": As already noted, the usage of *še-* in Cant is typical of LBH and later post-classical Hebrew dialects. Additionally, Wagner (1966: 110-11) has collected Aramaic analogs for most of the uses of *še-* in BH,[180] which, when combined with the known fact of Aramaic's influence on LBH more generally,[181] suggests the likelihood that the Aramaic relative (*zy/dy*) had a direct and/or indirect impact on the rise and use of *še-* in the later Hebrew dialects.[182] This can be seen more specifically with regard to Cant in several places. First, *šallāmâ* "lest" in 1:7, like *'ăšer lāmâ* in Dan 1:10,[183] is a calque of the common Aramaic idiom *dî* + *lmāh*.[184] *lmāh* "lest" is only known in Aramaic from OffA and later (Segert §7.5.9.8), though BH attests the use of *lāmâ* "why?" in rhetorical questions introducing undesirable alternatives (1Sam 19:17; Qoh 5:5; 7:16; Neh 6:3).[185] Pérez Fernández (1999: 231) also relates it to MH *šemmā'* which replaces BH *pēn*.[186] Second, though the possessive proclitc *šel-* of LBH (and its independent heir in MH, *šel*) is to be understood as an outgrowth of BH *'ăšer lĕ-*,[187] this need not preclude the likelihood of Aramaic influence as well.[188] For example, as Hurvitz notes,[189] *miššellānû* placed in the mouth of an Aramaic king in 2Reg 6:11 functions as a calque on Aramaic *zyl/dyl* in order to capture the foreignness of the monarch's native speech. In Cant 3:7 *miṭṭātô šelliššlōmōh* "the couch of Solomon" looks very much like the genitive construction with proleptic pronominal suffix

180 In particular, the use of *še-* as a clausal conjunction has especially good parallels in Egyptian Aramaic from the Persian period, see Muraoka and Porten 1998: 272, 327, 331-32.

181 E.g., Kutscher 1982: 71-73; Sáenz-Badillos 1993: 114.

182 cf. Peursen 2004: 301-2, 313, 327, 380.It may be affirmed, nevertheless, that the particle itself is indigenous (at least dialectically) to Hebrew (see similarly Pérez Fernández 1999: 6).

183 See Collins 1993: 128.

184 Cf. BA *dî-lĕmāh*, Ezra 7:32; JBA *dylm'/dlm'*; JPA *dlmh/dylmh*; CPA *dm'/dlm'*; Syr *dalmā'*; so Wagner 1966: 110; Fox 1985: 103; cf. 189; Murphy 1990: 4, n. 10; cf. Driver 1956: 448; Robert, Tournay, and Feuillet 1963: 21.

185 Though this usage is also known in Aramaic (e.g., *TAD* C1.1.36), I wonder whether the Qohelet and Nehemiah passages may not also be calques of Aram *lmh* "lest" (cf. *TAD* C1.1.126).

186 Significantly, *šallāmâ* does not continue in later Hebrew in this form, underscoring its borrowed status.

187 So Segal 1927: 189; cf. Givón 1974: 20-21.

188 *Contra* Segal; see Pérez Fernández 1999: 6.

189 Cited in Rendsburg 2002: 103-4, n. 31.

common in Aramaic.[190] Indeed, despite Polzin's protests to the contrary,[191] it is only in Aramaic that we have a close parallel to the *šel* genitive with proleptic suffix found in Cant 3:7 (and later very commonly in MH, see Pérez Fernández 1999: 32).[192] Third, the use of the temporal preposition *ʿad še-* in 1:12 meaning "as long as" likely reflects later (not in OA) Aramaic *ʿd* and *ʿd dy*, which has this sense (e.g., *T. Levi* 42.9; TgOnq Gen 25:6; cf. van Peursen 2004: 327). This sense is found as well with *ʿd ʾšr* in Ben Sira (13:7[193]) and with *ʿd š-* in MH.[194]

šĕwāqîm (3:2): That BH *šûq* "street, market" must ultimately derive from Akkadian *sūqu* "street" seems all but certain.[195] As S. KAUFMAN observes, it is only in Akkadian that a compelling etymology is available: **ḍyq* "to be narrow, straits" which becomes *siāqu* in Akkadian by Geers' Law.[196] The more immediate source of the Hebrew lexeme – whether borrowed from NA where it was pronounced [*šūqu*],[197] Aramaic, or LB where *šūqu* represents a reborrowing from Aramaic[198] – theoretically is an open question. The likelihood, however, is that Heb *šûq* represents a trans-Aramaic borrowing.[199] The word is very common in Aramaic from OffA period on and appears elsewhere in BH only in late poetic texts.[200] Indeed, the Qohelet passages appear to reflect the extended sense of *šûq* as "market" or "street-bazaar" that will later typify its usage in MH (e.g., *m. Demai* 3:2; *m. Šeb.* 7:3; *m. Pesa˙.* 2:5; *m. Sanh.* 7:4; see Seow 1997: 356-57). And the phrasing in Cant, *baššĕwāqîm ûbārĕḥōbôt* "in the streets and squares," appears to contrast with the more common (and earlier?) pairing of *ḥûṣ* and *rĕḥōb*, such as in Am 5:16: "In all the squares (*bĕkol-rĕḥōbôt*) there shall be wailing,/ and in all the streets (*ûbĕkol-ḥûṣôt*) they shall say, 'Alas! Alas!'" (cf. Is 15:3; Jer 5:1; 9:20; Nah 2:5;

190 Gordis 1974: 22; cf. Rosenthal 1995: 29.

191 Polzin 1976: 38-40, following Segal; see also Gordis 1974: 22-23.

192 The closest parallel outside of Aramaic appears in Akkadian, where a third person pronoun may be added to the governing noun preceding the relative *ša* in order to denote marked determination, though this is "a rare construction" (Huehnergard 1997: 363) and still not precisely analogous to the *dyl/šel* circumlocutions in Aramaic, LBH, and MH.

193 Peursen 2004: 327.

194 Pérez Fernández 1997: 208.

195 Ellenbogen 1962: 158; Kaufman 1974: 93-94; Mankowski 2000: 140-42. As with Aram *šūq*, ultimately one cannot completely rule out the possibility that BH *šûq* is a cognate to Akk *sūqu*.

196 Kaufman 1974: 94; cf. Mankowski 2000: 141-42.

197 Kaufman 1974: 93-94; 140-42.

198 Mankowski 2000: 141.

199 Robert, Tournay, and Feuillet 1963: 21; von Soden 1981: 164; Mankowski 2000: 141.

200 Prov 7:8; on the date of Proverbs 1-9, 31, see Yoder 2001: 15-38; Qoh 12: 4, 5; on the date of Qohelet, see Seow 1996: 650-54.

Prov 1:20; 5:16; 7:12; 22:13) – though admittedly the evidence of a single occurrence cannot be pressed too far.[201]

A good many other possible Aramaic loanwords are identified in the literature, including *ʾibbê* (6:11),[202] *ʾommān* (7:2),[203] *ginnat* (6:11),[204] *ḥărûzîm* (1:10),[205] *ḥărakkîm* (2:9),[206] *ṭōʿiyyâ* (Symm, Syr, Vg, Tg) (1:7),[207] *mitrappeqet*

---

201 The lexeme *ḥûṣ* appears in the phrase *baḥūš* in Cant 8:1, which can be construed quite literally, viz. "in the street" (Pope 1977: 653; Fox 1985: 165), or taken in its prepositional or adverbial sense, viz. "outside" (cf. Gen 9:22). The latter is quite common in MH (Jastrow, I, 438; Segal 1927: 135; Pérez Fernández 1999: 172) and would comprise an additional late feature in Cant. However, the context allows for both construals.

202 R. Tournay (Robert, Tournay, and Feuillet 1963: 21) lists *ʾibbê* in 6:11 as a possible Aramaism, though neither Wagner nor E. Kautzsch treat it as such. Against the hypothesis is the word's meaning in Job 8:12 and in MH (Jastrow, I, 2), "blossom" or the like instead of "fruit" as commonly in Aramaic (from Akk *inbu* "fruit," cf. Kaufman 1974: 58), and the absence of the *nun*, as in BA (*ʾinbēh*, cf. Akk; though see Syr *ʾebbāʾ* and TA *ʾibbāʾ*, *ʾîbbāʾ*). Moreover, the root *ʾbb* is reconstructible to PNWS (cf. BH *ʾābîb* "ripe wheat"; Amh *abāba* "flower"; see Fox 2003: 72 n6). The specific semantic sense intended in 6:11 is not certain; both "fruit" (Fox 1985: 155) and "blossom, bud" (Murphy 1990: 180; cf. Pope 1977: 582-83) are appropriate in the context.

203 The word is a *hapax legomenon* (though see *ʾāmôn* in Prov 8:30). It is considered to be an Aramaism by both Kautzsch (1902: 22) and Wagner (1966: 26; Fox 1985: 189), but this is far from certain. The ultimate origin of the word in Sumerian u m m e a "master," with Akkadian *ummânu* "craftsman" as the conduit into WS, is beyond dispute (Kaufman 1974: 109; Mankowski 2000: 33-34). Whether, in addition, the lexeme came into BH specifically via Aramaic must remain an open question, as there are no telltale (phonological, morphological, or semantic) signs of Aramaic derivation. Nevertheless, the word persists in MH (*ʾûmān*) and later Jewish Aramaic dialects (TA, JPA, JBA; cf. the contrast with SBH *ḥārāš* "artisan").

204 *ginnat* is sometimes listed among the Aramaisms in Cant (so Driver 1956: 448; Fox 1985: 189), presumably with forms such as JBA *gînnĕtāʾ* and TA *ginnĕtāʾ* in mind. However, it may well be that the influence runs in the opposite direction, namely, from Hebrew to Aramaic (so Sokoloff 1990: 133). Moreover, it should be noted that the original form is *qatl*-based (i.e., **gann(-at)*, Fox 2003: 75) and that in BH the form with an initial *i* vowel is restricted paradigmatically to the construct form of the feminine singular (Cant 6:11; Esth 1:5; 7:7, 8). Therefore, it is not obvious that the presumption of borrowing from Aramaic is the best or only means for explaining the *i* vowel in *ginnat*, nor in fact should too much stress be placed on the late distribution of the form (as does Tournay in Robert, Tournay, and Feuillet 1963: 21), given its paradigmatic restrictiveness.

205 So Robert, Tournay, and Feuillet 1963: 21.

206 Though sometimes identified as an Aramaism (e.g., Driver 1956: 448; Robert, Tournay, and Feuillet 1963: 21; Gordis 1974: 22, n. 78), this is far from certain. The etymology is not obvious and cognates appear only in TA and JPA (*ḥărakkāʾ* "window, lattice") and MH (*ḥărāk* "window").

207 Some number *ṭōʿiyyâ* (reading with Symm, Syr, Vg, and Tg against *ʿôtĕyâ* of MT and LXX) among the Aramaisms to be found in Cant (e.g., Driver 1956: 448; Rudolph 1962: 125; Wagner 1966: 61). The root occurs in Ezek 13:10 and appears to be the Aramaic (Syr, Palm) counterpart to BH *ṭʿh* "to wander." However, whether or not *ṭʿyh* was ever actually in the *Vorlage* of these versions remains an open question (cf.

(8:5),[208] *sansinnāyw* (7:9),[209] *paggeyhā* (2:13),[210] *mĕqappēṣ* (2:8),[211] *rhb* (6:5),[212] *rĕsîsê* (5:2),[213] *šzp* (1:6),[214] *šḥr* (1:5, 6; 5:11),[215] *šalhebetyāh* (8:6),[216] and *talpiyyôt* (4:4).[217] In most of these instances the word in question is extremely rare or

---

Alexander 2003: 84, n. 53; *BHQ*). The versions here (as often when confronted by a problematic passage in Cant, e.g., 3:9; 6:4) look as if they are simply translating according to their understanding of the larger context. This is especially evident in TgCant which recasts the verse (allegorically) to speak of Israel's exile and "wandering." MT (and LXX), on this view, then, preserve the more difficult reading, and thus *ʿôtĕyâ* should probably be retained (cf. Fox 1985: 103; Murphy 1990: 131). But in any event the reading is sufficiently problematic to warrant not counting *ṭōʿiyyâ* as a part of the evidence of typologically late Aramaisms in Cant.

208 So Robert, Tournay, and Feuillet 1963: 21.

209 Though sometimes listed as an Aramaism (e.g., Driver 1956: 448; Gordis 1974: 22-23, n. 78; Fox 1985: 189), the lexeme appears in Arabic (*sinsin*), Ugaritic (*ssnm*), and especially Akkadian (*sissinnu*, *CAD* S, 325-28), as well as in several Aramaic dialects (JPA and Syr).

210 Another *hapax legomenon*. Though frequently cited as a possible Aramaism (Driver 1956: 448; Robert, Tournay, and Feuillet 1963: 21; Gordis 1974: 22, n. 78), this remains uncertain. The root does appear in several Aramaic dialects (e.g., JPA *pgg* "to be unripe," Syr *paggāʾ* "unripe fig"), but it also occurs in MH (*paggîn*), Ar (*fijj* "unripe fruit"), and Eth (*fagaga* "to stink").

211 This *hapax legomenon* is frequently listed as an Aramaism (e.g., Driver 1956: 448; Gordis 1974: 22, n. 78; Fox 1985: 189). Verbs and nominals from the root are attested in TA, JPA, JBA, and MH.

212 *hirhîbūnî* in 6:5 must mean "to frighten, trouble, disquiet" or the like (Fox 1985: 152), a meaning well attested for the Aphel in Syriac (cf. CPA), but apparently not for the Hiphil in MH (Jastrow, II, 1453; MH shares the general semantic field associated with the root elsewhere in BH, viz. "arrogance, pride"). Therefore, this usage is sometimes counted as an Aramaism (e.g., Driver 1956: 448; Gordis 1974: 22, n. 78). However, the causative forms of the relevant cognate verbs in both Akkadian (*raʾābu, CAD* R, 1-3; *AHw*, 932) and Arabic (*rahibu/rābu*) have similar meanings, raising the possibility that the meaning "to frighten" (in the causative) is common Semitic.

213 Driver (1956: 448) lists *rĕsîsê* "drops of" in 5:2 as a possible Aramaism. The word is specifically attested in JPA, CPA, and Syr, but the root appears in Arabic (*rašša* "to sprinkle"), and perhaps Akkadian (*russû*, see *CAD* R, 425), and is used verbally in Ez 46:14.

214 Though usually associated with *šdp* "to burn, scorch, darken" (see Pope 1977: 322), the etymology of *šzp* is unknown and its attribution as an Aramaism (so Robert, Tournay, and Feuillet 1963: 21; Murphy 1990: 126) is hardly justifiable on present evidence.

215 Wagner (1966: 112-13) raises the possibility that the various BH lexemes derived from the root *šḥr* "to be black" (in Cant: *šĕḥôrâ*, 1:5; *šĕḥarḥōret*, 1:6; *šĕḥōrôt*, 5:11) are all Aramaisms. But beyond the fact that the root is attested in various of the Aramaic dialects (e.g., JBA, Syr, Mand), there is little warrant for the contention.

216 *šalhebetyāh* (8:6) is sometimes listed among the possible Aramaisms in Cant (so Driver 1956: 448; Fox 1985: 188; cf. JBA *šalhābîtāʾ*, Syr *šalhēbîtāʾ*, etc.), but the passage remains enigmatic and thus is not taken into consideration here.

217 Since A. Honeyman's seminal note (1949: 50-51), this notorious crux has been explained with reference to Ar *lafaʾa* "to arrange in order" (see Pope 1977: 465-69). Whether it can be classified more particularly as an Aramaism (so Robert, Tournay, and Feuillet 1963: 21; cf. Murphy 1990: 155) is more dubious. The root in Aramaic occurs at most only once (in TgLev 6:5, so Jastrow, I, 715) and clearly was not understood in the

lacks the telltale signs (phonology. morphology, syntactic use) that would identify it as deriving explicitly from Aramaic, and, as often as not, exhibits a distribution pattern outside of Cant that is not uniquely indicative of Aramaic. Therefore, while some of these words are surely Aramaic loans in Cant, the warrant for identifying them as such is generally weak or (mostly) lacking.

In sum, not every Aramaism posited as such in the literature is equally compelling – and not a few are mistaken. Still, the number of genuine Aramaisms in Cant is substantial, especially given the relatively brief compass of this sequence of poems. More importantly, a significant proportion of the latter are diagnostically late, i.e., date roughly from the late seventh or early sixth centuries at the earliest (e.g., *ʾêkâ, bĕrôtîm, kotlēnû, nota objecti l-, min-lĕbānôn, nṭr, sĕtāw, šallāmâ, šĕwāqîm*). This fact, combined with the evidence reviewed above for distinct LBH features in Cant, makes the case for the lateness of Cant's language compelling.

The one reason for possibly resisting this finding would be, as Hurvitz notes (1968: 240), the "plausible" presence of "circumstances which may have given the text a peculiar and highly distinctive Aramaizing character as early as the pre-exilic period." He proceeds to imagine just such a set of circumstances (possibly) pertaining to Cant:

> It is possible that this book [Song of Songs] stems, at least in origin, from the North. Now in the northern dialect as a whole there may have been numerous linguistic features which were also common to Aramaic, but which were unknown in the classical language of Jerusalem (i.e. standard biblical Hebrew). Consequently, the Aramaisms in Song of Songs – many of them being at the same time "Mishnaisms" as well –may not be helpful for our purpose [i.e., counted as criteria for lateness]" (1968: 236).

The possibility of a northern provenance for Cant is now routinely canvassed in the secondary literature. In fact, already by the end of the nineteenth century, Driver, whom Hurvitz references, surmised that the "many words" in Cant "found never or rarely besides in Biblical Hebrew, but common in Aramaic" show either that Cant "must be a late work (post-exilic), or, if early, that it belongs to *North* Israel" (1956: 448-49). But the thesis of Cant as a northern composition, however *possible* (and alluring), on present evidence is not very *plausible* and not defensible. It is not defensible chiefly because we lack the kind of empirical data needed to establish the thesis (cf. Fox 1985: 189). As much is implied by the warrants Driver himself offers for preferring the northern hypothesis (1956: 449): "the general purity and lightness of the style" and "the acquaintance shown by the author with localities in North

---

present passage by either of the Aramaic speaking translators of the Targum or Peshitta.

Palestine."[218] He cannot make a judgment on the basis of the linguistic data, which is the principal focus of his comments here, because he cannot control for them. There, of course, is no question about the reality of dialectical variation in ancient Hebrew – this much is shown (though only to a very limited extent) by the epigraphic remains from Iron II Judah and Israel (see Garr 1985). But currently we have no indisputably northern source (biblical or extra-biblical) with the linguistic profile supposed by Driver (and others).[219]

---

218 Driver's attempt to circumvent our linguistic ignorance by asserting a northern provenance for Cant based on "the acquaintance shown by the author with localities in North Palestine" (1956: 449) – another bias that seems to have entrenched itself in the scholarly literature (Keel, 1994: 36, even provides a map situating these northern sites!) – fairs no better. Fox is emphatic here and right on target (1985: 189): The content does not suggest a northern provenance. The incidental mention of northern place names (Lebanon, Hermon, Damascus, etc.) no more proves a northern provenience than the reference to Heshbon in Transjordan proves an eastern one. The events of Cant take place in Jerusalem. The heroine lives in a walled city, and since she converses with the girls of Jerusalem, it is fair to conclude that Jerusalem is her home. And it would be more natural for a Judean than a northerner to choose Jerusalem as the setting for the poem. One could elaborate on Fox's arguments in a myriad of ways, but several brief observations will suffice. First, as Murphy notes (1990: 4), "none of the geographical references betrays an interest in concrete political history" – or, one might add, requires first-hand, historical knowledge of the places in question. That is to say, the geographical references as a whole look to be employed for specifically literary purposes. This is perhaps corroborated (at least partially) by the frequency with which the poet plays on geographical names, e.g., *kĕʾōhŏlê qēdār* "the tents of Kedar" (1:5) coming immediately after the woman's assertion of her sun-darkened skin surely trades on the notion of "darkness" associated with verb *qādar* "to become dark" (Fox 1985: 101; cf. Murphy 1990: 128); *rêaḥ lĕbānôn* "the scent of Lebanon" (4:11) likely involves a play on the fragrance of "frankincense" (*lĕbônâ*, as explicitly in Vg: *odor turis*, cf. Vg. at 3:6; 4:6) just as *gibʿat hallĕbônâ* "the hill of frankincense" (4:6) surely plays on "the Lebanon" (*hallĕbānôn*, 3:9; note the reference to "mountains of Bether" in the echoing passage in 2:17). Second, the number of geographical references in Cant is actually quite small, totaling only thirteen in all, and out of these, not including the more general geographic designations such as Sharon, Gilead, Carmel, Hermon, and the like, for which no specialized knowledged would have been required, there is only one specific northern site mentioned, Tirzah (6:4). And third, with exception again of Tirzah, all of the sites mentioned have extant Persian period occupation layers (where this is a relevant datum; cf. Stern 1982; 2001).

219 As mentioned earlier, it is precisely the lack of control that most bedevils Rendsburg's otherwise stimulating research into "Israelian Hebrew" (1990; 2002). In lieu of outstanding northern linguistic sources Rendsburg is forced to rely on posited isoglosses with other NWS dialects (e.g., Aramaic, Phoenician, and the like) and on biblical compositions whose putative northern provenance is often little more than asserted. His use of Cant as source material for identifying northernism in the Psalms and Kings is a case in point (cf. Zevit 1992: 128). He simply states that the "Song of Songs is another book whose northern affinities have long been noticed" (1990: 11). Of course, he no more than Driver (who is his chief authority) is able to actually demonstrate this assertion (and certainly not on linguistic grounds, a possibility implied by his remark about the lack of a full scale study of Cant's language). The circularity endemic to this practice, in turn, means that much of Rendsburg's enterprise must be taken as a heuristic until such a time that his arguments can be empirically tested.

What we can control for at present is precisely the subject of this essay, the diachronic variation in Biblical Hebrew. And it is on the basis of this body of knowledge that one may posit that "the Aramaic usages" in Cant are "likely a sign of lateness".[220]

3. Foreign Loanwords

3.1. Persianisms

If the combination of diagnostically late linguistic features and (late) Aramaisms mark the language of Cant as LBH, it is the existence of Persian loanwords, or of loans from other languages that were likely to have been mediated through Persian, that allows us to fine-tune our estimate of Cant's likely chronological horizons more precisely. As Seow has observed, "there is no clear evidence of [commonly recognized] Persianisms prior to the Achaemenid period".[221] The appearance, then, of any Persianisms in Cant is strong evidence for a specifically Persian period or later date.[222] There are four likely Persianisms in Cant.

pardēs (4:13): As is widely recognized, *pardēs* "park, orchard," which appears outside of Cant in BH only in the late Qoh 2:5 and Neh 2:8, is ultimately of Persian origin, deriving from Old Persian **pardaiḏa* (Hinz 1975: 179; Kent 1953: 195).[223] The Old Persian term was borrowed into a number of languages, including Akkadian (perhaps the intermediate source for the word in Hebrew[224]) and Greek, but nowhere earlier than the second half of the sixth century.[225]

ʾĕgôz (6:11): A *hapax legomenon*. The term was recognized as a Persian loanword (< **gauz* "to hide," cf. *gauzaina* [Hinz 1975: 106]) early on.[226] Pope (1977: 574-79) and Murphy (1990: 176) are less certain. Wagner (1966: 18), who also notes the uncertainty of the word's origin, nonetheless suspects that Aramaic is the immediate source of the word in Cant.[227] The word is used more commonally in MH (Jastrow, I, 11). And, indeed, with the exception of the problematic Ug *ʿrgz*, all of the probable reflexes of this word in the various languages (Semitic and otherwise) are late. Thus, despite the uncertainty as to

220 Fox 1985: 189.
221 Seow 1996: 648.
222 Cf. Albright 1963: 1.
223 E.g., Graetz 1871: 52-53; Ellenbogen 1962: 136; *HALOT*, 3, 963.
224 See Seow 1996: 649-50, n. 38.
225 Seow 1996: 649.
226 Driver 1956: 449; cf. Seow 1996: 647; *HALOT* 1, 10.
227 Cf. Fox 1985: 189.

its ultimate origin, it would seem relatively certain that *'ĕgôz* is a late lexeme.[228]

nērd (1:12; 4:13, 14): Presumably, the reference here is to spikenard (often just "nard"; *Nardostachys jatamansi*), an aromatic that was imported from the mountains of India.[229] The term itself is non-Hebrew (and non-Semitic) in origin, as indicated by its morphological shape, a monosyllabic noun with a word-final consonant cluster. The latter is generally not tolerated in Semitic. Most understand the Hebrew term as deriving from Sanskrit *nalada* and borrowed more immediately from Persian (*nardin*[230]). The word continues in MH and is reflected as well in TA *nirdā'* (cf. Gk *nardos;* Ar. *nardīn*; Akk. *lardu* [only SB, NB]).

karkōm (4:14): a *hapax legomenon* in BH, appears to designate the aromatic spice saffron (*Crocus sativus*[231]), which was also used for medicinal purposes in Mesopotamia (*CAD* K, 560-61) and as a dye in Egypt.[232] The term itself is non-Hebrew, as suggested most tellingly by its quadrilateral base. In its attested form, *karkōm* looks to be derived ultimately from Sanskrit *kurkum*,[233] as mediated most likely through Persian (*kurkum*).[234] The hypothesis of *karkōm* as a possible loan from Akkadian (*kurkānû* = Sum Ú.KUR.GI.RIN/RÍN.NA [Ú.KUR$_4$.GI.RIN.NA]) is less attractive, chiefly for phonological reasons.[235] The term is used in MH (*karkôm/karqôm*) and appears in Syriac (*kûrkāmā'*). As a species, saffron now appears to have originated in eastern Greece (Gk *krokos*), though whether it was ever cultivated in the hinterland of the Near East during antiquity is an open question.[236]

228 Curiously, J. Fox (2003: 75) sees BH *'ĕgôz* as reflecting (and thus derivative of) a PS isolated noun **gawz* "nut, walnut" cf Ar *jawz*; Ge'ez *gawz*; Syr *gawztā'*).

229 Loew 1928, III: 482; Zohary 1982: 205; Jacob and Jacob 1992: 813.

230 E.g., Pope 1977: 348; Brenner 1983: 77.

231 Cf. Loew 1928, II: 7; Zohary 1982: 206.

232 Jacob and Jacob 1992: 815.

233 Ellenbogen 1962: 93.

234 So Brenner 1983: 76.

235 Nasals are generally preserved in Akkadian loans in BH (Mankowski 2000: 158-59), and thus the *-n-* in the Akkadian word would be expected to carry over into Hebrew, but it does not in this instance. Also the realization of Akk *ā* as BH *ō* is unexpected (though not wholly unexceptional, see Mankowski 2000: 159-60). On both counts, compare BH *'ommān* which ultimately is derived from Akk *ummānu* (see above). Moreover, loans from Akkadian in BH are relatively few in number (approximately only seventy as estimated by Mankowski 2000: 157).

236 For Syria-Palestine, see Brenner 1983: 76; Fox 1985: 138. A number of the other terms for imported aromatics that recur in Cant – such as *qinnāmôn* (4:14), *qāneh* (4:14), *'ăhālôt* (4:14), and *môr* (1:13; 3:6; 4:6, 14; 5:1.5.13) – however, though clearly attested in late sources, also appear slightly earlier (end of the seventh century, so Brenner 1983: 75-81), and therefore a pre-Persian period date for Cant cannot be ruled out on the baisis of these terms. Still, given the overall commonality of subject matter and the

3.2. Grecisms

The only possible Grecism in Cant is the *hapax legomenon* *ʾappiryôn* in 3:9,[237] which many understand as deriving from Gk *phoreion* "litter, sedan-chair".[238] However, phonological considerations, the strongest linguistic evidence for loan identification, are against the equation. As Pope notes, "the phonetic similarity between the Greek and Hebrew ... is somewhat vague".[239] In particular, the prothetic *aleph*, doubling of the *pe*, and presence of the *i* vowel all require some explanation. They do not seem to reflect a close approximation of the Greek, This is shown most tellingly by comparing the Hebrew term with JBA *pûryāʾ* "bed" (and related lexemes) and Syr *pûryāʾ/pûryōn* "couch, litter," both of which are (phonetically) more obvious and straightforward

---

clustering of these terms in only a handful of verses (Cant 1:13-14; 4:13-14), it is likely that *nērd* and *karkōm* are the best guages for the date of usage of these terms in Cant.

237 No one has pursued the question of possible Grecisms in Cant more broadly than H. Graetz (1871). He identified a host of possible Greek loanwords in Cant (1871: 54-60), reflexes of Greek customs and culture (1871: 60-67), and Greek literary parallels (1971: 67-91). Given such an abundance of posited Grecisms, it is not surprising that Graetz dates Cant most securely to the Hellenistic period – to the last part of the third century (1871: 90-91). Our chief interest here lies with the putative Greek loanwords posited by Graetz. As for these, with the possible exception of his seeing *ʾappiryôn* as a borrowing of Gk *phoreion* into Hebrew (1871: 54-55) discussed above, none are compelling. So, for example, Heb *mezeg*, which Graetz would understands as a borrowing of Gk *misgein* (1871: 55-56), is more likely an Aramaism (Aram *mzag* "to mix wine," cf. Wagner 1966: 73-74). If anything, instead of Heb *kōper* being a reflex of Gk *kupros* (Graetz 1871: 56), the direction of the borrowing is the reverse: Gk *kupos* is more likely a loan from Semitic (Lewy 1970: 40-41). And as for Heb *talpîyyôt,* another *hapax legomenon*, most today doubt Graetz's (1871: 57-58) equation with Gk *tēlōpis* (cf. esp. Rudolph 1962: 144-5; Garbini 1992: 219-20) – and indeed if it is a Greek loanword then it was not recognized as such by the translator of LXX – preferring instead to make recourse to one or another Semitic cognate, especially **lpy* "to arrange in courses" (Honeyman 1949: 50-52; cf.Fox 1985: 130-31; Murphy 1990: 155; Keel 1994: 138). While the cultural and literary parallels posited by Graetz deserve sustained discussion, I cannot help but agree with Fox's assessment that (the content of) Cant does not "seem to grow out of any specific artistic or historical environment" (1985: 191). Therefore, while comparison with Hellenistic literary parallels may be incredibly valuable for the larger appreciation of Cant, they are not of a kind that would demand a Hellenistic setting for Cant.

238 Liddell and Scott, 1950; cf. Rundgren 1962: 70-72; Rudolph 1962: 139-40; Fox 1985: 125; Müller 1992: 36, n. 99; Garbini 1992: 212; Keel 1994: 130. Intriguingly, Fox raises the possibility that the borrowing of Gk *phoreion* may have been mediated through Aramaic (cf. Wagner 1966: 28). However, the same kinds of phonetic problems that bedevil the supposition of a Greek loan in the first place – what is the motivation for the addition of the prothetic *aleph*? why an *i*-class instead of a *u*-class vowel? (see Robert, Tournay, and Feuillet 1963: 148) – recur under this hypothesis. The standard Aramaic forms (*pûryāʾ* and the like) look like loans from Gk *phoreion*, while the Hebrew is not a close match for either the Greek or the Aramaic. Therefore, however intriguing Fox's thesis, it does not circumvent the phonetic difficulties associated with a direct borrowing from Greek (see above).

239 Pope 1977: 31, cf. Robert, Tournay, and Feuillet 1963: 148.

borrowings of Gk *phoreion*[240] – and independent of BH *ʾappiryôn* (cf. MH *ʾappiryôn*; JBA *ʾpwryʾ*). Neither does the Hebrew look like an accommodation ("nativization") of the Greek to common Hebrew phonological or morphological structures. Therefore, from a purely linguistic perspective the equation of Hebrew *ʾappiryôn* with Greek *phoreion* remains problematic.

As it turns out, the linguistic fit between *ʾappiryôn* and other commonly posited etymons is equally troublesome. So, for example, Sanskrit *paryanka* (and *palki*) "palanquin, sedan-chair"[241] has also been suggested as a possible etymon.[242] But it, too, involves phonetic inconsistencies, e.g., uncertainty again as to the rationale for the prothetic *aleph* and no Hebrew reflex of the Sanskrit *k*.[243] W.F. ALBRIGHT, who was adamant that there was not a single Greek loanword in Cant (1963: 1), preferred instead to see *ʾappiryôn* as a loan from Old Persian, following G. WIDENGREN (< **upari-yāna*, 1955: 122, n. 80). However, the existence of the Persian term in question is now disputed,[244] though it continues to be cited as a possible source for the Hebrew word.[245] Given these kinds of linguistic complications, therefore, it is not surprising to find among contemporary commentators many agnostics who resist coming down strongly in favor of one or another of the posited etymons for *ʾappiryôn* and are content to translate in light of the general sense demanded by the larger literary context.[246]

240 Cf. Krauss 1899: 433

241 Monier-Williams 1960: 554.

242 So Gordis 1974: 21, 85

243 Moreover, it seems doubtful that such a term would be borrowed into Hebrew in the first place. To be sure, other Indian derived terms are attested in Hebrew (and in Semitic more generally), but these are restricted (for the most part) to items acquired commonly through trade (so *nērd*, *karkōm*, and the like, cf. Fox 1985: 125). A litter or sedan-chair is hardly the kind of commodity that was traded with any regularity in antiquity. Besides, even if it could be established with full confidence that the etymon is in fact Sanskrit, there is no evidence that the term (Hebrew or otherwise) became so common in the Levant that it could be used to describe a locally made litter or chair (from "the wood of Lebanon").

244 See Rundgren 1962: 70-72; Rudolph 1962: 139-40; Fox 1985: 125. Borrowing can also result in lexemes made up of disparate elements (e.g., morphemes) that are combined in ways not attested in the donor language (see Trask 1996: 21-22), though I know of no other evidence for such a practice involving Hebrew and Persian.

245 E.g., Murphy 1990: 149; *HALOT*, 1, 80. Other suggestions, such as that of G. Gerleman (1965: 139, 140-41), who posits a loan from Egyptian (*pr* "house"), seem even less likely. Although Gerleman's suspicion that what may be in view here is a structure and not a mobile vehicle is shared by ancient (Ibn Ezra, "magnificent building") and modern (Fox 1985: 125; Bloch and Bloch 1995: 163; for the emendation *ʾappeden* "palace," as in Dan 11:45, see Robert, Tournay, and Feuillet, 1963: 149-50) interpreters alike. And interestingly, litters were used in Egypt from the third millennium onwards (Keel 1994: 130-32, esp. Fig. 72).

246 E.g., Murphy 1990: 149; Longman 2001: 136.

That *phoreion* is found in the LXX of 3:9 undoubtedly has strengthened the appeal of a putative Greek etymology for Hebrew *ʾappiryôn*. However, that the substance of LXX's reading in this instance is an accurate reflection of the Hebrew is (at least) open to question. While LXX evidences a *Vorlage* close to that of MT (a little more expansive in places), the variants it preserves are as often as not trivial, as Rudolph says (1962: 80), and, like the other versions, it generally struggles to make sense of the many *hapax legomena* and other rare and exotic words that make up much of Cant's vocabulary. As a consequence of the latter, in particular, the specifics of LXX's readings, even when witnessing to the same *Vorlage* as MT (or the other versions), are frequently mistaken. Examples of LXX's misconstruals would include Gk *mastoi sou* "your breasts" for MT *dōdeykā* "your love" (1:2), Gk *deuto* "come!" for MT *ʾittî* "with me" (4:8), *siōpēseōs sou* "your silence" for MT *ṣammātēk* "your veil" (4:1, 3; 6:7), and Gk *trugones* "turtledove" for MT *tōrîm* "ornaments" in 1:10 and Gk *omoiōmata* "likeness" in 1:11 (MT *tôrê*). Similarly, LXX often fails to recognize geographical names, e.g., *rōʾš ʾămānâ* (4:8) is rendered as *archē pisteōs* "top of faith", *tirṣâ* (6:4) as *eudokia* "pleasure". And in several places LXX simply transliterates the Hebrew (e.g., 4:4.14; 5:11.14). As a general rule, then, the semantics of specific readings in LXX – especially where the Hebrew is obscure or problematic – are often not trustworthy (cf. *BHQ*,*10).

Moreover, it is often the case as well in Cant that troublesome Hebrew words and phrases cause translational turbulence in the versions more generally (e.g., *talpiyyôt*, 4:4; *šalhebetyâ*, 8:6). And such turbulence is in evidence in 3:9, as all of the versions appear to be struggling to make sense of MT here (cf. 4QCant^{b} II2i.7: [ʾ]*p̊r̊yw*[*n*]), guessing (it would appear) from their sense of the context. Vg (*ferculum* "a carrier"), if not simply following LXX here, would appear to take its clue from *miṭṭâ* "couch" in 3:7 and the sense of mobility implied in 3:6. P. ALEXANDER (2003: 126, n. 47) construes the reading in TgCant (*hykl qwdšʾ* "holy Temple") similarly, though obviously the latter is far more interpretive, as is this (late) targum's character. The reading of *magdlāʾ* "tower" in Syr (*kwrsyʾ* in some mss) moves in a rather different direction, presuming a more solid structure (so also Ibn Ezra, see Fox 1985: 122-24, 125-26). This reading is all the more intriguing as it does not gloss the Hebrew with either *pûryāʾ* or *pûryōn*, despite the (putative) resemblances of the latter with Hebrew *ʾappiryôn* and the explicit example of LXX's *phoreion*.[247]

Therefore, that LXX in 3:9 would manage to nail the Hebrew, where the Hebrew itself is problematic and where the other versions (and later interpreters) have difficulties, is at least surprising and somewhat contrary to expectation given the general translation tendencies of the versions (including LXX) in Cant. My own suspicion is that LXX, like the other versions, is

247 Cf. Fox 1985: 125.

guessing at the Hebrew based on context, and thus its use of *phoreion* here may be nothing more than happenstance. But whether or not I am right is beside the point. What seems evident is that on any analysis the textual issues in 3:9 are sufficiently problematic to forestall an easy use of LXX to bolster what are otherwise weak linguistic arguments in favor of seeing *ʾappiryôn* as a Greek loanword.

What is at stake in determining whether BH *ʾappiryôn* is in fact a Greek loanword was already seen by Greatz, namely, the very real likelihood, if true, that Cant could date to the Hellenistic period. Indeed, the earliest that *phoreion* appears in Greek literature is during this general period (in the work of Dinarchus, fourth-third century, cf. Liddell and Scott, 1950). Pope, however, resists this logic. He maintains to the contrary that "even acceptance of these words (i.e., *ʾappiryôn* and *talpiyyôt*) as Greek does not necessitate a late dating for Song of Songs, since Mycenaean Greek antedates the Exodus" (Pope 1977: 31). To be sure, there is no doubting the existence of Greek prior to the Hellenistic period, and, in fact, the evidence of early cultural contact between Greece and the Near East is not insubstantial (e.g., West 1997). And more to the point, there is considerable archaeological evidence from the Levant itself for contacts with the Aegean world during Iron II[248] and especially during the Persian period.[249] Indeed, one of the principal markers of Persian period strata at Levantine sites is the presence of black- and red-figured Attic ware (Stern 1982: xvii). However, what is most striking about the Greek material remains from these periods is the near complete absence of evidence for the use of Greek writing. This is especially striking for the Persian period, for which the written remains are abundant and multilingual, but, as E. STERN observes, "almost none are written in Greek" (2001: 366).[250] When this datum is combined with the knowledge that undisputed Greek loanwords start appearing commonly in Hellenistic-period literary works such as Daniel,[251] Pope's (and others') resistance to the chronological consequences of a Greek loanword in Cant – namely, as a likely indicator of a Hellenistic date – is hard to understand except as a case of special pleading. It seems to me, rather, on the basis of current knowledge, that the presence of Greek loans – aside perhaps from the technical language of trade and the like[252] – must be considered as a potentially good indicator of a Hellenistic date. We, of course, are not to imagine this as an exceptionless law, but more like a heuristic rule of thumb, which, in light of compelling evidence to the contrary, can always be

248 Waldbaum 1994: 53-66; Stern 2001: 217-27.

249 Stern 1982; 2001: 517-22, 552-54, 555, 556, 558-59.

250 Most of the evidence for Greek writing during this period comes from the northern coast, where there was a heavy concentration of Greek settlements.

251 See esp. Seow 1996: 657.

252 For example, in Egyptian Aramaic loans from Gk *statēr* (*TAD* C3.7Ar2:2) and *pinax* (*TAD* D7.57:8) are attested.

overturned. The point here is that Pope's thesis should not be the default perspective from which to frame the issue. The question, then, becomes for our present interest just how plausible is the construal of *ʾappiyrôn* as a Greek loan? And here, for the linguistic and text critical reasons noted above, I find myself agreeing with Pope (and others) that the attribution is "unlikely" (1977: 31) – or, at least, not nearly substantial enough linguistically to warrant placing of these poems and/or their editing in the Hellenistic period.[253] That is, the linguistic profile of Cant, while compatible with a Hellenistic dating,[254] does not require it, and therefore, the supposition that Cant is a Hellenistic work will need to be funded and moved on other than linguistic grounds.[255]

Conclusion

In conclusion, the late linguistic features and genuine Aramaisms isolated above show the language of Cant – as reflected in its extant textual embodiment (MT) – to be very much akin to that of the other late books of the Bible (e.g., Ezra, Nehemiah, Chronicles, Esther, Qohelet, and the like), a variety of what has become known as late Biblical Hebrew. The presence of several Persianisms provide our most sensitive linguistic barometer for gauging the actual date of Cant's language, pointing rather concretely to the two centuries of Achaemenid rule in the Near East (539-323 B.C.E.), and it is here that I am most inclined to place the composition of the poems themselves.[256] This position is not incontrovertible, of course, as Pope rightly observes, "The dating game as played with biblical books like Job and Song of Songs, as well as with many of the Psalms, remains imprecise and the score is difficult to compute."[257] Nonetheless, the language of Cant is by far its most tractable datum, and its lateness, as noted, is beyond doubt.

The consequences for an early (pre-exilic) dating of Cant (or some of its component poems) are severe and can only be sidestepped by presuming a rather prolonged period of transmission involving much revision of the language, the positive evidence for which is minimal and late at best (e.g.,

253 E.g., as does Müller 1992: 36 n99; cf. 3 nn2-3.

254 Cf. Fox 1985: 190.

255 Again this is not to say that comparative literary studies involving Hellenistic Greek literature, especially love poetry, cannot be informative and illuminating. They can be. But that this is so need not have any consequence for the question of date. In fact, all of the best parallels for Cant – Mesopotamian, Egyptian, Arabic, and Greek – come, as far as I can determine, from different historical epochs.

256 So also Albright 1963: 1; Greenfield and Naveh 1984: 120; cf. Rudolph 1962: 110-11. A hard *terminus ad quem* for Cant is established by the several Herodian period Song manuscripts from Caves 4 and 6 at Qumran (see esp. Tov 2000).

257 Pope 1977: 27.

1:1).[258] Even the geographical localities referenced in Cant, which have often been supposed to indicate an early date and a northern provenance, mostly all evidence Persian period occupation strata (esp. En-Gedi, Jerusalem, Heshbon) or were otherwise known to have existed during the period (e.g., Damascus, Kedar – a North Arabian tribal group known to have flourished into the Hellenistic period).[259] The outstanding exception is Tirzah (6:4), now commonly identified with Tell el-Far'ah (N), a large site that (so far) appears to have been abandoned at some point during the sixth century.[260] But no chronological implications necessarily entail from this reference. It may have been motivated for any number of reasons,[261] but, more to the point, it is simply a fallacy to assume that the mere mention of the site requires an early dating of Cant solely because Tirzah was the capital of the northern kingdom for only a relatively brief period of time – Omri having moved the capital to Samaria during the early part of the ninth century. Late anachronisms implicate lateness, but the reverse does not hold.[262] And thus there is nothing

---

258 The nature of lyric sequences is such that it allows quite easily for revision, recomposition, and editing (for example, witness 4QCant[b]), so it may well be that all signs of any early editorial intervention would remain invisible to us. But against the idea of updating are those instances in Cant where the presumed presence of an earlier linguistic element would destroy the literary effect of the received text (cf. Greenstein 2003). This is most obvious with the use of *še-*. For example, in the couplet

šekkullām mat'îmôt *wĕšakkūlâ 'ên bāhem* (4:2)

All of them twins and none among them miscarries

to assume that *'ăšer* once stood in place of *še-* (**'ăšer kullām*) destroys the play between *šekkullām* and *wĕšakkūlâ*. Another example involves euphony:

qōrôt bātênû 'ărāzîm *raḥîtēnû bĕrôtîm* (1:17)

The rafters of our house are cedars, our beams are cypresses

Groups of segments rhyme and chime throughout this couplet: the voiceless and emphatic dentals (*t, ṭ*), *-ôt*, /*-ēnū*/, and *-îm*. The euphony of the first three sets would be destroyed (or reduced) had the poet originally used either the SBH form of the construct chain (**qōrōt bêtĕnû*) or the Hebrew term for "cypresses" (*bĕrôšîm*).

259 Many of the geographical references, in fact, are to broad regions (e.g., Sharon, 2:1; Gilead, 4:1; 6:5) or mountain ranges (e.g., Lebanon, 3:9; 4:8, 11, 15; 5:15; 7:5; Carmel, 7:6) that require no premise of occupation in order to have been known during the period. Nevertheless, the Sharon plain was abundantly inhabited at this time (Stern 2001: 385-407), including Shiqmona along the Carmel coast (Stern 2001: 389), and while little is known of the Gilead during the period, there are Persian period strata at sites such as Tell es-Sa'idiyeh and Tell el-Mazar (Stern 2001: 455). Furthermore, though the speculation about a northern provenance for Cant cannot be supported linguistically or on the basis of the geographical references themselves, it should be pointed out that even if such a provenance for Cant could be shown, it would not then also entail the specification of a pre-exilic date for Cant. Large portions of the north (e.g., the provinces of Megiddo [Stern 2001: 373-79] and Samaria [Stern 2001: 422-28]) were well populated and even prospered during the Persian period.

260 Stern 2001: 320.

261 E.g., as a word play, so Fox 1985: 151; Murphy 1990: 4.

262 By the same principle, in comparative linguistics one guages family resemblance chiefly on the basis of shared innovations and not shared retentions.

against assuming with Fox that "Tirzah was probably half-legendary by the time Cant was composed, and probably little was known about it except that it was once the capital of the northern kingdom and thus offered an appropriate parallel to Jerusalem".[263] By contrast, the supposition of a Hellenistic date for Cant's composition (and/or editing) cannot be proscribed on the basis of the linguistic evidence. Our diachronic linguistic controls remain fairly blunt and are not well disposed to making such finer distinctions. Still, the absence of undisputed Grecisms in Cant does rob the thesis of any *positive* linguistic support and thus necessitates that it be moved on the strength of other considerations. In sum, then, the linguistic profile of Cant favors a Persian period or (possibly) later date for the composition and/or editing of these poems.

Bibliography

ALBRIGHT, W.F. (1963): Archaic Survivals in the Text of Canticles, in: D.W. Thomas and W.D. McHardy (eds.), Hebrew and Semitic Studies Presented to Godfrey Rolles Driver, Oxford, 1-7.

ALEXANDER, P. (2003): The Targum Canticles. The Aramaic Bible 17A, Collegeville.

ANDERSEN, F.I./FORBES, A.D. (1986): Spelling in the Hebrew Bible, BiOr 41, Rome.

BARR, J. (1989): The Variable Spellings of the Hebrew Bible, Oxford.

BENDAVID, A. (1967-71): Biblical Hebrew and Mishnaic Hebrew, 2nd ed. Tel Aviv [in Hebrew].

BERGEY, R. (1984): Late Linguistic Features in Esther, JQR 75, 66-78.

BEYER, K. (1984): Die aramäischen Texte vom Toten Meer samt den Inschriften aus Palästina, dem Testament Levis aus der Kairoer Genisa, der Fastenrolle und den alten talmudischen Zitaten, Göttingen.

BLOCH, A./BLOCH, C. (1995): Song of Songs, New York.

BRENNER, A. (1983): Aromatics and Perfumes in Song of Songs, JSOT 25, 75-81.

COGAN, M. (2000): 1 Kings, AB 10, New York.

COLLINS, J.J. (1993): Daniel, Hermeneia, Minneapolis.

COOPER, J.S. (1971): New Cuneiform Parallels to Song of Songs, JBL 90, 157-162.

CROSS, F.M./FREEDMAN, D.N. (1952): Early Hebrew Orthography, AOS 32, New Haven.

– (1975): Studies in Ancient Yahwistic Poetry, SBLDS 21, Missoula.

DEGEN, R. (1969): Altaramäische Grammatik der Inschriften des 10.-8. Jh. v. Chr., Wiesbaden.

DOBBS-ALLSOPP, F.W. (1998): Linguistic Evidence for the Date of Lamen-tations, JANES 26, 1-36.

DRIVER, S.R. (1892): A Treatise on the Use of the Tenses in Hebrew and Some Other Syntactical Questions, Oxford.

– (1897): An Introduction to the Literature of the Old Testament, Cleveland/ New York [repr. ed. 1956].

EHRENSVÄRD, M. (1997): Once Again: The Problem of Dating Biblical Hebrew, SJOT 11, 29-40.

---

263 Fox 1985: 151. Or to put it slightly differently, a good deal of other evidence pointing to an early date would be required in order to count the reference to Tirzah as a corroborating datum. On its own it is moot.

ELLENBOGEN, M. (1962): Foreign Words in the Old Testament: Their Origin and Etymology, London.
ERMAN, A./GRAPOW, H. (1926-50): Wörterbuch der ägyptischen Sprache I-VI, Leipzig.
ESKHULT, M. (2000): Verbal Syntax in Late Biblical Hebrew, in: T. Muraoka/J.F. Elwolde (eds.), Diggers at the Well. Proceedings of a Third International Symposium on the Hebrew of the Dead Sea Scrolls and Ben Sira, STDJ 36, Leiden, 84-93.
FALES, F.M. (1986): Aramaic Epigraphs on Clay Tablets of the Neo-Assyrian Period, Rome.
FASSBERG, S.D. (1996): The Pronominal Suffix of the Second Feminine Singular in the Aramaic Texts from the Judean Desert, DSD 3,10-19.
FITZMYER, J.A. (1995): The Aramaic Inscriptions of Sefire, BibOr 19A, rev. ed. Rome.
FOLMER, M.L. (1995): The Aramaic Language in Achaemenid Period: A Study in Linguistic Variation, Leuven.
FOX, J. (2003): Semitic Noun Patterns, HSS 52, Winona Lake.
FOX, M.V. (1985): Song of Songs and the Ancient Egyptian Love Songs, Madison.
FREEDMAN, D.N. (1983): The Spelling of the Name 'David' in the Hebrew Bible, HAR 7, 89-104.
FREEDMAN, D.N./FORBES, A.D./ANDERSEN, F.I. eds. (1992): Studies in Hebrew and Aramaic Orthography, Biblical and Judaic Studies 2 Winona Lake.
GARBINI, G. (1992): Cantico dei Cantici, Biblica Testi e studi 2, Brescia.
GARR, W.R. (1985): Dialect Geography of Syria-Palestine, 1000-586 B.C.E., Philadelphia.
GERLEMAN, G. (1965): Ruth, Das Hohelied, BK 18, Neukirchen-Vluyn.
GEVIRTZ, S. (1986): Of Syntax and Style in the 'Late Biblical Hebrew' – 'Old Canaanite' Connection, JANES 18, 25-29.
GINSBERG, H.L. (1969): Introduction to Song of Songs, in: Jewish Publication Society Version: The Five Megilloth and Jonah, Philadelphia, 3-4.
– (1970): The Northwest Semitic Languages, in: B. Mazar (ed.), The World History of the Jewish People, Vol. 2, New Brunswick, 102-124.
GIVÓN, T. (1974): Verb Complements and Relative Clauses: A Diachronic Case Study in Biblical Hebrew, Afroasiatic Linguistics 1/4, 1-22.
– (1977): The Drift from VSO to SVO in Biblical Hebrew: The Pragmatics of Tense-Aspect, in: C. Li (ed.), Mechanisms in Syntactic Change, Austin, 181-254.
GOLDENBERG, G. (1998): Studies in Semitic Linguistics, Jerusalem.
GORDIS, R. (1974): Song of Songs and Lamentations, 3rd ed., New York.
GRAETZ, H. (1871): Schir Ha-Schirim oder das Salomonische Hohelied, Breslau.
GREENFIELD, J.C. (1964): Ugaritc *mdl* and Its cognates, Bib, 527-534.
GREENFIELD, J.C./NAVEH, J. (1984): Hebrew and Aramaic in the Persian Period, in: W.D. Davies/L. Finkelstein (eds.), The Cambridge History of Judaism, Vol. 1, Cambridge, 115-129.
GREENSTEIN, E.L. (1974): Two Variations of Grammatical Parallelism in Canaanite Poetry and their Psycholinguistic Background, JANES 6, 87-105.
– (2003): The Language of Job and Its Poetic Function, JBL 122, 651-666.
HILL, A. (1983): Dating the Book of Malachi: A Linguistic Reexamination, in: C.L. Meyers/M. O'Connor (eds.), The Word of the Lord Shall Go Forth Essays in Honor of David Noel Freedman in Celebration of His Sixtieth Birthday, American Schools of Oriental Research, Special Volume Series 1, Winona Lake, 77-89.
HILLERS, D.R. (1992): Lamentations, AB 7A, New York.
HINZ, W. (1975): Altiranisches Sprachgut der Nebenüberlieferungen, Wiesbaden.
HOFTIJZER, J. (1985): The Function and Use of Imperfect Forms with Nun Paragogicum in Classical Hebrew, Assen.
HONEYMAN, A.M. (1949): Two Contributions to Canaanite Toponomy, JThS 50, 50-52.
HUEHNERGARD, J. (1991): Remarks on the Classification of the Northwest Semitic Languages, in: J. Hoftijzer/C. van der Kooij (eds.), The Balaam Text from Deir 'Alla Re-evaluated, Leiden, 282-293.
– (1995): What is Aramaic?, Aram 7, 261-282.

– (1997): A Grammar of Akkadian, HSM 45, Atlanta.
HUG, V. (1993): Altaramäische Grammatik der Texte des 7. und 6. Jh.s v. Chr., Heidelberg.
HURVITZ, A. (1968): The Chronological Significance of 'Aramaisms' in Biblical Hebrew, IEJ 18, 234-240.
– (1972): The Transition Period in Biblical Hebrew: A Study in Post-Exilic Hebrew and Its Implications for the Dating of Psalms, Jerusalem [in Hebrew].
– (1973): Linguistic Criteria for Dating Problematic Biblical Texts, Hebrew Abstracts 14, 74-79.
– (1974): The Evidence of Language in Dating the Priestly Code, RB 81, 24-56.
– (1982): A Linguistic Study of the Relationship between the Priestly Source and the Book of Ezekiel, Paris.
– (1995): Continuity and Innovation in Biblical Hebrew – The Case of 'Semantic Change' in Post-Exilic Writings, in: T. Muraoka (ed.), Studies in Ancient Hebrew Semantics, Abr-Nahrain Supplement Series 6, Louvain, 1-10.
– (1997): The Historical Quest for 'Ancient Israel' and the Linguistic Evidence of the Hebrew Bible: Some Methodological Observations, VT 47, 301-315.
– (2003): Hebrew and Aramaic in the Biblical Period: The Problem of 'Aramaisms' in Linguistic Research on the Hebrew Bible" in: I. Young (ed.), Biblical Hebrew: Studies in Chronology and Typology, JSOTS 369, London, 24-37.
JACOB, I./JACOB, W. (1992): Flora, in: ABD, Vol. 2, New York, 803-817.
JASTROW, M. (1967): A Dictionary of the Targumim, the Talmud Babli and Yerushalmi, and the Midrashic Literature, Brooklyn.
JOÜON, P./MURAOKA, T. (1991): A Grammar of Biblical Hebrew, SubBib 14/1-2, Rome (= JM).
KAUFMAN, S.A. (1974): The Akkadian Influence on Aramaic, Chicago.
– (1984): On Vowel Reduction in Aramaic, JAOS 104, 87-95.
– (1992): Aramaic, in: ABD, Vol. 4, New York, 173-178.
KAUTZSCH, E. (1902): Die Aramaismen im Alten Testament, Halle.
KEEL, O. (1994): Song of Songs, Continental Commentaries, Minneapolis.
KENT, R.G. (1953): Old Persian Texts, Grammar, Lexicon, New Haven.
KING, P.J./STAGER, L.E. (2001): Life in Biblical Israel, Library of Ancient Israel, Louisville.
KNOWLES, M. (2001): The Centrality of the Jerusalem Temple in the Religious Practice of Yehud in the Persian Period, Unpublished dissertation. Princeton Theological Seminary.
KÖNIG, F.E. (1881-97): Historisch-kritisches Lehrgebäude der Hebräischen Sprache, Leipzig.
KRAUSS, S. (1899): Griechische und lateinische Lehnwörter im Talmud, Midrasch und Targum, Vol. 2, Berlin.
KROPAT, A. (1909): Die Syntax des Autors der Chronik, BZAW 16, Giessen.
KUTSCHER, E.Y. (1974): The Language and Linguistic Background of the Isaiah Scroll (1QIsa[a]), STDJ 6, Leiden.
– (1977): Hebrew and Aramaic Studies, Jerusalem.
– (1982): A History of the Hebrew Language, Leiden.
LANDES, G.M. (1982): Linguistic Criteria and the Date of the Book of Jonah, EI 16, *147-*170.
LEANDER, P. (1928): Laut- und Formenlehre des Ägyptisch-Aramäischen, Göteborg.
LEMAIRE, A. (1994): 'House of David' Restored in Moabite Inscription, BAR 20, 30-37.
LEWY, H. (1895): Die semitischen Fremdwörter im Griechischen, Hildesheim/New York [repr. ed. 1970].
LOEW, I. (1928): Die Flora der Juden I-IV, Vienna, 1928.
LONGMAN, T. (2001): Song of Songs, NICOT, Grand Rapids.
MANKOWSKI, P.V. (2000): Akkadian Loanwords in Biblical Hebrew, Winona Lake.
MEYERS, C.L./MEYERS, E.M. (1994): Demography and Diatribes: Yehud's Population and the Prophecy of Second Zechariah, in: M.D. Coogan et al. (eds.), Scripture and Other Artifacts, Louisville, 268-285.

MILLER, C.L. (1996): The Representation of Speech in Biblical Hebrew Narrative, HSM 55, Atlanta.
MONIER-WILLIAMS, M. (1960): A Sanskrit-English Dictionary, New ed., Oxford.
MÜLLER, H.-P. (1992): Das Hohelied, in: id./O. Kaiser/J.A. Loader, Das Hohelied-Klagelieder-Das Buch Ester, ATD 16/2, 4th ed., Göttingen, 3-90.
MURAOKA, T. (1985): Emphatic Words and Structures in Biblical Hebrew, Leiden.
– (1987): Classical Syriac for Hebraists, Wiesbaden.
– (2000): An Approach to the Morphosyntax and Syntax of Qumran Hebrew, in: T. Muraoka/J. F. Elwolde (eds.), Diggers at the Well, Proceedings of a Third International Symposium on the Hebrew of the Dead Sea Scrolls and Ben Sira, STDJ 36, Leiden, 193-214.
MURAOKA, T./PORTEN, B. (1998): A Grammar of Egyptian Aramaic, Leiden.
MURPHY, R. (1990): Song of Songs, Hermeneia, Minneapolis.
NAVEH, J. (1970): The Development of the Aramaic Script, Jerusalem.
NICCACCI, A. (1990): The Syntax of the Verb in Classical Hebrew Prose, Trans. W.G.E. Watson, JSOTS 86, Sheffield.
NÖLDEKE, T. (2001): Compendious Syriac Grammar, Trans., J. Crichton. Winona Lake [1904].
PÉREZ FERNÁNDEZ, M. (1999): An Introductory Grammar of Rabbinic Hebrew, Trans. J. Elwolde, Leiden.
POLZIN, R. (1976): Late Biblical Hebrew: Toward an Historical Typology of Biblical Hebrew Prose, HSM 12, Missoula.
POPE, M.H. (1977): Song of Songs, AB 7C, New York.
QIMRON, E. (1986): The Hebrew of the Dead Sea Scrolls, HSS 29, Atlanta.
– (1992): Observations on the History of Early Hebrew (1000 B.C.E.-200 C.E.) in the Light of the Dead Sea Documents, in: D. Diamant/U. Rappaport (eds.), The Dead Sea Scrolls: Forty Years of Research, STDJ 10, Leiden, 349-361.
RENDSBURG, G.A. (1980): Late Biblical Hebrew and the Date of 'P', JANES 12, 65-80.
– (1990): Linguistic Evidence for the Northern Origin of Selected Psalms, SBLMS, Atlanta.
– (2002): Israelian Hebrew in the Book of Kings, Bethesda.
ROBERT, A./TOURNAY, R./Feuillet, A. (1963): Le Cantique des Cantiques, Études Bibliques, Paris.
ROOKER, M.F. (1990): Biblical Hebrew in Transition: The Language of the Book of Ezekiel, JSOTS 90, Sheffield.
ROSENTHAL, F. (1995): A Grammar of Biblical Aramaic, 6th rev. ed. Wiesbaden.
RUDOLPH, W. (1962): Das Buch Ruth, Das Hohe Lied, Die Klagelieder, KAT XVII/1-3, Gütersloh.
RUNDGREN, F. (1962): 'appirjon, Tragessel, Sänfte, ZAW 74, 70-72.
SÁENZ-BADILLOS, A. (1993): A History of the Hebrew Language, Trans. J. Elwolde, Cambridge.
SEGAL, M.H. (1927): A Grammar of Mishnaic Hebrew, Oxford.
SEGERT, S. (1975): Altaramäische Grammatik, Leipzig.
SEOW, S.L. (1993): Review of Linguistic Evidence for the Northern Origin of Selected Psalms, JBL 112, 334-337.
– (1996): Linguistic Evidence and the Dating of Qoheleth, JBL 115, 643-666.
SMITH, M.S. (1991): The Origins and Development of the waw-Consecutive. HSS 39, Atlanta.
– (2000): The Infinitive Absolute as Predicative Verb in Ben Sira and the Dead Sea Scrolls: A Preliminary Survey, in: T. Muraoka/J.F. Elwolde, (eds.), Diggers at the Well. Proceedings of a Third International Symposium on the Hebrew of the Dead Sea Scrolls and Ben Sira, STDJ 36, Leiden, 256-267.
SOKOLOFF, M. (1990): A Dictionary of Jewish Palestinian Aramaic, Ramat-Gan.
– (2002): A Dictionary of Jewish Babylonian Aramaic, Baltimore/London.

STERN, E. (1982): Material Culture of the Land of the Bible in the Persian Period 538-332 B.C., Jerusalem.
– (2001): Archaeology of the Land of the Bible, Vol. 2. The Assyrian, Babylonian, and Persian Periods 732-332 BCE, ABRL, New York.
TOV, E. (2000): 4QCant[a-c], in: E. Ulrich et al. (eds.), Qumran Cave 4/XI: Psalms to Chronicles, DJD 16, Oxford, 195-219.
TRASK, R.L. (1996): Historical Linguistics, London.
VAN PEURSEN, W. Th. (2004): The Verbal System in the Hebrew Text of Ben Sira, StSLL 41, Leiden.
VON SODEN, W. (1981): Zum hebräischen Wörterbuch, UF 13, 157-164.
WAGNER, M. (1966): Die lexikalischen und grammatikalischen Aramaismen im alttestamentlichen Hebräisch, BZAW 96, Berlin.
WALDBAUM, J.C. (1994): Early Greek Contact with the Southern Levant, ca. 1000-600 BC, BASOR 293, 53-66.
WALSH, C.E. (2000): Exquisite Desire. Religion, the Erotic, and the Song of Songs, Minneapolis.
WALTKE, B.K./O'CONNOR, M. (1990): An Introduction to Biblical Hebrew Syntax, Winona Lake (= WOC).
WEST, M.L. (1997): The East Face of Helicon. West Asiatic Elements in Greek Poetry and Myth, Oxford.
WIDENGREN, G. (1955): Sacrales Königtum im Alten Testament und im Judentum, Stuttgart, 1955.
WILDBERGER, H. (1991): Isaiah 1-12, Continental Commentary, Minneapolis.
YODER, C.R. (2001): Wisdom as a Woman of Substance: A Socioeconomic Reading of Proverbs 1-9 and 31:10-31, BZAW 304, Berlin/New York.
ZEVIT, Z. (1980): Matres Lectiones in Ancient Hebrew Epigraphs, ASORMS 2, Cambridge.
– (1992): Review of Linguistic Evidence for the Northern Origin of Selected Psalms, CBQ 54, 126-129.
ZOHARY, M. (1982): Plants of the Bible, New York.

The Poetic Genius of the Song of Songs

J. Cheryl Exum

... love is strong as death,
  jealousy as fierce as Sheol.
Its flames are flames of fire,
  an almighty flame.
Floods cannot quench love,
  nor rivers sweep it away.
Should a man offer all his wealth for love,
  it would be utterly scorned

(Cant 8:6-7).[1]

These verses, in the view of many scholars, form the climax of the Song of Songs, its 'message' so to speak. Taken on their own, they express a lofty sentiment, but I suspect we would not be inclined to call them gripping or stunningly profound. If we encountered them in the book of Proverbs, we would no doubt praise the affirmation that love is strong as death as an inspired insight, and we might wonder whether the second half of the first couplet is essentially synonymous with or antithetic to the first.[2] We might also comment appreciatively on the way allusions to chthonic and cosmic powers lend grand proportions to the struggle between love and death (e.g., Mot and Resheph, Nahar and the cosmic waters of chaos that only God can subdue,[3] the virtual personification of Sheol, and a possible reference to God in

---

This article is a revised version of the Ethel M. Wood lecture delivered in the University of London on 11 March, 2004; it was researched with assistance from a grant from the Arts and Humanities Research Board, October 2000-January 2001.

1 Translations in this essay are mine; for discussion, see my forthcoming commentary.

2 This is an issue for interpretation of the Song, too, though commentators tend to underplay the difficulty by translating קנאה as 'ardor' or 'passion'.

3 Of Resheph we know little, but he seems to have been associated with the underworld, fiery arrows, and pestilence; on מים רבים as an allusion to the cosmic waters, see Ps 24:2; 77:20; 93:4; Is 51:10; May 1955; Murphy 1987: 118-19; נהרות, recalling Yam's epithet 'Prince River', may also refer to the chaotic primeval waters, though some take it more specifically as the rivers of the underworld (Pope, Keel; cf. Ez 31:15).

שלהבתיה).[4] We could say more about these verses, but probably not a great deal more, before moving on to the next proverb, perhaps observing in conclusion that the final sentiment here, that money cannot buy love, is rather lame in comparison to the grandiose beginning.[5]

These verses would not be out of place in Proverbs, and, significantly, they stand out as the only didactic statement in the Song of Songs, the only time in this love poem that we are told anything about the nature of love in general. The poet places these words, like everything else that is said in the Song, in the mouth of one of the characters in the poem, for our poet is too good a poet, too subtle and too sophisticated, to preach to us directly about love. Here in these verses, near the poem's end, the female protagonist speaks to her lover not, as she has up till now, about their love, but about love itself. The significance of these verses in the context of the Song of Songs, the Bible's only love poem, far exceeds any meaning they have on their own, for they hold the key to the poem's raison-d'être. It is, I suggest, the poet's desire to immortalise a particular vision of love that gives rise to the poem. The proof that love is strong as death is the poem itself, a lasting testimony to the poet's vision of love, addressed to its readers throughout time, and preserved for us through centuries thanks to its inclusion in the Bible – the circumstances of which we know little.[6] So long as the poem is read, the love it celebrates lives on.

It is not quite right, then, to say that the message of the poem is found in the climactic affirmation of these few verses. If we can speak at all of a message, then the medium is the message. The message is the poem itself, the work of art, a literary creation by which the poet strives to make present, through language, what cannot be captured on the page, the lovers whose multiple identities enable them to stand for all lovers, and ultimately for love itself. Although the Song is routinely praised for its poetic achievement and various of its poetic features subjected to scrutiny,[7] the real genius of the Song has, in

---

4 Hebrew שלהבת, meaning 'flame', appears in Ez 21:3 and Job 15:30. The word here is שלהבתיה, with an affixed יָה according to the Ben Asher text (שלהבת יה, with a mappiq in the ה in Ben Naphtali), which some take as a short form of the divine name (e.g., Delitzsch; Rudolph; Murphy, 'flames of Yah') and others as a way of expressing the superlative (Meek, Krinetzki, Ringgren, Gerleman, Gordis, Keel, Snaith, Bloch and Bloch, Longman). Some find this line too short. Given the repetition in the previous line ('its flashes are flashes of fire'), it is possible that the text has suffered haplography and originally read 'its flames are the flames of Yah' (cf. BHS [Horst]; so Budde, Rudolph, Ringgren, Würthwein; see also Murphy; Pope simply ignores the word as a gloss).

5 Indeed, some scholars speculate whether or not v. 7b in the context of the Song is anticlimactic (Pope; Murphy) or out of place (Bergant); Landy speaks of a return to 'petty social discriminations with which we started [in 8:1]' (1983:132).

6 Surely its power as a poem contributed to its popularity, which must have played some role in its preservation.

7 E.g., metaphor (Good 1970; Müller 1984; Alter 1985), imagery (Munro 1995), sound patterns (Krinetzki 1964), prosody (Murphy 1990: 85-91), chiasmus, inclusio, and other

my view, gone virtually unnoticed.[8] The poetic genius of the Song of Songs, as I see it, is twofold: it lies (1) in the way the poet shows us, as well as tells us, that love is strong as death and (2) in the way the poet explores the nature of love, looking at what it is like to be in love from both a woman's and a man's point of view (the latter a striking feature in view of the Bible's androcentrism). These two aspects of the poet's artistry are intimately related; in what follows, I separate them for the purposes of exposition.

Showing that Love Is Strong as Death

How does the poem immortalise the love of which it speaks? First and foremost by presenting love as always in progress.[9] The Song offers its readers a vision of love not in the abstract but in the concrete, through showing us what lovers do, or, more precisely, by telling us what they say. Unlike other biblical texts, there is no narrative description, only dialogue. Through the exclusive use of direct speech, the poet creates an illusion of immediacy: the impression that, far from being simply reported, the action is taking place in the present. Voices that seem to reach us unmediated lend immediacy to what is actually reported speech, a written text whose author is brilliantly effaced. By presenting the lovers in the act of addressing each other, the poem gives us the impression that we are overhearing them and observing their love unfold.

The love that unfolds before us in the Song as the lovers speak is a love that is being celebrated in the here and now. The lovers are always taking their pleasure or just about to do so. The erotic imperative – the call to love by means of imperatives, jussives, and cohortatives – lends urgency to the moment: 'draw me after you', 'let us run' (1:4), 'tell me' (1:7), 'rise up', 'come away' (2:10.13), 'turn' (2:17), 'open to me' (5:2), 'let me see' (2:14), 'let me hear' (2:14; 8:13) and so on. The Song begins with the erotic imperative ('let him kiss

structural features (Exum 1973; Shea 1980; Webster 1982; Heinevetter 1988; Elliott 1989; Dorsey 1990; Wendland 1995; Bergant 2001; Davidson 2003).

8 Broader questions about poetics and meaning are not entirely neglected. The most perceptive poetic analysis remains, in my view, that of Landy (1983); important observations about imagery are offered by Munro 1995; Fox's discussion of modes of presentation, themes, and the Song's attitude to love is unrivaled (1985: 253-331); see also the questions of poetics addressed by Fisch 1988; Pelletier 2002; Sonnet 2002. Part of the reason the Song's genius has gone unnoticed may be the fact that a number of commentators view the Song as a collection of unrelated love poems, and thus do not explore their deeper poetic relationship. This is not the place to discuss the vexed question of the Song's unity; my views have changed since I argued for unity on the basis of literary structure (Exum 1973), but, as the present study makes clear, I am persuaded that an inspired poetic vision of love has guided the final composition of the Song and that only by reading the Song as a whole can we do justice to its poetic genius.

9 A preliminary investigation of some of the poetic techniques discussed here appears in Exum 1999a.

me', 1:2) and ends with it ('bolt away .. be like a gazelle or young deer', 8:14). Not least, the climactic affirmation of love in 8:6-7 is grounded in the erotic imperative ('Set me as the seal upon your heart ... for love is strong as death'). Coupled with imperatives, vocatives strengthen the impression of the lovers' presence at the moment of utterance: 'my soul's beloved', 'my sister, bride', 'most beautiful of women', etc.

Typical of the Song's emphasis on the present moment is the woman's dramatic description of her lover as he comes courting:

> Listen! My lover!
> Look! He's coming,
> leaping over the mountains,
> bounding over the hills.
> My lover is like a gazelle
> or young deer.
> Look! He's standing outside our wall,
> peering in through the windows,
> peeking through the lattice (Cant 2:8-9).

'Listen!' and 'Look!' focus our attention on the action in progress before us.[10] The present is vividly captured by participles: the man is approaching, bounding over hills, standing, looking – his activity arrested in time and space.

A related technique for immortalizing love is conjuring. By 'conjuring' I refer to the way that, through seductively beautiful poetry, the lovers materialise and dematerialise in a continual play of seeking and finding. Conjuring seeks to make immanent through language what is absent, the lovers – to bring them to life before us over and over again. The man conjures his lover up repeatedly by describing her, part by part, in densely metaphorical language, building up a picture of her so that she materialises before us, a body clothed in metaphor (4:1-5.12-15; 6:4-10; 7:1-8). She calls her lover forth through her poetic powers of representation only to let him disappear so that she can conjure him up again (2:8-17; 3:1-5; 3:6-11; 5:2-6:3). As an example of this technique, let us consider the remarkable feat of conjuring in Song 5:2-6:3 (about the metaphoric descriptions I will have more to say below).[11]

As the narrator of the opening verses of this unit, the woman conjures her lover up as a suitor begging entry to her chamber.

> I was sleeping but my heart was awake.
> Listen! My lover is knocking!
> 'Open to me, my sister, my friend,

10 For this usage of קול, see GKC §146b; Joüon/Muraoka §162e; Pope, Fox, Murphy; in vv. 8 and 9, זה reinforces הנה to emphasise the present action; see also 1Kgs 19,5; Isa 21,9. Some give the construction an adverbial sense: 'da kommt er!' (Loretz); 'There he comes' (Pope); 'he's coming now!' (Fox); cf. GKC §136d, Joüon/Muraoka §143a.

11 For an example of conjuring in Song 3:6-11, see Exum 2003a.

my dove, my perfect one,
for my head is drenched with dew,
my locks with mist of the night' (Cant 5:2).

(The presence of double entendre here bears mentioning. The verb 'open' never has an object in these verses; there is no door, as some translations have it, and so 'open to me' [v. 2], 'I rose to open to my lover' [v. 5], and 'I opened to my lover' [v. 6] clearly have erotic overtones.)[12]

She responds in v. 3 by claiming that she does not want to get up again, to get dressed and dirty her feet. Her excuse is not to be taken any more seriously than the reason he gives for wanting to be admitted: because he is wet. This is lovers' banter. All of a sudden he disappears into the night, dematerializing as suddenly as he had appeared.

I opened to my lover,
but my lover had turned and gone ... (v. 6).

The rest of v. 6 and v. 7 narrate a setback – she searches for him in the streets and is found and beaten by the city watchmen – but she is not deterred, and in v. 8 she enlists the aid of the women of Jerusalem, who ask her what is so special about her lover. She answers by describing him metaphorically from head to foot, which serves to conjure him up again before us on the page, a technique aptly described by A. Cook as 'finding-by-praise' (1968: 134). Thus when the women ask her where her lover is, it should come as no surprise that she knows:

My lover has gone down to his garden,
to the beds of spices,
to graze in the gardens
and to gather lilies.
I am my lover's and my lover is mine,
he who grazes among the lilies (Cant 6:2-3).

This is another double entendre. He is with her. To appreciate the sexual innuendo we need only recall that elsewhere in the Song she is described as a lily and as his pleasure garden of choice spices where he grazes or browses (2:1-2; 2:16; 4:12-5:1).

For the poet's vision of love to live on, the poem must be read. It needs us, its readers, in order to be actualised here and now in the present, in the acts of reading and of appreciation. Indeed, having an audience is so important that the poet provides one within the poem. In addition to the voices of the lovers, there is a third speaking voice, that of the women of Jerusalem, who function as an audience and whose presence facilitates the reader's entry into the lovers'

12 On double entendre in these verses, see Exum 1999b.

seemingly private world of erotic intimacy. The women of Jerusalem are especially important because, for readers, there is a certain element of voyeurism involved in overhearing the intimate exchanges of lovers. Presenting the lovers as aware of and in conversation with an audience is a poetic strategy that makes the relationship between the lovers less private, less closed (and the Song less voyeuristic).

The lovers do not view the presence of these women as either intrusive or embarrassing. By addressing them – as, for example, when she places them under oath not to arouse love before it wishes (2:7; 3:5; 8:4), or asks them to tell her lover that she is lovesick (5:8) – the woman invites their active participation. The invitation to the women of Jerusalem to participate in the lovers' bliss is also an invitation to the reader. The women's presence, especially when the lovers seem to be enjoying the most intimate pleasures (2:4-7; 3:4-5; 5:1; 6:1-3; 8:3-4), is always a reminder that what seems to be a closed dialogue between two perpetually desiring lovers is addressed to us, for our pleasure and possibly our enlightenment. And so the poem encourages us to join the women in their approbation of the lovers when they exclaim, 'Eat, friends, drink yourselves drunk on caresses!' (5:1). By showing us how marvellous it is to be in love, the Song of Songs invites us to become lovers too. Readers keep the poet's vision of love alive when, by overhearing the lovers, they observe love unfold and when they answer the poem's invitation to participate in the lovers' joy.[13]

Another way the Song involves its readers so that its vision of love may live on is by encouraging readers to identify with the lovers. The Song is not about specific lovers; its lovers are archetypal lovers, types of lovers.[14] The poet does not identify them either by name or by association with any particular time or place (except for the vaguest connections to Solomon and Jerusalem). In the course of the poem, they take on various guises or personalities and assume different roles. The man is a king and a shepherd; the woman is a member of the royal court and an outsider who tends vineyards or keeps sheep. She is black (1:5), as well as like the white moon and radiant sun (6:10), with a neck like an ivory tower (7:5) – an impossible combination in one person according to many commentators.

---

13 Obviously nothing compels readers to accept the poem's invitation or to accept it on the poet's terms. To judge from the admiration, and even adoration, it has elicited over the centuries, the Song is very effective in seducing most readers with its poetic vision of desire, though recently the number of resistant readers seems to be increasing; e.g., Clines 1995; Polaski 1997; Black 1999, 2000; Boer 2000, Burrus and Moore 2003.

14 Although they are types, they seem to take on distinct personalities as we get to know them, primarily because of the consistency of their character portrayal (see, e.g., below, on their different and distinct ways of talking about love). On consistency of character portrayal in the Song, see Fox 1985: 217, 221-22, 295-331 *passim*; Elliott 1989: 252-53; Murphy 1990: 80-85; even some commentators who view the Song as an anthology find consistency in character portrayal; e.g., Longman 2001: 15-17; Bergant 2001: xv.

By providing access to only the voices of the lovers, to what they say not who they are, the poet is able to identify them with all lovers. This, in turn, makes it easier for readers to relate the Song's lovers' experience to their own experience of love, real or fantasised. This strategy has been very successful, as can be seen in the way readers over the centuries have responded to the vision of love they find here as a description of human love or divine love or both. I doubt that allegorical interpretation of the Song would have been so widespread and influential for centuries if the poem were about specific lovers of the past, say, Solomon and the queen of Sheba, or Solomon and a country maid, as the two- and three-character dramatic theory popular in the late nineteenth and early twentieth century had it.

The Song gives the impression that the lovers are young because they often appear to be courting and because of the way love seems to take them by surprise, so amazed are they by its power. But the Song is not about young love only, for its lovers are also conversant in the art of love. The Song captures the excitement of being in love as though for the first time – the way that being in love makes one feel young (as in the lyrics of the popular song 'you make me feel so young, you make me feel like spring has sprung') and the romance and nostalgia associated with first love (a feeling William Butler Yeats captures in his poem 'A Dream of Death' with the line, 'She was more beautiful than thy first love'). The lovers are not to be confused with the poet, who presents them to us both as explorers discovering the delights of intimacy and as knowing all there is to know about love.

In the Song, desire is always on the brink of fulfilment, it has an urgency about it (come!, tell me!, make haste!). Fulfilment is simultaneously assured, deferred, and, on a figurative level, enjoyed. There is assurance because love is mutual; each seeks the other, and there is never any doubt about their mutual desire and devotion. There is no 'he loves me, he loves me not'; for the Song, there is only 'my lover is mine and I am his' (2:16; cf. 6:3; 7:11). Fulfilment may be deferred. For example, the woman invites her beloved to come out to the countryside, where she will give him her love (8:11-13), but this is something yet to take place. He takes her to the house of wine (2:4); she brings him to her mother's chamber (3:4). But do they consummate their love there? Or anywhere else in the poem? Yes, on the figurative level. Sexual union is represented in the poem through the indirection of language, through innuendo, double entendre and metaphor.[15] The man is an apple tree whose fruit is sweet to his lover's taste (2:3). The woman is a lily (2:1) and a garden (4:12.15), and her beloved goes down to his garden to feed among the lilies

15 This aspect of the Song is discussed in detail by Cook 1968: 99-151. As he perceptively points out, 'coition, the center of desire in the poem, is veiled by circumlocution, by metaphor, or by roundabout description of the delights of love play' (110). Thus I do not agree with Walsh (2000: 29, 34-35 *et passim*) that love is not represented as consummated in the Song.

(6:2-3). Honey and milk are under her tongue, and her body is a pleasure garden of choice fruits and spices (4:11-14). She invites him to come to his garden and eat its choice fruits (4:16), and he responds by laying claim to the garden – spices, honey, milk, and all:

> I come to my garden, my sister bride;
> I gather my myrrh with my spice,
> I eat my honeycomb with my honey,
> I drink my wine with my milk (Cant 5:1).

The slippage in the Song from one mode to another, the blurring of distinctions between the more literal level of wishing and desiring and the figurative level of consummation is also a blurring between past, present, and future, and is central to the Song's poetic artistry and erotic persuasiveness.[16] It is one of the ways the poem immortalises love by representing it as always in progress. We do not hear of a time when the lovers were not in love; they are in love now; and they are always just about to experience future bliss. Since love is always in progress, the poem, not surprisingly, does not progress in a linear fashion. It meanders. It surges forward and circles back upon itself, continuously and effortlessly repeating its acts of conjuring and reissuing its invitation to the reader. Just as the harmony of the male and female voices represents, on the poetic plane, their sexual union, so the poetic rhythm of the Song, ever forward and then returning, reflects the repetitive pattern of seeking and finding in which the lovers engage, which is the basic pattern of sexual love: longing – satisfaction – renewed longing – and so on. The prolonging of desire and of fulfilment stretching across the span of the poem plays an essential part in the Song's effectiveness – its power – as a love poem.

Significantly, there is no closure to this poem about desire. The concluding verses of the Song have perplexed, and sometimes disappointed, commentators. To deem the ending 'abrupt' (Pope) or 'an odd way to end a poem' (Longman)[17] or 'a peculiar ending for a love song' (Fox) is to underestimate the poetic genius of the Song of Songs. The Song's resistance to closure is perhaps its most important means of immortalizing love. Closure would mean the end of desiring, the silence of the text, the death of love.[18] Resistance to closure is an attempt to keep love always in progress on the page

16 On temporal and spatial shifts and their poetic effects, cf. Munro 1995: 117-42.

17 Similarly, Bergant. Both Longman and Bergant thus find it necessary to appeal to what love is like in the 'real' world to explain the inconclusiveness of the ending.

18 Brooks (1993: 20) writes about 'the way in which narrative desire simultaneously seeks and puts off the erotic dénouement that signifies both its fulfilment and its end: the death of desiring, the silence of the text'. See also Landy (1983: 113): 'The tension in the Song between the desire of the lovers to unite and the inevitability of their parting is that also between their voice and the silence into which it vanishes, and between love and death – the ultimate parting, the unbroken silence.'

before us. Moreover, not only does the Song end without closure, it begins *in medias res*, 'let him kiss me' – a design that makes the Song, in effect, a poem without beginning or end. Like the love it celebrates, the Song of Songs strives to be ongoing, never-ending (cf. Munro 1995: 89). In 8:13 the man addresses his beloved: 'You who dwell in the gardens, companions are listening for your voice. Let me hear it!' She replies, 'Bolt away, my love, and be like a gazelle or young deer upon the mountains of spices' – seemingly sending him away and calling him to her in the same breath: he as a gazelle and she as the mountains of spices where he will cavort. This answer also, because it signals both the lovers' separation and their union, brings the poem round full circle to desire's first articulation, 'let him kiss me', desire that is never sated because it folds back upon itself.

Exploring Love from Different Perspectives

The fact that the Song is a dialogue creates, as discussed above, the impression of immediacy so important to the poet's vision of love. The dialogue format also enables the poet to explore the nature of love and longing from both points of view, a woman's and a man's, and this inclusive vision is a measure of the poem's genius. On the one hand, the female and male voices are in harmony, both desirous and both rejoicing in the pleasures of sexual intimacy. On the other, the poet has given the lovers distinct perspectives. (This is, of course, no less than we would expect from any good writer.) The differences in the way the poet portrays the female and male lovers reveal the poet's remarkable sensitivity to differences between women and men – differences that, in turn, reflect cultural assumptions about gender differences and roles (which is not to say the poem does not challenge certain of these assumptions as well).[19]

There are differences in emphasis in the way the male and female lovers talk about love. They do not look at love or at each other in quite the same way. She expresses her desire and explores her feelings for him, and his for her, through stories, stories in which she and he are characters.[20] They both play roles, as themselves (2:8-17; 3:1-5; 5:2-6:3) or in fantasy guises (1:12; 3:6-11). Her stories have a narrative movement and a sense of closure, a tension and a resolution. They are the only parts of the Song that display narrative development, or what we might call a plot. For example, she tells two stories in

19 Feminist studies of the 70s, 80s and 90s focused largely on the Song's challenges to gender stereotypes (e.g. Trible 1978; Meyers 1986, 1991; Falk 1988; see also the articles in Brenner [ed.] 1993 and Brenner and Fontaine [eds.] 2000). More recent assessments have been more critical; e.g., Clines 1995; Polaski 1997; Black 2000; Exum 2000; Burrus and Moore 2003.

20 See, e.g., Exum 2003b.

which her lover comes courting: in one, he invites her to join him outside to enjoy the springtime (2:8-17), and in the other, which takes place at night, he asks to be admitted to her chamber (5:2-7). Twice she recounts how she goes out in the city streets searching for him: the first time, she is immediately successful in finding him; the second, she encounters a distressing setback before achieving her goal (3:1-5; 5:6b-6:3).

The man does not tell stories. His way of talking about love is to look at her, tell her what he sees and how it affects him. He describes what he sees metaphorically (4:1-5; 6:4-10; 7:2-10). Her effect on him is captivating ('You have captured my heart, my sister, bride', 4:9; '...the hair of your head is like purple; a king is held captive by the tresses', 7:6). He finds her awesome ('You are beautiful, my friend, like Tirzah, lovely as Jerusalem, as awesome in splendour as they', 6:4),[21] and, when her gaze meets his, he is overwhelmed ('Turn your eyes away from me, for they overwhelm me', 6:5).

The difference in the way the man and woman talk about love extends to a contrast on the poetic level between sight and speech. The man constructs the woman, he creates a picture of her for us, through the gaze, through seeing. We follow his gaze as he progressively builds up a metaphorical picture of her, bit by bit, until she materialises before us. The woman constructs the man primarily through the voice. She quotes him speaking to her (2:10-14; 5:2), but he never quotes her. Through putting words in his mouth when she tells stories in which he courts her, she controls the way we view him. We see him as a lover who comes courting by day and by night, who woos her with sweet words – and as a somewhat elusive lover she must seek, but one who is never difficult to find. She looks at him too, but when she describes him she pictures his body differently from the way he depicts hers (see below).

The lovers describe differently what it is like to be in love. The difference is subtle, for both feel wondrously overwhelmed by the other. The woman speaks about herself, about being in love and how she experiences it: 'I am faint with love' or 'I am lovesick' (2:5; 5:8). Her condition, lovesickness, is a malady to which lovers are prone, a state of intense longing that feeds on love and leaves one languid and in need of the sustenance only love can bring. In Song 2:5, she is lovesick when he is with her. He has brought her to the house of wine, which is also the house of love, where she calls for raisin-cakes and apples (as if they would help), because she is lovesick. She is also lovesick when they are apart. After a missed encounter, when she goes seeking him in the streets at night, she calls on the women of Jerusalem to tell him of her condition, since

21 Literally, 'awesome as the(se) distinguished sights'; i.e., the beautiful cities of Tirzah and Jerusalem. The niphal participle of דגל, נדגלות, appears only here and in the identical phrase in v. 10. It is related to דֶּגֶל (2:4) and דָּגוּל (5:10). Both דגל I, 'to raise a banner', and דגל II, 'to look', in the passive could connote being conspicuous or prominent (see DCH II: 414b), a combination I have tried to indicate in the word 'splendour'.

he is both the cause and the cure: 'if you find my lover, tell him that I am lovesick' (5:8).

The woman tells others, the women of Jerusalem, what *love* does to her; the man speaks to her about what *she* does to him. He thinks in terms of conquest, of power relations: '*you* have captured my heart' (4:9). Unlike the woman, who expresses her feelings subjectively, he does not say 'I am overwhelmed' but rather describes the way *he* feels as something *she* has done to him: '*You* have captured my heart'; 'Turn *your eyes* away from me, for *they* overwhelm me' (6:5). It appears that, in ancient Israelite culture as in many others, autonomy is part of the dynamic of male eroticism. As a man, he is used to feeling in control. But love makes him feel as though he is losing control. He is powerless to resist; his autonomy is challenged. He welcomes this, to be sure, but these feelings are disconcerting. He is – and he admits it – awestruck: 'You are beautiful, my friend, like Tirzah, lovely as Jerusalem, as awesome in splendour as they' (6:4).

He is awestruck; she is lovesick. As a woman, she is used to a world in which men are in control, and to a version of love according to which women surrender to men. Her autonomy is not challenged because she does not have the kind of autonomy a man has (even though she is the most autonomous of biblical women). She is not in awe of him; she is in need of him. She longs passionately for him and cannot do without him.

It is interesting to note that *she* does not think of him as being in awe of her. In her version of love, he thinks of her as shy and reticent.

> Rise up, my friend, my fair one,
>   and come away,
> my dove in the clefts of the rock,
>   in the covert of the cliff.
> Let me see you,
>   let me hear your voice,
> for your voice is sweet,
>   and you are lovely (Cant 2:13b-14).

When she puts words in his mouth, he calls her 'my dove in the clefts of the rock, in the covert of the cliff', an image that suggests shyness. But when he speaks for himself, he imagines her as dwelling among lions and leopards on remote mountaintops.

> With me from Lebanon, bride,
>   come with me from Lebanon.
> Come forth from the peak of Amanah,
>   from the peak of Senir and Hermon,
> from the dens of lions,
>   from the lairs of leopards (Cant 4:8).

He does not associate her with the domestic security of the house, as she had presented him doing, but rather with powerful, untamed animals whose abode in dangerous places she shares. Both these images convey the idea that he perceives her as inaccessible, but her inaccessibility seems vastly more daunting in his version.

The ability to capture such subtle differences between men and women is a mark of the genius of the Song of Songs. The differences also extend to the different ways the lovers have of speaking metaphorically about the body of the other. There are in the Song four descriptions that construct the lovers' sexuality through a series of metaphors for various body parts (4:1-5; 5:10-16; 6:4-7; 7:2-6). On the one hand, these descriptions are intimate, suggestive, and even explicit. On the other, the metaphors function as much to hide the body as to display it. The man pictures the woman's body part by part, with a striking simile or metaphor for each part, three times – twice from her head downwards (though he stops midway), and once, from her feet to her head. She describes his body in a similar fashion, from head to foot, only once, but the fact that she too owns the gaze is important for the Song's picture of gender relations, for traditionally women are looked at and men do the looking.

Song 4:1-7 is the man's first description of his lover, a description that leads to his admission, in v. 9, of the powerful effect she has on him.

> Look at you! You are beautiful, my friend!
>   Look at you! You are beautiful.
> Your eyes are doves
>   behind your veil.
> Your hair, like a flock of goats
>   winding down Mount Gilead.
> Your teeth, like a flock of shorn sheep
>   that have come up from the washing,
> all of them in pairs,
>   none bereft of its twin.
> Like a scarlet thread, your lips,
>   and your mouth is lovely.
> Like a slice of pomegranate, your cheeks
>   behind your veil.
> Your neck, like David's tower,
>   built in courses,
> a thousand shields hung on it,
>   all sorts of warriors' bucklers.
> Your two breasts, like two fawns,
>   twins of a gazelle,
>   grazing among the lilies (Cant 4:1-5).

Looking at his lover and describing what he sees and its effect on him, as I have indicated, is the man's primary mode of speaking about love. Her effect on him is a crucial feature. The sight of her stirs up within him a depth of passion that alarms him, a disturbance in his psyche, a threat to his equanimity that is both exhilarating and scary. The totality of her overwhelms him.

Lingering over the details of her body provides him with a way of dealing with the powerful feelings she arouses in him. In the verses quoted above he surveys her body part by part – eyes, hair, teeth, lips, mouth, cheeks, neck, and breasts – each tentatively anticipating a successful assemblage. Then, as if to make the parts less threatening, he compares them to familiar things. Each part is *like* something in the everyday world he knows, things that do not arouse such strong and disturbing emotions in him, such as a flock of goats moving down the mountainside, sheep that have come up from the washing. The closest he comes to describing something potentially awe-inspiring is the image of the tower with shields hung upon it for her neck – an image that yields to the tranquil, non-threatening image of fawns feeding among lilies for her breasts. (And, moreover, the shields hung on the tower, and thus not in use, give an impression of peace and security; she wears symbols of military might like trappings.)[22]

His second description (6:4-7) is virtually identical, but the third time, he describes his beloved more intimately. Song 7:2-7 deals with parts of the body not normally exposed to view: the navel, which some exegetes see as a euphemism for the vulva, the belly, and the breasts (which he described in 4:5 in the same terms). Some critics consider this description to be more controlled than his other two.[23] The metaphors here are not so elaborate; typically they consist of two clauses each whereas his other descriptions are more detailed. This description is like her description of him in that both consider the body from top to toe in ways that are intimate and erotically suggestive.

The inventories of body parts are presented for the visual pleasure they offer to the onlookers, who include the poem's readers. The degree to which they objectify the loved one is counterbalanced by the extent to which the lover is affected. The man does not just look. He loses himself in the vision of beauty he sees before him when he surveys the body of the woman he loves. He is overwhelmed by her eyes and held captive in her tresses – overcome by the very features he contemplates. If he distances himself from the whole person by perceiving her body in parts, he does not remain distanced. He always puts himself in the picture.[24] His first description reaches a climax in a

22 Landy (1983: 74-78, 87-89) and Meyers (1986) discuss the application of military and architectural imagery to the woman, and see it as a sign of the woman's power. The question is, what kind of power? Meyers takes images of power applied to the woman in the Song as a sign that women exercised power in rural, domestic settings in ancient Israel. It is hard to see how this reference in the Song can be used to support such a claim. As Landy rightly perceives, the power the woman has here is erotic. It is the kind of power the Bible conventionally ascribes to women, though outside the Song it is usually viewed with suspicion (e.g., Proverbs, the Samson story, the story of David and Bathsheba).

23 Landy 1983: 305 n. 46; Keel describes 7:2-6 as 'knapper und klarer' than the other descriptions of the woman, and sees them as 'kühler' and more aristocratic in tone.

24 Whereas the man participates in that which is seen, the woman does not include herself in what is seen in the same way. The circumstances, however, are different. She conjures him

metaphor of the woman as a pleasure garden, which he enters, at her invitation, to feast upon its exotic fruits (4:10-5:1). His metaphoric description of her body in Song 7:2-7 gives way to a metaphor for his desire when he compares her to a palm tree that he will climb, and whose clusters – her breasts – he will take hold of.

Putting himself in the picture he constructs of her is not unlike her telling stories in which both he and she are characters. Neither lover constructs the other without being affected themselves – without becoming part of the story or entering the picture.

What about the way she looks at him?

> My lover is radiant and ruddy,
> he stands out among ten thousand.
> His head is gold, pure gold,
> his locks, palm fronds,
> black as a raven.
> His eyes, like doves
> by watercourses,
> bathing in milk,
> sitting upon brimming pools.
> His cheeks, like beds of spices,
> pouring forth perfumes.
> His lips, lilies,
> dripping liquid myrrh.
> His hands, rods of gold,
> inlaid with Tarshish stones.
> His body, an ivory bar,
> covered with lapis lazuli.
> His legs, marble pillars
> set on gold pedestals.
> His form, like Lebanon,
> distinguished as the cedars.
> His mouth is sweet,
> and all of him desirable (Cant 5:10-16).

Some exegetes find her portrait of him more static or artificial or less imaginative than his portraits of her (e.g., Soulen 1967). This difference is often exaggerated, and the real differences, in my opinion, lie elsewhere. If, on the whole, his imagery is more picturesque than hers, hers is more relational than his. His statuesque body of precious materials is less an engrossing visual image than a comment on his value to her. His head, hands, and legs do not look like gold in the way that, say, wavy hair resembles goats winding down a mountainside; rather he shares qualities with gold. Like gold he is rare and precious, and dazzling. She describes some of the same features he did in 4:1-7

---

up by praising him, whereas he is looking at her and describing what he sees (see, further, below).

(eyes, hair, lips, cheeks, mouth), but some of her comparisons are different in emphasis from his. Whereas he says, 'your mouth is lovely' (4:3), she says, 'his mouth is sweet' (5:16). His 'all of you is beautiful' (4:7) is matched by her 'all of him is desirable' (5:16). He concentrates on the outward appearance (lovely, beautiful); she, on what he is to her. His mouth is sweet *to her*, and to say that he is desirable means that *she* desires him.

Each lover delights in the other's body. Each describes the loved one part by part, organizing the body in an effort to know and possess it, and investing each part with meaning through a simile or metaphor whose import cannot be reduced to prose paraphrase. An important difference is that, unlike his descriptions of her, her description of him is textually motivated. She describes him in answer to a question raised by the women of Jerusalem, who ask, 'What sets your lover apart from other lovers?' His descriptions, in contrast, are represented by the poet as spontaneous outbursts inspired by the sight of her. She is not looking at him when she pictures his body. Her description is based not on looking but, presumably, on having looked, and this may help to explain why her reaction to his body is different from his to hers. She is not so unsettled by his body as he is by hers. He deals with her body in parts to cope with her devastating presence. She treats his by parts to cope with his absence and to conjure him up through the evocative power of language.[25]

The fact that he describes her body more often than she describes his may reflect a cultural convention of reticence about depicting the male body (Brenner 1997: 31-43). It appears that the female body is the more likely object of the look, as it is in our culture. But the poet portrays the woman as looking too, and this has far-reaching implications for the Song's picture of the relationship between the sexes. That pleasure in visualizing the beloved's body is mutual is an important aspect of the poet's vision of love as mutual desire and mutual gratification[26] – a vision of love immortalised by a poet whose genius in portraying desire as mutual and love as always in progress has given us one of the great love poems of all time.[27]

---

25 The poet gives the woman and the man a different status with respect to the look or gaze: the man is presented as looking; the woman as having looked. Though her description of him indicates that she has intimate knowledge of his body, he nevertheless does not offer himself to her gaze in the same way she offers herself to his. She is not represented as looking at him and speaks of him as 'he' when she describes him to the women of Jerusalem. He, in contrast, is represented as looking at her when he describes her body and he addresses her as 'you'. Readers see the man in the same way as we see the woman, through an inventory of the body parts described metaphorically.

26 An aspect of the poet's vision of love as mutual that I have not discussed here is the way both lovers take the initiative in love; not unexpectedly, however, the man takes the more active role (for further discussion, see my forthcoming commentary).

27 This is not to suggest that the poet's vision is completely original; the poet worked within a cultural heritage, influenced and inspired by a distinguished succession of poetic precursors (we need only compare the Egyptian and Mesopotamian love poems that have come down

Bibliography

References to commentaries without page numbers in the article are *ad loc.*

ALTER, R. (1985): The Garden of Metaphor, in: The Art of Biblical Poetry. New York, 185-203.
BERGANT, D. (2001): The Song of Songs, Berit Olam, Collegeville.
BLACK, F.C. (1999): What Is My Beloved? On Erotic Reading and the Song of Songs, in: F.C. Black/R. Boer/E. Runions (eds.), The Labour of Reading: Desire, Alienation and Biblical Interpretation, Semeia Studies, Atlanta, 35-52.
– (2000): Beauty or the Beast? The Grotesque Body in the Song of Songs, BibInt 8, 302-323.
BLOCH, A./BLOCH, C. (1995): The Song of Songs: A New Translation with an Introduction and Commentary, New York.
BLOOM, H. (1973): The Anxiety of Influence. A Theory of Poetry, Oxford.
BOER, R. (2000): The Second Coming: Repetition and Insatiable Desire in the Song of Songs, BibInt 8, 276-301.
BRENNER, A. (1997): The Intercourse of Knowledge: On Gendering Desire and 'Sexuality' in the Hebrew Bible, BibIntS 26, Leiden.
BRENNER, A. ed. (1993): A Feminist Companion to the Song of Songs, The Feminist Companion to the Bible 1, Sheffield.
BRENNER, A./FONTAINE, C.R. eds. (2000): The Song of Songs: A Feminist Companion to the Bible (2nd Series), Sheffield.
BROOKS, P. (1993): Body Work: Objects of Desire in Modern Narrative, Cambridge/MA.
BUDDE, K. (1898): Das Hohelied, KHAT 17, Freiburg i.B.
BURRUS, V./MOORE, S.D. (2003): Unsafe Sex: Feminism, Pornography, and the Song of Songs, BibInt 11, 24-52.
CLINES, D.J.A. (1995): Why Is There a Song of Songs and What Does It Do to You If You Read It?, in: id., Interested Parties: The Ideology of Writers and Readers of the Hebrew Bible, JSOTS 205/Gender, Culture, Theory 1, Sheffield, 94-121.
COOK, A. (1968): The Root of the Thing: A Study of Job and the Song of Songs, Bloomington.
DAVIDSON, R.M. (2003): The Literary Structure of the Song of Songs *Redivivus*, Journal of the Adventist Theological Society 14, 44-65.
DCH = Clines, D.J.A. ed. (1993-): The Dictionary of Classical Hebrew. Sheffield.
DELITZSCH, F. (1980 [1872]): Proverbs, Ecclesiastes, Song of Solomon, trans. J. Martin, Commentary on the Old Testament VI, Grand Rapids.
DORSEY, D.A. (1990): Literary Structuring in the Song of Songs, JSOT 46, 81-96.
ELLIOTT, M.T. (1989): The Literary Unity of the Canticle, Europäische Hochschulschriften Reihe XIII Theologie 371, Frankfurt a.M.
EXUM, J.C. (1973): A Literary and Structural Analysis of the Song of Songs, ZAW 85, 47-79.
– (1999a): How Does the Song of Songs Mean? On Reading the Poetry of Desire, SEÅ 64, 47-63.
– (1999b): In the Eye of the Beholder: Wishing, Dreaming, and *double entendre* in the Song of Songs, in F.C. Black/R. Boer/E. Runions (eds.), The Labour of Reading: Desire, Alienation, and Biblical Interpretation, Semeia Studies, Atlanta, 71-86.

to us). But I would suggest that the poet responsible for שיר השירים, 'the best of songs', is a strong poet in Harold Bloom's sense, one who has overwritten the tradition with a fresh vision of desire (Bloom 1973).

– (2000): Ten Things Every Feminist Should Know about the Song of Songs, in A. Brenner/C.R. Fontaine (eds.), The Song of Songs: A Feminist Companion to the Bible (Second Series), Sheffield, 24-35.
– (2003a): Seeing Solomon's Palanquin (Song of Songs 3:6-11), BibInt 11, 301-16.
– (2003b): 'The Voice of My Lover': Double Voice and Poetic Illusion in Song of Songs 2.8-3.5', in: J.C. Exum/H.G.M. Williamson (eds.), Reading from Right to Left: Essays in Honour of David J.A. Clines, JSOTS 373, Sheffield, 141-152.
– (forthcoming): The Song of Songs, OTL, Louisville.
FALK, M. (1988): The Song of Songs, in: J.L. Mays (ed.), Harper's Bible Commentary, San Francisco, 525-28.
FISCH, H. (1988): Song of Solomon: The Allegorical Imperative, in: id., Poetry with a Purpose: Biblical Poetics and Interpretation. Bloomington, 80-103.
FOX, M.V. (1985): The Song of Songs and the Ancient Egyptian Love Songs, Madison.
GERLEMAN, G. (1965): Ruth. Das Hohelied, BK 18. Neukirchen-Vluyn.
GOOD, E.M. (1970): Ezekiel's Ship: Some Extended Metaphors in the Old Testament, Semitics 1, 79-102.
GORDIS, R. (1974): The Song of Songs and Lamentations: A Study, Modern Translation and Commentary, rev. and augmented ed., New York.
HEINEVETTER, H-J. (1988): 'Komm nun, mein Liebster, Dein Garten ruft Dich!' Das Hohelied als programmatische Komposition, BBB 69, Frankfurt a.M.
JOÜON, P. (1991-93): A Grammar of Biblical Hebrew, trans. and revised by T. Muraoka, SubBib 14/I–II, Rome.
KEEL, O. (1986): Das Hohelied, ZBK 18, Zürich.
KRINETZKI, L. (1964): Das Hohe Lied. Kommentar zu Gestalt und Kerygma eines alttestamentarischen Liebesliedes, Düsseldorf.
LANDY, F. (1983): Paradoxes of Paradise: Identity and Difference in the Song of Songs, BiLiSe 7, Sheffield.
LONGMAN III, T. (2001): The Song of Songs, NICOT, Grand Rapids.
LORETZ, O. (1971): Das althebräische Liebeslied, AOAT 14/1, Neukirchen-Vluyn.
MAY, H.G. (1955): Some Cosmic Connotations of Mayim Rabbîm, "Many Waters", JBL 74, 9-21.
MEEK, T.J. (1956): The Song of Songs: Introduction and Exegesis, IB 5, 91-148.
MEYERS, C. (1986): Gender Imagery in the Song of Songs, HAR 10, 209-223.
– (1991): 'To Her Mother's House: Considering a Counterpart to the Israelite Bet 'ab, in: D. Jobling/P.L. Day/G.T. Sheppard (eds.), The Bible and the Politics of Exegesis: Essays in Honor of N.K. Gottwald on His Sixty-fifth Birthday, Cleveland, 39-51.
MÜLLER, H.-P. (1984): Vergleich und Metapher im Hohenlied, OBO 56. Fribourg/Göttingen.
MUNRO, J.M. (1995): Spikenard and Saffron: A Study in the Poetic Language of the Song of Songs, JSOTS 203, Sheffield.
MURPHY, R.E. (1987): Dance and Death in the Song of Songs, in: J.H. Marks/R.M. Good (eds.), Love and Death in the Ancient Near East: Essays in Honor of Marvin H. Pope, Guilford, 117-119.
– (1990): The Song of Songs: A Commentary on the Book of Canticles or the Song of Songs, Hermeneia, Minneapolis.
PELLETIER, A.-M. (2002): Le Cantique des cantiques: un texte et ses lectures, in: J. Nieuviarts/P. Debergé (eds.), Les Nouvelles voies de l'exégèse: En lisant le Cantique des cantiques, XIXe congrès de l'Association catholique pour l'étude de la Bible (Toulouse, Septembre 2001), Lectio Divina 190, Paris, 75-101.
POLASKI, D.C. (1997): 'What Will Ye See in the Shulammite?' Women, Power and Panopticism in the Song of Songs, BibInt 5, 64-81.

POPE, M.H. (1977): Song of Songs: A New Translation with Introduction and Commentary, AB 7C, Garden City.

RINGGREN, H. (1967): Das Hohe Lied, ATD 16, Göttingen.

RUDOLPH, W. (1962): Das Buch Ruth. Das Hohe Lied. Die Klagelieder, KAT XVII/1-3, Gütersloh.

SHEA, W.H. (1980): The Chiastic Structure of the Song of Songs, ZAW 92, 378-396.

SNAITH, J.G. (1993): The Song of Songs, NCeB, Grand Rapids.

SONNET, J.-P. (2002): 'Le Cantique: la fabrique poétique', in: J. Nieuviarts/P. Debergé (eds.), Les Nouvelles voies de l'exégèse: En lisant le Cantique des cantiques, XIXe congrès de l'Association catholique pour l'étude de la Bible (Toulouse, Septembre 2001), Lectio Divina 190, Paris, 159-184.

SOULEN, R.N. (1967): The *waṣfs* of the Song of Songs and Hermeneutic, JBL 86, 183-190.

TRIBLE, P. (1978): Love's Lyrics Redeemed, in: ead., God and the Rhetoric of Sexuality, Philadelphia, 144-165.

WALSH, C.E. (2000): Exquisite Desire: Religion, the Erotic and the Song of Songs, Minneapolis.

WEBSTER, E.C. (1982): Pattern in the Song of Songs, JSOT 22, 73-93.

WENDLAND, E.R. (1995): Seeking the Path through a Forest of Symbols: A Figurative and Structural Survey of the Song of Songs, Journal of Translation and Textlinguistics 7, 13-59.

WÜRTHWEIN, E. (1969): Das Hohelied, in: E. Würthwein/K. Galling/O.Plöger, Die Fünf Megilloth, HAT 18, Tübingen, 25-71.

The Book of Canticles (Song of Songs) in the Dead Sea Scrolls

Peter W. Flint

1. Introduction

This essay surveys and discusses the scrolls of Canticles (Song of Songs) that were discovered at Qumran in the Judean Desert.[1] Following an overview of four the manuscripts, I shall offer several observations arising from this ancient material, comment the text of Canticles at Qumran, present a selection of significant readings, and close with a bibliography. The essay includes a table with data on the Canticles Scrolls, an index of contents by manuscript, and an index of contents by chapter and verse.

2. The Canticles Scrolls found at Qumran

2.1 Description of the Manuscripts:

Siglum	*Number*	*Content Range*[2]	*Date Copied*	*Edition (DJD Volume)*
4QCant[a]	4Q106	3:4 - 7:7	Early Herodian	XVI, 199-204 + pl. xxiV
4Cant[b]	4Q107	2:9 - 5:1	End 1st Century BCE	XVI, 205-18 + pl. xxv
4Cant[c]	4Q108	3:7-8	(Herodian?)[3]	XVI,219 + pl. xxv
6Cant	6Q6	1:1-7	ca. 50 CE	III, 112-3 + pl. xxiii

Four scrolls of Canticles were found at Qumran: three in Cave 4 (4Cant[a],

1 For a translation and general discussion of the Canticles scrolls, see Abegg/Flint/Ulrich 1999: 611-18.

2 In the Table, *Content Range* denotes the first and last preserved verses in the manuscript, without necessarily assuming that all the intervening text is preserved.

3 4Cant[c] contains too little text on which to base a firm conclusion.

4Cant^{b}, and 4Cant^{c}), and the fourth in Cave 6 (6QCant). At least three of these manuscripts – most likely all – were copied in the Herodian period (i.e. 30 BCE to 70 CE), the latest being 6QCant (cf. Table).

Between them, these four scrolls preserve portions of seven of the eight chapters of Canticles. Two manuscripts – 4Cant^{a} and 4Cant^{b} – will be discussed more fully in section 3 below, both because they are the best preserved and because each has a number of interesting features.

Contents in Traditional Order		*Contents by Manuscript*	
1:1-7	6QCant	4QCant^{a}	3:4-5, 7-11
2:9-17	4QCant^{b}		4:1-6, 7
3:1-2	4QCant^{b}		+6:11?-12
3:4-5	4QCant^{a}		7:1-7
3:5+9	4QCant^{b}		unidentified frg.
3:7-8	4QCant^{c}	4QCant^{b}	2:9-17
3:7-11	4QCant^{a}		3:1-2.5+9
4:1-3+8-11a	4QCant^{b}		4:1-3+8-11a, 14-16
4:1-6.7	4QCant^{a}		5:1
4:14-16	4QCant^{b}	4QCant^{c}	3:7-8
5:1	4QCant^{b}	6QCant	1:1-7
6:11?-12	4QCant^{a}		
7:1-7	4QCant^{a}		
unidentified frg.	4QCant^{a}		

***4Cant^{a}:** The extant fragments preserve a top margin, a bottom margin, and an intercolumnar margin. The orthography of 4Cant^{a} is very close to that of the MT, but once it is fuller (3:7, מ[ג̊בורי] מגברי MT), and in two instances it is more sparing (4:5, רעים] הרועים MT; 7:5, צפׄה] צופה MT). The most striking feature of 4Cant^{a} is its lack or omission of the text between 4:7 and 6:11 (see section 3.1 below). The editor of the scroll, Emmanuel Tov, describes it as an "abbreviated text",[4] but see the discussion below (cf. section 3.3 below).

***4Cant^{b}:** The three fragments preserve the bottom part of four consecutive columns, together with the bottom margins. The orthography is very close to that of the MT, but on some occasions it is more sparing (e.g. 4:2, מתאמות] מתאימות MT), and in other instances it is fuller (e.g. 4:3, שפתותיך] שפתתיך MT). In 3:1 the quiescent *aleph* has been omitted by the scribe (מצתיהו] מצאתיו MT). The scroll also features several scribal errors (e.g. 3:1, בשקתי] בקשתי MT). Although it is written in Hebrew, 4Cant^{b} contains several Aramaic word forms that reveal Aramaic influence on the scribe. The manuscript omits two large segments (3:6-8 and 4:4-7), possibly ended at 5:1, and features several

4 Tov, DJD XVI, 194-5.

unusual scribal markings (see section 3.2). Like 4QCant^a, the editor of 4QCant^b sees it as an "abbreviated text",[5] but see below.

**4Cant^c*: single small fragment is all that remains of the third Canticles manuscript from Cave 4. It preserves some of Cant 3:7-8, which is part of a section of text that was not included here in 4QCant^b (where v. 9 directly follows v. 5). Despite this feature, the fragment belongs to a distinct manuscript and is clearly not part of 4QCant^b. There is one variant reading at 3:8: אחוזי] אחזי MT. For this form functioning in an active meaning, see Ezek 43:6 and other parallels in Hebrew and cognate languages.[6]

**6Cant:* Parts of two adjoining columns are preserved, including the top and bottom margins preserved in col. I. It is possible that this scroll contained only part of Canticles, since the columns were short at only 7 lines each, with Cant 1:1-6 (to שאני֯) and 1:6-7 (from ש]חר[חרת֯) represented.

2.2 A Selection of Variant Readings

Some interesting or significant variant readings preserved in the Canticles Leviticus scrolls appear below. Many more may be found in the critical editions of these manuscripts (see the Bibliography).

Cant 2:15 ש]ועלים (one occurrence, based on letter count) 4QCant^b 𝔐^{mss} 𝔊 𝔙 | שועלים שועלים 𝔐

In this case 4QCant^b agrees with some Masoretic manuscripts, the Septuagint, and the Vulgate by mentioning *the foxes* that ruin the vineyards only once. In contrast, the MT repeats this word.

Cant 3:11 מ֯בנות ירושלים 4QCant^b | בנות ציון 4QCant^a 𝔐 𝔊

In a verse dealing with King Solomon, 4QCant^a mentions the *daughters of Jerusalem*, whereas the MT addresses the *daughters of Zion* (the phrase is not found in the LXX). It is noteworthy that *daughters of Zion* occurs only here in the Hebrew Bible, whereas *daughters of Jerusalem* (thus 4QCant^a) occurs elsewhere (e.g. v. 10). For a reverse interchange, see 4QLam 1:17.

Cant 4:3 מזקנתך 4QCant^a | רקתך 4QCant^b 𝔐 𝔊

The reading in 4QCant^a is not found elsewhere. מזקנתך is most likely connected with the root זקן. This term signifies an area of the body different from the רקה (*temple*) found in the MT, but nevertheless seems to indicate a section of the face (*your chin*).

---

5 Tov, DJD XVI, 194-5.

6 Y. Blau, *Leshonenu* 18 (1950-1952) 67-81, esp. 71, n. 3 and 72 [Hebrew]. See E. Tov, "108. 4QCant^c," in DJD XVI, 219.

Cant 4:3 מזקנתך 4QCant[a]] רקתך 4QCant[b] 𝔐 𝔊
The reading in 4QCant[a] is not found elsewhere. מזקנתך is most likely connected with the root זקן. This term signifies an area of the body different from the רקה (*temple*) found in the MT, but nevertheless seems to indicate a section of the face (*your chin*).

Cant 4:8 אומנון 4QCant[b]] אמנה 𝔐 𝔖 𝔗 (𝔊)
Omnon is apparently an alternative name for *Amanah*, a mountain peak in the Anti-lebanon range. The form found in 4QCant[b] is known from rabbinic literature, in several variations. Examples include: אמנון (*b. Gittin* 8a) and אמנוס ($𝔗^J$ in Num 20:22, 25).[7]

Cant 4:1 אחותי 4QCant[b]] > 𝔐
As occurs frequently elsewhere (Cant 4:9.10.12; 5:1), אחותי precedes כלה in 4QCant[b]. In contrast, the MT and LXX lack *my sister* in this verse.

Cant 5:1 [באתי לגני אחותי כלה] aα \ אריתי מרי עם בש]מי aβ \
שתיתי ייני עם חלבי[ן bβ \ אכלתי יערי עם דבשי]ן ba \
באתי לגני aβ אריתי מורי עם בשמי \ ] 4QCant[b] cα אכלו רעים בש שתו ושכרו דו]דים
aα אחותי כלה
𝔐 𝔊 cα אכלו רעים \ cβ שתו ושכרו דודים \
bα אכלתי יערי עם דבשי \ bβ שתיתי ייני עם חלבי \
Here the text of 4QCant[b] differs from the sequence found in the MT and the LXX. The reconstruction of this scroll (see section 3.2 below) may account for the rather puzzling interval following אריתי מרי עם בש]מי (Cant 5:1ab). According to the editor,[8] the different sequence of hemistichs in MT and LXX explains this interval by creating a parallel pattern (*abab*), whereas 4QCant[b] contains a chiastic pattern (*abba*). Although examination of the hemistichs and their contents renders this reasoning less than conclusive, the reconstruction in DJD XVI is most reasonable and may be accepted.

Cant 7:1 [שובי שובי] 4QCant[a]] שובי שובי ... שובי שובי 𝔐 𝔊
The relevant line in 4QCant[b] is col. III 5: מ̊ר̊כ̊]בות [7:1]שובי שובי השולמית ונחזה בך] עמי נדיב. Although very little of this line is actually preserved, there is insufficient space for the text found in the MT and LXX. The most likely explanation is that the second sequence שובי שובי was omitted in 4QCant[b].

3. Major Features of 4QCant[a] and 4QCant[b]

3.1 The Omission of Cant 4:8 to 6:10 in 4QCant[a]

4Cant[a] omits a large block of text, the passage between Cant 4:7 and 6:11. This sequence is definite because the end of 4:6 is extant in the last line of col. II and part of the first word of 4:7 is preserved in the first line of col. III. See the transcription below, which presents the last 8 lines of col. II and the first 8 lines of col. III.

---

7 For literature, see HAL *s.v.*
8 Tov, DJD XVI, 218.

Col. II (frgs. 2 i-5) Cant 4:1-6[9]

7] *vac[at*

8]4:1הנך יפה רעיתי הנך יפ]ה עיניך יונים [מ]בעד לצמתך כעדר

9]העזים שערך שגלש]ות מהר גלעד 2כעדר הקצובות שניך עלו

10]מן הרחצה שכלם מת]אימות ושכלה אינה בהם 3כחוט [ה]שני

11]שפתתיך ומדבריך נאוה]כפלח הרמון מזקנתך מבעד לצמ[ת]ך

12]4כמגדל דויד צוארך בנוי לתלפיות]אלף המגן תלוי בו כל שלטי הגבורים

13]5שני שדיך כשני עפרים תאומי צביה] רעים בשושנים 6עד שיפוח

14]היום ונסו הצללים אלך לי אל הר המו]ר אל גבעת הלבונה

bottom margin

Col. III (frg. 2 ii) Cant 4:7 + 6:11?-12 + 7:1-3[10]

top margin

1 4:7כל]ך יפה רעיתי ומום אין בך *vacat?* [

2] *vacat?* [

3]6:11אל גנת אגוז ירדתי לראות באבי הנחל לראות אם[

4 פרחה] הגפן הנצו הרמנים 12לא ידעתי נפשי שמתני[

5 מרכ]בות עמי נדיב 7:1שובי שובי השולמית ונחזה בך[

6 מה תח]זו בשולמית כמחלת המחנים 2מה יפו פעמיך[

7 בנ[ע]לים] בת נדיב חמוקי ירכיך כמו חלאים[

8 מע]שה ידי אמן 3שררך אגן הסהר אל יחסר[

When compared with the size of the book as a whole, the section missing in 4QCant[a] is very large (about 30%). One possibility is that 4QCant[a] preserves a shorter edition of the book, while the MT perseveres a longer edition. On the other hand, in the MT Cant 4:7 forms the end of a content unit (note the ס [*setuma*] in MT), and Cant 6:11 starts the beginning of another unit (note the ס in MT at the end of v. 10). So a second possible explanation is that the absence of chapters 4:8 to 6:10 in 4QCant[a] may be no mere accident, and that this material may have been deliberately omitted by the scribe or his source. As mentioned above, the editor of the scroll describes it as an "abbreviated text" (Tov, DJD XVI, 19f.).

---

9 The excerpt is based on the critical edition (E. Tov, "108. 4QCant[c]," DJD XVI, 200).
10 For the complete preserved column (lines 1-14), see DJD XVI, 202.

Cant 4:8-6:10 included in MT (omitted in 4QCant[a])	
Traditional Text (MT)	Translation (*RSV*)
4:6 עַד שֶׁיָּפוּחַ הַיּוֹם וְנָסוּ הַצְּלָלִים אֵלֶךְ לִי אֶל־הַר הַמּוֹר וְאֶל־גִּבְעַת הַלְּבוֹנָה	4:6 Until the day breathes and the shadows flee, I will hide me to the mountain of myrrh and the hill of frankincense.
7 כֻּלָּךְ יָפָה רַעְיָתִי וּמוּם אֵין בָּךְ ס (end of unit)	7 You are all fair, my love; there is no flaw in you. (end of unit ס)
8 אִתִּי מִלְּבָנוֹן כַּלָּה אִתִּי מִלְּבָנוֹן תָּבוֹאִי תָּשׁוּרִי מֵרֹאשׁ אֲמָנָה מֵרֹאשׁ שְׂנִיר וְחֶרְמוֹן מִמְּעֹנוֹת אֲרָיוֹת מֵהַרְרֵי נְמֵרִים	8 Come with me from Lebanon, my bride; come with me from Lebanon. Depart from the peak of Amana, from the peak of Senir and Hermon, from the dens of lions, from the mountains of leopards.
(Cant 4:10 to 6:10 included)	*(Cant 4:10 to 6:10 included)*
6:10 מִי־זֹאת הַנִּשְׁקָפָה כְּמוֹ־שָׁחַר יָפָה כַלְּבָנָה בָּרָה כַּחַמָּה אֲיֻמָּה כַּנִּדְגָּלוֹת ס (end of unit)	6:10 "Who is this that looks forth like the dawn, fair as the moon, bright as the sun, terrible as an army with banners?" (end of unit s)
11 אֶל־גִּנַּת אֱגוֹז יָרַדְתִּי לִרְאוֹת בְּאִבֵּי הַנָּחַל לִרְאוֹת הֲפָרְחָה הַגֶּפֶן הֵנֵצוּ הָרִמֹּנִים	11 I went down to the nut orchard, to look at the blossoms of the valley, to see whether the vines had budded, whether the pomegranates were in bloom.

If 4QCant[a] is indeed an abbreviated text rather than a shorter edition of the book, one explanation for the long glaring omission is the sensual language and erotic imagery found in much of Cant 4:8 to 6:10. Perhaps an ancient scribe or copyist wished to limit the amount of material that was no doubt controversial to some. Another possible explanation relates the similar content of the material before and after the break in Cant 4:7 to the shortening of the text. Note, for example, the closeness in content between 4:1-3 (included) and 6:5-7 (excluded). Moreover, the sections that are juxtaposed in 4QCanta describe several identical parts of the body or use similar motifs: pomegranates (4:3; 6:11), breasts, twins (4:5 = 7:4), neck (4:4; 7:5), eyes (4:1; 7:5), and tower (4:4; 7:5).[11]

3.2 Three Major Features in 4QCant[b]

4QCant[b] omits two large segments (3:6-8 and 4:4-7), as is evident in the following two extracts from the edition. The first omission (3:6-8) eliminates the description of King Solomon's dramatic arrival found in the MT. One possible reason for the second omission (4:4-7) is the parallels between descriptions of the female body in this chapter and in chapter 6; note that in

11 For further details, see DJD XVI, 203.

6:7 the description of the body ends at exactly the same point where it stops in 4:3. Another explanation is that the mention of breasts in v. 5 could have triggered the omission of the section as a whole

In the second case, it is interesting to note that both 4QCant^b and 4QCant^a lack material at exactly the same point (Cant 4:7). But while 4QCant^a omits a large piece of text (Cant 4:8 to 6:10) that *starts* after 4:7, 4QCant^b omits the three verses (4:4-7) that *end* with 4:7.

Col. II (frg. 2 i) Cant 3:5 + 9[12]

5]אל בית אמי ואל חדר הורתי 5השבעתי אתכ[מׄה
6]בנות ירושלם בצבאות או באילות השדה אם תע֯י[רו
7]ואם תעוררו את האהבה עד שתחפץ 9א[פׄרׄיון[
8]עשה לו המלך שלמה מן עצי הלבנון[*vacat*

Col. III (frg. 2 ii) Cant 4:2-3 + 8[13]

3 2שניך כעדר הקׄצׄ[ובות שעלו]מׄןׄ הׄ[רחצה]
4 שכלם מתאמות ו[שכלה אין]בהם 3כחוט
5 השני שפתותיך ומדברך נאוה כפלח הׄרמון
6 רקתך ומבעד לׄצׄמׄתך *vacat*
7 *vacat* 8את מן לבנון כלה את מן לבנון
8 אבאי תשורי מן ראשי אומנון ממענׄות
9 ארׄיׄוׄתׄ מן הררי נמרים 9לבבתני אחׄוׄתׄיׄ

The final fragment of 4QCant^b ends with 5:1, which is followed by blank space and a bottom margin; in the MT the final word of the verse is followed by a פ (*petuḥa*); see the extract below. Although the final three lines of the manuscript present some challenges, it is very possible that the full manuscript ended with the final word 5:1 (דׄוׄם or דׄיׄם, cf. MT דודים). If so, 4QCant^b represents a shorter version of Canticles than the eight-chapter version that is found in modern Bibles. Although the editor of the scroll describes it as an "abbreviated text,"[14] 4QCant^b may well be a shorter edition of Canticles.

12 For the complete preserved column (lines 1-14), see DJD XVI, 213.

13 For the complete preserved column (lines 1-14), see DJD XVI, 214-15.

14 Tov, DJD XVI, 194-5.

Col. IV (frg. 3) Cant 4:15 -5:1[15]

9 [באר מים חיי]ם ונוזלים מ[ן לבנון [16]עורי צפון]

10 [ובואי תימן]הׄפיחׄי גני י̊[זלו בשמיו יבא דודי]

11 [ל]גׄנו ויאכל מן ג[דיו [5:1]באתי לגני אחותי כלה]

12 אריתי מרי עם בש[מי *vacat* ?

13 אכלׄתי יערי עם דׄבשׄ[י ? ?

14 דׄיׄוׄם ¿ ?

bottom margin

Yet another interesting characteristic of 4QCant[b] is its unusual scribal markings. One example is at the end of col. I line 4, where הגיע וקל in Cant 2:9 is followed by the siglum , with the rest of the verse continuing on line 5. A second example is at line 7 of the same column, where the end of 2:13 (not preserved) is followed by an interval (mostly preserved) and the siglum . Note also the  in the last line of frg. 3, beneath the apparent final word (דׄום or דׄיׄם) at the end of Cant 5:1.

According to the editor of this scroll,[16] these scribal markings seem to represent letters either in the Paleo-Hebrew script, or the Cryptic A script (found in 4Q185, 4Q249, 4Q298, and 4Q317), or a combination of several scripts including Greek. They may also point to a sectarian scribal background or a special function of this manuscript among the Qumran community, since the Cryptic A script was used in Qumran sectarian writings. The actual purpose of the unusual letters is difficult to ascertain. One clue is that they appear in lines that were slightly or much shorter than the surrounding lines; perhaps the unusual letters served as line-fillers written in the spaces at the end of the lines to prevent such lines from being mistaken as "open sections."

15 For the complete extant column (lines 1-6 [not preserved], 7-14), see DJD 16.217.
16 E. Tov, DJD XVI, 204-5.

Select Bibliography

ABEGG, M./FLINT, P./ULRICH, E.C. (1999): The Dead Sea Scrolls Bible, San Francisco.

BAILLET, M./MILIK, J.T./DE VAUX, R. (1962): Les 'Petites Grottes' de Qumran: Exploration de la falaise Les grottes 2Q, 3Q, 5Q, 6Q, 7Q, à 10Q, Le rouleau de cuivre. 1. Texte, 2. Planches, DJD 3, Oxford, 112-13 + pl. XXIII.

CRAWFORD, S.W. (2000): Five Scrolls, in: L. Schiffman/J.C. VanderKam (eds.). Encyclopedia of the Dead Sea Scrolls, 2 vols., New York/Oxford, 295-297.

NEBE, G.W. (1994): Qumranica I: Zu unveröffentlichten Handschriften aus Höhle 4 von Qumran, ZAW 106, 307-322.

TOV, E. (1995): Three Manuscripts (Abbreviated Texts?) of Canticles from Cave 4, JJS 46, 88-111.

– (2000): Canticles, in: E.C. Ulrich et al. (eds.), Qumran Cave 4/XI: Psalms to Chronicles, DJD XVI, Oxford, 195-219 + pls. xxiv-xxv.

VANDERKAM, J.C./Flint, P.W. (2002): The Meaning of the Dead Sea Scrolls, San Francisco, 129-131.

Searching for a common background:
Egyptian love poetry and the Biblical Song of Songs

Antonio Loprieno

1. Introduction

In many respects, love lyrics could be seen as a unique phenomenon of Egyptian literature. At first sight, Egyptian love poetry seems idiosyncratic from the point of view of its forms, since it consists of scattered gatherings without apparent cohesion, of its historical emergence, which is limited to about one century of written evidence, of its motifs, that are less formal than in most literary compositions, and also of its presumable *Sitz im Leben*, for which we do not possess explicit collateral evidence. This does not mean, of course, that the ancient Egyptians experienced love in a radically different way from other human beings. Indeed their family structure, their emotional expressions, and their individual feelings do display many similarities with features we also encounter in other ancient and modern societies. The putative uniqueness of Egyptian love poetry is motivated, rather, by the rigidity of the filters usually adopted by ancient Egyptian culture in the visual or written display of the emotional sphere. These filters are generally subsumed under the heading of 'decorum': Egyptian artistic expressions and writing conventions were controlled by a highly formalized set of rules, most of which remained implicit and were rarely challenged in a dialectic manner (Baines 1990: 1-23). Not all human experiences were considered to be a legitimate topic for visual or written representation, but different time periods exhibited dramatic shifts in the hierarchies of decorum. There is more variety in the history of Egyptian discourse of love than we are usually inclined to assume.

The Biblical world, on the other hand, offers us a far more compact picture. This is not due to the fact that the authors of Old Testament books read their world in a homogeneous way, but rather to the relatively one-sided picture we are doomed to derive from a canonized set of texts. Biblical books were selected out of a great number of Hebrew (and Greek) writings in order to become the 'portative fatherland' of Judaism (Crüsemann 1987: 63-79). They are not just the traces of the intellectual history of the Jewish people over a millennium of literacy, but also – and more importantly – the carriers of a message with profound ideological, cohesive function. Although we can certainly recognize theological trends, cultural battles, and individual interests behind the written mirror offered by the Biblical books, it is fair to state that the early rabbis – and the ensuing Christian reception – interpreted a book on the basis of an explicit programmatic agenda. This agenda may or may not have been identical with the concerns that prompted the emergence of the texts themselves. In most cases, it probably was not, at the very least because of the time gap between the emergence of the text (in most cases sometime between the eighth and the third century BC) and its adoption into the canon at the end of the first century AD. But regardless of the convergence or divergence of ideological intents, through their very canonical status, Biblical texts have been read and transmitted over two millennia, conditioning Western readers to expectations that even modern scholars may find difficult to transcend.[1] From the point of view of a modern reader or exegete, therefore, Egyptian and Biblical texts are culturally antithetical: Egyptian texts are the more or less accidental result of a rediscovery; we read them as 'traces', as archaeological remnants. Biblical texts, on the other hand, partake of our common cultural heritage and experience; we are encyclopaedically (i.e., inadvertently) forced to read them as 'messages', as everlasting components of our classification of the world.

We could opt, of course, for an 'objective' (some would say: naïve) approach which consists in behaving as if the different cognitive status of the two sets of texts – a different cognitive status dictated by their radically different reception – could be disregarded. In fact, we probably do have to address the material evidence in this way, by reducing the mythical connotations of a purposeful message to the status of an information conveyed by a haphazard trace, if we want to achieve a scholarly reconstruction of Israelite cultural features in the first millennium at all. This is the approach that informs Biblical scholarship, and I shall of course adopt it in the following pages. But we should remain alert of the fact that, inevitably, the images of the Biblical text are doomed to appear to us more modern or less ideological than their Egyptian counterparts. Conversely, we should not let the archaeological context of the recovery of Egypt's cultural traces lead us to underestimate their intended role as message: because of the rigid set of decorum rules that underlay written production in Ancient Egypt, any Egyptian text, even the most private-looking, displayed a real-life embedding that may not always be evident at first sight. In one way or the other, all Egyptian texts were meant to serve a functional purpose.

To be sure, many historical and typological nuances do apply, and they will indeed guide the following comparative discussion of Egyptian and Israelite

---

1 A thoughtful analysis of the dilemma of interpretation in the history of Biblical reception – and to a certain extent of Biblical scholarship – is offered by Kugel 1997: 1-49.

love poetry. Historically and typologically, these two textual sources fill an eccentric slot within their respective cultural traditions. Within three thousand years of documented written history, Egyptian love poetry is a literary genre which only appeared in Dynasties XIX-XX, available sources coming from the second half of the thirteenth and the twelfth century BC. It does not denounce an explicit linkage to a formal setting and confronts the reader with far more lexical and semantic problems than the rest of contemporary Ramesside literature. The Biblical 'Song of Songs', whose dating is putative but most probably Hellenistic, is so unique that its place in the Biblical canon has always prompted some surprise. The rabbis at Yabneh accepted the Song into the canon[2] – to believe Rabbi Aqiba, without much hesitation[3] – because they read it both pseudepigraphically, as stemming from King Solomon himself, and allegorically, as a depiction of God's love for Israel rather than of man's love of sexual partnership.[4] At first sight, therefore, we might be content with classifying both sources as idiosyncratic, avoiding a confrontation with the issue of how they fit into their respective literary experience. Yet, two (broadly speaking) philological reasons prevent us from opting for this simplistic solution: on the one hand, Egyptian love poetry partakes of a global literary evolution which took place during the Ramesside era and which helps us frame its apparent singularity within a broader cultural analysis; as for the 'Song of Songs', it is so ostensibly related to the scope and the motifs of Egyptian love poetry that the question of a cultural *koiné* shared by Mediterranean literary traditions from the Late Bronze Age down to the first millennium BC demands to be addressed when discussing these two non-religious textual genres.[5]

2. *Chronological issues*

As it seems, the main problem associated with a comparative study of Egyptian love poetry and the Biblical Song of Songs remains that of the enormous time span – presumably a full millennium – that separates their textual documentation. While a serious handicap, this chronological gap can be very well explained in view of the radically different status enjoyed by literature in these two Mediterranean civilizations. If we do not possess true Egyptian lyrics from the Late Period, closest relatives being perhaps a Demotic satire of an incompetent and unappealing harper (Thissen 1992) and an invective on different human types in the context of drinking delights (Hoffmann 2000:

2 Bloch 1995: 27-29; Fox 1985: 250-256.
3 Mishnah, *Yadayim* 3,5.
4 Pope 1977: 18-19; Kuhn 1986; Köpf and Vincent 1986.
5 The issue of the documented cultural contacts between Egypt and Israel is addressed at length by Schipper (1999).

223-225), it is because in the Late Period, in spite of the unequivocal presence of a continuity of functional settings such as funerals, religious festivals, or wedding celebrations, 'poetry' in the narrower sense is not a major component of literary activity. Texts from these periods that might be possibly classified as 'lyric' (Kitchen 1999: 459-468) do not come from the literary, but rather from the funerary sphere. In Demotic literature, the emotional sphere appears alluded to in narrative as well as instructional texts, but it does not inspire dedicated genres as was the case in the Late Bronze Age. Also, during the second part of the first millennium BC, private autobiographical texts remained in productive use, and – in spite of the abundant use of codified expressions – they partly addressed the emotional needs and feelings of the individual, for example by emphasizing more than their Bronze Age predecessors the sense of loss caused by the death of a close relative (Gnirs 1996: 238-241). It is fair to state, however, that during the Late and Hellenistic periods Egyptian literary activity focussed primarily on tales, discourses, instructions, and myths, and did not include specific lyrical genres.

Israelite *literature* in the narrower sense, on the other hand – canonical *Ketubim* being the result of an ideological selection out of a certainly much larger body of texts – was composed during the Second Temple (Schniedewind 2004: 178-187) and displays, relatively speaking, a profound chronological cohesion; moreover, it does not generally confront us with issues related to the philological transmission or the intertextual reception of earlier texts and genres. This means that potential symmetries of contents or forms between the two literary traditions are hardly the result of a direct knowledge of the corresponding *texts*, but rather of cultural exposure to similar *contexts*. This probably already applies to the correspondences between Egyptian hymns and Israelite psalms,[6] and certainly to the Song of Songs: the similarities that we encounter rely on the exposure of Israelite (and then Jewish) authors to Egyptian cultural features as one of the dominating discourses in Ancient Near Eastern civilization and on the direct impact they exerted on emerging North-West Semitic literacy, but not – as far as our evidence suggests – on a formal schooling of Israelite scribes in Egyptian textual techniques: 'To a mare in Pharaoh's chariotry I compare you, my darling', says the boy in Cant 1:9, thus showing once more the associative power held by Egyptian icons in Israelite and then Jewish culture.

In this respect, the much debated issue of the 'unity' vs. 'disunity' of the compositions – whether each Egyptian collections of love songs and the Song of Songs itself are to be seen as a gathering of isolated stanzas or as a cohesive book – proves to be a false alternative. Egyptian love poetry represents a literary translation of non-literary public performances rooted in the reality of Egyptian festivals (Wimmer 2000: 25-33). A telling example is offered by

6 Auffret 1981: 14-16, 301-302.

Papyrus Chester Beatty I, which together with a collection of love songs contains a mythological text read on the occasion of king Ramses V's coronation and an encomium of the same king.

The Song of Songs' dialogical structure also points to the 'dramatic' context of real-life celebrations. That the two literary products date to quite different chronological frames is motivated by the discrepancy in the emergence of specific *literary* forms, not of the underlying *performative* settings. These can be considered to have remained relatively stable from the Late Bronze to the Iron Age in Near Eastern cultures, regardless of their being embedded into a continuous literary tradition or not. Even after the destruction of the Temple, the Song continued to be performed at 'banqueting houses' (*battey hammišta'ōt*) (Fox 1985: 249). An example for the presence of Egyptian singers in Canaan is offered by the dedicatory inscription of Karkar, a songstress of Ptah from the time of Ramses III (early twelfth century BC), among the Megiddo ivories (Kitchen 1968-90: V 256, 5-11), with a text that also points to the importance of the cult of Ptah in Palestine.[7] While it is unclear whether Karkar's activity was confined to the religious setting or also involved performing for a Palestinian prince, two clear references to the sphere of entertainment are on the one hand the mention of the Egyptian songstress Tentne at the court of the ruler of Byblos in the 'Tale of Wenamun' (eleventh century BC):[8]

> "And he had Tentne, an Egyptian songstress who was with him, be brought to me saying: 'Sing for him! Do not let his heart be sad!'" (Wenamun 2-68-69),

and on the other hand the representation of an Egyptian performer (with a flowery headdress that sometimes led to her being interpreted as a crowned Egyptian princess) in front of a Canaanite ruler on a vase from the Levante (Desroches-Noblecourt 1956: 179-220).

Late Bronze Egypt did not only act as exporter, but also as importer of entertainment migrants from the Syro-Palestinian world: we know of the presence of Levantine musicians in Amarna (Green 1992: 215-220), where they are sometimes represented in private tombs:

7 Wimmer 1990: 1091-1093; Wimmer 1998: 102-103.

8 Gardiner 1932: 74, 5-7. For the literary figure of the singer cf. Moers 2001: 95; Schipper 1999: 113.

Figure 1: Egyptian and Canaanite musicians from the tomb of Huya at Amarna: N. de Garis Davies, The Rock Tombs of El Amarna, Part III: The Tombs of Huya and Ahmes, London 1905, Pl. VII (Courtesy of the Egypt Exploration Society)

All these references to a common Egyptian-Canaanite milieu of musical performance remind us of the evocation of the dancing Shulamite in Cant 7:1-7:

> "Again, dance again, o Shulamite, that we may watch you dancing! Why do you look at the Shulamite as she whirls through the rows of dancers?"

It is a fact that the Egyptian literature of the Late and Hellenistic Period undertook a rather strict selection of accepted genres and that love poetry did not belong to the spectrum of productive forms. This does not imply that during the Late Period love songs were not sung in festive gatherings, as we know from Herodotus (II, 78) and other Greek authors as well as from Egyptian texts which stem from the religious or funerary context but emphasize the joy of love, both sexual (Kitchen 1999: 459-462):

> "Most beautiful among women, a girl whose like was never seen,
> blacker is her hair than the black of night, than the grapes of the river-bank;
> whiter are her teeth than flakes of plaster, than a slice of papyrus:
> her breasts are firm on her bosom."

and affectionate (Kitchen 1999: 465-468):

> "His beloved wife is a lady of charm, sweet of love, effective in speech and pleasing in words, effective in counsel in her writings: whatever passes her lips is like a work of truth".

Symmetrically, a selection of accepted, i.e. 'canonical' texts (not genres!) was not undertaken in the Jewish world before the end of the first century AD within the frame of the reorganization of Judaism into a religion of the 'text', rather than of the 'cult', which again does not imply that the performative reality at the roots of the Song of Songs had not already been present during earlier periods of Israelite culture. In fact, the pseudepigraphic reference to Solomon as the Song's author, a reference confirmed by 1Reg 5,12 and by

Ben Sira's wisdom text (47:15-17), suggests the existence of an informal continuous tradition which goes back to the very roots of Israelite civilization.[9]

Thus, we must presumably refrain from positing a direct *literary* continuity from the Egyptian love poetry of the Late Bronze Age to its Israelite Second Temple counterpart, while at the same time recognizing that the explicit formal parallels between two poetic traditions of celebrating love find their common denominator in the festive settings of ancient Mediterranean societies. That performatively founded literary forms may not be concomitant with the period of their pristine oral emergence is a very well-known phenomenon of Mediterranean cultures documented, for example, by the three formative stages of Homeric poems: the Late Bronze Mycenean setting, their oral transmission during the so-called Dark Age and their performance at festivals in Archaic Greece, and the philological codification of the text in Hellenistic times (Latacz 2001: 292-331).

3. How did Egyptian and Israelite love poetry emerge?

The two main periods of productive literary activity in Egypt, namely the Middle Bronze Age (ca. 2000-1600 BC) and the second part of the Late Bronze Age (i.e., from ca. 1300 to 1050 BC), are characterized by very different cultural contexts, which have a profound impact on their textual and stylistic choices. The former is strongly 'nilocentric' and monolingual: classical Middle Egyptian is the language used in literary genres – mainly wisdom texts, discourses[10] and tales – with a varying reception of expressions drawn from the spoken language. The latter is more 'international' and explicitly diglossic: classical Egyptian continues to be used in the transmission of earlier literary texts and in the production of new compositions modelled upon classical antecedents, but a new literary language, Late Egyptian, provides a vehicle for an expansion of the corpus of instructional and narrative literature as well as for the creation of textual genres hitherto excluded from literary 'decorum'. Very significant examples of these new genres that enter the domain of Egyptian literature are *mythology*, i.e. narratives with divine protagonists, and *lyrics*, i.e. poetry with emotional (including erotic) contents.

While the contextual setting of mythological texts is related to the performance of magical rites ranging from the king's burial (as in the 'Destruction of Mankind' on the internal walls of three early Ramesside royal

9 While pseudepigraphic references – such as the figures of Ptahhotep or Khety in Egyptian wisdom texts of the Middle and the New Kingdom respectively – cannot be taken as indicating a direct authorship, they do identify specific individuals as the source of functional 'myths' surrounding the emergence of literary texts and contexts (Parkinson 2002: 90-91).

10 Here and in the following in the meaning indicated by Parkinson 2002: 108-112.

tombs) to the ceremony of inthronization (as in the 'Contendings of Horus and Seth' on Papyrus Chester Beatty I), the *Sitz im Leben* of love poetry is opaque. The magical sphere does play a certain role (Davis 1980: 111-114), but it rather applies to the non-literary setting of the so-called 'love spells', which are intended to cause someone to fall in love or symmetrically, to damage someone else and prevent him from coming after the beloved person (Mathieu 1996: 226-232).[11] Love spells remain a constant component of Egyptian magic down to the Hellenistic period,[12] but they do not belong properly speaking to the domain of love lyrics.

The textual corpus of love poetry consists of three papyri and two dozen ostraca (Mathieu 1996: 19-23) and thus mirrors the situation of other sources which I have tentatively subsumed under the heading of 'proletarian literature' (Loprieno 1996: 227-231). Stylistic features and tropes are similar, but one hardly finds repetitions of sentences or expressions. This means that the texts were neither codified in a canonical manner nor compiled out of an inventory of established formulae, but rather the result of immediate individual creativity.

We can identify two literary genres, which shed some light on the emergence and the setting of Egyptian love poetry. The first genre is a peculiar type of discourse that is already documented in the Middle Kingdom and combines mythical and pastoral traits and praises the joys of life in the countryside: the 'Tale of the Herdsman' of Dyn. XII or the 'Pleasures of Fishing and Fowling' of Dyn. XVIII emphasize the benefits of agriculture as a source of life but also of pleasure (Parkinson 2002: 226-232). Many of the bucolic tableaus described in these texts find a corresponding setting in Ramesside love poetry:

11 For a Ramesside example of love spell cf. Smither 1941: 131-132.
12 For some examples in Greek and Demotic cf. Betz 1986: 169-172.

Figure 2: Fishing and fowling from the Dyn. XVIII tomb of Menena (TT 69): Alan H. Gardiner, N. M. Davies, La peinture égyptienne ancienne, vol. I, Paris 1953.

The second genre, the so-called 'harpers' songs',[13] display – as we shall see – more immediate connections with love poetry (Buchberger 1983: 11-43): framed as Epicurean comments on the ephemeral character of human life, the harpers' songs – again a post-Amarna innovation that frequently claims pseudepigraphic ancestry back to the early Middle Kingdom[14] – are rooted in the burial celebration and represent the literary transformation of actual performances that presumably occurred during these events in real life (Bochi 1998: 89-95):

13 Lichtheim 1945: 178-212; Assmann 1977: 55-84.

14 The king named Antef from whose tomb the author of the harper's song in pHarris 500, 6,2-7,3 putatively copied his text is usually taken to be one of the Antefs of Dyn. XI, whereas a recent proposal (Polz 2003: 75-87) suggests a background in Dyn. XVII which, however, would confront us with some cultural historical difficulties.

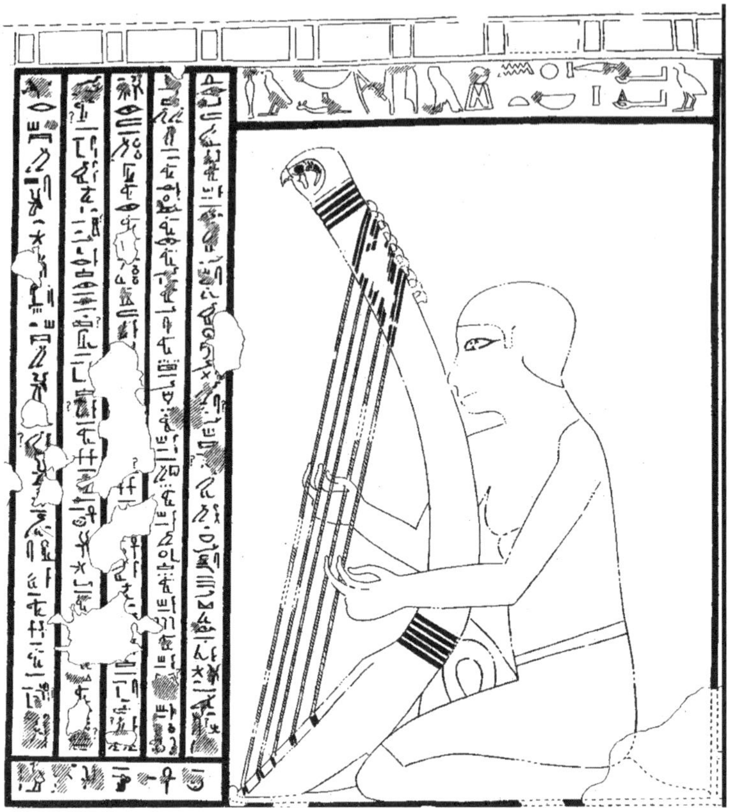

Figure 3: Male harper from the Middle Kingdom tomb of Antefiqer: N. de Garis Davies, The Tomb of Antefoker, Vizier of Sesostris I and of his wife Senet (No. 60), London 1920, Pl. XXVII.

Here, we should probably draw a distinction between two forms of representational dialogue between the funerary and the festive context. On the one hand, we have the deceased's 'funerary meal', which stresses his family and social ties beyond the crisis of death and is more properly rooted in the funerary cult.[15] This funerary meal is also archaeologically documented through materials used for Tutankhamun's burial as well as from private tombs of Dyn. XVIII.[16] On the other hand, scenes of entertainment in form of dancing, singing, or playing music are a constant component of the representation of 'ideal life' from the Old Kingdom on.

15 Fitzenreiter 1995: 112-116; Assmann 2001: 432-452

16 Cf. the collars or the ceramic jars from KV 54 (Winlock 1973); for evidence of cultic activity in private Theban tombs cf. Seiler 1995: 185-203.

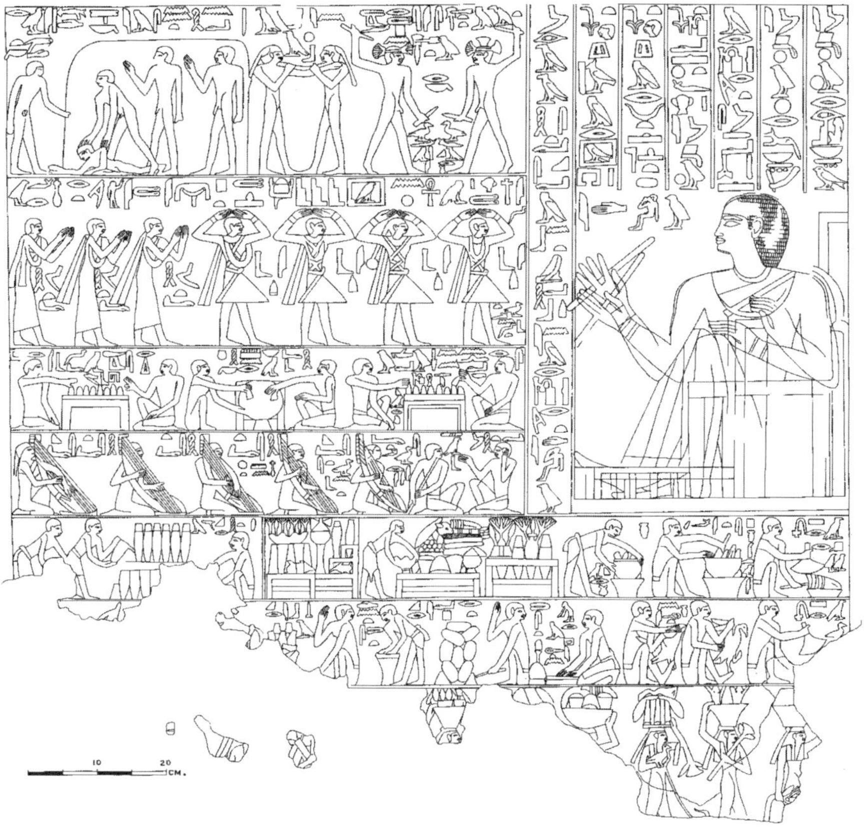

Figure 4: Music and dance performances in the Old Kingdom tomb of Idu: W. K. Simpson, *The Mastabas of Qar and Idu G 7101 and 7102*. Giza Mastabas 2, Boston 1976, Pl. 38 (Drawing © 1976 Museum of Fine Arts, Boston).

During Dyn. XVIII, entertainment scenes begin to emphasize the corporality of the female actors and convey explicitly erotic connotations hitherto unknown in Egypt's artistic experience.

Figure 5: Music and eroticism from the Dyn. XVIII tomb of Djeserkareseneb (TT 38): Alan H. Gardiner and N. M. Davies, La peinture égyptienne ancienne, vol. II, Paris 1953.

Dancing and singing scenes are accompanied by textual captions, which combine elements of the harpers' songs with motifs later found in Ramesside love poetry. We can assume, therefore, that festive celebrations – including visits to the relatives' tombs during the Beautiful Festival of the Valley (Schott 1953) and probably weddings[17] – provided a frame for oral performances which find in harpers' songs and love poetry their written, literary complement. This breadth of cultural expressions in which the oral and the written sphere are dialectically intertwined is a specific trait of Ramesside Egypt: in the preceding epochs, more rigid rules of decorum hindered the development of this textual variety; in the following Iron Age, an overall renegotiation of the domains of scribal activity led to a drastic reduction of literary activity (Loprieno 2003a: 141-143).

For Ancient Israel, we cannot remotely achieve such a detailed perception of functional contexts (Fox 1985: 186-193). We must rely on the rabbinic reception to possibly identify the wedding celebrations as the original setting of

17 There is very little Egyptian evidence for wedding celebrations, the main source being a reference to a wedding banquet in front of Pharaoh in the first Demotic tale of Setne Khaemwaset (third century BC). The legal status of marriage was probably formalized in a contract after the two young people had been living together for some time (Allam 1981: 116-135; Meskell 2002: 94-97).

love songs, including the 'Song of Songs'.[18] This reconstruction is also made likely by Cant 3:11:

> "Go forth and look, girls of Zion, king Solomon with the crown that his mother crowned him with on the day of his wedding, on the day of his heart's joy (*śimḥat libbō*)!"

The iconoclastic culture of the Biblical world, however, has left us bereft of visual traces that would allow us to place written evidence into a broader interpretative context. We do possess, however, an Egyptian literary reference to a Canaanite love adventure in a Ramesside school text, a satirical letter in which two fictive scribes make ostentatious display of their rhetorical talents by using foreign (mostly Semitic) vocabulary and alluding to exotic landscapes (Fischer-Elfert 1986: 212-222):

> "You now went to Joppa and found the meadows verdant in their season. You forced your way in with laments but encountered the beautiful girl who was tending the vineyards. She seduced you to be with her and showed you the colour of her bosom. But you were caught und had to confess. You were fined to pay the *mohar*, so that you had to sell your shirt of good fine linen" (pAnastasi I 25,2-6).

The fictive Egyptian protagonist has to pay a *mohar* for his abuse of the Canaanite girl, thus providing a Late Bronze Age literary echo of the entertainment context at the root of the later textual genre documented by the Song of Songs.

4. *Religious and secular aspects*

Within a primarily historical perspective, both Egyptian and Israelite love poetry exhibit intriguing connections between the religious and the erotic sphere (Fox 1985: 227-250). On the Egyptian side, we have referred to the ceremonies that celebrated the solidarity between the dead and the living and noticed how, during Dyn. XVIII, funerary paintings and texts pay increased attention to the domain of emotions, including erotic allusions (Meskell 2002: 126-147).[19] During the Ramesside period, the most explicit – almost pornographic – references, which Ancient Egypt has transmitted to us are represented on the so-called 'satirical-erotic papyrus' from Turin[20] and described iconically and textually as the sexual activity of a Theban priest in a

18 Mishnah, *Sanhedrin* 101a. For a broad study of the sacralization of the Song cf. Fox 1985: 250-256.

19 The same emphasis on eroticism is also found in contemporary objects of everyday life such as mirrors or other cosmetic objects and vessels (Bosse-Griffiths 1980: 70-82; Quack 2003: 44-64).

20 Omlin 1973; Kessler 1988: 171-196.

sequence of scenes organized according to the pattern of a religious ritual. In general, the locus of the goddess Hathor at the crossroads of celestial and material love and the mythological background of the depiction of the *hieròs gámos* represented on temples walls during Dyn. XVIII (Assmann 1982: 13-61) show that Egyptian culture did in fact recognize the presence of a dialogue between 'Love' as a motor of cosmic events and 'love' as a core feature of human life:

> "I shall call to Hathor that she may hear my prayers, and my lady will decree her for me. She came on her own to see me: how great is what happened to me! I became happy, glad and powerful when I could say: Here she is! See, lovers came to her bowed down because of the greatness of her Love. I shall pray to my goddess that she might give me my lover as a gift" (pChester Beatty I 3,6-9).

> "Sitting down and rejoicing on a beautiful day in his house in the West. It is the eternal house that lies in the region of Hathor, Mistress of Deir el-Bahri. May she let you come from the earth and open the Hereafter in order to see the sun god shine and hear the lowing of cattle (...) Take and drink: celebrate a beautiful day in your eternal house by the hand of your beloved one, Henut-nefret."[21]

And also on the Jewish side, even if the allegorical reception of the 'Song of Songs' was ultimately motivated by apologetic concerns, it was certainly favoured by the view that love had a role to play within the context of a religiously structured life.

Sexual attraction being one of man's most basic experiences, we can reasonably expect the relatively high degree of 'naturalness' of love poetry (Fox 1985: 295-298) to generate a broader spectrum of interculturally common features than is the case, for example, in religious or didactic poetry. A certain number of connotations, allusions, comparisons, expressions are doomed to be shared by a very high number of literary traditions. The praise of the scent of the beloved or of his or her physical attractiveness would probably turn out to be a literary universal. On a similar vein, longing for the beloved or trying to catch his or her attention by eluding strict surveillance is neither a typical trait of Bronze Age nor a singularity of the Shulamite's dialogue with the girls of Jerusalem. What characterizes Egyptian love songs and the Israelite Song of Songs, however, are two distinct qualities worthy of some attention: their use of religious associations on the one hand and their embedding into a dialogical, narrative frame on the other.

For Egyptian love songs, we can easily visualize the origin of these religious associations. On the walls of the private tombs (the so-called mastabas) of Old Kingdom's officials we find numerous scenes of human activities ranging from agriculture to handicraft, from working to singing, that are frequently accompanied by textual passages of varying length. These scenes fulfil the

21 From the tomb of Nebamun and Ipuky, TT 181 (Schott 1953: 126-27; Davies 1925: Pl. 5).

paradigmatic ('ideal') function of maintaining the solidarity between the deceased and his social milieu beyond the crisis of death. Since they are located at the crossroads between life and death, they are intended to be both real and fictive, with a base both in this world and in the realm of the dead: they are simultaneously a token of memory of this world and an emblem of departure from this world.[22] One of the frequent motifs is that of playing the harp,[23] sometimes in a setting which emphasizes private ties, and in what is the most concise form of love song, represented in the tomb of Inti from Dyn. VI (24th century BC), we see a harper in front of a clapping man accompanied by the inscription (Vachala 2003: 429-431):

ḥꜣꜣ ṯrꜣꜣ mrj=j dy=j r ẖr nfr=ṯ

"Music and dance: I love to be overwhelmed by your beauty".

Figure 6: Mereruka's wife playing the harp in front of her husband: J. A. Wilson and Th. G. Allen (eds.), *The Mastaba of Mereruka, Part I*, Chicago 1938, Pl. 94 (Courtesy of the Oriental Institute of the University of Chicago).

In the Middle Kingdom Theban tomb of Antefiqer and Senet (TT 60), we find representations of a male (Figure 3) and of a female harper (Figure 7) accompanied by the text of the hymns they sing in cursive hieroglyphs, not in

22 Assmann 2001: 299-318; Baines 1999: 34-37.
23 Altenmüller 1978: 1-24; Buchberger 1995: 93-123.

the monumental writing which is used for texts such as offering formulae that are more directly related to the funerary context.[24]

Figure 7: Female harper from the Middle Kingdom tomb of Antefiqer: N. de Garis Davies, The Tomb of Antefoker, Vizier of Sesostris I and of his wife Senet (No. 60), London 1920, Pl. XXVII.

This discrepancy in writing styles points to the different cultural significance of the two textual genres – on the one hand the mortuary setting, on the other hand the sphere of entertainment, and eventually of literature – and conveys a further proof of the claim that the Egyptian tomb was the locus of a complex cultural interaction between the living and the funerary level.

These early documents of a representational genre that will come to literary fruition several centuries later conveys to us a sense of the osmotic contamination between two discourses that modern readers are trained to regard as rigidly distinguished: 'religious' and 'secular' are not antithetic terms,

24 Morenz 1996: 58-77; Loprieno 2003: 32.

but rather complementary aspects of a homogeneous cultural reality in which the levels appear constantly superimposed. Transitional events such as birth, circumcision, marriage or death, regardless of their more or less pronounced legal dimension, were accompanied by social – both secular and religious – *rites de passage*. The celebratory atmosphere of these and similar events is conveyed in Egyptian by the term *hrww nfr* 'good day',[25] a concept which may equally apply to the religious aspect of ritual festivals and to the secular dimension of physical, including sexual, wellness and pleasure (Assmann 1989: 3-28).

Within this general frame, scenes on tomb walls as well as the literary genres that gradually develop out of functional contexts – 'tomb' and 'school' being among the most pregnant in generating the two basic literary types, i.e. narratives and instructions – may themselves be taken as a mirror of contextual realities and social expectations. In the Middle and the early New Kingdom, as we saw in the case of the 'Tale of the Herdsman' and of the 'Pleasures of Fishing and Fowling', the joys of a fictive pastoral life in which religious myths and real-life ideals appear to overlap, invaded the domain of literature. During Dyn. XVIII, the development of the tomb's decorative programme leads to an expansion of the festive setting;[26] the 'ideal life' as conveyed by Old and Middle Kingdom representations of professional activities is expanded by a focus on the convivial setting marked by explicit sensual, erotic connotations (Quack 2003: 60-61), and it may prove inappropriate to recognize in them only regenerative, mortuary functions.[27]

Rather, the periodical, ritualized meetings with the dead (Wiebach 1986: 263-291), for example during the Beautiful Festival of the Valley (*ḥȝb nfr n jn.t*), are also occasions for worldly celebration, and the border between the display of individual – including sexual – love and the praise to Hathor as its divine manifestation is doomed to remain as fuzzy as the one between the hope for an Epicurean *hrww nfr* and the call for a regeneration of the deceased in the Hereafter. In the Theban tomb TT 82, which belongs to Amenemhet (Davies-Gardiner 1915: Pl. 15), singers and musicians say (Schott 1953: 129-130):

> "You shine, the heads of Amun-Re shine!"
> "O beautiful day, waking up in the beautiful morning!"
> "You embrace eternity and enjoy the future!"
> "How beautiful is the house of Amun-Re that spends the day celebrating with the king of the gods who dwells in it!"

---

25 Cf. Hebrew *yōm ṭōb*, a compound in which the religious connotations were eventually privileged: 'festival, Holy Day' (Jastrow 1971: 569).

26 Conveniently called the '*sḫmḫ-jb* (i.e., entertainment) segment' of the tomb decoration by Engelmann-von Carnap (1999: 384-393).

27 Cf. the short, insightful discussion in Kampp 1996: 116-117.

"The goddess is like a woman who sits inebriated outside her room: locks of hair fall on her beautiful breast!"

This juxtaposition of divine and erotic traits in the figure of Hathor remains a feature of Egyptian culture until the Late Period, as demonstrated by hymns linking a princess to the divine beauty of the goddess (see above) or celebrating the return the goddess to the temple which display a continuity of performative settings (Darnell 1995: 49-50):

"Come, o Golden One, who eats of praise, for the food she wishes is dance, who shines on the festival at the time of lighting the lamps, who is happy with dancing at night! Come, the procession is in the place of inebriation, namely that hall of going through the marshes! Its performance stands, its order is set, and nothing is lacking for me there!"

But it is in the Ramesside era that specific *literary* developments take place. Harpers' songs and love poems in the vernacular language – Late Egyptian – are extrapolated from their *Sitz im Leben* and recorded on papyri for the entertainment of literate elites:

"Beginning of the sweet verses found in a book container and written by the scribe of the Necropolis Nakhtsobek" (pChester Beatty I 16,9).

'Sweet verses' (*ṯz.w nḏm*) is a synonym of 'entertainment' (*sẖmẖ-jb*, cf. *śimḥat libbō* in Cant 3:10) and the symmetrical counterpart of 'instruction' (*sbꜣ.yt*): the latter is founded on the scholarly reception of classical 'books' in Middle Egyptian, the former on the episodic writing of 'proletarian' compositions rooted in oral transmission. In this literary process, Late Egyptian texts keep their original features of individual poetic creativity – they never become 'books', but remain *rꜣ.w* 'words' (Mathieu 1996: 135), i.e. collections of 'songs of entertainment'. Sometimes the two genres can appear combined, as in the case of Papyrus Harris 500 (BM 10060), which presents 'the songs that are in the tomb of Antef, justified, in front of the harper' within a collection of love songs (6:2-7,3) and thus offers a textual counterpart to the tomb scenes where erotic representations are embedded into the funeral procession. Eventually, with the crisis that characterized the end of the Bronze Age (Liverani 1988: 629-660), literary discourse ceased to be productive and was resumed several centuries later, during the so-called 'axial age', under new historical and cultural premises. The *hrww nfr*-theme, however, continued to be echoed in private autobiographies (Gnirs 1996: 238-241).

It is not difficult to posit for Ancient Israel the existence of comparable festive settings enriched by the entertainment of oral compositions, although this hypothesis must remain speculative. Nonetheless, the Bible itself alludes to personal satisfaction at the crossroads between religious embedding and secular pleasure with expressions that seem to echo earlier Egyptian wisdom texts:[28]

> "Let your fountain be blessed: take delight in your youthful wife, a loving doe, a pleasant gazelle: let her breasts fill you with pleasure at all times, be always ravished with her love" (Prov 5:18-19)

> "Go and eat your bread with joy, and drink your wine with a happy heart, for God has already approved your doing. Your clothes should always be white and oil to anoint your head should never be missing. Enjoy life with the woman you love, all the fleeting days that are granted you under the sun. For this is your share in life and in your work which you perform under the sun" (Qoh 9:7-9).

and to a certain extent to the performance of texts in which the religious and the erotic sphere are allegorically combined and which may have been sung on specific occasions:

> "I want to sing to my beloved one the song of his love for his vineyard. My beloved one had a vineyard in a fruitful hill; he fenced it, gathered out its stones, planted it with the best vine, built in it a tower and also a winepress. He expected it to bring forth grapes, but it produced wild grapes. And now, inhabitants of Jerusalem and people of Judah, judge between me and my vineyard: what more could I have done to my vineyard that I failed to do there? Why did it produce wild grapes, although I expected it to bring forth grapes? But now I shall tell you what I will do to my vineyard: take away its hedge and it shall be eaten up, break down its wall and it will be trodden upon. I shall lay it waste, and it will not be pruned or digged, but briers and thorns will come up, and I shall order to the clouds that they not rain on it. For the vineyard of the Lord of Hosts is the House of Israel and the people of Judah are the planting in which he delights" (Is 5:1-7).

> "My people will come to you as to a public event and sit before you. They will listen to your words but not do them. For they have a taste for attractive things, and their heart goes after their desire. As far as they are concerned, you are just a singer of love songs who sings pleasantly and plays well. So they will hear your words, but will not do them" (Ez 33:31-32).

It is clear, therefore, that Egypt and Israel shared a common performative culture that expressed itself in particular during festivals and celebrations. The royal milieu and the royal palace, particularly during the Amarna era with its iconic emphasis on the king's multifunctional presence (Figure 8), but also during the Ramesside period (Figure 9) provides many examples of the crucial connection between power display and the erotic sphere.

While Egyptian festivals, however, appear frequently embedded in the remembrance of the deceased – whether in the context of funerals or of visits to the tomb –, this sphere seems to be altogether absent from Israelite love poetry. In general, two opposite trends are at work here: on the one hand,

28 Cf. Ptahhotep 325-338 (Junge 2003: 52-53, 196-197).

Israelite religion is overall less concerned with the cult of the deceased, specific expectations about life *post mortem* being the result of post-exilic developments that are thematized in wisdom texts such as Job or Qohelet (Qoh 12:7: 'The dust returns to the earth, as it was before, while the breath returns to God, who had given it'); on the other hand, the fuzzy status of marriage in Egyptian sources does not allow us to identify a specific setting for wedding celebrations. This situation shows us in an ideal way how difficult it is to recognize a direct textual dependence between the two traditions in spite of their explicit harmony in treating love as a central component of a hierarchically structured religious as well as festive life.

Figure 8: Queen Nefertiti filling king Akhenaten's cup from the tomb of Merire II at Amarna: N. de Garis Davies, The Rock Tombs of El Amarna, Part II: The Tombs of Panehesy and Meryra II, London 1905, Pl. XXXII (Courtesy of the Egypt Exploration Society).

5. *The dramatic frame*

The second aspect in which I would like to see a shared cultural experience as the motor of similarities between Egyptian love poetry and the Song of Songs is the dramatic setting. By 'dramatic' I mean here the dialogical structure whereby individual songs (and texts) are sung (or read?) by the two love partners in alternating sequences.

Figure 9: King Ramses III playing draughts with a princess and attended by another: The Epigraphic Survey, The Eastern High Gate with Translations of Texts. Medinet Habu VIII, Chicago 1970, pl. 640 (Courtesy of the Oriental Institute of the University of Chicago).

In this respect, the Israelite composition is less equivocal than Egyptian love poems. In fact, one can indeed recognize – at least in some sections of the Song of Songs – a narrative dialectic that is absent from Egyptian texts, where the boy's or the girl's speeches seem to elude a predictable succession. Also, the boy's and the girl's monologues are frequently similar and sexually undistinguishable:[29]

> "(Boy) I am sailing downstream in the boat by the captain's strokes, with my bundle of reeds on my shoulder, headed for Ankh-Tawy, and I shall say to Ptah, Lord of Truth: 'Give me my lover tonight. The river is like wine, its reeds are like Ptah, its lotus leaves are Sakhmet, its lotus buds are Yadet, its lotus blossoms are Nefertem, so that the country shines through her beauty. Memphis is a jar of mandrakes set before the god whose face is pleasant" (pHarris 500 2,5-9)

> "(Girl) I am sailing downstream on the Canal of the Ruler and I have entered that of Re. My desire is to go and prepare the booths for the opening of the canal's entrance. I shall set out to hurry and will not pause, for my heart thinks of Re. Then I will see my lover's entry when he heads toward the park. I shall stand with you at the entrance of the Ity Canal, for you have taken my heart to Heliopolis" (pHarris 500 3,1-8).

The contents of the stanzas in the Song of Songs, on the contrary, are both more dramatically pregnant and more immediately gender-related (Cant 2:8-14):

> "(Girl) Listen, the voice of my beloved – he is now bounding over the mountains, leaping over the hills. My beloved is like a gazelle, a young roe; there he stands behind our wall, gazing through the windows, glancing in through the lattice. My beloved spoke and said to me: '(Boy) Arise, my darling, my beauty, and come away! See, the winter is over, the rain has passed and gone its way. Blossoms have appeared in the land, the time of song has approached and the voice of the turtledove can be heard in our land. The fig tree sweetens its young fruit, and the budded vines smell fragrant. Arise, my darling, my beauty, and come away, my dove in the clefts of the rock, in the shadow of the cliff: let me see your form, let me hear your voice, for your voice is sweet and your form is pleasing."

Here, one can recognize connections with fertility festivals known from Mesopotamia, and students of the Song of Songs have indeed, in different forms, posited a ritual function within the context of the celebration of the Sacred Marriage between Tammuz and Ishtar (Fox 1985: 239-243). Be it as it may, the text of the Song of Songs was certainly directly rooted in actual festive performances: the succession of repetends generates a high degree of dialogic homogeneity (Fox 1985: 220), whereas Egyptian love poems always represent the result of a literary reformulation and thus give preference to stylistic requirements. I shall give two examples, which witness an explicit literarization process. One is the use of wordplay: in the Song of Songs, it is a more distinctly *oral* feature which emphasizes rhythmic *sound* sequences: Cant 1:2 *yiššaqeni minnĕšiqōt pihu* ... 1:3 *lĕreaḥ šĕmaneyka ṭōbim šemen turaq šĕmeka* ... 4:11 *nōpet tiṭṭōpnāh śiptōtayk kallāh* (Alter 1995: 123). Alliteration and

29 A certain similarity in the lovers' verbal behaviour, however, is a general feature of Ancient Near Eastern love poetry, which should not be misinterpreted as an egalitarian rejection of sex roles (Fox 1985: 305-310).

paronomasia are also documented in Egyptian love poetry (Mathieu 1996: 203-204), but a more frequent recourse to wordplay involves the cognitive, *semantic* associations. A most frequent pun revolves around the concept of 'love'. The Egyptian root is *mrj*, and the same sequence of consonants *mr(j)* is common to a variety of words which often appear, especially in love poetry, in paronomastic association with the concept of 'love': the 'sickness' (*mr*) caused by love:

> "I will lie down inside and then forge illness (*mr*): my neighbours will come to visit and my lover with them: she will make the doctors dumb, for she understands my illness (*mr*)" (pHarris 500 2,9-11),

or the 'bundle' (*mrw*) of reeds on which the lover sleeps during his journey to the beloved:

> "I am sailing downstream in the boat by the captain's strokes, with my bundle (*mrw*) of reeds on my shoulder, headed for Ankh-Tawy" (pHarris 500 2,5-6),

or the fragrant /reddish wood/ (*mrj*), which called our attention above in a wordplay involving an empty space on a scribal palette (Seidlmayer 1991: 319-330) and is here compared to the lover's seductive head:

> "My lover is a whole lotus: her breasts are like mandrakes, [...], her head like a bush of reddish wood (*mrj*) – and I am like a wild-goose!" (pHarris 500 1,11-2,1).

In a similar vein, the number of successive stanzas or the name of a flower or a plant is resumed in the first verse of the poem, expanding on its connotational potential:

> "Fifth (*djw*) stanza: I shall pray (*dwꜣ=j*) to the Golden One and praise her Majesty, I shall exalt the Mistress of Heaven and give homage to Hathor and thanks to my lady" (pChester Beatty I 3,4-6).

> "The *mẖmẖ*-flower: my heart is in balance (*mẖꜣ*) with you" (pHarris 500 7,3-4).

The other example is the presence, in one of the papyri and in two ostraca, of a mysterious figure called Mehy (Fox 1985: 64-66), who frequently has royal or aristocratic associations and plays the role of a trickster or *arbiter amoris* (Hermann 1959: 106-107). Mehy has been identified with various figures ranging from one of the kings or princes of Dyn. XVIII (Schott 1950: 35) to king Sethy I's charioteer during the Palestinian campaigns (Helck 1988: 143-148), which reminds of the tableau in Cant 3:7-8:

> "Look, Solomon's own couch! Around it are the best sixty warriors of Israel, all of them swordsmen skilled in warfare, each with his sword along his thigh because of the fear of night".

Whatever the origin or the function of this figure may be, it is clear that we are dealing with a fictional device that points to literary discourse rather than actual performance as its most appropriate context:

> "My heart wanted to see her beauty while sitting at her place, but on the way I found Mehy in his chariot together with his lovers. I do not know if I should take myself away from him or pass freely by him" (pChester Beatty I 2,5-6).

Finally, dialogical structure definitely does not entail cross-gender authorship. The attribution of specific stanzas to the boy or to the girl is not always unequivocal, as is shown by the variability in the use of determinatives of personal pronouns (Fox 1985: 265).[30] Egyptian love songs were certainly copied by male scribes: sources on female literacy are elusive,[31] the most direct source being the depiction of Qenamun's wife with a scribal palette beneath her chair in TT 162 (Porter-Moss 1960: 276), and the case for female literary authorship of any sort is altogether weak. Although recent provocative suggestions point into different directions (Bloom-Rosenberg 1990), the same situation is most likely to have occurred in Israel.[32] In the performances that are at the core of the evolution of these literary forms, female roles were probably filled by women. The agents of literary discourse, on the contrary, were members of a Theban elite that could enjoy an appropriate schooling (Meskell 2002: 84-85).

6. *Punctual correspondences*

Nature. We have observed that Egyptian love poetry is typologically linked to an earlier form of discourse that emphasizes pastoral pleasures. Love poems on both sides of the Sinai peninsula display attention for what we might call 'tamed nature' in a threefold way: first, by directly associating the lover's sexual attractiveness to the pleasures of nature:[33]

> "The plants of the marsh are intoxicating, the mouth of the beloved is a lotus, her breasts are mandrakes" (pHarris 500 1,11-12)

> "Thus is your stature: it resembles a palm tree, and your breasts are like clusters. I said to myself: I shall climb the palm and get hold of its branches" (Cant 7:8-9)

---

30 The equivocal status of first person pronouns is a feature of other late Ramesside texts (Sweeney 2001: 180), including Butehamun's 'love' letter to his dead wife's coffin (Frandsen 1992: 31-49; Goldwasser 1995: 191-205).

31 Sweeney 1998: 1009-1017; Sweeney 2001: 6

32 For feminist readings of the Song of Songs cf. Brenner-Fontaine 2000.

33 For the erotic connotations of fruits cf. Bosse-Griffiths 1983: 62-74.

secondly, by letting trees, flowers and gardens become *dramatis personae* directly involved in the dialogue between lovers:

> "The fig tree opens his mouth and comes to speak: ‚Listen to what I will do: I shall come to the lady. Is there anyone as noble as me, although I have no slaves?" (pTurin 1966 1,11)

and thirdly, by presenting the countryside or the garden as an ideal place for the erotic encounter:[34]

> "My heart desires you: let us release it together, I am alone with you. I shall let you hear the sound of my myrrh-anointed bird. Were you here with me as I set the snare: it is pleasant for lovers to go to the field" (pHarris 500 4,5-7)

> "I am headed to the Garden of Lovemaking, my bosom full of persea branches, my hair laden with balm" (pHarris 500 3,12-4,1)

> "Come, my beloved, let us go to the field and pass the night in the countryside, we'll go early to the vineyards" (Cant 7:12-13a).

In Egyptian love poetry, pastoral references are frequently associated with exotic countries such as Syria or Punt, whereas the Song shows a distinct preference for Palestinian landscapes such as Sharon or Bether. To a certain extent, this is rooted in the more 'international' character of Late Bronze Age Egyptian culture as opposed to the closer Palestinian scope of Second Temple Jewish society.

Water. The 'feminine' associations of water are known to Egyptian literature since the early wisdom texts,[35] but it is in love poetry that the direct connections between water landscapes[36] and the freedom of individual emotions appear emphasized:

> "I am the servant [brought from Syria] as a loving girl's prisoner.
> She had me placed in her orchard, but did not spend water for me.
> When it comes to drinking, my body cannot fill itself with the water of the waterskins.
> One comes to see me just for entertainment, [but leaves me] without drinking.
> As my Ka lives, beloved girl, [this] will get back at you!" (pTurin 1966 1,13-15).

But even in this literature, in which protagonists indulge primarily in romantic exchanges, we find signs of the fear of water so typical of Egyptian literature;

34 Hugonot 1989: 165-168; Wilkinson 1998: 50-62

35 For example, in the Middle Kingdom Ptahhotep compares to water a woman who is allowed to behave according to her own judgement, whereas in the New Kingdom Ani regards as a 'deep, inscrutable water' a woman who is separated from her husband (Moers 2001: 211-219).

36 Mathieu 1996: 152; Moens 1984: 11-53.

the two feelings – fear of the dangers of water and longing for the beauty of its settings – sometimes appear in dialectic tension; thus for example in the Cairo Love Songs:[37]

> "My beloved sister is over there, on the other side,
> the river pervades my limbs, and the Flood is powerful in its season:
> a crocodile stands on the sandbank.
> Yet, I have descended to the water to wade across the inundation,
> with a brave heart in the channel".[38]

In love poetry, however, the traditional emphasis on water landscapes as a source of pleasure appears enhanced, and to a certain extent even corrected, by a new perspective in which water is presented as a paradigm of purification, not only with religious overtones but also with emotional prominence. Verbs such as *wᶜb* 'to purify', but also 'to bathe' are ideally suited to express this dialectic of semantic spheres and contextual associations, as again in the Cairo Love Songs:[39]

> "I desire to go down and bathe myself before you,
> in order to show you my beauty in a tunic of finest royal linen,
> soaked in perfume, [with my hair woven] in reeds.
> I shall go down to the water with you
> And come out bringing you a red fish,
> which would be just right in my fingers.
> I shall set it before you while [watching your beauty],
> My beloved, look at me!"

While in general less concerned with the significance of water in connection with love, the Song of Songs does not refrain from presenting water as a component of bucolic tableaus and using its associations in the praise of the beloved (Fox 1985: 298-300):

> "Your fields are an orchard of pomegranates heavy with fruits, henna with spikenards, spikenard and saffron, cane and cinnamon, with every frankincense tree, myrrh and aloes with all the best spices. You are a garden fountain, a well of living water streaming from Lebanon" (Cant 4:13-15).

37 Fox 1985: 32, 384; Mathieu 1996: 98, Pl. 18.

38 We have here an ostensible wordplay between *mr* 'channel' and *mr(w.t)* 'love' and a possible connotation 'with my heart full of love'.

39 Fox 1985: 32, 384; Mathieu 1996: 98, Pl. 18.

Physical love. Love poetry is relatively explicit in its sexual allusions and bears witness to a cultural context which precedes the marginalization of sexuality documented in later, especially Christian traditions (Meskell 2002: 134-140):[40]

> "My heart is not yet done with your love, my little wolf cub; your lovemaking (*dd*) is intoxicating and I shall not abandon it" (pHarris 500 2,2-3)

> "How beautiful is your lovemaking, my sister, my bride; your lovemaking (*dōdim*) is sweeter than wine and the scent of your oil more fragrant than all spices" (Cant 4:10).

On the other hand, the view that love can be assimilated to a disease (Griffiths 1990: 349-364), expressed in the seventh stanza of pChester Beatty I (4,6-8):

> "Yesterday for the seventh day I did not see my beloved, and illness has entered me: my limbs have grown heavy, and I lost sense of my own body. If the chief physicians came to me, their medicines could not ease my heart; the lector-priests have no remedy, for one cannot diagnose my disease"

finds a close parallel in the 'love-sickness' (*ḥōlat 'ahabāh*) of Cant 2:5 and 5:8.

Divine associations. We have referred more than once to the correlations between the literary description of the beloved one and the divine features he or she personifies. From the parallels the lover sees between the beloved and Hathor[41] to the description of the beloved one's body with the precious attributes of divine images, both Egyptian love poetry and the Song of Songs betray the presence of representative models drawn from the religious praxis (Mathieu 1996: 233-241):

> "She resembles the Star that shines at the beginning of a beautiful year. Her perfection is brilliant, her complexion radiant ... her neck is high, her throat dazzling, her hair true lapis lazuli" (pChester Beatty I 1,2-4).

> "My beloved is white and reddish, distinguishable among a myriad. His head is finest gold, his locks fronds of a palm, black as a raven ... (5,14-15) His arms are cylinders of gold, inlaid with jaspers. His belly is an ivory bar, adorned with lapis lazuli. His thighs are marble pillars, set on pedestals of gold" (Cant 5:10-11)

---

40 Interestingly, the Egyptian term for 'lovemaking' (*dd*), determined by the phallus, is a borrowing from the same Semitic root we find in Hebrew *dōdim*, whereas the general root *mrj*, to judge from the determinative of a man who touches his mouth, rather addresses the emotional sphere.

41 Darnell 1995: 50-51, 82-83.

7. Conclusion

Rooted in performances held at festivals and celebrations, which display a historical continuity from the Late Bronze Age to the Hellenistic period, the literary treatment of love in Egypt and Israel emerges in different time periods and cultural settings. Ramesside Egypt sees the development of new textual genres, among them love poetry, which unlike classical literature are written in a lower linguistic register and address the sphere of public as well as private entertainment. During the Second Temple period, a similar textual form appears in Jewish literature, as documented by the Song of Songs, which shares many of the conceptual and stylistic features of Egyptian love poetry. However, rather than on a direct textual transmission, made unlikely by the disappearance of a written tradition of love poems after the end of the Bronze Age, this continuity of forms and contents finds its origin in the common festive background of the genre in Egypt and Israel: the continuity in underlying performances, rooted in a dialectic between the sphere of periodic religious festivals and the context of episodic social events, proves to be much more stable than their impact on literary discourse.

Bibliography

ALLAM, SH. (1981): Quelques aspects du mariage dans l'Egypte ancienne, JEA 67, 116-135.

ALTENMÜLLER, H. (1978): Zur Bedeutung der Harfnerlieder des Alten Reiches, SAK 6, 1-24.

ALTER, R. (1995): Afterword, in: A. Bloch/C. Bloch, The song of Songs, New York, 119-131.

ASSMANN, J. (1977): Fest des Augenblicks, Verheißung der Dauer. Die Kontroverse der ägyptischen Harfnerlieder, in: J. Assmann et al. (eds.), Fragen an die altägyptische Literatur. Gedenkschrift Eberhard Otto, Wiesbaden, 55-84.

– (1982): Die Zeugung des Sohnes, in: J. Assmann/W. Burkert/F. Stolz, Funktionen und Leistungen des Mythos. Drei altorientalische Beispiele, OBO 48, Fribourg/Göttingen, 13-61.

– (1989): Der schöne Tag. Sinnlichkeit und Vergänglichkeit im altägyptischen Fest, in: W. Haug/R. Warning (eds.), Das Fest, München, 3-28.

– (2001): Tod und Jenseits im Alten Ägypten, München.

AUFFRET, P. (1981): Hymnes d'Egyptes et d'Israel, OBO 34, Fribourg/Göttingen.

BAINES, J. (1990): Restricted Knowledge, Hierarchy, and Decorum: Modern Perceptions and Ancient Institutions, JARCE 27, 1-23.

– (1999): Forerunners of narrative biographies, in: A. Leahy/J. Tait (eds.), Studies on Ancient Egypt in Honour of H.S. Smith, London, 23-37.

BETZ, H.D. (1986): The Greek Magical Papyri in Translation Including the Demotic Spells, Chicago/London.

BLOCH, A./BLOCH, C. (1995): The Song of Songs, New York.

BLOOM, H./ROSENBERG, D. (1990): The Book of J, New York.

BOCHI, P.A. (1998): Gender and Genre in Ancient Egyptian Poetry: The Rhetoric of Performance in the Harpers' Songs, JARCE 35, 89-95.

BOSSE-GRIFFITHS, K. (1980): Two Lute-Players of the Amarna Age, JEA 66, 70-82.

– (1983): The fruit of the mandrake, in: M. Görg (ed.), Fontes atque Pontes. Eine Festgabe für Hellmut Brunner, ÄAT 5, Wiesbaden, 62-74.

BRENNER, A./FONTAINE, C.R. eds. (2000): The Song of Songs, A Feminist Companion to the Bible, Sheffield.

BUCHBERGER, H. (1983): Sexualität und Harfenspiel. Notizen zur 'sexuellen' Konnotation der altägyptischen Ikonographie, GM 66, 11-43.

– (1995): Das Harfnerlied im Grab des *Kꜣ (=i)-m-ꜥnḫ* oder die Riten des *sn nṯrw*, in: D. Kessler/R. Schulz (eds.), Gedenkschrift für W. Barta, Münchner Ägyptologische Untersuchungen 4 , 93-123.

CRÜSEMANN, F. (1987): Das 'portative Vaterland'. Struktur und Genese des alttestamentlichen Kanons, in: A. and J. Assmann (eds.), Kanon und Zensur, Archäologie der literarischen Kommunikation 2, München, 63-79.

DARNELL, J. C. (1995): Hathor Returns to Medamud, SAK 22, 47-94.

DAVIES, N. de G. (1905a): The Rock Tombs of El Amarna, Part II: The Tombs of Panehesy and Meryra II, London.

– (1905b): The Rock Tombs of El Amarna, Part III: The Tombs of Huya and Ahmes, London.

– (1920): The Tomb of Antefoker, Vizier of Sesostris I and of his wife Senet (No. 60), London.

– (1925): The Tomb of Two Sculptors at Thebes, New York.

DAVIES, N. DE G./GARDINER, A.H. (1915): The Tomb of Amenemhet, London.

DAVIS, V.L. (1980): Remarks on Michael V. Fox's 'The Cairo Love Songs', JAOS 100, 111-114.

DESROCHES-NOBLECOURT, C. (1956): Interprétation et datation d'une scène gravée sur deux fragments de récipients en albâtre provenant des fouilles du palais d'Ugarit, Ugaritica 3, 179-220.

ENGELMANN-VON CARNAP, B. (1999): Die Struktur des thebanischen Beamtenfriedhofs in der ersten Hälfte der 18. Dynastie, ADAIK, Ägyptologische Reihe 15, Berlin.

EPIGRAPHIC SURVEY (1970): The Eastern High Gate with Translations of Texts, Medinet Habu VIII, Chicago.

FISCHER-ELFERT, H.W. (1986): Die satirische Streitschrift des Papyrus Anastasi I: Übersetzung und Kommentar, ÄgAbh 44, Wiesbaden.

FITZENREITER, M. (1995): Totenverehrung und soziale Repräsentation im thebanischen Beamtengrab der 18. Dynastie, SAÄK 22, 95-130.

FOX, M.V. (1985): The Song of Songs and the Ancient Egyptian Love Songs, Madison.

FRANDSEN, P.J. (1992): The Letter to Ikhtay's Coffin: oLouvre Inv. No. 698, in: R.J. Demarée/A. Egberts (eds.), Village Voices, Leiden, 31-49.

GARDINER, A.H. (1932): Late Egyptian Stories, Bibliotheca Aegyptiaca 1, Bruxelles.

GARDINER, A.H./DAVIES, N.M. (1953): La peinture égyptienne ancienne, Paris.

GNIRS, A.M. (1996): Die ägyptische Autobiographie, in: A. Loprieno (ed.), Ancient Egyptian Literature. History and Forms, Probleme der Ägyptologie 10, Leiden, 191-241.

GOLDWASSER, O. (1995): On the Conception of the Poetic Form: A Love Letter to a departed Wife, IOS 15, 191-205.

GREEN, L. (1992): Asiatic Musicians and the Court of Akhenaten, in: Contacts between Cultures: West Asia and North Africa, Selected Papers from the 33rd International Congress of Asian and North African Studies, Toronto, August 15-25, 1990, Lewiston, 215-220.

GRIFFITHS, J.G. (1990): Love as a Disease, in: S. Israelit-Groll (ed.), Studies in Egyptology Presented to Miriam Lichtheim, Jerusalem, 349-364.

HELCK, W. (1988): Der 'geheimnisvolle' Mehi, SAK 15, 143-148.

HERMANN, A. (1959): Altägyptische Liebesdichtung, Wiesbaden.

HOFFMANN, F. (2000): Ägypten: Kultur und Lebenswelt in griechisch-römischer Zeit, Berlin.

HUGONOT, J.-C. (1989): Le jardin dans l'Egypte ancienne, Publications Universitaires Européennes 38/27, Frankfurt a.M.

JASTROW, M. (1971): A Dictionary of the Targumim, Talmud Babli, Yerushalmi and Midrashic Literature, New York.

JUNGE, F. (2003): Die Lehre Ptahhoteps und die Tugenden der ägyptischen Welt, OBO 193, Fribourg/Göttingen.

KAMPP, F. (1996): Die Thebanische Nekropole, vol. I, Theben XIII, Mainz.

KESSLER, D. (1988): Der satirisch-erotische Papyrus Turin 55001 und das 'Verbringen des schönen Tages', SAK 15, 171-196.

KITCHEN, K.A. (1968-90): Ramesside Inscriptions, Oxford, Vol. V, 256, 5-11.

– (1999): Poetry of Ancient Egypt, Documenta Muni Aegyptica 1, Jonsered.

KÖPF, U./VINCENT, J.M. (1986): Art. Hoheslied. Auslegungsgeschichte im Christentum, TRE 15, Berlin/New York, 508-514.

KUGEL, J.L. (1997): The Bible as It Was, Cambridge/MA.

KUHN, P. (1986): Art. Hoheslied. Auslegungsgeschichte im Judentum, TRE 15, Berlin/New York, 503-508.

LATACZ, J. (2001): Troia und Homer. Der Weg zur Lösung eines alten Rätsels, München/Berlin.

LICHTHEIM, M. (1945): The Songs of the Harpers, JNES 4, 178-212.

LIVERANI, M. (1988): Antico Oriente. Storia, società, economia, Bari.

LOPRIENO, A. (1996): Defining Egyptian Literature: Ancient Texts and Modern Literary Theory, in: J.S. Cooper/G.M. Schwartz (eds.), The Study of the Ancient Near East in the Twenty-First Century. The William Foxwell Albright Centennial Conference, Winona Lake, 209-232.

– (2003a): Von der Stimme zur Schrift, in: N. Bolz/A. Münkel (eds.), Was ist der Mensch?, München, 119-152.

– (2003b): Travel and Fiction in Egyptian Literature, in: D. O'Connor/S. Quirke, Mysterious Lands, Encounters With Ancient Egypt 5, London, 31-51.

MATHIEU, B. (1996): La poésie amoureuse de l'Egypte ancienne, BdE 115, Le Caire.

MESKELL, L. (2002): Private Life in New Kingdom Egypt, Princeton, 94-97.

MOENS, M.-F. (1984): The Ancient Egyptian Garden in the New Kingdom, OLP 15, 11-53.

MOERS, G. (2001): Fingierte Welten in der ägyptischen Literatur des 2. Jahrtausends v.Chr., Probleme der Ägyptologie 19, Leiden.

MORENZ, L.D. (1996): Beiträge zur Schriftlichkeitskultur im Mittleren Reich und in der 2. Zwischenzeit, ÄAT 29, Wiesbaden.

OMLIN, J.A. (1973): Der Papyrus 55001 und seine satirisch-erotischen Zeichnungen und Inschriften, Torino.

PARKINSON, R.B. (2002): Poetry and Culture in Middle Kingdom Egypt, London.

POLZ, D. (2003): 'Ihre Mauern sind verfallen … ihre Stätte ist nicht mehr'. Der Aufwand für den Toten im Theben der Zweiten Zwischenzeit, in: H. Guksch et al. (eds.), Grab und Totenkult im Alten Ägypten, München, 75-87.

POPE, M.H. (1977): Song of Songs, AB 7c, New York.

PORTER, B./MOSS, R. (1960): Topographical Bibliography of Ancient Egyptian Hieroglyphic Texts, Reliefs and Painting. Vol. I: The Theban Necropolis, Part 1: Private Tombs, 2nd ed., Oxford.

QUACK, J.F. (2003): Das nackte Mädchen im Griff halten. Zur Deutung der ägyptischen Karyatidenspiegel, WdO 33, 44-64.

SCHIPPER, B.U. (1999): Israel und Ägypten in der Königszeit, OBO 170, Fribourg/Göttingen.

SCHNIEDEWIND, W.M. (2004): How the Bible Became a Book. The Textualization of Ancient Israel, Cambridge.

SCHOTT, S. (1950): Altägyptische Liebeslieder, Zürich.

– (1953): Das Schöne Fest vom Wüstentale, Abhandlungen der Akademie der Wissenschaften zu Göttingen, Wiesbaden.

SEIDLMAYER, S.J. (1991): Eine Schreiberpalette mit änigmatischer Aufschrift, MDAIK 47, 319-330.

SEILER, A. (1995): Archäologisch fassbare Kultpraktiken in Grabkontexten der frühen 18. Dynastie in Dra' Abu el-Naga/Theben, in: J. Assmann et al. (eds.), Thebanische Beamtennekropolen, SAGA 12, Heidelberg, 185-203.

SIMPSON, W.K. (1976): The Mastabas of Qar and Idu G 7101 and 7102. Giza Mastabas 2, Boston.

SMITHER, P. (1941): A Ramesside love charm, JEA 27, 131-132.

SWEENEY, D. (1998): Women and language in the Ramesside Period, or, Why Women Don't Say Please, in: C.J. Eyre (ed.), Proceedings of the Seventh International Congress of Egyptologists, Cambridge, 3-9 September 1995, OLA 82, Leuven, 1009-1017.

– (2001): Correspondence and Dialogue, ÄAT 49, Wiesbaden.

THISSEN, H.J. (1992): Der verkommene Harfnerspieler. Eine altägyptische Invektive (P. Wien KM 3877), Demotische Studien 11, Sommerhausen.

VACHALA, B. (2003): Das älteste Liebeslied?, in: N. Kloth/K. Martin/E. Pardey (eds.), Es werde niedergelegt als Schriftstück. FS für Hartwig Altenmüller zum 65. Geburtstag, BSAK 9, Hamburg, 429-431.

WIEBACH, S. (1986): Die Begegnung von Lebenden und Verstorbenen im Rahmen des Thebanischen Talfestes, SAK 13, 263-291.

WILKINSON, A. (1998): The Garden in Ancient Egypt, London.

WILSON, J.A./ALLEN, T.G. eds. (1938): The Mastaba of Mereruka, Part I, Chicago.

WIMMER, St. (1990): Egyptian Temples in Canaan and Sinai, in: S. Israelit-Groll (ed.), Studies in Egyptology Presented to Miriam Lichtheim, Jerusalem, 1065-1106.

– (1998): (No) more Egyptian Temples in Canaan and Sinai, in: I. Shirun-Grumach (ed.), Jerusalem Studies in Egyptology, ÄAT 40, Wiesbaden, 87-123.

– (2000): Ancient Egyptian Love Songs: Papyrus Harris 500, in: K. Modras (ed.), The Art of Love Lyrics. In Memory of Bernard Couroyer, OP and Hans Jacob Polotsky, First Egyptologists in Jerusalem, Cahiers de la Revue Biblique 49, Paris, 25-33.

WINLOCK, H.E. (1973): Materials Used at the Embalming of King Tut-'Ankh-Amun, New York.

Kursorisches zur Konstruktion liebender Körper im pharaonischen Ägypten

Hans-Hubertus Münch und Gerald Moers

In den modernen Gesellschaften steht die Liebe im Prinzip außerhalb des Netzes sozialer Beziehungen. Menschen kommen "in Liebe" zusammen aufgrund emotionaler Affinität beschließen miteinander durchs Leben zu gehen, und trennen sich dann nicht selten auch wieder infolge persönlicher Differenzen. Liebe heute, um es kurz zu fassen, ist eine Privatangelegenheit zwischen zwei – oder manchmal auch mehreren – Personen. Der Gedanke, daß Liebe dagegen ein hauptsächlich sozialer Akt ist, der nicht vom Individuum selbst bestimmt wird, sondern sich aus seinem Status innerhalb der jeweiligen Gruppe ergibt, über die es in die Gesellschaft eingebunden ist, ist heutigen Menschen weitgehend fremd. Und beinahe unbegreiflich scheint ihnen in diesem Zusammenhang die Möglichkeit zu sein, daß eine Liebesbeziehung sämtliche sozialen Bande, die ein Mensch unterhält, in Frage stellen, gar bis hin zu seiner physischen Vernichtung führen kann. Man denke hier nur an die heute noch oft in traditionellen Gesellschaften praktizierte Hinrichtung der Frau im Falle eigenmächtiger Beziehungen zum anderen Geschlecht. Der letzte derart konzipierte Fall, den die westlichen Gesellschaften der Moderne kannten, war die Liebe zwischen zwei Männern. Aber auch das scheint heute ein mehr oder weniger abgeschlossenes Kapitel der Sozialgeschichte zu sein.

In den vergangenen zwanzig Jahren ist viel sowohl über die Genese als auch über die Konstruktion der Vorstellung von privater Liebe geschrieben worden. Je nach theoretischem Rüstzeug und Fragestellung sind hierbei verschiedene Aspekte thematisiert worden – mit zum Teil divergierenden Ergebnissen. Trotz derartiger Unterschiede ist allerdings fast allen diesen Untersuchungen gemein, daß der Aufstieg der bürgerlichen Klasse und ihren mehr das Individuum als den Stand und die Herkunft eines Menschen in den Vordergrund stellenden Wertvorstellungen im Verlaufe des Übergangs zur Moderne als wesentlich für den Erfolgszug dessen ausgemacht wird, was wir heute allgemein als Liebe definieren. Wie das empirische Material deutlich zeigt, ist eine solche Argumentation nicht von der Hand zu weisen. Aus soziologischer Perspektive – und hier besonders aus Sicht der Systemtheorie – greift ein solcher Erklärungsansatz gleichwohl zu kurz, sind doch Umformungen im überlieferten Ideengut zumeist an gesellschaftsstrukturelle Transformationen gebunden. Dieses trifft, wie Niklas Luhmann eindrucksvoll zeigen konnte, auch und in ganz besonderer Weise auf die Semantik der Liebe im neuzeitlichen Europa zu.[1] Im Klartext: In Folge einer grundlegenden Änderung in der Sozialstruktur der europäischen Gesellschaften im Übergang vom Mittelalter zur Moderne – und zwar von einer stratifikatorischen zu einer funktionalen Gesellschaftsdifferenzierung – ändert sich auch die Liebe von einer sozialen Institution, die vornehmlich dem Zwecke der Reproduktion und der gesellschaftlichen Abgrenzung diente, hin zu einem an unverwechselbaren Personen orientierten Gefühl, das zum einzig legitimen Grund der Partnerwahl jenseits aller existierenden sozialen Faktoren wird.

Wie wir im folgenden begründen werden, war unserer Ansicht nach auch die Liebe im pharaonischen Ägypten zur Zeit des Neuen Reiches keine Privatangelegenheit zwischen zwei Menschen, sondern, wie in anderen vormodernen Gesellschaften auch, zuallererst ein sozialer Akt. Um etwaigen Mißverständnissen an dieser Stelle gleich vorzubeugen: Wir behaupten nicht, daß die Menschen in der Vergangenheit sich nicht liebten, sich zueinander hingezogen fühlten, oder gar einander nicht begehrten. Ganz im Gegenteil, wie im zweiten Teil dieses Artikels noch deutlich werden wird. Aber um erfolgreich zu sein – das heißt, Liebe in die Tat umzusetzen – mußte sich das Gefühlsleben an der omnipräsenten gesellschaftlichen Ordnung orientieren. Andernfalls liefen die Liebenden Gefahr, nicht nur nicht das zu bekommen, was sie sich ersehnten, sondern zugleich auch ihre gesamte soziale Existenz aufs Spiel zu setzen. Privat sein, respektive Individualität in Anspruch zu nehmen, und zwar im Sinne eines sich frei Entscheidens ohne jedwede Rücksichtnahme auf etwaige Herkunft und Status innerhalb des eigenen sozialen Umfeldes und der damit verbundener Erwartungshaltungen, bedeutete und bedeutet in Gesellschaften dieses Typus erfahrungsgemäß immer noch, aus der Ordnung zu fallen. "Privatus heißt inordinatus".[2] Diese Prinzip galt nach allem, was wir wissen können, auch für die Bevölkerung des pharaonischen Ägypten zur Zeit des Neuen Reiches.

1. Der theoretische Rahmen

Alle Hochkulturen der Vormoderne beruhten auf dem Prinzip der sozialen Stratifikation. Jede Person gehörte hierbei grundsätzlich nur einer Schicht, einem Stand oder einer Kaste an, in die sie, meist über die Zugehörigkeit zu einer bestimmten Familie, hineingeboren wurde. Dabei galt die Regel, daß nur in der jeweiligen Gesellschaftsschicht geheiratet wurde, so daß diese Einheiten

1 Luhmann 1982.
2 Luhmann 1980: 72.

rekrutierungsmäßig autonom waren.[3] Zusammengehalten wurden diese sozialen Systeme hierbei durch eine zumeist religiös fundierte Weltsicht, nach der jeder Mensch durch göttliche Fügung an seinen Platz gesetzt war und diesen Platz durch Rollenkonformität behauptete.[4] Diese Plazierung nicht zu akzeptieren bedeutete dementsprechend, gegen göttlichen Ratschluß zu rebellieren und sich dadurch nicht nur aus der eigenen Gemeinschaft, sondern aus sämtlichen dem jeweiligen Individuum zur Verfügung stehenden Sinn- und Ordnungszusammenhängen selbst auszuschließen. Es ist daher nicht, wie Luhmann in Blick auf die Oberschicht formulierte, die Fremdbestimmung, die Menschen in stratifizierten Gesellschaften disziplinierte, sondern in erster Linie ihre eigene Ausweglosigkeit.[5] Anders ausgedrückt: Eine soziale Existenz außerhalb der eigenen Schicht war für niemanden – gleichgültig welchen Standes – denkbar, denn es war eben gerade die Schicht, der man angehörte, die jemanden zur Person machte. Wir werden später noch einmal darauf zurückkommen.

Es gehört aus Sicht der Systemtheorie zu den wesentlichen Merkmalen stratifizierter Gesellschaften, daß, indem sich diese in der Sozialdimension differenzierten, also Personen alternativlos und in aller Regel lebenslang unterschiedlichen Schichten zuordneten, ausnahmslos alles, was sich in ihnen ereignete – jedes Erleben, jede Interaktion, jedwede Sinn- und Entscheidungsmuster – daran orientiert war, wie es die hierarchische Ordnung, in der die Menschen lebten, berührte.[6] Für die frühmittelalterlichen Gesellschaften Europas beispielsweise gilt, daß der Platz an der Tafel des Königs oder in der Kirche weder zufällig noch aufgrund des Wohlwollens anderer besetzt wurde, sondern nach dem Rang der jeweiligen Person innerhalb der Gruppe.[7] Das galt etwa auch für den Umgang der Mitglieder des französischen Königshofes im 17. Jahrhundert: Ob man einer Person hier nun freundlich, unfreundlich oder gar mißachtend entgegentrat, stützte sich nicht auf persönliche Erwägungen von Sympathie oder Antipathie, als vielmehr auf die soziale Stellung desjenigen, dem man begegnete, das heißt ob er/sie in der sozialen Hierarchie über oder unter einem selbst stand.[8] Auch die Identität einer

---

3 Das Prinzip der festen Inklusion von Personen in die Gesellschaft über ihre Familie gilt auch für diejenigen geschichtlichen Fälle, in denen eine gewisse soziale Mobilität zwischen den Schichten nachgewiesen werden kann. Vgl. hierzu Luhmann 1980: 30.

4 Kneer/Nassehi 1993: 127-129.

5 Luhmann 1980: 77.

6 Kneer/Nassehi 1993: 126.

7 Fichtenau 1992: 11-47.

8 Als weiteres Beispiel ließe sich in diesem Zusammenhang das unbekümmerte Verhalten der Oberschicht gegenüber Untergebenen wie beispielsweise das sich An- und Auskleiden, Baden und die Verrichtung der Notdurft nennen, die Norbert Elias als Ergebnis einer "Gleichgültigkeit" der Herren gegenüber ihrer Dienerschaft erklärt (Elias 1994: 76-78). Aus systemtheoretischer Perspektive ließe sich dieser Gedanke dahingehend weiterentwickeln, daß man sich als Mitglied der Oberschicht vor seinen Dienern anders verhalten konnte als im Verhältnis zu seinesgleichen, da diese eben nicht sozial gleich und

Person basiert in Gesellschaften dieses Typus zuallererst auf ihrem jeweiligen Stand, das heißt direkt auf dem Prinzip sozialer Differenzierung, und nicht, wie in heutigen Gesellschaften allgemein angenommen, auf einer individuellen Einzigartigkeit im Sinne einer Abgrenzung zu anderen.[9] Man könnte auch sagen, daß die Identität einer Person und damit ihre jeweilige Individualität nach einem festen Schichtindex mit in der Gesellschaftsstruktur tief verankerten "Identifikationssymbolen", wie beispielsweise Bauer, Kleriker oder Adeliger, gesellschaftlich zugewiesen wurde.[10] Aber dieses ist noch nicht alles und vielleicht auch noch nicht einmal das Wichtigste. Zu denjenigen Phänomenen, die in stratifizierten Systemen darüber hinaus fest mit der Sozialdimension verbunden waren, gehörte auch das Fühlen und die damit verbundenen Handlungen. Dieses wird neben den Emotionen Scham und Ehre ganz besonders an der Liebe deutlich.[11] Nicht primär ein romantisches, an einzigartigen Individuen orientiertes Gefühl brachte Personen beiderlei Geschlechtes zusammen, sondern ihr gemeinsamer Stand.[12] Dieses galt wesentlich für alle Ehebeziehungen, jedoch auch für etwaige außereheliche Verhältnisse jenseits der sexuellen Triebbefriedigung.[13] "Partner" konnten in diesem Sinne immer nur diejenigen Männer oder Frauen sein, die vergleichbarer Herkunft waren. Alle anderen Personen waren demgegenüber schlichtweg Herren oder Untergebene. Ein weiteres Beispiel für die Bedeutung des Status innerhalb des Liebeslebens in Gesellschaften der Vormoderne, auch wenn wir von ihnen ausführlicher erst relativ spät erfahren, sind Liebeserklärungen.[14] Diese sind in ihrer Art nämlich grundverschieden und zwar je nachdem, ob sie "von oben nach unten" ergehen oder umgekehrt von einer untergeordneten Person an eine ihr im Rang höhergestellte. Konkret: Von oben her sind sie "offen" und "direkt". In umgekehrter Richtung müssen sie dagegen mit viel Geschick und Umsicht auf den Weg gebracht werden, weil eine solche Avance sich im Falle der Nichterwiderung seitens des Adressaten als eine extreme Form der Anmaßung und des Hochmuts darstellt, die von der Gesellschaft dann mit entsprechenden Mitteln sanktioniert wird. Intimität zwischen verschiedenen Rängen war somit also durchaus denkbar, hatte sich allerdings auf das primäre soziale Ordnungsprinzip einzustellen, um in die Tat umgesetzt zu werden und dabei nicht gleichzeitig aus der gegebenen Ordnung – und damit der Gesellschaft per se – heraus zu fallen. Abschließend sei an dieser

damit Partner waren. In diesem Sinne steht das Verhalten klar in Bezug auf die Schichtung der Gesellschaft und kaum in Abhängigkeit auf eine irgendwie gelagerte Individualität der beteiligten Personen. Vgl. hierzu auch Le Roy Ladurie 2001: 23-61.

9 Luhmann 1980: 30.

10 Kneer/Nassehi 1993: 129, 159; Luhmann 1994: 22.

11 Zum Aspekt der Scham und Ehre in stratifizierten Gesellschaften mit weiterführender Literatur siehe im besonderen Neckel 1991 und Frevert 1995.

12 van Dülmen 1999: 134-197.

13 Zum Ehebruch in der höfischen Gesellschaft des Mittelalters vgl. Bumke 1983.

14 Luhmann 1980: 26-27.

Stelle noch auf einen anderen Bereich hingewiesen, der später noch einmal in Bezug auf das ägyptische Material eine Rolle spielen wird: das Liebesspiel oder das Liebesethos. Je nachdem, welcher Schicht eine Person angehörte, unterschied sich der "Code", mit dem Liebe zum Ausdruck gebracht werden konnte und wie auf entsprechende Offerten zu reagieren war.[15] Dieses Phänomen ist besonders gut für Oberschichten dokumentiert mit ihrem ausgeprägten Wunsch, sich von der als vulgär geltenden, auf direkte sexuelle Befriedigung hin orientierten Liebe des "gemeinen Volkes" zu distanzieren.[16] Ein umfassender, alle Schichten der Gesellschaft gleichermaßen durchdringender "Code der Liebe", wie wir ihn heute allgemein annehmen, ist eine Errungenschaft späterer Zeit und untrennbar mit der zunehmenden Verbreitung von Liebesromanen zu Beginn des 19. Jahrhunderts verbunden.[17]

Diese von uns im vorhergehenden beschriebene Idee einer umfassenden Wirkung der Sozialdimension auf die ihr unterworfenen Menschen, ihr Denken und Handeln, ist innerhalb der Geisteswissenschaften gelegentlich in Zweifel gezogen worden – scheint diese doch auf den ersten Blick denjenigen Aspekten zu widersprechen, die den Menschen gemeinhin zu dem werden lassen, was er ist: seiner Autonomie, seiner Willenskraft und seinem Verstand.[18] Bei genauerer Betrachtung erweist sich diese Kritik allerdings in den meisten Fällen als unbegründet, ist doch die Vorstellung einer Form der totalen und allumfassenden Selbstbestimmung des Menschen reine Fiktion. Seit Max Weber und Georg Simmel gehört es zum festen Wissensbestand der Soziologie, daß der Mensch sein Menschsein nur innerhalb gesellschaftlicher Beziehungen und ihrer jeweiligen Sinn- und Erkenntnisstrukturen realisieren kann – und dies gilt dann selbst noch für die freisten Formen der Liebe: "Wer zweimal mit derselben pennt gehört schon zum Establishment". Ein Leben außerhalb dieser Strukturen ist für ihn unmöglich. Außerdem: psychische Systeme akzeptieren und internalisieren in der Regel nun einmal schnell und unbewußt die jeweiligen Rollen und Ordnungsprinzipien, denen sie unterworfen sind, werden sie doch andernfalls allzuleicht Außenseiter und infolgedessen Opfer andauernder Diskriminierung durch ihre Umwelt. Die Beispiele hierfür sind Legion. Auch der in diesem Zusammenhang bisweilen geäußerte Vorwurf, systemtheoretisch orientierte Arbeiten würden die Vergangenheit verklären, weil sich in ihnen scheinbar alles einer Ordnung fügt, geht meist fehl, ist es doch nicht Ziel wissenschaftlichen Bemühens, Gesellschaften der

15 Luhmann 1982; Mason 1994: 105-173. Zum Phänomen der schichtspezifischen Kommunikation insbesondere Luhmann 1980: 95; Kelso 1929 und Kelso 1956.

16 van Dülmen 1999: 184-197.

17 Luhmann 1982; Smith 2001.

18 Die Liste der von uns gegebenen Beispiele ließe sich noch beliebig verlängern und bliebe auch nicht auf den europäischen Kulturkreis beschränkt. Ähnliche sich aus der Sozialdimension ergebende Phänomene aus dem Bereich des menschlichen Zusammenlebens sind unter anderem auch aus den historischen Gesellschaften Indiens, Japans oder Chinas bekannt. Vgl. hierzu insbesondere Dumont 1976.

Vormoderne und deren soziale Phänomene zu rechtfertigen oder abzulehnen, sondern vielmehr, diese analytisch zu durchdringen.[19] In diesem Sinne geht es entsprechenden Untersuchungen auch nicht primär darum, das Leben, Denken oder Handeln fernliegender Zeiten, Gesellschaften oder einzelner Individuen zu erschließen, sondern auf Grund moderner Prämissen die Distanz zu dieser fremden Welt zu begreifen und damit einen Beitrag zu dem zu leisten, was unserer Ansicht nach zu den vordringlichsten Aufgaben der kulturhistorischen Wissenschaften gehört: die Menschen der Vergangenheit in ihren spezifisch historisch-sozialen Kontexten zu sehen und damit in ihren vielfältigen Entscheidungslagen besser erfassen zu können. Um die Diskussion ein wenig von der Last des allzu Theoretischen zu befreien, wollen wir in der Folge anhand einer ausgewählten Textpassage aus den Liebesliedern des Neuen Reiches exemplifizieren, worum es uns geht. Allerdings müssen wir auch hier zunächst ein wenig weiter ausholen und über Umwege argumentieren, da das zu besprechende Beispiel nur im Kontext schichtenspezifischer Identitätsvorstellungen dieser Epoche zu verstehen ist und obendrein bei "unvoreingenommener", d.h. methodisch uninformierter Lektüre wie selbstverständlich das Gegenteil von dem zu belegen scheint, was wir einführend entworfen haben.[20]

2. Fallbeispiel

Bei unserem Textbeispiel handelt es sich um die vierte Stanze (äg. *ḥw.t*, "Haus") des aus insgesamt sieben Stanzen bestehenden ersten Zyklus von Liebesliedern, die uns unter dem Titel 'Sprüche der großen Herzensfreude' im ramessidischen *pChester Beatty I* überliefert sind. Der Zyklus ist in Form eines geschlossenen Männer-Frauen-Wechsels gestaltet, der mit einer männlichen Stimme beginnt und auch mit dieser endet. In der zentralen vierten Stanze nun macht eine ägyptische Dame, die laut gängiger Meinung ein authentisches weibliches Gefühl kommuniziert und deswegen als verschriftete authentische weibliche Stimme angesehen wird, im Rahmen eines Zwiegesprächs mit ihrem Herzen folgende Aussage:[21]

> Es hüpft (*jfd*) mein Herz vor Unrast (*ꜣs*),
> wenn ich an Deine Liebe (*mrw.t*) denke.

---

19 Luhmann 1980: 75; Kneer/Nassehi 1993: 129.

20 Wir möchten damit auch eine Diskussion fortsetzen, die Gillam 2000 am Beispiel der dritten Stanze des Zyklus angestoßen hat und in der sie die ägyptologische Unbefangenheit gegenüber der Herausforderung der interkulturellen Übersetzung problematisiert.

21 pChester Beatty I vso. C2,9-C3,4, vgl. Mathieu 1996: 28, 39-40 m. pl. 2,9-3,4; siehe auch Fecht 1963: 54-96, hier 72-77. Die Verseinteilung der Übersetzung folgt den in Rot gehaltenen Gliederungspunkten der Handschrift.

Es verwehrt mir menschliche Umgangsformen (*šm mj rmṯ*),[22]
denn es ist fortgerissen <von> seinem rechten Platz.
Es verhindert, daß ich mein Gewand anlege,
und auch bin ich nicht in der Lage, meinen Fächer zur Hand zu nehmen.
Es verhindert, daß ich meine Augen schminke,
und bloß[23] mich zu salben, bin ich nicht in der Lage.
„Verharre (*ꜥḥꜥ*) nicht, damit Du das Ziel erreichst (*pḥ*)!"
sagt es zu mir, wann immer ich an ihn denke.
"Mach mir, mein Herz, nicht Kummer!
Warum handelst Du töricht?
Warte (*ḥms*) geduldig (*qb*), dann kommt der Bruder zu Dir
und zahlreiche Augen ebenso.
Laß nicht die Menschen (*rmṯ*) über mich sagen:
'Das ist eine Frau, die der Liebe (*mrw.t*) verfallen (*hꜣj*) ist.'
Sei standhaft (*s.mn*) wann immer Du an ihn denkst!
Mein Herz, hüpfe (*jfd*) nicht!"

Wir wollen nun anhand dieser Stanze argumentieren, daß eine ägyptische Passage wie die vorliegende bei aller vordergründig unvermittelten Selbstverständlichkeit[24] für den modernen Interpreten gerade nicht einen im Sinne einer anthropologischen Konstante zu verstehenden "zutiefst menschlichen" und damit universalen Gefühlszustand eines autonom gesetzten eigenen Begehrens beschreibt,[25] das nach Erfüllung drängt und für welches durch Veröffentlichung um Verständnis geworben werden könnte. Natürlich kann man mit Hinweis auf Stellen wie diese oder generell auf die Liebeslieder auf die Möglichkeit eines Gefühls von emotionalem Verlangen nach einem anderen Menschen auch im pharaonischen Ägypten schließen. Nur heißt das nicht, daß die soziale Interpretation eines solchen Gefühls in der antiken Kultur damit automatisch identisch ist mit unseren zeitgenössisch-neuzeitlichen Vorstellungen dieser Form emotionaler Affektiertheit.[26] Um diesen Punkt ver-

22 Wörtl.: "Es verhindert, daß ich wie ein Mensch gehe". Wir haben die Übersetzung "Umgangsform" gewählt, weil sie das in *šm* enthaltene Moment der Bewegung am besten wiedergibt.

23 Diese Form der Übersetzung erhält die Möglichkeit, die Passage auch im Deutschen so zweideutig zu lesen, wie sie im Ägyptischen ist. *bw wrḥ=j m kfꜣ* kann ebenso "Ich salbe mich überhaupt nicht" wie auch "Ich salbe meine Blöße nicht" bedeuten. Die Möglichkeit einer sexuellen Konnotation von *kfꜣ* als Vagina diskutiert *in extenso* Fecht 1963: 75-76 m. Anm. 1.

24 Sowohl ältere Bearbeitungen wie die von Fecht 1963: 72 als auch jüngere Studien wie die von Gillam 2000: 207 bemerken, daß es im Gegensatz zu vielen anderen ägyptischen Texten auch dieses Genres vergleichsweise wenig philologische Schwierigkeiten mit dem ersten Zyklus des pChester Beatty I gibt, die einem modernen ad-hoc Verständnis im Wege stehen.

25 In diesem Sinne grundsätzlich für die Liebeslieder etwa Meskell 2002: 126-147 und Manniche 1997: 7-12. 52-117.

26 Man wird – zumal aus konstruktivistischer Perspektive – ohnehin davon ausgehen müssen, daß selbst dieses angeblich so unhintergehbare Gefühl von "Liebe" sozial konstruiert ist, daß also Liebe sekundär zu den historisch je differenten gesellschaftlichen Vorstellungen von ihr ist.

ständlich machen zu können, beginnen wir mit einem Blick auf die spezifische Semantik des Begriffs *rmṯ* "Mensch", der in der vorgestellten Stanze zweimal Verwendung findet.

Im dritten Vers ist davon die Rede, daß das "hüpfende" Herz der Dame "menschliche Umgangsformen" verwehre, während diese selbst am Ende der Stanze dem eigenen Herzen gegenüber ihrem Wunsch Ausdruck verleiht, vor "den Menschen" nicht als jemand dazustehen, der der Liebe "verfallen" ist. Man kann nun aber bei aller bildlichen Kraft der Passage, in der dem Rezipienten durch die Wahl des Terminus *jfd* "hüpfen wie ein Tier" eine gewisse Brutalisierung der Dame suggeriert wird, kaum annehmen, daß das Nicht-mehr-Menschliche, welches die Dame in der Selbstbeschreibung ihres Zustandes von "den Menschen" unterscheidet, in dem Sinne interpretierbar wäre, daß sie ihre biologische Klassenzugehörigkeit und damit ihre Menschlichkeit an sich verloren hätte – Menschen sind und bleiben immer als Menschen erkennbar, zumal die Mitglieder einer Gruppe, die sich nicht im ethnologischen Sinne fremd sind. Vielmehr muß man davon ausgehen, daß der Begriff hier als Träger von Vorstellungen dient, die jenseits des Natürlich-Biologischen liegen und damit aller Wahrscheinlichkeit sozialen Ursprungs sind. In der Tat handelt es sich bei der vorliegenden Passage um einen der sehr wenigen Belege, in denen diese andere Seite des Menschseins überhaupt thematisiert wird und zur Sprache kommt. Wir wollen deshalb zur Verdeutlichung ein weiteres plakatives Beispiel anführen, das sich in der etwa zeitgleichen Schulliteratur des Neuen Reiches, den sogenannten *Miscellanies*, findet. Im Rahmen einer in dieser Textsorte häufig auftretenden Subgattung "Schülersatire" argumentiert ein Lehrer in recht drastischen Farben gegen die aufsässige Vergnügungssucht seines Schülers und seine daraus resultierende Entmenschlichung:[27]

> Mir wurde berichtet, daß du die Schriften vernachlässigst und hinter Vergnügungen her bist. Du ziehst von Viertel zu Viertel und es stinkt nach Bier, wann immer man dir nahekommt. Bier läßt ihn aufhören (*rwj*), Mensch (*rmṯ*) zu sein und deinen Geist unstet werden. Du bist wie ein krummes Steuerruder in einem Schiff, das zu keiner Seite reagiert, wie ein gottleerer Schrein und wie ein Haus ohne Brot. Man erwischte dich beim Übersteigen der Mauer, nachdem du ausge<büchst> bist und die Menschen (*rmṯ*) vor dir flohen, weil du ihnen Wunden geschlagen hast. Wüßtest du doch, daß Wein ein Greuel ist, dann würdest du dem *šdḥ*-Getränk abschwören, hättest nicht nur Bierkrüge im Sinn und würdest das *tnrk*-Getränk vergessen. Man lehrte dich, nach der Flöte zu singen und nach dem *wꜣr*-Instrument zu trällern, nach der Leier zu intonieren und nach dem *nṯḫ*-Instrument zu singen. Du sitzt auf der Straße, Freudenmädchen um dich herum. Dann stehst du auf und springst herum. Es [...] dich. Du hast dich vor der Hure niedergelassen und bist tropfnaß vom Öl, deinen Kranz Vergißmeinnicht(?)[28] um deinen Hals. Du trommelst auf deinem Bauch und torkelst, fällst lang hin und bist mit Scheiße beschmiert.

---

27 pAnastasi IV 11,8-12,5; vgl. Gardiner 1937: 47,6-48,3.
28 Zur Diskussion vgl. Müller 2002: Sp. 42-43.

Im ersten Beispiel steht ein blockiertes *šm mj rmṯ* "sich bewegen wie ein Mensch" einem durch "Liebestaumel" (*hꜣj m mrw.t*) hervorgerufenen aktuellen *jfd* "tierisch hüpfen" gegenüber.[29] Diese Antithese bezieht sich als Metapher auf eine Verhinderung der, wie Gerhard Fecht es dereinst formulierte, "selbstverständlichsten und alltäglichsten Beschäftigungen der ägyptischen Dame".[30] Im zweiten Beispiel sind es die unkontrollierten Bewegungen des besoffenen Hurenbocks, die diesen vom Mensch-Sein (*rmṯ*) "abhalten" (*rwj*). Für unseren Zusammenhang reformuliert heißt das, daß Ankleiden, Ausstaffieren, Schminken und Salben auf der einen bzw. ein unauffälliger, nüchtern getragener Bewegungsablauf auf der anderen Seite eine offensichtlich distinkte Form von Körperlichkeit produzieren, die es einem Gegenüber im nicht durch Liebe oder Suff verhinderten Normalfall erlaubt, ein biologisch ohnehin menschliches Wesen als besonderen Typ Mensch zu erkennen. Stellen wie diese machen klar, daß die Erkennbarkeit eines voll individuierten Körpers als menschlich in bestimmten kommunikativen Kontexten also keinesfalls ausreicht, um als "Mensch" durchzugehen. Vielmehr erscheint der biologische Körper des Menschen in diesen Passagen als Projektionsfläche von ganz offensichtlich normierten und normierenden kulturellen "Manipulationen", die aus einem biologisch ohnehin menschlichen Organismus einen Typ von Menschen machen, den man im heutigen, mit Hilfe des Mensch-Begriffs auf Distinktionen *zwischen* Menschen zielenden Umgangssprachgebrauch dann als einen "wahren" Menschen bezeichnen würde.[31] Solches spezifisches Mensch-Sein ist das Ergebnis eines normorientierten Verhaltens, welches von denjenigen, die die eingeforderten Normen als Trägergruppe kommunizieren – in unserem Falle genau diejenigen Menschen (*rmṯ.w*), die sich über den Liebestaumel der Dame mokieren würden, sowie diejenigen, die vor dem gewalttätigen Trunkenbold Reißaus nehmen – als prozessualer Ausweis sozialer Veredlung verstanden wird. Mensch-Sein (*rmṯ*) in diesem Sinne heißt also nichts anderes als sich im Sinne gruppenspezifischer Normvorstellungen "vernünftig" zu verhalten.[32] Über dieses als vernünftig normierte Verhalten erwirbt man sich Gruppenzugehörigkeit, da es für die, die bereits Gruppenmitglieder sind, als "eigen" im Sinne des von ihnen kommunizierten Norminventars wiedererkannt wird. Ein solches spezifisch definiertes Mensch-Sein dient also als je gruppen- oder schichtenspezifischer Zugehörigkeits-

29 Fecht 1963: 76 m. Forts. v. Anm. 1.

30 Fecht 1963: 75; zu *mj rmṯ* als "selbstverständlich, angemessen, normkonform" siehe auch Mathieu 1996: 39, Anm. 62 sowie Blackman 1933: 203: "properly", "as I (you or she) should".

31 So gesehen handelt es sich bei dem ägyptischen Terminus *rmṯ* um einen (implizit) *asymmetrischen Gegenbegriff*, vgl. Koselleck 1979: 211-259, bes. 212-213 und 244-245.

32 Guglielmi 1985: 140 m. Anm. b.

ausweis.[33] Man wird für den Fall der Liebeslieder, die aus dem Umfeld der höfischen Kultur des Neuen Reiches stammen,[34] mit Sicherheit nicht fehlgehen, wenn man diesen Zugehörigkeitshorizont mit dem Oberschichtenstratum der Zeit identifiziert.

Hier liegt unser entscheidender Punkt: Ganz offensichtlich befürchtet die Dame, durch die Veröffentlichung ihres durch Liebe hervorgerufenen Zustands ihre soziale Akzeptanz und eventuell sogar ihre schichtenspezifische Identität zu verlieren, da sie, wie wir vermuten,[35] weiß, daß niemandem verborgen bleiben würde, daß sie aussieht wie eine der karikierenden Darstellungen sexuell aggressiver "Damen" aus dem sogenannten *Erotischen pTurin 55001*. Aus diesem Grund verharrt sie im Gegensatz zu ihrem Herzen in Passivität. Die Termini, mit denen diese Passivität zum Ausdruck kommt, sind *ꜥḥꜥ* "stehen bleiben" (vom Herzen an die Dame gerichteter negativer Imperativ in Vers 9) sowie *ḥms qb* "geduldig warten" und *s.mn* "standhaft bleiben" (von der Dame an ihr Herz gerichtete Imperative in den Versen 12 und 17). Die Spannung zwischen der Passivität der Dame und dem aktiven Drängen (*jfd*; *ꜣs*; *pḥ*) ihres Herzens nun läßt sich abbilden auf den Begriff der Passion, an dem laut Luhmann "im Keim [...] die Chance enthalten [ist], sich in Angelegenheiten der Liebe von gesellschaftlicher und moralischer Verantwortung freizuzeichnen".[36] Das Herz jedenfalls plädiert eindeutig für die Autonomisierung des eigenen Begehrens,[37] während die Dame ganz offensichtlich nicht primär auf Erfüllung durch individuelle Befriedigung aus ist, sondern beabsichtigt, im Einklang mit einer moralischen Ordnungsvorstellung zu handeln, "die regelt, was Achtung und was Mißachtung einbringt".[38] Und diese schreibt nun einmal vor, daß man Liebe – gäbe es einen ägyptischen Begriff mit identischer historischer Semantik wie das europäische "Passion" – nur im Sinne eines vormodernen *passiven* Passionsbegriffs aufzufassen hat, über den geregelt ist, daß man sie leidend erduldet und nicht aktiv betreibt.[39] Liebe im Sinne eines passiven Passionsbegriffs wird dem Liebenden nachgerade aufgezwungen durch die Vollkommenheit des geliebten Objektes, die nicht nur

33 Daß der ausstaffierte Körper selbst schon Zeichen von Zugehörigkeit ist, ist keinesfalls ungewöhnlich, besonders typisch aber eben für Gesellschaften der Vormoderne, vgl. Luhmann 1991: 172.

34 Guglielmi 1996: 340-341.

35 Wir simulieren an dieser Stelle natürlich eine kulturelle Kompetenz, die wir nicht haben, und begeben uns durch die Postulierung einer intertextuellen Verbindung zwischen unserem Liebeslied und dem pTurin 55001 in die Gefahr einer Hyperkontextualisierung.

36 Luhmann 1982: 71-96, Zitat: 73.

37 Interessanterweise spielt hier das Herz genau jene Rolle, die Junge 2003 vornehmlich anhand der 14. Maxime des Lehre des Ptahhotep aus dem Mittleren Reich als die Rolle des Leibes herausgearbeitet hat. Man müßte schauen, ob es sich bei dieser Verschiebung um einen Zufall, um eine Textsortenspezifik oder um einen kulturhistorisch bedeutsamen Konzeptwandel handelt.

38 Luhmann 1982: 58.

39 Luhmann 1982: 73-74.

diesem teils überirdische und damit in vormodernen Gesellschaften zwangsläufig göttliche Züge verleiht, sondern auch schon die Vorstellung von der Liebe mit höheren, mithin göttlichen Zügen überformt.[40] Ägyptische Belege für die Ver-göttlichung des Objektes gleichwie der Vorstellung von Liebe wären Legion. Hier soll je ein Beispiel aus unserem Zyklus hinreichen. Auf den bereits oben zitierten Titel folgt als Beginn der ersten (Männer-)Stanze: "Die Einzigartige, die Schwester, ohne ihrer Gleichen/ die Schönste von allen/ Schau, sie gleicht einer aufgehenden Sternengöttin".[41] Für die spirituelle Überformung der Vorstellung von der Liebe können wir auf die fünfte (Männer-)Stanze verweisen, die wir ausführlich zitieren wollen. Im Prinzip handelt es sich hier um einen Hymnus an die Göttin Hathor, die aber im Begriff der "Herrin" (*ḥnw.t*) im weiteren Verlauf der Stanze durchaus mit der Geliebten des Mannes verschmilzt.[42]

Ich verehrte Die-Goldene und pries ihre Majestät.
Ich rühmte die Gebieterin des Himmels.
Ich gab Lobpreis der Hathor
und Glorie <meiner> Herrin (*ḥnw.t*).
Ich flehte zu ihr und sie erhörte mein Bitten
und sie sandte <meine> Herrin (*ḥnw.t*) zu mir.
Von selbst kam sie, mich zu sehen.
Wie groß ist das, was mir geschah!
Gejubelt habe ich, mich gefreut und groß gefühlt,
als man sagte: "Schau, hier ist sie!
Schau, sie ist gekommen!"
und sich die Jünglinge verbeugten
aus großer Liebe zu ihr.
Ich machte meiner Göttin ein Gelübde,
denn sie gab mir die Schwester als Geschenk.
Drei Tage waren es bis gestern, seit meinen Bitten
um ihretwillen. Sie verließ mich vor fünf Tagen.

Die Erfüllung des Liebeswunsches bleibt also bei aller Sehnsucht nach Überwindung der Distanz zwischen den Liebenden und der Befriedigung des körperlichen Begehrens, die in unseren Texten durchaus thematisiert werden, an Vorstellungen gebunden, die jenseits autonomer Selbstverwirklichung durch individuelle Lustbefriedigung angesiedelt sind. Im Einklang mit Gott und der Welt, was nichts anderes heißt als im Einklang mit den Vorstellungen der Menschen (*rmṯ.w*), die die Liebenden beobachten, haben sich diese zueinander zu finden. So ist denn auch die Passion des liebenden Herzens, wie sie uns in der vierten Stanze des pChester Beatty I vorliegt, keinesfalls als pharaonischer Beleg für die Möglichkeit eines ahistorischen und universellen

40 Luhmann 1982: 57-59; das Faktum, nicht aber seine Bedeutung bemerkt ägyptologisch zuletzt Gillam 2000: 214-215.

41 pChester Beatty I vso. C1,1-2; Mathieu 1996: pl. 1,1-2.

42 pChester Beatty I vso. C3,4-9; Mathieu 1996: pl. 3,4-9, siehe auch Fecht 1963: 77-80.

Verständnisses von Liebe zu werten, das sich dem modernen Interpreten methodisch unvermittelt aus einem ägyptischen Text dartut. Es handelt sich hier nicht um die Präsentation einer leicht nachvollziehbaren individuellen Gefühlslage, für die durch die Veröffentlichung gleichzeitig ein institutionalisierter Raum von Privatheit eingefordert werden kann, der dann trotzdem frei von sozialer Determination bliebe. Im Gegenteil präsentiert unser Beispiel das Prinzip gesellschaftlich gesteuerter Affektkontrolle, die im pharaonischen Ägypten selbst noch in den Räumen hochwirksam war, die wir heute als einen Bereich sensibelster Privatheit ansehen würden. Wir hoffen damit klargemacht zu haben, daß menschelnde Intuition allein ebensowenig als Bedingung der Möglichkeit zu einem adäquaten Verständnis ägyptischer Texte ausreicht wie philologischer Sachverstand.

Die Texte sperren sich aber auch noch aus anderen Gründen dem intuitiven Zugriff des modernen Interpreten. Wenn es nämlich sozial gar nicht möglich ist, einen Gefühlszustand wie den von der Dame in der vierten Stanze beschriebenen in der Öffentlichkeit ohne Gesichtsverlust zu präsentieren, eine weibliche Stimme solchen Inhaltes also wahrscheinlich außerhalb des Schlafzimmers gar keinen konkreten kommunikativen Ort hatte, dann könnte dies auch darauf hindeuten, daß wir es hier gar nicht, wie bisher angenommen, mit einer realen, sondern höchstwahrscheinlich mit einer fingierten weiblichen Stimme zu tun haben, die den weiblichen Körper als Projektionsfläche männlicher Vorstellungen einer durch Männer ausgelösten weiblichen Passion imaginiert. Wenn dem so wäre, ließen sich einige immer wieder an den Liebesliedern beobachtete und bisher ausschließlich philologisch interpretierte Probleme lösen, die in der angeblich recht unmotivierten Verteilung der Graphien für feminine und maskuline Suffixpronomen der 1. Person begründet liegen.[43]

Wenn man nämlich vor dem Hintergrund komparatistischen Materials und historischer Wahrscheinlichkeit die Möglichkeit auch für die ägyptischen Liebeslieder in Betracht zieht, daß – wie etwa aus dem mittelalterlichen Minnesang bekannt – sowohl die Männer- als auch die Frauenstimmen während ihrer Aufführung komplett von einer männlichen Person vorgetragen worden sind, dann ist die "Verwechslung" von femininen und maskulinen Suffixpronomen der 1. Person nicht in erster Linie ein beim Kompilationsvorgang von Handschriften wie der des pChester Beatty I aus Unachtsamkeit oder aus Gründen des lautlichen Gleichklangs beider Pronomen produziertes Problem, sondern hängt mit der Notwendigkeit zusammen, den performativen Körper, der sich beim Vortrag selbst seinen eigenen Repräsentationskontext schaffte, auch im Manuskript zu repräsentieren. So könnte es denn durchaus sein, daß es dem Textkompilator als zukünftiger Benutzer der von ihm kompilierten Handschrift schon beim Kopieren nicht mehr gelang, zwischen den verschiedenen Ichs zu

43 Vgl. zuletzt Gillam 2000: 213.

differenzieren, denen er als männlicher Kopist und männlicher Vorleser im späteren Vortrag sowohl männliche wie weibliche Stimmen verleihen wird. In der Tat wäre aus der Perspektive einer solchen kulturhistorischen Kontextualisierung jedes der bisher als philologisch fehlerhaft angesehenen Suffixpronomen genau an der Stelle motivierbar, an der es auftaucht, nicht zuletzt also auch als Reflex des männlichen Körpers, der der Frauenstimme im Vortrag einen physikalischen Stimmkörper verleihen wird.

3. Schluß

Wir hoffen, daß wir auch anhand dieser nur kursorischen Bemerkungen einen Eindruck davon vermitteln konnten, was die Historisierung eines zunächst aus heutiger alltagshermeneutischer Perspektive ins Auge gefaßten Phänomens wie Liebe zum adäquateren Verständnis des angeblich identischen Phänomens in einer vormodernen Kultur beitragen kann. Über die dergestalt konstruierte und aus geschichtswissenschaftlichem Blickwinkel ohnehin plausiblere Widerständigkeit des vormodernen Objekts gegen eine intuitive Vereinnahmung durch den modernen Bearbeiter kann der erwartbaren historischen und interkulturellen Differenz nicht nur Rechnung getragen werden, vielmehr ist es erst die Konstruktion des Objekts als Widerständiges, die die Differenzen zwischen aktiver und passiver Passion (s.o.) als solche faßbar werden läßt und damit klar macht, daß in einer Kultur wie der pharaonischen nicht damit zu rechnen ist, daß Liebe ausschließlich eine passionierte Privatangelegenheit hätte sein können.

Bibliographie

BLACKMAN, A.M. (1933): The Library of A. Chester Beatty. The Chester Beatty Papyri No.1, Oxford 1931, JEA 19, 200-204.

BUMKE, J. (1983): Liebe und Ehebruch in der höfischen Gesellschaft, in: R. Krohn (Hg.), Liebe als Literatur. Aufsätze zur erotischen Dichtung in Deutschland, München, 25-45.

DUMONT, L. (1976): Gesellschaft in Indien. Die Soziologie des Kastenwesens, Wien.

ELIAS, N. (1994): Die höfische Gesellschaft, Frankfurt a.M.

FECHT, G. (1963): Die Wiedergewinnung der altägyptischen Verskunst, MDAIK 19, 54-96.

FICHTENAU, H. (1992): Lebensordnungen des 10. Jahrhunderts. Studien über Denkart und Existenz im einstigen Karolingerreich, München.

FREVERT, U. (1995): Ehrenmänner. Das Duell in der bürgerlichen Gesellschaft, München.

GARDINER, A.H. (1937): Late Egyptian Miscellanies, Bibliotheca Aegyptiaca 7, Brüssel.

GILLAM, R.A. (2000): The Mehy Papers: Text and Lifestyle in Translation, CdÉ 75, 207-216.

GUGLIELMI, W. (1985): Das Ostrakon Gardiner 25 verso und seine hyperbolischen Vergleiche, ZÄS 112, 139-143.

– (1996): Die ägyptische Liebespoesie, in: A. Loprieno (Hg.), Ancient Egyptian Literature. History and Forms, PdÄ 10, Leiden, 335-347.

JUNGE, F. (2003): Die Lehre Ptahhoteps und die Tugenden der ägyptischen Welt, OBO 193, Fribourg/Göttingen.

KELSO, R. (1929): The Doctrine of the English Gentleman in the 16th Century, Urban.

– (1956): Doctrine of the Lady of the Renaissance, Urban.

KNEER, G./NASSEHI, A. (1993): Niklas Luhmanns Theorie sozialer Systeme, München.

KOSELLECK, R. (1979): Vergangene Zukunft. Zur Semantik geschichtlicher Zeiten, Frankfurt a.M.

LE ROY LADURIE, E. (2002): Saint-Simon and the Court of Louis XIV, Chicago.

LUHMANN, N. (1980): Gesellschaftsstruktur und Semantik. Studien zur Wissenssoziologie der modernen Gesellschaft 1, Frankfurt a.M.

– (1980-95): Gesellschaftsstruktur und Semantik. Studien zur Wissens-soziologie der modernen Gesellschaft 1-4, Frankfurt a.M.

– (1982): Liebe als Passion: zur Codierung von Intimität, Frankfurt a.M.

– (1991): Die Form "Person", Soziale Welt 42, 166-175.

MANNICHE, L. (1997): Sexual Life in Ancient Egypt, London.

MASON, M. (1992): The Making of Victorian Sexuality, Oxford.

MATHIEU, B. (1996): La poésie amoureuse de l'Égypte ancienne. Recherches sur en genre littéraire au Nouvel Empire, BdÉ 115, Le Caire.

MESKELL, L. (2002): Private Life in New Kingdom Egypt, Princeton.

MÜLLER, M. (2002): Rezension zu J.E. Hoch "Semitic Words", OLZ 97, Sp. 29-43.

NECKEL, S. (1991): Status und Scham. Zur symbolischen Reproduktion sozialer Ungleichheit, Frankfurt a.M.

SMITH, A. (2001): Exposed – the Victorian Nude, London.

VAN DÜLMEN, R. (1999): Kultur und Alltag in der Frühen Neuzeit: Das Haus und seine Menschen 16.-18. Jahrhundert, München.

Le *Cantique des Cantiques* et l'Egypte pharaonique. Etat de la question

Pascal Vernus

Face aux problèmes ardus que suscite le *Cantique des cantiques*, les biblistes ont plus que jamais senti le besoin de faire appel aux cultures voisines dans le temps et l'espace. Leurs quêtes anxieuses d'éléments de comparaison ne pouvaient manquer de les conduire sur les bords du Nil, étant donné le beau corpus de poésie amoureuse que nous a légué la civilisation pharaonique.[1] De fait, plusieurs contributions récentes ont visé à confronter ce corpus au *Cantique des cantiques*.[2]

S'agissant d'apprécier les relations entre la civilisation pharaonique et les écrits vétéro-testamentaires, une distinction première s'impose entre:

I. Les références *explicites* à l'Egypte.
II. Les références *implicites*, parfois conscientes, le plus souvent inconscientes, à des traits propres à la civilisation égyptienne.

Contrairement à ce qu'on pourrait penser superficiellement, le premier cas (références *explicites*) ne témoigne pas nécessairement *a priori* d'une influence plus authentique que le second cas (références *implicites*). L'Egypte qu'on convoque *explicitement* pour les besoins de l'argumentation est en fait souvent – pas toujours, toutefois – une reconstruction factice opérée dans l'imaginaire du peuple hébreu à partir de souvenirs lointains, hétérogènes, revisités et transformée au gré de différentes traditions; ainsi, entre autres, l'Egypte de l'Exode. Inversement, les références *implicites*, et très probablement

1 Les indications qui suivent se bornent aux travaux fondamentaux récents. Mises au point: Meeks 1979: 1047-1052; Guglielmi 1996: 335-347. L'étude d'ensemble Hermann 1959 conserve quelque intérêt. L'édition philologique la plus récente du corpus a été donnée par Mathieu 1996, où on trouvera une bibliographie quasi exhaustive. Traduction complète du corpus avec un choix de textes relatifs à la femme: Vernus 1992. Traduction complète aussi dans Foster 1974, et dans Kitchen 1999: 315-420. Par ailleurs, nombre de recueils de textes d'anthologies de la littérature (au sens large ou au sens étroit) pharaonique comportent souvent, bien sûr, un choix plus ou moins fourni de pièces tirées de ce corpus. Parmi les contributions trop récentes pour avoir été prises en compte dans les travaux cités précédemment, citons Haikal 1997: 79-85; Derchain 1997: 79-80; Gillam 2000: 207-216.

2 Tournay 1963: 340-362; White 1978; Fox 1985 et Fox 1983: 219-228.

inconscientes, aux traditions administratives pharaoniques à travers plusieurs termes d'origine égyptienne, même si leur utilisateur pouvait souvent ne pas être au fait de leur étymologie, comme *'ēpō*, "mesure" (< ég. *jp.t*), *hīn*, "mesure" (< ég. *hnw*), *qeset*, "ustensile de scribe" (< ég. *gstj*), *ṭabba'at*, "sceau" (< ég. *ðb'.t*),[3] pourraient bien être les marques d'une inspiration égyptienne beaucoup plus authentique. En effet, l'utilisation de chiffres et de sigles métrologiques égyptiens, prouvée au VIIe siècle avant notre ère par des ostraca didactiques trouvés sur des sites israélites,[4] vient recouper ces indications dans la mesure où ils illustrent indiscutablement une influence égyptienne sur la comptabilité. A comparer le recours dans nos cultures européennes à chiffres dits "arabes", en fait. Qui plus est, les rapprochements très discutés, mais difficilement négligeables entre certains passages des *Proverbes* et *L'enseignement d'Aménemopé*,[5] produit typique de l'idéologie des scribes et bureaucrates égyptiens, convergent avec ces trouvailles archéologiques pour suggérer que les références implicites, apparemment dérisoires, à travers des mots d'emprunts qui n'étaient déjà sans doute plus perçus comme tels, peuvent en fait se révéler l'indice d'une influence culturelle égyptienne profonde dans un domaine important, celui de la pratique administrative et comptable.

Bien entendu, il serait caricatural de poser en règle absolue ce genre de hiérarchisation entre références explicites et références implicites à l'Egypte dans la Bible. On en retiendra simplement un *caveat*, suggérant que la précaution n'est jamais excessive en ce domaine, et que l'ostensible n'est pas nécessairement gage d'authentique.

Ces prolégomènes étaient nécessaire à l'appréciation raisonnable des éventuelles points de contact entre le *Cantique des cantiques* et l'Egypte. Dans la composition biblique, il existe une référence explicite à la civilisation pharaonique:

> A ma (/une) cavale, attelée au char (parmi les destriers[6]) de Pharaon,
> Je te compare ma bien-aimée
> et ton cou dans les colliers.
> Tes joues restent belles, entre les pendeloques,
> Nous te ferons des pendants d'or
> et des globules d'argent.

Pour décrire la beauté de la jeune fille, plus particulièrement la beauté de son visage et de son cou mise en valeur par les parures, le point de comparaison est une cavale avec son harnachement. Le cou et le port de tête de l'animal, il est

---

3 Lambdin 1953: 149-150; Hoffmeier1996: 92; Williams 1971: 257-29; Redford 1992: 383-386; Schneider 2001:162.
4 Lemaire/Vernus 1978: 53-8; Lemaire 1980: 341-45 et Lemaire 1983: 302–326.
5 Vernus 2001: 306-308. Voir aussi, dans une perspective plus large, Shupak 1993.
6 Les deux variations dans la traduction reflètent l'interprétation du texte hébreu proposée par Keel 1986: 60.

vrai particulièrement élégants et altiers, sont considérés comme une référence gratifiante pour la jeune fille. Mais il y a plus: ce point de comparaison est en quelque sorte exalté par le fait qu'il s'agit plus particulièrement de la cavale de Pharaon. S'il y a référence au souverain d'Egypte ici, c'est clairement d'abord en tant que parangon du luxe somptueux et raffiné, valorisation bien connue dans l'imaginaire biblique, à côté d'autres valorisations différentes. On observera que le texte biblique évoque, comme souvent "Pharaon" en général et non un pharaon particulier comme il peut arriver parfois. Cela posé, ce luxe somptueux et raffiné se manifeste plus particulièrement à travers l'apparat équestre. Quelques précision s'imposent donc pour pleinement apprécier la référence.

Le cheval est introduit relativement tardivement, vers le dix-septième siècle ou la seconde moitié du XVIIIe siècle avant J.C.,[7] en Egypte très probablement par l'intermédiaire des populations à prédominance sémitique, dont les Hyksôs sont les plus célèbres représentants.

Dès le Nouvel Empire (1550 avant J.-C. environ), il est intégré dans l'apparat matériel et idéologique qui entoure le pharaon. Mais s'il est utilisé, c'est comme animal de trait attelé au char. Même si les luttes féodales du premier millénaire ont popularisé la monte du cheval à la guerre, à l'Epoque Ethiopienne encore (715-856 avant J.-C.), par souci de la dignité de sa fonction le pharaon conduit son cheval plutôt qu'il ne l'enfourche.[8] L'habileté à conduire le char, et la rapidité des chevaux, passent dès le début de la XVIIIe dynastie dans les stéréotypes de la fonction monarchique, exprimés aussi bien à travers les textes que l'iconographie.[9] Le cheval est très clairement considéré comme un élément précieux du standing pharaonique. Ramsès III s'est fait représenter dans la première cour de son temple funéraire de Médinet Habou "inspectant les grands attelages de la grande écurie. Le roi d'apparaître à l'instar de Montou, sa force étant à la mesure du fils de Nout (= Seth) pour contempler les chevaux que ses soins (litt.: ses bras) avaient élevés pour la grande écurie du château qu'a faite le maître des deux pays Ramsès-meryamon."[10] Ce sont les chevaux du pharaon qui sont érigés en référence; un des poèmes d'amour du Nouvel Empire est sans ambiguité:

7 La date ressort du long débat ouvert à propos des plus anciens restes trouvés en Egypte et en Nubie; voir Anthony/Brown 1989: 111-115; Boessneck 1970: 43-47; Clutton-Brock 1974: 89–100. Pour d'aures restes anciens trouvés récemment, voir Houlihan 1996: 33.

8 Le fait de monter sur son cheval plutôt que de l'atteler à un char est une marque d'affolement et de couardise dans le récit de la conqête d'Egypte par Piânkhi. Pour le cheval dans l'apparat guerrier de Taharqa, voir Altenmüller/Moussa 1981: 64.72-73 aa.

9 Decker 1971: 125-135; Hofmann 1989; Schade-Busch 1992: 198-199; Kruchten 1982: 41-42.

10 *The University of Chicago Oriental Institute Publications. Medinet Habu II*, Chicago 1930, pl. 109.

Le cheval du roi
Le meilleur de tous les destriers
Le premier des écuries
Il est l'objet d'une attention particulière dans sa nourriture.
Son maître reconnaît son pas.
S'il entend le son de la cravache,
Il ne saurait se traîner.[11]

Les chevaux du pharaon reçoivent un harnachement approprié à l'éminence de leur maître. La crinière, impeccablement peignée, se termine par une coiffure faite de hautes plumes d'autruches maintenues par des rondelles d'or ou par un mortier orné de têtes de lions. Une résille fine, ponctuée elle aussi de rondelles, couvre leur dos tandis qu'une mince guirlande de perles d'or souligne l'élégante courbure de leurs queues.[12]

Ajoutons, les poèmes d'amour égyptiens évoquent les chevaux avant tout en tant parangon de célérité. C'est au demeurant le cas dans la précédente citation, l'insistance sur la qualité du cheval visant avant tout à mettre en exergue sa vitesse, c'est encore plus manifestement le cas dans les deux exemples suivants

"Si seulement tu te précipitais pour (voir) la "soeur" (= l'amante)"
Comme le cheval sur le champ de bataille"[13]

"Si seulement tu te précipitais pour voir la "soeur"
Comme le messager du roi qui se hâte." [14]

Dans ce troisième exemple, le cheval n'est pas réduit à un simple terme de comparaison, mais utilisé réellement par le jeune homme pour plus vite rejoindre sa dulcinée. Le travail littéraire déplace le statut de l'animal: il sert à montrer que si impérieux est l'amour du jeune homme que c'est lui qui, en fait, tient les rênes:

"J'ai pris un cheval devançant le vent
C'est son (= la belle) amour qui me dirige"[15]

Bien évidemment, il n'y a rien dans ces citations16 qui puissent servir d'élément de référence au texte même du *Cantique des cantiques*. Certes, comme lui, les poèmes d'amour égyptiens utilisent la comparaison équestre, mais c'est dans une perspective différente.

---

11 P. Chester Beatty I, v° G1, 5-7 = Vernus 1992: 69.
12 Voir l'ouvrage fondamental sur ce point de Rommelaere 1991; Spruytte 1999: 77-82.
13 P. Harris 500, r° 1, 8 = Vernus 1992: 75.
14 P.Chester Beatty I, v° G 1 = Vernus1992: 69.
15 O DM 1078 r° 3 = Vernus 1992: 95.
16 Autre exemple du cheval, parangon de course éperdue: Helck 1955-1958: 1541.

Un dernier point mérite attention: le *Cantique des cantiques* évoque plus précisément une cavale et non un cheval. La raison première en est évidemment qu'il s'agit d'une comparaison dont le centre est la jeune fille. Toutefois, on ne saurait passer sous silence deux faits dignes d'attention, suggérant quelque valorisation particulière de la jument dans la civlisation pharaonique. Le premier fait est de nature archéologique. On a retrouvé à proximité de la tombe de Senenmout, le célèbre homme de confiance de la reine Hatshepsout, une sépulture que se partageaient, entre autres, un cynocéphale et une jument.[17] La jument reposait dans un sarcophage, enveloppée de bandelettes, avec une selle de tissu et de cuir. C'est assurément en tant qu'animal familier que l'animal avait été enterré. Reste à déterminer si le choix d'une jument dans ce statut était motivé par quelque appréciation différente entre le mâle et la femelle.

L'autre fait est de nature philologique. Le terme égyptien pour le cheval en général ssmt, emprunté au sémitique selon des modalités en partie obscure, peut être masculin ou féminin, le genre étant explicité par les déterminants du substantif ou les pronoms qui y réfèrent. La plupart des du temps, c'est le masculin qui est utilisé dans les textes égyptiens pour désigner le générique ou le mâle. Les cas où une jument est spécifiquement désignée par des accords aux féminin sont d'autant plus notables. En particulier celui-ci:

> "Alors le chef de Qadesh fit sortir une jument [qui se trouvait être rapide] sur ses pattes. Elle pénétra à l'intérieur des lignes (litt.: de l'armée). Je courus à sa poursuite à pieds, avec mon coutelas. Je lui ouvris le ventre. Avais-je coupé sa queue que je la déposai devant le roi. On me remercia pour cela."[18]

D'après ce récit d'un lieutenant de l'armée qui participa aux expéditions de Thoutmosis III au Proche Orient, on croit comprendre que l'armée égyptienne dut faire face à un stratagème de l'ennemi asiatique et qui consistait à envoyer une jument dans ses rangs. Si bien des éléments nous échappent, on en retient l'attention portée au sexe de l'animal, alors qu'*a priori*, son importance en la circonstance n'apparaît pas clairement.

Même si ces exemples pourraient suggérer quelque valorisation particulière de la jument dans la civilisation pharaonique, il n'y a rien qui puisse être directement mis en rapport avec l'allusion à la jument de Pharaon dans le *Cantique des cantiques*. C'était la seule mention explicite à l'Egypte dans le livre biblique. Mais, par ailleurs, on a cru y discerner la présence implicite de traits de sa civilisation.

A coup sûr, ce qui contribue à ce genre de rapprochements, c'est avant tout la place que tient la nature autant dans le *Cantique des cantiques* que dans les

---

17 Lansing/Hayes 1935-1936: 4-39; Ikram/Iskander 2002: 45 (momie = CGC 29897; selle en tissu et cuir: Caire JE 66250). Voir encore Clutton-Brock 1974: 94.

18 Sethe 1927-1930: 894, l. 5-13.

poèmes d'amour égyptiens du Nouvel Empire. Dans l'un comme dans les autres, elle est très présente, c'est indéniable.

D'abord comme cadre favorisant l'expression de l'expression de l'amour. "*aller aux champs: comble du bien pour celui qui est aimé*" dit un poème égyptien.[19] Les amants y trouvent tout à la fois une intimité propre à accroître le plaisir d'être ensemble et un environnement en accord, en symbiose même, avec leurs entiments: "... *tandis que je me mettrai à l'écart avec toi parmi les arbres du domaine ....tandis que mon visage sera tourné vers le jardin.*"[20] Présence analogue de la nature dans le *Cantique des cantiques*; par exemple, la passion de l'amant s'exalte "*sous le pommier où je t'ai réveillée*" (8,5), ou tandis que "*les mandragores exhalent leur parfum*" (7,14). Cela posé, la nature n'est pas exactement le même. Dans le livre biblique, elle est convoquée dans une perspective avant tout pastorale: "*Mon Bien-aimé est descendu à son jardin, aux parterres embaumés, pour paître son troupeau dans les jardins et pour cueillir des lis*" (6,2); de même: "(le *Bien-aimé*) *mène paître tes troupeaux*" (1,8). C'est une nature parfois laissée à elle-même, mal accessible: "*Viens donc ... ma colombe, cachée au creux des rochers, en des retraites escarpées*" (2,13-14). En revanche, dans la poésie égyptienne, prévaut une nature assujettie, artificielle sous forme d'arbres et de plantes ordonnées comme éléments d'un jardin d'agrément dont un bassin est le centre:

> "Agréable y est une pièce d'eau que ta main a creusée pour nous rafraîchir à la faveur du vent du nord; c'est un bel endroit de promenade, quand ta main est sur ma main et mon coeur revigoré de plaisir pendant notre commune déambulation."[21]

> "J'ai rencontré le frère dans l'accès au bassin."[22]

Au delà d'un simple cadre, dans le texte biblique comme dans les textes égyptiens, la nature prodigue aux poètes une profusion de comparaisons susceptibles de d'agrémenter l'expression des épanchements amoureux. Par exemple

> "Comme le pommier parmi les arbres d'un verger,
> ainsi mon Bien-aimé parmi les jeuns hommes;
> A son ombre désirée je me suis assise
> et son fruit est doux à mon palais " (Cant 2,3).

La comparaison peut-être élargie: l'amante n'est plus seulement un arbre mais un verger entier: "*Elle est un jardin bien clos, ma soeur, ma fiancée.*" (Cant 4,12). Même élargissement dans les poèmes égyptiens: "*Je suis à toi comme l'arpent de terre où sont cultivées pour moi toute sorte de fleurs, au parfum agréable.*"[23] La nature peut

19 P. Harris 500 r° 4, 6-7 = Vernus 1992: 79
20 P. Harris 500 r° 3, 8-9 = Vernus 1992: 77.
21 P. Harris 500 r° 7, 8-9 = Vernus 1992: 82.
22 P. Chester Beatty I r° 17, 4-5 = Vernus 1992: 72.
23 P. Harris 500 r° 7, 7-8 = Vernus 1992: 82.

être sollicitée plus directement dans la vie des amants. Dans le *Cantique des cantiques* (2,5), les fruits des arbres servent de remède: "*ranimez-moi avec des pommes car je suis malade d'amour.*" L'élaboration la plus sophistiquée des comparaisons florales et végétales se manifestent par leur prolongement en *double-entendre* érotique "*dans ton élan tu ressembles au palmier, tes seins en sont les grappes. J'ai dit: Je monterai au palmier*" (Cant 7,8-9). Les textes égyptiens montrent un autre type de sophistication en ce domaine: une oeuvre est fondée sur une véritable prosopopée des arbres du jardin, qui non seulement prennent la parole pour commenter les rapports des jeunes gens, mais encore interviennent directement dans leur histoire: "*Le jeune sycomore ... il a mis un message dans la main d'une domestique ... Il l' a fait courir auprès de l'Aimée.*"[24]

Bien entendu, la faune fournit, elle aussi, son lot de comparaisons. Il y a même un terme commun à la Bible (1) et aux poèmes égyptiens (2), la gazelle comme référence de la hâte mise par l'amant à rejoindre sa dulcinée:

(1) "J'entends mon bien aimé
voici qu'il arrive bondissant sur les collines
mon bien aimé semblable à une gazelle
à un jeune faon." (Cant 2,17)

(2) "Si seulement tu te hâtais de venir auprès de la "soeur" comme une gazelle bondissant sur le plateau désertique."[25]

Cela posé, la composition biblique fait, par ailleurs, un usage bien plus large de la gazelle comme terme de comparaison pour chanter l'amant: "*Sois sembable mon Bien-aimé à une gazelle, à un jeune faon.*" (Cant 2,1) et, inversement, à propos de la Bien-aimée: "*Tes deux seins, deux faons jumeaux d'une gazelle qui paissent parmi les lis*" (Cant 4,5 et 7,4). Il y a donc une certaine convergence entre textes égyptiens et texte biblique, mais sans plus.

Une autre allusion à la faune mérite grande attention. Dans le *Cantique des cantiques*, voici que référence est faite à un canidé sauvage:

"Attrapez-nous les renards
les petits renards ravageurs des vignes
car nos vignes sont en fleur." (2,15)

On a fait valoir que terme hébreu dénommant l'animal peut s'appliquer au renard comme au chacal.[26] Une telle ambiguité se retrouve dans l'Egypte pharaonique. Il y a deux termes principaux désignant les canidés sauvages, mais "anthropohiles", c'est-à-dire n'hésitant pas à venir rôder près des établissement humains, par opposition aux canidés totalement à l'écart comme

---

24 P. Turin 1996 r° 2, 5-6 = Vernus 1992: 85.
25 P. Chester Beatty I v° G 2,1-2 = Vernus 1992: 79.
26 Keel 1998: 102-106.

le lycaon. Le premier de ces termes *z'b*, qui a un apparentement sémitique,[27] pourrait avoir comme représentant prototypique le chacal doré (*Canis aureus*). Le second *wânish*, copte *ouônsh* (*wnš*), qui a un apparentement en berbère et en sémitique d'Ethiopie,[28] pourrait avoir comme représentant protoypique la sous-espèce *Canis aureus lupaster*. En tout cas l'un[29] comme l'autre[30] semblent pouvoir s'appliquer au renard, même s'il existe sans doute un terme plus spécifique.[31]. Cela posé, ce qui mérite d'être souligné, c'est que la canidé sauvage est convoqué dans la thématique amoureuse. On en fait un parangon de frénésie sexuelle. On connaît une fable animalière intitulée "*Copulation de deux chacals*-wânish".[32] On l'a rapprochée d'une illustration représentant deux chacals copulant; ce serait alors le cas exemplaire d'une fable connue et par une version purement picturale et par une version écrite.[33] Dans un poème d'amour, la belle, encore sous le coup de sa nuit de passion, évoque son très brillant partenaire, en soupirant: "*Mon jeune chacal*-wânish *qui suscite le plaisir*".[34] Il y a plus: la même expression "*chacal*-wânish *qui suscite le plaisir*" apparaît dans deux hymnes hélas lacuneux,[35] ce qui ne permet pas d'être totalement sûr qu'elle s'applique au dieu, bien que cela soit probable. Voici le mieux conservé:

> "Amon-Rê sonther, le taureau [de] l'Egypte
> ... de tout le monde. Amon, ne m'abandonne pas
> chacal lubrique. Tu es celui qui fait advenir ...
> Viens à moi!"

Une telle transposition du domaine de l'amour à celui de la piété personnelle serait évidemment à méditer dans une perspective comparatiste avec le *Cantique des cantiques*. En tout cas, on notera que l'attrait des canidés sauvages pour la vigne, épinglé dans le *Cantique des cantiques*, est relevé aussi dans un

---

27 La relation entre *z'b* et les formes sémitiques est difficilement réfutable, mais elle suppose des correspondances phonétiques particulières, ce qui n'est pas *a priori* invraisemblable pour ce enre de mot d'emprunt; voir Vicychl 1958: 383; Takàcs 1999: 73-74, où les rapprochements hors du sémitique laissent perplexe.

28 Vernus 2000: 181; Vychichl 1983: 235.

29 Une argumentation visant à établir que *z'b* s'applique au renard a été dévéloppée par Osborn/Osbornova 1998: 68.

30 Dans *The Battle Reliefs of King Sety I, Translation and Commentary Booklet*, 1986, p. 97 (g), est proposé le sens de "*fox*" pour *wnš*. Les peaux du même animal sont très recherchées, voir Edel 1975: 29 et Janssen 1975: 178-179. Cela suggère que le terme englobe parfois le renard.

31 Pour le renard, voir Janssen 1990: 43-51; Darnell 1995: 80.87-88; Lacau 1970: 65; Vycichl 1958: 33; Westendorf 1965-1977: 29.

32 Fischer-Elfert 1997: 160-161 (O DM 1598).

33 Quirke 1996: 274. Beaucoup plus tard, dans la littérature démotique, deux chacals-*wânish* sont derechef les protagonistes d'une histoire.

34 P. Harris 500 r° 2, 2, cf. Mathieu1996: 173, n. 578.

35 O DM 1038 r° 2-v° 1 et O DM 1406, 3 = Fischer-Elfert 1997: 121-123.

traité compilant les mythes relatifs à la région de Harday, en Moyenne Egypte. Son dieu principal Anoubis, un canidé conciliant des traits du chien sauvage, du renard et du chacal, y est décrit entassant les raisins pour son père Osiris.[36] En dehors de la mise en oeuvre de la nature, quelques convergences méritent d'être signalées entre le *Cantique des cantiques* (a) et les poèmes égyptiens (b).

D'abord dans l'exaltation du pouvoir exercé par les charmes de la belle:

(1)

a) "je suis malade d'amour" (Cant 2,5)
"que je suis malade d'amour" (Cant 5,8)

b) "jusqu'à faire qu'une maladie s'empare de moi"[37]

"On ne peut identifier ma maladie. Il n'y a que le fait de dire "La voici!" qui me guérisse."[38]

"car elle connaît ma maladie."[39]

"étant donné qu'elle se trouve être maladie."[40]

(2)

a) "Un roi est pris à tes boucles." (Cant 7,6)

b) "Qu'elle est experte à lancer le lasso, la "soeur",
Quoiqu'un chasseur de taureau ne l'ait pas mise au monde!
Si elle lance le lasso contre moi, c'est avec ses cheveux."

(3)

a) "Pose-moi comme un sceau sur ton coeur, comme un sceau sur ton bras" (Cant 7,6).

b) "Si elle marque au fer, c'est avec sa bague."[41]

On a aussi souligné dans la composition des textes bibliques et égyptiens, la convergence de certaines situations cadres à partir desquelles se développe l'expression lyrique de l'amour.[42] Convergence, certes, mais à un haut niveau de généralité. Fort significatif, en particulier, se révèle le thème de l'amoureux à la porte de sa dulcinée. Là où les poèmes égyptiens tirent partie de cette situation jusqu'à susciter l'invocation par le jeune homme des parties constitutives de la porte[43] pour réduire l'obstacle qu'elle dresse, dans le texte hébreu, c'est du point de vue de la jeune fille que la porte devient un bref moment sujet d'intérêt. Sitôt qu'elle l'a ouverte, l'amant a disparu (Cant 5,4-6).

36 Vandier s.d.: 78-79.
37 P. Chester Beatty I v° C 1, 8 = Vernus 1992: 64.
38 P. Chester Beatty I v° C 4, 8-9 = Vernus 1992: 68.
39 P. Harris 500 r° 2, 11 = Vernus, o.c., p. 76.
40 O. Nash 12 = Vernus 1992: 94.
41 P. Chester Beatty I, r° 17, 2 et r° 17, 3 = Vernus 1992: 71.
42 White1978: 148-151.
43 Vernus 1992: 37.

Au demeurant, la convergence est d'autant moins significative que la porte fournira un thème convenu de la littérature amoureuse gréco-romaine sous le nom de *paraklausithyron*.

Convergence phraséologique, encore. La relation des deux amants est systématiquement exprimée en Egypte par des termes qui signifient fondamentalement "frère" et "soeur". Bien entendu, rien d'incestueux là-dedans, mais simplement un élargisssement sémantique pour faire saillir la solidarité de génération et de sentiment. On n'a pas manqué de faire valoir que "the Egyptian custom of employing the terms 'brother' and 'sister' for one's beloved is reflected also in the Hebrew work (4:9-12; 5:1f.)."[44]

Si on tente un bilan d'ensemble des ressemblances possibles entre le *Cantique des cantiques* et la poésie amoureuse égyptienne pharaonique, qui date essentiellement du Nouvel Empire, plus particulièrement du XIIIe au XIe siècle avant J.-C., on ne parvient guère à produire d'éléments suggérant de manière convaincante une influence directe de la seconde sur le premier. A vrai dire, l'écart chronologique l'eût faite difficilement attendre. On en peut guère aller plus loin que le constat d'une certaine affinité d'atmosphère et de sensibilité entre les textes égyptiens et le texte biblique. Que l'amour affronte des situations semblables partout et produit des sentiments universels rend en grande partie compte de cette affinité. Cela posé, on ne déniera pas qu'elle puisse reflèter aussi, à moindre degré sans doute, la proximité géographique et le long voisinage historique du monde israélite et du monde égyptien, et, par ce biais, on ne peut exclure absolument que la culture du premier ait pu avoir été effleurée par la littérature amoureuse du second, dans la mesure où elle a été touchée par ses traditions administratives et sapientiales (voir ci-dessus). Mais, ce serait en tout cas de manière trop ténue pour parler de "sources" ou des "racines" égyptiennes du texte biblique ou d'influences directes sur lui.

Annexe

Les commentateurs sont divisés sur la nature des rapports entre poésie amoureuses égyptienne et le *Cantique des cantiques*. Voici quelques jugements récents émis par des égyptologues.

Affinité marquée:

R.J. WILLIAMS:[45]

"The marked resemblance of these poems to their Egyptian counterparts is unmistakable."

44 Williams 1971: 284-285.
45 Williams 1971: 284.

D. B. REDFORD:[46]
"...similarity in genre and treatment between extant New Kingdom love poetry and the Song of Songs. Although the latter is Exilic or post Exilic in date, the form harks back to Egyptian love poetry one thousand years earlier ... the origin remains an erotic though discreet creation ..."

M. GÖRG:[47]
"... reveals metaphors and similes strongly familiar with Egyptian illustrations, despite problems in determining its date of origin, the song in part remember some early imagery of international peace (as between King Solomon and his beloved, a royal woman from an African land). There may have been a collective memory of peace, as described by the two lovers."

Affinité lâche:

B. WHITE:[48]
"The Hebrew Song of Song shares in the design, languages and literary genres expressing the human joy of love. An analysis of the egyptian poems provides the interpreter of the Song of the Song with what he may expect in terms of themes, literary fictions, and atmosphere in Canticles ... but the commonality of love-language denotes archetypal vehicles through which human, sexual love was celebrated in the ancient world ... To paint with bold strokes and contend that the Song's structure, setting, genre, and meaning coincide with that of the Egyptian songs would be unwarranted."

D. MEEKS:[49]
"L'influence de cette poésie sur la littérature vétéro-testamentaire n'est pas évidente quand bien même certaines similitudes la rapprochent du Cantique des Cantiques."

K.A. KITCHEN:[50]
"Song of Songs which shares many features with our Egyptian poems alternate speakers (boys; girl, bystanders), portic descriptions of the other's anatomy, background themes of flowers and fruits, garden and orchard, etc. But it would be imprudent to view the Song of Songs as merely appendage to the late-2nd millenium Egyptia poems. For all these features and other, they both share also with lyric poetry frm Mesopotamia that is in part older than either the Eyptian or Hebrew examples."

46 Redford 1992: 389.
47 Görg 2001: 183.
48 White 1978: 162-163.
49 Meeks 1979: 1047.
50 Kitchen 1999: 316.

Bibliographie

ALTENMÜLLER, H./MOUSSA, A. (1981): Die Inschriften der Taharqastele von der Dahschurstrasse, Studien zur altägyptischen Kultur 9, 64-73.

ANTHONY, D./BROWN, D. (1989): Looking a Gift Horse in the Mouth. Identification of the Earliest Bitted Equids and the Microscopic Analysis of Wear, dans P.J. Crabtree/D.Campana/K. Ryan (eds.), Early Animal Domestication and its Cultural Context, Philadelphia, 111-115.

BOESSNECK, J. (1970): Ein altägyptisches Pferdeskelett, MDAIK 27, 43-47.

CLUTTON-BROCK, J. (1974): The Buhenhorse, Journal of the Archaeological Science 1, 89-100.

DARNELL, J.C. (1995): Hathor returns to Medamud, Studien zur altägyptischen Kultur 22, 47-94.

DECKER, W. (1971): Die physische Leistung Pharaos, Cologne.

DERCHAIN, P. (1997): Art. Miette (IV), Revue d'Egyptologie 48, 79-80.

EDEL, E. (1975): Beiträge zum ägyptischen Lexikon VI, ZÄS 102, 29.

FISCHER-ELFERT, H.-W. (1997): Lesefunde im literarischen Steinbruch von Deir el Medineh, Kleine ägyptische Texte 12, Wiesbaden.

FOSTER, J.L. (1974): Love Songs of the New Kingdom, New York.

FOX, M.V. (1982): Love, Passion and Perception in Israelite and Egyptian Love Poetry, JBL 102, 219-228.

– (1985): The Song of Songs and Ancient Egyptian Love Songs, Madison.

GILLAM, R. (2000): The Mehy Papers. Texts and Lifestyle in Translation, Chronique d'Egypte 75, 207-216.

GÖRG, M. (2001): Biblical Tradition, dans: D.B. Redford (ed.), The Oxford Encyclopedia of Ancient Egypt , Vol 1, Oxford, 181-184.

GUGLIELMI, W. (1996): Die ägyptische Liebespoesie, dans: A. Loprieno (ed.), Ancient Egyptian Literature. History and Forms, Probleme der Ägyptologie 10, Leyde, 335-347.

HAIKAL, F. (1997): Thoughts and Reflexions on the Love Songs in Ancient Egypt, dans L'imperio Ramesside. Convegno internazionale in onore di Sergio Donadoni, Vicino Oriente Quaderno 1, Rome, 79-85.

HELCK, W. (1955-8): Urkunden der 18. Dynastie, Urkunden des ägyptischen Altertums, Berlin.

HERMANN, A. (1959): Altägyptische Liebesdichtung, Wiesbaden.

HOFFMEIER, J.K. (1996): Israel in Egypt. The Evidence for the Authenticity of the Exodus Tradition, Oxford.

HOFMANN, U. (1989): Führerwesen und Pferdehaltung im Alten Ägypten, Diss. Bonn.

HOULIHAN, P. (1996): The animal World of the Pharaohs, Londres.

IKRAM, S./ISKANDER, N. (2002): Catalogue général of Egyptian Antiquities in the Cairo Museum Nos 24048-24056; 29504-29903 (selected); 51084-51101; 61089 Non-Human Mummies, Le Caire.

JANSSEN, J.J. (1975): Commodity Prices from the Ramessid Period. An Economic Study of the Village of Necropolis Workmen at Thebes, Leyde.

– (1990): On the Scent of a Fox, Discussions in Egyptology 16, 43-51.

KEEL, O. (1986): Das Hohelied, ZBK 18, Zurich.

KITCHEN, K.A. (1999): Poetry of Ancient Egypt, Documenta Mundi Aegyptiaca 1, Jonsered 1999, 315-420.

KRUCHTEN, J.-M. (1982): Convention er innovation dans un texte royal du début de l'Epoque Ramesside. La stèle de l'an de Séthy I découverte à Jérusalem, Annuaire de l'IPHOS 26, 41-42.

LACAU, P. (1970): Les noms de parties du corps en égyptien et en sémitique, Memoires de l'Académie des Inscriptions et Bellles-Lettres, Paris.

LAMBDIN, T.O. (1953): Egyptian Loan Words in the Old Testament, JAOS 73, 149-150.

LANSING, A./HAYES, W. (1935-36): The Museum Excavations at Thebes, BMMA, 4-39.
LEMAIRE, A. (1980): Les ostraca paléo-hébreux de Qadesh-Barnéa, Orientalia 49, 341-345.
– (1983): L'ostracon paléo-hébreu n° 6 de Tell Qudeirat (Qadesh-Barnéa), dans: M. Görg (ed), Fontes atque Pontes. Eine Festgabe für Hellmut Brunner, ÄAT 5, Wiesbaden, 302-326.
LEMAIRE, A./VERNUS, P. (1978): L'origine égyptienne du signe ǧ des poids inscrits de l'époque royale israélite, Semitica 28, 53-58.
MATTHIEU, B. (1996): La poésie amoureuse de l'Egypte ancienne. Recherches sur un genre littéraire au Nouvel Empire, Bibliothéque d'Etudes 115, Le Caire.
MEEKS, D. (1979): Art. Liebeslieder, Lexikon der Ägyptologie III, Wiesbaden, 1047-1052.
OSBORNOVA, J. (1998): The Mammals of Ancient Egypt, Warminster.
QUIRKE, S. (1996): Narrative Literature, dans: A. Loprieno (ed.), Ancient Egyptian Literature. History and Forms, Probleme der Ägyptologie 10, Leyde, 263-276.
REDFORD, D.B. (1992): Egypt, Canaan, and Israel in Ancient Times, Princeton.
ROMMELAERE, C. (1991): Les chevaux du Nouvel Empire égyptien. Origines, races, harnachement, Connaisance de l'Egypte ancienne Etude n° 3, Bruxelles.
SCHADE-BUSCH, M. (1992): Zur Königsideologie Amenophis III. Analyse der Phraseologie hisartorischer Texte der Voramarnazeit, HÄB 35, Hildesheim.
SCHNEIDER, T. (2001): Review Essay: Y. Muchiki, Egyptian Proper Names and Loanwords in North-West Semitic, SBLDS 17, Atlanta 1999, JQR 92, 151-161.
SETHE, K. (1927-30): Urkunden der 18. Dynastie, historisch-biographische Urkunden, Urkunden des ägyptischen Altertums, 2me ed. Leipzig.
SHUPAK, N. (1993): Where can Wisdom be found? The Sage's Language in the Bible and in Ancient Egyptian Literature, OBO 130, Fribourg/ Göttingen.
SPRUYTTE, J. (1999): L'attelage égyptien sous la XVIIIe dynastie. Étude technique et technologique, Kyphy Bulletin du Cercle Lyonnais d'égyptologie Victor Loret 2, 77-82.
TAKÀCS, G. (1999): Etymological Dictionary of Egyptian Volume I. A Phonological Introduction, HdO 48, Leyde/Boston/Cologne.
TOURNAY, R.J. (1963): Egypte, dans A. Robert/R.J. Tournay (ed.), Le Cantique des cantiques. Traduction et commentaire, Paris, 340-362.
VANDIER, J. (n.d.): Le papyrus Jumilhac, CNRS, Paris.
VERNUS, P. (1992): Chants d'amour de l'Egypte antique, La Salamandre, Paris.
– (2000): Situation de l'égyptien dans les langues du monde, dans: F.-X. Fauvelle-Aymar/J.P. Chrétien/C.-H. Perrot (eds.), Afrocentrismes. L'histoire des Africains entre Egypte et Amérique, Paris.
– (2001): Sagasses de l'Egypte pharaonique, La Salamandre, Paris.
VICYCHL, W. (1958): Grundlage der ägyptisch-semitischen Wortvergleichung, Mitteilungen des Deutschen Archäologischen Instituts. Abt. Kairo 16, Mainz.
– (1983): Dictionaire étymologique de la langue copte, Louvain.
WESTENDORF, W. (1965-77): Koptisches Handwörterbuch, Heidelberg.
WHITE, B. (1978): A Study of the Language of Love in the Song of Songs and the Ancient Egyptian Poetry, Missoula.
WILLIAMS, R.J. (1971): Egypt and Israel, dans J.R. Harris (ed.), The Legacy of Egypt, 2nd ed. Oxford, 257-290.

„Kundbar werde mir deine Sehnsucht ...“
Eros und Liebe im Alten Orient

Karl Hecker

Wer sich intensiver mit dem kuneiformen Schrifttum des Alten Orients zu befassen und darin dann literarische Schätze zu suchen beginnt, den wird unweigerlich bald eine gewisse Verzweiflung überkommen angesichts der unüberschaubaren Massen von Rechts- und Verwaltungsurkunden, Geschäftsnotizen und Briefen, die zwar mannigfaltige Einblicke in das altorientalische Sozialverhalten vermitteln, aber nur selten etwas über persönliche menschliche Empfindungen und Gefühle mitteilen. Und wendet man sich dann den ungleich weniger zahlreichen Produkten und Skripten der Keilschriftgelehrten zu, die uns aus Tempel-, Palast- oder vereinzelt auch Privatbibliotheken erhalten sind und die in der Assyriologie für gewöhnlich als „literarische Texte“ oder „keilschriftliche Literatur“ zusammengefaßt werden,[1] dann findet man verschiedenartige Listen[2] oder Omen- und Beschwörungssammlungen, astronomische Kompendia und auch einige Dichtwerke erzählenden oder reflektie-

1 Der Begriff „Literatur“ wird in der Altorientalistik unterschiedlich interpretiert. Borger 1967-75 verstand darunter alles keilschriftlich Geschriebene, Krecher und Reiner (1978) schließen Listenwerke, Omen und Ritualsammlungen aus und kommen zu einem relativ kleinem Korpus hauptsächlich poetisch strukturierter Texte, während Edzard und Röllig (1987-90) zwar Strukturkriterien in den Vordergrund stellen, dann aber in die von ihnen zusammengestellten Kataloge doch wieder z.B. magische Texte und Rituale aufnehmen (dafür aber die ebenfalls oft kunstvoll strukturierten Königsinschriften ausschließen). Eine Vorstellung vom Umfang des literarischen Korpus des 1. Jahrtausends vermitteln die Berechnungen von Oppenheim (1977: 16-17) zur Größe der Bibliothek des Assurbanipal in Ninive, für die im Auftrag des Königs im ganzen Land Tafeln gesammelt wurden und die daher einen für ihre Zeit gewiß repräsentativen Bestand aufwies. Oppenheim zufolge umfaßte sie maximal 1500 Tafeln, davon nur etwa 200 mit (im engeren Sinn) literarischem Inhalt.

2 Als typische Beispiele seien Götter-, Königs- oder lexikalische Listen genannt. Vgl. dazu RlA Bd. III, 1957-71, 473-479 und Bd. VI, 1980-83, 77-135 und 609-641 für eine Übersicht über die jeweilige Subspezies. Die Listen können als eine Art frühwissenschaftlicher Phänomenologie verstanden werden, vgl. von Soden 1936 und von Soden 1985: 138-164.

renden Inhalts, Hymnen auf Götter, Gebete und anderes mehr,[3] aber Lieder um Liebeslust und Liebesleid, Lob des oder der Geliebten oder Sehnsucht nach ihm oder ihr? Man muß schon eine Weile suchen, ehe man derartiges in dem kaum noch überschaubaren Wust der auf uns überkommenen keilschriftlichen Quellen findet. Man kommt schließlich auf kaum mehr als eine Handvoll meist fragmentarischer Texte, die sich zudem auf einen Zeitraum von mehr als einem Jahrtausend verteilen; kurz: das Genre scheint nicht zu den großen und beliebten Gattungen der keilschriftlichen Literatur zu gehören. Dies gilt zumindest für die akkadischsprachige Überlieferung; das im allgemeinen ältere sumerische Korpus ist um einiges umfangreicher als das akkadische.[4]

Natürlich war die Liebe selbst auch im Alten Orient kein unbekanntes Phänomen. Die akkadischen Wörterbücher verzeichnen unter dem Stichwort *ramû* 'lieben' und seinen Derivaten[5] zahlreiche Belege für mannigfaltige Nuancen zwischen rein gefühlsmäßiger Zuneigung und bloßer sexueller Aktion. Liebe als erotisches Phänomen kann Götter und Menschen gleichermaßen ergreifen, Objekte können andere Götter bzw. Göttinnen, Menschen oder auch Tiere sein. Dem ninevitischen Gilgameš-Epos zufolge hatte die Liebesgöttin Ištar bereits den Dumuzi, die Mandelkrähe, den Löwen, das Pferd, den Hirten und den Gärtner Išullānu geliebt, ehe sie Gilgameš die Ehe anbot.[6] Diese Szene ist geprägt von einem auffälligen Wechsel der Diktion. Während Ištar sich bei ihrem Antrag der wohl aus einem profanen Eheschließungszeremoniell stammenden Formel ‚Du sollst mein Mann, ich will deine Frau sein' bedient,[7] führt Gilgameš die Namen der verflossenen Liebhaber der Göttin jeweils mit *tarāmī-ma* „du liebtest den ..." ein. Dabei ist deutlich, daß die Ištar von ihren jeweiligen Geliebten keine nurmehr platonische Liebeserfüllung erwartete, äußerte sie doch unverblümt sexuelle Begierden:

> „Mein lieber Išullānu, laßt uns deine Kraft genießen,
> strecke auch deine Hand aus und berühre unsere Scham!"[8]

3 Für eine Zusammenstellung der wichtigsten Gattungen und ihrer (sumerischen und akkadischen) Texte vgl. RlA VII: 35-66.

4 Sefati 1998: 18 zählt 38 sumerische Lieder mit rund 1700 Zeilen zum Thema Liebe und Hochzeit von Dumuzi und Inanna, schließt darunter aber das Zwiegesprächs (a-da-mìn-du$_{11}$-ga)-Gedicht „Hirte und Bauer" (Dumuzi und Enkimdu) sowie offensichtlich auch Königshymnen wie Šulgi X (Klein 1981: 135-66) mit als Beleg für das Ritual des *Hieros Gamos* gedeuteten erotischen Passagen ein.

5 Für das sumerische Äquivalent k i . a g , ursprünglich vielleicht mit der Bedeutung „Land (ver)messen", gibt es leider keine bequem benutzbare Belegzusammenstellung.

6 Ninive-Rezension, Tafel VI, 6ff. Vgl. George 2003: 618-23, für eine deutsche Übersetzung auch Hecker 1994 (TUAT III): 699-701.

7 Gilg.nin. VI, 9. Die Formel ist auch in Z. 82 der Tell el-Amarna-Fassung des Mythos von Nergal und Ereškigal belegt. Vgl. Müller 1994 (TUAT III): 766-9 für eine Übersetzung.

8 Ältere Übersetzungen emendieren das akkadische *ḫurdat-ni* (zu akkadisch *ḫurdatu* „weibliche Scham") zu *ḫurdatī* „meine Scham" und übersehen dabei, daß Ištar mit der von ihr

Das Berühren der (weiblichen) Scham ist schon in den ältesten akkadischen Liebesliedern ein Topos[9] und findet sich – eigentlich wenig überraschend – auch in sumerischen Liedern, die dem Umfeld der Heiligen Hochzeit zugerechnet werden.[10]

Mit *ramû* werden, wie schon angedeutet, aber auch Affekte ohne sexuelle Konnotation beschrieben: Die Götter lieben ihre Stadt oder Tempel, den König oder dessen Regierung, Eltern (göttliche und menschliche) ihre Kinder, der König liebt Wahrheit und Gerechtigkeit oder ein Kaufmann das Geld mehr als sein Leben.[11] Obwohl Kaufleute eher Geschäfts- als Liebesbriefe schreiben und Richter nüchtern und emotionslos Rechtsfälle protokollieren, liefern auch in derartig unromantischem Umfeld beheimatete Texte gelegentlich Hinweise auf Liebesbeziehungen. So bittet ein Assyrer im anatolischen Kaniš seine Zweitfrau mit Bezug auf ihre Liebe brieflich, zu ihm zu kommen;[12] fast schon rührend ist die vor Gericht abgegebene Liebeserklärung einer jungen Frau, deren 'Ehe in der Schwebe' geschieden werden soll.[13] Meist allerdings stehen in Rechtsurkunden und Briefen andere Motive als gegenseitige Zuneigung im Vordergrund, der Wunsch nach hausfraulicher Versorgung zum Beispiel,[14] und vor allem nach Kindern, die die Betreuung im

---

gewählten Formulierung dem Išullānu ihren Körper als gemeinsamen Besitz anbietet. Vgl. auch Anm. 9 und 10 für Parallelbeispiele.

9 Vgl. *bilam-ma šumēlik luput ḫurdat-ni* „strecke deine Linke aus und berühre unsere Scham" (gesprochen von der Frau) in Kol. I, 13' des aus Kiš stammenden altbabylonischen Liedes Westenholz 1987 und – von einem Mann zur Ištar gesprochen – in einem mittelbabylonischen (oder eher Abschrift eines altbabylonischen?) Lied auf die Göttin: *alkī lulappit ḫurdat-ki* „Komm, ich will deine Scham berühren" (von Soden 1991: 11). Die altakkadische Liebesbeschwörung Gelb 1970, Nr. 8 (neu bearbeitet von J. und A. Westenholz 1977) benutzt andere Worte, sagte aber Ähnliches: *a-ḫu-uz*$_x$ *ur*$_4$*-ki* [16)] *ša ši-na-tim* „ich faßte deine Urin-Scham".

10 Z.B. in dem schon in Anm. 4 erwähnten Hymnus auf König Šulgi von Ur: „... weil er (Šulgi) meine reine Scham berührte" (Šulgi X, 30. Vgl. Klein 1981: 136-7).

11 Contenau 1920, Nr. 5: 8-10 *kaspam ta-ra-am* [9)]*na-pá-áš-ta-kà* [10)]*ta*$^!$*-ze-ar* „du liebst das Geld (und) mißachtest dein Leben". Es handelt sich um einen Brief zweier in Assur lebender Damen an einen in Anatolien tätigen Kaufmann. Die Absenderinnen lassen keinen Zweifel daran, daß sie das Verhalten des Adressaten für nicht gottgefällig halten. Für eine vollständige Übersetzung des Briefes vgl. Michel 2001, Nr. 348.

12 *šu-ma ke-na-tim ta-ra-i-mì-ni tí-ib-e-ma a-tal-ki-im* „wenn du mich wirklich liebst, dann mach dich auf und komm her!" Garelli 1957: 6, 30-31, Neubearbeitung bei Larsen 2002: 184-186. Der Briefschreiber hatte noch eine Hauptfrau (*aššatum*, die Adressatin wird in der Briefhülle als *amtum*, wörtlich „Sklavin", angesprochen.

13 Pinches 1964, Nr. 86: 16-26: „Vor diesen (den in Z. 1-15 aufgelisteten) Zeugen fragten sie den Aḫam-nirši: ‚Ist diese Frau deine Ehefrau?' Er antwortete: ‚Hängt mich an einen Pflock, schneidet meine Glieder ab: ich werde sie nicht heiraten!'. Sie fragten seine Frau, sie sagte: ‚Ich liebe meinen Mann.' Er aber weigerte sich weiter ..." Es handelt sich um die Auflösung einer abgesprochenen, aber noch nicht vollzogenen Ehe. Diese einzigartige Urkunde ist wiederholt, zuletzt von Pientka-Hinz, TUAT NF I (S. 29), behandelt worden.

14 Sehr schön in dem altassyrischen Brief eines Puzur-Aššur an die in Assur wohnende

Alter übernehmen und nach dem Tode das Totenopfer darbringen. Der Wunsch nach Kindern ist dabei so bestimmend, daß Eheverträge vorsehen können, daß der Mann im Falle ungewollter oder, wenn die Ehefrau eine zur Kinderlosigkeit verpflichtete *nadītum*-Priesterin ist, auch gewollter Unfruchtbarkeit eine Zweit- und bisweilen sogar eine Drittfrau nehmen kann.[15] Ein kurioses Beispiel für die Versorgung eines jungen Mädchens aus Nuzi hat G.G.W. Müller 1998, Nr. 18 veröffentlicht. Das Mädchen wird adoptiert, um mit einem Sklaven des Adoptivvaters verheiratet zu werden. Stirbt dieser, soll sie den 2. usw. bis zum 5. Sklaven heiraten. Sie behält außerdem lebenslanges Wohnrecht im Hause des Adoptivvaters. Daß bei einer der beteiligten Personen tiefere Gefühle von Zuneigung und Liebe entstanden sein könnten, kann man sich kaum vorstellen.

Es ist hier nicht der Platz, weitere keilschriftliche Äußerungen zum Thema Liebe und Sexualität zusammenzustellen, zumal sich damit erst unlängst eine *Rencontre Assyriologique* beschäftigt hat.[16] Ganz kurz sollte aber wenigstens noch auf magische Beschwörungen und Rituale eingegangen werden, mit denen Liebeszauber und Potenzgewinnung angestrebt wurde.[17] Die Durchführung

---

Nuḫšatum (Clay 1927, Nr.104): [3)]*a-bu-ki* / *ašu-mì-ki* [*a-na*] [4)]*ṣé-ri-a a-na a-ḫa-*[*zi-ki*] [5)]*iš-pu-ra-am ù a-na-ku* [6)]*ṣú-ḫa-ri-a ù na-áš-pé-er-tí* [7)]*a-ṣé-er* / *a-bi-ki* / *a-šu-mì-ki* [8)]*a-šé-ṣú-i-ki* [9)]*áš-ta-áp-ra-am a-pu-tum* [10)]*i-na* ^{d}UTU^{ši} *ṭup-pí* [11)]*ta-ša-me-i-ni* / *a-ma-k*[*am*] [12)]*a-na a-bi-ki* / *pu-nu-*⌈*i-ma*⌉ [13)]*iš-tí ṣ*[*ú-ḫ*]*a-ri-a* [14)]*tí-ib-e-ma a-tal-ki-im* [15)]*we-da-ku* / *ma-ma-an* / *ša i-na* [16)]*re-šé-e-a* / *i-za-zu-ma* [17)]*pá-šu-ra-am* / *i-ša-kà-na=ni* [18)]*lá-šu* / *šu-ma iš-tí* [19)]*ṣú-ḫa-ri-a* / *lá ta-li-ki-*[*im*] [20)]*i-na Wa-aḫ-šu-ša-na* [21)]DU[MU.SAL] *Wa-aḫ-šu-ša-*[*na*] [22)]*a-ḫa-az* (3 Zz. Spuren): „[3-5)]Dein Vater schrieb mir deinetwegen wegen einer Heirat [mit dir], [5-9)]und ich schickte jetzt meine Diener und einen Brief von mir zu deinem Vater, um dich herzuholen. [9-12)]Also, am Tage, da du meine Tafel hörst, wende dich dort an deinen Vater, dann [13-14)] mach dich auf und komm mit meinen Dienern her! [15-18)]Ich bin allein und habe niemanden, der mir zur Seite (wörtlich „zu Häupten") steht und mir den Tisch vorsetzt. [18-22)]Wenn du nicht mit meinen Dienern kommst, werde ich in Waḫšušana eine Waḫšušaniterin heiraten ..." Von Liebe ist in diesem Brief keine Rede, und eine Absage der Nuḫšatum scheint dem Puzur-Aššur nicht sonderlich zu Herzen zu gehen, vielmehr ist er bereit, sich auch mit einer anderen Dame zu trösten.

15 Ein Beispiel für eine Drittfrau findet sich in dem Kültepe-Text I 490 in Hecker/Kryszat/Matouš 1998, wo allerdings als Besonderheit hervorzuheben ist, daß der Ehemann für längere Zeit außerhalb seiner Heimatstadt Assur lebte. Die hier interessierenden Zeilen lauten: (1-4) „Puzur-Ištar heiratete die Ištar-lamassī als Zweitfrau." ... (16-22) „Außer seiner Ehefrau in der Stadt Assur wird er keine andere heiraten. Wenn Ištar-lamassī bis in 3 Jahren kein Kind bekommt, wird er eine Sklavin kaufen und heiraten." Zu beachten die Terminologie, die zwischen *aššatum* „Ehefrau", *amtum* „Zweitfrau" (eigentlich „Sklavin") und dem Ideogramm GÉME für die 3. Frau unterscheidet. Letzteres wird zwar gewöhnlich mit *amtum* geglichen, doch könnte man sich für diese Stelle auch andere Lesungen vorstellen (etwa *ṣuḫartum* „Kleine", *wardatum* „Mädchen" oder *šāwītum* etwa „Nebenfrau"?).

16 Kongreßbeiträge veröffentlicht durch Parpola/Whiting 2002.

17 Hauptsächlich die sog. ŠÀ.ZI.GA (etwa „Erektions")-Beschwörungen. Zu diesen vgl. Biggs 1967 (Edition) und 2002 (Nachträge und Interpretation).

des Rituals oblag dem Beschwörungspriester (*āšipu*), die Beschwörung aber wurde meist von der auf Liebeserfüllung hoffenden Frau rezitiert. Die Sprache ist teils bildhaft, teils von unmittelbarer und drastischer Direktheit[18] und vermittelt erheblich deutlicher noch als die bereits zitierten Einzelbeispiele den Eindruck eines sehr unbekümmerten und tabulosen[19] Sexualverständnisses, in das nicht nur die Menschen, sondern auch die Götter einbezogen sind.[20]

Wenden wir uns nun den keilschriftlichen Liebesliedern zu, so werden wir davon ausgehen dürfen, daß sie nicht in einem grundlegend abweichenden Sexualethos verwurzelt sind. Tatsächlich verwenden sie teilweise ganz ähnliche Bilder und Ausdrücke wie die ŠÀ.ZI.GA-Beschwörungen oder erotische Passagen in anderen Texten.[21] Allerdings ist das Liebesliedkorpus keinesfalls in sich einheitlich. Aus der benutzten Sprache läßt sich ein wenn auch nur ungefähres Datierungskriterium gewinnen: Sumerisches ist verbunden mit Namen wie Šulgi von Ur (2029-1982 v. Chr.[22]) oder Iddin-Dagān von Isin (1910-1890), Rīm-Sîn von Larsa (1758-1699) und die Könige ab der 1. Dynastie von Babylon schreiben akkadisch.[23] Für die sumerischen Lieder lassen sich vom Inhalt her 3 Typen unterscheiden:[24]

---

18 Vgl. etwa Wilcke 1985, Z. 14-22:
„... Ich halte dich fest, wie Ištar den Dumuzi festhielt,
und Zeraš (die Biergöttin) den Trinker bindet.
Ich band dich mit meinem haarigen Mund,
mit meiner Urin-Scham,
mit meinem Speichel-Mund,
mit meiner Urin-Scham.
Nicht soll die Nebenbuhlerin zu dir gehen!
Gelagert ist der Hund, gelagert ist der Eber,
du lagere dich immer wieder auf meinen Schenkeln!"
Für weitere Beispiele vgl. Biggs 2002: 72-73.

19 Dies schließt nicht aus, daß es soziale Tabus gab, deren Einhaltung durch gesetzliche Sanktionen wie z.B. Codex Ḫammurapi § 128ff. (Übersetzung Borger (TUAT I) 1982: 58) geregelt war.

20 Ergänzend sei noch auf die zahlreichen bildhaften Darstellungen erotischer Szenen verwiesen, die oft öffentlich sichtbar angebracht waren (dazu Assante 2002: 28) oder als Votivgabe im Tempel aufbewahrt waren. Für ein beschriftetes Beispiel vgl. das von Jakob-Rost/Freydank 1981 veröffentlichte bronzene Schamdreieck aus Assur. Die Inschrift lautet: „Zur Zeit von Šarrum-kēn, Stadtfürst von Assur, hat Ḫadītum, die Gattin von Bēlum-nādā, der Ištar von Assur (dies) geweiht. Für das Leben ihres Gatten, ihr Leben und das Leben ihrer Kinder brachte sie die(se) Scham ein."

21 Für ein Beispiel vgl. die Zitate aus der 6. Tafel des Gilgameš-Epos und die Parallelen dazu oben S. 170f.

22 Alle Datierungen nach der Kurzen Chronologie: Ḫammurapi 1728-1686 v. Chr. Der Zusatz „v. Chr." bleibt im folgenden weg.

23 Die sumerische Tradition reißt aber nicht ab. Das Inanna-Lied ba-lam ba-lam-lam (Sefati 1998: 165ff.) lag noch dem Kompilator des Hymnenkatalogs Ebeling 1919-23: 158 II 52 vor.

24 Vgl. Alster 1985: 127-8.

1. Lieder, in denen die Liebenden Götterpaare (Inanna und Dumuzi bzw. Amaušumgalanna) sind,[25]
2 Lieder, in denen Könige als Liebespartner der Göttin Inanna oder ihrer Frau oder Konkubine fungieren,[26] und
3. allgemeine Liebeslieder,[27]

wobei aber die Abgrenzungen, wie allgemein in der altorientalischen Literatur, fließend sind und auch erzählende Partien eingeflochten sein können. Beliebtes Stilelement ist das auch sonst in der sumerisch-akkadischen Literatur gut bezeugte Zwiegespräch, wobei sich die Liebenden oft als Bruder und Schwester anreden.[28] Daneben finden sich auch Passagen, die offenbar von einem Chor oder von Einzelsängern vorgetragen wurden, so daß dann der Eindruck des Librettos für ein kultisches Schauspiel entsteht. Da keine „Regieanweisungen" überliefert sind, sind verschiedene Szenarien vorstellbar. Denkbar wäre ein Ritual mit einer nurmehr symbolischen Vereinigung der beiden Gottheiten durch Zusammenführung ihrer Kultstatuen, wie dies in späterer Zeit offenbar üblich war.[29] Wenn aber der König in Vertretung des Gottes den Part des Liebenden übernimmt, ist ein derartiges Ritual wenig wahrscheinlich. Die erzählenden Partien der bereits erwähnten Šulgi- und Iddin-Dagān-Lieder[30] liefern zum Ablauf dieser in der Literatur unter dem Stichwort „Heilige Hochzeit"[31] zusammengefaßten Ereignisse zahlreiche Einzelheiten wie das Schmücken der 'Braut', den Eintritt des Königs in das Brautgemach oder das Beilager.[32] Wichtige Einzelheiten aber bleiben unbekannt und spekulativ. Ungeklärt ist vor allem, wer die Göttin vertrat, wie die Vereinigung stattfand – etwa realiter und vor aller Augen? – und bei welcher Gelegenheit – an jedem Neujahrsfest oder nur an dem auf die Thronbesteigung folgenden? – sowie schließlich, aus welcher Vorstellungswelt das Ganze erwuchs. Bei der Beantwortung dieser Fragen stehen sich Positivisten, die ein öffentlich durchgeführtes Ritual für möglich halten, und Skeptiker gegenüber.[33] Letztere führen u.a. als Argument ins Feld, daß echte Ritualtexte, die den Ritus beschreiben, und Hinweise auf seine Ausführung in zeitnahen Verwaltungstexten fehlen, daß die Hohenprie-

25 Bearbeitet von Sefati 1998.

26 Hierher gehören die Königslieder wie „Šulgi X" (Klein 1981: 124-55), „Šu-Sîn A-C" (Sefati 1998: 344-64 [Nr. 25-7]) oder auf Iddin-Dagān (Übersetzung Römer 1989 (TUAT II/5): 659-73).

27 Alster nennt keine Beispiele. Man könnte auf die ‚anonymen' Lieder Sefati 1998: 132-50 [Nr. 3]. 165-70 [Nr. 5]. 177-184 [Nr. 7] verweisen, auch wenn sie die Unterschrift „balbale-Lied der Inanna" haben.

28 Für weitere Einzelheiten, poetischen Stil, Benutzung des eme.sal genannten Sonderdialekts durch weibliche Sprecher etc. vgl. Sefati 1998: 50-116.

29 Vgl. unten S. 181 zur Hochzeitsfeier für Nabû und Tašmētu.

30 Vgl. Anm. 26.

31 Vgl. zusammenfassend Renger 1975, speziell § 13 zu älteren Vorstellungen zum Ritualablauf.

32 Vgl. die Iddin-Dagān-Hymne (Anm. 26), Z. 185-91.

33 Vgl. zusammenfassend J.S. Cooper in: Matsushima 1993: 81-96.

sterin der Göttin als Partnerin kaum in Frage kommt, da sie wohl eine Tochter des Königs (oder seines Vorgängers) war, und neigen dann dazu, wenigstens einen Teil der Lieder als im königlichen Harem beheimatete Kompositionen zu interpretieren. Wie dem auch sei: Ob man einzelne Lieder als profan oder kultgebunden versteht, so scheint doch, wenn auch oft unausgesprochen, in allen der König die zentrale Gestalt zu sein, auf die sich das Interesse fokussiert. Nur er erhält durch den Liebesgenuß über diesen hinaus weiteren Gewinn: Er darf sich mit vollem Recht „geliebter Gatte der Inanna" nennen,[34] und das Schicksal, das ihm die Götter während des Neujahrsfestes zubestimmen, kann nur positiv sein und ihm eine lange Regierungsdauer und seinem Land Wohlstand und Prosperität verheißen. Königskult, nicht Fruchtbarkeitsritus ist also der Boden, aus dem die Lieder erwachsen sind.

Akkadischsprachige Liebesdichtung stammt zumeist aus der altbabylonischen Zeit und ist, wie eingangs angedeutet, mit nur wenigen Beispielen erhalten. Anders als bei den sumerischen Liedern, von denen oft mehrere Textzeugen erhalten sind, liegt von den akkadischen jeweils nur eine einzige und dann gewöhnlich stark fragmentarisierte Tafel vor.

1. Lied mit Nennung von Rīm-Sîn von Larsa (1758-1699). Kopie bei van Dijk et al. 1985, Nr. 24. Unfertiger und teilweise unverständlicher Entwurfs- oder Schülertext mit 44(?) Zeilen in zwei Kolumnen. Der Text bricht mitten im Wort ab, die Rückseite ist unbeschrieben. Übersetzungen: K. Hecker in: Kaiser et alii 1982-2001 (Bd. II): 747-50, Foster 1993 (Bd. I): 89-99,

2. „Der getreue Liebhaber", Lied mit Nennung Ḫammurapis von Babylon (1728-1686) mit etwa 107(?) erhaltenen Zeilen, publiziert durch von Soden 1950. Neuedition durch Held 1961 und 1962 (Nachträge). Neuere Übersetzungen: K. Hecker (TUAT II) 1989: 743-477, Foster 1993: 92-95, Groneberg 2002: 165-183,

3. Zwei fragmentarische Lieder aus Babylon, publiziert durch Lambert 1966. a) „Nanāja und Muati", nennt Abī-ešuḫ (1647-1620), 38 z.T. beschädigte Zeilen erhalten, Übersetzungen auch von K. Hecker (TUAT II) 1989: 741-743, Foster 1993: 96-97, b) 44 (von ursprünglich 100) Zeilen, keine komplett erhalten, mittelbaylonisch, vom Inhalt her eher ein Klage- als ein Liebeslied,[35]

---

34 Ein vergleichbarer weiblicher Titel (etwa 'Gattin des Dumuzi') fehlt bezeichnenderweise.

35 Vgl. Rückseite 12-19 (angeredet ist eine Dame):

[*i-dam-m*]*a-am ma-áš-ta-ku*	*i-ba-ak-ki ur-šu*
[*ša i*]*-na lib-bi*	*ni-te-ep-pu-šu ši-pir kal-lu-ti*
[*ú*]*-ta-an-na-aḫ ki-sa-al-lu*	*ut-taḫ-ḫa-su a-bu-us-su*
[*ša*] *i-na lib-bi*	*ni-te-ep-pu-šu ši-pir tar-ta-mi*
[*e*]*-ne-nam ki-i ma-li*	*ga-ni-nu ú-ṣi-rù*
[*š*]*a i-na qer-bu-uš-šu*	*ni-it-ta-aš-ša-bu-nim re-ši-iš*
[*x*] *x ba-a-bu*	*qut-tu-ru si-ip-pu-šu*
[*a-šar te-e*]*n-ne-em-di-ma*	*ta-ad-bu-bi it-ti-ja*

4. Fragment eines altbabylonischen Liedes aus Kiš mit 38 großenteils beschädigten Zeilen: Westenholz 1987: 415-25,[36]

5. die mittelbabylonische ‚Ballade': Black 1983 mit 39 Zeilen; das Lied war dem Hymnenkatalog aus Assur (vgl. unter 7.) zufolge Teil einer größeren Serie,[37]

6. ein neuassyrisches Lied zur Hochzeit der Götter Nabû und Tašmētu, Keilschrifttext publiziert von van Dijk 1976, Nr. 54. 12. Tafel einer größeren Sammlung, 53 Zeilen erhalten, wobei aber die zahlreichen refrainartigen Wiederholungen nur durch das Ditto-Zeichen angezeigt sind. Übersetzung bei Livingstone 1989, Nr. 14, ausführliche Analyse durch Nissinnen 1998: 585-634.

7. Wenigstens erwähnt werden muß auch der Hymnenkatalog aus Assur (Ebeling 1919-1923, Nr. 158). Von den etwa 400 ursprünglich in ihm aufgelisteten Liedanfängen sind rund 275 erhalten. Davon sind etwas über 100 sumerisch, der Rest akkadisch. Eines der sumerischen Lieder ist das Inanna-Dumuzi-Lied ba-lam ba-lam-lam, wenn auch in unorthographischer Schreibung,[38] man wird daher vermuten dürfen, daß sich auch unter den akkadischen über die oben unter 5. genannte hinaus Kompositionen finden, die dem Thema „Liebe" gewidmet sind. Tatsächlich finden sich neben typischen Kultliedanfängen[39] auch entsprechende Titel, z.B.:

„Es klagt die Wohnung, weint das Schlafgemach,
worin wir bräutliche Verrichtung pflegten.

Es seufzt der Vorhof, bedrückt sind die Kammern,
in denen wir Liebesgeflüster pflegten.

Wie voll ist an Strafe der Raum, den ich so prachtvoll machte,
worin wir froh beisammensaßen!

[Zerbrochen] ist das Tor, rauchgeschwärzt seine Pfosten,
[wo du] dich anlehntest, (wenn) du mit mir sprachst."

36 Für Kol. I,13' vgl. schon Anm. 9.

37 Der Liedanfang/Titel *erbam-ma rē'û ḫarmi Ištar-ma* „Tritt ein, Hirte, Buhle der Ištar" ist im Hymnenkatalog als Kol. I, 6, die Fangzeile *uršāna rē'â azammur-ma* „Den heldenhaften Hirten besinge ich" ebd. Z. 7' und der im Kolophon genannte Serientitel *mārum-ma rā'im-ni* „Knabe, der uns liebt" in der Serienzusammenfassung Z. 43 und Kol. VIII, 3 aufgeführt. Die Serie umfaßte laut Kol. I, 42 [6] Unterserien mit 31 „Liedern in akkadischen Manier" *zamārū akkadīta*.

38 Siehe schon Anm. 23.

39 Vgl. etwa Kol. I, 20-22:
bu-kur bi-in ^{d}*A-nim lu-uz-mur du-un-na-ka*
lu-uz-mur ^{d}*Ér-ra du-un-na-šu lu-ul-li*
be-e-lu lu-uz-mur za-mar i-lu-ti-ka
„Erstgeborener Sohn Anus, ich will deine Stärke besingen.
Erra will ich besingen, seine Stärke hochpreisen.
Herr, ich will ein Lied deiner Gottheit besingen."

ù re-'-i [a-n]a É *ru-'-a-am*
„Mein Hirte, nun bring mich ins Haus!" (II, 8)[40]

ḫi-i-pa-a-ku a-na da-di-ka
„Ich habe mich herausgeputzt für deine (mask.) Liebe" (VII, 11)

mu-ú-ša ma-a-ru ú-šàm-ša-a-ku (VII, 13)
„Die Nacht werde ich, Knabe, (mit) dir verbringen"

uru*ni-ip-pu-ri-ti la-ḫa-na-tu da-šu-up-tu* (VII, 18)
„Mein Mädchen aus Nippur, süßer *Spatz*".

Insgesamt listet die unter der Bezeichnung *i-ra-a-tu ša ki-it-me* „Brust(lieder) in *kitmu*-Stimmung"[41] zusammengefaßte Rubrik (Kol. VII, 7-24) 17 derartige Liednamen auf und auch in anderen Rubriken lassen sich 'verdächtige' Titel finden.[42]

Die große räumliche und zeitliche Streuung der wenigen Texte läßt eine gleichbleibende Thematik und formale Ausgestaltung von vorneherein wenig wahrscheinlich erscheinen, auch wenn das Festhalten an überkommenen Traditionen wie allgemein im Alten Orient auch in der Liebesdichtung erkennbar ist. Die aus den sumerischen Liedern bekannte Kompositionsweise des Zwiegesprächs mit eingestreutem Chorgesang oder Erzählabschnitt lebt in den akkadischen weiter, und auch die Bindung zum Neujahrsfest ist wenigstens in dem Rīm-Sîn-Text, dem ältesten der fünf akkadischen Lieder, noch deutlich gegeben, fehlt dann aber in den anderen Texten. Auffällige Veränderungen sind dann aber mit der Person der Liebenden verbunden. Rīm-Sîns Partnerin ist offensichtlich keine Göttin, sondern eine Frau aus Larsa, die er aus der Schar ihrer Gefährtinnen auserwählt hat (Z. 8-13):

te-el-qí un-ne-ni-ja li-ib-<ba>-ka li-ip-pa-aš-ra-am
i-na pu-úḫ-ri-im <ša> a-li ù ni-ši ba-aš-tim
šu-mi dam-qá-am ta-az-kur-ma
ki ma-ṣi-ma-an tu-ša-[qá]-an-ni
i-na i-in ta-ap-pa-ti [e-li š]a pa-na e-qì-ir ⌈*da-an*⌉ *-ni-iš*

„Du nahmst meine Bitten an: möge sich dein Herz beruhigen!
in der Versammlung der Stadt und der Leute von Würde
nanntest du mich mit gutem Namen und
ehrtest mein Haupt, o Herr!
Wie sehr doch erhöhtest du mich!
Im Auge der Gefährtinnen wurde ich [mehr als] früher sehr wertvoll."

---

40 In der Zusammenfassung Z. 11 als „Ištar-Lied" bezeichnet.
41 Für *kitmu* als musikalischem Begriff vgl. Kümmel 1970, besonders S. 257f.
42 Das Bruchstück eines weiteren Kataloges (Finkel 1988) gibt die Anfänge von 4 „Brust"-Liedern mit zugehöriger Antiphon, von denen das 3. den Namen des Ammī-ṣaduqa von Babylon nennt, und zweier weiterer, unklassifizierter Lieder.

Der Chor verrät dann in Z. 14-19 den Namen des mit „mein Herr“ Angeredeten:

an-na ni-sa-nu-um ša ni-nu ni-ik-ta-na-ra-bu-šum
a-na a-ma-ri-šu ni-ṣa-me-ru iš-tu ul-la
ú-mi ma-du-tim a-na da-ar ba-la-{du}-ṭam
na-ši me-le-eṣ li-ib-bi-im a-na ^{d}*Ri-im-*^{d}EN.ZU ^{d}UTU^{ši} *-ni*
a-na ša-tim eš-še$_{20}$*-tim ka-ra-nam*
i-qí-a-ši-im ša ta-ṣa-ru-ra im-ni

„Ja, es ist der Frühlingsmonat,[43] in dem wir immer für ihn beten (und)
ihn zu sehen wünschen seit eh
viele Tage lang, (und) auf ewig zu leben!
Er[44] bringt Herzensfreude zu Rīm-Sîn, unserem Sonnengott.
Zum neuen Jahr[45] gießt ihr Wein ein,[46] mit dem ihr zu meiner Rechten
funkelt.“

In den folgenden Zeilen 20-25 bittet die Frau den König um Liebeserfüllung:

al-kam lu-ne-ed-ra-am ki-ma li-ib-bi iq-bi-a-am lu né-pu-uš
ši-ip-ra-am ša mu-ur-ta-mi ka-al mu-ši-im e ni-iṣ-la-al
lu-uḫ-ta-al-ṣa ṣú-ḫi-iš i-na ma-a-a-lim ki-la-al-la-ni
i-ta-ap-la-al e-li in-bi ù da-di ba-la-ṭam et-pi-ir
i-na ṣe-ri-ja ṣú-ru-up la-la-ka
ta-bi-ik-kum ra-mi ta-ap-ḫa-ra-am le-qe ma-la ḫa-aš-ḫa-ti

„Komm, wir wollen einander umarmen! Wie es mein Herz mir befahl, wollen wir tun
das Werk der Liebenden, die ganze Nacht nicht schlafen!
Wir wollen uns beide auf dem Bett *aneinanderpressen*.[47]
Wache[48] über Potenz und Liebreiz, versorge dich mit Leben!
Bring deine Sehnsucht zu mir zum Ausdruck!
Ausgegossen ist dir meine Liebe zur Gänze, nimm davon, soviel du willst!“[49]

---

43 Wörtlich „der Nisan (der 1. Monat des Jahres, entsprechend März/April)“.

44 Der Frühlingsmonat. Foster 1993 verbindet anders.

45 Ergänze auch Z. 1 entsprechend [*a-na eš-še*$_{20}$*-ti*]*m ša-tim a-ri-a-tum it-ba-la ḫi-ib-ši* „[Zum Neu]en Jahr trugen die Schwangeren mein ... fort.“ (*ḫi-ib-ši* bleibt unklar; kaum mit *ḫabāšu* I „anschwellen“, II „zerkleinern“ zu verbinden).

46 *i-qí-a-šim* läßt sich als *iqiaš-šim*/*iqiāšim* (= Imp. Sg. + Ventiv/Pl. zu *naqû* „opfern, ausgießen“), *iqqiaš-šim* (3. Sg. Prt. gleiches Verb) oder *iqīaš-šim* (3. Sg. Prs. *qiāšu* „schenken“), jeweils mit Suffix -*šim*, normalisieren. Für die erste der drei Lösungen spricht, daß *ta-ṣa-ru-ra* ebenfalls 2. Person ist (Sg. + Ventiv/Pl.).

47 *lu-úḫ-ta-al-ṣa* zu *ḫalāṣu* „kämmen, (aus)drücken“? Foster 1993 leitet offenbar von *elēṣu* „jauchzen“ ab.

48 Oder lies *i-ta-ab-la-al* „mische dich“? Schwierigkeiten bereitet dann die Verbindung mit *eli* „über“.

49 Nach Foster 1993 spricht in Z. 25 der König zur Frau. Er begründet dies offenbar damit, daß *ḫa-aš-ḫa-ti* im Babylonischen gewöhnlich feminin ist. Im älteren Altbabylonischen ist die Endung -*āti* aber auch als maskulin belegt, und das Suffix in *ta-bi-ik-kum* kann nur maskulin sein.

Auch wenn der Rest des Textes auf Grund seiner schlechten Erhaltung großenteils unverständlich bleibt,[50] so wird doch deutlich, daß auch Rīm-Sîn menschlich und nicht mehr als gottähnlicher Dumuzi-Vertreter im Ritual der Heiligen Hochzeit gesehen wird:[51] Für ihn wird gebetet, ihm wünscht man, was nur bei Menschen nötig ist, langes Leben, und er genießt die Freuden des Neujahrsfestes statt Teil des Festrituals zu sein. In den Texten Nr. 2 („Der getreue Liebhaber") und 3 („Dialog zwischen Nanāja und Muati") sind die Könige Ḫammurapi und Abī-ešuḫ gar nur dritte oder Nebenfigur und zwar noch wichtige, aber eben doch nicht mehr liebesaktive oder selbst redende Person. Am deutlichsten ist dies in Text Nr. 2, einem Dialog eines wenigstens in den erhaltenen Textteilen anonym bleibenden Liebespaares.[52] Ḫammurapi dient dort zusammen mit Nanāja lediglich als Schwurzeuge des männlichen Partners (Kol. IV, 6'-7'):

at-ma-ki-im ᵈ*Na-na-a ù Ḫa-am-mu-ra-pí* LUGAL
ša ki-na-ti-ja lu a-qá-ab-bi-ki-im

„Ich schwöre[53] dir bei Nanāja und König Ḫammurapi,
(daß) ich dir meine wahren (Gedanken) sage!"

Auch in Text Nr. 3a („Nanāja und Muati"), in dem Abī-ešuḫ mehrfach genannt wird, bleiben wieder zahlreiche wichtige Einzelheiten wegen der schlechten Erhaltung der Tafel unklar. Dies gilt auch für die Frage, wem ein bestimmter Vers in den Mund gelegt und wer angeredet ist. Der Schreiber der Tafel hat aber mehrmals Zeilen durch Absatzlinierungen als Sinneinheit zusammengefaßt. Die von Lambert als „Obverse" bezeichnete Seite[54] beginnt mit einer Anrede an die Nanāja (Z. 1):

... ... *l*]*a-la-ki* ᵈ*Na-na-a ša-ap-ta*⁾*-ki du-uš-*[*šu-pa*
„[*Ich will mich sättigen an*] deiner Schönheit, Nanāja, deine Lippen sind honig[süß]!"

Sprecher ist offenbar Muati; ein Chor oder Sänger kommt wegen *lu-ur-ta-*⌈*a-ma*⌉ „laßt uns einander lieben" (Z. 3) nicht in Frage. Es kann daher auch nur der Gott sein, der für den König Gutes erbittet (Z. 5-6, danach Absatzlinie):

---

50 Aus dem Wechsel maskuliner und femininer Formen läßt sich aber die Vermutung ableiten, daß der Dialog der Liebenden sich weiter fortsetzt.

51 Dies schließt nicht aus, daß sein Name Z.17 mit Gottesdeterminativ geschrieben ist.

52 Der von von Soden 1950 gewählte, ursprüngliche Titel „Ein Zwiegespräch Ḫammurapis mit einer Frau" trifft also nicht das Richtige.

53 Akkadisch Präteritum. Der Eid bei Gott und König ist im babylonischen Rechtsbrauch verwurzelt. Vgl. etwa die in den Wörterbüchern s.v. *nīšu* notierten Belege.

54 Foster 1993: 96-7 vertauscht die Seiten, wohl weil am Schluß der „Reverse" ein Kolophon fehlt, was aber auch sonst häufiger vorkommt. Daß die an die auf der „Obverse" an die Göttin gerichteten Bitten auf der „Reverse" erfüllt worden sind, spricht eher für Lamberts Seitenanordnung.

[. . .] *x* [. . .] *x x x-šu šu-ul-ma a-na da-a-ar li-re um*[!]*-ma-an-šu*
[. . . . . .] ⌈*a-na*⌉ *A-bi-*⌈*e-šu*⌉*-uḫ lu-te-ep-pu-uš*

„[. . . . . .] . . . Heil, auf ewig möge er sein Volk weiden,
[. . . . . .] will ich immer *für* Abī-ešuḫ tun!"

Im darauf folgenden Abschnitt werden sowohl Muati – z.B. in dem Doppelvers Z. 10 (mit strophischer Repetion von Z. 9)

Mu-ù'-a-ti du-uš-šu-pu da-du-ú-ka
di-iš-pa i-še-e[*b-bi ku-zu*]*-ub ra-mi-ka*

„Muati, honigsüß sind deine (mask.) Schamteile,
an Honig wird satt der Scharm deiner Liebe!" —

als auch Nanāja, jetzt mit einer Bitte für den König, angesprochen (Z. 14):

šar-rum lu da-ri i-na qá-bé-e-ki
A-bi-e-šu-uḫ lu d[*a-ri i-na qá-bé-e-ki*]

„Der König sei ewig auf dein (fem.) Wort hin,
Abī-ešuḫ sei ewig auf dein Wort hin!"

Man wird daher die Zeilen 7-14 einem Sänger oder Chor in den Mund zu legen haben. Gleiches gilt auch für die Zeilen 3-7 der „Reverse", die die Segnungen der Nanāja für Babylon und seinen König als eingetroffen schildern:

ta-ap-pa-l [*i-is* K]Á.DINGIR.RA.KI *i-na i-ni-ša dam-*[*qá-tim*]
ta-ak-ru-ub-[*šu t*]*a-aq-ta-bi du-mu-uq-šu*
u_4-mi-ša ba-la-ṭa[*am a-na*] *šar-ri a-ši-bi-šu t*[*a-*. . .] *x x* [. . .]
^{d}*Na-na-a ba-la-ṭ*[*am a-n*]*a šar-ri A-bi-e-š*[*u-uḫ*. . .]
tu-šu-ši-ib i-na šu-pa-at ni-iḫ-ti li-x-[*x x*]*-im-ma*

„Sie blickte mit ihren guten Augen auf Babylon,
segnete es und sagte Gutes für es.
Täglich [schenkte sie] dem König, der darin wohnt, Leben.
Nanāja [schenkte] dem König Abī-ešuḫ Leben
Sie setzte ihn in eine ruhige Wohnstatt, auf daß er [. . .]."

Der Rest der „Reverse" ist wieder ganz schlecht erhalten, scheint im großen und ganzen aber ganz ähnlich gegliedert zu sein: Z. 10-13 und wohl auch 16 spricht der Sänger, Z. 14-15, vielleicht auch Z. 22,[55] Muati. Auch wenn unbekannt bleibt, wieviel der Tafel und damit des Gesamttextes fehlt, drängt sich der Eindruck auf, als sei das zentrale Thema des Liedes nicht die Liebe zweier Götter zueinander, sondern der Wunsch nach Leben und Wohlfahrt für König

55 *ra-am-ki* „deine (fem.) Liebe", Kontext aber zerstört.

und Land. Dabei ist die Liebe der beiden Götter jedoch mehr als bloße Staffage, sie ist vielmehr als die Quelle gnädigen Wohlwollens gegenüber den bittenden Menschen und ermöglicht es diesen, sich in Vertrauen und Hoffnung mit Bitten an die Gottheit zu wenden.

Obwohl im Aufbau den sumerischen und älterakkadischen Liebesliedern vergleichbar – wir haben es wieder mit einem von Drittsprecherpartien durchsetzten Zwiegespräch zu tun – reflektiert das 'Lied' für Nabû und Tašmētu (Nr. 6) ein ganz anderes Gottesverständnis. Die Götter waren ja (einst) Menschen[56] und hatten zahlreiche menschliche Eigenschaften: Sie aßen und tranken, liebten und haßten, heirateten und bekamen Kinder. Hochzeitsfeiern von Göttern wurden im 1. Jtd. bis in die seleukidische und arsakidische Zeit hinein[57] an manchen Orten jährlich begangen, für Marduk und seine Gattin Ṣarpānītu in Babylons Haupttempel Esagila, wo womöglich ein Eifersuchtsdrama ablief, bei dem die Göttin Ištar involviert war,[58] für Anu und Antu in Uruk[59] und eben auch für Nabû und Tašmētu.[60] Die Statuen der beiden Götter wurden bei diesen Festen von Priestern in feierlicher Prozession unter Musik und Gesang in das Brautgemach überführt. Auch andere Götter reisten zu der Zeremonie an.[61] Dem König oblag die Herstellung des Brautbettes, ansonsten war er nur ein – wenn auch herausgehobenes – Mitglied der Kultgemeinde.[62]

Die Liebe von Nabû und Tašmētu spielt in einer idyllischen Umgebung, in einem Garten mit Zedern und Obstbäumen, in denen Vögel zwitschern, und die Schönheit der Göttin wird verglichen mit Gazellen und Edelsteinen. Ganz

---

56 Dies ist ein Quasi-Zitat der Eingangszeile des akkadischen Atram-ḫasīs-Epos: *i-nu-ma i-lu a-wi-lum* „Als die Götter Mensch waren" (Lambert-Millard 1969; neue Übersetzung von Soden (TUAT III) 1994: 612-45).

57 Vgl. Hibbert 1984.

58 Vgl. Lambert 1975 und die Neuinterpretation von Edzard 1987.

59 Hier fand das Fest am *akītu*-Fest im 7. Monat statt. Dies wurde in Uruk zweimal, einmal im Nisan (als Neujahrsfest) und einmal im Tešrīt begangen.

60 Der Ort, wo das Fest gefeiert wurde, ist unbekannt. Nabûs Hauptkultstätte war der Tempel Ezida im babylonischen Borsippa, er hatte aber auch Tempel in Ninive und Kalaḫ. Der assyrische Dialekt des Textes spricht am ehesten für eine dieser beiden Städte.

61 Für Einzelheiten vgl. Matsushima 1988.

62 Das Gemeinschaftsgefühl der Gemeinde kommt sehr schön in den 5 Eingangszeilen des Nabû-Tašmētum-Textes zum Ausdruck:

man-nu ana šá ta-kil-ú lu ta-kil
a-ni-nu a-na ^{d}AG *tak-la-a-ni*
a-na ^{d}*Taš-me-tum šur-bu-ba-a-ni-ma*
ša at-tu-u-ni at-tu-u-ni ^{d}AG EN-*a-ni*
^{d}*Taš-me-tum šad-du-ú ša tuk-la-te-ni* KI.MIN

„Wem er vertraut, mag (jed)er vertrauen,
wir vertrauen auf Nabû!
Der Tašmētu sind wir zugetan!
Was unser ist, ist unser: Nabû ist unser Herr,
Tašmētu ist der Berg unseres Vertrauens."

anders, nämlich äußerst vulgär, ist die Atmosphäre in Babylon, jedenfalls wenn man die Liedanfänge betrachtet, die in dem von Lambert 1975 publizierten Ritual für Marduk und Ṣarpānītu aufgeführt sind.[63] Diese Lieder sind bei den Prozessionen, d.h. mehr oder weniger öffentlich, vorgetragen worden, und auch wenn aus ihnen die eifersüchtige Feindschaft der Ṣarpānītu gegen die Ištar von Babylon sprechen mag,[64] ist die häufige Erwähnung der Schamteile im Kultablauf zwar nicht singulär,[65] wohl aber einigermaßen befremdlich.

Zum Abschluß wäre noch kurz auf die Frage einzugehen, ob denn alle bekannten Liebeslieder kultverbunden sind und gegebenenfalls, welche nicht. Für die sumerischen Inanna-Dumuzi-Lieder war bereits oben die Vermutung geäußert worden, daß es sich teilweise um Lieder des königlichen Harems handele,[66] das hieße, daß wir es mit profanen Gesängen zu tun hätten. Für das Akkadische verneint Reiner (1978: 186) die Existenz von „Liebesdichtung mit menschlichen Liebenden als Akteuren“, und tatsächlich spricht einiges dafür, auch die ‘weltlich’ klingenden Liedanfänge des Hymnenkatalogs (Ebeling 1919-23 Nr. 158) als religiöse Texte zu verstehen, enthält er doch nicht nur typische Götterhymnenanfänge, sondern auch eine große Anzahl von Liedern in sumerischer Sprache, die dem Laien nicht mehr verständlich waren und nur von gelehrten Priester im Tempelritual rezitiert wurden. Dem Katalog lag demnach wohl eine Tafelsammlung einer Tempelbibliothek zugrunde. Am ehesten noch ließe sich „Der getreue Liebhaber“ als profanes Lied verstehen, da in ihm keine liebenden Götter auftreten[67] und Eifersucht bei der liebenden Frau eine Rolle spielt, die man als eine typisch menschliche Erscheinung ansehen möchte, wäre da nicht die ebenfalls eifersüchtige Ṣarpānītu. So lassen sich die „divine love lyrics“ wegen der Menschenähnlichkeit der Götter am besten

---

63 Vgl. etwa l.c. 104 III, 7ff. (teilweise gleichlautend ebd. 122, Z. 4ff.):
ana bi-iṣ-ṣu-ri-ka šá tak-la-a-tú kalba ú-še-reb bāba a-ra-ak-kás
a-na bi-iṣ-ṣu-ri-ka šá tak-la-a-tú kīma abnī-ka aq-ri ina pānī-ka
bi-iṣ-ṣu-ru-ú šá tap-pat-ti-i am-me-ni ki-ki-i te-te-né-pu-uš
bi-iṣ-ṣu-ru-ú šá tap-pat-ti-i pi-rik Bābili[ki] *sin-gu i-saḫ-ḫur*
bi-iṣ-ṣu-ru-ú šá šitta[ta] *ubānāti am-me-ni ṣa-la-a-tú tug-da-nar-ri*
„In deine Vulva, auf die du vertraust, lasse ich einen Hund eintreten und verschließe die Tür,
in deine Vulva, auf die du vertraust wie (auf) ein(en) Edelstein vor dir.
Vulva meiner Freundin, warum tust du immer so?
Vulva meiner Freundin, der Bezirk von Babylon sucht einen Lumpen (zum Abwischen).
Vulva von zwei Fingern, warum suchst du immer wieder Streit?“

64 Vgl. Lambert 1975: 108, Z. 11: *i-na šá-ni-ti-ja a-na* [d]*Ištar* ... „in meiner Feindschaft gegen Ištar.“

65 Vgl. schon Anm. 9 für das Zitat aus von Soden 1991.

66 S. XXX.

67 Der Schwur bei Nanāja und Ḫammurapi (oben S. 173) bleibt ohne Bedeutung.

als ein Spiegelbild jener menschlicher Lust und Leidenschaft verstehen, die uns in so manch einem anderen Keilschrifttext so unverblümt entgegentreten.

Bibliographie

ALSTER, B. (1985): Sumerian Love Songs, RA 79, 127-159.
– (1992): The Manchester Tammuz, ASJ 14, Hiroshima, 1-46.
– (1993): Marriage and Love in Sumerian Love Songs, in: M.E. Cohen/D.C. Snell/D.B. Weisberg (Hgg.), The Tablet and The Scroll. Near Eastern Studies in Honor of William W. Hallo, Bethesda (MD), 15-27.
ASSANTE, J. (2002): Sex Magic and the Liminal Body in the Erotic Art and Texts from the Old Babylonian Period, in: S. Parpola/R.M. Whiting (Hgg.), Sex and Gender in the Ancient Near East. Proceedings of the 47th Rencontre Assyriologique Internationale, Helsinki, July 2-6, 2001, CRRAI 47/II, Helsinki, 27-52.
BIGGS, R.D. (1967): šà.zi.ga. Ancient Mesopotamian Potency Incantations, Texts from Cuneiform Sources II, Locust Valley.
– (2002): The Babylonian Sexual Potency Texts, in: S. Parpola/R.M. Whiting (Hgg.), Sex and Gender in the Ancient Near East. Proceedings of the 47th Rencontre Assyriologique Internationale, Helsinki, July 2-6, 2001, CRRAI 47/II, Helsinki, 71-78.
BLACK, J.A. (1983): Babylonian Ballads: A New Genre, JAOS 103, 26-34.
BORGER, R. (1967-75): Handbuch der Keilschriftliteratur, Berlin.
CLAY, A.T. (1927): Letters and Transactions from Cappadocia, Babylonian Inscriptions in the Collection of James B. Nies, Yale University IV, New Haven/London/Oxford.
CONTENAU, G. (1920): Tablettes cappadociennes, Textes cunéiformes du Louvre IV, Paris (Neudruck 1973).
COOPER, J.S. (1997): Gendered Sexuality in Sumerian Love Poetry, in: I.L. Finkel/M.J. Geller (Hgg.), Sumerian Gods and their Representations, Cuneiform Monographs 7, Groningen, 85-97.
EBELING, E. (1919-23): Keilschrifttexte aus Assur religiösen Inhalts, Wissenschaftliche Veröffentlichung der Deutschen Orient-Gesellschaft 28 und 34, Leipzig.
EDZARD, D.O. (1987): Zur Ritualtafel der sog. 'Love Lyrics', in: F. Rochberg-Halton (Hg.), Language, Literature, and History: Philological and Historical Studies Presented to Erica Reiner, American Oriental Series 67, New Haven, 57-69.
FINKEL, I.L. (1988): A Fragmentary Catalogue of Love Songs, Acta Sumerologica 10, 17-18.
FOSTER, B. (1993): Before the Muses. An Anthology of Akkadian Literature, Bethesda.
GARELLI, P. (1957): Trois tablettes cappadociennes du Musée du Rouen, Revue Assyriologique 51, 1-10.
GELB, I.J. (1970): Sargonic Texts in the Ashmolean Museum Oxford, Materials for the Assyrian Dictionary 5, Chicago.
GEORGE, A.R. (2003): The Babylonian Gilgamesh Epic. Introduction, Critical Edition and Cuneiform Texts, Oxford.
GRONEBERG, B. (2002): „The Faithfull Lover" reconsidered. Towards Establishing a New Genre, in: S. Parpola/R.M. Whiting (Hgg.), Sex and Gender in the Ancient Near East. Proceedings of the 47th Rencontre Assyriologique Internationale, Helsinki, July 2-6, 2001, CRRAI 47/II, Helsinki, 165-183.
HECKER, K./KRYSZAT, G./MATOUŠ, L. (1998): Kappadokische Keilschrifttafeln aus den Sammlungen der Prager Karlsuniversität, Prag.
HELD, M. (1961): A Faithful Lover in an Old Babylonian Dialogue, JCS 15, 1-26.
– (1962): A Faithful Lover in an Old Babylonian Dialogue. Addenda et Corrigenda, JCS 16, 37-39.

HIBBERT, P.H. (1984): Liebeslyrik in der arsakischen Zeit, WdO 15, 93-95.
HRUŠKA, B. (1997): Das Hohelied und die Sumerer, eine negative Zwischenbilanz, in: P. Zemánek (Hg.), Studies in Near Eastern Languages and Literatures. Memorial Volume of Karel Petráček, Prag, 287-295.
JACOBSEN, T. (1975): Religious Drama in Ancient Mesopotamia, in: H. Goedicke/J.J.M. Roberts (Hgg.), Unity and Diversity. Essays in the History, Literature and Religion of the Ancient Near East, Baltimore/London, 65-97.
JAKOB-ROST, L./FREYDANK, H. (1981): Eine altassyrische Votivinschrift, Altorientalische Forschungen 8, 325-326, Pl. I.
KLEIN, J. (1981): Three Šulgi Hymns. Sumerian Royal Hymns glorifying King Šulgi of Ur, Ramat Gan.
KRAMER, S.N. (1969): The Sacred Marriage Rite. Aspects of Faith, Myth and Ritual in Ancient Sumer, Bloomington/London.
KRECHER, J. (1978): Die sumerische Literatur, in: W. Röllig et al. (Hgg.), Altorientalische Literaturen, Neues Handbuch der Literatur, Wiesbaden, 101-150.
KÜMMEL, H.M. (1970): Zur Stimmung der babylonischen Harfe, Or 39, 252-263.
LAMBERT, W.G. (1966): Divine Love Lyrics from the Reign of Abiešuḫ, Mitteilungen des Instituts für Orientforschung 12, Berlin, 41-55.
– (1975): The Problem of the Love Lyrics, in: H. Goedicke/J.J.M. Roberts (Hgg.), Unity and Diversity. Essays in the History, Literature and Religion of the Ancient Near East, Baltimore/London, 98-135.
LAMBERT, W.G./MILLARD, A. (1969): Atra-ḫasīs. The Babylonian Story of the Flood, Oxford.
LARSEN, M.T. (2002): The Aššur-nādā Archive, Old Assyrian Archives I, Publications de L'institut historique archéologique néerlandais de Stamboul 96, Leiden.
LEICK, G. (1994): Sex and Eroticism in Mesopotamian Literature, London/New York.
LIVINGSTONE, A. (1989): Court Poetry and Literary Miscellanea, State Archives of Assyria 3, Helsinki.
– (1997): Love Lyrics of Nabû and Tashmetu, in: W.W. Hallo/K.K. Lawson Jr. (Hgg.), The Context of Scripture. Vol. I. Canonical Compositions from the Biblical World, Leiden, 445-446.
MATSUSHIMA, E. (1987): Le rituel hiérogamique de Nabû, AS 9, 131-175.
– (1988): Les Rituels du marriage divin dans les Documents Accadiennes, AS 10, 95-128.
– (1993): Official Cult and Popular Religion in the Ancient Near East, Heidelberg.
MICHEL, C. (2001): Correspondance des marchands de Kanish au début du IIe millénaire avant J.-C., LAPO 19, Paris.
MÜLLER, G.G.W. (1998): Londoner Nuzi-Texte, SANTAG 4, Wiesbaden.
NISSINEN, M. (1998): Love Lyrics of Nabû and Tašmetu. An Assyrian Song of Songs?, in: M. Dietrich/I. Kottsieper (Hgg.), „Und Moses schrieb dieses Lied auf". Studien zum Alten Testament und zum Alten Orient. Festschrift für Oswald Loretz zur Vollendung seines 70. Lebensjahres, AOAT 250, Münster, 585-634.
OPPENHEIM, A.L. (1977): Ancient Mesopotamia. Portrait of a Dead Civilisation, 2. Aufl. Chicago.
PARPOLA, S./WHITING, R.M. (2002): Sex and Gender in the Ancient Near East. Proceedings of the 47th Rencontre Assyriologique Internationale, Helsinki, July 2-6, 2001, CRRAI 47/II, Helsinki.
PINCHES, T.G. (1964): Old Babylonian Business Documents, Cuneiform Texts from Babylonian Tablets in the British Museum XLV, London.
REINER, E. (1978): Die akkadische Literatur, in: W. Röllig et al. (Hgg.) Altorientalische Literaturen, Neues Handbuch der Literatur, Wiesbaden, 151-210.
REISMAN, D. (1973): Iddin-Dagan's Sacred Marriage Hymn, JCS 25, 185-202.
RENGER, J. (1972-75): Heilige Hochzeit. A. Philologisch, in: RlA IV, 251-259.
RÖMER, W.H.PH. (1982) Einige Überlegungen zur „Heiligen Hochzeit", in: W.C. Delsman et

al. (Hgg.), Von Kanaan bis Kerala, Festschrift für Prof. Mag. Dr.Dr. J.P.M. van der Ploeg O.P., AOAT 211, Kevelaer-Neukirchen-Vluyn, 411-427.

RUBIO, G. (2001): Inanna and Dumuzi: A Sumerian Love Story, JAOS 121, 268-274.

SEFATI, Y. (1998): Love Songs in Sumerian Literature, Bar-Ilan Studies in Near Eastern Languages and Cultures, Publications of The Samuel N. Kramer Institute of Assyriology, Ramat Gan.

VON SODEN, W. (1936): Leistungen und Grenze sumerischer und babylonischer Wissenschaft, Die Welt als Geschichte 2, 411-464, 509-557 [Neudruck Darmstadt 1965].

– (1950): Ein Zwiegespräch Ḫammurabis mit einer Frau, ZA 49, 151-194.

– (1985): Einführung in die Altorientalistik, Orientalistische Einführungen, Darmstadt.

– (1991): Ein spät-altbabylonisches *pārum*-Lied auf Ištar, Or 60, 339-343, Tab. CVI.

WESTENHOLZ, A./WESTENHOLZ, J. (1977): Help for Rejected Suitors. The Old Akkadian Love Incantation MAD V 8, Or 46, 198-219.

WESTENHOLZ, J.G. (1987): A Forgotten Love Song, in: F. Rochberg-Halton (Hg.), Language, Literature, and History: Philological and Historical Studies Presented to Erica Reiner, AOS 67, New Haven, 415-425.

WILCKE, C. (1985): Liebesbeschwörungen aus Isin, ZA 75, 188-209.

Themes of Female Desire and Self-Assertion in the Song of Songs and Hellenistic Poetry

Joan B. Burton

The Song of Songs includes the theme of female self-assertion against the efforts of watchmen and brothers to control a woman's sexuality and access to the public space. Even in this patriarchal context, a woman claims control over her own body and the right to bestow her favors where she chooses; she asserts her own erotic perspective and gaze. In the midst of textual uncertainties regarding speakers, content, verse division, even form, a thematic focal point persists: the positioning of a female as a desiring subject.

Some scholars argue that the Song of Songs as we have it may well date to the Hellenistic period, and even more specifically the third-century BCE.[1] Bloch and Bloch offer several reasons for looking to the Hellenistic Greek world for the Song's composition (1995: 27): 'It is clear that much of the Song is anomalous in the biblical context, and calls for explanation: the concern with the private life as opposed to the public and communal, the frank interest in sexual experience, the idealization of pastoral innocence, the aesthetic appreciation of the human body. All of this would suggest that the Song was composed in a Hellenized atmosphere'. Strong parallels for each of these themes can be cited from third-century Greek literature. Theocritus in particular has been prominent in discussions of a possible third-century date for the Song: scholars have adduced parallels in Theocritus's pastoral imagery

1 Bloch and Bloch 1995: 24-25 ('All these factors taken together – the Aramaic influence, the similarity to Mishnaic Hebrew, the influence of the spoken idiom, the foreign loan-words – suggest that the Song was written down in post-Exilic times, most likely in the Hellenistic period, around the third century BCE'); Fox 1985: 190 ('*This* song is, to judge from its linguistic characteristics, postexilic and probably Hellenistic'); Hengel 1974: 129 ('from about 300 BC one can speak of a certain accumulation of "Solomonic writings": the final recension of Proverbs and the Song of Songs are to be put at about the same time as Koheleth, and at best a few decades earlier'); Blank 1970: xxix ('If Carl Gebhardt . . . is right in comparing the Song with the mimes of Theocritus [*cir.* 275 B.C.], this parallel in Hellenistic literature would also suggest the third century. And this indeed is the tendency among interpreters today'); Ginsberg 1969: 3 ('The language of the Song of Songs shows that in its present form it is late, perhaps as late as the third century B.C.E.').

and themes, as well as the form of his literary mimes.[2] Theocritus's representations of relationships between women and men, particularly in his urban mimes (Idylls 2, 14, and 15), offer other intriguing parallels, not least their positioning of a woman as a self-assertive, desiring subject. This paper focuses on parallels in social and gender themes between the Song and Hellenistic poetry, with special attention to representations of female desire.

A Social and Cultural Context in the Hellenistic World

Alexander's conquests changed the social and political landscape dramatically for the Greeks: the boundaries of the Hellenic world expanded to include Macedonia, Asia, and Egypt. Royal dynasties were established on a scale not seen before in the Hellenic world, and together with them massive governmental bureaucracies. Wealth and power shifted outward from the old mainland Hellenic world to massive new city centers such as Alexandria and Antioch. With Greek as the language of administration and Greeks comprising the ruling class in these new centers, the prospect of privilege attracted many Greeks to move away from home and family to seek advantage abroad. Mobility was not a new phenomenon for Greeks, but it was an important factor in the Hellenistic world and actively encouraged by its rulers. Elite Greek men could assert themselves in new communities through such ubiquitous Greek institutions as gymnasia and symposia, at which it had long been customary for elite males to gather and mingle.[3] Greek women had to find other ways to establish themselves in new environments and adjust to altered circumstances.

Under traditional Greek law codes, women needed male guardians (typically fathers, husbands, sons, or other male kin) to transact legal business[4] – easy enough when the family lives mostly in the same town or city-state. When relocated far from family, however, women often needed to find new sources of legal protection. Egypt offered a relatively egalitarian model of legal relations between males and females.[5] Since the Dynastic

---

2 See Graetz 1871: 68-73; Gebhardt 1931: 17-21; Bloch and Bloch 1995: 25-27.

3 On the role of the gymnasium in maintaining cultural values and establishing social communities in the Hellenistic world, see Marrou 1950: 148-64; Giovannini 1993: 270-73. For a historical overview of Greek symposia, with attention to the Hellenistic period, see Burton 1992: 228-35, 243-44 (with references).

4 See Schaps 1979: 48-60; Sealey 1990: 154-55.

5 For a Greek historian's first-century BCE vantage on power relations between males and females in Egypt, see Diod. Sic. 1.27.1-2: 'In sum, she [Isis] was responsible for the most and greatest benefactions to all mankind. This, they say, is the reason that it was handed down that the queen should receive greater power and respect than the king and that, among private individuals, the woman should be master of the man, and in the dowry-

period, Egyptian women had been able to own, sell, and manage property without the help of male guardians; they had been able to represent themselves in court and enter into marriage agreements.[6] Such legal independence would have offered benefits for Greek women in a world of ready mobility. Indeed, under Egyptian influence Greeks began to write their own marriage contracts, and papyri show Greek women even permitted to transact marriages for themselves or their daughters.[7] Further, elite Greek women in Hellenistic Egypt and elsewhere were gaining public visibility as money-lenders, benefactors of public works, patrons of building projects, and so forth.[8] Thus, during the Hellenistic period, and particularly in Egypt, traditional legal and social restrictions on Greek women were relaxing.[9]

Yet while Greek women were gaining in visibility and independence in an expanded Hellenistic world, Greek men had lost some traditional avenues for male self-definition. For example, the civic ideal of a citizen-soldier fighting for an autonomous city-state was no longer a Greek reality; instead, huge autocratic hegemonies dominated the political landscape, and mercenary soldiers fought the wars.[10] Changes in social conditions and political institutions were challenging traditional assumptions about gender roles. There was also an intensified interest in exploring female sexuality in art, as reflected in the large number of Hellenistic statues of naked Aphrodites after the model of Praxiteles' famous Aphrodite of Knidos.[11]

Greek establishment of important new political and commercial centers and the expansion of existing eastern Mediterranean communities also attracted non-Greek settlers, including Jews.[12] In Ptolemaic Alexandria, a primary center of Hellenistic culture, Jews were present early on and participated significantly in the cultural and economic activities of the city as well as the surrounding *chora*.[13] Further, in Ptolemaic-controlled Palestine, Greek cities were established, and Jews and Greeks interacted with one another in these cities as well.[14] Thus there was an intensification of contact

---

contract husbands should agree to obey the wife in all matters' (translation in Rowlandson 1998: 50-51). On how interactions with other societies, and particularly Egypt, helped loosen constraints on Hellenistic Greek women, see, e.g., Ahmed 1992: 29-33; cf. Rowlandson 1995: see esp. 301-302; for documentation from Greek and Roman Egypt, see Rowlandson 1998: e.g., 167-69.

6 See, e.g., Robins 1993: 136-37; Tyldesley 1994: 37, 40-44.

7 See Pomeroy 1984: 90 (on marriage contracts: 83-98); Rowlandson 1998: 168-69.

8 For evidence of economic activities of Hellenistic women, see Rowlandson 1998: 218-30, 245-51; on women as principal legatees, see Pomeroy 1997: 223-24.

9 See further Burton 1998b: 149-50, 156-57 (with references).

10 See, e.g., Baker 2003: 378-79.

11 See Smith 1991: 79-83.

12 On this Jewish diaspora, see Gruen 2002b: 77-78.

13 See Barclay 1996: esp. 20-30, 103-4; Gruen 2002a: 68-71, 83.

14 See Tcherikover 1961: 90-116; Hengel 1974: e.g., 1:14-17, 22-23, 56-57.

between Jews and Greeks from the early Hellenistic period.[15] Indeed, some Jews became so deeply engaged with Greek culture and language as to require a Greek version of Hebrew scriptures (which became known as the Septuagint).[16]

During the third century, Alexandria, with its strong state support for the arts and literature, attracted such stylish Greek poets as Callimachus, Theocritus, and Apollonius of Rhodes. Educated Jews also drawn to the luminous cultural world of Alexandria would have doubtless been impressed with the striking literary experimentation characteristic of the leading contemporary Greek authors. Indeed Gruen has recently stressed ways in which Jewish writings of the Hellenistic period show active, self-assertive engagement with the Greek language and its literature: 'the capacity to compose such works demonstrates that their composers had access to higher education and to the Hellenic cultural traditions available in Ptolemaic Alexandria'.[17] Recent scholars have also argued that Greek literature associated with the court at Alexandria resonates with Egyptian motifs, as did the practices at court – for example, the Ptolemies' adoption of full brother-sister marriage (reminiscent of the pharaohs).[18] Egypt also had a Ramesside tradition of expressions of male and female desire in love songs and poetry,[19] which, as Tyldesley points out, '[made] it quite clear that a woman can desire a man just as a man desires a woman' (Tyldesley 1994: 36). Indeed, the multi-cultural context of a Hellenistic kingdom centered in Egypt and extending to Palestine would have offered Jewish writers a multiplicity of literary traditions – including not only Greek poetry but also Egyptian love songs – as possible background for the Song.

15 On Jewish access to Greek education, including the gymnasium, see Hengel 1974: 1:68-77; Gruen 2002a: 123-26. On Jews resorting to Greek laws and Greek courts, see Tcherikover 1957: 33-36 (with documentation).

16 On the likely origin of the Septuagint in Hellenistic Alexandria, see Fraser 1972, 1:689-90; see also Gruen 2002b: 78-79.

17 Gruen 2002a: 69; cf. Gruen 1997; 1998; on Alexandria's attractions cf. Barclay 1996: 30.

18 On the 'double face' (Greek and Egyptian) of Ptolemaic kingship, with attention also to brother-sister marriage, see Koenen 1983, 1993. For a book-length treatment of Egyptian influence on Alexandrian Greek literature, see Stephens 2003.

19 For English translations, with commentary, see Fox 1985: 3-81.

Assertion of Female Desire in the Song

Here is a brief summary of themes and motifs of the Song, with attention to themes of female desire and self-assertion.[20] The Song is presented in the voices of the internal characters: there is no intervention by an external narrator. Female voices dominate, taking up nearly three-fifths of the verses. A young woman speaks aloud her desire, expresses her sexuality, and claims the right to love whom she pleases.[21] She describes her beloved at length; he is the object of her gaze (e.g., 5:10-16), as she is of his (e.g., 4:1-5). In the context of a patriarchal world, the Song's close matching of male and female expressions of desire, as well as the repeated exchange of erotic invitations, suggests reciprocity, a balance of erotic feeling and power.[22] In this patriarchal society, a woman says no to male control: her brothers made her 'keeper of the vineyards', but she did not keep her own vineyard (1:6). A woman claims her right to pursue her desire despite male dominance and control (represented variously in the Song by brothers, watchmen, King Solomon and his soldiers). When seeking her beloved through city streets, she encounters watchmen and proceeds to question them (3:2-3). Later, watchmen strike a woman searching for her beloved, and strip her of her mantle (5:6-7).[23] A women's community seems to balance the censorious presence of brothers and watchmen in the Song, as repeated appeals to the daughters of Jerusalem suggest. With this as a backdrop, let us consider parallel themes of female self-assertion and desire in Hellenistic poetry.

Female Desire and Self-Assertion in Theocritus

Idylls 2 and 15, two of Theocritus's urban mimes, are of special interest in relation to the Song. They both directly represent women's voices, again without the intervention of a narrator, and include the theme of female self-assertion on city streets in a context of male privilege and dominance.

Idyll 2 represents a young woman's private world of desire; the entire poem is presented through Simaetha's voice. With the help of a female servant,

20 For the Song of Songs, I consulted a number of texts, translations, and commentaries, including Rahlfs 1935, Ginsberg 1974, Pope 1977, Fox 1985, Keel 1986, Murphy 1990, Bloch and Bloch 1995. All the Scripture quotations are from the New Revised Standard Version Bible.

21 E.g., Cant 1:2-3; 2:3; 4:16; 5:4-6.

22 For example, see the matching descriptions of a man and a woman at Cant 1:15; 4:1; 5:12 (eyes like doves); and at 1:3.12-13; 4:14; 5:1 (fragrant with spices, perfumes).

23 Whether the street episodes are dream visions or reality (see, e.g., Pope 1977: 415, 418), they show desire empowering a woman to take bold action.

Simaetha performs magic rituals to bring back her lover Delphis, who has evidently abandoned her (1-63); then Simaetha, alone, tells the Moon the story of her love affair (64-166). In making the woman the passionate, desiring subject, and the man the desired object, Theocritus reverses a normative gender pattern for representations of heteroerotic desire among Greeks. Idyll 2 also explores how a young woman constructs identities for herself when left to her own devices in a patriarchal world. While Simaetha's world is full of female friends who invite her to festivals, loan her clothing to wear, and gossip, parents or other protectors are conspicuously absent. During the early Hellenistic period, with rulers attracting Greeks away from their homes to new cities and settlements (e.g., for social or economic advancement), the situation of a Greek woman left without male protection must have been not unfamiliar.[24]

One day, on her way with a female friend to a festival of the goddess Artemis, Simaetha sees Delphis fresh from a wrestling-school, and the sight of his golden beard and glistening breast transfixes her, changes her. Like the woman in the Song of Songs (5:8), Simaetha too becomes lovesick with yearning for her beloved (Id. 2.85). Eros drains all the dark blood from her body (55-56); she goes mad; her looks fade (82-83). Simaetha's descriptions of the physical effects of her passion (82-90, 106-10) recall a tradition stemming from Sappho fr. 31 of representations of symptoms of female desire.[25] That Sapphic language becomes also part of the language of male desire.[26] Theocritus stresses the feminine quality of Simaetha's desire by having her use distinctly feminine imagery: she describes her muteness as an inability to make even the whimpering sound of babes calling for their mothers in their sleep; she likens the stiffness of her body to that of a wax doll (Id. 2.108-10). Yet Simaetha also constructs a masculine self from her desire. Feeling pain and loss, she adopts masculine manners and agency to attain her aim. A woman (in the absence of a male guardian), having fallen in love with an elite outlander Greek, finds her own way to satisfy her desire. In other literary contexts, parents might have made inquiries of oracles (as in Callimachus's *Akontios and Kydippe* or the novel of Xenophon of Ephesus); a nurse might have approached the languishing woman (as in Euripides' *Hippolytus*). In Idyll 2, after ten days and nights in bed, Simaetha arises and finds herself a cure for her

---

24 On 'migrant widows without kinsmen' as 'a new feature of the Hellenistic period', see Pomeroy 1997: 205-6. Cf. Herodas *Mime* 1, in which a Greek man's departure for Ptolemaic Egypt five months earlier has left his woman vulnerable to bawds.

25 Cf. the lovesickness of Euripides' Phaedra (*Hipp.* 131-34).

26 For male and female versions of love fever: Theoc. Idd. 2.85-86 (female), 30.1-2 (male). For male and female versions of love reducing one to skin and bones: Theoc. Id. 2.89-90 (female); Callim. Ep. 30.3 Pf = *Anth. Pal.* 12.71.3 (male); cf. Theoc. Id. 14.3 (male). See also Catull. 51 (male).

desire. With no family or guardian to protect or help her, she empowers herself by recognizing and speaking her desire for Delphis.

The poem also suggests equivalencies between male and female desire by using traditionally homoerotic language and motifs to represent Simaetha's desire. Simaetha falls in love at her first sight of Delphis, with his muscles glistening after exercising at the wrestling-school; yet traditionally Greek men were attracted to handsome boys with well-oiled muscles glistening from wrestling.[27] Similarly to the female voices of the Song of Songs, Simaetha claims for herself, in her narration of her story, the motifs of the erotic gaze and love at first sight.

Both in the Song and in Idyll 2, a woman claims her right to the public streets, and it is her erotic desire that moves her to do so. In the Song, a woman twice enters public streets to search for her beloved (Cant 3:2-3; 5:6-7). In Idyll 2, while seeking a cure for her love, Simaetha took to the streets to visit the houses of workers of magic (90-91). Also, whether from autopsy or hearsay, she knew Delphis frequented Timagetus's wrestling-school (96-98). In fact, Idyll 2 begins with Simaetha's assertion of her right to walk the streets, approach an exclusively male institution (the wrestling-school), and there proclaim her desire, for she declares she will go to the wrestling-school the next day to reproach Delphis (8-9). As in the Song, Simaetha's desire has moved her to defiance of traditional norms of feminine behavior (whereby a woman might send a servant to summon a lover but not go herself, Id. 2.96-98). Then, after inviting Delphis (through a servant girl) to her house, Simaetha draws him down onto her bed. In both the Song and Idyll 2, a woman usurps the masculine role by issuing the invitation and initiating the lovemaking (Id. 2.100-101, 138-43; Cant 4:16; 7:13). In Idyll 2, Delphis's suggestion that Simaetha barely anticipated his own advances to her (114-16) underscores the gender inversion in Simaetha's behavior (her unconventional boldness in courtship).

Just as there is gender ambiguity in Simaetha's self-representations and actions, so too in Delphis's. Delphis assesses his own attractiveness within a homoerotic frame, as shown by his self-description to Simaetha (Id. 2.124-25):

καί κ', εἰ μέν μ' ἐδέχεσθε, τάδ' ἧς φίλα (καὶ γὰρ ἐλαφρός
καὶ καλὸς πάντεσσι μετ' ἠιθέοισι καλεῦμαι)

'And if you had received me, that would have been pleasing (for I'm considered agile and fair among all the young men)'.[28]

---

27 See, e.g., Plat. *Symp.* 217c, *Chrm.* 154a-c; Ar. *Pax* 762-63, *Av.* 139-42 (for discussion see Dover 1978: 54-56).

28 Theocritus's text is cited from Gow 1952, vol. 1; all translations of Theoc. Idd. 2, 14, and 15 are taken from Burton 1995: 161-72.

There is a contiguity of male and female desire in this poem. By having Delphis describe the boy he beat in a close race as 'graceful' (115, τὸν χαρίεντα ... Φιλῖνον), the poet reinforces Delphis's own gender and sexual ambiguity.[29] Twice Simaetha expresses uncertainty whether Delphis's new beloved is male or female (44, 150). By having Delphis claim to have intended to perform the customary active role of masculine courtship at the beloved's door (118-28), the poet highlights by contrast the actual passivity of Delphis's initial involvement with Simaetha. Complicating this picture is the fact that Simaetha herself is the one re-presenting the male's speech to her (his expressions of desire for her). Simaetha's narrative emphasizes her appropriation of the masculine role in her courtship of Delphis. This appropriation continues after Delphis deserts her, in her self-assertive use of magic to bring him back under her power.[30] Another parallel between the Song and Idyll 2 is that both include the motif of a woman re-presenting a male's speech of courtship to her (Id. 2.114-38; Cant 2:10-14; 5:2).[31]

Theocritus Idyll 15, set in the city of Alexandria, also highlights themes of female self-assertion and the right to a female erotic gaze. In the course of the poem, two Syracusan women, Praxinoa and Gorgo, with their maids, walk through the streets of Alexandria to the Ptolemaic palace to attend an Adonis festival sponsored by Queen Arsinoe in honor of her mother. The poem is presented entirely through direct speech: the women exchange words with one another and with people they encounter, and at the palace a female hymnist performs an Adonis hymn. As in the Song, in Idyll 15 women claim their right to be on the streets despite a heavy patriarchal presence, represented in this poem by men in cloaks and heavy shoes (6), other males (52-54, 70-75, 87-88), and the king's horses (52). In both the Song and Idyll 15, the vulnerability of a woman on the streets is represented by a piece of clothing being torn or taken: at Cant 5:7, watchmen tear a mantle from a woman; at Idyll 15.69-70, Praxinoa has her shawl torn in half. In both the Song and Idyll 15, women talk back to male figures who confront them (in Cant 3:3, a woman addresses watchmen she encounters on the streets; in Id. 15.89-95, Praxinoa confronts a male bystander).

29 Nine of the eleven more instances of the adjective χαρίεις (charming) in Theocritus's idylls modify an object of desire: a female beloved at 3.6, 45; 4.38; 10.26, 36; 11.30; 14.8; a male beloved at 12.20, 13.7; not a beloved at 15.79, 18.38 (cf. *Ep.* 4.13).

30 On how 'in her magic rites Simaetha appropriates symbols of Delphis's patriarchal world and uses them against him', see Burton 1995: 65-67 (quotation from 65). On 'Simaetha's apparent appropriation of traditionally male forms of erotic magic', see Faraone 2002: 408.

31 On Simaetha's embedding of Delphis's speech in Idyll 2, see Andrews 1996 (with attention to Homeric allusion).

As in the Song, Idyll 15's women claim the right to admire youthful male beauty and articulate that admiration publicly and unhindered. When the women arrive at the Ptolemaic palace, they praise works of art on display, including an Adonis-figure reclining on a couch. The language in which Praxinoa expresses admiration for this figure coincides with the language of homoerotic desire (Id. 15.84-86):

αὐτὸς δ' ὡς θαητὸς ἐπ' ἀργυρέας κατάκειται
κλισμῶ, πρᾶτον ἴουλον ἀπὸ κροτάφων καταβάλλων,
ὁ τριφίλητος Ἄδωνις, ὁ κἠν Ἀχέροντι φιληθείς.

'Adonis himself, how marvelous he is, reclining on a silver couch, with the first youthful down spreading from his temples, thrice-loved Adonis, loved even in Acheron'.

Thus her eroticized gaze may seem to place her in the position of an *erastes* (older male lover) regarding an *eromenos* (beloved boy).[32] When a male bystander tries to silence the women (Id. 15.87-88), Praxinoa vehemently claims their right to speech in the public space (94-95): μὴ φύη, Μελιτῶδες, ὃς ἁμῶν καρτερὸς εἴη, | πλὰν ἑνός ('Let there be no master over us, honey-goddess, | except one'). Whoever the one master is meant to be, Praxinoa's statement denies normative rules of male dominance: she denies an anonymous male stranger's right to exert power and control over Gorgo and herself.

Idylls 2 and 15 both show women reconstructing their gendered identities through talking with others and expressing their desires aloud. Both poems also include the theme of female desire accompanied by separation and loss, as does the Song of Songs. In Idyll 2 Simaetha finds, desires, and loses her beloved; the poem leaves her intending to seek him the next day at the wrestling-school. In Idyll 15, the endless cycle of desire is institutionalized in the Adonia, an annual festival commemorating desire, return, and separation: Aphrodite recovers and loses the youthful Adonis yearly, as do the women who attend the Adonis-festival. Desire brings these women onto the public streets; they claim their right to the streets, to a space filled with patriarchal institutions and control. In the Song too are passages of a woman repeatedly losing her beloved and searching for him through public streets controlled by watchmen (Cant 3:1-4; 5:6-7). The lover's flight, his loss, is symbolized in a gazelle's flight, a stag's running on the mountains, with the return also implied therein (Cant 2:17; 8:14).

32 On the high value set on the beloved's 'youthfulness' (and 'youthful down') in homoerotic relations, see Halperin 1990: 90; also Headlam and Knox 1922: 38 n. 52. On correspondences between male and female desire in Hellenistic poetry, see Burton 1995: 83-92. Cf. Reed 1995: 342-45, on the sexual ambiguity of late fifth-century vase-paintings of Adonis.

Heightened attention to the possibility of symmetry between male and female desire is another aspect of Hellenistic poetry with parallels in the Song of Songs. Throughout the Song, male and female voices echo each other's descriptions of the beloved. Theocritus too highlights symmetries between male and female desire, for example through role reversals, as in Idyll 6, where the sea nymph Galateia is represented playing the excluded lover, a reversal of her role in Idyll 11, where the cyclops Polyphemus is in the position of excluded lover. In Idyll 15, Aphrodite and Adonis's embrace is described reciprocally (128): τὸν μὲν Κύπρις ἔχει, τὰν δ' ὁ ῥοδόπαχυς Ἄδωνις ('Cypris embraces him; the rosy-armed Adonis holds her').[33] So also in Idyll 2 Theocritus shows Simaetha's expressions of desire borrowing language and imagery not only from Sappho's realm of female desire but also from the male world of the symposium and the gymnasium.[34] Such borrowings may naturally reflect the poet's ready familiarity and interest in the sympotic world of males desiring one another, but they also suggest an interest in female erotic desires, and a corresponding attempt to discover a language adequate for expressing those desires.

Other Theocritean poems focus on the effects on males when females act according to their own desires. Like Idylls 2 and 15, Idyll 14 includes the theme of a woman asserting her right to act on her own desire, choose her own lover, govern her own speech and movement. The poem is presented entirely through the male voices of Aeschinas and a friend. The poem centers on the theme of loss and desire: Cynisca, Aeschinas's former girlfriend, left his symposium and his life about two months earlier, after making it clear that she was in love with another, and Aeschinas has been suffering from feelings of pain and loss ever since. At the symposium, when toasts of love were being made, Cynisca refused to speak (she was now in love with another); when Aeschinas struck her with his fist in anger, she left the party. She refused to be intimidated and controlled; she claimed her freedom to direct her desire where she wished. Similarly in the Song a woman repeatedly defies males (e.g., brothers, watchmen) who try to control her sexuality, her freedom to bestow her love where she chooses. Idyll 14 highlights how Cynisca's demonstration of amatory independence and self-empowerment unsettles Aeschinas's sense of gendered self-identity. Thus, for example, in a radical inversion of gendered imagery, Aeschinas redescribes Cynisca as a bull running through the woods (Id. 14.43) and himself as a mouse caught in pitch (51). As the poem begins, Aeschinas's friend describes him as thin, shaggy, and dirty (3-4). Like Idyll 2, Idyll 14 focuses on how *eros* can isolate individuals from the normative society

---

33 Cf. the reciprocity asserted by a female voice at Cant 2:16: 'My beloved is mine and I am his'; 6:3: 'I am my beloved's and my beloved is mine'; cf. 7:10.

34 See Burton 1995: esp. 43-46, 64-69, 83-84.

and how through talk, males and females can strive to remake their gendered selves: Idyll 14's Aeschinas resolves to leave home and become a mercenary soldier; his friend suggests seeking employment with Ptolemy in Egypt.[35]

King Ptolemy's presence in Theocritus Idylls 14 and 15 offers a parallel to King Solomon's presence in the Song of Songs.[36] In the Song, Solomon's wealth and power serve as foils for values outside the hegemonic elite: for example, Solomon's vineyard tended by many keepers contrasts with a vineyard that has a single keeper (8:11-12); a multiplicity of queens, concubines, and maidens contrasts with a single beloved (6:8-9). The Song thus evokes Solomon's legendary prowess as a lover,[37] with stress also given to the luxuriant (amatory) setting at his disposal (3:7-11). In Theocritus Idyll 15, from the vantage of immigrant women, one of Ptolemy's great accomplishments was to make the streets safe from evildoers (46-50); yet as they walk through the streets, the king's horses threaten the women (51-54). Similarly in the Song, intimidating authority figures (watchmen) threaten women on the streets. Further, in Idyll 15, Ptolemy's wealth contrasts with the women's spend-thrift husbands: the Adonis-festival is held in rich King Ptolemy's palace (22), which features a luxurious lover's bower constructed for Adonis and Aphrodite, with couch and purple coverlets (119-27). Theocritus's poems also highlight Ptolemy's prowess as a lover. Idyll 17, for example, an encomium of Ptolemy, stresses passionate love as characteristic of Ptolemy and his wife Arsinoe (128-30), as well as their parents (38-40).[38] In Idyll 14, Aeschinas's friend praises Ptolemy as *erotikos*, "amorous" (61-62); Ptolemy's discernment in love contrasts with Aeschinas's initial failure to realize that his beloved no longer loved him. Ptolemy, like Solomon, was also famous for his numerous mistresses[39] and for the scores of warriors surrounding him (Id. 17.93-94):

πολλοὶ δ' ἱππῆες, πολλοὶ δέ μιν ἀσπιδιῶται
χαλκῷ μαρμαίροντι σεσαγμένοι ἀμφαγέρονται

35 On Theocritus's urban mimes (Idd. 2, 14, 15) in relation to issues of gender and mobility in the Hellenistic world, see further Burton 1995.

36 On 'the emphasis on Solomon in the Hellenistic period' see Hengel 1974, 1:129-30: 'the riches and the wisdom of Solomon form a pendant to the splendour of the Ptolemaic kings . . . Solomon was, so to speak, their Jewish counterpart' (quotation from p. 130).

37 See 1Reg11:1-3.

38 For the suggestion that literary themes of erotic reciprocity in marriage may reflect a Ptolemaic policy to validate 'the sharing of monarchic power by husband and wife, a condition of royalty customary for the native Egyptians but radically new to the Greeks', see Gutzwiller 1992: esp. 363-69 (quotation from p. 364).

39 On Ptolemy's mistresses, see *FGrH* 234 F4 (=Ath. 13.576e-f); Polyb. 14.11; Ath. 10.425e-f, 13.576f; Plut. *Mor.* 753e; see also Pomeroy 1984: 53-55.

'Round about him gather huge numbers of horsemen and huge numbers of shield-bearing soldiers, burdened with glittering bronze'.[40]

Similarly the Song of Songs highlights the large number of warriors surrounding Solomon's couch (3:7-8): 'Around it are sixty mighty men of the mighty men of Israel, all equipped with swords and expert in war'.

Another parallel is the attention paid to mothers both in the Song and in Theocritean poetry. Although the Song includes brothers, watchmen, a male beloved, Solomon, and warriors surrounding Solomon, fathers are absent – mothers are featured instead. When a woman finds her beloved in the city, she brings him to her mother's house: 'I held him, and would not let him go until I brought him into my mother's house, and into the chamber of her that conceived me' (3:4; cf. 8:1-2). When a woman is described as uniquely deserving of love, she is 'the darling of her mother, flawless to her that bore her' (6:9). A woman identifies the apple tree beneath which she seduced her beloved as the place where 'your mother was in labor with you; there she who bore you was in labor' (8:5).[41] In Theocritus's poetry, the prominence of mothers (and not fathers) in amatory contexts is similarly noteworthy. For example, in Idyll 11, Polyphemus fell in love with his beloved Galateia when she first went flower-gathering with his mother (25-29); later in the poem he blames his mother for not furthering his cause with Galateia, and when suffering physical symptoms from love, he wishes that his mother might suffer the same (67-71). Idyll 10 ends with Milon's recommendation to the lovelorn Bucaeus to tell of his love to his mother when she rises in the morning (57-58). Idyll 12's narrator reports that the winner of a boys' kissing contest would return, garlanded, to his mother (32-33). Also, repeatedly in Theocritus's poems, males and females are identified by their mothers' names.[42] Further, in Idyll 24, Herakles' mother, not his father, arranges his training in the 'manly arts'.[43]

In the context of Ptolemaic Egypt, the Song's repeated amatory references to the beloved female as sister would not seem out-of-place (4:9: 'You have ravished my heart, my sister, my bride'; 4:10: 'How sweet is your love, my sister, my bride!'; 4:12: 'A garden locked is my sister, my bride'; and esp. 5:1: 'I come to my garden, my sister, my bride; I gather my myrrh with my spice, I eat my honeycomb with my honey, I drink my wine with my milk'). Although

---

40 All translations of Theoc. Id. 17 are taken from Hunter 2003.

41 On the emphasis on mothers in the Song, cf. Bloch and Bloch 1995: 5-6.

42 Females at Theoc. Idd. 17.36, 61; 15.97, 110-11, 106; males at 13.20, 15.139; cf. 17.53-57.

43 Cf. Gow 1952, 2:435: 'we might have expected the choice of instructors in these manly arts to rest with his father'.

in the Song a woman does not call her beloved her brother, a woman does express a specific wish that her beloved were like a brother (8:1-2):

> O that you were like a brother to me,
> who nursed at my mother's breast!
> If I met you outside, I would kiss you,
> and no one would despise me.
> I would lead you and bring you
> into the house of my mother,
> and into the chamber of the one who bore me.
> I would give you spiced wine to drink,
> the juice of my pomegranates.

Egypt had a tradition of erotic addresses to siblings and the usage need not be related to sibling marriage;[44] yet Egypt also had a long pharaonic tradition of brother-sister marriage as well as a strong mythic tradition of reciprocal love between Isis and Osiris, full brother and sister. The Greeks too had a mythic tradition of marriage between full brother and sister (Zeus and Hera). In the early-third-century BCE, the marriage of Ptolemy II to his full sister Arsinoe II brought this tradition (with its parallels in pharaonic practice and mythology) into the Greek political landscape as well.[45] Emphasis is placed in Hellenistic poetry on this brother-sister marriage at the heart of the Ptolemaic state, e.g., Theocritus Idyll 17.128-30:

> αὐτός τ' ἰφθίμα τ' ἄλοχος, τᾶς οὔτις ἀρείων
> νυμφίον ἐν μεγάροισι γυνὰ περιβάλλετ' ἀγοστῷ,
> ἐκ θυμοῦ στέργοισα κασίγνητόν τε πόσιν τε

> 'both he [Ptolemy II] and his noble partner [Arsinoe II], than whom no better wife embraces her young husband in the halls, loving with all her heart her brother and her husband'

Arsinoe in fact received the title of Philadelphus, 'brother-loving'.[46] Thus the eroticized language of brother-sister love in the Song could have naturally arisen in the context of Ptolemaic Egypt.

---

44 In Egyptian love songs, the lover and beloved are addressed as brother and sister. See Fox 1985: 8 n.l: 'The usage does not derive from the supposed custom of sibling marriage'.

45 For discussion see, e.g., Griffiths 1979: 77; Koenen 1983: esp. 157-60; Stephens 2003: 168; Hunter 2003: 192-93. See also Diod. Sic. 1.27.

46 For discussion see Fraser 1972, 1:217.

Female Desire and Self-Assertion in Other Hellenistic Literature

Key examples of themes of female desire and self-assertion in other Hellenistic literature help fill out a picture of a welcoming cultural context for such themes in the Song of Songs. In Hellenistic poetry, fictive women repeatedly express their right to their own critical standards, their own desire. Thus in Herodas Mime 4, two women assert their right to feel desire when they gaze at a painting and to express that desire regardless of the function or overall subject of the painting. When they see in Asclepius's temple a painting evidently of a sacrifice scene, one of the women fixates on the figure of a naked boy, observing that 'the flesh seems to pulse warmly as it lies on him in the picture' (πρὸς γάρ οἱ κεῖνται | αἱ σάρκες οἷα †θερμα† πηδῶσαι | ἐν τῆι σανίσκηι, 60-62).[47] Regardless of the obvious humor in this representation of women responding to art, still the poem shows women asserting their right to express their desire out loud in public situations. Specifically, they are asserting their right to interpret the art in terms of their own desires rather than as serving a specific function in a temple.[48] So too in Theocritus Idyll 15, when the Syracusan women gaze upon a work of art, they express out loud their admiration of the Adonis figure's youthful eroticism (84-86); they do this in a public venue, in the presence of men, and they refuse to let a man silence their speech (87-95).[49] Similarly in the Song, despite male attempts to control and limit female choice and self-expression (e.g., 1:6; 5:7; 8:8-9), female voices claim the right to speak and act on female desire. Herodas Mime 6 also shows two women asserting their right to fulfill their desire as they wish and to admire art wherever they choose to find it: thus they praise the craftsmanship of well-made dildoes in terms that echo admiration given elsewhere in Hellenistic poetry to fine works of art.[50]

Representations of female desire are also prevalent in Apollonius's epic, the *Argonautica*: it is Jason's sexual attractiveness (not Medea's) that is the object of gaze. Apollonius presents Medea's lovesickness, her erotic gaze, her longing in response to Jason's beauty – and also her assertiveness, her willingness to leave home and family with him. Thus, the sight of Jason fills Medea with desire (3.287-98):

---

47 The text is cited from Cunningham 1987: 15; translation according to Headlam 1922: 171.

48 On the kind of 'ritual-centered visuality' Mime 4's women are rejecting, see Elsner 2000: 62.

49 For discussion of the women's responses to art in Herodas Mime 4 and Theocritus Idyll 15, see, e.g., Burton 1995: 97-108; Skinner 2001.

50 Herod. 6.65-67; cf. Theoc. Id. 15.80-81, Herod. 4.57-58. For discussion see Burton 1995: 110-12.

ἀντία δ' αἰεί
βάλλεν ἐπ' Αἰσονίδην ἀμαρύγματα, καί οἱ ἄηντο
στηθέων ἐκ πυκιναὶ καμάτῳ φρένες, οὐδέ τιν' ἄλλην
μνῆστιν ἔχεν, γλυκερῇ δὲ κατείβετο θυμὸν ἀνίῃ·
...
ἁπαλὰς δὲ μετετρωπᾶτο παρειάς
ἐς χλόον, ἄλλοτ' ἔρευθος, ἀκηδείῃσι νόοιο.[51]

'Full at Jason her glances shot, and the wearying pain scattered all prudent thoughts from her chest; she could think of nothing else, and her spirit was flooded with a sweet aching ... At one moment her soft cheeks were drained of colour, at another they blushed red, the control of her mind now gone'.

Just as in Theocritus Idyll 2, a woman's erotic gaze is the narrative focus (3.443-47):

θεσπέσιον δ' ἐν πᾶσι μετέπρεπεν Αἴσονος υἱός
κάλλεϊ καὶ χαρίτεσσιν. ἐπ' αὐτῷ δ' ὄμματα κούρη
λοξὰ παρὰ λιπαρὴν σχομένη θηεῖτο καλύπτρην,
κῆρ ἄχεϊ σμύχουσα, νόος δέ οἱ ἠύτ' ὄνειρος
ἑρπύζων πεπότητο μετ' ἴχνια νισσομένοιο.

'Among them all the son of Aison stood out for his divine beauty and grace. The young girl kept her eyes on him, looking sideways behind her shining veil, and she wondered at him; her heart smouldered with pain, and her mind fluttered after his departing footsteps, creeping like a dream'.

So too, like women of the Sapphic tradition, Medea suffers physical symptoms of lovesickness (e.g., 3.761-65):

ἔνδοθι δ' αἰεί
τεῖρ' ὀδύνη, σμύχουσα διὰ χροὸς ἀμφί τ' ἀραιάς
ἶνας καὶ κεφαλῆς ὑπὸ νείατον ἰνίον ἄχρις,
ἔνθ' ἀλεγεινότατον δύνει ἄχος, ὁππότ' ἀνίας
ἀκάματοι πραπίδεσσιν ἐνισκίμψωσιν ἔρωτες.

'within her the pain wore her away, smouldering through her flesh, around her fine nerves and deep into the very base of the neck where the ache and hurt drive deepest, whenever the tireless Loves shoot their pains into the heart'.

When Jason finally meets Medea alone, as she desires, the physical effect of his sight on her is again a narrative focus (3.961-65). Apollonius also puts emphasis on the mutuality of Jason and Medea's desire for one another (3.1022-24):

ἄμφω δ' ἄλλοτε μέν τε κατ' οὔδεος ὄμματ' ἔρειδον
αἰδόμενοι, ὁτὲ δ' αὖτις ἐπὶ σφίσι βάλλον ὀπωπάς
ἱμερόεν φαιδρῇσιν ὑπ' ὀφρύσι μειδιόωντες.

---

51 All citations of the text of Ap. Rhod. *Argon.* are taken from Fränkel 1961; all translations according to Hunter 1993.

'At one moment they both stared coyly at the ground, at the next they cast glances at each other, smiling with desire, their faces lit up'.

Later, Medea runs through the streets, alone on foot, to Jason's ships. So too, in the Song, a woman goes through the streets, seeking her beloved. As in the Song, Medea's movement through the public space is articulated by the presence of watchmen (4.43-49):

γυμνοῖσιν δὲ πόδεσσιν ἀνὰ στεινὰς θέεν οἴμους,
...
καρπαλίμως δ' ἀίδηλον ἀνὰ στίβον ἔκτοθι πύργων
ἄστεος εὐρυχόροιο φόβῳ ἵκετ', οὐδέ τις ἔγνω
τήνγε φυλακτήρων.

'On naked feet she ran through the narrow streets . . . Swiftly she passed in terror out of the walls of the broad city by a lonely path; none of the guards recognized her'.

Here too a female pursues her desire in defiance of male figures seeking to control her: Medea eludes her father to follow her passion.

The gender ambiguity of Apollonius's descriptions of Jason is also striking. At the moment of attaining the golden fleece, the object of his heroic quest, Jason is described as lifting the fleece in his hands thus (4.167-70):

ὡς δὲ σεληναίης διχομήνιδα παρθένος αἴγλην
ὑψόθεν †ἀνέχουσαν ὑπωρόφιον θαλάμοιο
λεπταλέῳ ἑανῷ ὑποΐσχεται, ἐν δέ οἱ ἦτορ
χαίρει δερκομένης καλὸν σέλας.

'As when a young girl catches in her fine dress the gleam of the full moon hanging high over her bedroom under the roof, and her heart is delighted at the sight of the lovely radiance'.

Callimachus too highlights gender ambiguity in young males. Thus in the story of Akontios and Kydippe (frr. 67-75 Pf.), the poet highlights the beauty of Akontios by describing how male lovers noticed him on his way to school or the bath (fr. 68), and toasted him at the symposium (fr. 69).[52] As in the Song, Akontios's female lover, Kydippe, becomes lovesick (Callim. fr. 75.12-19); her sickness 'wastes her even to Hades' halls' (14-15). The motifs of female lovesickness and the linkage between love and death also find parallels in the Song of Songs (e.g., 8:6: 'love is strong as death, passion fierce as the grave').

Hellenistic epigrams, particularly the erotic epigrams of Asclepiades as well as the epigrams of certain women poets, reinforce a perception that themes of female independence in the realm of love were prominent during the

52 Cf. in Theoc. Id. 2, the descriptions of Simaetha's beloved Delphis in the contexts of the wrestling-school (79-80, 97-98), athletics (114-16), and the symposium (150-53; cf. 118-22).

Hellenistic period.[53] Asclepiades' epigrams repeatedly express unhappiness about women who assert erotic autonomy, claiming their right to love as they please (e.g., *Anth. Pal.* 5.164):[54]

Νύξ, σὲ γάρ, οὐκ ἄλλην, μαρτύρομαι, οἷά μ' ὑβρίζει
  Πυθιὰς ἡ Νικοῦς οὖσα φιλεξαπάτις.
κληθείς, οὐκ ἄκλητος, ἐλήλυθα· ταῦτα παθοῦσα
  σοὶ μέμψαιτ' ἔτ' ἐμοῖς στᾶσα παρὰ προθύροις.

'Night, I call upon you, no other, to witness how Nico's Pythias, lover of deceit, mistreats me. I came at her invitation, not uninvited. May she suffer the like as she stands at my door and complains to you'.[55]

The male speaker's vengeful desire to see Pythias forced into the role of komastically courting him (customarily a male activity), with him barring the door against her, further highlights the theme of gender inversion.[56]

Asclepiades also represents women as feeling passion and desire. For example, in *Anth. Pal.* 5.153, a man at her door attracts a woman's erotic gaze:

Νικαρέτης τὸ πόθοισι βεβλημένον ἡδὺ πρόσωπον
  πυκνὰ δι' ὑψηλῶν φαινόμενον θυρίδων
αἱ χαροπαὶ Κλεοφῶντος ἐπὶ προθύροισι μάραναν,
  Κύπρι φίλη, γλυκεροῦ βλέμματος ἀστεροπαί.[57]

'Nicarete's sweet face, smitten by desire, appearing often through her high windows, was blasted by the bright lightning of the sweet eye of Cleophon, dear Cypris, as he stood before her door'.

This is a change from themes of earlier Greek poetry in which amatory relations were depicted instead primarily as matters of male control and pursuit.[58] Now Asclepiades represents a male in a state of Sapphic anguish and desire before a beloved girl (*Anth. Pal.* 5.210.1-2):

†Τῷ θαλλῷ† Διδύμη με συνήρπασεν, ὤμοι ἐγὼ δέ
  τήκομαι ὡς κηρὸς πὰρ πυρὶ κάλλος ὁρῶν.

---

53 For important discussions see Gutzwiller 1998: esp. 54-58 (Anyte and Nossis), 122-50 (Asclepiades).

54 See also, e.g., *Anth. Pal.* 5.7, 150, 158.

55 The text of the epigrams is cited from Gow/Page 1965, vol. 1; translations are my own unless otherwise noted.

56 Cf. Galateia in the role of excluded lover (Theoc. Id. 6); Simaetha's strategies of inverted revenge (Id. 2); Aeschinas, upset over how Cynisa "shamefully mistreated" him (Id. 14.8-9). See also the woman's complaint in Fragmentum Grenfellianum (Powell 1925: 177-80; Cunningham 1987: 36-38). For the motif of *paraclausithyron* (lover's complaint at beloved's door) in the Song of Songs, see 5:2-6 (Pope 1977: 522-24).

57 *Anth. Pal.* 5.153.1: I print the manuscript's βεβλημένον rather than Wilamowitz's βεβαμμένον (accepted in Gow/Page 1965, 1:45; 2:119). For defense of βεβλημένον see Cameron 1995: 498; Gutzwiller 1998: 131 n. 38.

58 Gutzwiller 1998: 130-31; see also Williamson 1998.

'Didyme has carried me off with her bloom, alas, and I melt like wax before the fire, as I behold her beauty'.

As in the Song of Songs, the theme of a continuum of male and female desire comes into play. The rest of this epigram suggests a further parallel (5.210.3-4):

εἰ δὲ μέλαινα, τί τοῦτο; καὶ ἄνθρακες· ἀλλ' ὅτε κείνους
  θάλψωμεν λάμπουσ' ὡς ῥόδεαι κάλυκες.

'If she is dark, what of this? So are coals, but when we heat them, they gleam like rosebuds'.

The theme of the beauty of women of dark complexion is also prominent in the Song (1:5-6):

I am black and beautiful,
  O daughters of Jerusalem,
like the tents of Kedar,
  like the curtains of Solomon.
Do not gaze at me because I am dark,
  because the sun has gazed on me.

Similarly, in Theocritus Idyll 10, the lovelorn reaper expresses admiration for a dark-complexioned woman (26-29):

  Βομβύκα χαρίεσσα, Σύραν καλέοντί τυ πάντες,
ἰσχνάν, ἁλιόκαυστον, ἐγὼ δὲ μόνος μελίχλωρον.
  καὶ τὸ ἴον μέλαν ἐστί, καὶ ἁ γραπτὰ ὑάκινθος·
ἀλλ' ἔμπας ἐν τοῖς στεφάνοις τὰ πρᾶτα λέγονται.

'Charming Bombyca, all call you the Syrian, lean and sun-scorched, and I alone, honey hued. Dark is the violet and the lettered hyacinth, yet in garlands these are accounted first'.[59]

Cameron suggests a linkage between Asclepiades' dark-skinned Didyme and one of Ptolemy's mistresses, a native Egyptian also called Didyme (Ath. 13.576e-f); Theocritus Idyll 10's assertion of dark-skinned beauty might suggest a similar orientation toward the Ptolemaic court.[60] Suggestions of linkages of this theme with the Ptolemaic court remain speculative. Nonetheless, interest in the theme of dark-complexioned female beauty offers another strong parallel between the Song and Hellenistic poetry.

While men in Hellenistic literature may be represented as disempowered in love, women are often explicitly empowered. Thus an epigram of Asclepiades

59 Translation according to Gow 1952, 1:83, rev.
60 Cameron 1995: 233-37; Burton 1995: 130-32; cf. Gutzwiller 1998: 136.

offers another take on the theme of gender crossing: a woman exercises sexual power by dressing as a boy and seducing young men (*Anth. Pal.* 12.161). Asclepiades represents a female voice also, in *Anth. Pal.* 12.153 (an abandoned woman's vantage on love):

Πρόσθε μοι Ἀρχεάδης ἐθλίβετο, νῦν δέ, τάλαινα,
 οὐδ' ὅσσον παίζων εἰς ἔμ' ἐπιστρέφεται.
οὐδ' ὁ μελιχρὸς Ἔρως αἰεὶ γλυκύς, ἀλλ' ἀνιήσας
 πολλάκις ἡδίων γίνετ' ἐρῶσι θεός.

'Once Archeades used to be oppressed with passion for me; now, alas, he does not turn to me even in sportive mood. Not even sweet Love is sweet always; yet often, after giving pain, the god becomes more pleasant to lovers'.[61]

The new value that Hellenistic literature was placing on an ideal of mutual passion in heteroerotic relationships, both within and also outside marriage, is also evident in the epigrams. Thus an epigram attributed to Posidippus sets a value on the reciprocal, symmetrical love that develops between a man and the woman he sees swimming in the sea (*Anth. Pal.* 5.209, lines 7-8 of an eight-line epigram):

νῦν δ' ἴσος ἀμφοτέροις φιλίης πόθος, οὐκ ἀτελεῖς γάρ
 εὐχαὶ τὰς κείνης εὔξατ' ἐπ' ἠιόνος.

'Now they are both equally in love, for not unfulfilled were the prayers he made on that shore'.[62]

Further, this ending to the epigram makes it clear that the woman previously had more power than the man (not less).

Not much remains of the writings of Hellenistic women poets such as Moero, Nossis, and Anyte, but enough to show some shared themes with the Song of Songs. Nossis's poems, for example, seem to reflect the changing roles and expectations of women in Hellenistic society. She asserts her right to set a high value on love and to voice such an opinion publicly, with her name attached (*Anth. Pal.* 5.170):

Ἅδιον οὐδὲν ἔρωτος, ἃ δ' ὄλβια δεύτερα πάντα
 ἐστίν· ἀπὸ στόματος δ' ἔπτυσα καὶ τὸ μέλι.
τοῦτο λέγει Νοσσίς· τίνα δ' ἁ Κύπρις οὐκ ἐφίλασεν
 οὐκ οἶδεν †κῆνα τ'† ἄνθεα ποῖα ῥόδα.

'Nothing is sweeter than love. Everything desirable is second to it. I spit even honey from my mouth. Nossis says this: The one who has never been loved by Aphrodite, that woman does not know what sort of flowers roses are'.[63]

---

61 Translation according to Hutchinson 1988: 272.
62 Translation according to Austin and Bastianini 2002: 165 (*Epigr.* 128.7-8).
63 Translation according to Gutzwiller 1998: 76, reformatted.

So too Nossis has fictive women visit a temple to admire a work of art (*Anth. Pal.* 9.332):

Ἐλθοῖσαι ποτὶ ναὸν ἰδώμεθα τᾶς Ἀφροδίτας
  τὸ βρέτας ὡς χρυσῷ δαιδαλόεν τελέθει.
εἵσατό μιν Πολυαρχὶς ἐπαυρομένα μάλα πολλὰν
  κτῆσιν ἀπ' οἰκείου σώματος ἀγλαΐας.

'Let us go to the temple and see Aphrodite's statue, how intricately it is adorned with gold. Polyarchis set it up, enjoying the great wealth she has from the beauty of her own body'.[64]

Like the women of Herodas Mime 4 and Theocritus Idyll 15, these women too claim the right to express admiration of a gilt statue of Aphrodite on their own terms, from the vantage of what they know or appreciate (e.g., making money from prostitution).

The poet Anyte's literary subjects include animals, children, and young women. Her poems also feature (perhaps even before Theocritus's bucolic poetry) the rural landscape, as shown, for example, by the bucolic invitation issued in *Anth. Pal.* 9.313:

Ἵζε' ἅπας ὑπὸ καλὰ δάφνας εὐθαλέα φύλλα
  ὡραίου τ' ἄρυσαι νάματος ἁδὺ πόμα
ὄφρα τοι ἀσθμαίνοντα πόνοις θέρεος φίλα γυῖα
  ἀμπαύσῃς πνοιᾷ τυπτόμενα Ζεφύρου.

'Sit beneath the laurel's beautiful, luxuriant foliage, and draw a sweet drink from the lovely spring, that your limbs – weary from the harvest's labours – may rest, buffeted by the Zephyr's breeze'.[65]

Although few poems have survived from the Hellenistic women poets, and explicitly amatory poems are rare, one of Moero's epigrams, on a cluster of grapes dedicated in Aphrodite's temple, is filled with lush, sensual imagery (*Anth. Pal.* 6.119):

Κεῖσαι δὴ χρυσέαν ὑπὸ παστάδα τὰν Ἀφροδίτας,
  βότρυ, Διωνύσου πληθόμενος σταγόνι,
οὐδ' ἔτι τοι μάτηρ ἐρατὸν περὶ κλῆμα βαλοῦσα
  φύσει ὑπὲρ κρατὸς νεκτάρεον πέταλον.

'You lie within Aphrodite's golden chamber, O grape cluster, full of Dionysus's liquid. No longer will your mother throw a lovely vine-branch around you and put forth a nectarous leaf above your head.'

Like Sappho, these Hellenistic women poets open up a world of women's aesthetics and desires in their epigrams; this world also emerges centrally in

64 Translation according to Gutzwiller 1998: 81, reformatted.
65 See also *Anth. Plan.* 228 (Anyte); cf. Theoc. Id. 5.31-34, 45-49.

the Song of Songs. The following exchange between male and female voices epitomizes the Song's lush, sensual imagery. First the male (Cant 7:8-9):

Oh, may your breasts be like clusters of the vine
  and the scent of your breath like apples,
and your kisses like the best wine
  that goes down smoothly,
  gliding over lips and teeth.

Then the female (Cant 7:12):

Let us go early to the vineyards,
  and see whether the vines have budded,
whether the grape blossoms have opened
  and the pomegranates are in bloom.
There I will give you my love.

Theocritus too is famous for sensual bucolic settings, of which the most luxuriant (and fruitful) is the harvest celebration at the close of Idyll 7 (132-34, 143-46):

ἔν τε βαθείαις
ἁδείας σχοίνοιο χαμευνίσιν ἐκλίνθημες
ἔν τε νεοτμάτοισι γεγαθότες οἰναρέοισι.
...
πάντ' ὦσδεν θέρεος μάλα πίονος, ὦσδε δ' ὀπώρας.
ὄχναι μὲν πὰρ ποσσί, παρὰ πλευραῖσι δὲ μᾶλα
δαψιλέως ἁμῖν ἐκυλίνδετο, τοὶ δ' ἐκέχυντο
ὄρπακες βραβίλοισι καταβρίθοντες ἔραζε.

'We laid ourselves down rejoicing on deep couches of sweet rush and in the fresh-stripped vine-leaves . . . All things were fragrant of rich harvest and of fruit-time. Pears at our feet and apples at our sides were rolling plentifully, and the branches hung down to the ground with their burden of sloes'.[66]

The readily available apples may reinforce the impression of sensuality in this passage. Apples are traditional love tokens among the Greeks.[67] Further, the easy accessibility of these apples contrasts with Sappho's single (chaste) apple left at the top of a tree – unreachable by the apple-pickers (fr. 105 a). Apples figure too in the erotic imagery of the Song of Songs, notably 2:3: 'As an apple tree among the trees of the wood, so is my beloved among young men. With great delight I sat in his shadow, and his fruit was sweet to my taste'.[68] Thus the Song's sensual pastoral imagery, although more extended and densely

66 Translation according to Gow 1952, 1:65, 67, reformatted.
67 See, e.g., Theoc. Idd. 2.120, 3.10, 5.88, 6.6-7, 11.10; Littlewood 1968.
68 Cf. Cant 2:5; Sappho fr. 2.

erotic, also finds parallels amidst the lushness and sensuality of the bucolic imagery found in Hellenistic literature.

Conclusion

In the early Hellenistic age, there was a general poetic engagement with changing gender roles. This engagement seems related to the unsettling of social roles and expectations that naturally accompanied the increased mobility of the Hellenistic age and the changed political landscape, as well as the interactions of different cultures with different gender mores. Themes of female desire and self-assertion as well as male helplessness and erotic passivity become prominent, and themes of erotic reciprocity and mutual passion also come into play. There are parallels in social and gender themes between Hellenistic poetry and the Song of Songs: for example, Theocritus Idylls 2 and 15, both of them mimes, show women feeling and expressing desire and claiming their right to enter the streets if they wish. Not only the form – that of mime – but also the content help suggest a congenial context for the creation of the Song of Songs in the third century BCE.

A preeminent characteristic of the Song is the abundance of pastoral and alimentary erotic imagery throughout: breasts like clusters of grapes, breath like apples, kisses like wine, and so forth. Parallels between the Song and Theocritus's bucolic imagery have often been adduced. The Song focuses similarly on the pastoral world, uses pastoral imagery for the beloved, features carefully balanced speeches and luxuriant settings. Such thematic parallels corroborate the often-remarked parallel motifs: the foxes threatening the vineyards (Cant 2:15; Theoc. Idd. 1.45-49, 5.112-13), the dark skin of the beloved (Cant 1:5-6; Theoc. Id. 10.26-29), the frequent comparisons of the beloved to the bucolic world. There is also a rich tradition in Greek literature of the use of food and garden imagery to describe the beloved. Much of this erotic nature imagery (the comparisons to flowers, trees, and a vineyard, the honeyed mouth, and so forth) has a long history among the Greeks and can be traced even to archaic poetry.[69] Even the love duet finds parallels in earlier Greek literature.[70] If indeed the Song was composed in the vibrant, multicultural Hellenistic world, it could have drawn not only on Egyptian love poetry and songs, but also on Greek, Hebraic, and Near Eastern songs and poetry – a rich mix to be refashioned and recreated as the magnificent, distinctive Song of Songs.

---

69 E.g., Sappho frr. 105a, 105b (cf. fr. 96); Hom. *Od.* 6.162-69 (Nausicaa as a shoot of a palm tree; cf. Cant 7:7), *Il.* 14.347-51 (the blossoming of earth that accompanies Hera and Zeus's lovemaking).

70 E.g., Ar. *Eccl.* 952-75 (for discussion see Bowra 1958).

The pastoral, erotic imagery is more fully developed in the Song of Songs than in Theocritus: in the Song the imagery is luxuriant, concentrated, distinctive in its elaborateness, with the female extensively describing her own desire for the male, her erotic gaze. The themes of female desire, self-assertion, and erotic reciprocity are also strongly present in the novels of the Second Sophistic period (a time of rising Christianity and therefore perhaps [re]acquaintance with the Song of Songs).[71] Among the ancient Greek novelists, Achilles Tatius and Longus show the most lush erotic nature imagery (including erotic food imagery).[72] (Erotic imagery drawn from the realms of nature and food is prominent also in the Greek epigrams.)

Later, in the Byzantine world, the imagery of the Song of Songs is again used to articulate female desire. Indeed, with the revival of the novel in twelfth-century Byzantium, pastoral and alimentary imagery emerges full-blown in the texts of Niketas Eugenianos and Eustathios Makrembolites: the flowers and trees, the images of erotic consumption, the enclosed garden, the extended expressions of female desire. One episode in particular of Eugenianos's romance novel directly recalls the erotic imagery of the Song of Songs. A short excerpt will suffice. Here are the words the hero gives to an amorous woman, the keeper of an enclosed garden, as she invites the hero within (4.285-88):

ἐγὼ τὸ δένδρον· δεῦρο, προσπλάκηθί μοι·
ἀντὶ κλάδων ἐμὰς γὰρ ὠλένας ἔχεις·
ἐγὼ τὸ δένδρον· καὶ προσανάβηθί μοι
δρέπου τε καρπὸν τὸν γλυκὺν ὑπὲρ μέλι.

'I am the tree: come cling to me, for you have my arms in place of branches. I am the tree: climb me and pluck my fruit, which is sweeter than honey'.[73]

Compare a male lover's amatory address to a woman in the Song (7:7-8):

You are stately as a palm tree,
and your breasts are like its clusters.
I say I will climb the palm tree
and lay hold of its branches.

By casting the female gardener's erotic invitation in the amorous language of the Song's male lover, Eugenianos highlights the role reversal implied in this woman's self-assertive sexuality and also evokes a tradition of symmetries between male and female desire. Eugenianos's passage shows that in the deeply Christian world of twelfth-century Byzantium, an author was reading

71 On the theme of 'sexual symmetry' in the Greek novels, see Konstan 1994.
72 For discussion, with references, see 'Eugenianos, themes of erotic consumption, and the Song of Solomon', in Burton 1998a: 200-203.
73 The text is cited from Conca 1990; translation according to Burton 2004: 77, 79.

the Song of Songs in a literal, sexual way, in defiance of the orthodox reading of the Song as spiritual allegory.[74] In a Christian world, Eugenianos's rewriting of the Song of Songs also involves separating female desire from the institution of marriage and thoughts of procreation. Eugenianos's novel, rich in pastoral motifs, is notable also for its density of allusions to Theocritus's poetry.[75] Thus Eugenianos's novel demonstrates an appreciation early on of the strong parallels in sensual bucolic imagery as well as themes of female desire and self-assertion between Theocritus's poetry and the Song of Songs.[76]

Bibliography

AHMED, L. (1992): Women and Gender in Islam: Historical roots of a modern debate, New Haven.
ANDREWS, N.E. (1996): Narrative and Allusion in Theocritus, Idyll 2, in: M.A. Harder/ R. F. Regtuit/G. C. Wakker (eds.), Theocritus, Groningen, 21-53.
AUSTIN, C./BASTIANINI, G. eds. (2002): Posidippi Pellaei quae supersunt omnia, Milan.
BAKER, P. (2003): Warfare, in: A. Erskine, (ed.), A Companion to the Hellenistic World, Malden, 373-388.
BARCLAY, J.M.G. (1996): Jews in the Mediterranean Diaspora: From Alexander to Trajan (323 BCE-117 CE), Edinburgh.
BLANK, S.H. (1970): Prolegomenon to The Song of Songs and Coheleth (commonly called the Book of Ecclesiastes). Translated from the original Hebrew, with a commentary, historical and critical, by C.D. Ginsburg, New York, ix-xliv.
BLOCH, A./BLOCH, C. (1995): The Song of Songs, New York.
BOWRA, C.M. (1958): A Love-Duet, AJPh 79, 376-391.
BURTON, J.B. (1992): The Function of the Symposium Theme in Theocritus' Idyll 14, GRBS 33, 227-45.
– (1995): Theocritus's Urban Mimes: Mobility, Gender, and Patronage, Berkeley/Los Angeles.
– (1998a): Reviving the Pagan Greek Novel in a Christian World, GRBS 39, 179-216.
– (1998b): Women's Commensality in the Ancient Greek World, GaR 45, 143-165.
– (2003): A Reemergence of Theocritean Poetry in the Byzantine Novel, CP 98, 251-273.
– (2004): A Byzantine Novel: 'Drosilla and Charikles' by Niketas Eugenianos. A Bilingual Edition, Translated with an introduction and explanatory notes, Wauconda.
CAMERON, A. (1995): Callimachus and His Critics, Princeton.
CONCA, F. (1990): Nicetas Eugenianus. De Drosillae et Chariclis amoribus, Amsterdam.
CUNNINGHAM, I.C. (1987): Herodae Mimiambi cum appendice fragmentorum mimorum papyraceorum, Leipzig.
DOVER, K.J. (1978): Greek Homosexuality, Cambridge/MA.

74 Burton 1998a: 201-3.
75 See Burton 2003, with references.
76 I should like to thank Anselm C. Hagedorn for encouraging me to explore Hellenistic expressions of female desire in the context of a volume on the Song of Songs and for hios generous editorial support. I owe thanks also to Erwin Cook, Thomas Jenkins and David Stinchcomb for their valuable suggestions and comments.

ELSNER, J. (2000): Between Mimesis and Divine Power. Visuality in the Greco-Roman World, in: R.S. Nelson (ed.), Visuality before and beyond the Renaissance: Seeing as Others Saw, Cambridge, 45-69.
FARAONE, C.A. (2002): Agents and Victims. Constructions of Gender and Desire in Ancient Greek Love Magic, in: M.C. Nussbaum/J. Sihvola (eds.), The Sleep of Reason: Erotic Experience and Sexual Ethics in Ancient Greece and Rome, Chicago, 400-426.
FOX, M.V. (1985): The Song of Songs and the Ancient Egyptian Love Songs, Madison.
FRÄNKEL, H. (1961): Apollonii Rhodii 'Argonautica', Oxford.
FRASER, P.M. (1972): Ptolemaic Alexandria, 3 vols., Oxford.
GEBHARDT, C. (1931): Das Lied der Lieder. Übertragen mit Einführung und Kommentar, Berlin.
GINSBERG, H.L. (1974): The Five Megilloth and Jonah. A new translation, 2nd ed., Philadelphia.
GIOVANNINI, A. (1993): Greek Cities and Greek Commonwealth, in: A. Bulloch/E.S. Gruen/A.A. Long/A. Stewart (eds.), Images and Ideologies: Self-definition in the Hellenistic World, Berkeley/Los Angeles, 265-286.
GOW, A.S.F. (1952): Theocritus, 2 vols., 2nd ed., Cambridge.
GOW, A.S.F./Page, D.L. (1965): The Greek Anthology: Hellenistic Epigrams. 2 vols., Cambridge.
GRAETZ, H. (1871): Schir Ha-Schirim, oder das Salomonische Hohelied. Übersetzt und kritisch erläutert, Vienna.
GRIFFITHS, F.T. (1979): Theocritus at Court, Leiden.
GRUEN, E.S. (1997): Fact and Fiction. Jewish Legends in a Hellenistic Context, in: P. Cartledge/P. Garnsey/E. Gruen (eds.), Hellenistic Constructs: Essays in Culture, History, and Historiography, Berkeley and Los Angeles, 72-88.
– (1998): Heritage and Hellenism: The Reinvention of Jewish Tradition, Berkeley/Los Angeles.
– (2002a): Diaspora: Jews amidst Greeks and Romans, Cambridge/MA.
– (2002b): Hellenistic Judaism, in: D. Biale (ed.), Cultures of the Jews: A New History, New York, 77-132.
GUTZWILLER, K.J. (1992): Callimachus' Lock of Berenice: Fantasy, Romance, and Propaganda, AJPh 113, 359-385.
– (1998): Poetic Garlands: Hellenistic Epigrams in Context, Berkeley/Los Angeles.
HALPERIN, D.M. (1990): One Hundred Years of Homosexuality, and Other Essays on Greek Love, New York.
HEADLAM, W./KNOX, A.D. (1922): Herodas: The Mimes and Fragments, Cambridge.
HENGEL, M. (1974): Judaism and Hellenism: Studies in Their Encounter in Palestine during the Early Hellenistic Period, 2 vols., Philadelphia.
HUNTER, R. (1993): Apollonius of Rhodes, Jason and the Golden Fleece (the Argonautica): Translated with an introduction and explanatory notes, Oxford.
– (2003): Theocritus, Encomium of Ptolemy Philadelphus: Text and translation with introduction and commentary, Berkeley/Los Angeles.
HUTCHINSON, G.O. (1988): Hellenistic Poetry, Oxford.
KEEL, O. (1986): Das Hohelied, ZBK 18, Zürich.
KOENEN, L. (1983): Die Adaptation ägyptischer Königsideologie am Ptolemäerhof, in: E. van't Dack/E.P. van Dessel/W. van Gucht (eds.), Eygpt and the Hellenistic World. Proceedings of the International Colloquium, Leuven, 24-26 May 1982, Louvain, 143-190.
– (1993): The Ptolemaic King as a Religious Figure, in: A. Bulloch/E.S. Gruen/A.A. Long/A. Stewart (eds.), Images and Ideologies: Self-definition in the Hellenistic World, Berkeley/Los Angeles, 25-115.
KONSTAN, D. (1994): Sexual Symmetry: Love in the Ancient Novel and Related Genres, Princeton.

LITTLEWOOD, A.R. (1968): The Symbolism of the Apple in Greek and Roman Literature, HSCP 72, 147-181.
MARROU, H.I. (1950): Histoire de l'éducation dans l'antiquité, 2nd ed., Paris.
MURPHY, R.E. (1990): The Song of Songs, Hermeneia, Minneapolis.
POMEROY, S.B. (1984): Women in Hellenistic Egypt: From Alexander to Cleopatra, New York.
– (1997): Families in Classical and Hellenistic Greece: Representations and Reality, Oxford.
POPE, M.H. (1977): Song of Songs, AB 7C, Garden City.
POWELL, J.U. (1925): Collectanea Alexandrina, Oxford.
RAHLFS, A. (1935): Septuaginta. Id est Vetus Testamentum Graece iuxta LXX interpretes, 2 vols., Stuttgart.
REED, J.D. (1995): The Sexuality of Adonis, ClAnt 14, 317-347.
ROBINS, G. (1993): Women in Ancient Egypt, Cambridge/MA.
ROWLANDSON, J. (1995): Beyond the Polis. Women and Economic Opportunity in Early Ptolemaic Egypt, in: A. Powell (ed.), The Greek World, London, 301-322.
ROWLANDSON, J. et al. (1998): Women and Society in Greek and Roman Egypt. A Sourcebook, Cambridge.
SCHAPS, D.M. (1979): Economic Rights of Women in Ancient Greece, Edinburgh.
SEALEY, R. (1990): Women and Law in Classical Greece, Chapel Hill.
SKINNER, M.B. (2001): Ladies' Day at the Art Institute. Theocritus, Herodas, and the Gendered Gaze, in: A. Lardinois/L. McClure (eds.), Making Silence Speak: Women's Voices in Greek Literature and Society, Princeton, 201-222.
SMITH, R.R.R. (1991): Hellenistic Sculpture. A Handbook, New York.
SNYDER, J.M. (1989): The Woman and the Lyre: Women Writers in Classical Greece and Rome, Carbondale.
STEPHENS, S.A. (2003): Seeing Double: Intercultural Poetics in Ptolemaic Alexandria, Berkeley/Los Angeles.
TCHERIKOVER, V.A. (1957): Corpus papyrorum Judaicarum. Vol. 1. Cambridge/MA.
– (1961): Hellenistic Civilization and the Jews, Trans. S. Applebaum, Philadelphia.
TYLDESLEY, J. (1994): Daughters of Isis: Women of Ancient Egypt, London.
WILLIAMSON, M. (1998): Eros the Blacksmith. Performing Masculinity in Anakreon's Love Lyrics, in: L. Foxhall/J. Salmon (eds.), Thinking men: Masculinity and Its Self-representation in the Classical Tradition, London, 71-82.

Jealousy and Desire at Night
Fragmentum Grenfellianum and Song of Songs

Anselm C. Hagedorn

In Cant 3:1-5 and 5:2-8 we encounter an inner monologue of the woman, spoken at night and in utter the privacy of her own chamber.[1] In the following we will take a closer look at these 'private' expressions of (sexual) desire and compare them to the so called *Fragmentum Grenfellianum* thus hoping to offer yet another parallel text to the Song of Songs from the realm of the Eastern Mediterranean world.[2]

Cant 3:1-5 and 5:2-8

In Cant 3:1 we meet the woman laying at night (בלילות)[3] on her bed (על־משכבי), yearning for her beloved (בקשתי את שאהבה נפשי). Older commentators generally viewed this passage (together with Cant 5:2) as a report of a dream dreamt by the woman.[4] However, the Hebrew text does not allow to jump to such a conclusion and one cannot help getting the impression that

My sincere thanks to Mr. A. Hollis (Keble College, Oxford) for drawing my attention to the fragment and to Prof. P.J. Parsons (Christ Church, Oxford), Dr. Elena Esposito (Turin) and Prof. F.W. Dobbs-Allsopp (Princeton) for invaluable help – all remaining faults are of course my own. Unless otherwise stated all translations of Greek texts are taken from the Loeb Classical Library.

1 Exum 2000: 32 has drawn attention to the fact that the passages invite us "to become voyeurs"; in the following she distinguishes "between the voyeuristic gaze that intrudes upon that which is seen and the erotic gaze, looking that participates in that which is seen".

2 In the following we will assume that the poems of the Song of Songs were collected during the Hellenistic period and that a certain knowledge of Greek literature has been a strong possibility; cf. *int. al.* Müller 1992; Bosshard-Nepustil 1996: 67-71; Garbini 1992.

3 The plural is generally understood as having a singular meaning (cf. JM §136b and most commentators) but it could also refer to a longing in consecutive nights (Fox 1985: 60; Garbini 1992: 209, 'un fatto ricorrente').

4 Ewald 1826: 92; Hitzig 1855: 35 and again Longmann III 2001: 129 who states "that this is poetry and not the account of an actual event"; Exum 1999: 73 uses the terms 'wishing' or 'dreaming' as referring "to all the ways desire is expressed in the Song, and not as a literary category ... or as a state of consciousness ... to be decided upon."

scholars transfer moral values of the 19th century to the biblical text. Thus for example F. DELITZSCH is able to ask:

> "Wie ist dieses nächtliche Sehnen bei aller Stärke der Liebe mit der jungfräulichen Zucht vereinbar?" (Delitzsch 1852: 103)

In the inner time-sequence of Song of Songs, the pericope Cant 3:1-5 follows the preceding couplet which places the statement of belonging to each other (דודי לי ואני לו) at the time of the later afternoon (עד שיפוח היום ונסו הצללים). Thus Cant 3:1 has to follow Cant 2:16-17 due to the catchword לילה.[5] Just as in Cant 2:7 and Cant 8:4 (here without בצבאות או באילות השדה), Cant 3:5 forms an *inclusio* to the poem, emphasising that love should not be disturbed.[6] At the same time the adjuration moves the private desire once more in the public realm,[7] a feature to which we will have to return.

The place of the women is described as being על־משכב a phrase that occurs elsewhere in the Bible to describe the place where one lays down.[8] Naturally it is associated with sleeping and can – together with מטה – denote the bed-chamber (cf. 2Sam 4:7). Texts such as 2Reg 6:12 suggest that this chamber was situated in the upper part of a house.

> The exact place of the 'female quarters' in an Israelite house is difficult to determine,[9] and the parallel text in Cant 5:2-8 does not allow us to draw any conclusions whether the woman is upstairs. If we however go by analogy with archaeological evidence from Greece, it might be possible to argue for a certain seclusion of the rooms inhabited by the (unmarried) women of the household.[10] This is supported by the following advice given by Ben Sira (42:11):
>
> ἐπὶ θυγατρὶ ἀδιατρέπτῳ στερέωσον φυλακήν,
> μήποτε ποιήσῃ σε ἐπίχαρμα ἐχθροῖς,
> λαλιὰν ἐν πόλει καὶ ἔκκλητον λαοῦ,
> καὶ καταισχύνῃ σε ἐν πλήθει πολλῶν.
>
> In similar vein Ps-Phocylides (215-6) advises parents to keep a virgin in locked rooms but fails to state explicitly where these rooms might have been:
>
> παρθενικὴν δὲ φύλασσε πολυκλείστοις θαλάμοισιν,
> μὴ δέ μιν ἄρχι γάμων πρὸ δόμων ὀφθῆμεν ἐάσῃς.

---

5 Keel 1992: 113.
6 Keel 1992: 114.
7 Different Murphy 1990: 147 who thinks that "the adjuration to the Daughters does not demand their physical presence; they could be merely a foil for the woman. Only when they are clearly represented as speaking ... is their physical presence necessary."
8 Cf. 2Sam 4:11; 11:2; 13:5; Is 57:2; Hos 7:14; Mi 2:1; Ps 4:5; 36:5; 149:5; Jb 33:15.19.
9 Cf. the discussion in de Geus 1992: 75-86.
10 On the archaeological evidence from Greece cf. Walker 1993: 81-91 and Lewis 2002.

Despite the rich evidence for a total seclusion of women in antiquity,[11] D. COHEN has demonstrated convincingly that much confusion exists between ideology and reality as well as between separation and seclusion.[12] We will see below that the Song of Songs thought it indeed possible and even acceptable for a woman to leave the house (at night!).

Ezekiel can describe the marriage bed of adulterous Oholibah as משכב דודים (Ez 23:17). Due to the obvious connection with שכב the term evokes certain sexual connotations.[13] However, we should note that the verb שכב never occurs in Song of Songs and even in those passages where sexual intercourse is clearly envisaged (e.g. Cant 2:6; 4:16b etc.) other descriptions are favoured, carefully avoiding the blunt expression.[14]

As in Cant 5:2 (אני ישנה ולבי ער), a text that "also blurs distinctions, the nebulous boundary between sleep and wakefulness",[15] we do not know whether the woman is asleep but the setting seems to suggest that the woman is awake, tossing and turning, yearning for her beloved. The *Palatine Anthology* can describe such doings as follows:

καὶ μ᾽ ἔτι νῦν θάλπει μνήμης πόθος· ὄμμασι δ᾽ ὕπνον
  ἀγευτὴν πτηνοῦ φάσματος αἰὲν ἔχω.
ὦ δύσερως ψυχή, παῦσαί ποτε καὶ δι᾽ ὀνείρων
  εἰδώλοις κάλλευς κωφὰ χλιαινομένη.

[Still does the desire of the memory heat me, and in my eyes still abideth sleep that caught for me in the chase that winged phantom. O soul, ill-starved in love, cease at last even in dreams to be warned all in vain by beauty's image.][16]

Sleeplessness is of course known to the Bible but generally the lack of sleep is associated with distress (cf. Ps 77:4-5; 102:8; Est 6:1; Dan 6:19) – of course distress also provides the background for Cant 3:1, however not a distress in the view of the enemies or illness but simply because of the absence of the beloved. By being awake the woman allows us to partake in her innermost thoughts, while laying on her bed. This view would fit well with other passages from the Hebrew Bible where the bed is mentioned as the place to ponder words or thoughts in utter privacy, Thus for example we read in the book of Psalms (Ps 4:5): רגזו ואל־תחטאו אמרו בלבבכם על־משכבכם ודמו

11 The best example remains Euripides, *Troades* 645ff.

12 Cohen 1989: 134-145.

13 Cf. the phrase אהבת משכבים in Is 57:8 which according to DCH V, 527 is an expression of 'sexual deire'.

14 In this respect the Song of Songs is far more subtle than Boer's pornographic interpretation wants us to believe (Boer 1999: 53-70); cf. the critique of his approach in Burrus/Moore 2003: 24-52; Exum 1999: 72 rightly states that sexual union takes place "on the level of *double entendre*"in the Song of Songs; different Clines 1994: 3-27 who altogether denies any sexual relation within the Song of Songs.

15 Exum 1999: 78.

16 *Anth. Pal.* 12.125.

In a similar vein, Qoheleth (10:20) urges his reader to be careful what one says in the bedroom (בחדר), i.e. in 'privacy' since even here it is possible to be overheard:

גם במדעך מלך אל־תקלל ובחדרי משכבך
אל־תקלל עשיר כי עוף השמים יוליך את־הקול
ובעל הכנפים יגיד דבר

All this shows, that next to the bed as an obvious place for sleeping (or sexual activities), it was also the place for private thoughts and maybe the only true place of privacy in the world of the eastern Mediterranean.

Only in passing we will note that in Babylonia and Assyria beds were in general associated with the domains of women.[17] Furthermore there are administrative text that state explicitly that a bed is part of the dowry or note that female deportees possessed bed.[18] "Textual references indicate in addition that beds were typically placed in the sections of the house known as the bedchamber ... and the *maštaku*, the rooms that appear to have constituted the women's quarters in the house and to have served as centres of family life."[19] Also it seems that having a (solid) bed-stand in Mesopotamia indicated a certain degree of wealth and status.

The whole passage is dominated by a deep expression of desire manifested in the quadruple repetition of the phrase את שאהבה נפשי. It is interesting that the woman uses this description not only in her own thoughts but also in her inquiry of the whereabouts of her beloved when speaking to the guards of the city. It is one of the rare instances where the woman describes her beloved in terms other than דוד (cf. also שאהבה נפשי in Cant 1:7). The male on the other hand seems to be more imaginative when addressing the woman and can call her רעיה as in Cant 1:9.15; 2:2.10.13; 4:1.7; 5:2; 6:4 or כלה (Cant 4:8.9.10. 11.12; 5:1) and אחות (Cant 4:9.10.12; 5:1.2; 8:8). However, we should note that in the male parts of Song of Songs, the נפש is never mentioned, whereas the term is used when describing female desire (Cant 1:7; 3:1-4; 5:6; 6:12). This use is hardly surprising since נפש can be used to describe desire and passion (cf. Ps 103:3; Prov 19:2). Without making too much of this use it might be possible to argue that in general the expressions of female desire are more an inward reflection whereas the male speaker prefers descriptions.

The expression of desire (את שאהבה נפשי) corresponds to the seeking (and not finding) of the beloved. The first occurrence of the phrase בקשתיו ולא מצאתיו is still spoken in the bedroom of the women but will be the trigger for the following actions in Cant 3:2. בקש is the classic biblical term for seeking and seems to imply a finding (מצא) of the object or person one is looking for.

---

17 Neveling Porter 2002: 526.
18 *ibid.* citing SAA 11, No. 169.
19 *ibid.*

In Song of Songs it is only used to describe the seeking of the male by the woman (Cant 3:1-2; 5:6; 6:1 [the daughters of Jerusalem help the woman to look for the beloved]).[20]

Of course it is possible to seek (בקש) love (אהבה) in the Bible but the two passages where אהבה is the object to בקש are ambiguous. In Jer 2:33 the overtones are clearly negative and in Prov 17:9 the term is used more like 'friendship'.

The double not finding (לא מצאתיו) is set opposite a double finding in Cant 3:1-4: first the woman is fund by the watchmen (מצאוני השמרים) and then she herself is finding the beloved (עד שמצאתי). In contrast to that Cant 5:2-8 only mentions בקש once (Cant 5:6) – the seeking of the beloved is not successful here and this is probably most clearly demonstrated by the different behaviour or attitude of the watchmen in Cant 5:7 (interestingly enough the women does not or is not able to ask the watchmen in this passage for the whereabouts of her beloved): הכוני פצעוני נשאו את־רדידי מעלי. Both texts indicate what can happen – in the positive as well as in the negative way – if a woman is outside alone 'after hours'.[21]

While the male lover in Cant 3:1-5 remains strangely passive so that we are only able to speculate whether he himself was seeking his beloved too, in Cant 5:2-8 he assumes a more active role, since his appearance at the door of the house of the woman prompts her finally to go out and look for him. Throughout Cant 3:1-5 the male seems to be absently present and even when he is finally being found (עד שמצאתי) the woman remains the active one, who grabs him and does not let him go (אחזתיו ולא ארפנו). In contrast to that, in Cant 5:2-8 the woman simply reacts to his pleading (פתחו־לי... שראשי נמלא־טל קוצותי רסיסי לילה).

It is striking that the male in Cant 5:2-8 seems to behave like any good Greek *komastes*, performing a *paraklausithyron*. He even attacks the door, albeit in a very subtle way: דודי שלח ידו מן־החר (Cant 5:4a). This behaviour, certainly a sign of frustration, is attested elsewhere in Greek literature:

> καὶ ἐρῶν ἑταίρας καὶ κριοὺς προσβάλλων ταῖς θύραις πληγὰς εἰληφὼς ὑπ' ἀντεραστοῦ διακάζεσθαι.
>
> [He becomes infatuated with a prostitute, uses a battering ram on her door and gets a beating from her other lover – then takes him to court.][22]

---

20 The seeking (בקש) of a man (איש) is well attested, cf. Jud 4:22; 1Sam 13:14; 16:16; 24:3; 2Sam 17:3; 2Reg 6:19; Is 41:12; Ez 22:30.

21 Cf. Carr 2003: 120 who stresses the vulnerability of the woman.

22 Theoprastus, *Characters* 27.9; cf. also Herodas, *Mime* 2. 34-37 (οὐδεὶς πολίττης ἠλόησεν οὐδ' ἦλθεν | πρὸς τὰς θύρας μευ νυκτὸς οὐδ' ἔχων δᾶιδας | τὴν οἰκίην ὑφῆψεν οὐδὲ τῶν πορνέων | βίηι λαβὼν οἴχωκεν).

Of course, he is not admitted since the woman uses all kind of, admittedly feeble, excuses – probably an attempt to preserve her propriety.[23] The mentioning of dew (טל), normally a blessing to humans (Deut 33:13.28; Ps 133:3 etc.) is seen here as part of the difficulties the lover has to face on the way to his beloved. Again in Hellenistic epigrams the difficult way to the beloved is a literary topos, expressing that nothing can stop the desire:

> Νὺξ μακρὴ καὶ χεῖμα, μέσην δ᾽ ἐπὶ Πλειάδα δύνει·
> κἀγὼ πὰρ προθύροις νίσσομαι ὑόμενος,
> τρωθεὶς τῆς δολίης κείνης πόθῳ· οὐ γὰρ ἔρωτα
> Κύπρις, ἀνιηρὸν δ᾽ ἐκ πυρὸς ἧκε βέλος.

> [The night is long, and it is winter weather, and night sets when the Pleiads are half-way up the sky. I pass and repass her door, drenched by the rain, smitten by desire of her, the deceiver. It is not love that Cypris smote me with, but a tormenting arrow red-hot from the fire.][24]

In a further variation of the singing of a song in front of the door of the beloved, desire itself (ἔρως) can appear an assume the role of the *exclusus amor*, who is standing outside being wet after wandering about at night:

> μεσονυκτίοις ποτ᾽ ὥραις,
> στρέφετ᾽ ἡνίκ᾽ Ἄρκτος ἤδη
> κατὰ χεῖρα τὴν Βοώτου,
> μερόπων δὲ φῦλα πάντα
> κέαται κόπῳ δαμέντα,
> τότ᾽ Ἔρως ἐπισταθείς μευ
> θυρέων ἔκοπτ᾽ ὀχῆας.
> τίς ἔφην θύρας ἀράσσει
> κατά μευ σχίσας ὀνείρους;
> ὁ δ᾽ Ἔρως ἄνοιγε φησίν·
> βρέφος εἰμί, μὴ φόβησαι·
> βρέχομαι δὲ κἀσλέηνον
> κατὰ νύκτα πεπλάνημαι.

> [Once in the middle of the night, at the hour when the Bear is already turning by the Ploughman's hand and all the tribes of mortals lie overcome by exhaustion, Love stood at by bolted door and began knocking. 'Who is banging on my door?' I said: 'You've shattered my dreams.' Love said, 'Open up! I'm a baby: don't be afraid. I am getting wet, and have been wandering about in the moonless night'.][25]

Finally, let us briefly consider the possibility of a certain notion of jealousy in the Song of Songs. Despite the fact that obvious language of jealousy such –

---

23 Keel 1992: 176 seems to have problems in regard to the wherabouts of the woman, when he says: "Allein schon die Tatsache, daß ein Mädchen oder eine Frau allein in einem Zimmer zur Straße schläft, ist unwahrscheinlich." However, nothing in the text states that the door through which the beloved attempts to seek entry leads directly to the woman's room; even in an upstairs room קול דודי דופק would have been possible to hear.

24 *Anth. Pal.* 5.189 (Asklepiades).

25 Anacreonta, *fr.* 33 [Preisendanz].

with the notable exception of the noun קנאה in Cant 8:6 – is totally absent in Song of Songs scholars have tried to find hidden signs of (sexual) jealousy in the text.[26] For example the 18th century commentator T. HARMER who regards Cant as a document depicting the marriage arrangements and relationships of Solomon with his wives, remarks on the basis of Cant 3:4 (אל־בית אמי) – a text he sees as documenting some friction between the first wife and Solomon because of the imminent arrival of the new Egyptian queen – that the being in her mother's house is a sure indication that some jealousy must have occurred:[27]

> "Is it not natural to interpret the being in a *Mother's house*, in the life-time of an husband, as signifying a being parted in Displeasure from that husband? And are we not thus to understand Cant. iii. 4?" (263)

Thus, he is able to conclude on the longing of the woman in Cant 3:1-4:

> "It should seem indeed, that they were the Remains of this Jealousy that made her take his absence so heavily, that night in which she expected him, and was disappointed" (278).

Of course almost all of Harmer's presuppositions have to be abandoned in the light of recent research, however his observations might be a possible starting point for investigating the problem of jealousy in Song of Songs. If jealousy is indeed defined as being "the state of mind arising from the suspicion, apprehension, or knowledge of rivalry ... in love" that will ultimately lead to the "fear of being supplanted in the affection ... of a beloved person",[28] we need to look for possible rivals within the text. This is of course difficult since any member of a 'third party' is pushed into the background in favour of the 'privacy' of the loving couple. However, the frequent appeal to the 'daughters of Jerusalem' (בנות ירושלם in Cant 1:5; 2:7; 3:5.10; 5:8.16; 8:4) by the woman,[29] who describes herself as being שחורה אני ונאוה (Cant 1:5), may allow

26 The most obvious example is probably the 1535 translation of the Bible by Miles Coverdale, who renders כי־עזה כמות אהבה קשה כשאול קנאה in Cant 8:6aβ as 'for louve is mightie as the death, gelousy as the hell'.

27 For similar instances cf. the study of Bedouin society by Abu-Lughod 1999. The mentioning of the mother's house is indeed puzzling and much has been specualted about it (Murphy 1990: 146 calls it "a haven to which the woman can bring the man"; similar Keel 1992: 128); however other occurances of the phrase in the Bible (Gen 24:28; Rt 1:8) seem to suggest that speaking of the mother's house is part of the female dicourse; Gen 24:22-28 are especially illuminating in this respect: when the servant Rebekah, asking for a place to say the night, he speaks about בית־אביך (Gen 24:23), Rebekah on the other hand when reporting back home is said to talk לבית אמה (Gen 24:28).

28 The definition follows the second edition of Oxford English Dictionary, Vol. VIII, 207.

29 Heinevetter 1988: 179 calls the daughters 'antipodes'.

for the speculation that the city-girls can be perceived as possible rivals.[30] This notion of rivalry is further expressed in Cant 1:3, when the woman concludes her praise of the man with the words על־כן עלמות אהבוך.[31] The man, on the other hand, generally refrains from such statements (with the possible exception of Cant 2:15). Along this lines it is hardly surprising that the woman utters one of the most powerful phrases in Song of Songs that allows for an interpretation along the lines of 'jealousy': קשה כשאול קנאה (Cant 8:6).[32] What such jealousy can do is most aptly expressed in Prov 6:34 (in reference to the cuckolded husband): כי־קנאה חמת־גבר ולא־יחמול ביום נקם.

Admittedly, in comparison to the powerful statements of jealousy which we will encounter in *Fragmentum Grenfellianum*, the signs in Song of Songs are sparse, but it might not be too far fetched to assume that it probably wasn't only the desire for the beloved that led the woman to leave her room at night in Cant 3:1-5. If we regard the appearance of the daughters of Jerusalem as a (small) indication for possible rivalry – their mentioning in Cant 3:5 might not be incidental.

Fragmentum Grenfellianum

Fragmentum Grenfellianum[33] is the name commonly given to an erotic papyrus discovered in 1895 by the English papyrologist BERNHARD PYNE GRENFELL (1869-1926)[34] and now housed in the British Library (Inv. No. 605). It is written on the verso of a contract that can be dated to the eighth year of the reign of Ptolemaios VI. 'Philometor' (181-145 BCE), i.e. 174/3 BCE. The fragment is 6,5 x 7in in size and according to Grenfell himself "written in a small cursive hand, which is in some places difficult to read owing to its

30 Longmann 2001: 16 describes them as "city girls, young and naïve, inexperienced in matters of love"; unfortunately he fails to tell his reader on which eveidence he bases such conclusion.

31 Different Murphy 1990: 127 who states that "[t]he woman shows a generous and non-jealous attitude toward her lover."

32 Cf. Graetz 1885: 207, "hart wie das Grab die Eifersucht" and Robert/Tournay 1963: 300, "la jalousie inflexible comme le shéol"; Longmann 2001: 207, "tenacious like the grave is jealousy"

33 Other designations are P.Grenf. 1^{v} or P. Lit. Lond. 50; the first edition of the papyrus can be found in Grenfell 1896: 1-6, cf. also the corrections and additions in Grenfell/Hunt 1897: 209-17 and the edition in Powell 1925: 177-80.

34 B.P. Grenfell was since 1899 scholar of Queen's College/Oxford and since 1908 the first professor of papyrology at Oxford. He was part of the team that discovered the Oxyrhynchus Papyri and mostly responsible (together with A.S. Hunt) for the publication of the initial volumes; for more details of his life cf. the entry by H.I. Bell in the *Dictionary of National Biography 1922-1930*, 361-62.

minuteness and the roughness of the papyrus" (Grenfell 1896: 1).[35] Two columns of text have been preserved but there might have been a third. The text of the fragment runs as follows:[36]

col. 1 ἐξ ἀμφοτέρων γέγον᾽ αἵρεσις·
ἐζευγνίσμεθα· τῆς φιλίης Κύπρις
ἐστ᾽ ἀνάδοχος. ὀδύνη μ᾽ ἔχει,
ὅταν ἀναμνησθῶ
ὥς με καταφίλει ᾽πιβούλως μέλλων
με καταλιμπαν[ει]ν
ἀκαταστασίης εὑρετὴς
καὶ ὁ τὴν φιλίην ἐκτικώς.
ἔλαβέ μ᾽ ἔρως,
οὐκ ἀπαναίναμαι, αὐτὸν ἔχουσ᾽ ἐν τῆι διανοίαι.
ἄστρα φίλα καὶ συνερῶσα πότνια νύξ μοι
παράπεμψον ἔτι με νῦν πρὸς ὅν ἡ Κύπρις
ἔκδοτον ἄγει με καὶ ὁ
πολὺς ἔρως παραλαβών.
συνοδηγὸν ἔχω τὸ πολὺ πῦρ
τὸ ἐν τῆι ψυχῆι μου καιόμενον.
ταῦτά μ᾽ ἀδικεῖ, ταῦτά μ᾽ ὀδυνᾶι.
ὁ φρεναπάτης,
ὁ πρὸ τοῦ μέγα φρονῶν, καὶ ὁ τὴν Κύπριν οὐ
φάμενος εἰναι τοῦ ἐρᾶν μεταιτίαν
οὐκ ἤνεγκε νῦν
τὴν τυχοῦσαν ἀδικίην.
μέλλω μαίνεσθαι· ζῆλος γάρ μ᾽ ἔχει,
καὶ κατακα‹ί›ομαι καταλελειμμένη.
αὐτὸ δὲ τοῦτ[ό] μοι τοὺς στεφάνους βάλε,
οἷς μεμονωμένη χρωτισθήσομαι.
κύριε, μή μ᾽ ἀμφῆις ἀποκεκλειμένην·
δέξαι με· εὐδοκῶ ζήλωι δουλεύειν.
†επιμανουσοραν† μέγαν ἔχει πόνον.
ζηλοτυπεῖν γὰρ δεῖ, στέγειν, καρτερεῖν.
ἐὰν δ᾽ ἑνὶ προσκάθει μόνον ἄφρων ἔσει.
ὁ γὰρ μονιὸς ἔρως μαίνεσθαι ποιεῖ.
γίνωσχ᾽ ὅτι θυμὸν ἀνίκητον ἔχω
ὅταν ἔρις λάβηι με· μαίνομ᾽ ὅταν ἀναμ[νή]σωμ᾽
εἰ μονοκοιτήσω,
σὺ δὲ χρωτίζεσθ᾽ ἀποτρέχεις.
νῦν ἂν ὀργισθῶμεν, εὐθὺ δεῖ
καὶ διαλύεσθαι.
οὐχὶ διὰ τοῦτο φίλους ἔχομεν
οἳ κρινοῦσι τίς ἀδικεῖ;
col. 2 νῦν [ἂ]ν μὴ ἐπι[
ἐρῶ, κύριε, τὸν [
νῦν μὲν ουθε[

35 Wilamowitz 1896: 95-120 – whose article remains the most fundamental discussion and anlysis of the text – is even more explicit about the person who wrote down the text when he says: "Der Schreiber war Dillettant; er schrieb sich auf die Rückseite einer Rechnung einen literarischen Text ab. Schäden des Papiers zwangen ihn namentlich gegen Ende größere Räume unbeschrieben zu lassen, was den täuschenden Eindruck absichtlich verkürzter Zeilen macht" (97).

36 Text according to I.C. Cunningham, *Herodiae Mimiambi cum appendice fragmentorum Mimorum papyraceorum*, Bibliotheca Teubneriana, Leipzig 1987, 36-38.

πλυτης ο[
δυνήσομαι [
κοίτασον ἧς ἐχ[
ἱκανῶς σου εν[
κύριε, πῶς μ᾽ α.[
πρῶτος μεπειρ[
κύρι᾽ ὃν ἀτυχῶς ου[..].[
ὀπυασθαώμεθα ἐμὴν [..]εδε[ἐπι-
τηδείως αἰσθέσθω μ[..]ταν[
ἐγὼ δὲ μέλλω ζηλοῦν τω[
δουλ[....]ταν διαφορου. η[
ἀνθρ[ωπο.]ς ἀκρίτως θαυμάζει [
με. [   ].[.]φ[.]ρη. προσίκου δω[
θαυ[μα].ξριαν κατεῖδεν ο[
σξω[   ]τωι τοιντα η ετυ[
κου[ἐ]νόσησα νηπία· σὺ δέ, κύρ[ιε
και[   ]μμεν ..[
λελαλ[ηκ   ]ριεμη. [

The English translation reads:[37]

The choice was made by both:
we were united; Aphrodite
is surety for our love. Pain holds me,
when I remember
how he kissed me while treacherously intending
to leave me,
inventor of inconstancy
and creator of love.
Desire has seized me,
I do not deny it, having him in my thoughts
Loving stars and Lady Night who shares desire with me,
escort me even now to him to whom Aphrodite
delivers and drives me, and the
great desire that has taken hold of me.
As guide I have the great fire
that burns in my heart.
These things hurt me, these things pain me.
The mind-deceiver,
he who formerly had high thoughts, and he who denies that [Aphrodite
shares responsibility for desire
has not now borne
the present hurt.
I am about to go mad; for jealousy holds me,
and I am burning at being deserted.
For this reason throw the garlands to me,
with which I shall be bedded in my loneliness.
My lord, do not exclude me and put me away;
receive me; I accept to be a slave to jealousy.

---

37 Quoted from J. Rusten and I.C. Cunningham, *Theophrastus, Characters. Herodas,Mimes. Sophron and other Mime Fragments*, Loeb Classical Library 225, Cambridge/MA 2002, 363-367.

To be madly in love (?) brings great trouble.
For one must be jealous, conceal endure.
And if you devote yourself to only one man, you will be senseless.
For single-minded desire makes one mad.
Recognise that I have an undefeated spirit
When strife takes me: I am mad when I remember
that I sleep alone,
while you go off to be bedded.
Now if we have quarrelled, we must at once
also to be reconciled.
Is it not for this that we have friends
who will judge who is at fault?
Now if not [
I desire my lord, the [
Now [
[
I shall be able [
sleep with whom [
sufficiently of you [
my lord, how [do you put] me away [
you were the first to seduce me [
my lord, whom unfortunately [
that we be married my [
let him fittingly perceive [
but I am going to be jealous [
slave [ ] different [
men uncritically you admire [
approach [
admir[e] he (?) saw [
[
I was sick like a child; but you, my lord, [
[
spoke [

As far as the genre is concerned, the fragment has been described as being a song of "a woman who has been spurned by her former lover and now complains bitterly outside his house" (Hunter 1996: 8). The setting defines it as a *paraklausithyron*[38] (and indeed, J.U. POWELL (1925: 177) in his edition of the fragment adds the heading 'Παρακλαυσίθυρον' which is not found in the papyrus),[39] but deviates from the general form in that it is the woman who stands this time outside her lover's house. The setting might be perceived as unusual, however Greek epigram can envisage such a scenario, thus we read for example:

Νύξ· σὲ γὰρ οὐκ ἄλλην μαρτύρομαι, οἷά μ᾽ ὑβρίζει
  Πυθιὰς ἡ Νικοῦς, οὖσα φιλεξαπάτις·

38 One of the earliest forms of a *paraklausithyron* can be found in Alcaeus, *fr.* 374 [L-P]: δέξαι με κωμάσδοντα, δέχαι, λίσσομαί σε, λίσσομαι.

39 On this literary form see Canter 1920: 355-68 and Copley 1956: 1-6.

κληθεὶς, οὐκ ἄκλητος, ἐλήλυθα. ταὐτα παθοῦσα
σοὶ μέμψαιτ' ἔτ' ἐμοῖς στᾶσα παρὰ προθύροις.

[Night, I call thee alone to witness, look how shamefully Nico's Pythias, ever loving to deceive, treats me. I came at her call and not uninvited. May she one day stand at my door and complain to thee that she suffered the like at my hands.][40]

"The language of the *Fragmentum* is marked by a striking number of words and usages familiar from Hellenistic prose, but not found elsewhere in poetry."[41]

The Fragment starts without providing its reader with any setting or sense of place. However, line 12 (παράπεμψον ἔτι με νῦν πρὸς ὄν) seems to suggest that the first part is probably spoken away from the door of the beloved and thus one might be allowed to postulate that the woman is at home when the text begins. As far as the time is concerned, *Fragmentum Grenfellianum* suggests the present and due to the appeal to the 'loving stars and Lady Night' (ἄστρα φίλα καὶ πότνια νύξ) in line 11 we are able to locate the proceedings at night. As we have already seen in Song of Songs, the sleeplessness at night prompted by a longing for the beloved seems to be a fairly standard feature of love-poetry.[42] In addition, the protagonists (apart from Aphrodite who is mentioned by name several times) remain anonymous. In a similar way, Song of Songs does provide several epithets for the beloved but never gives a concrete name.

The poem as a whole is spoken by a woman. This has puzzled commentators despite the evidence for women's voice in poetry as for example in the following line from Anacreon:

ἐκ ποταμοῦ 'πανέρχομαι πάντα φέρουσα λαμπρά.

[I come up from the river bringing (the washing) all bright.][43]

On the basis of Athenaeus explanation of the behaviour of the *magodos*, R. HUNTER, for example, argued that "the *Fragmentum* was indeed presumably performed by a man."[44] However, a closer look at the passage from Athenaeus in question reveals certain differences that do not necessarily allow to jump to such a conclusion:

ὁ δὲ μαγῳδὸς καλούμενος τύμπανα ἔχει καὶ κύμβαλα καὶ πάντα τὰ περὶ αὐτὸν ἐνδύματα γυναικεῖα· σχινίζεταί τε καὶ πάντα ποιεῖ τὰ ἔξω κόσμου, ὑποκρινόμενος ποτὲ μὲν γυναῖκας καὶ μοιχοὺς καὶ μαστροπούς, ποτὲ δὲ ἄνδρα μεθύοντα καὶ ἐπὶ κῶμον παραγινόμενον πρὸς τὴν ἐρωμένην.

40 *Anth. Pal.* 5.164 (Asklepiades).

41 Hunter 1996: 9-10, cf. also Wilamowitz 1896: 107 ("Im Ganzen ist die Sprache ausgesprochen hellenistisch").

42 Cf. *Anth. Pal.* 5.166, lines 1-2: ὦ νύξ, ὦ φιλάγρυπνος ἐμοὶ πόθος Ἡλιοδώρας, | καὶ σκολιῶν ὄρθων κνίσματα δακρυχαρῆ.

43 Anacreon, *fr.* 385 [PMG] = *fr.* 73 [Diehl].

44 Hunter 1996: 8.

[The magodist, as he is called, has tambourines and cymbals, and all his garments are feminine; he not only makes indecent gestures, he does everything that is shameless, at one time acting part of women as adulteresses or pimps, at another, a drunken man going to meet his mistress in a revel rout.][45]

If indecent gestures (σχινίζεται) and shameless behaviour are, according to Athenaeus, part of such a performance, it is difficult to assign the contents of *Fragmentum Grenfellianum* to such a performance. Of course, males acting as females are well known from Greek literature and performance and we certainly do not deny this transsexual element, but for our interpretation we will maintain that a woman speaks. A further question, however – that cannot be addressed in this context – remains how male writers tend to construct female identity and desire.[46]

The scene opens with a statement stressing the mutual agreement of both lovers to be united (ἐξ ἀμφοτέρων γέγον' αἵρεσις· | ἐζευγνίσμεθα·). The term used for the union (ζεύγνυμι) should not be interpreted as being joined together in wedlock,[47] but rather to stress a union between two previously unlinked persons, now connected by love.[48] The first two lines of *Fragmentum Grenfellianum* distantly echo the expression of belonging דודי לי ואני לו in Cant 2:16a. The following sentence introduces a divine element by directly appealing to Aphrodite, the goddess of love (τῆς φιλίης Κύπρις| ἐστ' ἀνάδοχος). Aphrodite is mentioned two times further (l. 12 and l. 19) and always in connection with longing or desire (ἡ Κύπρις | ἔκδοτον ἄγει με καί).

Aphrodite is always called Κύπρις in the Fragment, thus alluding to her place of home: ἡ δ' ἄρα Κύπριν ἵκανε φιλομμειδὴς Ἀφροδιτὴ | ἐς Πάφον· ἔνθα δέ οἱ τέμενος βωμός τε θυήεις.[49] This designation aptly demonstrates the Near Eastern characteristics and the place of origin of the goddess already known in antiquity.[50] Generally speaking Aphrodite is the impersonation of (sexual) desire and 'beguilement that steals the wits even of the wise' (ἥ τ' ἔκλεψε νόον πύκα περ φρονεόντων [Homer, *Il.* 14.217]) and can be rightly called an 'enchantress of men':

λίπον χλωραύχενα
ἐν δώμασι Δαϊάνειραν,
νῆιν ἔτι χρυσέας
Κύπριδος θελξιμβρότου[51]

45 Athenaeus 14.621c-d.

46 Cf. the contribution by J.B. Burton and R. Hunter in this volume note that both Attic tragedy and Hellenistic poetry broke the silence of the women in discourses on love; for the Bible cf. the study by Goitein 1998: 1-33 and the discussion in Exum 2000: 28-29.

47 Euripides, *Trachiniae* 676 (παρθένιον ἐζευξω λέχος).

48 For such a use see Homer, *Il.* 18.276 (joining of two doors by a bolt); Herodotus, *Hist.* 1.206 (a bridge joins two banks).

49 Homer, *Od.* 8.363 [but she, the laughter-loving Aphrodite, went to Cyprus, to Paphos where she has precinct and fragrant altar].

50 Cf. Herodotus, *Hist.* 1.105,131.

51 Bacchylides, *fr.* 5.172-5.

[I left in my home Deianeira, the bloom of youth on her neck, still without experience of golden Cypris, that enchantress of men]

In an interesting parallel to the Song of Songs, the dove is generally regarded as the sign of Aphrodite.[52]

Furthermore, the use of the word Κύπρις allows for the possibility that the goddess of love merges with the concept of 'Love', since Κύπρις can be used as an appellative for love or passion.[53] Thus for example Euripides can state

οἴνου δὲ μηκέτ' ὄντος οὐκ ἔστιν Κύπρις
οὐδ' ἄλλο τερπνὸν οὐδὲν ἀνθρώποις ἔτι.

[If there is no wine, there is no Aphrodite or any other pleasure for mortals.][54]

and Bacchylides is able to link wine and love in a similar way:

εὖτε νέων ἁ[παλὸν γλυκεῖ' ἀ]νάγκα
σευομενᾶν κ[υλίκων θάλπη]σι θυμ[όν
Κύπριδος τ' ἐλπ[ὶς <δι>αιθύσσῃ φρέ]νας,
ἀμμειγνυμέν[α Διονυσίοισι] δώροις·

[when the sweet compulsion of the speeding cups warms the tender hearts of the young men, and hope of the Cyprian, mingling with the gifts of Dionysius, makes their hearts flutter.][55]

In a fragment of Mimnermus, one gets the impression that Aphrodite (or Love) is associated with youthful and virile behaviour and set opposite to the horrors of old age (ὀδυνερὸν γῆρας):

τίς δὲ βίος, τί δὲ τερπνὸν ἄτερ χρυσέης Ἀφροδίτης;
τεθναίην, ὅτε μοι μηκέτι ταῦτα μέλοι,
κρυπταδίη φιλότης καὶ μείλιχα δῶρα καὶ εὐνή,
οἷ' ἥβης ἄνθεα γίνεται ἁρπαλέα
ἀνδράσιν ἠδὲ γυναιξίν.

[What life is there, what pleasure without golden Aphrodite? May I die when I no longer care about secret intrigues persuasive gifts, and the bed, those blossoms of youth that men and women find alluring.][56]

Here in *Fragmentum Grenfellianum* Aphrodite serves as a witness or better surety (ἀνάδοχος) for the loving union of the couple.[57] The term ἀνάδοχος is rare in

52 *LSAM* no. 86 and Lucian, *de Dea Syria* 54; cf. Keel 1984: 59-60.

53 Cf. also Aristophanes, *Ecclesiazusae* 721-4: καὶ τάς γε δούλας οὐχὶ δεῖ κοσμουμένας | τὴν τῶν ἐλευθέρων ὑφαρπάζειν Κύπριν, | ἀλλὰ παρὰ τοῖς δούλοισι κοιμᾶσθαι μόνον | κατωνάκην τὸν χοῖρον ἀποτετιλμένας.

54 Euripides, *Bacchae* 773-4.

55 Bacchylides *fr.* 20b 6-9 [Snell-Maehler].

56 Mimnermus, *fr.* 1.1-5

the Greek language. However, its Cretan derivate ἀνδοκά already occurs in the Gortyn Code.[58] This appeal to a higher, i.e. divine authority for love is missing in the Song of Songs as are direct references to the divine sphere as such with the possible exception of the 'flame of Yah' (שלהבתיה) in Cant 8:6[59] if one does not want to regard the phrase as a way to express the superlative.[60] This however does not imply that the numinous is missing entirely from the Song of Songs. Especially H.-P. MÜLLER – in taking up the concept of theomorphy from H. Blumenberg – has shown that several of the comparisons and descriptions found in the Song of Songs echo the divine sphere and can indeed be described as remnants of a religious memory (*religiöse Erinnerungsreste*).[61] All this does not change the fact that in the two passages we are concerned with here, no appeal is made to a higher authority.

Rather abruptly the pain at being deserted by her lover is introduced in the third line (ὀδύνη μ' ἔχει) using a construction that will be repeated in line 23, when the aspect of jealousy is first mentioned by name (ζῆλος γάρ μ' ἔχει); in contrast to that the seizure by 'desire' (ἔρως, l. 9) and 'strife' (ἔρις, l. 34) are expressed with the verb λαμβάνω. The word for 'pain' (ὀδύνη) can either refer to the pain of the body (Homer, *Il.* 11.398; *Od.* 9.440) or to the pain of mind (Homer, *Il.* 15.25, cf. Xeneophon, *Symposium* 1.15). Generally it is used in the plural but the singular is also found.[62] The pain is prompted by the remembrance (ὅταν ἀναμνησθῶ) of the kisses received from the lover, here expressed by the verb καταφίλει that can be used to describe the courteous or humble kissing of hand or feet by a person of lower status (Xenophon, *Cyr.* 7.5.32) but should probably be understood here as the amorous kiss.[63]

The aspect of jealousy is introduced in line 5 with the phrase 'πιβούλως μέλλων and is immediately connected with the aspect of leaving her.[64] In l. 6 καταλιμπάνω is used actively to describe the treacherous intend of the man, while in l. 24 the woman describes herself as 'burning at being deserted' (καὶ κατακα‹ί›ομαι καταλελειμμένη). We note that the text uses a certain degree of intensification, when speaking about the women's feeling. In l. 16 the burning within her heart is described simply using καίω, while the 'burning at being

57 Crusius 1896: 361-2 translates 'Bürge'.

58 Cf. *ICr* IV 72 IX.34-7: ... ἀνδοκ- | ᾶδ <δ>ε κἐνκοιοτᾶν καὶ διαβολᾶς κ- | αἰ δι<αρ>ρέσιος μαίτυρες οἱ ἐπιβ- | άλλοντες ἀποπονιότον.

59 Robert/Tournay 1962: 301-2; Murphy 1990: 196-8; Garbini 1992: 276 with reference to Theocritus, *Id.* 2.133-4.

60 Thus Pope 1977: 670-1; Keel 1992: 250; Longman 2001: 212-3.

61 Cf. Müller 1976: 23-41 (reference to Blumenberg's work on p. 24); 1988: 112-121 and 1994: 375-395.

62 ὀδύνη in pl.: Homer, *Od.* 1.242; Sophocles, *Trachiniae* 959; 986; Aristophanes, *Acharnes* 526; in sg.: Sophocles, *Trachiniae* 975.

63 Cf. Lucian, *Amores* 13 καὶ ἅμα προσδραμὼν λιπαρέσι τοῖς χείλεσιν ἐφ' ὅσον ἦν δυνατὸν ἐκτείνων τὸν αὐχένα κατεφίλει.

64 καταλιμπάνω as in Gen 39,16 [LXX] and Thuycidides, 8.17 instead of καταλείπω.

deserted' is expressed with κατακαίω, a word that usually denotes the complete consumption by fire (cf. Homer, *Il.* 7.333).[65]

As in Cant 3:1-4; 5:2-8 the desire for the beloved prompts the woman to leave her home to look for him (l.11-13):

ἄστρα φίλα καὶ συνερῶσα πότνια νύξ μοι
παράπεμψον ἔτι με νῦν πρὸς ὅν ἡ Κύπρις
ἔκδοτον ἄγει με

The mentioning of ἄστρα φίλα and πότνια νύξ indicate that it is night-time when the women commences her wanderings (cf. בלילות in Cant 3:1).[66] As in the Bible, so Greek literature can envisage the possibility of a woman leaving home at night; thus we read, for example, in another epigram by Asklepiades:

Ὡμολόγησ' ἥξειν εἰς νύκτα μοι ἡ 'πιβόητος
 Νικώ, καὶ σεμνὴν ὤμοσε Θεσμοφόρον·
κοὐχ ἥκει, φυλακὴ δὲ παροίχεται. ἆρ' ἐπιορκεῖν
 ἤθελε; τὸν λύχνον, παῖδες, ἀποσβέσατε.

[The celebrated Niko promised to come to me for to-night and swore by solemn Demeter. She comes not and the first watch of the night is past. Did she mean then to forswear herself? Servants, put out the light.][67]

Here however, we should note that the promise of Niko is not fulfilled (κοὐχ ἥκει), prompting dissapointment. Did the women in Cant 3:1 simply state that she was seeking 'him whom my soul (נפש) loves', the speaker of the *Fragmentum* is much more explicit when she says to be guided by a great fire that burns in her heart:

τὸ πολὺ πῦρ
τὸ ἐν τῆι ψυχῆι μου καιόμενον

This links well with the frequent mentioning of ἔρως in the fragment (l. 9.14.32 and most likely also the unclear reading επιμανουσοραν in l. 29[68]); in contrast to Κύπρις, ἔρως does not describe a godhead here but points to sexual desire.[69] This desire has – so we learn from the woman – a maddening power:

†επιμανουσοραν† μέγαν ἔχει πόνον.
ζηλοτυπεῖν γὰρ δεῖ, στέγειν, καρτερεῖν (lines 29-30)

65 Cf. the intersting parallel to such metaphorical use of κατακαίω in *Lyrica Adespota* 8c (Powell 1925: 186) πίνοντ[ες ....? π]οτοῦ μ[εμεθύ]σμεθα κοὐκέστι φρονοῦμμεν, | ὁ δ' ἔρως ἐμὲ π[υρί]ναις ταῖς ... κατακέκαυκεν.

66 πότνια νύξ is also found in Euripides, *Orestes* 174 (πότνια, πότνια νύξ); Theocritus, *Id.* 18.26-7 (ἀὼς ἀντέλλοισα καλὸν διέφανε πρόσωπον, | πότνια Νύξ, τό τε λευκὸν ἔαρ χειμῶνος ἀνέντος); *Anth. Pal.* 5.165, line 2 (ναὶ λίτομαι, κώμων σύμπλανε, πότνια Νύξ).

67 *Anth. Pal.* 5.150.

68 Wilamowitz 1896: 98 and other propose to read ἐπιμανοῦς ἐρᾶν.

69 Cf. Aeschylus, *Choephori* 600; Euripides, *Hippolytus* 32 etc.

She describes her pains in three infinitives. The first one (ζηλοτυπεῖν) echoes the theme of jealousy that drove her to the house of her beloved in the first place, while the other two sound like attempts to exercise self-control. Love (here paired with jealousy) can of course have a maddening nature as the following fragment from Sappho shows:

> Ἔρος δηὖτέ μ᾽ ὁ λυσιμέλης δόνει,
> γλυκύπικρον ἀμάχανον ὄρπετον
>
> [Once again limb-loosening Love makes me tremble, the bitter-sweet, irresistible creature][70]

A few lines later, this madness will stressed once more (μαίνομ᾽ ὅταν ἀναμ[νή]σωμ᾽, line 34),[71] this time connected with the fear of loneliness at night, or more precisely the prospect of having to sleep alone (εἰ μονοκοιτήσω),[72] while the beloved possibly sleeps with somebody else (σὺ δὲ χρωτίζεσθ᾽ ἀποτρέχεις).[73] The loneliness at night is another well known topos from Greek literature and also reflected in the Song of Songs. Again, we turn to Sappho as one of the first poetic voices to describe it:

> δέδυκε μὲν ἁ σελάννα
> καὶ Πλήϊαδες· μέσαι δὲ
> νύκτες, παρὰ δ᾽ ἔρχετ᾽ ὤρα,
> ἔγω δὲ μόνα κατεύδω.
>
> [The moon has set and the Pleiades; it is midnight, and time goes by, and I lie alone.][74]

Furthermore we find similar expressions in Theocritus' second Idyll, a text which bears many similarities to *Fragementum Grenfellianum*.[75] One gets the

70 Sappho, *fr.* 130 [L-P].

71 μαίνομαι can be used to described the state of mind, cf. Homer, *Od.* 21.297-8 (ὁ δ᾽ ἐπεὶ φένας ἄασεν οἴνῳ, | μαινόμενος κάκ᾽ ἔρεξε δόμον κατα Πειριθόοιο; 'mad with wine', i.e. drunk); Aristophanes, *Frogs* 751 (μᾶλλα πλεῖν ἢ μαίνομαι;'mad of joy') and Theocritus, *Id.* 10.31 ἐγὼ δ᾽ ἐπὶ τὶν μεμάνημαι (mad with love).

72 The verb is rare in Greek, cf. Aristophanes, *Lysistrata* 592 (μονοκοιτοῦμεν διὰ τὰς στρατίας καὶ θἠμέτερον μὲν ἐάσω) and *Anth. Pal.* 11.196 (εἰμι, λέγει, σώφρων, Λουκίλλιε, καὶ μονοκοιτῶ); however, the few references we have seem to point to a lack of sexual activity.

73 χρωτίζομαι is another rare and difficult word. Grenfell 1896: 5 himself thought that the word refers to ointments and concludes that the beloved man might have been an athlete, different Wilamowitz 1896: 107 who thinks of the Theocritean χρὼς ἐπὶ χρωτὶ πεπαίνετο (*Id.* 2.140), a view reflected in Cunningham's translation of the term in the Loeb edition and also adopted in this paper. Further occurances for example are: Aristophanes, *Clouds* 516 (τοῦ πράγμασιν χρωτίζεται) and Plutarch, *Table Talk* 693c6 (οὐκοῦν καὶ τὸν οἶνον οἱ μὲν ἀλόαις χρωτίζοντες ἢ κιναμώμοις καὶ κρόκοις ἐφηδύνοντες ὥσπερ γυναῖκα καλλωπίζουσιν κτλ.).

74 Sappho, *fr.* 168B (Voigt) = *fr.* 94 (Diehl); on the fragment and its parallels cf. Müller 2001: 206-218.

impression that the loneliness at night prompts the woman to reflect on her situation and her love.

A certain shift happens in line 25 (αὐτὸ δὲ τοῦτ[ό] μοι τοὺς στεφάνους βάλε). Now the man is addressed directly and within the performance of the *Fragmentum* the reader (or hearer) realises the woman must have arrived in front of the door of the house of the beloved man – strictly speaking the genre of the paraklausithyron only starts here. The garlands are normally left by the male lover at the door of the beloved.[76] Here it seems that the woman must have presented him a garland. The following line reveals that she will use the garlands (στεφάνοι) as a substitute for her lover (οἷς μεμονωμένη χρωτισθήσομαι), again using the difficult verb χρωτίζομαι. The beloved is addressed as κύριε (as again in line 42 and 51) which is set in opposition to εὐδοκῶ ζήλωι δουλεύειν in line 28, clearly denoting some sort of submission of the woman.[77] However, it is not possible to draw any conclusions about different social status, since the woman makes it quite explicit that she is only a slave due to her jealousy. Why she feels like that is revealed in line 50 when the woman states that her beloved was the first one to seduce her (πρῶτος μεπειρ[]).[78]

How the situation is resolved we do not know, since the *Fragmentum* breaks off – the last complete statement from the woman again refers to her torment, this time employing illness: κου[ἐ]νόσησα νηπία· We are reminded of Cant 2:5b (כי־חולת אהבה אני). As the love-sickness of the woman in Song of Songs can only be cured by the love of her desired partner,[79] so can the sickness due to jealousy only be healed by a change in the attitude of the man who left her.

Fragmentum Grenfellianum represents an innovation in Greek poetry as being one of the few examples that explicitly states the psychological condition of a lover. By doing so it moves significantly beyond the modes of expression we know from Sappho which are focussed solely on the physical torment evoked by love.[80] Song of Songs seems to move in the same direction when linking an

75 Hunter 1996: 8-11 who, however, notes one major difference: "Idyll 2 is actively engaged with its own literary history; the *Fragmentum* is concerned only with the considerable power of its immediate performance" (10).

76 Canter 1920: 356.

77 Wilamowitz 1896: 111.

78 Powell 1925 reads πρῶτος μ' ἐπείρ[ασας. The verb used (πειρᾶ or πειράω/πειράζω) generally refers to an (indecent) attempt of seduction cf. Aristophanes, *Knights* 517 (πολλῶν γὰρ δὴ πειρασάντων αὐτὴν ὀλίγοις χαρίσασθαι); *Peace* 763 (παῖδας ἐπείρων, ἀλλ' ἀράμενος τὴν σκευὴν εὐθὺς ἐχώρουν); *Wasps* 1025 (οὐδὲ παλαίστρας περικωμάζειν πειρῶν).

79 Murphy 1990: 137.

80 Cf. Sappho, *fr.* 31 [Voigt].: φαίνεταί μοι κῆνος ἴσος θέοισιν | ἔμμεν' ὤνηρ, ὄττις ἐνάντιός τοι | ἰσδάνει καὶ πλάσιον ἆδυ φωνεί-|σας ὐπακούει | καὶ γελαίσας ἰμέροεν· τό μ' ἦ μὰν | καρδίαν ἐν στήθεσιν ἐπτόαισεν. | ὡς γὰρ <ἔς> σ' ἴδω βρόχε', ὤς με φώνης | οὐδὲν ἔτ' εἴκει· | ἀλλὰ κὰμ μὲν γλῶσσά †ἔαγε†, λέπτον | δ' αὔτικα χρῷ πῦρ ὐπαδεδρόμακεν, | ὀππάτεσσι δ' οὐδὲν ὄρημμ', ἐπιρρόμ-| βεισι δ' ἄκουαι, | †έκαδε μ' ἴδρως ψῦχρος κακχέεται†, τρόμος δὲ |

obvious awareness of the body with mental pain caused by the longing for the beloved.

Conclusion

What can we conclude from the two texts we looked at in this study? Cant 3:1-5; 5:2-8 and *Fragmentum Grenfellianum* belong to the group of texts that assume the female voice to make it heard. If they were indeed written by female authors we cannot say but, nevertheless, they are part of the literary expression of female desire. LILA ABU-LUGHOD in her study on the role of poetry in a contemporary Bedouin society has shown how poetic devices are used to express sentiments that would otherwise be regarded as unacceptable in society:

> "It is clear that individuals are shielded from the consequences or making statements and expressing sentiments that contravene the moral system if they do so in poetry." (Abu-Lughod 1999: 248).

As such poetry forms an integral part on the discourse on the 'politics of sentiment'. The behaviour of female (and male) protagonists in poetry is not condemned but rather appreciated as an expression of the feelings of the lovers.[81] Furthermore, poetry – in Bedouin society – is mostly sung by women (and youths), thus reflecting a certain opposition and anti-structure to the prevalent moral and societal system.[82] I would argue that much of the female (and probably also the male) voice in Song of Songs has to be seen as part of this anti-structure to surrounding moral values. In similar veins, *Fragmentum Grenfellianum* serves as such an anti-structure: the author deliberately employs literary conventions that are normally associated with the male sphere and transforms them to become the expression of the jealous desire of an abandoned woman.

Due to the relative scarcity of expressions of female desire in the Hebrew Bible,[83] the texts from (Hellenistic) Greece employing women's voices serve as an convenient set of comparative data that can be utilised to illuminate the

παῖσαν ἄγρει, χλωροτέρα δὲ ποίας | ἔμμι, τεθνάκην δ' ὀλίγω 'πιδεύης | φαίνομ' ἔμ' αὔται | ἀλλὰ πὰν τόλματον, ἐπεὶ †καὶ πένητα†

81 Abu-Lughod 1999: 250.

82 "Poetry is, in so many ways, the discourse of opposition to the systemn and of difiance of those who represent it: it is antistructure just as it is antimorality" (Abu-Lughod 1999: 251).

83 Dijk-Hemmes 1993: 108 in conclusion to her survey of possible women-texts in the Bible states: "Asking whether women did contribute to the writtentraditions of the Bible is sure to be relevant, but it is far from clear which texts are actually implicated. In view of this situation and in view of the complex history of biblical tradition 'women's texts' the also acquired the emaning of 'texts transmitted orally by women but (probably) written down by male authors'".

poems from the Song of Songs. However, despite all the parallels in structure and contents one should not disregard the differences. As far as our look at *Fragmentum Grenfellianum* was concerned, it became clear that expressions of desire, often similar to the two passages Cant 3:1-5 and 5:2-8 are utilised in the Fragment to shape a powerful expression of jealousy and to point the reader to the pains caused by abandonment. This notion is missing in Song of Songs, but the desire for the beloved partner is equally strong expressed.

Bibliography

ABU-LUGHOD, L. (1999): Veiled Sentiments. Honor and Poetry in a Bedouin Society, rev. ed. Berkeley/Los Angeles/London.

BERGANT, D. (2001): The Song of Songs, Berit Olam, Collegeville.

BOER, R. (1999): Night sprinkle(s): Pornography and the Song of Songs, in: id. Knockin' on Heaven's Door. The Bible and Popular Culture, Biblical Limits, London, 53-70.

BOWRA, C.M. (1958): A Love Duet, AJPh 79, 376-391.

BRENNER, A. (1997): The Intercourse of Knowledge. On Gendering Desire and 'Sexuality' in the Hebrew Bible, BibIntS 26, Leiden/New York/Cologne.

BURRUS, V./MOORE, S.D. (2003): Unsafe Sex: Feminism, Pornography, and the Song of Songs, BibInt 11, 24-52.

CANTER, H.V. (1920): The Paraclausithyron as a Literary Theme, AJPh 41, 355-368.

CARR, D.M. (2003): The Erotic Word. Sexuality, Spirituality, and the Bible, Oxford/New York.

CLINES, D.J.A. (1994): Why Is There a Song of Songs and What Does It Do to you if you read it?, Jian Dao 1, 3-27 (= id., Interested Parties. The Ideology of Writers and Readers of the Hebrew Bible, JSOTS 205/Gender Culture Theory 1, Sheffield 1995, 94-121).

COHEN, D. (1989): Seclusion, Separation, and the Status of Women in Classical Athens, in: I. McAuslan/P. Walcot (eds.), Women in Antiquity, GaR Studies, Oxford 1996, 134-145.

COPLEY, F.O. (1956): Exclusus Amor. A Study in Latin Love Poetry, Philological Monographs 17, Oxford.

CRUSIUS, O. (1896): Grenfells Erotic fragment und seine litterarische Stellung, Philologus 55, 356-384.

DEAN-JONES, L. (1992): The Politics of Pleasure: Female Sexual Appetite in the Hippocratic Corpus, Helios 19, 72-91.

DE GEUS, C.H.J. (1992): The City of Women: Women's Place in Ancient Israelite Cities, in: J.A. Emerton (ed.), Congress Volume Paris 1992, VT.S 61, Leiden/New York/Cologne, 75-86.

DELITZSCH, F. (1851): Das Hohelied, Leipzig.

DIJK-HEMMES, F. (1993): Traces of Women's Texts in the Hebrew Bible, in A. Brenner/F. Dijk-Hemmes (eds.), On Gendering Texts. Female and Male Voices in the Hebrew Bible, BibIntS 1, Leiden/New York/Cologne, 17-109.

EWALD, H. (1826): Das Hohelied Salomos, Göttingen.

EXUM, J.C. (1999): In the Eye of the Beholder: Wishing, Dreaming, and Double Entendre in the Song of Songs, in: F.C. Black/R. Boer/E. Runions (eds.), The Labour of Reading. Desire, Alienation, and Biblical Interpretation, SBL Semeia Studies 36, Atlanta, 71-86.

– (2000): Ten Things Every Feminist Should Know About the Song of Songs, in: A. Brenner/C.R. Fontaine (eds.), The Song of Songs. The Feminist Companion to the Bible (2nd Series) 6, Sheffield, 24-35.

FARAONE, C.A. (1999): Ancient Greek Love Magic, Cambridge/MA.

FOX, M.V. (1985): The Song of Songs and the Ancient Egyptian Love Songs, Madison.
GARBINI, G. (1992): Cantico dei cantici, Biblica Testi e studi 2, Brescia.
GERLEMAN, G. (1981): Ruth. Das Hohelied, BK XVIII, 2nd ed. Neukirchen-Vluyn.
GOITEIN, S.D. (1988): Women as Creators of Biblical Genres, Prooftexts 8, 1-33.
GRAETZ, H. (1885): Shir Ha-Shirim oder das salomonische Hohelied, Berslau.
GRENFELL, B.P. (1896): An Alexandrian Erotic Fragment and other Greek Papyri chiefly Ptolemaic, Oxford.
GRENFELL, B.P./HUNT, A.S. (1897): New Classical Fragments and other Greek and Latin Papyri, Greek Papyri Series 2, Oxford.
GUTZWILLER, K.J. (1998): Poetic Garlands. Hellenistic Epigrams in Context, Hellenistic Culture and Society 18, Berkeley/London.
HARMER, T. (1748): The Outline of a New Commentary on Solomon's Song drawn by the help of instructions from the East, London.
HEINEVETTER, H.-J. (1988): 'Komm nun, mein Liebster, Dein Garten ruft Dich!' Das Hohelied als programmatische Komposition, BBB 69, Frankfurt a.M.
HITZIG, F. (1855): Das Hohe Lied, Kurzgefaßtes exegetisches Handbuch zum Alten Testament 16, Leipzig.
HUNTER, R. (1996): Theocritus and the Archaeology of Greek Poetry, Cambridge.
HUTCHINSON, G.O. (1988): Hellenistic Poetry, Oxford.
KEEL, O. (1984): Deine Blicke sind Tauben. Zur Metaphorik des Hohen Liedes, SBS 114/115, Stuttgart.
– (1992): Das Hohelied, ZBK.AT 18, 2nd ed., Zurich.
LEWIS, S. (2002): The Athenian Woman. An Iconographic Handbook, London/New York.
LONGMANN, T. (2001): Song of Songs, NICOT, Grand Rapids/Cambridge.
MÜLLER, H.-P. (1976): Die lyrische Reproduktion des Mythischen im Hohenlied, ZThK 73, 23-41.
– (1984): Vergleich und Metapher im Hohenlied, OBO 56, Göttingen/Fribourg.
– (1988): Begriffe menschlicher Theomorphie. Zu einigen cruces interpretum in Hld 6,10, ZAH 1, 112-121.
– (1992): Das Hohelied, in: id./O. Kaiser/J.A. Loader, Das Hohelied-Klagelieder-Das Buch Ester, ATD 16/2, 4th ed., Göttingen, 3-90.
– (1994): Menschen, Landschaften und religiöse Erinnerungsreste. Anschluß-erörterungen zum Hohenlied, ZThK 91, 375-395.
– (2001): Der Mond und die Plejaden. Griechisch-orientalische Parallelen, VT 51, 206-218.
MURPHY, R.E. (1990): The Song of Songs, Hermeneia, Minneapolis.
NEVLING PORTER, B. (2002): Beds, Sex, and Politics: The Return of Marduk's Bed to Babylon, in: S. Parpola/R.M. Whiting (eds.), Sex and Gender in the Ancient Near East, CRRAI 47/II, Helsinki, 523-535.
PAUL, S.M. (2002): The Shared Legacy of Sexual Metaphors and Euphemisms in Mesopotamian and Biblical Literature, in: S. Parpola/R.M. Whiting (eds.), Sex and Gender in the Ancient Near East, CRRAI 47/II, Helsinki, 489-489.
PIRAS, A. (1994): At ille declinaverat atque transierat (Cant 5,2-8), ZAW 106, 487-490.
POPE, M.H. (1977): Song of Songs, AB 7c, New York.
POWELL, J.U. (1925): Collectanea Alexandrina. Reliquiae minores Poetarum Graecorum Aetatis Ptolemaicae 323-146 A.C. Epicorum, Elegiacorum, Lyricorum, Ethicorum, Oxford.
ROBERT, A./TOURNAY, R. (1963): Le Cantique des Cantiques, Etudes Bibliques, Paris.
RUDOLPH, W. (1962): Das Buch Ruth. Das Hohelied. Die Klagelieder, KAT XVII/1-3, Gütersloh.
STEWART, C. (2002): Erotic Dreams and nightmares from antiquity to the present, Journal of the Royal Anthropological Institute 8, 279-309.
USSHER, R.G. (1973): Aristophanes. Ecclesiazusae, Oxford.

V. WILAMOWITZ-MOELLENDORFF, U. (1896): 'Des Mädchens Klage – eine alexandrinische Arie', in: id., Kleine Schriften 2, Berlin 1941, 95-120.

WALKER, S. (1993): Women and Housing in Classical Greece: the Archaeological Evidence, in: A. Cameron/A. Kuhrt (eds.), Images of Women in Antiquity, rev. ed. Detroit, 81-91.

WINKLER, J.J. (1990): The Constraints of Desire. The Anthropology of Sex and Gender in Ancient Greece, The New Ancient World, London/New York.

'Sweet Talk'
Song of Songs and the Traditions of Greek Poetry

Richard Hunter

I.

In the twenty-second book of the *Iliad* Hector considers whether he should plead for peace with Achilles by offering him all the wealth of Troy in return for an end to the killing; he realises, however, that such a course would be fruitless:

> ἀλλὰ τίη μοι ταῦτα φίλος διελέξατο θυμός;
> μή μιν ἐγὼ μὲν ἵκωμαι ἰών, ὃ δέ μ᾽ οὐκ ἐλεήσει
> οὐδέ τί μ᾽ αἰδέσεται, κτενέει δέ με γυμνὸν ἐόντα
> αὔτως ὥς τε γυναῖκα, ἐπεί κ᾽ ἀπὸ τεύχεα δύω.
> οὐ μέν πως νῦν ἐστιν ἀπὸ δρυὸς οὐδ᾽ ἀπὸ πέτρης
> τῶι ὀαριζέμεναι, ἅ τε παρθένος ἠίθεός τε,
> παρθένος ἠιθεός τ᾽ ὀαρίζετον ἀλλήλοιιν.
> βέλτερον αὖτ᾽ ἔριδι ξυνελαυνέμεν ὅττι τάχιστα·
> εἴδομεν, ὁπποτέρωι κεν Ὀλύμπιος εὖχος ὀρέξηι.

> 'But what need for this debate in my heart? I fear that if I go up to him he will not show me any pity or regard for my appeal, but will simply kill me unarmed like a woman, when I have taken off my armour. There can be no sweet murmuring with him now from tree or rock[1] like a girl and a boy, as a girl and boy murmur sweetly together. Better to close and fight as soon as can be. We can see then to which of us the Olympian is giving the victory.' (Homer, *Iliad* 22.122-30, trans. M. Hammond, adapted).

Achilles will slay the defenceless Hector 'like a woman' (perhaps raped and killed as her city is sacked); he will not deal with the Trojan hero as a lovestruck youth will exchange 'sweet talk' with a young maiden. The poignant contrast between the γυνή 'married woman' and the παρθένος 'young girl/virgin' differentiates this passage from other real and imagined scenes of supplication, such as that of Lykaon who pleads with Achilles for 'respect' and 'pity', but is killed 'unarmed' (γυμνός) and utterly exposed (*Iliad* 21.49-125). Erotic encounters and the deadly encounters of warfare are crucially both like

---

1 On this mysterious phrase see M.L. West's note on Hesiod, *Theogony* 35.

and unlike each other throughout Greek and Latin poetic traditions; Hector himself expresses this truth with memorable concision:[2]

τῷ τις νῦν ἰθὺς τετραμμένος ἢ ἀπολέσθω
ἠὲ σαωθήτω· ἣ γὰρ πολέμου ὀαριστύς.

'Therefore let each of you turn to face the enemy and be killed or survive: for this is the sweet talk of war' (Homer, *Iliad* 17.227-8).

For the implicit contrast in Hector's words in Book 22 between the 'exchanges' of war and the 'exchanges' of peacetime, we might perhaps compare the effect of the killing of the unsuspecting herdsmen, 'while they took pleasure in the playing of the Pan-pipes', on the Shield of Achilles (*Iliad* 18.525-9). If it is true that these herdsmen 'are straight out of later pastoral poetry' (M.W. Edwards on vv. 525-6), the repetition ('epanalepsis') of the final three metra of 22.127 at the head of the following verse might also remind us of the repetitions and echoing effects of pastoral poetry.[3] Ancient scholars offered various explanations for this rare[4] trope in *Iliad* 22, including seeing in it a representation of the talkativeness (πολυλογία) of the young 'flirting' couple (cf. bT-scholia *ad loc.*). In late antiquity, however, Macrobius (*Saturnalia* 5.14.6) adduced these Homeric verses as an example of 'lovely repetition' (*amoena repetitio*), such as Virgil imitated, and he illustrated his point from the pastoral *Eclogues*:

Pan etiam Arcadia mecum si iudice certet
Pan etiam Arcadia dicet se iudice uictum

Pan too, if he were to compete with me and Arcadia were to judge, Pan too would admit that he was beaten, if Arcadia were to judge (Virgil, *Eclogues* 4.58-9).

Both subject-matter and style explain Macrobius' choice. It is indeed tempting to think that Hector's words conjure up not merely two entirely different situations, one of peace and one of the most bitter war, but two contrasting types of 'performance', an epic supplication and a love-duet, perhaps a 'lyric-pastoral' exchange of the kind which is so central to the *Song of Songs*. Hector's acknowledgement of the realities of his situation would be expressed with a generic self-consciousness marking the high seriousness of the coming duel.

Early Greek poetry cannot in fact offer clear parallels to the type of semi-dramatic exchanges between young lovers familiar from the Hebrew poems. Certain motifs and images are, of course, shared between the poetic traditions (for example, the association of fruitfulness and gardens with love), but – as with the striking parallels between Greek and Egyptian and between Hebrew

2 For sexual language in the *Iliad* cf. R. Janko's note on 13.290-1, with further bibliography.
3 For a quite different approach to these verses cf. Martin 1989: 138.
4 The other Homeric examples are *Iliad* 20.371-2 and 23.641-2, cf. Wills 1996: 178-9.

and Egyptian love-poetry[5] – claims of transmission from one culture to another are always vulnerable to assertions that such ideas might easily arise independently in many places and/or that we should rather be thinking of a broad Mediterranean *Gemeingut* of images, motifs, and poetic structures (such as the *paraklausithyron*), which have their basis in shared cultural features. Let us consider a specific example. Here is the first stanza of the first Egyptian 'love-song' on P. Chester Beatty 1 (20th dynasty) in Michael Fox's translation:[6]

One alone is (my) sister, having no peer:
  More gracious than all other women.
Behold her, like Sothis rising
  At the beginning of a good year:
Shining, precious, white of skin,
  Lovely of eyes when gazing.
Sweet her lips <when> speaking:
  She has no excess of words.
Long of neck, white of breast,
  Her hair true lapis lazuli.
Her arms surpass gold,
  Her fingers are like lotuses.
Full (?) (her) derrière, narrow (?) her waist,
  Her thighs carry on her beauties.
Lovely of <walk> when she strides on the ground,
  She has captured my heart in her embrace.
She makes the heads of all (the) men
  Turn about when seeing her.
Fortunate is whoever embraces her –
  He is like the foremost of lovers.
Her coming forth appears
  Like (that of) her (yonder) – the (Unique) One.

This poem may, above all, call to mind for many readers Antonio Carlos Jobim's 'The Girl from Ipanema':

Tall and tan and young and lovely,
The girl from Ipanema goes walking,
And when she passes, each one she passes goes "a-a-ah!"

We will probably not wish to see here a borrowing by Jobim from the ancient Egyptian; multi-genesis would seem a more attractive explanation. If we turn to early Greek poetry, the 'parallels' to this Egyptian song are many and obvious. The comparison of a lovely (and beloved) girl to a star or heavenly phenomenon is very familiar: Sappho compares Atthis among Lydian women to

5 Cf. Fox 1985.
6 Fox 1985: 52; for other translations and discussions cf. Gardiner 1931: 30-1, Lichtheim 1976: 182. There are, needless to say, many uncertainties of translation, but I do not think that they affect the general point.

the moon far outshining all other stars in the heavens (*fr.* 96), and the chorus of Alcman's 'Louvre Partheneion' compare one of their leaders, Agido, to the sun (*PMG* 1.40-1), as they also compare their leader Hagesichora to a prize-winning horse (vv. 45-59), a comparison which may call to mind *Song of Songs* 1:9.[7] The summer rising of Sirius/Sothis is associated by Hesiod with female desire (*Works and Days* 586), but its most famous Greek occurrence is in the same book of the *Iliad* with which we have already been concerned. At 22.25-32 Priam sees Achilles advancing across the plain towards Hector, bright as Sirius; here it is a baleful brightness portending sickness and disaster, whereas of course in the Egyptian song it is complimentary and optimistic. A later epic poet, Apollonius of Rhodes (third century BCE), combined both resonances in describing how the beautiful Jason's appearance to Medea, 'like Sirius rising high from Ocean', brought 'the sickening distress of desire' (κάματος δυσίμερος) to the maiden (*Argonautica* 3.956-61); the following meeting and 'sweet murmuring' between them indeed rewrites the meeting of Hector and Achilles as precisely what Hector said it could not be, 'sweet talk' (ὀαριστύς) between a young man and a girl.[8]

The description of the beloved's loveliness in the Egyptian song is also of a very familiar kind in many poetic cultures, including that of the *Song of Songs*;[9] such descriptions commonly move from the head downwards (cf. Cant 4:1-7; 5:10-16; 6:4-10), but the reverse direction is also known (e.g. Cant 7:2-10). 'Parallels' for the individual items are too numerous to deserve listing, but the emphasis on the beloved's lovely walk may remind us of Sappho's desire to see Anaktoria's 'lovely step' (ἔρατον βᾶμα, *fr.* 16.17), as the lover's *makarismos* of the man who enjoys the girl's favours suggests the famous opening of Sappho *fr.* 31 ('That man seems to me equal to the gods ...') or, in a different register, the destitute Odysseus' flattery of Nausicaa, 'Thrice blessed are your parents and thrice blessed your brothers ... but most blessed of all above everyone is that man who, winning you with gifts, takes you to his house as wife' (*Odyssey* 6.154-9). As has long been recognised, Odysseus' meeting on the seashore with Nausicaa uses many of the tropes and motifs of explicitly erotic poetry, not merely to show how 'appealing' Odysseus actually was, but also (*inter alia*) to suggest the generic 'roads not taken', some of which will concern us

7 The standard Greek parallel adduced for Cant 1:9 is Theocritus 18.30-1, 'as a Thessalian horse for a chariot, so was rose-coloured Helen the glory of Sparta'. The comparison of women to horses is of course ubiquitous in the poetry of many cultures; for a Vedic parallel to the horse-imagery of Alcman's poem cf. Dunkel 1979: 259-64. In another context Alcman's song also illustrates, as does the Egyptian song, the poetic use of the brightness of Sirius (v. 62).

8 Cf. my notes on *Argonautica* 3.956-61, 964-5 (R. Hunter, *Apollonius of Rhodes, Argonautica III* (Cambridge 1989)), below. We might also think of Odysseus seen by Nausicaa 'gleaming (στίλβων) with beauty and graces' after a bath and new clothes (*Odyssey* 6.237).

9 Cf. Hermann 1959: 124-30, Fox 1985: 269-78; for Greek and Roman poetry cf., e.g., J. McKeown on Ovid, *Amores* 1.5.19-22.

presently.[10] When, for example, Odysseus (*Odyssey* 6.160-8) compares his admiration for the 'young shoot of a palm-tree' by Apollo's altar on Delos ('the earth had never sent forth a tree like it') to his admiration for the Phaeacian princess ('I have never before laid eyes on such a mortal'), we may be reminded of Cant 7:7-8 (*New English Bible*):

> You are stately as a palm-tree,
> And your breasts are the clusters of dates.
> I said, 'I will climb up into the palm
> To grasp its fronds'.

Odysseus' palm-tree image[11] does not, of course, suggest sexual possession, and he skilfully deflects its direction from consideration of Nausicaa's body to his own sense of wonder; our sense, however, of where the palm-tree image *could* be taken, of the poet's generic exclusions, is important in judging what is going on in this scene.

That early Greek poetry cannot produce clear analogues for the apparently mutual love of men and women celebrated in the *Song of Songs* will have more than one (overlapping) explanation in both cultural and literary practice. Explicit expressions of female sexual desire are notoriously rare in Greek literature of all periods, and Greek epic is coy even when it comes to male desire; the two exceptions proving the rule are Zeus (*Iliad* 14.312-28), who breaks every rule (although in *Iliad* 14 it is really his wife Hera who is in control), and Paris, the adulterous and unheroic prince, whose 'natural habitat' is the bedroom rather than the battlefield (*Iliad* 3.437-47). Outside epic, our evidence for early Greek song traditions is simply exiguous. Nevertheless, it is at least suggestive that the closest early Greek poetry comes to expressions of such mutual affection is the poetry of Sappho which is focused rather on love between women, and that it was not until much later in antiquity under the Roman empire that a literature with mutual heterosexual desire at its heart ('the Greek novel') flourished. Be that as it may, it is indeed upon epic 'encounters' that we must largely rely in the early period for a sense of what might have been.

In the *Homeric Hymn to Aphrodite* Zeus casts into the heart of the goddess of *erôs* 'sweet desire to lie with a mortal man' (vv. 45-6), so that she should be in the same boat as all the other gods and thus stop boasting of her power over them. The chosen mortal is Anchises, a divinely handsome (v.77) Trojan herdsman. Aphrodite presents herself to him in the guise of a lovely virgin, as he is playing his lyre alone on the mountainside, and tells him that Hermes had snatched her away from Phrygia where she was taking part in the dances of young women in honour of Artemis and told her that she was to be the

10 Cf. below on the *Homeric Hymn to Aphrodite* and Archilochus *fr.* 196A.
11 For similar examples in erotic praise cf., e.g., Petropoulos 2003: 33.

'wedded wife' (κουριδίη ἄλοχος) of Anchises and was to bear him glorious children. She begs him to present her, a young virgin with no previous experience of love-making (v.132), to his family so that the wedding can take place without delay. Anchises, like – or so it is popularly believed – many men in such situations, promises that he will indeed marry her, but declares that no force on heaven or earth will prevent him from making love to her there and then (αὐτίκα νῦν, 151), which he then indeed proceeds to do, right there by the ox-stalls (vv.155-67); the description of him leading Aphrodite to his bed is clearly presented as a 'transgressive' version of a Greek wedding-night, and one which matches the other inversions of the episode, such as the 'bride's' forwardness.[12] The 'pastoral' elements of this narrative have long attracted attention,[13] but it is in keeping with the epic mode that Aphrodite, who here embodies desire in two complementary senses, must present that desire as a wish for formal marriage; she, of course, knows what will happen (her control is marked by the smile of v.155), but the socially approved framework of marriage is the only language in which a desiring woman can offer herself to a man. We may compare again the sixth book of the *Odyssey* where Nausicaa, whose head has been filled with thoughts of marriage by Athena's dream appearance to her (*Odyssey* 6.1-40), can only express her thoughts about the handsome stranger who has turned up on her shores through the hope that he (or someone like him) might choose to remain on Scherie and marry her (6.244-5);[14] so too, Odysseus – driven not by sexual desire, but by needs of another kind – appeals for her help in the only way in which a man alone in the countryside with a young girl can speak to her (at least in epic poetry), namely in terms of marriage (6.15-9, 180-5). Odysseus, of course, does not, unlike Anchises in a similar situation, offer to marry Nausicaa himself, another 'road not taken', but he certainly allows her to entertain hope, as the poet evokes in us memories of the other directions in which this delicate situation could be developed.

The closest parallel to these exchanges outside epic, and one which allows us to appreciate some of the parameters within which different genres operated, is the famous 'Cologne Epode' of Archilochus (*fr.* 196A West), which was first published in 1974. Only the final part of this first-person narration survives, and interpretation is inevitably disputed. When our unfortunately fragmentary text opens, a girl seems to be buying herself time by suggesting to the narrator, who wants to have sex with her (cf. v. 15), that he could satisfy himself with someone else (and then marry the speaker herself later?):

---

12 Cf. Bergren 1982.

13 Cf., e.g., Bergren 1982: 9, Griffin 1992: 199-200.

14 Aristarchus athetised these verses and it is clear from the scholia that some critics found them shockingly blunt for a young virgin.

πάμπαν ἀποσχόμενος·
ἶσον τολμ[
εἰ δ' ὦν ἐπείγεαι καί σε θυμὸς ἰθύει,
ἔστιν ἐν ἡμετέρου
ἣ νῦν μέγ' ἱμείρ[ει
καλὴ τέρεινα παρθένος· δοκέω δέ μι[ν
εἶδος ἄμωμον ἔχειν·
τὴν δὴ σὺ ποίη[

'... holding back completely; equally endure ... But if you are in a hurry and your heart spurs you on, we have a beautiful tender maiden who now greatly desires ... I think her beauty is faultless. Make her [your lover?]' (Archilochus *fr.* 196A 1-8 West).[15]

The loss of the early sections of the poem makes uncertainty inevitable, but it is likely enough that, in this poem also, the girl expressed any desire on her own part through the socially approved code of marriage, whereas male desire will brook no delay to its satisfaction.[16] This is the last we hear from the girl in this conversation, for she is answered by a long speech from the narrator, full of abuse of Neoboule, apparently the other girl offered to him, because she is aging and 'overripe', a condition brought on (so we are to understand) by too much sexual activity; as for the girl the narrator wants, he offers her some ambiguous promises about the limits of the sexual activity he has in mind, and then the time for words is over:

τοσ]αῦτ' ἐφώνεον· παρθένον δ' ἐν ἄνθε[σιν
τηλ]εθάεσσι λαβὼν
ἔκλινα· μαλθακῇ δ[έ μιν
χλαί]νῃ καλύψας, αὐχέν' ἀγκάλῃς ἔχω[ν,
...]ματι παυσαμένην
τὼς ὥστε νεβρ[
μαζ]ῶν τε χερσὶν ἠπίως ἐφηψάμην
...]ρέφηνε νέον
ἥβης ἐπήλυσιν χρόα
ἅπαν τ]ε σῶμα καλὸν ἀμφαφώμενος
...]ον ἀφῆκα μένος
ξανθῆς ἐπιψαύ[ων τριχός.

'This is what I said. I took the maiden and laid her down amidst the blooming flowers; I covered her with a soft cloak, cradled her neck in my arms ... ceasing like a fawn ... gently my hands felt her breasts ... the approach of her youthful beauty,[17] and stroking her [whole] beautiful body I released my [?white] force, touching her blond [hair]'[18] (Archilochus *fr.* 196A 42-53 West).

---

15 There are, of course, textual uncertainties, but not such as to affect the present limited discussion.

16 Helpful discussion and comparison with the relevant epic scenes in van Sickle 1975 and Henderson 1976. For a full bibliographical survey to 1989 cf. Gerber 1991: 80-93.

17 The meaning of this passage is particularly vexed.

18 Much critical ink has been spilled over the nature of the sex act with which the poem ends (vv. 51-3); it is too often forgotten in such discussions, as also in discussions of the imagery of vv. 21-4, that the narrator is hardly an impartial or trustworthy reporter either of what

In place of an expected answer from the girl,[19] she is wordlessly enjoyed 'among the blooming flowers'. Such silence stands in strong contrast to the traditions of Egyptian and Hebrew love-poetry.[20]

Both Attic tragedy, most notably Euripides, and Hellenistic poetry broke that silence. In *Idyll* 2 Theocritus wrote his version of 'boy encounters girl', but the narrator is now the girl, Simaitha, who is trying by magic to win back the young man with whom she has had 'an affair' but who now appears to have abandoned her. In this poem it is the girl who has fallen into *erôs*, and she who makes the first move by sending a message to the beloved; much of the poem's force derives from its many reversals of normal cultural and literary protocols. When 'the object of desire' arrives at Simaitha's house, he – or at least in the speech which Simaitha puts in his mouth[21] – professes that her summons only just preceded his own coming, i.e. he claims that he feels *erôs* for the woman with whom he is about to have sex, as do Paris and Zeus in similar situations in the *Iliad*, and as probably did the narrator of the 'Cologne Epode'.[22] His speech ends abruptly after one foot of a hexameter, leaving the highly charged words 'husband' to hang in the air:

> ... ἀνέρος·' ὣς ὃ μὲν εἶπεν· ἐγὼ δέ νιν ἁ ταχυπειθής
> χειρὸς ἐφαψαμένα μαλακῶν ἔκλιν' ἐπὶ λέκτρων·
> καὶ ταχὺ χρὼς ἐπὶ χρωτὶ πεπαίνετο καὶ τὰ πρόσωπα
> θερμότερ' ἦς ἢ πρόσθε, καὶ ἐψιθυρίσδομες ἁδύ.
> ὡς καί τοι μὴ μακρὰ φίλα θρυλέοιμι Σελάνα,
> ἐπράχθη τὰ μέγιστα, καὶ ἐς πόθον ἤνθομες ἄμφω.

'... [the bed of a] husband." So he spoke, And I, the gullible one, took him by the hand and laid him down on the soft bed. Quickly body grew warm on body and our faces were hotter than before and we whispered sweet things together. So as not to detain you with a long story, dear Moon-goddess, the highest thing was done, and we both reached fulfilment of our desires' (Theocritus, *Id.* 2.138-43).

It is at least tempting to believe that Simaitha's narrative echoes and reverses that of Archilochus' 'Cologne Epode', a poem that Theocritus elsewhere

---

he wanted or of what he got. How would the girl have described what is alleged to have happened? The presumably male and élite identity of the audience of the poem is crucial here.

19 The expectation is encouraged by the parallel structure of v.9, τοσαῦτ' ἐφώνει, τὴν δ' ἐγὼνταμειβόμην.

20 There are, of course, female speakers in early lyric (cf., e.g., Alcaeus *fr.* 10 LP-Voigt), as in other forms of archaic poetry (cf. Theognis 257-60, 579-82) but the general point is, I think, unaffected. Of particular interest is Anacreon, *PMG* 432 'through your lustfulness I have become wrinkled and overripe' which sounds almost like 'Neoboule's reply'; on this fragment cf. Brown 1984.

21 On Simaitha's manipulation of the narrative and the speeches within it cf. Andrews 1996.

22 It is tempting to supplement v. 20 as πολλόν μ' ἔρως, as suggested by Merkelbach and West in the *editio princeps* (Merkelbach-West 1974).

clearly knows,[23] though the matter must remain open. The woman now takes the man by the hand (contrast, e.g., *Homeric Hymn to Aphrodite* 155, Euripides, *Ion* 891) and it is she who does the 'laying down'. To what extent Simaitha's stress on the exchange of sweet 'pillow talk' (contrast Archilochus!) and the mutuality of the sexual pleasure is mimetic of female concerns and attitudes is a subject that need not be pursued here.

II.

Archilochus' 'Cologne Epode' can also serve as a reminder of how little early Greek élite poetry seems to take the form of a mimetic or semi-dramatic exchange, such as is the dominant form in *Song of Songs*, as opposed to 'contests', such as 'The Contest of Homer and Hesiod'. We must, of course, always reckon with the very broken state of the transmission,[24] and the exchange of snatches of song, often involving impersonation, was a familiar part of the entertainment of the male symposium.[25] Thus, for example, a fragment such as Archilochus *fr.* 193 West,

δύστηνος ἔγκειμαι πόθωι
ἄψυχος, χαλεπῆισι θεῶν ὀδύνηισιν ἕκητι
πεπαρμένος δι᾽ ὀστέων

'I am gripped by desire, wretched, without life, pierced through the bones with terrible pains from the gods' (Archilochus *fr.* 193 West).

could certainly have met with an answer and/or taken its place in a Greek 'Song', but – as so often – we know nothing of the context. So too, a famous fragment of disputed date and authorship, *PMG* 976 (= Sappho *fr.* 168 B Voigt), in which a female voice laments the loneliness of the night, might well call the *Song* to mind:

δέδυκε μὲν ἁ σελάννα
καὶ Πληίαδες· μέσαι δὲ
νύκτες, παρὰ δ᾽ ἔρχετ᾽ ὤρα,
ἔγω δὲ μόνα κατεύδω.[26]

23 7.121, cf. Henrichs 1980. The coy euphemism τὰ μέγιστα 'the highest thing' for sexual intercourse would then vary 'the divine thing' τὸ θεῖον χρῆμα in Archilochus (v.15).

24 It would, for example, be very nice to know more of the context of Sappho *fr.* 121: 'but if you [masculine] are my friend (φίλος), find a younger bed-partner; for I [feminine] will not endure life together, when I am the older'.

25 Cf., e.g., Ferrari 1988.

26 If this song is in fact Hellenistic, rather than archaic, the chances that it was part of a song-exchange are perhaps increased. Paul Maas understood ὤρα as the 'watch' which patrolled the city at night and makes two important appearances in the *Song* (Cant 3:3;

The moon and the Pleiades have disappeared; it is the middle of the night – the hour passes, and I sleep alone.

Catullus might well have had real or believed archaic Greek forebears for the choral exchange of Poem 62 (a wedding-song), and Sappho seems to have written an exchange between a bride and the personified virginity which she is leaving behind (*fr.* 114). Both Attic comedy and the later biographical tradition were, of course, free to invent meetings and song-exchanges between poets; the comic poet Diphilus (late fourth century BCE), for example, wrote a *Sappho* (*frr.* 70-71 K-A) in which Archilochus and Hipponax were the Lesbian poet's 'lovers' (ἐρασταί) and may have competed in song for her affections.

It is in representations of the semi-dramatic poetry of a lower social level that we can find the nearest Greek equivalents to the traditions represented by the *Song of Songs*. A brief 'summoning' song by a young girl in Aristophanes' *Ekklesiazousai* seems not far from both 'Sappho *fr.* 168B' (above) and from the Hebrew traditions:

αἰαῖ, τί ποτε πείσομαι;
οὐχ ἥκει μοὐταῖρος
μόνη δ' αὐτοῦ λείπομ'· ἡ
        γάρ μοι μήτηρ ἄλλῃ βέβηκεν.

Alas, what will become of me? My lover has not come and I am left here alone; my mother has gone off somewhere (Aristophanes, *Ekklesiazousai* 911-14).

In the same play, the song-exchange (a form of *paraklausithyron* familiar also from Cant) between this girl and her 'suitor' brings us as close to Hebrew traditions, albeit in a genuinely dramatic mode, as Greek poetry allows:[27]

Girl δεῦρο δή, δεῦρο δή,
φίλον ἐμόν, δεῦρό μοι
πρόσελθε καὶ ξύνευνέ μοι
τὴν εὐφρόνην ὅπως ἔσει.
πάνυ γάρ τις ἔρως με δονεῖ
τῶνδε τῶν σῶν βοστρύχων·
ἄτοπος δ' ἔγκειταί μοί τις πόθος,
ὅς με διακναίσας ἔχει.
μέθες, ἱκνοῦμαι σ', Ἔρως,
καὶ ποίησον τόνδ' ἐς εὐνὴν
τὴν ἐμὴν ἱκέσθαι.

Man δεῦρο δή, δεῦρο δή,
φίλον ἐμόν, καὶ σύ μοι
καταδραμοῦσα τὴν θύραν
ἄνοιξον τήνδ'· εἰ δὲ μή, καταπεσὼν κείσομαι.

5:7), but this interpretation appears to have fallen from favour, cf. Maas 1973: 199-20, Longo 1953.

27 I have not marked uncertainties in the text or colometry, as they do not affect what is at issue here.

ἀλλ᾽ ἐν τῶι σῶι βούλομαι κόλπωι
πληκτίζεσθαι μετὰ τῆς σῆς πυγῆς.
Κύπρι, τί μ᾽ ἐκμαίνεις ἐπὶ ταύτηι;
μέθες, ἱκνοῦμαι σ᾽, Ἔρως,
καὶ ποίησον τήνδ᾽ ἐς εὐνὴν
τὴν ἐμὴν ἱκέσθαι.

καὶ ταῦτα μέντοι μετρίως πρὸς τὴν ἐμὴν ἀνάγκην
εἰρημέν᾽ ἐστίν. σὺ δέ μοι, φίλτατον, ὢ ἱκετεύω,
ἄνοιξον, ἀσπάζου με.
διά τοι σὲ πόνους ἔχω.
ὦ χρυσοδαίδαλτον ἐμὸν μέλημα, Κύπριδος ἔρνος,
μέλιττα Μούσης, Χαρίτων θρέμμα, Τρυφῆς πρόσωπον,
ἄνοιξον, ἀσπάζου με.
διά τοι σὲ πόνους ἔχω.

Girl: 'Here, here to me, my love, and spend the night in my bed. Passion for these locks of yours has set me awhirl. No ordinary desire has me in its grip of destruction. Let me go, Eros, I beg you, and make him come to my bed.'
Man: "Here, here to me, my love; please run down and open this door! If not, I shall fall to the ground and not get up. I would lie in your lap and engage with your bum! Cyprian One, why do you drive me mad for her? Let me go, Eros, I beg you, and make her come to my bed.'
In comparison with my need, this song has been moderate enough. But now, dearest, I beg you, open up and receive me: it is for you that I suffer. O gold-wrought love of my life, offshoot of Kypris, bee of the Muse, nursling of the Graces, Pleasure's image, open up and receive me: it is for you that I suffer' (Aristophanes, *Ekklesiazousai* 952-75).

J. DAVIDSON has recently made the attractive suggestion that we are to recognise this exchange as a comic representation of a familiar kind of 'entertainment' or *paignion*, of a kind that might regularly accompany symposia.[28] Its tone and style – reminiscent in places of that of the popular love-magic preserved from both Greece and Egypt – is indeed rather 'lower' than that of the erotic exchanges of *Song of Songs*, and the frank expression of female sexual desire finds, as we have seen, few earlier Greek parallels, but there is little reason to doubt that this song represents a very long Greek tradition which has largely been suppressed by the modes of élite poetry. From the later Hellenistic period survive snatches of 'semi-dramatic' song which give us brief glimpses of what we have been missing. One is an example of a 'naughty' (μοιχικόν) 'Locrian' song which survives in Athenaeus' *Deipnosophistai* (second century CE):

28 Davidson 2000: 50-1; for criticism of Davidson's suggestion cf. Hordern 2003: 609. On this exchange see also Bowra 1958, Slater 2002: 224-5. It is not improbable that an earlier reflection of such exchanges is to be seen in the desperate pleas of Kinesias to his wife Myrrhine in the *Lysistrata*: he too is 'locked out' and pleads with his 'sweetest little Myrrhine' to 'come down' (from the Acropolis), vv. 872-3. Kinesias is suffering from a very taut phallus which requires relief, and it is indeed 'likely, though not certain' (Sommerstein on v. 969) that the man in the *Ekklesiazousai* is wearing an erect phallus; if so, ἀνάγκη (v. 969) and πόνοι (vv. 972, 975) present a typically Aristophanic mixture of the emotional and the physical.

ὢ τί πάσχεις; μὴ προδῶις ἄμμ', ἱκετεύω·
πρὶν καὶ μολεῖν κεῖνον, ἀνίστω,
μὴ κακόν ‹σε› μέγα ποιήσηι
    κἀμὲ τὰν δειλάκραν.
ἁμέρα καὶ ἤδη· τὸ φῶς
    διὰ τᾶς θυρίδος οὐκ εἰσορῆις;

Oh, what are you doing? Don't betray us, I beg you! Get up, before he comes, lest he do great harm to you and wretched me. The day is already with us. Don't you see the light through the window? (*Poetae Melici Graeci* ed. D.L. Page, 853)[29]

This song could be considerably earlier than the later Hellenistic period,[30] but its mimetic form suggests affinities with 'popular', non-élite poetry. It is a form of *Tagelied*,[31] in which however the lovers must part because the husband is about to return; as such, it has an obvious relation to the very popular 'adultery mime' of Graeco-Roman antiquity, in which the cuckolded husband returns to find his wife's lover at home.[32] Athenaeus tells us that 'all of Phoenicia' was full of such songs (15.697c), and though no influence from eastern, non-Greek traditions is necessary to explain such poems, this geographical information at least sparks thoughts of the cross-fertilisation of poetic traditions. So too, a snatch of mimetic exchange between two lovers was inscribed in the middle of the second century BCE on a temple at Marisa in Judaea:

οὐχ ἔχω τί σοι πάθω ἢ τί χαρίσωμαι·
καῖτα κεῖμαι μεθ' ἑτέρου, σὲ μέγα φιλοῦσα;
ἀλλὰ ναὶ τὴν Ἀφροδίτην μέγα τι χαίρω
ὅττι ‹τοι› σου θοἰμάτιον ἐνέχυρα κεῖται.

ἀλλ' ἐγὼ μὲν ἀποτρέχω, σοὶ δὲ καταλείπω
εὐρυχωρίην πολλήν κτλ.

Woman: 'I do not know what to do or what I can offer you. Am I to lie with another, when I love you so much? By Aphrodite, it is a very good thing that I have your cloak as a pledge. *Man*: 'I shall leave and give you a great deal of space ... (*Collectanea Alexandrina* ed. J.U. Powell, p. 184).[33]

Such a script, whatever scenario we reconstruct from this snatch of dialogue, takes us deep into the extremely flexible 'mime' traditions of the Hellenistic world where indeed we would expect cross-cultural transfusion of more than one kind. The semi-dramatic or mimetic mode of such Greek poetry may well owe something to non-Greek traditions.

---

29 For the metre cf. West 1982: 149.

30 Cf. Ath. 14.639a: the peripatetic Clearchus of Soli discussed 'Locrian songs'. For a recent discussion of this and the 'Marisa song' (below) cf. Petropoulos 2003: 131-3.

31 Cf., e.g., Hermann 1959: 130-2, Hatto 1965.

32 Cf. Reynolds 1946, McKeown 197.

33 On this song cf. Crönert 1909, Wilamowitz 1921: 344-5, Garrod 1923.

III.

The links between Greek pastoral and the poetic traditions of the Near East have been catalogued more than once,[34] and it is indeed to bucolic poetry, and particularly the *Idylls* of Theocritus, which combine traditions of mime and 'popular' song with the élite mode of the hexameter, that those interested in analogies between the *Song of Songs* and Greek poetry have normally turned.[35] Common to both traditions are not merely pastoral elements and imagery, but also a mimetic structure in which characters speak directly with each other. We can in fact trace through the Theocritean corpus different narrative and mimetic modes which shed an interesting light upon how Greek poetic tradition viewed the relation to 'popular' forms.

Of the *Idylls* which are normally accepted as 'genuine Theocritus', only *Idyll* 6 and *Idyll* 18 mix simple third-person narration (in the first case an enclosing frame of five-verse proem and five-verse closure, and in *Idyll* 18 an eight-verse introduction only) and mimetic impersonation involving more than one character. *Idylls* 1-5, 10, 14, and 15, like the 'mimiambs' of Herodas, offer 'pure' mimesis without explanatory narrative. *Idyll* 7 is a first-person narrative, into which conversation and songs are woven, and *Idyll* 11 offers a first-person introductory address to a named friend, followed by the impersonated song of the young, lovesick Cyclops. Of the two 'mixed' cases, *Idyll* 18 presents itself as the archaic wedding-song of Helen and Menelaus, and in *Idyll* 6, the songs of Daphnis, who impersonates a nameless 'adviser' of Polyphemus,[36] and of Damoitas, impersonating the Cyclops himself, are framed and separated by third-person narrative from 'the poet'. Although the 'adviser' seeks to attract the Cyclops' attention to the alleged 'off-stage' actions of his beloved Galateia, there is no necessary 'action' or change in the course of the song; the two characters may be presumed to remain stationary, and there is no interchange between them. Moreover, although, as critics have often pointed out, we are invited by the poem to wonder to what extent the relationship of Daphnis and Damoitas is similar to and/or different from that of Galateia and the Cyclops, there is no direct intervention by the narrator within the songs – the two parts of the poem remain formally distinct.[37]

In *Idyll* 8, however, which on other grounds is now accepted as the work of a relatively early imitator of Theocritus,[38] we have a rather more complicated

34 Cf. particularly Halperin 1983: 85-117, Griffin 1992.

35 Cf., e.g., Graetz 1871: 67-74, Seiple 1902/3, Dornseiff 1936. The tradition goes back at least to Erasmus' scorn for *Theocriti naeniae* ('Theocritus' 'ditties') in comparison to the *Song* (*Opera Omnia Desiderii Erasmi Roterodami* I.2, Amsterdam 1971, 645).

36 For the possible identity of this adviser cf. Hunter 1999: 245-6.

37 For some general considerations of Theocritus' two-part structures cf. Pretagostini 1980.

38 Important discussions include Perrotta 1925 and Rossi 1971. Both *Idyll* 8 and 9 offer difficult and interesting problems of interpretation, but my concern here is solely with their structural shape.

structure. The opening third-person narrative (vv. 1-10), for which the opening of *Idyll* 6 was perhaps the main model, contains the first exchange of hexameter couplets in which Daphnis and Menalcas agree to compete in song; each couplet of direct speech is preceded by a third-person introductory verse ('First spoke Menalcas ... Daphnis then answered him ...'). After Daphnis' answering couplet, it comes as a shock to find him answered in turn by Menalcas, though without any introductory verse, and we now find ourselves in a passage of seventeen verses of mixed 'stichomythia'. Theocritus himself experiments elsewhere with such slides between narrative and mimetic modes – stichomythia in the midst of 'heroic' narrative in *Idyll* 22 and unintroduced direct speech in *Idyll* 24[39] – but the mode of *Idyll* 8 must be seen against the background of many Hellenistic attempts to destabilise the boundary between narrative and *mimesis*. Moreover, the poem itself now has a narrative: Menalcas and Daphnis agree to have a nearby goatherd as their judge (vv. 25-7), and the narrator tells us that the goatherd indeed answered the call. After this second third-person intervention by the narrator (vv. 28-32), we get the first exchanges of the song contest (vv. 33-60) which follow each other with narratorial introduction. The text and arrangement of verses here present a set of very thorny problems, but the fact that this first set of exchanges is in elegiac couplets is worth a moment's pause. Whatever the reason for and resonance of the changed metre,[40] by their variation from pastoral tradition the elegiacs call attention to the rôle of the poet who is ringing the changes both structurally and rhythmically: we are never to be allowed to forget what kind of a performance we are hearing or reading. The variety (ποικιλία) continues with the second set of exchanges, for here two matched sets of hexameters are introduced, separated (v.71), and concluded by interventions from the narrator; we are then given the (introduced) judgement of the goatherd, again in direct speech (vv. 82-7), and then the narrator's conclusion to the whole scene (vv. 88-93). The move away from the simplicity of Theocritean structures, though under the impulse of Theocritus' own experiments, may be seen as a recognition, and incorporation into 'literature', of the mimetic-dramatic origins of pastoral and/or part of a gradual break from the formal 'classicising' structures of the poetry of the high Hellenistic period.[41] With either (or both) explanations it may be thought likely that the resulting poetry of mixed mode was, at least in spirit, close to the flexibility of popular performative modes.

Idyll 9, as transmitted, presents a curious structure. The poet addresses Daphnis and Menalcas directly in the second person, inviting them to engage in bucolic song (βουκολιάζεο, Δάφνι κτλ. vv. 1-6); after Daphnis' performance (vv. 7-13), however, we are apparently back in a narration of a past contest,

39 Cf. Hunter in Fantuzzi-Hunter 2004: 208-210.

40 I hope to discuss this elsewhere.

41 Cf. Hunter in Fantuzzi-Hunter 2004: 485.

'thus did Daphnis sing to me, and thus Menalcas ...' (v.14). Menalcas then sings seven verses to match Daphnis' seven, and the poet narrates his reaction to the songs, with the singers again in the third person (vv. 22-7). We then, however, move to a present invocation by the poet to the 'bucolic Muses' to remember a past song (vv. 28-36). This poem has prompted much speculation, for its peculiarities are by no means limited to its structure; many critics have wanted to separate the song-exchange and the narrator's reaction from the proem and epilogue.[42] Great caution is of course needed in drawing conclusions from what may be a freak of transmission, but at the very least we should note that *Idyll* 9 could be understood as a further step down the road of weakening the barriers between narration and mimesis and/or of experiments with the mixing of modes. Here again, at any rate, it seems likely that the poet of *Idyll* 9 was reacting to and innovating in an already well established tradition of bucolic song.

Virgil's *Seventh Eclogue* in which a song-contest between two shepherds from the (recent) past is related as a reminiscence by another rustic, Meliboeus, takes the innovations of *Idylls* 8 and 9 a stage further:

forte sub arguta consederat ilice Daphnis,
compulerantque greges Corydon et Thyrsis in unum,
Thyrsis ouis, Corydon distentas lacte capellas,
ambo florentes aetatibus, Arcades ambo,
et cantare pares et respondere parati.
huc mihi, dum teneras defendo a frigore myrtos,
uir gregis ipse caper deerrauerat; atque Daphnin
aspicio etc.

'By chance Daphnis had settled under a rustling oak, and Corydon and Thyrsis had driven their flocks together, Thyrsis his sheep, Corydon his goats swollen with milk; both in the bloom of youth, both Arcadians, ready to sing and prepared to respond. While I was trying to protect my myrtles from the cold, my he-goat himself, lord of the flock, had roamed in that direction and I caught sight of Daphnis ...' (Virgil, *Eclogue* 7.1-8).

Meliboeus' memories have no addressee, and in the opening five verses we have no reason (other perhaps than a list of characters inscribed above the text) to think that anyone other than 'the poet' is speaking (cf. *Idylls* 6 and 8); it comes as a shock when we discover in v.6 that the speaker himself is engaged in rustic tasks. What Virgil has done is to move from the suggestions in *Idyll* 9 that 'the poet' is himself a rustic and a bucolic singer (*Idyll* 9.28-36) to an explicit identification of 'the poetic voice' as that of a named herdsman. As such, *Eclogue* 7 occupies an important place in the development of pastoral conventions and in biographical interpretations of the poetic voice.

42 The details may be pursued in Gow's commentary. Comparison with, say, Callimachus' 'mimetic' hymns (cf., e.g., White 1980: 42) does not help, as these do not show the variety of mode of *Idyll* 9.

Of particular interest for this survey, in view both of Hector's words from which we began and of its similarity of situation to Archilochus' 'Cologne Epode',[43] is the ὀαριστύς (though there is no reason to think that that was its original title) of *Idyll* 27. This mimetic, stichomythic seduction of a goat-herding girl by the cowherd Daphnis has lost its beginning, but it has a narrative conclusion, though one which is apparently broken (vv. 67-71b), followed by a two line address by the poet to a 'happy shepherd' (vv. 72-3). Once again, we need not be concerned with the difficult textual issues raised by the end of this poem,[44] but if we were to assume the loss of an opening piece of third-person scene-setting, a stichomythic exchange framed by a narrative is not very far from the structure of *Idyll* 6. It is, however, worthy of note that the conversation within the narration clearly contains 'action' (kissing, vv. 2-6, fondling and love-making vv. 49-66) and a change of scene after v.48, both phenomena of the performative mimetic-dramatic tradition. Such a combination of the narrative and mimetic traditions would represent a further significant step down the road we have been following.

Bibliography

ANDREWS, N.E. (1996): Narrative and allusion in Theocritus, Idyll 2, in: M.A. Harder/R.F. Regtuit/G.C. Wakker (eds.), Theocritus (Groningen) 21-51.

BERGREN, A. (1982): Sacred apostrophe: representation and imitation in the Homeric Hymns, Arethusa 15, 83-108.

BROWN, C. (1984): Ruined by lust: Anacreon, fr. 44 Gentili (432 PMG), CQ 34, 37-42.

BOWRA, C.M. (1958): 'A love-duet' AJPh 79, 376-91 [= C.M. Bowra, On Greek Margins (Oxford 1970) 149-63].

CRÖNERT, W. (1909): Das Lied von Marisa, RM 64, 433-448.

DAVIDSON, J. (2000): Gnesippus paigniagraphos: the comic poets and the erotic mime, in: D. Harvey/J. Wilkins (eds.), The Rivals of Aristophanes, London, 41-64.

DEGANI, E. (1974): Il nuovo Archiloco, Atene & Roma 19, 113-28.

DORNSEIFF, F. (1936): Ägyptische Liebeslieder, Hoheslied, Sappho, Theokrit, ZDMG 90, 589-601.

DUNKEL, G. (1979): Fighting words, Alcman Partheneion 63 μάχονται, JIES 7, 249-272.

FANTUZZI, M./HUNTER, R. (2004): Tradition and Innovation in Hellensitic Poetry, Cambridge.

FERRARI, F. (1988): P. Berol. Inv. 13270. I canti di Elefantina, SCO 38, 181-227.

FOX, M.V. (1985): The Song of Songs and the Ancient Egyptian Love Songs, Madison.

GARDINER, A.H. (1931): The Library of A. Chester Beatty, London.

GARROD, H.W. (1923): Locrica, CR 37, 161-162.

GERBER, D.E. (1991): Early Greek elegy and iambus, Lustrum 33, 7-225.

GRAETZ, H. (1871): Schir Ha-Schirim oder das salomonische Hohelied, Vienna.

GRIFFIN, J. (1992): Theocritus, the Iliad, and the East, AJPh 113, 189-211.

43 That the poet of *Idyll* 27 was indebted to the 'Cologne Epode' has been argued more than once, cf., e.g., Degani 1974: 128 n.12.

44 Gow's note usefully rehearses the arguments which have been brought to bear. For a more recent defence of the poem's integrity cf. White 1980: 41-51; cf. also Sider 2001.

HALPERIN, D.M. (1983): Before Pastoral: Theocritus and the Ancient Tradition of Bucolic Poetry, New Haven/London.
HATTO, A.T. ed. (1965): Eos. An enquiry into the theme of lovers' meetings and partings at dawn in poetry, London/The Hague/Paris.
HENDERSON, J. (1976): The Cologne Epode and the Conventions of Early Greek Erotic Poetry, Arethusa 9, 159-79.
HENRICHS, A. (1980): Riper than a Pear: Parian Invective in Theokritos, ZPE 39, 7-27.
HERMANN, A. (1959): Altägyptische Liebesdichtung, Wiesbaden.
HORDERN, J.H. (2003): Gnesippus and the Rivals of Aristophanes, CQ 53, 608-613.
HUNTER, R. (1999): Theocritus. A Selection, Cambridge Greek and Latin Classics, Cambridge.
LICHTHEIM, M. (1976): Ancient Egyptian Literature, A Book of Readings. Vol. II: The New Kingdom, Berkeley.
LONGO, V. (1953): Aristofane e un' interpretazione di Saffo, Maia 6, 220-23.
MAAS, P. (1973): Kleine Schriften, Munich.
MARTIN, R.P. (1989): The Language of Heroes, Ithaca.
MCKEOWN, J.C. (1979): Augustan Elegy and Mime, PCPS 25, 71-84.
MERKELBACH, R./WEST, M.L. (1974): Ein Archilochos-Papyrus, ZPE 14, 97-112.
PERROTTA, G.P. (1925): Teocrito e il poeta dell'Idillio VIII, Atene e Roma 6, 62-80 [= Poesia ellenistica. Scritti minori II (Rome 1978) 9-32].
PETROPOULOS, J.C.B. (2003): Eroticism in Ancient and Medieval Greek, London.
PRETAGOSTINI, R. (1980): La struttura compositiva dei carmi teocritei, QUCC 34, 57-74.
REYNOLDS, R.W. (1946): The adultery mime, CQ 4, 77-84.
ROSSI, L.E. (1971): Mondo pastorale e poesia bucolica di maniera: l'idillio ottavo del corpus teocriteo, SIFC 43, 5-25.
SEIPLE, W.G. (1902-3): Theocritean parallels to the Song of Songs, AJSL 19, 108-115.
SIDER, D. (2001): Theokritos 27: *Oaristys*, WJA 25, 99-105.
SLATER, N.W. (2002): Spectator Politics, Philadelphia.
VAN SICKLE, J. (1975): The new Erotic Fragment of Archilochus, QUCC 20, 123-55.
WILAMOWITZ-MOELLENDORFF, U. V. (1921): Griechische Verskunst, Berlin.
WEST, M.L. (1982): Greek Metre, Oxford.
WHITE, H. (1980): Essays in Hellenistic Poetry, Amsterdam.
WILLS, J. (1996): Repetition in Latin Poetry, Oxford.

Zum Werden des Lyrischen
Am Beispiel des Hohenliedes und frühgriechischer Lyrik

Hans-Peter Müller †

Warum produziert der menschliche Geist Gebilde, die nicht unmittelbar nützlich sind? Welche Bedingungen tragen dazu bei, Dichtung zu ermöglichen? Welche Lebensfunktionen hat speziell die Lyrik oder – beiläufig in anderen Grundformen der Poesie (Epik, Dramatik)[1] – das Lyrische?

I.

Was ermächtigt dazu, die Frage nach dem Werden des Lyrischen sowohl am Beispiel des Hohenliedes als auch dem frühgriechischer Lyrik zu stellen? Beide stehen geographisch, auch was die Kulturgemeinschaften angeht, dazu zeitlich sowie sozial- und geistesgeschichtlich weit auseinander.

Denken wir zur frühgriechischen Lyrik an Archilochos sowie an die Mytilener Sappho und Alkaios, so befinden wir uns im 7./6. Jh. v. Chr.; die Sammlung des der semitischen Kulturgemeinschaft angehörenden Hohenliedes, jedoch nicht die Entstehung aller seiner Einzelstücke, fand dagegen im 3. Jh. v. Chr. statt, das freilich für Juda, insbesondere Jerusalem,[2] als das hellenistische zu gelten hat. Dazu kommt die sozialgeschichtliche Differenz: während die frühgriechische Lyrik in der Spätgestalt der alten agrarisch-kriegerischen Adelswelt wurzelt, deren Blüte wir aus Homer kennen,[3] entstammt die Sammlung des Hohenliedes eher einem urban-‚bürgerlichen' Milieu.[4] Was die geistesgeschichtliche Stellung angeht, so bilden den Hintergrund der früh-

---

1 Zu den drei Grundformen der Poesie vgl. die ‚klassisch' gewordene Monographie von Staiger 1946. Einen konsistenten Begriff des Lyrischen hat die Antike nicht gebildet; vgl. neben der ebenfalls ‚klassischen' Untersuchung von Färber (1936: 3-28) zuletzt Robbins 1999: 586.

2 Zur Entstehung der Sammlung im Jerusalem des 3. Jh.s v. Chr. vgl. Vf. 1992: 3f.8f.16 et passim; 2000: 421f.; Kaiser 1994: 35f.; Bosshard-Nepustil 1996: 67-71 u.v.a. sowie zuletzt Hagedorn 2003: 351f., jeweils mit Lit.

3 Vgl. Schadewaldt 1989: 12.59.96.99.

4 Zum sozioökonomischen und geistesgeschichtlichen Hintergrund Kohelets und des Hohenliedes, der mit dem der frühgriechischen Lyrik einige Ähnlichkeit hat, vgl. Vf. 1978; 2003a: 27f.; 2003b: 68f.

griechischen Lyrik nur die Epik, die wir mit dem Namen Homer verbinden, und die Dichtungen Hesiods; die Sammlung des Hohenliedes aber markiert beinahe das Ende der altisraelitischen Literaturgeschichte, soweit sie durch das Alte Testament bezeugt ist. Vor allem: der Wurzelboden der Lyrik etwa Sapphos ist institutionell und inhaltlich der Kult der Aphrodite;[5] im Hohenlied dagegen gibt es allenfalls noch mythische Reminiszenzen,[6] die sich dem Verdikt eines monotheistischen Rigorismus entziehen konnten.

Was also verbindet das Hohelied mit der frühgriechischen Lyrik, so daß beide als signifikante Paradigmen für das Werden des Lyrischen – zumindest im orientalisch-abendländischen Kulturbereich – gelten können? Unsere engere Thematik freilich betrifft das Hohelied, für dessen Interpretation wir die frühgriechische Lyrik im Vergleich heranziehen.

Wenn die Sammlung des Hohenliedes im 3., dem hellenistischen Jahrhundert erfolgte, so mag die Anregung dazu von dem übermächtigen Kultureinfluß Alexandrias, insbesondere der literaturbeflissenen, auch an Lyrik interessierten Gelehrten[7] seiner Bibliothek seit der Zeit Ptolemaios' I. (305-283) ausgegangen sein. Ihrem Sammlerfleiß wollten ‚Weise' aus Jerusalem etwas atmosphärisch Ähnliches aus der eigenen Überlieferung entgegensetzen, auch wenn dieses in Inhalt und Stil verschieden war; daß das Hohelied im Kanon innerhalb des Kontexts von Weisheitsbüchern erscheint, wird kein Zufall sein.[8] Griechische Papyri, die in Ägypten gefunden wurden, sind dort frühestens im ausgehenden 4. Jh. v. Chr. geschrieben worden;[9] da sie z.T. Älteres enthalten, zeigt dessen Vorkommen, daß griechische Literatur hier überhaupt seit dem Frühhellenismus wirksam wird. Dies erklärt zugleich einen mutmaßlichen Einfluß griechischer, auch vorsokratischer Philosophie auf den Weisheitslehrer Kohelet, der ebenfalls dem 3. Jh. v. Chr. angehört.[10]

Allgemein mit altorientalischem Einfluß auf frühgriechische Religion, Denken und Dichtung wird heute vermehrt gerechnet;[11] dessen Spuren lassen sich bis in früharchaische Zeit,[12] archäologische Befunde, die auf einen umfassenden ostmediterranen Kulturzusammenhang hinweisen, bis tief ins 2. Jt. verfolgen.[13] Zumindest für Sappho und Alkaios von

---

5 Vgl. Burkert 1977: 242.

6 Vgl. Vf. 1976.

7 Die Alexandriner stellten einen ‚Kanon' von neun lyrischen Dichtern auf und teilten deren Texte nach Versmaß bzw. Gattung ein.

8 Auch Sappho wurde nach Aelian, Var. hist. 12, 19, von Platon „die Weise" (σοφή) genannt; Treu 1991: 116f. Vgl. σοφία für Dichtkunst Sappho 60, 3 D.; Treu 1991: 201.

9 Vgl. Fränkel 1962: 3. Ebenfalls dem 4. Jh. gehört im griechisch-sprachigen Raum ein biographisch-anekdotisches Interesse an Dichtern an; Schadewaldt 1989: 61.

10 Vgl. Anm. 5. – Die Ausbreitung des griechischen Liebesromans auch im Orient scheint im 2. Jh. v. Chr. einzusetzen; Musche 1999: 89.

11 Vgl. Cornford 1952; Hölscher 1953; West 1971, 1997; Kaiser 2000, bes. 309-313 (Lit.); Prayon/Röllig 2000; Ribichini 2001; Witte/Alkier 2003; Hagedorn 2003, ferner unsere Anm. 46.

12 Vgl. Burkert 1992.

13 Vgl. Buchholz 1999.

der Insel Lesbos, aber auch für Archilochos, der aus Paros, von den Kykladen, stammt und bei seinem Abenteurerleben weit herumgekommen ist, wird man an kleinasiatischen Einfluß denken müssen, der seinerseits altorientalisches, vielleicht speziell babylonisches Kulturgut vermittelte, wozu u.a. die Verwendung der Keilschrift durch Hurriter und Hethiter Veranlassung gab.[14] Im Fall von Sappho und Alkaios mag die Bewunderung, die die Bewohner von Lesbos für das nahe Lydien mit seiner überlegenen urbanen Kultur hegten,[15] das um die Wende des 1. Jt.s mehrheitlich griechisch besiedelt war und zur Zeit Sapphos eine Blüte erlebte, den Kulturtransfer erleichtert haben; vollends soll der etwa gleichzeitige, in Sparta wirkende Chorlyriker Alkman aus dem lydischen Sardes gebürtig sein.[16] Zu den Importgütern aus Kleinasien, die im 8. oder 7. Jh. die griechische Welt erreichten, gehört die kunstmäßige Flötenmusik.[17] Speziell der *Aulós* stammt nach der Überlieferung aus Phrygien,[18] woher sie der Kulturheros Olympos eingeführt haben soll;[19] er diente der Begleitung der Elegie sowie von Arbeitsliedern u.ä.[20]

II.

1. Ähnlich der ägyptischen Liebeslyrik der Amarnazeit[21] erreicht die frühgriechische Lyrik bei ihrem ersten uns bekannten Auftreten sogleich eine stupende Vollkommenheit. In bezug auf das Hohelied, dessen sprachlich offenbar einem Idiom des 3. Jh.s v. Chr. angepaßte Einzeltexte aus verschiedenen Zeiten stammen, läßt sich das Gleiche nicht mit derselben Sicherheit sagen. Gesamtorientalisch gesehen, steht das Hohelied zweifellos nicht am Anfang;[22] was die althebräische Literatur angeht, so kennen wir an früheren Zeugnissen von Liebeslyrik aber allenfalls Fragmente.[23] Bezeugt der späte Zeitpunkt der Sammlung, daß man in Spätzeiten den Reiz, wenn schon nicht des Volkstümlichen,[24] so doch des Elementaren entdeckt?

---

14 Daß nicht das europäische, sondern das kleinasiatisch-ionische Griechentum die für Hellas prägenden Kulturgüter hervorbrachte, wobei ein pluraler Sprachverband in Ionien unter dem Einfluß der altorientalischen Kultur gestanden habe, betont Högemann 2003.

15 Vgl. Sappho 98, 1.6 D.; 98ab, 11 D.

16 Vgl. zur Problematik dieser antiken Angabe Calame 1996: 512.

17 Vgl. Dihle 1967: 46.

18 Vgl. Fränkel 1962: 181f.

19 Zaminer 2000a: 522; 2000b: 547-549; Harmon 2000: 1192-4. Zum orientalischen Einfluß auf die griechische Musik allgemein vgl. Kranz 1992: 67f.

20 Vgl. Boetticher 1979: 494; zum antiken Lyrikbegriff Robbins 1999.

21 Vgl. Hermann 1959; Fox 1985.

22 Vgl., mit einer gelegentlichen Zurückhaltung in bezug auf Einzelurteile, Musche 1999.

23 Loretz 1993 meint, ein solches Fragment in Hos 2,7b zu finden.

24 Die Grenze zwischen dem Volkstümlichen und dem Anspruch hoher Literatur ist im Alten Israel wohl noch weithin fließend. Für den volksliedhaften Ursprung der im Hohenlied vereinigten Texte sind die Wiederholungen von Motiven und Wendungen, ja ganzer Verse charakteristisch. So etwas wie ein Bildungsanspruch dokumentiert sich dagegen im gewählten, z.T. manierierten Vokabular des Hohenliedes (soweit wir angesichts mangelnden Vergleichsmaterials urteilen können), u.a. mit wohlstands- und luxusorientierten Kulturwörtern (vgl. zu indischen Lehnwörtern Powels 1992, zu *qinnamôn* „Zimt" als malaiischem Lehnwort u.ä. Vf. 1988: 197f.) und teilweise ungewöhnlicher Syntax, wäh-

Im Falle der Liebeslyrik der Amarnazeit und der betr. frühgriechischen Dichtung kann der Eindruck, bereits Vollkommenes vor sich zu haben, freilich darauf beruhen, daß ältere Texte, wenn sie etwa den alexandrinischen Sammlern und Editoren als geringerwertig galten, von der Überlieferung ausgeschieden wurden und zufällig auch durch Papyrusfunde o.ä. nicht bezeugt sind. Immerhin hat es im Orient und in Hellas Zaubersprüche,[25] Arbeitslieder,[26] Hochzeitsgesänge (ὑμέναιος, ἐπιθαλάμιον),[27] Trinklieder,[28] Siegeslieder (ἐπίνικιον),[29] Spottlieder (σκολιόν),[30] Totenklagen (ἐπικήδειον, θρῆνος),[31] auch als Klagen um einen toten Gott,[32] etc. gegeben, volkstümliche Gattungen, auf deren Formenbestand derjenige der Lyrik aufbauen konnte; das Lyrische scheint aus ältesten menschlichen Ausdrucksformen hervorgegangen zu sein. Wenn die Überlieferung und alexandrinische Gelehrsamkeit[33] im Falle der frühgriechischen Lyrik Älteres verdrängte und dazu die althebräische Literatur den Reiz des Liebesliedes spät entdeckte, so bewirkt dies, daß alle diese Dichtungen unter den übrigen genres, aber auch gegenüber Philosophie bzw. Religion[34] weithin isoliert blieben.

2. Da wir das Aufkommen lyrischer Dichtung weder für Hellas, noch für Israel beobachten können, müssen wir die Spuren ihres Werdens dem Gewordenen absehen. Dieses ist um so leichter möglich, als die stark traditionsgebundenen Dichter der Antike nicht originär sein wollten. Zwar werden für die frühgriechische Zeit Dichternamen und biographische Daten von Dichtern überliefert, denen die einzelnen Texte zugeordnet werden; beim Hohenlied zeigt sich die Nähe zum Volkstümlichen umgekehrt auch daran, daß hier Entsprechendes fehlt.[35] Die für frühe Kulturen charakteristische Begrenztheit des Interesses am

---

rend die aiolische Lyrik der Alltagssprache näher blieb. - Dafür, daß es sich um abgesunkene Kunstdichtung handelt, gibt es keinen Hinweis. Vgl. Anm. 36.

25 Num 21,17f., offenbar beim Brunnengraben als Arbeitslied zu singen; zum Ägyptischen Hermann 1959: 66f., zum Hohenlied Vf. 2000.

26 Vgl. zum Ägyptischen Hermann 1959: 68, zum Griechischen Boetticher 1979; Schadewaldt 1989: 11.42f. (mit Hinweis auf Ilias 18, 569ff.); Robbins 1996.

27 Vgl. Sappho 115-136 D., dazu vielleicht 55a/b D. Zu Hochzeitsgesängen allgemein Färber 1936: 37f.63f.; Schadewaldt 1989: 9.42 (mit Hinweis auf Ilias 18, 492ff.); Robbins 1998.

28 Jes 22,13; 56,12; vgl. Ilias 1, 603f. Zur frühgriechischen Gelagepoesie etwa Fränkel 1962: 222f.

29 Färber 1936: 36.57; Schadewaldt 1989: 43. – Jud 5; 16,23f.; 1 Sam 18,7; vgl. Ilias 22, 393f. und natürlich Pindar.

30 Färber 1936: 36f.57-63. – Num 21,27-30 (Textvariante Jer 48,45f.); Jes 23,16.

31 Färber 1936: 38f.65f.; Keydell 1979; Schadewaldt 1989: 41f.; Robbins 1997; 2002.

32 Vgl. Vf., Adonis und Adonisgärtchen, demnächst in ZDMG; Der tote König Jojakim und der Gott Adonis, demnächst in FS K. Stähler (AOAT). – Zu den u.a. beim Totenzeremoniell aufgeführten ‚Linos-Liedern' vgl. Ilias 18, 569f.; Hesiod, Fr. 305f. M.-W.; Pindar, Fr. 128c,6 u.a.; weiteres Material bei Eißfeldt 1939 (vgl. Färber 1936: 43f.71) sowie in KP und Der Neue Pauly s.vv. ‚Arbeitslieder', ‚Linos' und ‚Ailinos'. Der Linus wurde wie Hymen(aios) und Ialemos sekundär als sterbender Heros personifiziert.

33 Vgl. Robbins 1999: 587f.

34 Anders Schadewaldt 1978: 18 et passim; vgl. Fränkel 1962.

35 Obwohl auch Volkslieder Verfasser haben, werden deren Namen nicht überliefert – ein Merkmal mündlicher Dichtung, das wie der Übergang von der Alltagssprache zur Dichtersprache (s. Anm. 25) im Hohenlied nachwirkt, vgl. Vf. 2003a: 27. Zum volkstümlichen Charakter des Hohenliedes auch Vf. 2000: 423.

nur-Individuellen[36] wirkt hier wie dort im Grunde weiter. Wie sich das Ich des frühen lyrischen (Chor-)Dichters zu dem des (der) Vortragenden verhält, ist ohnehin umstritten.[37] Insbesondere auch in bezug auf das Hohelied sollte man mit der Voraussetzung von kontingent-einmaligen Erlebnissen hinter den Texten vorsichtig sein; das Ich des Dichters will immer den Kreis seiner Adressaten in das Gesagte einbeziehen können und wird insofern vom Publikum mitkonstituiert, was eine gewisse Allgemeingültigkeit dessen voraussetzt, das jeweils zur Sprache kommt.

Indem wir das Werden von Lyrik am Aufkommen einzelner seiner Strukturelemente abzulesen suchen, werden wir gleichzeitig seines Wesens inne, soweit es sich in diesen Strukturelementen entfaltet.

3. Die Spuren des Werdens von Lyrik und somit die Merkmale seines Wesens sind am Hohenlied relativ leicht zu erkennen.

a. Auf einen letzten *kultischen Hintergrund* verweist die Gattung des Beschreibungsliedes, das in Cant 2,2; 4,12-15; 6,10 einer Frau, in 2,3.8f.14b; 3,9-11; 5,10-16 einem Manne gilt: es wurzelt in der einer Göttin oder einem Gott dargebrachten kultischen Beschreibungshymne; geschieht die Beschreibung in der Anrede – so für die Frau 1,9-11.15; 4,1-7.9-11; 6,4-7; 7,1-7.8-10, für den Mann 1,16f. –, mag man von einem ‚Bewunderungslied' sprechen.[38] Der Verwandtschaft von Gottesbildbeschreibung und statuarischer erotischer Beschreibung entspricht es, wenn die Menschendarstellungen offenbar volkstümliche theomorphe Steigerungen erfahren, wie sie für die Frau mit besonderer Intensität in 6,10 begegnen (vgl. u. sub II 3c),[39] während die Travestie-nach-oben für den Mann in 3,9-11[40] den sagenhaften König Salomo (vgl. zum Mann als „König" 1,4.12; 7,6) zum Modell wählt;[41] Vergöttlichungen der Liebenden gibt es auch in der griechisch-römischen Antike.[42]

Daß das erotische Beschreibungslied die kultische Beschreibungshymne ablöst und die theomorphe Steigerung des Menschen geradezu eine quasi religiöse Ersatzfunktion hat, ist offenkundig: das Bild der Gottheit wird beim Menschen gesucht, wie umgekehrt wohl schon immer die Gottheit der Ideal-

36 Vgl. zu Homer Schadewaldt 1978: 79.

37 Vgl. Lardinois 1996; Robbins 1999: 587.

38 Vgl. Herrmann 1963; Keel 1986: 185ff.; Vf. 1992: 59, zum Bewunderungslied 7. Daß es auch in Ugarit auf Gottheiten bezogene erotische Lieder gab, zeigen entsprechende Wendungen in KTU 1.3 III: 5-8; 1.101: 17.

39 Vgl. Vf. 1988; 1992: 67-69, dazu Anm. 52. Von einer ‚aufgeklärten' Tendenz des Hohenlieds sollte man also nicht reden.

40 In 1,5 ist statt שְׁלֹמֹה besser שַׁלְמָה, d.h. die parallel zu קדר gebrauchte Bezeichnung einer Landschaft, zu lesen; vgl. Vf. 1992: 14f.

41 Auch „der Wagen Amminadabs" 6,12 gehört wohl in den weiteren Zusammenhang der Königstravestie; vgl. Vf. 1996. – Dagegen distanziert sich 8,11f. von den Werturteilen „Salomos"; vgl. 6,8f.

42 vgl. etwa Sappho 2, 1 D. (= Catull 51, 1); Sappho 123, 5f.; 132b D. und den freilich nicht ganz eindeutig lesbaren Vers 98, 4 D. Dazu etwa Fränkel 1962: 197.199.209.

typ des menschlichen Erospartners war; daraus ergibt sich beiläufig, daß, anders als in der althebräischen Sage und im griechischen Epos, in der Lyrik das Gegenwärtige als preiswürdig erscheint.[43] Der Nachklang des traditionell Gottheitlichen bedingt zugleich eine gewisse Erlebnisferne der betr. Texte. Diese zeigt sich auch in anderen Travestien – nach oben zum König (s.o.) und entsprechend zur Königin 7,1-7,[44] nach unten zum Hirten 1,7f.[45] und wohl auch zum Gärtner 4,16; 8,13f.[46] Allgemein ermöglicht gerade der Schwund des Religiösen ein Hervortreten des Ästhetischen mit einer Beimischung von Anscheinhaftigkeit in bezug auf die Objekte der Beschreibung und zugleich von subjektiver Maskerade, sofern sich die *mens auctoris* wie auch im Fall Kohelets hinter einer Konventionskulisse verbirgt.[47] Zu den postreligiösen Merkmalen der Dichtkunst gehört auch, daß sich Dichter seit frühester Zeit einen Hörer- bzw. Leserkreis bilden, der, wie bereits oben sub II 2 angedeutet, dem Kollektiv-Ich einer religiösen Gemeinde ähnlich ist.[48]

b. Ein weiteres Strukturelement des Lyrischen ist die *Integration des Menschen* und des Geschehens, an dem er beteiligt ist, *in Naturvorgänge*, wofür Cant 2,8-14 das treffendste Beispiel bietet.[49] Der Schwund des Religiösen bewirkt wie überall auf der Welt auch das ersatzweise Hervortreten einer Naturfrömmigkeit, die in Hellas schon ursprünglich gegeben war – noch weit entfernt von der Teilnahmslosigkeit, die die wissenschaftliche Sicht an einer entgöttlichten Natur erlebt. Allerdings geht es nicht um Natur in bloßer Natürlichkeit;[50] dar-

43 Daß echte religiöse Empfindung in der frühgriechischen Lyrik schwindet, zeigt u.a. der ironisch-spielerische Zug der Gebetsparodie Sappho 1 D.; vgl. Vf. 2003a: 28-34. Im Hohenlied fehlt eine entsprechende ironisch-parodistische Haltung.

44 Falls שולמית mit „Salomonin" wiederzugeben ist; vgl. Rudolph 1962: 101.170f.; Vf. 1992: 11.74.

45 Schon in der Ilias scheint gelegentlich eine leicht romantisierende Vorstellung vom Hirtendasein vorausgesetzt; so in Il. 8, 555-559, vielleicht auch in Il. 18, 526b (vgl. 4, 452-455); dazu Vf. 1997: 566; 2002: 78f. Man denke auch an den „göttlichen" Schweinehirten Eumaios von Od. 14. – Zu den bildnerischen Vorbildern des Schilds des Achilleus von Ilias 18 bemerkt Schadewaldt 1959: 359, „daß dieser Dekorationsstil dem Vorderen Orient entstammt".

46 Entsprechend der vermutlichen Gärtnertravestie erscheint die Frau als Garten 4,12-5,1; 6,2.11 oder Weingarten 1,6; 8,11. Vgl. zur Liebe in Weingärten 1,14; 7,13, ferner 2,8-14; 7,12.14; 8,13f.; Hagedorn 2003: 342-348. Zu einem möglicherweise planvollen Gegensatz von „Hofmilieu" und „Landmilieu" in Cant vgl. Bosshard-Nepustil 1996: 50-52 et passim.

47 Zur Funktion verfremdender Fiktionen, insbesondere in nicht-alltäglichen Erfahrungszusammenhängen, vgl. insbesondere im Bezug auf Kohelet Lux 1990, der auch von Signalen spricht, die Fiktionen kenntlich machen.

48 Vgl. zu den frühgriechischen Lyrikern Fränkel 1962: 210.223f.; Franyó 1976: 12; Schadewaldt 1989: 86.89.95. – Zum Kontinuum von Religion und Dichtung Vf. 2003a: 39-42.

49 Vgl. Vf. 1994, dazu die stimmungsorientierte Erwähnung von Gärten und Balsambeeten 6,2 sowie von Lilien 2,16; 4,5; 6,3.

50 Sappho 96, 25-30 D. erwähnt den Klang von Liedern im Zusammenhang mit Fest(-Reigen?) im frühlingshaften Hain – offenbar Äußerungen eines bodenständigen kultisch gere-

gestellt wird vielmehr eine Gartenlandschaft, ja eine traumhafte Wunschlandschaft, die der Verwandlung der menschlichen Aktanten in Travestien entspricht. Zu den namentlich genannten Landschaften, die für die Liebenden eher eine schaurig-unwirtliche Feindwelt mit Löwen und Panthern sind, aus der sie an den Ort der Liebe gleichsam heimkehren, gehört – neben der „Wüste" von 3,6 – der Libanon zusammen mit Amana, Senir und Hermon 4,8. Daneben finden sich positiv-wertige Erwähnungen des Libanon (3,9b; 4,11.15), auch als Vergleichsspender (5,15b, vgl. „Libanonturm" 7,5b [s.u. sub II 3c]). – Eine dem Naturenthusiasmus entsprechende Philosophie der Lebensfreude, in ähnlichen gartenhaften Phantasielandschaften und Travestien, bietet Kohelet – auf dem Hintergrund vor allem eines gleichzeitigen hellenistischen Eudämonismus.[51]

Der Einklang mit der Natur scheint in der Dichtung in dem Maße gesucht zu werden, wie er in Wirklichkeit verloren geht. Die im hellenistischen Jerusalem gesammelten Stücke des Hohenliedes setzen eine Urbanisierung des Lebens voraus, die – auch dieses wie überall in der Welt – eine Lockerung ehemals strenger Sitten mit sich brachte.[52] Umgekehrt wird die aus einer Sehnsuchtsperspektive besungene Natur, wie wohl auch in Sappho 5/6, 3-13; 98, 5-11 D., phantasievoll überhöht; aus kulturellem, vielleicht auch politischem Wirklichkeitsüberdruß flieht die Dichtung in ein ästhetisiertes Weltsurrogat, das mit den harten Bedingungen der palästinischen Natur und der hellenistischen Gesellschaften wenig zu tun hat.

c. Eine der Sprachgebärden, der die frühe Lyrik Wesentliches verdankt, ist die *Metapher* samt dem ihr zugrunde liegenden Vergleich. Vergleichsspender wie שחר „die Morgenröte", Mond, Sonne und die rätselhaften נדגלות „Himmelsbilder(?)"[53] Cant 6,10 mit ihren theomorphen Konnotationen, aber auch

gelten Naturenthusiasmus, wie wir ihn auch aus Ägypten im Zusammenhang des Hathor- und Isiskultes kennen (Hermann 1959:19). Vgl., auch zum Folgenden, Vf. 2001.

51 Vgl. Anm. 40, dazu Vf. 1997; 2002: 77f.; 2003b: 75-77.

52 Daß die im Hohenlied besungene Liebe allermeist nicht die in der Ehe ist (so vor allem Budde 1898, vgl. Childs 1979: 578; vermittelnd Rudolph 1962: 105), geht schon daraus hervor, daß von Fruchtbarkeit und Kindern nirgends die Rede ist; was zur Sprache kommt, ist eine ungebunden-spielerische Gefühlswelt. Von der Hochzeit handelt Cant 3, 6-11; vgl. 3,4bb; 8,2a. In 4,8-5,1 wird die Geliebte, vielleicht verschleiernd, כלה „Braut" bzw. אחתי כלה „meine Schwester (und) Braut" genannt (dazu Vf. 1992: 18.46.47f.51), sonst heißt sie רעיתי „meine Freundin" 1,9 u.ö.

53 Die auch von Rudolph 1962: 162.164 vorgeschlagene versuchsweise Übersetzung ergibt sich bei einem Verständnis von נדגלות als zustandsbeschreibende adjektivisch-intransitive *niqtal*-Bildung von einer Wurzel דגל „sehen" u.ä. in der primären Bedeutung „Sichtbare" (vgl. דגול „sichtbar" Cant 5,10); gedacht wäre, passend zu Morgenröte, Mond, Sonne, an einen Sternenkranz als Majestätsmerkmal, das das Prädikat אימה „furchtbar" in V. 4 und V. 10 rechtfertigt (vgl. V. 5a). Zum Einzelnen und zu einer alternativen Deutung vgl. Keel 1984: 43-53; 1986: 295f.; Vf. 1988: 118-121; 1992: 68f. – Der Reiz des uranisch-siderischen Vergleichs von Cant 6,4.10 liegt darin, daß – wie bei einer Göttin des Ischtar-Typs – Schönheit (יפה//נאוה V. 4a [10aβ]) und Schrecklichkeit (אימה 4b.10bβ) ineinander übergehen, das *mysterium fascinosum* also mit dem *mysterium tremendum* übereinkommt.

die zahlreichen Tiervergleiche u.ä. eignen dem Vergleichsempfänger einen Mehrwert zu, der seiner gegenständlichen Realität abgeht;[54] traditionelle Vergleichsspender wie Gazelle, Hirsch und Taube[55] waren einst Göttertrabanten, so daß auch ihnen etwas Gotthaltiges anhaftete. Die Metaphern geben der Darstellung aber auch etwas Vieldeutiges, Gebrochenes: viele der Vergleiche und Metaphern lassen sich nicht auf ein *tertium comparationis* festlegen, was man geradezu als Andeutung eines Bedeutungsdefizits des Bezeichneten auffassen kann, insofern die Dinge in ihrer bloßen Gegenständlichkeit nichts Sinnhaltiges besagen. So bezeichnen die Metaphern etwas die Gegenständlichkeit des Metaphorisierten Überschreitendes und mit unmittelbaren Sprachmitteln nicht-Darstellbares; indem sie aus Resten mythischer Erinnerung einen Transzendenzbezug ahnen lassen, tritt die metaphorisierte Gestalt in einen gewissen Gegensatz zur Realität. Wenn mit Metaphern oft determinierte Spezifikationen oder Lokalisierungen verbunden sind, so darum, weil an diesen diffuse Stimmungsreste haften, die sie dem Metaphorisierten mitteilen: man denke an die Vergleiche כמגדל השן „wie der Elfenbeinturm", ברכות בחשבון על־שער בת־רבים „,wie' Teiche in Hesbon beim volkreichen (?) Tor", כמגדל חלבנון צופה פני דמשק „wie der Libanonturm, der gen Damaskus späht" 7,5. Ähnlich verhält es sich in 2,14, wonach der Vergleich der jungen Frau mit der Taube durch die determinierten Lokalisierungen בחגוי הסלע „in den Felsenklüften" und בסתר המדרגה „im Versteck der Felsenstiege" erweitert wird, ohne daß wir sagen könnten, welche Assoziation diese Adverbiale wecken sollen.

In einen Widerspruch zur Realität des Metaphorisierten tritt eine prädikative Metapher auch in dem Oxymoron „Deine Augen / Blicke sind Tauben" (1,15; 4,1, vgl. 5,12), worin die Metapher der prädizierten Größe eine Bedeutung geradezu aufzunötigen scheint.[56] Verständlich wird die unauflösbare (‚absolute') Metapher[57] allenfalls durch den Tatbestand, daß die Taube der Vogel der Astarte bzw. später der Aphrodite und Venus war,[58] wodurch dem Meta-

54 Vgl. Jüngel 1974: 78-81. Zum Gegensatz von Realität und nachmagischen Sprachspielen im Hohenlied vgl. Vf. 2000: 421f.

55 Vgl. Keel 1984: 89-100; zur Taubenmetapher auch Anm. 57.

56 Es bleibt der Phantasie des Hörers überlassen, zu entscheiden, was Augen bzw. Blicke taubenhaft macht; wir erfahren nicht einmal, ob die Augen mit den Tauben oder nur mit deren Augen bzw. Blicken verglichen werden (vgl. Keel 1984: 53-62). Das Fehlen eines stringenten *tertium comparationis* (anders 2,14; 5,2; 6,9?) führt insofern zu einer logischen Ellipse; das Fehlen der Vergleichspartikel כ – „wie" (anders 5,12) trägt offenbar zum Verzicht auch auf syntaktische Stringenz bei – im lyrischen Verschweben des Gedankens, das eine semantisch festlegende Deutung, wie sie auch Keel sucht, eher verbietet. Auch das Adverbial על־אפיקי מים (ohne Determination) „an Wasserbächen" (5,12) deutet kein *tertium comparationis* an, sondern bezeichnet ein atmosphärehaltiges Requisit und einen damit verbundenen Stimmungsgehalt, den man schwerlich auf den Begriff bringen kann.

57 Zur ‚absoluten Metapher' vgl. Blumenberg 1960: 9 u.ö.; Stoellger 2000: 87-94 (und Register).

58 Vgl. KP und Der Neue Pauly s.v. ‚Taube'; Keel 1984: 55.

phorisierten wieder ein sonst halb vergessener religiöser Stimmungsrest zuwächst, der im Grunde außerhalb des Vergleichs liegt; Bedeutung wird also, wie H. Friedrich[59] im Blick auf zeitgenössische Lyrik formulierte, nur durch „Einblendung eines zweiten Bereichs in die Erscheinung" gewonnen, nämlich in Cant des mythischen. Die Polysemie der Metapher ist hier und in ähnlichen Fällen entsprechend weitreichend. Im Maße ihres metaphorischen Gehalts wird die Bedeutung lyrischer Texte weithin erst durch deren jeweilige Rezeption im semantischen System des Empfängers konstituiert.

Nicht in gleicher Weise verrätselnd ist die Metaphorik, wenn wie in 2,14 die junge Frau selbst als Taube angeredet wird und durch den Hinweis auf die angenehme Stimme und die liebliche Gestalt anders als im Blick auf die eben genannten Lokalisierungen *tertia comparationis* angegeben zu sein scheinen; ähnlich 5,2; 6,9, wo die junge Frau durch die Taubenmetapher als תמה „makellos" dargestellt werden soll (vgl. ומום אין בך „und kein Makel ist an dir" 4,7b).

d. Formale Merkmale nicht nur des Lyrischen, sondern des Dichterischen überhaupt sind dyadische und rhythmische Strukturen.

Wir stoßen hier auf eine humanethologische Dimension des Dichterischen samt dessen neurobiologischem Hintergrund.[60] Die *dyadische Struktur* als eines der Kennzeichen des Poetischen, die sich in stilistischen Merkmalen wie Merismen und Dichotomien,[61] im Semitischen dazu im *parallelismus membrorum* manifestiert, mag auf einem entsprechenden dyadischen Instinkt beruhen, der unserer Vernunft angeboren zu sein scheint; in einer Welt voller Asymmetrien gelingt es auf diese Weise, semantische Gegensätze aufzustellen, die untereinander in eine sich gegenseitig bedingende Polarität und in einen komplementären Ausgleich gebracht zu sein scheinen.[62] Offenbar ist die ästhetische Höherwertung symmetrischer Beziehungen auf zentralnervöse Verschaltungen zurückzuführen, die auf solche Beziehungen bevorzugt in Resonanz geraten.

Mutatis mutandis gilt Ähnliches von der *rhythmischen Struktur* der Poesie, die der Lyrik von Arbeitsliedern, aus dem Tanz, dem Spiel u.ä. zugeflossen ist.[63] Das Miterleben von Lyrik gewinnt so etwas Leibliches und dabei einen regelmäßigen Wechsel von Spannung und Entspannung als etwas Nicht-Alltägliches, Festliches, ja Beschwörendes, das tiefe Dimensionen unserer Psyche anrührt: ebensowenig wie der lyrische Dichter eigentlich ein Wollen zu verwirklichen sucht, kommt bei der Einfühlung in Lyrik in erster Linie das Bewußtsein in Aktion; der Hörer bzw. Leser wird ‚unwillkürlich' mitgenommen.

59 Friedrich 1975: 206. Hier wird ein ‚dekonstruktivistischer' Standpunkt vorweggenommen.

60 Vgl. zu den neurobiologischen Befunden im Folgenden Singer 2002: 227. Schon nach C. Lévi-Strauss ist das menschliche Gehirn so ‚verdrahtet', daß binäre Gegensätze anziehend auf das Denken wirken; vgl. Harris 1989: 328.445f.

61 Vgl. Schadewaldt 1978: 56.58.60f.63-65 u.ö.

62 Daß auch die Sammlung des Hohenliedes, sein redaktioneller Aufbau, auf Polaritäten beruht, vermutet Heinevetter 1988: 66.171 u.ö.

63 Vgl. Schadewaldt 1989: 34f.

Ein Hindernis der Interpretation antiker Lyrik ist freilich der Tatbestand, daß wir – wie bei Texten in vielen anderen nicht mehr gesprochenen Sprachen – nur den semantischen, nicht auch den musikalischen (‚sprachmagischen') Gehalt erfassen können: wie Bedeutung und Klang ineinanderwirken, worauf also die sprachkünstlerische (phonetische) Stimmigkeit von Lyrik beruht, können wir allenfalls erahnen.[64] Daß wir in der griechisch-lateinischen Dichtung – anders als in der althebräischen – die Metrik kennen, ist nur ein geringer Ersatz; im Blick auf die althebräische Lyrik ist unsere weitgehende Unkenntnis des Vokalklanges ein erheblicher Mangel.

III.

1. Wir kehren zur Ausgangsfrage zurück: Wie kommt der an Lebensdienlichkeit orientierte menschliche Geist dazu, Lyrik zu produzieren?[65]

Da alle Lebewesen teilweise anachronistische Merkmale in sich tragen,[66] kann mit Vorsicht damit gerechnet werden, daß das Lyrische, insbesondere wenn wir die Entstehung von Lyrik früh in der Geistesgeschichte ansetzen, zu den eher archaischen Elementen der menschlichen Psyche gehört, zu den Medien, die vielleicht sogar einer evolutionär und/oder kulturgeschichtlich veralteten Gefühls- und Geistestätigkeit ein Reservat verschaffen. Es könnte sich in der Kunst überhaupt aber auch um das *Neben*produkt („fall out") einer im Gang der Evolution oder Kulturgeschichte benachbarten Entwicklung handeln, die ihrerseits einen hohen Selektionswert bietet oder einmal bot, nun aber als unschädliches oder doch ‚kostenneutrales' Epiphänomen einer anderen selektionsgünstigen Anpassung nicht eliminiert werden muß,[67] wie denn auch sonst nicht alle Eigenschaften von Organismen optimierte Ergebnisse evolutiver Selektionsmechanismen sind.[68]

Andere als nicht unmittelbar nützlich anzusehende Geistestätigkeiten mögen eine Disgruenz zwischen natürlichen Verhaltensstrukturen und sich verselbständigenden Kulturentwicklungen ausgleichen; Dichtung wird dann zum Kompensat eines sich seiner natürlichen Befindlichkeit, etwa infolge Überrationalisierung, entfremdenden Daseins. Dabei können obsolete Eigenschaften und Verhaltensformen, weil bewährte Strukturen ungern aufgegeben werden, zu Teilen eines umfassenderen Wirkungsgefüges geistiger und technischer Umweltbeziehungen werden, das seinerseits Selektionsvorteile bietet, vielleicht einer Verknüpfung phylogenetisch älterer mit jüngeren Elementen unseres neuronalen Systems entsprechend;[69] gleichzeitig entsteht ein Selektionsdruck

---

64 Einen neuen Weg zu diesem Ziel suchte von Soden 1990.

65 Vgl. zum Folgenden Roth 1996; Wilson 2000: 281-316; Singer 2002: 211-234.

66 Vgl. Voland 2000: 17-21.

67 Ein anderes Beispiel eines „kostenneutrale(n) Nebenprodukt(s) einer ganz anderen Angepasstheit" bietet Voland 2000: 283.

68 Ein Beispiel dafür ist die ‚Toleranz' von betr. Opfern gegenüber Schmarotzern, die sie zu Betrogenen macht, ohne daß dafür eine Kompensation erfahren würde.

69 Vgl. zum Einzelnen Wilson 2000: 143-147(-156), aber auch Roth 1996: 66-77.178-212.

zugunsten komplexer und subtilerer Verhaltensmuster, die gleichsam ‚Luxuriöses' zulassen, wenn es gegen Widrigkeiten des Daseins geistig und sozial resistent macht.[70]

2. Welche also sind die humanethologischen Funktionen des Lyrischen? – Ich vermute, daß sich in der Lyrik ein Vorgang isoliert, der auf dem Wege von der Sinneswahrnehmung zur Erkenntnis eine elementare, wenngleich sonst wenig beachtete Rolle spielt. Die wohl nie voll erklärliche ‚Übersetzung' eines sensorischen Reizes, der von Materiepartikeln oder Energiewellen ausgeht, in eine Vorstellung oder einen Begriff, eine Aneignung, die über mehrere Stufen der Metaphorisierung erfolgt,[71] unterliegt auf bestimmten Stufen offenbar einem ‚limbischen' Bewertungssystem, das die betreffenden Inhalte mit angenehmen, indifferenten oder schmerzlichen Empfindungen besetzt, um eine selektive Aufmerksamkeit zu steuern und so lebensdienliches Handeln zu ermöglichen. Solche Empfindung scheinen in der Kunst symbolisch kodiert zu werden, was zu einer teilautonomen Zwischenwelt sprachlicher und bildnerischer Figurationen in der Lücke von Objekt und Subjekt führt, einer Popperschen ‚Welt-Drei', mit der Hörer bzw. Leser oder Betrachter sich eine befriedigende Weltkonstruktion verschaffen. Eine solche Figurationenwelt ermöglicht angesichts der Veränderlichkeit von Wirklichkeit eine Ich-Kontinuität, – und zwar über eine Ich-Du-Identifikation, nämlich mit dem Du des Dichters oder Künstlers, oder doch wenigstens über eine Ich-Es-Identifikation mit dem Es des Werkes.[72]

---

70 Überlegungen wie die hier vorgelegten mögen als geistfeindlich erscheinen. Da das Erklärungspotential der Humanethologie bedeutend ist, wird man sie gleichwohl in der Hoffnung anstellen dürfen, daraus Wesentliches über die ursprüngliche, inzwischen ins ‚Vergessen' gedrängte Funktion gerade sublimer Geistesphänomene zu erfahren. Auch Lyrik darf, wenn wir nach ihrer Lebensdienlichkeit fragen, nicht vordergründig aus dem Abstand vom Kollektiv-Nützlichen oder gar aus einem rein individuellen l'art pour l'art begriffen werden; hier sind ältere Auffassungen zur griechischen Lyrik wie die von Snell 1993: 56-81 und, zur altägyptischen Lyrik, von Hermann 1959: 71f. zu korrigieren. Die biologischen und sozialen Zwecke höher differenzierter Kulturleistungen wie die der Dichtung sind freilich viel mittelbarer als die allermeist von der Humanethologie erörterten; nur so gesehen, sind auch die höchsten Kulturleistungen biosoziale Instrumente.

71 Vgl. die Definition von ‚Verstand' als „verschlüsselte Darstellung von Sinneseindrücken und der Erinnerung und Vorstellung von Sinneseindrücken", was ein „Verschlüsselungsnetzwerk" voller „virtueller Realitäten" ergibt, bei Wilson 2000: 147f.(83); zur entsprechenden ‚Metaphorisierung' Vf., Mythos und Metapher. Zur Ambivalenz des Mythischen in poetischer Gestaltung, demnächst in QD.

72 Vergleichbar ist die Funktionalität von Träumen: offenbar als ein Grenzfall des Bewußtseins bewirken sie mittels vorwiegend endogener Reize „eine besondere Form von *Selbst-Erzeugung*" des Träumenden im Zusammenhang simulatorischer ‚Welt'-Modelle, wie wir sie ähnlich in den ‚traumhaften' Wunschlandschaften und Travestien des Hohenlieds und Kohelets (1,12-2,12) finden (s.o. sub II 3b); dem Träumenden fehlt dabei die kritische Einsicht in das Wesen seines Traumzustands, er weiß nicht, daß er ‚nur' träumt. Von erkenntnistheoretischem Interesse ist dann die Frage, ob es dennoch „ein gemeinsames funktionales Substrat des Traum- und Wachbewußtseins geben könnte". Vgl. Metzinger 1993: 146-149 u.ö.; 2001: 455-458 (Zitate 457f.) zu O. Flamagan (daselbst 491-521).

Die einzelnen, oben sub II. 3 genannten Strukturelemente des Lyrischen wie kultischer Hintergrund, Integration des Menschen in eine sublimatorisch aufgewertete Natur, Metaphorik sowie dyadische und rhythmische Ordnung u.a. tragen je auf ihre Weise zu dieser figurativen Zwischenwelt bei, die die Erfahrungswelt als ‚poetische' Wahrnehmungseinheit erscheinen läßt. Um eine uns fremde, teilnahmslose Realität zu korrigieren, an die wir immer nur partiell angepaßt sind, werden gesellschaftlich approbierte ‚Gegenwelten' gepflegt,[73] deren ontologischen Status wir nicht bestimmen können.[74] Phylogenetisch entwickelte Anlagen werden dazu je nach einzelkulturellen Voraussetzungen sowie kollektiven und individuellen Erinnerungen aktiviert oder im Stillstand belassen. Allerdings kann nur einzelkulturell, kollektiv und individuell erweckt werden, was stammesgeschichtlich angelegt ist, wodurch eine transkulturelle Ähnlichkeit und Verständlichkeit des Dichterischen möglich wird. Umgekehrt entsprechen die unreduzierte Komplexität und die große Varianz des Lyrischen einer lebensdienlichen Fülle möglicher, Gegenwelten', die dadurch, daß sie als – teilweise – erklärbar erscheint, wie vieles andere, das erklärterweise das Mensch-Sein ausmacht, weder ihre Funktionen, noch ihren Wert verliert; sie trägt, indem sie selbst Teil eines äußerst komplexen Wirkungszusammenhanges ist, zur mentalen Konstruktion einer Wirklichkeit bei, durch die die Menschheit – bislang – in ihrer ‚Welt' trotz oder gerade wegen der Abweichungen solcher Konstruktionen von der physikalischen Realität überleben konnte.[75]

---

73 Natürlich tragen solche ‚Gegenwelten' umgekehrt zur Sozialisation bei. Gesellschaften entstehen überhaupt erst mit der Möglichkeit eines Informationsaustauschs. Je zahlreicher und heterogener die sozialisierenden Informationen insbesondere in größeren Zeiträumen werden, um so schwerer wird es, Effektives von ‚Authentischem' zu unterscheiden; ja, dieses ist im Grunde nicht einmal nötig, da ‚Erkenntnis' eine Handlung ist, die es dem Erkennenden erlaubt, sein Leben dadurch fortzusetzen und zu verbessern, daß er sich ein kommunikables, wenn auch nicht immer authentisches Bild seiner Welt macht, wobei auch un- und vorbewußte Antriebe einwirken.

74 Je weiter der Weg zwischen Sinneswahrnehmung und Erkenntnis ist, je mehr Metaphorisierungen erstere dabei durchläuft, um so mehr wächst ein erkenntnistheoretisch begründetes Mißtrauen gegenüber allen Vorstellungen und Begriffen, da sie den Bereich des Metaphorischen prinzipiell nicht verlassen. So ist die Frage nach dem ontologischen Status von ‚Gegenwelten' nur von relativer Relevanz. ‚Ding an sich' ist ohnehin ein ebenso erhabener wie leerer Begriff.

75 Ich danke Frau stud. theol. et phil. Friederike Niemeier für Recherchen, die Beschaffung von Literatur und die Erstellung der PC-Fassung dieses Artikels.

Bibliographie

BOETTICHER, W. (1979): Arbeitslieder, in: KP 1, 494-495.
BOSSHARD-NEPUSTIL, E. (1996): Zu Struktur und Sachprofil des Hohenlieds, BN 81, 45-71.
BLUMENBERG, H. (1960): Paradigmen zu einer Metaphorologie, ABG 6, 7-142.301-305.
BUCHHOLZ, H.-G. (1999): Ugarit, Zypern und Ägäis. Kulturbeziehungen im 2. Jt.v.Chr., AOAT 261, Münster.
BUDDE, K. (1898): Das Hohelied, in: id. et al., Die fünf Megillot, KHC 17, Freiburg i.Br., IX-XXIV. 1-48.
BURKERT, W. (1977): Griechische Religion der archaischen und klassischen Epoche, RM 15, Stuttgart u.a.
– (1992): The Orientalizing Revolution. Near Eastern Influence on Greek Culture in the Early Archaic Age, Cambridge/MA.
CALAME, C. (1996): Alkman, Der Neue Pauly 1, Stuttgart/Weimar, 512-515.
CHILDS, B.S. (1979): Introduction to the Old Testament as Scripture, London (6. Aufl. 1989).
CORNFORD, F. M. (1952): Principium Sapientiae. The Origins of Greek Philosophical Thought, Cambridge.
DIHLE, A. (1991): Griechische Literaturgeschichte, 2. Aufl. München.
EIßFELDT, O. (1939): Linos und Alijan, in: FS R. Dussaud, 161-170, Halle (= id., Kleine Schriften 2, Tübingen 1963, 150-159).
FÄRBER, H. (1936): Die Lyrik in der Kunsttheorie der Antike, München.
FOX, M.V. (1985): The Song of Songs and the Ancient Egyptian Love Songs, Madison.
FRANYÓ, Z./SNELL, B./MAEHLER, H. (1979): Frühgriechische Lyriker 1-4, SQAW 24, Berlin.
FRÄNKEL, H. (1962): Dichtung und Philosophie des frühen Griechentums, 2. Aufl. München.
FRIEDRICH, H. (1975): Die Struktur der modernen Lyrik, 7. Aufl. Hamburg.
HAGEDORN, A.C. (2003): Of Foxes and Vineyards: Greek Perspectives on the Song of Songs, VT 53, 337-352.
HARMON, R. (2000): Olympos 14, Der Neue Pauly 8, Stuttgart/Weimar, 1193-1194.
HEINEVETTER, H.-J. (1988): "Komm nun, mein Liebster, Dein Garten ruft Dich!" Das Hohelied als programmatische Komposition, BBB 69, Frankfurt a.M.
HERMANN, A. (1959): Altägyptische Liebesdichtung, Wiesbaden.
HERRMANN, W. (1963): Gedanken zur Geschichte des altorientalischen Beschreibungsliedes, ZAW 75, 176-197.
HÖGEMANN, P. (2003): Das ionische Griechentum und seine altanatolische Umwelt im Spiegel Homers, in: M. Witte/S. Alkier (edd.), Die Griechen und der Vordere Orient. Beiträge zum Kultur- und Religionskontakt zwischen Griechenland und dem Vorderen Orient im 1. Jahrtausend v. Chr., OBO 191, Fribourg/Göttingen, 1-24.
HÖLSCHER, U. (1953): Anaximander und die Anfänge der Philosophie, Hermes 81, 257-277.385-418.
JÜNGEL, E. (1974): Metaphorische Wahrheit, in: P. Ricoeur/E. Jüngel, Metapher, München 71-122 (= id., Entsprechungen. Gott – Wahrheit – Mensch, 2. Aufl. Tübingen 1986, 103-157).
KAISER, O. (1994): Grundriß der Einleitung in die kanonischen und deuterokanonischen Schriften des AT 3: Die poetischen und weisheitlichen Werke, Gütersloh.
– (2000): Die Bedeutung der griechischen Welt für die alttestamentliche Theologie, NAWG I, phil.-hist. Kl. Nr. 7, Göttingen [= id., Zwischen Athen und Jerusalem. Studien zur griechischen und biblischen Theologie, ihrer Eigenart und ihrem Verständnis, BZAW 320, Berlin/New York 2003, 1-38].
KEEL, O. (1984): Deine Blicke sind Tauben. Zur Metaphorik des Hohenliedes, SBS 114/115, Stuttgart.
– (1986): Das Hohelied, ZBK.AT 18, Zürich.
KRANZ, W. (1998): Geschichte der griechischen Literatur, Nachdruck der 4. Aufl., Köln.

LANDINOIS, A. (1996): Who Sang Sappho's Songs?, in: E. Green (ed.), Reading Sappho. Contemporary Approaches, Berkeley.
LORETZ, O. (1993): Ein kanaanäisch-biblisches Liebeslied in Hos 2,7, UF 25, 311-318.
LUX, R. (1990): "Ich, Kohelet, bin König...". Die Fiktion als Schlüssel zur Wirklichkeit in Koh 1,12-2,26, EvTh 50, 331-342.
METZINGER, T. (1999): Subjekt und Selbstmodell, 2. Aufl. Paderborn.
METZINGER, T. ed. (2001): Bewußtsein. Beiträge aus der Gegenwartsphilosophie, 4. Aufl. Paderborn.
MÜLLER, H.-P. (1976): Die lyrische Reproduktion des Mythischen im Hohenlied, ZThK 73, 23-41 (= id., Mythos – Kerygma – Wahrheit, BZAW 200, Berlin/New York 1991, 152-171).
– (1978): Neige der althebräischen „Weisheit". Zum Denken Qohäläts, ZAW 90, 238-264 (= id., Mensch – Umwelt – Eigenwelt, Stuttgart u.a. 1992, 143-168).
– (1988): Begriffe menschlicher Theomorphie, ZAH 1, 112-121.
– (1992): Das Hohelied, in: H.P. Müller/O. Kaiser/J.A. Loader, Das Hohelied – Klagelieder – Das Buch Ester, ATD 16/2, 4. Aufl. Göttingen, 1-90.
– (1994): Menschen, Landschaften und religiöse Erinnerungsreste, ZThK 91, 375-395 (= id, Glauben, Denken und Hoffen, Altes Testament und Moderne 1, Münster 1998, 155-175).
– (1996): Kohelet und Amminadab, in: FS D. Michel, BZAW 241, Berlin/New York, 149-165.
– (1997): Travestien und geistige Landschaften. Zum Hintergrund einiger Motive bei Kohelet und im Hohenlied, ZAW 109, 557-574.
– (2000): Zum magischen Hintergrund des Hohenliedes, ZDMG 150, 409-424.
– (2001): Der Libanon in altorientalischen Quellen und im Hohenlied, ZDPV 117, 116-128.
– (2002): Die Kunst der Selbstverwandlung in imaginären Landschaften, in: J. Hahn et al. (edd.), Religiöse Landschaften, AOAT 301, Münster, 69-84.
– (2003a): Psalmen und frühgriechische Lyrik, BZ 47, 23-42.
– (2003b): Kohelet und die frühgriechische Philosophie, in: D.J.A. Clines et al. (edd.), Weisheit in Israel, Altes Testament und Moderne 12, Münster, 67-80.
MUSCHE, B. (1999): Die Liebe in der altorientalischen Dichtung, SHCANE 15, Leiden.
PRAYON, F./RÖLLIG, W. edd. (2000): Akten des Kolloquiums zum Thema "Der Orient und Etrurien". Zum Phänomen des 'Orientalisierens' im westlichen Mittelmeerraum (10.-6. Jh.v.Chr.), Tübingen 12.-13. Juni 1997, Biblioteca di Studi Etruschi 35, Pisa/Rom.
RIBICHINI, S. et al. edd. (2001): La questione delle influenze vicino-orientali sulla religione greca. Atti del Colloquio Internazionale, Roma, 20-22 maggio 1999, Rom.
ROBBINS, E. (1996): Arbeitslieder, Der Neue Pauly 1, Stuttgart/Weimar, 969-970.
– (1997): Epikedeion, Der Neue Pauly 3, Stuttgart/Weimar, 1116-1117.
– (1998): Hymenaios 2.1, Der Neue Pauly 5, Stuttgart/Weimar, 785-786.
– (1999): Lyrik I, Der Neue Pauly 7, Stuttgart/Weimar, 586-591.
– (2002): Threnos, Der Neue Pauly 12/1, Stuttgart/Weimar, 500.
ROTH, G. (1996): Das Gehirn und seine Wirklichkeit. Kognitive Neuro-biologie und ihre philosophischen Konsequenzen, 5. Aufl. Frankfurt a.M.
RUDOLPH, W. (1962): Das Buch Ruth. Das Hohe Lied. Die Klagelieder, KAT XVII/1-3, Gütersloh.
SCHADEWALDT, W. (1959): Von Homers Welt und Werk, 3. Aufl. Stuttgart.
– (1978): Die Anfänge der Philosophie bei den Griechen, Frankfurt a.M.
– (1989): Die frühgriechische Lyrik, Frankfurt a.M.
SINGER, W. (2002): Der Beobachter im Gehirn. Essays zur Hirnforschung, Frankfurt a.M.
SNELL, B. (1993): Die Entdeckung des Geistes, 7. Aufl. Göttingen.
STAIGER, E. (1946): Grundbegriffe der Poetik, Zürich/Freiburg i.B.
STOELLGER, Ph. (2000): Metapher und Lebenswelt, HWTh 39, Tübingen.
TREU, M. (1991): Sappho, 8. Aufl. München.

VOLAND, E. (2000): Grundriß der Soziobiologie, 2. Aufl. Heidelberg/Berlin.
WEST, M.L. (1971): Early Greek Philosophy and the Orient, Oxford.
– (1997): The East Face of Helicon. West Asiatic Elements in Greek Poetry and Myth, Oxford.
WILSON, E.O. (2000): Die Einheit des Wissens, München (englisch 1998).
WITTE, M./ALKIER, S. edd. (2003): Die Griechen und der Vordere Orient, Beiträge zum Kultur- und Religionskontakt zwischen Griechenland und dem Vorderen Orient im 1. Jahrtausend v. Chr., OBO 191, Fribourg/Göttingen.
ZAMINER, F. (2000a): Musik IV, Der Neue Pauly 8, Stuttgart/Weimar, 520-533.
– (2000b) Musikinstrumente V, Der Neue Pauly 8, Stuttgart/Weimar, 543-551.

Pigs in the Camps and the Breasts of my Lambs. Song of Songs in the Syriac Tradition

Alison Salvesen

This essay is a general survey of the Syriac texts of Song of Songs and the surviving Syriac commentaries on the book, with some examples of its influence on wider literature. There is still much work to be done on the extant of Cant's influence on Syriac authors, a subject that is beyond the scope of this short article.

1. The Old Testament Text in Syriac

There are three continuous extant texts of the biblical book in Syriac. Two of them, the Peshitta and the Syrohexapla, are well known, but the third seems to have had a much more limited circulation.

1) The Peshitta text (PCant) is the most important and influential of the Syriac versions of Cant.[1] The usual superscription in Syriac *tešbḥaṯ tešbḥāṯā dšleymon* means, "the praise of praises of Solomon", i.e. "the greatest hymn", though a number of manuscripts and commentaries also use the more Aramaic-sounding title *šīraṯ šīrīn* "Song of Songs", which the manuscripts sometimes refer to as the "Hebrew" title.[2] PCant is based on the Hebrew text, and like the rest of the Peshitta books corresponding to the Jewish canon, the translation shows a good knowledge of Hebrew. Therefore, along with the rest of the Peshitta books, it is likely to have been the work of Jewish translators working in northern Mesopotamia around the end of the second century CE,[3] although it is difficult to rule out completely the possibility that

1 Textual references are to the Leiden Peshitta edition of 1979: see the article by John Emerton (1967), on the limitations of the earlier non-critical printed editions, and his caustic remarks on Bloch's 1921/22 plagiarism of Euringer's 1901 work. Also Baars 1968: 281-89 on the witness of the thirteenth century writer Barhebraeus to readings that may be older than those of the MSS of PCant.

2 Van den Eynde 1963: 256 n.4 thinks that this is a Hebrew title Syriacized, but it is close to the Jewish Aramaic form.

3 See the work of Weitzman 1999: 2.258-62. He dates the earliest books to c.150 CE, and the latest (Chronicles) no earlier than 200 CE, after which time he believes the translators'

the translators were recent converts from Judaism to Christianity at the same period. At the same time, it should be noted that there is no connection with the Aramaic Targum of Song of Songs, which in any case is an allegory of the history of God's relationship with Israel, and not a conventional rendering of the Hebrew text.[4]

The main features of the translation technique and manuscript tradition of PCant have been outlined in an excellent article by one of the editors of the Leiden edition, David Lane (1995: 71-84). More recently Michael Weitzman (1999: 76) argued that PCant showed evidence of sporadic but wide use of LXX, for instance at Cant. 4:1; 6:7, where צַמָּתֵךְ "your veil" is rendered as "your silence" by both P and LXX (*štqky* and σιώπησις), as if the etymology of the word were from the root צמת rather than צמם.[5] However, van Wyk (1977: 182)[6] and the present writer believe that both P and LXX arrived at their renderings independently. As Weitzman himself notes,[7] the Greek translator Symmachus[8] understands Ps 101(LXX 100):8 אַצְמִית as ἀφώνους ἐποίουν "I made them dumb" while the Peshitta has the similar rendering *'štq* "I will silence".[9] The translator of PPss would not have known of Symmachus's translation, since the two versions were produced more or less contemporaneously. Weitzman believes that the rendering "beyond your silence" is so unlikely that P's agreement with LXX cannot be accidental. But it is more likely that PCant, PPss, LXXCant and Symmachus all share a common etymological tradition. The Greek version of Cant is one of the latest renderings in LXX. It was probably translated in Palestine rather than Alexandria, perhaps as late as in the early first century CE, and with PCant tends to translate literally.[10]

---

community converted to Christianity, taking their Syriac translation of Hebrew Scripture with them.

4 Alexander 1988: 234-7 and 1994, especially p. 332.

5 Interestingly, it is in Arabic that the root *ṣmt* has the meaning "be silent", rather than in Hebrew or the known Aramaic dialects.

6 Also Shedinger in his review of Weitzman's book on the SBL website.

7 Weitzman 1999a: 76 and 1999b: 183. See also Lane 1995: 82.

8 I.e. the Jewish reviser of the Septuagint who lived at the end of the second century CE, not the Christian exegete of Song of Songs discussed below.

9 The same rendering occurs at PPs 18:41; 54:7; 88:17; 94:23; 101:8; 143:12; Job 23:17, but not for every use of צמת within those books, e.g. not at PPs 73:27; 101:5; 119:139 where it is rendered by *'wbd* "destroy", nor at PJob 6:17. Evidently the translator of PPss knew the meaning of the Hebrew word, but believed that silencing someone was a synonym for destroying them (this meaning is also possible in English), and since the Hebrew verb often occurs in parallelism with other verbs of destroying, the rendering "to silence" provided variety in the rendering.

10 See Barthélemy 1963: 33, 47.158, though his theories concerning the consistuents of the so-called *kaige* group of late, Hebraising translations in LXX continue to be disputed or refined.

Another place where dependence on LXX is possible occurs at Cant 3:2, where ברחבות "in the broad streets" is rendered in P by the Greek loan word *bplṭwtʾ* "in the broad ways", corresponding to the LXX reading ἐν πλατείαις. The commonest rendering of רחוב in other books of the Peshitta is in fact the native Syriac word *šwqʾ*, but Greek-derived *plṭyʾ* is found twice in Jeremiah[11] as well as in Cant, and on both occasions LXX has πλατείαι.[12] On the other hand, Cant, Jer and Dan appear to belong to a group of books that were translated later in the formation of the Peshitta Old Testament, at a time when Greek loan words were more likely to occur spontaneously. A further point of coincidence between P and LXX occurs ar 7:11, where תשוקתו "his desire" is translated by P as *pnyth*, "his turning", which is very similar to LXX ἡ ἐπιστροφή αὐτοῦ.[13] However, independent renderings should not be ruled out here, since the same Hebrew word is found at Gen 3:16 where it is rendered by P as *ttpnyn* "you will turn", and although LXX has ἀποστροφή, the Aramaic Targumim Onkelos and Neofiti also render as "your return". It seems that, as with צַמָּתֵךְ above, there was a widespread Jewish tradition of interpretation that connected תשוקה with the much commoner word תשובה, "return, repentance".

There are some features in PCant that reflect a desire to represent the difficult Hebrew text as closely as possible. One is the use of the particle *yt*, an old Aramaic object marker corresponding to Hebrew את. *yt* occurs at least four times in PCant[14] and only a further 14 times in the rest of the Peshitta, 11 of these in another literal translation, Ecclesiastes.[15] The particle *nʾ* for נא "I pray; please!" (PCant 3:2) looks suspiciously like a Hebraism, since there are more natural Syriac equivalents employed in other books of the Peshitta, such as *bbʿwtʾ*, *hšʾ*, *twb*, or *bʿʾ ʾnʾ*. However, the second occurrence of נא, in Cant 7:9, is not represented by PCant. Another example of literal rendering is the

11 Jer 5:1; 9:21(MT 20). The translation technique of both P and "Theodotion's" Greek Daniel with regard to the Hebrew original text does not permit firm conclusions about whether the appearance of *plṭwtʾ* in the Peshitta of Dan 9,25 corresponds to πλατεῖα in the same verse in Theod. Dan.

12 Πλατεῖα is in fact the commonest Greek rendering for רחוב in LXX books.

13 Van Wyk 1977: 185 overlooks P's resemblance to LXX here.

14 PCant 2:7; 3:4.5; 8:4, all for את. It may also be significant that all precede the verb or noun for "love". The particle is also found with 2nd fem. sg. suffix at 1:8 as *ytky* for לך, and Weitzman 1999a: 123 suggests that it may have been corrupted into *yhbt* from *yhb yt* in 8:11.

15 Weitzman 1999b: 203. He rejects the idea that it is a Western Aramaic feature, as the late seventh century Syriac writer Jacob of Edessa implies by his remarks on the phenomenon in his *Encheiridion* (see Wright 1871: 984b). Certainly it was already an archaism by the time of the Peshitta translators.

use of *ddy* for דודי:[16] unlike its Biblical Hebrew counterpart, *ddʾ* in native Syriac can only mean "uncle", and for this literalism we can compare LXXCant ἀδελφιδός. Another rendering is *qrybty* "my kinswoman" for רעיתי,[17] probably because the masculine form רע often means "companion, the next man", as in Lev 19:13. 16.18. LXX renders both words as πλησίον in Lev and Cant. Since the Hebrew of Cant itself uses "sister" as a term of endearment for the beloved, the translator may not have found these other renderings too odd. Both LXXCant and PCant belong to a movement of Jewish translation methodology when it was felt important to reflect certain details of the Hebrew text quite literally. Although LXX and P coincide on their renderings of דודי and רעיתי, unlike PCant, LXXCant never attempts to mark the particle את in a special way. LXXCant represents both occurrences of נא (Cant 3:2; 7:9) as δή, a rendering found frequently in other LXX books, especially in the more literally translated sections.

At most, the occasional coincidences between P and LXX could be explained by the hypothesis that P was aware of or consulted LXX from time to time, without actually relying on it in any significant way.[18] Yet it is likely that the two versions reflect their dependence on a common stream of Jewish interpretation. As we shall see below, PCant's independence with regard to LXX became a problem for later Syriac interpreters who wanted to draw on the Greek commentary tradition.

Of features exclusive to the Peshitta tradition, two are of note for their curious nature. The Hebrew of 8:1 reads "(O that you were like a brother to me) who nursed at my mother's breast! (NRSV)". PCant 8:1 originally read, "my mother's breasts suckled", translating the Hebrew Qal singular verb with a causative Aphʿel plural. An inner-Syriac corruption very early in the manuscript tradition has resulted in the reading "the breasts of my *lambs* suckled" where *ʾmy* "my mother" has become *ʾmry* "my lambs".[19] A later corruption in the transmission history of PCant occurs at 7:1 (NRSV 6:13b), where the conventional English translations have something such as "Why should you look upon the Shulammite, as upon a dance before two armies?". The majority of P manuscripts have the rendering "why will you look on the Shilomite [sic] who descends like joy, like the joy of the camps?" The sixth

---

16 PCant 1:13b.14; 2:3.8.9.10.16.17; 5:1.2.4.6.8.10.16; 6:32; 7:10.11.14; 8:5.14. See Weitzman's comments on the longer and less literal rendering *drḥm ly* "of the one who loves me" at 1:13a (1999b:83).

17 PCant 1:9; 2:2.10.13; 4:7; 5:8; 6:4

18 Cf. Lane 1995: 75: "resemblances between them do not show clear evidence of derivation, but simply of shared attitude." He gives another example at 6,4, where תרצה is rendered by P as *ʾyk ṣbynʾ* "according to pleasure"(cf. PLev 26:34) and by LXX as ὡς εὐδοκία.

19 The word is singular in 6h17. See Emerton 1967: 420, Lane 1995: 83.

century manuscript 6h17, noted for its peculiar readings,[20] has, "why will you look on the Shilomite descending like pigs, like the pigs of the camp?" It is unclear how *ḥdwt'* "joy" became corrupted into *ḥzyr'* "pigs", unless through the work of an unusually inattentive or playful scribe.

As for the use of Song of Songs in the liturgy, Emerton and Lane (1979: X-XI) note only two lectionaries, both dating from the ninth century, which incorporate readings from PCant. One has 1:2-12 (with the heading Wisdom of Solomon!), and the other has 1:2-14.

Otherwise no other part of Cant appears to be used in the Syriac lectionaries. This is not so unusual, however, for the shorter books among what the Syriac churches termed the Beth Mawthbe. Ecclesiastes, Wisdom, 1 Maccabees and Sirach feature very little in lectionaries, and Ruth does not appear at all.[21]

2) The Syrohexapla version of Cant (SyhCant) is part of the wider Syriac rendering of the Greek Septuagint text in Origen's revision, which was carried out by Paul of Tella at the Ennaton in Egypt in 616/7 CE. There is no one manuscript or modern edition covering the entire Syrohexapla, but SyhCant can be consulted in the edition of Ceriani, a photolithographic edition of the eighth century Codex Ambrosianus.[22] SyhCant influenced the manuscript tradition of PCant on occasion, for instance in 12a1 fam at Cant 3:9, which reads *kwrsy'* "chair, throne" with Syh (MT אפריון, LXX φορεῖον) instead of P *mgdl'* "tower", and in Cant 2:9 manuscript 12k3 adds the phrase "on the mountains of Beth El" from Syh.[23]

3) Rather less influential but certainly intriguing is the anonymous version of Song of Songs (AnonCant) found in what was originally a single manuscript containing in addition the Syriac version of Gregory of Nyssa's homilies on Cant.[24] Brock notes that AnonCant diverges from P, often agrees with LXX, and cannot be identified with the Syrohexapla, but neither does it correspond to the biblical citations in the Syriac version of Gregory's *Homilies* which it follows (1995: 41-42.46). One well known figure who tried to bridge the gap between P and LXX generally is the Syrian Orthodox bishop Jacob of Edessa (d. 708 CE), and Van den Eynde had suggested in passing that AnonCant could be Jacob's work, but then rejected the possibility on the ground of date (1939: 26.61). Brock pointed to differences between Jacob's style of rendering and that of the anonymous version of Cant (1995: 50). On the basis of its translational features Brock tentatively assigns to it a sixth century date, well before both the Syrohexapla and Jacob, and he also suggests a possible

20 Emerton and Lane 1979: III-IV.

21 See also Jenner 1993.

22 The same Milan manuscript is used for Middeldorpf's edition of 1835, but that of Ceriani (1874) is to be preferred.

23 See Lane 1995: 77.

24 See Brock 1995.

connection with the Syro-Lucianic (i.e. Philoxenian) version of Isaiah which dates from the early sixth century (1995: 41).

Although as Brock has shown, there is no connection between AnonCant and Jacob of Edessa, it is likely that the latter produced his own version of Cant in his revision of the Old Testament carried out in the early years of the eighth century. Jacob's Syriac version of the books of Samuel drew on the Peshitta, Septuagint (especially in the Lucianic and Hexaplaric recensions) and to a lesser extent the Syrohexapla[25] and any revision of Cant would probably have followed similar principles. We have manuscripts covering the Pentateuch, Samuel, Isaiah, Ezekiel, Daniel and Susanna, in Jacob's version, and a fragment of Wisdom was discovered and published by Baars (1968), so it is possible that further portions of Jacob's revision, including Cant, may yet surface.

2. *Commentaries*

A number of famous Syriac writers are reputed to have written commentaries covering much or all of the Old Testament, which would imply that they also wrote about Song of Songs. They include the major exegete St Ephrem (mid-fourth century) and Elias of Merv (fl. c. 660). The Eastern writer Henana of Adiabene (c. 590) is said to have written on Job, Proverbs, Ecclesiastes, the Minor Prophets and Cant. However, tradition tends to make exaggerated claims for the output of literary figures, and what little of their output survives does not suggest a great interest in Cant among native Syriac writers and those who transmitted their works. The late eighth century commentator of the Church of the East,[26] Theodore Bar Koni, dismisses Cant as an unprofitable work written by Solomon to defend himself when he was criticised for marrying Pharaoh's daughter. Moreover, he says, it lacks any divine name.[27] In this he was evidently influenced by the opinion of the Greek theologian Theodore of Mopsuestia (c.350-428), whose biblical scholarship was so revered in the Church of the East that he was often referred to simply as "the Interpreter".[28] It is unlikely that Bar Koni was the only influential

25 See Salvesen 1999.

26 The term "Nestorian" is more familiar to Western scholars, but one rejected by the Church of the East itself since the work of Nestorius is not at all influential in their tradition. See Brock 1996: 23-35.

27 Mimra V on the books of Solomon, in ed. Scher 1910: I.323 line 20-324 line 4 (French translation in Hespel and Draguet 1981: 273). Another exegete of the Church of the East who lived in the ninth century, Isho' bar Nun, does not comment on Cant, Wisdom, Job, Ruth or Chronicles in his *Selected Questions* (Van den Eynde 1963: XXXIII-XXXIV).

28 Theodore's opinion of Cant is recorded in a letter, of which some fragments survive in Latin (Migne, PG LXVI col. 699-700). Although Theodore appears very sceptical as to its religious genre, and comments on the lack of a Divine Name in the book, Amann

figure to regard the book with suspicion. The Syriac exegesis preceding the christological schisms of the fifth century tended to shy away from allegory in favour of typology, for which a "historical" or literal interpretation was a prerequisite. The strong eroticism of Song of Songs when read as a literal account was no doubt too earthy to lend itself easily to typological exegesis of the book, or to enhance its sacred character. Moreover, Jewish exegetical influence was strong in the early Syriac church: some rabbis of the Tannaitic period had had misgivings about Song of Songs themselves, and it was not until the period of the Babylonian Talmud that an allegorical interpretation indicating the relationship between God and Israel became dominant in Jewish exegesis.[29]

Probably for such reasons, the earliest surviving witness in Syriac to the exegesis of Cant is not a native Syriac work but fragments of the Greek writer Hippolytus in translation.[30] It represents an allegorical interpretation of Cant, and of course is based on LXX, not PCant.

Much more extensive, however, is the Syriac translation of Gregory of Nyssa's *Homilies* on Cant that was referred to above. This survives in what were originally three manuscripts, two of which also contain a copy of some correspondence concerning the translation. The first letter asks the recipient to produce a Syriac version of the *Homilies* on Cant, and the reply is a response that speaks of the difference between PCant and LXXCant, and of the

1946: 239, 245-47 wonders whether Theodore took a similar line to that he espoused on Psalm 45 (LXX 44). This psalm Theodore also categorised as a wedding song in its historical origins, but explained that it expressed the love of Christ for the Church. The sentiments expressed in Theodore's letter on Cant are very negative, however, and they would seem to preclude his acceptance of the book as canonical, unless the theological opponents who preserved excerpts of the letter have deliberately omitted more positive comments.

29 Mishnah Yadaim 3.5: R. Jose says that there is dissension as to whether reading Song of Songs renders the hands unclean, i.e. necessitates ritual washing afterwards, as would be the case with other books of Scripture. However, in the same passage R. 'Akiba (died 132 CE) declares that the day on which the book was given to Israel was worth all the ages, and it is the holiest part of all Scripture. The Babylonian Talmud cites Song of Songs many times, more than any other rabbinic source. See Newby 2002: 124-83 for the argument that there was no extended allegorization of the book in either Christianity or Judaism until Hippolytus of Rome (c. 170-c.236). Newby observes that the earliest example of allegorical exegesis of Cant attributed to R. 'Akiba is found in the late third century CE compilation Mekhilta de-Rabbi Ishmael, tractate Shirata 1:136-9, on Cant 5:10-15.

30 Pitra 1883: 36-41, Latin translation 306-310. Apart from the Syriac version, Hippolytus' commentary on Cant survives only in Georgian and in an abbreviated Greek form. A fragment preserved in Syriac (Pitra 1883: 26, Latin translation ibid. 299-300) mentions the interpretation of Cant by Irenaeus (130-200 CE), but what follows does not reveal much about the author's wider interpretation of Cant, since it involves only an allegorical understanding of "twin (fawns of a gazelle?)" (LXXCant 7:3).

difficulties in translating Gregory's work.[31] The date of the translation is estimated to be the end of the fifth or beginning of the sixth century. It should be noted that although Van den Eynde published a valuable monograph entitled *La version syriaque du commentaire de Grégoire de Nysse sur le Cantique des Cantiques,* he does not actually include an edition of the Syriac text of Gregory's *Homilies.*[32] He does discuss its form and influence, and refers to it in his 1963 work covering the section of Isho'dad of Merv's commentary on Song of Songs. To my knowledge, no one has yet edited the Syriac text of Gregory's *Homilies.*

Because Gregory's *Homilies* terminate at Cant 6,9, their Syriac translator says that he is providing a commentary for the remainder of Cant from the work of a certain Symmachus.[33] The style of the Syriac text shows that this Symmachus was a Christian writing in Greek and that the translation was made by the same person responsible for Gregory's *Homilies.*[34] Like Gregory, Symmachus adopts an allegorical approach to the text. For instance, at Cant 7,9 the phrase "the scent of your nostrils is like apples" is said to indicate the sweet smell of divine instruction. Since Symmachus refers to verses preceding the point where his work follows on from that of Gregory, it is likely that originally Symmachus's commentary covered the whole of Cant and was not written merely to supplement the missing part of Gregory's *Homilies.*

The combined commentary of Gregory and Symmachus was very influential in Syrian Orthodox circles. An anonymous seventh century catena uses scholia from it,[35] and the catena of the monk Severus depends entirely upon it. Material from it even entered the exegesis of the Church of the East, as will be seen below.[36]

One native Syriac writer some of whose comments on Cant survive is the Syrian Orthodox scholar John bar Aphtonia (d. 537). He founded the important monastery Qenneshre on the Euphrates, where Greek formed an important part of the syllabus, and this may be why he apparently wrote in Greek rather than Syriac.[37] Certainly the six surviving fragments of his commentary in a Syriac version appear to have been translated from Greek, as the biblical text they cite does not correspond completely to PCant.[38] The

31 Discussed by Van den Eynde 1939: 17-22. He gives the Syriac text (ibid. 69-76) and Latin translation (ibid. 97-102).

32 This may be because at the time there was less interest in translation Syriac for its own sake, in cases where the original Greek text had survived.

33 Van den Eynde 1939: 77.

34 Van den Eynde 1939: 34-42, who does provide the text of Symmachus's commentary (ibid. 77-89), and a Latin translation (ibid. 103-16).

35 BM Add.12.168.

36 Van den Eynde 1939: 43-60.

37 Watt 1999: 160.

38 The scholia occur in a manuscript in the British Museum dating to the eighth or ninth century, commenting on words or phrases in Cant 1:12; 2:4; 3:6-7; 4:9.13; 5:3; 7:7. See Krüger 1963.

nature of the commentary is typological and non-literal: for instance, John says that the spices and apples are the words and deeds of the prophets and apostles which the "bride"asks the holy angels to sustain her with.

The ninth century Church of the East writer Isho'dad of Merv[39] compiled commentaries on many books of the Bible, drawing heavily on the work of his predecessors, eastern and western, Syriac and Greek.[40] Unlike Theodore bar Koni, he does cover Cant, even though he recognises the lack of a divine name in it.[41] He also admits that there are different views concerning the book, which he proceeds to list. First he gives the judgement of Theodore of Mopsuestia and his followers, who say that Solomon had written Cant as a song to flatter Pharaoh's daughter whom he had married. It was to be performed before her at banquets to reassure her that, although the Israelite women mocked her ugliness, small stature and swarthy complexion, Solomon found her dark and beautiful and loved her. Thus he would prevent a diplomatic incident with Egypt.[42]

Isho'dad then presents the very different opinion of Gregory of Nyssa, John Chrysostom and others. They refute the idea that Cant was ever a secular song about Pharaoh's daughter, otherwise it would never have been received into sacred Scripture. This literal, historical sense is impossible anyway because it would denigrate, not praise her, since it describes a woman roving round the town and being roughly treated by the watchmen (PCant 5:7): no one but a prostitute would do this! The same people also object that only a madwoman would want to climb trees (PCant 7:9),[43] and point to the apparent inconsistency of the supposed daughter of Pharaoh being described as "black" in PCant 1,5 and then referred to as a "Shilomite" who is white and ruddy.[44] Therefore this second group of commentators interpret Cant as an allegory of Christ and the Church, who is the daughter of the gentile nations, though they uphold Solomonic authorship and connect it to Ps 45:1. Isho'dad then gives their identification of each of the protagonists in the Song.

The third opinion Isho'dad gives is that of the Jews, which is that Cant is about God and the "Israelite" Synagogue. However, he makes no further comment on this interpretation, and also refuses to pass judgment on any of the three opinions, since he says they are all those of "orthodox" teachers (surprisingly, since doctrinally he would have been a long way from Gregory

39 An oasis city on the silk route, now Mary in Turkmenistan.

40 The commentaries are edited by Van den Eynde (the volume on Genesis with J-M. Vosté) in the CSCO series. The Syriac text of Isho'dad's commentary on Cant appears in Van den Eynde 1962: 219-224.

41 See the full and very helpful notes by Van den Eynde on Isho'dad's sources in the volume containing the French translation (1963: 256-66).

42 This corresponds more or less to the content of Theodore's letter mentioned above (Migne PG LXVI cols. 699-700).

43 However, even in the Greek text it is clear that the speaker here is the male protagonist.

44 See Van den Eynde's note (1963: 259 n.1) on the Shulamite/Shunamite.

and John), and he leaves it to them to chew the Song over "with their iron jaws and Attic tongue." He, Isho'dad, will confine himself to explaining the difficult words.[45] Though he adopts a similar approach when commenting on other books, in the case of Cant, it enables him to preserve a certain agnosticism with regard to the book's sacred character, since he focuses on matters philological and botanical, and ignores completely Cant's voluptuous sensuality.

Surprisingly, elements of his commentary are dependent directly or indirectly on Gregory of Nyssa,[46] but shorn of the latter's allegorical interpretation. There are also parallels with material found in an anonymous commentary,[47] and with a collection of unattributed scholia of uncertain date that includes some details absent from Isho'dad's work.[48] Interestingly, the Syrian Orthodox writer Dionysius bar Salibi (d. 1171) is dependent on Isho'dad and not on the Syriac version of Gregory and Symmachus for his comments on Cant.[49]

The thirteenth century Syrian Orthodox catholicos Gregory Abul Faraj, better known as Barhebraeus, covered Cant in his commentary on the Old Testament, the *Auṣar Rāzē*, written in 1278.[50] However, there is little originality in his remarks: the beginning of the commentary refers immediately to Gregory of Nyssa, John Chrysostom, Theodore of Mopsuestia, and the Jews, presenting a succinct account of the various views on Cant that appeared in greater detail in Isho'dad of Merv's commentary. But in contrast to the explanations in Isho'dad's work, the scholia in Barhebraeus take an allegorical understanding of the text that originates (directly or indirectly) from the interpretations of Gregory and Symmachus. Barhebraeus's explicit reference to Theodore's view and his evident reliance on another "Nestorian", Isho'dad, is notable.

3. The use of Song of Songs in Syriac literature

Tracing the influence of Song of Songs in Syriac literature outside direct biblical exegesis is a hard task. In the absence of scriptural concordances to a wide range of literature it is difficult to produce a full account of the reception history of the book in the Syriac tradition. Remarkably, those authors for

---

45 This is particular feature of commentaries of this period in the Church of the East. Cf. Salvesen (forthcoming) on "Obscure Words in the Peshitta of Samuel, according to Theodore bar Koni".

46 Van den Eynde 1963: XXVIII and Euringer 1932: 51.

47 The section of this commentary that covers Cant has not yet been published.

48 Hoffmann 1880: 103-104, part of a larger collection of scholia on difficult words in Scripture. See Euringer 1901: 69 and Van den Eynde 1963: VII-VIII.

49 Van den Eynde 1939: 59 n.24 and 105.

50 Rahlfs 1887: 20-27.

whom citation indexes exist, such as the fourth century writers Aphrahat and Ephrem, rarely if ever refer to Song of Songs.

One early and unusual work is the collection of Syriac poems known as the *Odes of Solomon,* which may date from the late second century CE. Newby (2002: 144-48) refutes the idea that they allude to Cant (Cant 2:3 in Ode 7:1; Cant 3:4 in Ode 3:7; Cant 2:16 in Ode 3:5; Cant 1:2 (LXX) in Ode 19:2-4).[51] There are certainly some verbal parallels (e.g. "lover", "Beloved", "fruit", "breasts"), but these are rather vague, and it is hard to say whether or not the author of the *Odes of Solomon* had Cant in mind.[52]

In contrast, the single citation of PCant in Aphrahat's *Demonstration* 6 is very clear. *Dem.* 6.19 quotes Cant 2:12-13, "the time of summer is near, the fig tree has budded and its leaves have come out".[53] Far from taking an allegorical or typological approach, Aphrahat gives these verses an eschatological dimension, relating them to the sign of the fig tree given by Jesus in Mt 24:32. Since he does not cite Cant anywhere else in his work, it is hard to know what this renowned champion of celibacy and virginity made of the rest of the book.

Beck's edition of St. Ephrem's *Hymn on the Nativity* associates HNat 16.15 with Cant: "The blossom faded, for the fragrance of the Glorious Lily surpassed it. The Treasure of Spices did not need the flower or its scents ..." McVey also regards these lines as "loosely related" to Cant 1:3; 1:12-2:3.[54] Nevertheless, there is nothing uniquely reminiscent of Song of Songs in either ideas or vocabulary here. Ephrem has many biblical allusions in his poetry, but he also often refers to natural imagery, and we cannot discount the possibility that he did not have Song of Songs in mind at all here. The address to Christ, "Your lips distil the fragrance of Life while balsam flows from your fingertips" in the *Hymn on Mary* 10.13 may also be a rather loose allusion to Cant 4:11 and 5:5.[55] In general, Cant does not appear to feature much in Ephrem's poetry, noted for the richness of its biblical imagery.

The late fifth century writer Jacob of Serugh makes more direct use of Cant. In the *Hymn on the Ascension of our Lord* he prays, "Let your name be for me the oil of myrrh which delights me, for your mercy is better than wine".[56] Here

51 Charlesworth 1973: 33-35; 18-19; 81-82.

52 The suggested date of composition of the *Odes of Solomon* ranges from 1st century to third century CE, with the late second century being the most likely. They may also been written in Greek originally.

53 Parisot 1894: 309 lines 26-27: *zbn' dqyṭ' qrb lh wtt' 'prʿt wnpqw ṭrpyh* "the time of summer is near, the fig tree has budded and its leaves have come forth". This is not the same as the text of PCant, "the time of pruning has arrived ... the fig tree has produced its early fruit", perhaps through influence from the Syriac text of Matthew, "from the fig tree learn the parable: as soon as ... its leaves bud ... summer has arrived".

54 Ed. Beck, 1959: 86, German translation on p. 77, and English translation in K. McVey 1989: 151 n.368.

55 Brock 1994: 53. The full Syriac text is in ed. Lamy 1886: 519-90.

56 Kollamparampil 1997: 344 lines 299-30. Syriac text in ed. Bedjan 1902, Hom. 9, lines 822-23.

there is clear reference to PCant 1:2. Jacob also has an extended allusion in his *Homily on the Parable of the Vineyard*, connecting Cant with the gospel and seeing the fulfilment of both scriptural passages in the life of the Church:[57]

> "With them they worked it, and the vineyard was established and gave you the fruits.
> Your Name is oil of myrrh: see, it delights the congregations,
> and the young girls loved your sweet fragrance and worshipped it ... [58]
> Your sweet wine thrills the teeth of virgins[59]."

In contrast to such a communally-based interpretation, the fifth century spiritual writer John of Apamea (also known as John the Solitary) reformulates Cant 8:6 to express the idea that the love of God is stronger than death for the individual believer.[60]

Cant 1:1-12 was read at the consecration of the anointing oil (the *muron*), according to the important seventh century manuscript 7a1 and in the sixth century manuscript 6k2,[61] and the connection between Cant and the *muron* is frequently made. Moshe bar Kepha, a Syrian Orthodox writer who died in 903, wrote a series of questions and answers on the symbolism of the *muron*,[62] using the proof text of Cant 1,3 three times (in chapters 5, 6 and 41). Yet each time it appears in the form agreeing with the Septuagint, not PCant.[63]

These examples represent a mere handful of instances that came to light in the course of writing this chapter. A properly systematic exploration of the influence of Song of Songs on Syriac literature and the general trends of interpretations there, from the earliest times to the medieval period, would be a very worthwhile research project.

57 Syriac text in ed. Bedjan 1908: 760 lines 16-18. 21.
58 Cf. PCant 1:3.
59 Cf. PCant 7:11.
60 In his *Letter to Hesychius* §45, as yet unpublished in Syriac. See Brock's translation (1987: 92).
61 Jenner 1993: 388, 413.
62 Strothmann 1973: 107.
63 PCant has *mšḥ' dmwr' šmk* ("your name is oil of myrrh") whereas Moshe's text reads each time *mwrwn mspq' šmk* ("your name is myrrh poured out"), thus differing slightly from the Syrohexaplar version as well.

Bibliography

ALEXANDER, P.S. (1988): Jewish Aramaic Translations of Hebrew Scriptures, in: M.J. Mulder and H. Sysling (eds.), Miqra. Text, Translation, Reading and Interpretation of the Hebrew Bible in Ancient Judaism and Early Christianity, Assen/Maastricht/Philadelphia. 217-253.

– (1994): Tradition and Originality in the Targum of the Song of Songs, in: The Aramaic Bible, in: D.R.G. Beattie/M.J. McNamara (eds.), The Aramaic Bible. Targums in their Historical Context, JSOTS 166, Sheffield, 318-339.

AMANN, É. (1946): Théodore de Mopsueste, Dictionnaire de Théologie catholique XV/1, Paris, 235-79.

BAARS, W. (1968a): The Peshitta Text of Song of Songs in Barhebraeus' *Auṣar Rāzē"* VT 18, 281-289.

– (1968b): Ein neugefundenes Bruchstück aus der syrischen Bibelrevision des Jakob von Edessa, VT 18, 548-554.

BECK, E. (1959): Des Heiligen Ephraem des Syrers Hymnen de Nativitate (Epiphania). Texte CSCO 186-187 SS 82-83, Louvain.

BEDJAN, P. (1902): S. Martyrii qui et Sahdona, quae supersunt omnia, Paris.

– (1908): Homiliae Selectae Mar Jacobi Sarugensis. Tome IV, Paris.

BLOCH, J.S. (1921/22): A Critical Examination of the Text of the Syriac Version of the Song of Songs, AJSL 38, 103-139.

BROCK, S.P. (1987): The Syriac Fathers on Prayer and the Spiritual Life, Kalamazoo.

– (1994): Bride of Light. Hymns on Mary from the Syriac Churches, Moran Etho 6, Kottayam.

– (1995): Mingana Syr. 628: A folio from a revision of the Peshitta Song of Songs, JSS 40, 39-56.

– (1996): The 'Nestorian' Church: a Lamentable Misnomer, in: J.F. Coakley/K. Parry (eds.), The Church of the East. Life and Thought, BJRL 78/3, Manchester, 23-35.

CERIANI, A.M. (1874): Codex Syro-Hexaplaris photolithographice editus, MSP VII, Milan.

CHARLESWORTH, J.H. (1973): The Odes of Solomon, Oxford.

EMERTON, J.E. (1967): The Printed Editions of the Song of Songs in the Peshitta version, VT 17, 416-429.

EMERTON, J.E./LANE, D.J. (1979): The Old Testament in Syriac according to the Peshitta Version II,5. Song of Songs, Leiden.

EURINGER, S. (1901): Die Bedeutung der Peschitto für die Textkritik des Hohenliedes. Biblische Vorträge, BSt (F) 6, Freiburg i.Br., 117-128.

– (1932): Des Išô'dâd von Maru Kommentar zum Hohenlied, Oriens Christianus (3rd series) 7, 49-74.

HESPEL, R./DRAGUET, R. (1981): Théodore bar Koni, Livre des Scolies (recension de Séert) I. Mimré I–V, CSCO 431, SS 187, Louvain.

HOFFMANN, G. (1880): Opuscula Nestorian, Kiel.

JENNER, K.D. (1993): De Perikopentitels van de geïllustreerde Syrische kanselbijbel van Parijs (MS Paris, Bibliothèque Nationale, Syriaque 341). Een vergelijkend onderzoek naar de oudste Syrische perikopenstelsels, PhD thesis, Leiden.

KOLLAMPARAMPIL, Th. (1997): Jacob of Serugh. Select Festal Homiles, Rome/Bangalore.

KRÜGER, P. (1966): Johannes bar Aphthonaja und die syrische Übersetzung seines Kommentars zum Hohenliede, OrChr 50, 61-71.

LAMY, T.J. (1886): Sancti Ephraem Syri Hymni et Sermones II, Maines.

LANE, D.J. (1995): 'The Curtains of Solomon': some notes on the 'Syriacing' of *Šir Haššīrim*, in: P. Dirksen/A. Van der Kooij (eds.), The Peshitta as a Translation. Papers read at the II Peshitta Symposium held at Leiden 19-21 August 1993, Leiden, 73-84.

– (2001): 'Come here ... and let us sit and read': the use of Psalms in five Syriac authors, in: A. Rapoport-Albert/G. Greenberg (eds.), Biblical Hebrew, Biblical Texts. Essays in

Memory of Michael P. Weitzman, JSOTS 333/The Hebrew Bible and its Versions 2, Sheffield, 412-430.
McVEY, K.E. (1989): Ephrem the Syrian. Hymns, New York/Mahwah.
MIDDELDORPF, H. (1835): Codex Syriaco-Hexaplaris. Liber Quartus Regum e Codice Parisiensi; Iesaias, Duodecim Prophetae Minores, Proverbia, Iobus, Canticum, Threni, Ecclesiastes e Codice Mediolanensi. Pars I, Berlin.
NEWBY, M. (2002): The Song of Songs before Origen: Aspects of Canon and Hermeneutics, PhD thesis Birmingham.
PARISOT, J. (1894): Patrologia Syriaca. Pars Prima, Paris.
PITRA, J.B. (1883): Analecta Sacra Spicilegio Solesmensi Parata. Tom. 4, Patres Anteniceni, Paris.
RAHLFS, A. (1887): Des Gregorius Abulfarag gennant Bar Ebroyo Anmerkungen zu den salomonischen Schriften, (Diss. Göttingen), Leipzig.
SALEY, R.J. (1998): The Samuel Manuscript of Jacob of Edessa. A Study in its Underlying Textual Traditions. Monographs of the Peshitta Institute Leiden 9, Leiden.
SALVESEN, A. (1997): Hexaplaric Sources in Isho'dad of Merv, in: J. Frishman/L. Van Rompay (eds.), The Book of Genesis in Jewish and Oriental Christian Interpretation, Louvain. 229-253.
– (1999): The Books of Samuel in the Syriac version of Jacob of Edessa. Monographs of the Peshitta Institute Leiden 10, Leiden.
– (forthcoming): Obscure Words in the Peshitta of Samuel, according to Theodore bar Koni, in: K. Jenner (ed.), IIIrd Peshitta Symposium Volume (Leiden 2001) Leiden.
SCHER, A. (1910): Theodorus Bar Koni Liber Scholiorum I, CSCO 55, SS 19, Louvain.
STROTHMANN, W. (1973): Moses bar Kepha, Myron-Weihe, GOF 1. Syriaca, Band 7, Wiesbaden.
VAN DEN EYNDE, C. (1939): La version syriaque du commentaire de Grégoire de Nysse sur le Cantique des Cantiques, Bibliothèque du Muséon 10, Louvain.
– (1962): Commentaire d'Isô'dad de Merv sur l'ancien testament. III. Livre des Sessions. Texte, CSCO 229, SS 96, Louvain.
– (1963): Commentaire d'Isô'dad de Merv sur l'ancien testament. III. Livre des Sessions. Version, CSCO 230, SS 97, Louvain.
VAN WYK, W.C. (1977): The Peshitta of the Song of Songs, OTWSA 20, 181-189.
WATT, J.W. (1999): A Portrait of John Bar Aphtonia, Founder of the Monastery of Qenneshre, in: J.W. Drijvers/J.W. Watt (eds.), Portraits of Spiritual Authority: Religious Power in Early Christianity, Byzanium and the Christian Orient, Leiden, 155-169.
WEITZMAN, M.P. (1999a): The Syriac Version of the Old Testament. An Introduction, UCOP 36, Cambridge.
– (1999b): From Judaism to Christianity, in: A. Rapoport-Albert /G. Greenberg (eds.), Studies in the Hebrew and Syriac Bibles, JSS Suppl. 8, Oxford.
WRIGHT, W. (1871): Catalogue of Syriac Manuscripts in the British Museum acquired since the year 1838. Vol. II, London [Repr. ed. Piscataway 2002].

Origen, the Jews, and the Song of Songs:
Allegory and Polemic in Christian Antiquity

Elizabeth A. Clark

Introduction

Origen's *Commentary* and *Homilies* on the Song of Songs provided the inspiration for much later discussion of that biblical book[1] – despite the author's condemnation as a heretic.[2] Distinctive to Origen's interpretation was his deployment of the Song to illustrate Paul's hope, expressed especially in Romans 9-11, for the eventual union of Jews and Gentiles in the Christian Church. For Origen, the Song is a saga of Judaism's and paganism's progress to Christianity, a progress from the children's milk and weak man's vegetables to the solid food of Christ's athletes.[3] Whether or not Origen deemed likely the conversion of the Jews in his own time (the mid-third century), his unwavering conviction of the power of God's goodness and of the freedom of the human will to turn from unbelief to "faith" prompted him to champion Paul's vision.

Later spiritualizing interpretations of the Song of Songs, by contrast, centered largely on two aspects of Origen's interpretation that "traveled" well:

Some paragraphs of this essay are taken from Clark 1986. I thank the Edwin Mellen Press for permission to use them.

1 Although these two works were themselves copied and recopied through the centuries – in the twelfth century, the monastery library at Cluny possessed three copies of the *Commentary* – they also were incorporated into the writings of later, and widely-read, authors such as Gregory the Great, Bede, Isidore of Seville and the *Glossa ordinaris* (De Lubac 1959: 222-27; Scheper 1971: 325-34). It appears that the *Homilies*, shorter and relying on moral and spiritual, rather than theological argumentation, were better known in the Middle Ages than the *Commentary* (Riedlinger 1958: 24-25; Riedel 1898: 55). Of Bernard of Clairvaux's 86 sermons on the Song, for example, 39 are deemed dependent on Origen (Brésard 1982: 68).

2 Origen's views were somewhat unofficially condemned (for his speculations *in On First Principles*) by the bishop of Rome in 400; and officially, by an ecumenical council in 553 (Clark 1992: 32, 171-73; Vogt 1987: 78-99). The condemnation seemed not to effect his popularity as an exegete – although perhaps his fallen reputation accounts for why later authors sometimes disguise their source.

3 Origen, *Hom. in Lev.* 1.4 (GCS 29, 286).

the relation of the Church, or the individual soul, to Christ.[4] These chronologically-"transportable" motifs were deemed more significant than time-bound themes pertaining to Jews and Gentiles, seemingly irrelevant to many (but not to all[5]) later commentators. Gregory of Nyssa's *Sermons on the Song of Songs*, for example, display a "mystical" exegesis in which the soul is urged never to cease in her ascent to Christ, her transformation into an ever more perfect condition:[6] the theme of Jew and Gentile is here obscured. Fourth- and fifth-century Latin commentators, for their part, probed the Song of Songs for verses pertinent to their own religious disputes: to promote ascetic renunciation; to argue for Mary's virginity *in partu*; to claim the unity of the Catholic Church over against Donatist schismatics.[7] The pliability of allegorical interpretation in addressing ever-new religious and cultural situations is abundantly manifest in these later interpretations of the Song of Songs.

Origen as Exegete

Early twentieth-century scholars considered Origen the Alexandrian largely as mystic, spiritualist, Platonist, and "true Gnostic".[8] These interpretations, however important, tended to obscure Origen's contribution as exegete, a contribution that has been increasingly recognized in recent scholarship. Focusing on Origen's exegetical works, however, requires a shift in *Sitz im Leben* from Alexandria to Caesarea, where he composed most of his homilies and many of his commentaries on biblical books (Nautin 1977: chp. 10).

Textbook descriptions of Origen's exegetical methods often mislead by assuming that the scheme he outlines in *De principiis* IV reflects his actual practice. In that book, Origen describes a threefold exegesis: of the "flesh", the

4 For the development of interpretation of the Song of Songs in a Christological direction, see Elliott 2000.

5 For explications of the Song of Songs that retain Origen's interest in the reunion of the Jew and Gentile in the Christian Church, those of Apponius, Pseudo-Athanasius, and Gregory the Great are among the most striking. In some of these later commentaries, however, a more strident anti-Judaism emerges. Yet even the sympathetic Apponius, for example, interprets Cant 2:14 ("let me see your face, let me hear your voice") as Christ's call to the Jews that they should be cleansed of the blood they had shed; they should cease crying "Crucify him" and rather sing the praises of the redeemer (*In Canticum Canticorum* [PL Suppl. 1, 873]). And for later commentators such as Gregory of Elvira and Justus Urgellensis, the "sons of the mother who fought against me" (Cant 1:6) are identified as the Jews who persecuted the early Church (Gregory of Elvira, *Comm. in Cant.* II [Heine, pp. 141-42]; Justus Urgellensis (*In Cant. Canticorum* [PL 67, 965]).

6 Gregory of Nyssa, Oratio VIII, *Commentarius in Canticum Canticorum* (GNO 1960: 245-46).

7 Discussion of these uses can be found in my essay, "The Uses of the Song of Songs: Origen and the Later Latin Fathers", in Clark 1986: 386-427.

8 Bigg 1913; Daniélou 1948; Koch 1932; Völker 1931.

"soul", and the "spirit",[9] that is, "literal", "moral", and "spiritual/allegorical" interpretations. Yet even here, Origen notes that some passages of Scripture have no "bodily" sense, but only those pertaining to the "soul" or the "spirit".[10] His qualification more accurately represents his actual mode of exegesis, for many passages in his homilies in particular dwell on only one or two of the alleged three levels of interpretation (Torjesen 1986, 1989). In Origen's homilies, preached to church congregations, the "moral" interpretation of the text often dominates – unsurprisingly, since the purpose of Scriptural preaching is to transform the souls of the hearers. The commentaries, on the other hand, contain longer expositions and engage all three types of interpretation.

First, however, we might reflect on "why is commentary necessary?" Do not texts "speak for themselves" without the assistance of a commentator? Here, Michel Foucault's observations on the paradoxical character of commentary are helpful: although commentary claims merely to repeat the original source – a repetition of "the same" – in effect it operates quite differently. As Foucault puts it:

> By a paradox which it always displaces but never escapes, the commentary must say for the first time what had, nonetheless, already been said, and must tirelessly repeat what had, however, never been said ... it allows us to say something other than the text itself, but on the condition that it is this text itself which is said, and in a sense completed.[11]

In his treatment of the Song of Songs, Origen manifestly "say[s] something other than the text itself, but on the condition that it is this text itself which is said, and in a sense completed". The sexual dimensions of the Song of Songs in particular demanded a "resaying".

Allegorical exegesis, in which Origen's commentaries abound, also is a topic that has recently received reconsideration. D. DAWSON's *Allegorical Readers and Cultural Revision in Ancient Alexandria*, for example, provides new ways of understanding its function.[12] Allegory, Dawson argues, should not be considered an inert, passive method of interpretation in which an "obvious" meaning of a text is replaced by a "higher", usually abstract, one. Allegory, he claims, is not so much a "mental operation" as a social practice linked to power; it is a practice that does "work". Situating themselves and their communities with respect to the larger society via texts, ancient allegorists exercised power through setting "one text over other texts and the worldviews they represent" (Dawson 1992: 236, 5). In late antiquity, Dawson posits, allegory "stemmed from efforts by readers to secure for themselves and their communities social and cultural identity, authority, and power" (Dawson

9 Origen, *De principiis* IV.2.4 (GCS 22, 312-14).
10 Origen, *De principiis* IV.2.5 (GCS 22, 314).
11 Foucault 1981: 58, cf. Clark 1999: 6-9.
12 Dawson 1992; cf. Clark 1999: 73-78.

1992: 2). Allegorical readings can nonetheless function in diverse ways: they can "domesticate" earlier texts now found culturally shocking; or alternatively, they can critique the dominant culture "by giving cultural classics deviant meanings"; or, they can give Scripture a way "to absorb and reinterpret culture", thus bringing culture "into" the Scriptural text (Dawson 1992: 10). Allegory assists Origen's assignment of a "spiritual" message to the Song of Songs as well as his appropriation of it as a Christian book.

Solomon, Allegory, and the Dangers of the Song of Songs

In the case of Origen's reading of the Song of Songs, the "work" allegory must first perform is to "domesticate" the text: patristic interpreters could find no place in sacred Scripture for a poem celebrating sexual love.[13] To be sure, Jewish interpreters had likewise deemed that study of the Song of Songs should be reserved for more advanced, spiritually-oriented readers of a certain age – not for easily-aroused adolescents or vulgarly-minded readers. This caution Origen also knew, and reports in his Prologue to his *Commentary*:

> For they say that with the Hebrews also care is taken to allow no one even to hold the book in his hands, who has not reached a full and ripe age. And there is another practice too that we have received from them – namely, that all Scripture should be delivered to boys by teachers and wise men, while at the same time the four that they call *deuterôsis* – that is to say, the beginning of Genesis, in which the creation of the world is described; the first chapters of Ezekiel, which tell about the cherubim; the end of that same, which contains the building of the temple; and this book of the Song of Songs – should be reserved for study till the last.[14]

Origen supports his spiritualized interpretation of the Song by proposing that Solomon was the (alleged) author of Proverbs and Ecclesiastes, as well as this book. The messages of the three works form a graded course of instruction: Proverbs teaches ethics (providing rules for moral living in "short and pithy maxims"), while Ecclesiastes, a second stage, discusses natural science (counseling readers to "forsake vanity"). Only after these disciplines have been appropriated is the reader/hearer prepared to understand the last of Solomon's trilogy, his "inspective" book, the Song of Songs, which teaches the contemplation of divine and heavenly things.[15] The prestige of Solomon's

13 For an amusingly racy discussion of how "queer" the text looks in the hands of Christian commentators, especially Origen and Bernard of Clairvaux, see Moore 2000: 328-49.

14 Origen, *Commentary on the Song of Songs*, prologue 1, trans. Lawson 1956: 23; Latin text in GCS 33, 62. Section numbers for the Prologue are provided by Lawson and are not contained in the Latin text. For discussion of rabbinic treatments of this theme, see Halperin 1980: 38-39.

15 Origen, *Comm. Cant.*, prologus 3 (GCS 33, 75-76).

alleged authorship – his "author-function"[16] – goes far (as ANDREW JACOBS has put it) to "domesticate that text for fruitful interpretation." Ascribing authorship to Solomon "defines textual boundaries that will exclude not only certain readings, but also the egregious 'others' who attempt those readings (Jews, pagans, or 'unlearned' Christians)" (Jacobs 1998: 3), and curbs disturbing associations that might allow *eros* to spin free. For Origen, the "erotic body" of the text must remain a "spiritual" body.[17]

Origen's Commentary and Homilies on the Song of Songs

PIERRE NAUTIN, chronologist of Origen's writings, dates the *Homilies on the Song of Songs* to C.E. 239-242, years during which Origen was in Caesarea. Nautin posits that Origen composed the first books of the *Commentary* on a journey to Athens in 245 and completed the work upon his return to Caesarea in 246-247.[18] That Origen would write two separate treatments of varying difficulty on the same biblical book accords well with his belief that Christianity should be explicated in ways that meet the needs of both naïve believers and the more advanced. (Völker 1931: chp. 2). Some considered Origen's writings on the Song of Songs his crowning achievement; as Jerome famously commented, "While in his other books, Origen surpassed everyone else, in his Song of Songs he surpassed himself."[19]

Origen, to be sure, was not the first of the Greek-writing Fathers to comment on the Song of Songs. Hippolytus of Rome had preceded him by a few decades. Of Hippolytus' commentary, only fragments remain in Greek (Bonwetsch 1897: 1-2, 7-8, 81-85), although a Georgian version is extant.[20] Hippolytus' employment of the dialogue form,[21] his attention both to "the Synagogue" and the Gentiles as the constituency from which Christianity was drawn,[22] and his explanation of "Solomon's" purposes in his three books,[23] suggest that he established the general pattern that Origen followed in

16 Here, Jacobs borrows from Michel Foucault's famous essay, "What Is an Author?" (Foucault 1984: 101-20).

17 Miller 1986: 241-53; Jacobs 1998: 7.

18 Nautin 1977: 380-81, 403, 411; cf. Rousseau 1954: 8-9. There are also a few fragments of another treatise on the Song that Origen wrote in his youth: see Jerome, *ep.* 33.4 (CSEL 54, 256); Nautin 1977: 238; Baehrens 1916: 233-34; Riedel 1898: 52-53). Bammel 1995: 497 cautions that Nautin's chronology is not based on hard evidence and requires several assumptions.

19 Jerome, *Origenes*, *Hom. in Canticum Canticorum*, prologus (GCS 33, 26).

20 Translated into German in Bonwetsch 1903 (TU 23.2) and into Latin by Garitte 1965 (CSCO 263: 23-70 [Armenian]; CSCO 264: 23-53 [Latin]).

21 Meloni 1977: 98-100; Bonwetsch 1897: 53-56.

22 Hippolytus, *In Canticum Canticorum* 26-27 (CSCO 264, 49-53).

23 Hippolytus, *In Canticum Canticorum* 1.3 (CSCO 264, 23-24).

presenting the Song as a story of the reunion of Jews and Gentiles in the Christian faith.[24]

That Hippolytus and Origen construe the Song of Songs as a drama[25] was probably encouraged by the Septuagint version of the text (at least as preserved in Codex Sinaiticus) and some manuscripts of the Vetus Latina, which had assigned various verses to different characters: a bride, a groom, and choruses of young men and women.[26] Origen appropriates this scheme:[27] the Bride's longing for her absent Groom and their conversations with their companions comprise the narrative for the drama he stages. Although Origen himself admitted that the story itself was not profitable (it did not even offer a continuous narrative), he thought that this very lack, doubtless a defect to some, should prompt a deeper exploration of the story's hidden spiritual truth pertaining to Christ, the Church, and the individual soul.[28]

As with so many of Origen's writings, the Greek texts of his *Commentary* and *Homilies* on the Song of Songs have not survived.[29] Despite this loss, parts of the *Homilies* and *Commentary* are extant in Latin translations by Jerome and Rufinus, respectively. Although the standards by which Jerome and Rufinus translated are not ours (as Jerome was eager to repeat, "not word for word, but sense for sense"[30]), modern commentators,[31] unlike some older ones (deFaye 1923: I, 63), argue that their translations preserve the substance of Origen's exegesis. Jerome's translation of the *Homilies*, done at Rome around C.E. 383, predates Rufinus' translation of the *Commentary* by about twenty-seven years (Lawson 1957: 19, 4, 5). Jerome translated two of the *Homilies* for his patron Pope Damasus as a "sample" of Origen's exegesis, but declined attempting the longer and more complex *Commentary*[32] – perhaps a hint that Damasus' financial support would need to be more generous if he wished for more than a "sample"? Neither translation as we have it covers the entire Song of Songs: the Latin *Homilies* comment only up to 2:14, and the Latin *Commentary* covers a scant verse more, preserving less than half of the ten-book original.[33] Since

---

24 For discussion and some further points that bear similarity to Origen's exegesis, see DeSimone 2000: 30-37; Chappuzeau 1976.

25 Origen, *Comm. Cant.*, prologus 1; *Hom.in Cant.* 1.1 (GCS 33, 61, 29).

26 Ohly 1958: 19; de Bruyne 1926: 120, 122.

27 Origen, *Comm. in Cant.* I.1 (GCS 33, 89-90).

28 Origen, *Comm. in Cant.*, III (IV).15; *Comm. Cant.*, prologus, 1; *Hom. in Cant.* 1.1 (GCS 33, 229, 61, 29).

29 "Of the 574 known homilies only 21 have survived in Greek, and 388 no longer exist even in Latin translation" (Lawson 1957: 16). Of the NT Commentaries, eight books on Matthew remain in Greek, and nine on John.

30 Jerome, *ep.* 57.5 (CSEL 54, 508).

31 Chênevert 1969: 8; Crouzel 1962: 85, 87; Wilkelmann, 1970: II, 532-47.

32 Jerome, *Origenes, Hom. in Canticum Canticorum*, Prologus (GCS 33, 26).

33 Jerome notes that the *Commentary* was a ten-book work (*ep.* 33.4 [CSEL 54, 256]). Perhaps it was death that cut off Rufinus' translation efforts (Elliott 2000: 31).

only fragments remain of earlier Latin commentaries on the Song of Songs,[34] Jerome's translation of Origen's *Homilies* remains the first surviving Latin work on the Song – although Gregory of Elvira's *Commentary* may date to the same decade (Ohly 1958: 28-30).

Typical Origenist Themes

Themes familiar from other of Origen's writings, including his earlier Alexandrian works, appear in the *Commentary* and *Homelies on the Song of Songs* as well. Origen claims that just as pagan authors borrowed Hebrew wisdom, so Christians utilize, but surpass, the precepts of pagan natural and moral philosophy.[35] He strongly champions personal responsibility for sinful behavior: we, like Pharaoh, are to blame for our own "hardening."[36] Omnipresent is the theme of progress in the spiritual life: although the Church welcomes "simple believers," she encourages their advancement to a more "perfect" state. Thus in the *Homilies*, Origen asserts that although the maidens of the chorus (here, representing the "simple believers") do not yet enjoy the "breasts" of the Groom that contain treasures of wisdom and knowledge, he trusts that they will progress from their childish understanding.[37] Such is Origen's confidence in Christianity as *paideia*.[38]

Platonic themes, typical of Origen's writings, likewise abound in his *Commentary* and *Homilies* on the Song of Songs. The "likenesses of gold" (Cant 1:11), made by the Bridegroom's friends for the Bride, signify that the Law and the ritual of the Old Testament were mere shadows of truth, the genuine "gold" existing incorporeally in heaven.[39] Similarly, Genesis 1:26's claim that humans are created in "the image and likeness of God" implies (with Plato) that earthly things are copies of heavenly realities.[40] And Origen notes, alluding to Plato's *Symposium*, the Christian belief in the soul's yearning for the intelligible world above was prefigured by Greek sages who composed dialogues on the ascent of the soul through love.[41]

These points, however, are secondary to the distinguishing and particularizing motif of Origen's exegesis: the union of Jew and Gentile in the

34 Jerome notes a commentary by Reticius of Autun (*ep.* 37.1 [CSEL 54, 286-87]); in *De viris illustribus*, he mentions Latin commentaries on the work by Hilary of Poitiers (100; PL 23, 739), Reticius (82; PL 23, 727), and Victorinus of Pettau (74; PL 23, 722); also see Ohly 1958: 27.

35 Origen, *Comm. in Cant.*, prologus, 3; I.3; *Hom. in Cant. Cant.* 1.1 (GCS 33, 75, 100, 29).

36 Origen, *Comm. in Cant.* II.2 (GCS 33, 128-29); cf. *Hom. in Cant.* 1.6 (GCS 33, 36).

37 Origen, *Comm. in Cant.* I.1, 5; I.2 (GCS 33, 29, 34, 110-11, 94).

38 Koch 1932: 32-36; Pt. I, chp. 5; Chadwick 1966: chp. 3.

39 Origen, *Comm. in Cant.* II.8 (GCS 33, 160-61).

40 Origen, *Comm. in Cant.* III.12 (GCS 33, 208).

41 Origen, *Comm. in Cant.*, prologus, 2 (GCS 33, 63).

Christian Church. This does not, to be sure, mean that Origen believed that Judaism was on a par with Christianity. Yet when read with an historian's eye, Origen's *Commentary on the Song of Songs* resembles nothing so much as Romans 9-11, in which Paul's argument for the union of Jew and Gentile in Christianity reaches its climax.[42] Later generations, eager to press the "mystical" aspects of Origen's exegesis that would offer spiritual edification for audiences of their own time and place, downplayed or ignored the historical significance of this point.

Jews and Gentiles in the Song of Songs

Throughout his exposition of the Song of Songs, Origen argues for the superiority of the Gospel to the Law, yet strongly underscores the worth of the Hebrew tradition.[43] When heretics proclaim the Old Testament deity to be inferior to that of the New, Origen charges, they only manifest their own blindness, their inability to see the Trinity therein.[44] His interpretation of Cant 1:2 LXX ("Your breasts are better than wine") illustrates his view: the Groom's "breasts" (i.e., Christ's wisdom and knowledge) are indeed better than the "wine" of the Law and the Prophets, but the latter are nonetheless *good.* By drinking the "wine" of the Old Testament, the Bride readied herself to receive the even better drink offered by Christ.[45] That she is told to "keep the vineyard" (Cant 1:6b) signals to Origen that she was to keep the books of the Law and the Prophets – although, to be sure, she should abandon Jewish traditions after she receives the faith of Christ.[46]

The Bride's first request of God (the Bridegroom's Father) is that her Groom may "kiss me with the kisses of His mouth" (Cant 1:2a). The Prophets had showed her the Groom (the Son of God) to whom they wished to betroth her but he is "delayed."[47] (Here, Origen appeals to the intertext of Matt 25:5 [the "delay" of the bridegroom in the parable of the Wise and Foolish Virgins] to heighten the sense of anticipation he assigns to the drama.) Yet the Bridegroom remains "hidden like a treasure in the Law and the Prophets";[48] the Bride must patiently await her Spouse's coming. But he will come "leaping upon the mountains" (that is, upon the books of the Law) and "skipping over the hills" (that is, over the books of the Prophets) (Cant 2:8) to greet her.[49] He "stands behind the wall" (Cant 2:9b) of the Old Testament, not yet showing

---

42 Gorday 1983: chp. 3; Bietenhard 1974: chp. 8.
43 E.g., Origen, *Comm. in Cant.* III.1, III.13 (GCS 33, 205, 220).
44 Origen, *Comm. in Cant.* II.8 (GCS 33, 158).
45 Origen, *Comm. in Cant.* I.2 (GCS 33, 94, 96-97).
46 Origen, *Comm. in Cant.* II.3 (GCS 33, 132).
47 Origen, *Comm. in Cant.* I.2a (GCS 33, 89).
48 Origen, *Comm. in Cant.* I.2b (GCS 33, 97).
49 Origen, *Comm. in Cant.* III.11 (GCS 33, 204-05).

himself – although the Bride begins to glimpse him through the "windows" of the Law and the Prophets.[50]

Similar is Origen's treatment of Cant 1:3a, "The fragrance of thine ointments is above all spices." The Bride (representing the ancient Israelites) enjoys the use and knowledge of spices, that is, "the words of the Law and the Prophets", which served as her *paidagogus* (Gal 4:24) until the coming of the Bridegroom. While the "ointments of Aaron" (Ex 30:22ff.) were earthly and material, the ointment of her Spouse is spiritual and heavenly. Only at the Bridegroom's coming does she realize how "vastly inferior" were the spices she had previously enjoyed.[51]

Origen also affirms that the Law and the Prophets were "most fitting" betrothal gifts for the Bride, but claims that the veil that covers them must be removed if they are to be understood correctly (i.e., Christianly).[52] Christians should always remember that the "lily" (Cant 2:1) of the Church sprang up in a field that had been well-cultivated by the Law and the Prophets.[53] Origen even styles the Synagogue the "brother" or "sister" of the Church: since Christ in his human aspect was a son of the Synagogue, Cant 1:13 rightly calls him the "nephew" of the Bride.[54] To reach the mystic perfection of the Song of Songs, Christians must rehearse the experience of the ancient Israelites by marching through the Sea upon the dry land, escaping from the hands of the Egyptians, and so forth.[55] Such themes accord well with Origen's view that the "heretics" unjustly deprecate the Old Testament – and that contemporary Jews deserve censure for their failure to appreciate the New.

If we plot closely Origen's path through the Song of Songs, we see that it parallels Paul's movement in the Epistle to the Romans. The key lies in Origen's identification of the Bride: sometimes she represents Judaism, but elsewhere she symbolizes the Gentiles. The Bridegroom's wooing of her signifies Christ's desire to bring both Jews and Gentiles into his household. Throughout Book I of the *Commentary*, the Bride often signifies ancient Israel. Here, Origen claims that the angels gave her the Law as a betrothal gift and that she prepared herself for the "breasts" of Christ through imbibing the Law and the Prophets.[56] Near the end of Book II, the Bride is again identified with the Jews: she is the child who had the Law as her pedagogue before the coming of Christ her Groom.[57] Yet most of Book II depicts the Bride as the

50 Origen, *Comm. in Cant.* III.13 (GCS 33, 220).
51 Origen, *Comm. in Cant.* I.3 (GCS 33, 97-98).
52 Origen, *Comm. in Cant.* I.1; III.11 (GCS 33, 89, 91, 204-05).
53 Origen, *Comm. in Cant.* III.4 (GCS 33, 177-78).
54 Origen, *Comm. in Cant.* II.10 (GCS 33, 168-69); *Hom. in Cant.* 2.3 (GCS 33, 45). In the *Homelies*, *fratuelis* is the translation for the LXX's ἀδέλφιδος.
55 Origen, *Comm. in Cant.*, prologus 4 (GCS 33, 80-81).
56 Origen, *Comm. in Cant.* I.1 (GCS 33, 91, 96).
57 Origen, *Comm. in Cant.* II.8 (GCS 33, 157).

Gentiles now being drawn to Christianity.[58] Appropriating and adapting Paul's image in Galatians 4, Origen contrasts the Bride as the (Gentile) daughter of the "heavenly Jerusalem" with the Daughters of Jerusalem, the female chorus in the Song of Songs, that is, the "earthly Jerusalem" of the Jews.[59]

Most instructive is Origen's discussion of Cant 1:5: "I am dark but beautiful, O Daughters of Jerusalem." The Daughters of Jerusalem (the Jews) have called the Bride "dark" because she as a Gentile was not enlightened by the Patriarchs' teachings. Acknowledging their charge, the Bride pleads that she nonetheless was beautified by the Image of God at creation (Gen 1:26). Now she draws further adornment from the Logos, who chants to her Cant 2:11, "Lo, the winter is past" – the "winter" of her Gentile unbelief.[60] Furthermore, the Daughters of Jerusalem who mocked the Gentile Bride as "dark" are reminded that when Miriam (a type of the Synagogue) criticized the marriage of Moses (a type of Christ) to a black Ethiopian woman, she was struck with leprosy.[61] The story stands as a warning to the Daughters of Jerusalem (the Jews).[62]

The former "darkness" of the Gentiles and the Jews' present unbelief are understood by Origen to mean that Jew and Gentile share a heritage of disobedience, as Paul explicates in Romans. Nonetheless, the Bride testifies that Christ her Groom shall return her light to her and she shall be judged worthy to be called "the light of the world."[63] Not only the Gentiles shall be granted God's favor through Christ; Origen, following Paul, asserts that when the fullness of the Gentiles has come in, Israel shall receive a second call.[64]

To be sure, Origen's emphasis on the reconciliation of Jew and Gentile in Christianity does not obscure prominent themes such as Christ's relation to the soul or the Church (Dassmann 1966). In the *Commentary on the Song of Songs*, as other scholars have noted, it becomes an increasingly dominant theme as Origen proceeds through the text (Riedel 1898: 60). For example, Origen complements his description of the betrothal gifts the Bride as Church receives with a corresponding description of the gifts received by the individual soul, namely, natural law and reason.[65] When the Groom in Cant 1:8 warns the Bride, "Unless you know yourself, o fair one among women, go forth," Origen imagines that Christ here encourages the soul to self-knowledge, as Greek and Hebrew sages had earlier counseled.[66] Parallel to the progress of salvation history that he believed would culminate in the churchly union of Jew and

58 Origen, *Comm. in Cant.* II.1 (GCS 33, 113).
59 Origen, *Comm. in Cant.* II.3; II.1 (GCS 33, 131, 114).
60 Origen, *Comm. in Cant.* II.1; III(IV).14 (GCS 33, 114, 226).
61 Origen, *Comm. in Cant.* II.1 (GCS 33, 114).
62 Origen, *Comm. in Cant.* II.1 (GCS 33, 118); cf. *Hom. in Cant.* 1.6 (GCS 33, 36-37).
63 Origen, *Comm. in Cant.* II.2 (GCS 33, 127).
64 Origen, *Comm. in Cant.* III (IV).15 (GCS 33, 233-34).
65 Origen, *Comm. in Cant.* I.1 (GCS 33, 91).
66 Origen, *Comm. in Cant.* II.5 (GCS 33, 141, 143).

Gentile is the soul's progress: although she is a small child needing tutelage, not fed on the strong meat of the Word but instructed only through "likenesses and patterns," she will grow sufficiently to receive "the King reclining at his table" (Cant 1:12).[67] Later Christian commentators preferred Origen's exposition of the individual soul in relation to Christ: this was a "transportable" theme, suited to times when competition with Jewish and Gnostic beliefs and practices no longer occupied a central role in Christian debate.

Origen, Jews, and the Commentary on Romans

The movement between God's appeal to the Jews and that to the Gentiles also provides the structure for Origen's *Commentary on Romans*, preserved in the Latin translation of Rufinus.[68] P. GORDAY claims that Origen sees in Romans "an argument that is always in motion, now addressing one group or the other, now picking up on the objections or perspectives of one interlocutor or another," a style that lends a "dramatic quality" to his reading of Romans.[69] Since Origen wrote the *Homilies on the Song of Songs* either a few years before or simultaneously with the *Romans Commentary*, and his *Commentary on the Song of Songs* a few years later, it is less surprising that in all three works he testifies to a "drama" in which Jew and Gentile would be reconciled in Christianity.

In his *Commentary on Romans*, Origen replicates Paul's message that God came first to the Jew and then to the Gentile, a theme that culminates in Rom 9-11.[70] Discussing Rom 3:1-8, Origen comments that Paul presents himself as an *arbiter* who affirms both Jews and Gentiles: some pagans will come to salvation, and not all Israel will be cast out.[71] Commenting on Rom 11, Origen argues that although God is angry at the Jews' unbelief, he has not rejected them. Origen follows Paul in the hope that the Jews will be converted; like the woman of Hosea 2, the Jews will say, "it is better for me to return to my first husband."[72] God wishes for the salvation of all, eventually including that of the Jews.[73] Origen notes that Paul then moves back to the Gentiles in Rom 11:13ff. God's providence, his hope for universal salvation of all creatures at the time when he shall be "all in all" (I Cor 15:28), are sounded in

67 Origen, *Comm. in Cant.* II.8 (GCS 33, 164-65).
68 Gorday 1983: 45 dates the *Commentary on Romans* to 243, thus putting this work also in the Caesarean context.
69 Gorday 1983: 84.
70 Origen, *Comm. in Rom.* VII.11-VIII.12, on Rom 9-11 (Bammel 1998: 609-710).
71 Origen, *Comm. in Rom.* II.10-III.1, on Rom 3:1-8 (Bammel 1990: 177-203).
72 Origen, *Comm. in Rom.* VIII.6-12, on Rom 11 (Bammel 1998: 667-710, citation at VIII.11 [700]).
73 Origen, *Comm. in Rom.* VIII.8, on Rom 11:11-12 (Bammel 1998: 681-86)

Origen's comments on the final verses of Rom 11.[74] Because free will always remains as a human endowment despite sin and because God always acts for the good – two distinctive themes of Origenist theology – Origen holds out the hope that even the presently recalcitrant will find salvation.[75]

Origen's treatment of the Pauline theme of union of Jew and Gentle nonetheless raises questions for the modern interpreter.[76] Whereas Rom 9-11 presupposes an identifiable historical moment in the first decades of Christianity (the difficulties occasioned by Gentile recruitment into an initially Jewish sect), the situation confronting Origen is more difficult to assess: does he still believe that more Jews will convert to Christianity?

Rufinus' highly truncated translation of Origen's *Commentary on Romans* hinders an easy grasp of Origen's views on this point. C.H. BAMMEL proposes that Rufinus' abbreviated translation obscures the primarily Jewish-Christian audience to whom Paul wrote: dwelling on the Jewish character of the early Roman church, she posits, was "scarcely the sort of picture that would have appealed to early fifth-century Roman readers" (Bammel 1995: 508-09). Moreover, she here observes, it is not until Rufinus arrives at Book 3.2 that he highlights the Jewish-Christian character of Paul's audience with the observation that "we have already stated that in this epistle Paul regulates and weighs up his words like a mediator between those who have come to the faith from the circumcision and those from the Gentiles, rebuking and encouraging them in turn."[77] Bammel also proposes that Rufinus may have abbreviated Origen's Preface to his *Commentary*, thus eliminating the author's probable discussion of Paul's addressees who were converts from Judaism (Bammel 1995: 510). Yet elsewhere, Bammel notes that although Rufinus in the heat of polemic was not above casting anti-Jewish slurs, he does not use his translation of Origen's *Romans Commentary* to advance an anti-Jewish cause; rather, he appears (as far as we can tell) faithful to Origen's rendition of Paul's hope for the salvation of the Jews as well as the Gentiles (Bammel 1990: 145-56).[78] The theme emerges clearly in Origen's *Commentary on the Song of Songs* as well as that on Romans.

Bammel's claim that it was Rufinus who toned down Origen's acceptance of the Jewish-Christian audience of Paul's Letter to the Romans raises questions about an argument advanced by J. MCGUCKIN. McGuckin argues that the centrality of passages in Romans and other Pauline texts in which Paul

---

74 Origen, *Comm. in Rom.* VIII.12, on Rom 11:33-36 (Bammel 1998: 707-10).

75 Origen, *Comm. in Rom.* VIII.10, on Rom 11:16-24 (Bammel 1998: 692-98).

76 For a discussion of some of the differences between Paul's and Origen's situation, see Heither 1990: 279-82.

77 Origen, *Comm. in Rom.* III.2 on Rom 3:9 (Bammel 1998: 204).

78 Bammel mentions Rufinus' *Apology against Jerome* II.41, in which Rufinus accuses Jerome of having been "taken captive by the Jews" in his Biblical translations.

shows some "personal feeling" for Judaism,[79] have been "censored" by Origen, who rather emphasizes such passages as Rom 2:5 (the refusal of Jews to repent) and II Cor 3:13-15 (the veil covering the Jews' minds) (McGuckin 1992: 12). The question remains, however, whether the "censoring" was done by Origen or by Rufinus. In light of Bammel's construal, as noted above, it may be the case that it was later translators, not Origen himself, who downplayed the more positive role that Paul attributes to the Jews.

Two questions pertaining to Origen exegetical treatment of the Jews prompt further exploration: to what extent, if any, were Origen's assessment of Judaism and his exegesis of the Old Testament prompted by discussion and/or controversy with actual Jews of his day? And, second, was Origen's stress on the goodness of the Old Testament and its God at least in part motivated by his wish to counter a Gnostic or Marcionite threat?

Origen and Contemporary Jews

Scholars differ in their views of the extent to which debate with Jews stimulated Origen's work on the various points of Hebrew Scripture.[80] First, of course, we must register that Origen's work as a commentator was based on the Septuagint, not directly on the Hebrew text (Ulrich 1988: 3-33). Beyond that, we can note with P. NAUTIN that although Origen was indebted to Jews for points of Scriptural interpretation, we should not overemphasize the polemical nature of their relations: Origen's task at Caesarea was to instruct Christians, not convert Jews, and in any case, his relations with rabbis was "sporadic" (Nautin 1977: 346-47). John McGuckin concludes that Origen's dependence on Jewish traditions of third-century Caesarea them was slight, and that his dialogue with Jews there was "neither successful nor particularly happy" (McGuckin 1992: 2, 13). And J.S. O'LEARY argues that we should not ascribe to Origen an "ecumenical attitude" toward Jews that we *wish* he had endorsed; what might have been a "fraternal dialogue" between Jew and Gentile in Paul's day had by Origen's time hardened[81] (O'Leary 1995: 378).

---

79 McGuckin 1992: 12 lists as "laudatory texts" Rom 1:7; 3:2; 9:3; 10:1; 12:15; 12:28; of these, McGuckin argues, only 3:2 survives as a laudatory text in Origen's *Commentary on Romans*.

80 Roger Brooks, for example, thinks that Origen knew only a "few scraps of Jewish exegesis", that the "Jewish background and culture" available to Origen was "remarkably superficial" (Brooks 1988: 94), while Paul Blowers, writing in the same volume, presumes that Origen knew a great deal more about Jewish exegesis (Blowers 1988: 113). For Origen's *Homilies on Leviticus* in relation to the rabbinic *Vayikra Rabbah*, see Wilken 1995: 81-91. For J.S. O'Leary, arguing against Theresia Heither, "Anti-Judaism is a structural necessity of [Origen's] thought" (O'Leary 1995: 378).

81 O'Leary's critique is directed at what he considers Theresia Heither's overly-positive assessment (1990) of Origen's views on Jews.

Other scholars, however, emphasize the positive significance of Origen's contact with Jews – whether or not a "fraternal dialogue" – for the development of his exegesis. Building on ancient testimony (some from Origen himself) that at Alexandria a converted Jew served as his Hebrew teacher, that he held discussions with Jews, and that he cites the opinion of a contemporary Jewish teacher named "Hiullus",[82] modern commentators have taken considerable interest in Origen's involvement with Jews and Jewish literature. In part the debate centers on the depth of Origen's knowledge of Hebrew: those who think his Hebrew was weak posit that he must have employed either Jews or Jewish Christians to copy the columns of the Hexapla, for he would not have been able to judge correctly appropriate divisions in the Hebrew text or to match it with the parallel columns of Greek (de Lange 1976: 58, 22-23).

In addition, N.R.M. DE LANGE emphasizes the challenge that the Jewish presence in Caesarea posed to its Christian community. De Lange shows how Origen fought to counter the Jewish syncretism to which his congregation was prone: some members attended synagogue on Saturday as well as church on Sunday, and showed more than an antiquarian interest in Jewish holidays, fasts, and circumcision.[83] Origen himself rebuked Christians who observed Yom Kippur, celebrated Passover with unleavened bread, and adorned themselves for the Jewish Sabbath.[84] Evidence of these Judaizing tendencies among Origen's congregation supports Lee Levine's conviction that Judaism was an active force at Caesarea at this time.[85] And we know that the development of Caesarea as a center of rabbinic studies coincided closely with Origen's Caesarean sojourn: Rabbi Hoshaya's activities in Caesarea date to the 230's and beyond.[86]

Moreover, Reuven Kimelman and David Halperin strongly argue for the interplay between Origen's exegesis and Jewish commentary. Halperin claims that Origen used homilies employed at Pentecost in third-century Caesarean synagogues (Halperin 1981: 261-75), while Kimelman explores Origen's probable knowledge of at least some rabbinic interpretations of the Song of Songs (Kimelman 1980: 567-95). In Kimelman's view, there was a "cross-fertilization" between Jewish exegesis of the Song and Origen's interpretation that led to contested interpretations; Rabbi Yohanan, he argues, "led the exegetical battle against Origen's Christologization of the Song's allegory" (Kimelman 1980: 573, 569, 595).

Did the Jewish presence in Caesarea influence Origen's writings on the Song of Songs? Quite possibly. Scholars of ancient Judaism agree with

---

82 Origen, *De Principiis* I.3.4; IV.3.14 (GCS 22, 53, 346); *Sel. in Ezech.* 9.2 (PG 13, 800); *Ep. ad Africanum* 6 (PG 11, 61); *Contra Celsum* I.45; I.55; II.31 (GCS 2, 95, 106, 159); Jerome, *Apologia contra Rufinum* I.13 (PL 23, 408); and see deLange 1976: 23-28; Nautin 1977: 27-78.

83 de Lange 1976: 86-87; cf. Krauss 1893: 146-47; Bietenhard 1974: 50-51.

84 Origen, *Hom. in Lev.* 10.2 (GCS 29, 442-45); *Hom. in Jerem.* 12.13 (GCS 6, 99-100).

85 Levine 1975: chp. 5; cf. Bietenhard 1974: 8-11.

86 Levine 1975: 88; cf. Kimelman 1980: 572.

Kimelman that Jews before Origen's time had interpreted the Song of Songs as an allegory of God's love for Israel, and that points of Origen's exegesis may reflect his response to Jewish interpretations of the book.[87] An obvious parallel lies in the opening lines of Origen's first *Homily* that paraphrase Rabbi Akiba's maxim, "All the Writings are holy, but the Song of Songs is the Holy of Holies."[88] If Origen's discussion of the Song of Songs was part of a contemporary interpretive debate, his *Commentary* and *Homilies on the Song of Songs* may not stand as mere antiquarian excurses on mid-first century Christianity. In this regard, my assessment revives the insights, sometimes bypassed by later interpreters.[89]

The Old Testament in Origen's Anti-Gnostic Polemic

Another question: does Origen's stress on the unity of Jew and Gentile in the Church and God's "call" to each group stand as an attempt to counter a Gnostic or Marcionite threat? Was his exegesis a rebuke to those who severed the Old Testament from the New, degraded the Creator God, and mocked the history and customs of the ancient Israelites? If so, was this threat a contemporary problem, or merely of "historical" interest? Although Origen's contact with and dependence on actual Jewish teachers of his day can be variously assessed, his high estimation of the "Old Testament" as a bulwark against "heresy" is not in doubt.

Although Origen's earlier treatise, *On First Principles* (especially Books III and IV) surely has an anti-Gnostic thrust,[90] the question remains whether Origen there addressed a *contemporary* Gnostic challenge. His traditional arguments, amalgamation of Gnostic opinions, and imprecise allusions to his opponents' views have been cited as evidence that he there combated only an "attenuated image" of Gnosticism, not a present danger.[91] Yet Eusebius reports that Origen knew Gnostics, and Jerome, that he debated with the Gnostic Candidus.[92] Moreover, the evidence from Caesarea and from Origen's exegetical works written there suggests that Marcionites were active in the vicinity. Eusebius records that a Marcionite woman was martyred in Caesarea around 257, and that a Marcionite bishop, probably from Caesarea,

87 Baer 1961: 100-5; Loewe 1966: 161-62; Urbach 1971: 247-52, 255, 263-65.

88 Akiba, *m.Yadaim* 3,5; cited and discussed in de Lange 1976: 60.

89 See Harnack 1918: 22-30, 47-52 and 1919: 81-87, Bardy 1925: 217-252; Krauss 1893: 139-57; and Marmorstein 1920: 190-99 and 1935: 223-61.

90 Le Boulluec 1975: 47-61; Ruis-Camps 1975: 297-312.

91 Le Boulluec 1975: 55, 58-61; Harl 1981: 203

92 Eusebius, *Historia ecclesiastica* VI.18.1-2 (GCS 9.2, 556); Jerome, *Apologia contra Rufinum* II.19 (PL 23, 462-63).

was burned at the stake during Diocletian's persecution, more than a half-century after Origen's time.[93]

When the historical notices are supplemented by the exegetical, a reasonable case can be made that one feature of Origen's Scriptural interpretation was prompted not just by antiquarian interests, but also by a present concern, namely, to distinguish Catholic teaching from that of the "heretics." To be sure, in his various commentaries and homilies, Origen often lumps together Marcion, Basilides, and Valentinus and decries their theology and view of Scripture.[94] Yet numerous points in his exegesis suggest that he did not simply appropriate a general critique of Gnosticism from his Catholic predecessors, but knew details of Gnostic or Marcionite interpretation. Whether Origen himself countered actual Gnostics or Marcionites in Caesarea, the questions they posed were still commanding attention. Their objections to the Old Testament and their refusal to accept one God as the source of both Testaments still troubled Caesarean Christians.[95] Just as Origen hoped to forestall his community's adoption of Jewish practices, so he tried to expunge Marcionite interpretation as an option for his flock and provide alternative readings of Scriptural passages.[96] Such evidence suggests that Marcionite and Gnostic interpretation still confounded Caesareans in Origen's time, whatever assessment commentators may make of their "real" presence in Origen's time.

Origen attempts to refute these Marcionite and Gnostic criticisms by providing alternative explanations for the alleged (and even admitted) absurdities of Scripture,[97] the shocking behavior of Old Testament heroes,[98] and the unworthy depiction of God that his opponents alleged was everywhere present in the Hebrew books.[99] He warns Catholic Christians against the heretical penchant to divide the two Testaments and give deviant

93 Eusebius, *Historia ecclesiastica* VII.12 (GCS 9.2, 666); *De Martyribus Palaestinae* X.3 (GCS 9.2, 931); the bishop dies in the company of someone explicitly named as coming from Caesarea (X.2); see Levine 1975: 131.

94 For example, Origen, *Hom. in Ex.* 3.2 (GCS 29, 164); *Hom. in Num.* 9.1; 12.2 (GCS 30, 54-55, 98); *Hom. in Lev.* 8.9 (GCS 29, 407); *Hom. in Jesu Nave* 7.7; 12.3 (GCS 30, 335, 370); *Hom. in Matt.* 12.23 (GCS 40, 122).

95 Harnack 1918: 38; Harl 1981: 216.

96 I have detailed these in Clark 1986: 394. For passages, see Origen, *Hom. in Gen.* 2.2 (GCS 29, 27-30), cf. *Contra Celsum* V.54 (GCS 3, 58); *Hom. in Num.* 7.1, 27.2 (GCS 30, 38, 258), cf. *Contra Celsum* III.12 (GCS 2, 212); *Hom. in Jesu Nave* 10.2; 11.6 (GCS 30, 359, 366); *Hom. in Jerem.* 12.5 (GCS 6, 91); *Hom. in Luc.* 17 (4); 25 (5) (GCS 35, 115, 162); *Hom. in Matt.* 14.13 (GCS 40, 313-14).

97 E.g., Origen, *Comm. in Joan.* 10.26-27 (17-18); 40-41 (24-25) (GCS 10, 198-201, 217-19); *Hom. in Gen.* 2.2-5 (GCS 29, 27-36).

98 E.g., Origen, *Hom. in Num.* 7.1 (GCS 30, 38); *Hom. in Jesu Nave* 10.2; 11.6 (GCS 30, 359, 366).

99 E.g., Origen, *Hom. in Gen.* 4.6 (GCS 29, 56-57); *Hom. in Num.* 9.4; 19.2 (GCS 30, 58-59, 181); *Hom. in Lev.* 5.1; 11.2 (GCS 29, 333-34, 451); *Hom. in Jesu Nave* 12.3 (GCS 30, 370); *Hom. in Ezech.* 1.1 (PG 13, 667).

interpretations of their contents.[100] The frequency with which Origen addresses these issues in his exegetical writings suggests that something more was at stake than an antiquarian interest in past errors.[101]

Despite their evident differences, one point links Origen's criticisms of Jews and of Gnostics (as well as of "simple Christians"): to his mind, many of these read Hebrew Scripture too literally, albeit to very different ends. Origen's rebuttal rests on the acceptance of a spiritual meaning not only for the Bible as a whole, but also for every verse. As he puts it, it is an "old" Testament only for those who take it in the fleshly sense; for those of us (i.e., Christians) who read it spiritually, it is always "new" – and thus *both* Testaments are "New Testaments."[102] Without allegorical/spiritual interpretation of Scripture, Christians are left with a book that, on Origen's own admission, abounds in absurdities, contradictions, and matters too lowly for religious concern.[103] Origen's allegorical reading of the text thus appears directed against threats from several quarters.

However we weigh the relative degree to which Origen's exegesis reflects his own polemic against Jews (or Judaizers) and Marcionites, J. GRIBOMONT'S claim that the exegesis of the first three centuries was carried out between the poles of Judaism and Gnosticism is apt for Origen.[104] By the end of the fourth century, with the progressive Christianization of the Roman Empire, Gnosticism and Judaism posed fewer exegetical problems for Christians in many (if not all) areas of the Empire; by then, the debate had come to center largely on *inner*-Christian issues of theology, ethics, ecclesiology, and asceticism (Gribomont 1982: 359, noting some exceptions).

That Origen's interpretation of the Song of Songs (as well as his reading of Romans) emphasizes the Jewish-Gentile union in Christianity and the value of the Old Testament reveals both his faithfulness to Paul's vision as exemplified in Romans and his eagerness to claim the Jews' sacred books as a bulwark against Gnosticizing heresy. For readers of our own time, it also reveals how sharply early Christian biblical interpretation differed from that of modern historical biblical criticism.

---

100 Origen, *Hom. in Num.* 9.1; 9.4; 12.2 (GCS 30, 55-56, 59, 98); *Hom. in Lev.* 13.4 (GCS 29, 473-74); *Hom. in Jerem.* 10.5; 17.2 (GCS 6, 75-76, 144-45), and many other references. Origen's *Commentary on John* was written at least in part to refute the interpretations of the Gnostic Heracleon's commentary on that book: see Pagels 1973; Poffet 1985.

101 Harnack 1918: 38; Harl 1981: 216.

102 Origen, *Hom. in Num.* 9.4 (GCS30, 59); Harl 1981: 216-27; LeBoulluec 1975: 49; for critique, de Lange 1976: 82, 83, 105-06.

103 For a small sampling, see Origen, *Hom. in Gen.* 2.2-5; 3.5; 6.1-3; 11.1; 11.2 (GCS 29, 27-36, 44-46, 65-70, 100-4); *Hom. in Ex.* 22.1-4; 10.2-4; 11.2 (GCS 29, 154-61, 246-52, 253-54); *Hom. in Num.*7.1-2; 12.1-2; 26.3 (GCS 30, 37-41, 93-101, 246-49); *Hom. in Lev.* 4.7; 10.1; 16.2 (GCS 29, 326-27, 440-42, 246-49).

104 Gribomont 1982: 358; cf. Vogt 1974: 193.

Bibliography

BAEHRENS, W.A. (1916): Überlieferung und Textgeschichte der Lateinisch erhaltenen Origeneshomilien zum Alten Testament, Leipzig.

BAER, Y.F. (1961): Israel, the Christian Church, and the Roman Empire from the Time of Septimius Severus to the Edict of Toleration of A.D. 313, ScrHier 7, 79-149.

BAMMEL, C.P.H. (1990): Die Juden im Römerbriefkommentar des Origenes, in: H. Frohnhofen (ed.), Christlicher Antijudaismus und jüdischer Anti-paganismus: Ihre Motive und Hintergründe in den ersten drei Jahrhunderten, Hamburg, 145-151.

– (1995): Origen's Pauline Prefaces and the Chronology of his Pauline Commentaries, in: G. Dorival/A. Le Boulluec, (eds.), Origeniana Sexta, Origènee et la Bible/Origen and the Bible, Leuven, 495-514.

– (1990-98): Der Römerbriefkommentar des Origenes. Kritische Ausgabe der Übersetzung Rufins I–III, Freiburg.

BARDY, G. (1925): Les traditions juives dans l'oeuvre d'Origène, RB 34, 215-52.

BIETENHARD, H. (1974): Caesarea, Origenes und die Juden, Stuttgart/Berlin/Cologne/Mainz.

BIGG, C. (1913): The Christian Platonists of Alexandria, 2nd. ed, Oxford.

BLOWERS, P.M. (1988): Origen, the Rabbis, and the Bible: Toward a Picture of Judaism and Christianity in Third-Century Caesarea, in: C. Kannengiesser/ W.L. Petersen (eds.), Origen of Alexandria: His World and His Legacy, Notre Dame, 96-116.

BONWETSCH, G.N. (1897): Studien zu den Kommentaren Hippolyts zum Buche Daniel und Hohen Liede, Leipzig.

BRÉSARD, L. (1983): Bernard et Origène commentent le Cantique, Beernem.

BROOKS, R. (1988): Straw Dogs and Scholarly Ecumenism: The Appropriate Jewish Background for the Study of Origen, in: C. Kannengiesser/W.L. Petersen (eds.), Origen of Alexandria: His World and His Legacy, Notre Dame, 63-95.

CHADWICK, H. (1966): Early Christian Thought and the Classical Tradition: Studies in Justin, Clement, and Origen, New York.

CHAPPUZEAU, G. (1976): Die Auslegung des Hohenliedes durch Hippolyt von Rom, JAC 19, 45-81.

CHÍNEVERT, J. (1969): L'Eglise dans le Commentaire d'Origène sur les Cantique des Cantiques, Bruxelles/Paris.

CLARK, E.A. (1986): The Uses of the Song of Songs: Origen and the Later Latin Fathers, in: ead., Ascetic Piety and Women's Faith: Essays on Late Ancient Christianity, Lewiston/Queenston, 386-427.

– (1992): The Origenist Controversy: The Cultural Construction of an Early Christian Debate, Princeton.

– (1999): Reading Renunciation: Asceticism and Scripture in Early Christianity, Princeton.

CROUZEL, H. (1962): Origène. Homélies sur S. Luc, Paris.

CROUZEL, H. et al. eds (1975): Origeniana. Premier colloque internationale des Études origéniennes, Bari.

DANIÉLOU, J. (1948): Origéne, Paris.

DASSMANN, E. (1966): Ecclesia vel Anima. Die Kirche und ihre Glieder in der Hohenliederklärung bei Hippolyt, Origenes und Ambrosius von Mailand, RQ 61, 121-144.

DAWSON, D. (1991): Allegorical Readers and Cultural Revision in Ancient Alexandria, New Haven/London.

DE BRUNYE, D. (1926): Les Anciennes Versions latines du Cantique des Cantiques, RBen 38, 97-122.

DE FAYE, E. (1923): Origène: sa vie, son oeuvre, sa pensée, I-II, Paris.

DE LANGE, N.R.M. (1976): Origen and the Jews: Studies in Jewish-Christian Relations in Third-Century Palestine, Cambridge.

DE LUBAC, H. (1959): Exégèse médievale: Les quatres sens de l'écriture, I.1, Paris.
DE SIMONE, R.J. (2000): The Bride and the Bridegroom of the Fathers: An Anthology of Patristic Interpretations of the Song of Songs, Rome.
DORIVAL, G./LE BOULLUEC, A. eds. (1995): Origeniana Sexta. Origène et la Bible/Origen and the Bible, Leuven.
ELLIOTT, M.W. (2000): The Song of Songs and Christology in the Early Church, Studien und Texte zu Antike und Christentum 7, Tübingen, 381-451.
FOUCAULT, M. (1981): The Order of Discourse, in: R. Young (ed.), Untying the Text: A Post-Structuralist Reader, Boston/London/Henley, 48-78.
– (1984): What Is an Author? in: P. Rabinow (ed.), The Foucault Reader, New York, 101-120.
GORDAY, P. (1983): Principles of Patristic Exegesis: Romans 9-11 in Origen, John Chrysostom, and Augustine, New York/Toronto.
GREGORY OF ELVIRA (1848): Commentarium in Cantica Canticorum, ed. by G. Heine, Leipzig.
GRIBOMONT, J. (1982): Nouvelles perspectives sur l'exégèse de l'Ancien Testament la fin du IIIe siècle, Aug. 22, 357-363.
HALPERIN, D.J. (1981): Origen, Ezekiel's Merkabah, and the Ascension of Moses, Church History 50, 261-275.
HARL, M. (1981): Pointes antignostique d'Origène: le questionnement impie des ... ecritures, in: R. Van den Broek/M.J. Vermaseren (eds.), Studies in Gnosticism and Hellenistic Religions, Presented to Gilles Quispel on the Occasion of His 65th Birthday, Études préliminaires aux Religions Orientales dans l'Empire Romain 91, Leiden, 205-17.
HARNACK, A.v. (1918-19): Der kirchengeschichtliche Ertrag der exegetischen Arbeiten des Origenes I-II, Leipzig.
HEITHER, T. (1990): Translatio Religionis: Die Paulusdeutung des Origenes in seinem Kommentar zum Römerbrief, Cologne/Vienna.
JACOBS, A.S. (1998): Solomon's Salacious Song: Foucault's Author Function and the Early Christian Interpretation of the Canticum Canticorum, Medieval Encounters 4, 1-23.
KANNENGIESSER, C./PETERSEN, W.L. eds. (1988): Origen of Alexandria: His World and His Legacy, Notre Dame.
KIMELMAN, R. (1980): Rabbi Yohanan and Origen on the Song of Songs: A Third-Century Jewish-Christian Disputation, HThR 73, 567-595.
KOCH, H. (1932): Pronoia und Paideusis: Studien über Origenes und sein Verhältnis zum Platonismus, Berlin/Leipzig.
KRAUSS, S. (1893-94): The Jews in the Works of the Church Fathers, JQR 5, 122-57, JQR 6, 223-261.
LAWSON, R.P. (1957): Introduction, in: Origen, The Song of Songs: Commentary and Homilies, New York/Ramsey, 3-20.
LE BOULLUEC, A. (1975): La place de la polémique antignostique dans le Peri Archôn, in: H. Crouzel et al. (eds.), Origeniana. Premier colloque internationale des Études origéniennes, Bari, 47-61.
LEVINE, L. I. (1975): Caesarea Under Roman Rule, Leiden.
LOEWE, R. (1966): Apologetic Motifs in the Targum to the Song of Songs, in: A. Altmann (ed.), Biblical Motifs: Origins and Transformations, Cambridge, Mass, 159-196.
MARMORSTEIN, A. (1920): Deux Renseignements d'Origène concernant les juifs, REJ 71, 190-199.
– (1935): Judaism and Christianity in the Middle of the Third Century, HUCA 10, 223-261.
MELONI, P. (1977): Ippolito e il Cantico dei Cantici, in: Ricerche su Ippolito, Studia Ephemeridis 'Augustinianum' 13, Rome, 97-120.
MILLER, P.C. (1986): Pleasure of the Text, Text of Pleasure: Eros and Language in Origen's Commentary on the Song of Songs, JAAR 54, 241-253.

MOORE, S.D. (2000): The Song of Songs in the History of Sexuality, ChH 69, 328-349.
NAUTIN, P. (1977): Origène. Sa vie et son oeuvre, Paris.
OHLY, F. (1958): Hohelied-Studien. Grundzüge einer Geschichte der Hohenlied-auslegung des Abendlandes bis um 1200, Schriften der wissenschaftlichen Gesellschaft an der Johann Wolfgang Goethe-Universität Frankfurt am Main. Geisteswissenschaftliche Reihe 1, Wiesbaden.
O'LEARY, J.S. (1995): The Recuperation of Judaism, in: G. Dorival/A. Le Boulluec, (eds.), Origeniana Sexta, Origène et la Bible/Origen and the Bible, Leuven, 373-380.
RIEDEL, W. (1898): Die Auslegung des Hohenliedes in der jüdischen Gemeinde und der griechischen Kirche, Leipzig.
RIEDLINGER, H. (1958): Die Makellosigkeit der Kirche in den Lateinischen Hohenlied-kommentaren des Mittelalters, Münster.
ROUSSEAU, O. (1954): Introduction, in: Origène, Homélies sur le Cantique des Cantiques, Paris, 7-55.
RUIS-CAMPS, J. (1975): Origenes y Marciôn. Caracter preferentemente antimarcionita del Peri Archôn, in: H. Crouzel et al. (eds.), Origeniana, Premier colloque internationale des Études origéniennes, Bari, 297-312.
SCHEPER, G.L. (1971): The Spiritual Marriage: The Exegetic History and Literary Impact of the Song of Songs in the Middle Ages, PhD diss., Princeton.
TORJESEN, K.J. (1986): Hermeneutical Procedure and Theological Method in Origen's Exegesis, Berlin/New York.
– (1989): Hermenutics and Soteriology in Origen's Peri Archon, StPatr 21, 333-348.
URBACH, E.E. (1971): The Homiletical Interpretation of the Sages and the Expositions of Origen on Canticles, and the Jewish-Christian Disputation, ScrHier 22, 247-275.
ULRICH, E.C. (1988): Origen's Old Testament Text: The Transmission History of the Septuagint to the Third Century C.E., in: C. Kannengiesser/W.L. Petersen (eds.), Origen of Alexandria: His World and His Legacy, Notre Dame, 3-33.
VOGT, H.-J. (1974): Das Kirchenverständnis des Origenes, Cologne/Vienna.
– (1987): Warum wurde Origenes zum Häretiker erklärt?, in: L. Lies (ed.), Origeniana Quarta. Die Referate des 4. Internationalen Origeneskongresses, Innsbruck/Vienna, 78-99.
VÖLKER, W. (1931): Das Volkommenheitsideal des Origenes, Tübingen.
WILKEN, R.L. (1995): Origen's Homilies on Leviticus and Vayikra Rabbah, in: G. Dorival/A. Le Boulluec (eds.), Origeniana Sexta, Origène et la Bible/Origen and the Bible, Leuven, 81-91.
WINKELMANN, F. (1970): Einige Bemerkungen zu den Aussagen des Rufinus von Aquileia und des Hieronymus über ihre Übersetzungstheorie und -methode, in: P. Granfield/J.A. Jungman (eds.), Kyriakon. Festschrift Johannes Quasten Vol. 2, Münster, 532-547.

Middle High German Appropriations of the Song of Songs: Allegorical Interpretation and Narrative Extrapolation

Annette Volfing

The aim of this article is to examine the ways in which certain Middle High German writers responded to the particular hermeneutic and narratological problems posed by the Song of Songs. Section I sets out the nature of these problems: as will be shown, Latin exegetes of the twelfth century were only too aware that the standard method of interpreting the Bible, in accordance with the principle of *vierfacher Schriftsinn*, could only be applied with some difficulty to the Song of Songs, given that this text does not conform to the normative narrative model (best exemplified by Old Testament histories). In the drive to impose a coherent narrative framework on the supposedly disjointed fragments of dialogue, which make up the text, some attempts at allegorical interpretations essentially spiralled into independent myth-making – a development which ran entirely counter to the accepted opposition between the Bible and human *fabulae*. Furthermore, it will be argued that the exact nature of the myth or narrative framework is largely dependent on the particular *significatio* chosen for the figure of the *sponsa*, an ecclesiological reading of this figure being the most likely to trigger extravagant narrative extrapolation.

In Section II, two Middle High German "case studies" will be presented: Brun von Schönebeck's *Das Hohe Lied*, and the anonymous *Tochter Syon*-material. Although both of these have clearly identifiable Latin sources, each one recasts the Song of Songs for its own purposes and responds to the theoretical issues just outlined in ways which are sometimes controversial. Brun von Schönebeck's non-mystical work constitutes an idiosyncratic response to the Latin commentary tradition: by presenting mythic elements as historically true, Brun undermines the fundamental principle that layers of meaning are hermeneutically distinct. By contrast, the mystically oriented *Tochter Syon* represents the fusion of selected elements from the Song of Songs with an existing narrative pattern (that of Alan of Lille's *Anticlaudianus*) to create a fresh myth, which incorporates comment on aspects of contemporary female spirituality.

Any attempt at exhaustive historical coverage, either of the Latin exegetical tradition or of the reception of the Song of Songs into Middle High German, is clearly beyond the scope of this article. While there are several excellent monographs devoted precisely to providing an overview of the Latin exegetical tradition,[1] the impact of the Song of Songs on the full spectrum of Middle High German literature has not yet been studied systematically. Although the influence of the Song of Songs is not restricted to mystically oriented works, discussion of its reception into German tends to proceed either from a thematic engagement with bridal mysticism and female spirituality,[2] or else from the analysis and contextualization of individual, high-profile mystical texts, such as the *St. Trudpeter Hohelied* (12th cent.)[3] or Mechthild von Magdeburg's *Das fließende Licht der Gottheit* (13th cent.).[4] Such a primary association of the Song of Songs with bridal mysticism is a natural one,[5] but should not allow one to forget that the distinctive images and metaphors of this text, together with their allegorical interpretations, were also quarried for re-deployment in other kinds of religious writing – such as the mariological "Leich" or "Meisterlied".[6]

I.

In late classical and in medieval thought, the term *allegoria* has two distinct meanings, one rooted in rhetoric and the other in hermeneutics.[7] As a rhetorical term, *allegoria* refers to the use of figurative or non-literal statements in any context: the *Rhetorica ad Herennium* includes *allegoria* amongst the list of tropes or extended ornamental devices available to writers,[8] while Isidore of

1 Ohly 1958 remains the definitive study dealing with the tradition up to 1200. See also Riedlinger 1958, Astell 1990 and Matter 1990.

2 Most significantly, Keller 2000. Note also Bauer 1973, who sets out the importance of the Song of Songs for the development of the metaphor of the *claustrum animae* ("Herzklosterallegorie"; the soul as a spiritual convent).

3 E.g. Spitz 1986; Keller 1993 and 1995; Wisniewski 1995; and Küsters 1985 who focuses particularly on the importance of this text for the promulgation of the monastic ideal for women.

4 E.g. Haas 1975 and Köbele 1993: 74-96.

5 Cf. Köpf 1987. Ruh 1990-99 provides a comprehensive history of the Western mystical tradition. For a much shorter introduction to the essential concepts of mysticism, see Störmer-Caysa 1998.

6 The "Leich" is a formally irregular, *sequentia*-like lyric composition. For the reception of the Song of Songs within this genre, see Gärtner 1988 and Wachinger 1992. The "Meisterlied" may be described as the polystrophic successor to the to the "Spruch" (a didactic monostrophic lyric form); for discussion of one such mariological text containing extensive Song of Songs material, see the commentary by Stolz (1996) on Heinrich von Mügeln's *Der Tum* (Book VI of *Die kleineren Dichtungen Heinrichs von Mügeln*).

7 Cf. Krewitt 1971: 93-96; Zerfaß 1995: 46-61.

8 Pseudo-Cicero, *Rhetorica ad Herennium* IV.34.46. Cf Lausberg1960: vol. 1, 441-446.

Seville pithily sums it up as the technique of saying one thing to mean something else (*Allegoria est alienoloquium, aliud enim sonat, aliud intelligitur*).[9] By contrast, hermeneutic allegory concerns itself with the interpretation of whole texts which are deemed to operate with multiple levels of meaning. Starting with Philo of Alexandria in late antiquity and continuing throughout the medieval period, hermeneutic allegory constitutes a cornerstone of the approach to the Bible. Ostensibly justified by Paul's exposition in Gal 4:21-31 of how the "historical" figures of Hagar and Sarah also serve to signify respectively the Jewish and the Christian peoples,[10] the central element of this methodology is the belief that while every statement in the Bible is literally or historically true, it also contains further layers of meaning which complement the literal truth, and which are (usually) of greater ultimate significance. Sometimes all non-literal meanings are subsumed collectively under the blanket designation *sensus allegoricus*; while at other times, further gradations are introduced: so one finds *sensus allegoricus* in the narrower sense (limited to the typological relationship between events and figures in the Old and the New Testament), *sensus tropologicus* (spelling out the practical moral lesson of the passage in question) and *sensus anagogicus* (relating to eschatology).[11] Taken together with the *sensus litteralis*, these three make up the so-called "vierfacher Schriftsinn", or four standard levels of biblical interpretation.

The extension of the concept of hermeneutic allegory to other, non-biblical, texts, is more problematic. On the one hand, there are a number of late classical or medieval philosophical narratives (or "philosophical allegories", in modern terminology) which operate much more explicitly with multiple levels of meaning than does the Bible: notably, Prudentius' *Psychomachia*, Martianus Capella's *De nuptiis Philologiae et Mercurii*, Bernardus Silvestris' *Cosmographia*, and Alan of Lille's *De planctu naturae* and *Anticlaudianus*.[12] Indeed, the programmatic

9 Isidore of Seville, *Etymologiae* I.37.22.

10 Further justification is supposedly provided by the miracle at the Wedding in Cana. According to an exegetical tradition started by Augustine, the transformation of water into wine was taken to signify – and thus, by circular argumentation, to justify – the transition from the literal to the allegorical levels of scriptural interpretation for the Bible as a whole. Cf Augustine, *In Iohannis Evangelium* 9, pp. 90-100; furthermore Ohly 1958-59: 20; Spitz 1972: 145 and 151-154.

11 Cf. the famous mnemonic attributed to Augustine of Dacia: *Littera gesta docet, quid credas allegoria / Moralis quid agas, quo tendas anagogia* (here quoted from Zerfaß 1995: 55, note 47.) A particularly effective illustration of these four levels by reference to the departure of the Jewish people from Egypt is set out in Dante's letter to Can Grande della Scala (Epistola 13, *Opere*, 402-411, here p. 405): the *sensus litteralis* is what actually happened; the *sensus allegoricus* is the Redemption wrought by Christ; the *sensus tropologicus* is the conversion of the soul from a state of sin to a state of grace; and the *sensus anagogicus* is the departure of the soul from the body at the point of death.

12 The fact that these works tend now to be designated as "philosophical allegories" is due not only to their hermeutic complexity, but also to their extended use of personification (i.e. of allegory in the rhetorical sense).

statement in the prologue to *Anticlaudianus* setting out the different layers of meaning to be found in the text is conceptually not dissimilar to "vierfacher Schriftsinn":

> *In hoc etenim opere litteralis sensus suauitas puerilem demulcebit auditum, moralis instructio perficientim imbuet sensum, acutior allegorie subtilitas proficientem acuet intellectum.*[13]
>
> [For in this work the sweetness of the literal level will soothe the ears of boys, the moral instruction will inspire the mind on the road to perfection, the sharper subtlety of the allegory will whet the advanced intellect.]

Nonetheless, as a methodology, the allegorical interpretation of the Bible is predicated on an absolute distinction between it and other narrative texts (however intellectually or spiritually worthy these might be).[14] Other texts were essentially deemed to lack the guaranteed truth-value of the Bible,[15] and so the relationship between the literal and non-literal meanings within them could not be viewed as complementary, but rather as one of opposition: the inner truth was said to be cloaked or veiled with lies. The classic *locus* for this distinction occurs in Bernardus Silvestris' commentary on Martianus Capella's *De nuptiis Philologiae et Mercurii*:

> *Genus doctrine figura est. Figura autem est oratio quam involucrum dicere solunt. Hec autem bipertita est: partimur namque eam in allegoriam et integumentum. Est autem allegoria oratio sub historica narratione verum et ab exteriori diversum involvens intellectum, ut de lucta Iacob. Integumentum vero est oratio sub fabulosa narratione verum claudens intellectum, ut de Orpheo. Nam et ibi historia et hic fabula misterium habent occultum, qod alias discutiendum erit. Allegoria quidem divine pagine, integumentum vero philosophice competit.*[16]
>
> [The form [*genus*] of instruction is figurative [*figura*]. Figurative discourse (*figura*) is a manner of speaking (*oratio*) which is usually called a "veil". It is twofold for we divide it into *allegoria* and *integumentum* [literally, "covering"]. Allegory is a manner of speaking which covers a true meaning different from its exterior und an historical narrative (*historica narratione*), as in the case of Jacob's wrestling-match. *Integumentum*, however, is a manner of speaking which hides a true meaning under a fabulous narrative (*fabulosa narratione*), as in the case of Orpheus. For both there history and here fiction (*fabula*) contain a hidden mystery. Allegory pertains to divine writings (*divine pagine*), but *integumentum* pertains to philosophical.][17]

---

13 Alan of Lille, *Anticlaudianus*, Prologus (p. 56).

14 Brinkmann 1980: 169-198; Freytag 1982: 15-17; Copeland and Melville 1991: 159-187; Grünkorn 1994: 49-66.

15 Reservations occasionally expressed about the principle that all biblical statements are literally true. An extreme case is provided by the twelfth-century intellectual William of Conches, who treated as mythology the account of the creation of Eve from Adam's rib. Cf. Jeauneau 1964: 850; Dronke 1975: 173.

16 Quoted from Jeauneau 1964: 856.

17 Translation taken from Fulton 2002: 375-376, with minor alterations.

Notwithstanding the fact that the basic hermeneutic metaphor of veiling (*involucrum*) could be applied equally to the Bible and to other texts,[18] the fundamental difference in the truth-value of the literal level was marked by a terminological opposition: *integumentum* was normally used for non-biblical narrative texts (e.g. histories, pagan mythologies, philosophical allegories, or vernacular courtly romances),[19] and *allegoria* was normally reserved for the Bible.

While this distinction may seem unambiguous, there was inevitably some blurring around the edges – and as this article will seek to show, the Song of Songs does not fit as neatly into the "biblical" category as one might have thought. As the hermeneutic methodology just outlined is essentially designed to tease further levels of meaning out of clear-cut historical narratives, it works less well for those parts of the Bible – such as the Song of Songs, or the sapiential books – which lack the requisite narrative basis. In the case of books which did not purport to present factual information about the past, exegetes were often inclined to regard the literal or historical level simply as a non-issue and to proceed straight the inner or allegorical meaning.[20] As the Song of Songs was widely regarded as having been composed by Solomon as a record of his nuptials, it did possess a claim to historicity, albeit a tenuous one. Nonetheless, given the licentious nature of this "historical" material, exegetes tended to discount the significance (and even the truth-value) of this literal level, choosing instead to focus firmly on the allegorical level.

The first step in the allegorical interpretation of this text is to set out the "true" identities of the two principal speakers, the *sponsus* and the *sponsa*. There are almost no deviations from the standard view that the *sponsus* signifies Christ,[21] an approach which is supported by the widespread use of the image of Christ as bridegroom in the New Testament.[22] As far as the *sponsa* is concerned, three main approaches were current in the Middle Ages: the ecclesiological approach (I), whereby the sponsa is identified with the Church (or, as a minor variation, with *natura humana* or some other abstraction representing the collective human condition); the mariological approach (II),

18 For survey of the use of such metaphors in Christian writing, see Spitz 1972: 23-141.

19 Knapp 1980 argues that this hermeneutic model does not work for the symbolically structured Arthurian romances which feature so prominently in classical Middle High German literature; on this point, see also Wells 1992 and Grünkorn 1994.

20 Freytag 1982: 16.

21 A few Middle High German sermons on John the Evangelist take the highly unusual step of interpreting the figure of the bridegroom in the Song of Songs (esp. Cant 5:10) with reference to John rather than to Christ. This is part of a wider strategy of deification of John, whereby he is presented as the equal of Christ. Cf. Volfing 2001: 155-160. Note also Sense's strategy of representing himself in his spiritual "autobiography" as the bridegroom of Divine wisdom.

22 Mt 9:15; 22:1-14; 25,1-13, John 3:29, Acta 19:1-8. In this context, Eph 5:25-32, in which Paul compares the relationship between actual husbands and wives to that between Christ and the Church, is clearly also of relevance. Cf. Keller 2000: 19-20.

whereby the *sponsa* is identified with Mary; and finally the "mystical" approach (III), whereby the *sponsa* potentially signifies the soul of any believer aspiring to nuptial union with the Logos. Of these three, which are by no means mutually exclusive,[23] the ecclesiological approach is the oldest and most mainstream. The mariological one gained sudden popularity in the twelfth century, when it was promulgated by Rupert of Deutz and others.[24] The "mystical" approach (III), which had initially been proposed by Origen,[25] gained sudden popularity aften being relaunched in the twelfth century, primarily by Bernhard of Clairvaux in his highly influential series of sermons on the Song of Songs.[26] While this third approach to the interpretation of the Song of Songs clearly provides a valuable premise for bridal mysticism (i.e. for the aspiration of an individual believer to experience in this life a spiritual union or *connubium* with Christ which is as complete and intense as the physical one between husband and wife), it is important to separate intellectual position from experiential aspiration: it is perfectly possible for a thinker to regard the individual *anima* as a correct, or at least as a possible, *significatio* of the figure of the *sponsa*, without therefore necessarily showing much positive interest in the scope, methodology, and literary articulation of bridal mysticism. At this point it should be noted that active, experiential bridal mysticism was very much a female phenomenon. Few men chose the paradigm of bridal mysticism as a blueprint for expressing their own relationship with Christ.[27] To the extent that men engaged with phenomenon, this tended instead to be in the context of the spiritual direction of women (*cura monialium*). While bridal mysticism frequently formed the basis for vernacular sermons, treatises and other literary works produced by men for religious women, there are also indications of some hostility towards this form of radical piety; in particular, the combination of bridal mysticism with a cultivation of visionary experiences was considered potentially anarchic and liable to trigger an unacceptable spiritual solipsism, in which the female mystic withdraws from the communal religious life and rejects it authoritative framework.[28]

A further issue in the interpretation of the Song of Songs relates to the narrative coherence of the text. Adopting the notion of the "quest for

---

23 (I) and (III) are consistent, in that the Church is made up of individual souls; (II) and (III) are consistent, in that Mary constitutes a particular individual soul; and (I) and (II) are consistent, to the extent that Mary is identified with the "Mother Church".

24 Ohly 1958: 121-135; Fulton 2002: 309-350.

25 Ohly 1958: 19-21.

26 Ohly 1958: 135-158.

27 Friedrich Sunder (1254-1328) is a rare example is a male author engaging experientially with bridal mysticism. Cf. Ringler 1980: 144-380.

28 Langer 1987 discusses the general "problem" of unchecked female spirituality, with particular reference to the Dominican order in the early fourteenth century. For the rejection by the Dominican order of radical forms of piety for its female members in the fifteenth century, see Williams-Krapp 1990; for the on-going reception of bridal mysticism amongst Domincan reformed nuns, see also Schiewer 2000.

narrative" from Todorov, Matter claims that "Latin interpretation of the Song of Songs strives for narrative; the primary objective of breaking the [allegorical] code was to turn the text into a narrative plot".[29]

The different possible readings for the identity of the *sponsa* in turn generated different kinds to attempts to construct a satisfactory narrative framework. Particularly in the case of the ecclesiological approach, one senses the extent to which the tentative hints of narrativity in the Song of Songs tantalized and frustrated twelfth-century exegetes; notwithstanding the established opposition between the truthfulness of the Bible and the mendacity of *fabulae* and philosophical allegories, a common solution was to re-brand the Song of Songs precisely as this kind of *fabula* – and then to flesh out the narrative detail according to taste. Of the various fantastical results, special mention is due to William of St. Thierry (d. ca. 1148), who uses the terms *drama historiale*, *fabula* and *parabola* interchangeably to describe a story about a black bride (i.e. *nigra sed formosa*) who has to change her skin-colour before she is accepted back into the marriage-bed;[30] and to Honorius of Autun (d. ca. 1158), who in his *Expositio in Cantica canticorum* invents a myth according to which the bride is searching for the lost "jewel of obedience".[31] The following summary, taken from Fulton, gives a flavour of Honorius' invention:

> "The emperor of the heavenly republic, wishing to have an heir, bore to himself a co-equal son, whom he betrothed, in turn, to a queen and concubine, that is, to angelic and human nature, so that they might bear for him co-heirs to the kingdom. When, however, one of the princes attempted to seize the highest power the queen, who had consented to his tyranny, was polluted by her adultery and condemned to eternal exile along with the prince. Immediately, the concubine was raised to the royal dignity and given title to the crown of the kingdom; she could not at this time receive the crown herself, however, for it had not yet been ornamented with the jewels of obedience. When the exiled queen saw the crown being prepared . . . for her rival, she began to plot how she might deceive the *sponsa* to render her, rather than God, the jewel of her obedience. The *sponsus*, seeing his bridal gift thrown away, expelled the *sponsa* from the chamber of paradise, not to be restored until she had won back the lost jewel from the queen. And so . . the bride was forced to wander throughout the earth . . . set upon by giants, who, like thieves, polluted her with their vices ... At long last, however, the *sponsus* visited the *sponsa* and returned to her the lost jewel of her obedience . . . She was at once led to her coronation in the heavenly court, where she was made with her *sponsus* co-heir to the kingdom."[32]

In both cases, these myths provide the framework within which specific verses of the Song of Songs might plausibly have been spoken – and are therefore to be interpreted. Rather than inventing their own myths and *fabulae*, some writers also constructed links between the Song of Songs and established

29 Matter 1990: 56.

30 Cf. Astell 1990: 31; and, more generally, Ohly 1958: 158-170.

31 For discussion of this work, see Ohly 1958: 254-262; Flint 1974: 196-211; Astell 1990: 31-33; Matter 1990: 58-76.

32 Fulton 2002: 377.

philosophical allegories. For example, in his commentary on the Song of Songs (composed ca. 1170-1189), Thomas the Cistercian suggests that the *sponsus* and *sponsa* signify not only Christ and the Church, but also the two protagonists of Martianus Capella's nuptial romance recording the deification of the maiden Philology through marriage to the God Mercury (col. 17-18).[33] When a pagan fiction is thus presented as the "inner meaning" of biblical text, we are confronted with a complete reversal of the ordinary model of *integumentum*: instead of the truth being clothed in lies, it would seem that lies (or at least pure fiction) are clothed in biblical verses.[34]

By contrast with this tendency to achieve narrative cohesion through the invention or annexation of philosophical allegories, the mariological approach encourages the strategy of interpreting the text specifically by reference to the events of the Incarnation and to the relationship between Christ and Mary. Philip of Harvengt (d. 1183), for example, suggests that the Song of Songs should be read as a nuptial song marking the institution of the marriage between Christ and Mary within Mary's womb.[35] An even more overt attempt at "re-historicizing" the text is to be found in the commentary of William of Newburgh (d. after 1198) who presents the verses as an historically accurate record of a dialogue between Mary and Christ: the anachronism of this dialogue's having been written down by the prophet Solomon is not deemed to detract from its validity as a historical witness.[36]

Finally, in the case of the "mystical" approach to the Song of Songs, no single strategy emerges. On the one hand, the *Filia Syon* material to be discussed in the second case study illustrates the fact that myths could be written about the individual soul just as easily as they could about *Ecclesia* or *natura humana*. On the other hand, there is some indication that in texts which actually engage with the domain of experiential mysticism (as well as merely endorsing a particular *significatio* for the *sponsa*), the "quest for narrative" is much less pronounced. To take as an example a vernacular text written by a woman rather than a Latin text written by a man, Mechthild von Magdeburg's *Das fließende Licht der Gottheit* engages with the Song of Songs largely without recourse to mythic narratives of the type discussed above, and appears averse to promoting any single story-line or exegetical approach as the "key" to

33 For a general discussion of this text, see Ohly 1958: 188-197; Bell 1977. For further, less explicit analogies between Martianus' work and the Song of Songs, see Fulton 2002: 370-372.

34 Conversely, secular texts were sometimes credited with a biblical inner meaning: according to Allen 1971: 4, the friars of the fourteenth century "read literature in precisely the same way that was traditional for scripture" and understood Boethius' Philosophia and Alan of Lille's Natura to signify *Ecclesia* (Allen 1971: 21-24).

35 Fulton 2002: 356 (and 351-404 for Philip of Harvengt more generally); Ohly 1958: 206-212. For the mariologically oriented "re-historizing" of the Song of Songs, see also Fulton 1996 and 1998.

36 Fulton 2002: 438 (and 405-470 for William of Newburgh more generally).

understanding this text. *Das fließende Licht der Gottheit* does not even confine itself strictly to the "mystical" approach, going as far as to stage dialogues between different categories of "bride" (i.e. the historical bride from the Song of Songs, Mary, Christendom and the narrator's own soul), on the subjects of how to endure the bridegroom's apparent rejection after the initial bliss of erotic intimacy. Admittedly, there are slight hints of "heilsgeschichtliche" *fabula* implicit in the evocation of Christendom as the cast-off bride,[37] but the use of ecclesiological *fabula* is sustained and there is no indication that Mechthild is interested in imposing a single narrative structure either on the Song of Song or on her own work. On the contrary, from the perspective of Mechthild and of other female mystics, the particular attraction of the Song of Songs lies precisely in the way its dialogic (rather than the epic) form is underpinned by an indeterminate narrative development. These features encourage a focus on the quality of the subjective experience articulated rather than on logical progression or on objective facts: the important thing for the mystic is not to define what went wrong between the *sponsus* and *sponsa*, and to relate this to the "Heilsgeschichte", but rather to engage imaginatively the situation of the *sponsa* and to use this role to give expression to her own painful experiences of "Gottesferne" and spiritual aridity. The combination of dialogicity with narrative indeterminacy also allows the mystic (or her narrator) to adopt a wide range of sometimes disjointed voices or "Sprecherpositionen", the diversity of which serves not only to articulate particular aspects of mystical experience, but also to hint more broadly at the way in which the boundaries of personal identity dissolve at the point of *connubium* and are never quite restored.[38]

II.

Case Study I: Brun von Schönebeck

Brun von Schönebeck's *Das Hohe Lied*, written in 1267 by an aristocratic layman in Magdeburg, constitutes a unique and highly idiosyncratic response both to the Latin commentary tradition in general, and to the *Expositio in Cantica canticorum* by Honorius of Autun.[39] Although Brun ostensibly undertook his project in order to make the Song of Songs more "accessible" to other aristocratic laypeople who were unable to read Latin commentaries for

37 *Das fließende Licht der Gottheit* I 22 (pp. 18-19); cf. Kasten 1995; Volfing 2003a: 261-262.

38 Hasebrink 2000: 161; Volfing 2003a: 257-258. For the importance of dialogues for Mechhild, see also Haug 1984; Dicke 2003; Suerbaum 2003.

39 Brun's use of Honorius is established by Hübner 1963: 43-54, although the question of further sources remains open – cf. Hagenlocher, pp. 139-140.

themselves, one can only marvel at the hermeneutic confusion likely to beset anybody relying solely on this interpretation.[40]

While a number of twelfth-century Latin exegetes had simply discounted the historical level of the Song of Songs, choosing instead to treat the text as a kind of incomplete philosophical allegory which they could expand at will, Brun appears at first sight to take the historical level very seriously: as far as he is concerned, the text is, at least on one level, "about" the wedding of Solomon to the daughter of Pharaoh, and perfectly suited to interpretation according the methodology of the "vierfacher Schriftsinn". This stance is reflected in the structure of Brun's work, which opens (after a short prologue) with a narrative section constructed around a selection of verses from the Song of Songs. This first, bipartite, section (62-428; 429-1055) purports to represent the literal or historical meaning of the text, while a much longer second section (1056-12719) interprets the verses quoted in the first second in relation to Mary, to the individual soul, and to the end of the world (1056–12719).[41] Brun's apparent endorsement of the fundamental opposition between *sensus litteralis* and *sensus allegoricus* (in the broad sense) is underscored by his use of traditional hermeneutic metaphors which are essentially variations on that of *involucrum*:[42] as with a nut (919–920) or an egg (1024–1029), the hard shell of the narrative must be pierced if one wishes to savour that which is to be found inside.

The problem with this approach was that Brun was also clearly attracted by the exegetical use of allegorical *fabulae* – particularly by Honorius of Autun, his chief source – and had no compunction introducing "fabulous" elements, not only as allegory, but also as historical fact.

The most striking example of involves the treatment of *mandragora* (the mandrake), mentioned in Cant 7:13. Although the mandrake is simply a root, it was credited in the Middle Ages with various unusual properties, including certain anthropomorphic features.[43] Building on this tradition, both Honorius and Brun present the mandrake as a headless woman symbolizing the reign of Anti-Christ and forming part of a larger cavalcade of brides. Despite the fact that Honorius' overall approach to the Song of Songs is essentially the traditional ecclesiological one (i.e. the *sponsa* signifies the *Ecclesia / natura humana*), he also operates with four other biblical manifestations of the *sponsa*, two of which are treated as historically real (the daughter of Pharaoh and the daughter of the King of Babylon) and two of which as allegorical (Sunamitis

---

40 See for example *Das Hohe Lied* 814-817: *wie rou dise selben wort sint, / gibet mir sine hulfe gotis kint, / ich mache si ebene und slecht, / daz si vorsta ritter und knecht* [however rough these words may be, if God grants me his assistance, I will make the so smooth and simple that knights and pages will be able to understand them].

41 These three areas of concern correspond loosely to *sensus allegoricus* (in the narrow sense), *sensus tropologicus*, and *sensus anagogicus*. See footnote 11 above.

42 Cf. Spitz 1972: 61-67.

43 See Menhardt 1962.

and Mandragora).[44] Honorius uses these four figures as emblematic focal points for the structure of his commentary, rather than as full-scale participants within the myth of the lost jewel of obedience; they represent respectively the Chosen People, the Gentiles, the Jews, and pagans; and also four phases of the "Heilsgeschichte" (*ante legem*, *sub legem*, *sub gratia*, and *sub Antichristo*). The brides are iconographically striking, in terms of their appearance, provenance, and mode of transport; in particular, the headless woman Mandragora would be implausible on a literal level.[45] While Honorius divides the Song of Songs into four sections and interprets each one systematically with particular reference to one of these brides,[46] Brun only introduces the full cohort of brides at a late stage in the interpretative section. At this point, he follows Honorius in explaining that the first two *waren an der warheit also* (11556) and the last two *waren zu bedutunge / uns gegebin* (10557-8). However, at a much earlier point, he has already allowed Mandragora to make a solo intrusion into the supposedly literal, narrative section (875-909): a naked and headless lady is said to arrive at the wedding feast, carried by the wind, whereupon Solomon's bride (i.e. the daughter of Pharaoh) takes pity on her and persuades Solomon to make this woman a new head. No reference is made to the other two brides belonging to the four-part scheme.[47] Given that Mandragora exists solely *zu bedutunge*, her intrusion onto the literal level clearly undermines the historical credibility of the whole narrative.[48] Whereas in a traditional commentary, the interpretation essentially "serves" the literal level by elucidating it,[49] Brun's text suggests that the exegete is free to alter the literal level, if it suits his literary purposes.[50]

---

44 PL 172, 352. The daughter of Pharaoh is mentioned in 1Reg 3:1 as the bride of Solomon. The daughter of the King of Babylon is identified as the Queen of Sheba mentioned 1 Reg 10:1-13.

45 For the iconography of the brides (particularly Sunamitis), see Curschmann 1988: 153-160.

46 Cant 1:1-2.17 relates to the daughter of Pharaoh; 3:1-6.9 to the daughter of the King of Babylon, 6:10-7:10 to Sunamitis; and 7:11-8:14 to Mandragora.

47 The biblically attested visit of the Queen of Sheba (the second bride in Honorius' scheme) is mentioned at an earlier point (152-159).

48 Other details which undermine the verisimilitude of the narrative and suggest allegory rather than history include the points that Solomon uses the messenger Fortitudo to convey his love-letter (354); and that Pharaoh's daughter is given the unlikely name *oleum effusum* (196) / *uz gegozzin ole* (197) [oil which has been poured out].

49 While the allegorical levels may ultimately be more important, the commentator should nonetheless be bound by, and focused on, the literal manifestation of divine revelation. For a survey on what was thought to constitute good hermeneutic practice, see Freytag 1982: 17-22.

50 In the course of the text, Brun repeatedly underscores his right to create historical details which suit his interpretation. For example, one would expect the appearance of Solomon's litter (Cant 3:6-10) to be presented as a matter of historical fact, (even if the an author might use some discretion in embellishing the description of extra-biblical details). However, rather than simply describing or interpreting an object from the past, Brun's narrator takes the credit for building the litter himself, through his literary endeavours. Consequently, he is the one who decides which stones go where (*durch daz han ich desen stein*

Ultimately, Brun's maverick approach appears to stem from a preoccupation with what he regards as the unreliability of *schrift* (both in the sense of Holy Scripture, and of writing more generally). He is keen to stress the literal untruthfulness of figurative statements (of which there are many in the Song of Songs),[51] and to highlight the almost infinite open-endedness inherent traditional methods of exegesis. In view of its "accommodating" nature, *schrift* is compared, first to a harlot with many partners, and then to a pliable waxen figure:

iz ist um di schrift also geschaffen,
als um ein elich wip
daz do treit doch velen lip
und sich vremden mannen leget bi . . .
von der schrift ist noch me gelesen:
di schrift hat eine wechsene nesen.
daz wachs ist gel var und ouch wiz,
daz daz wachs behende is mit vliz
zu nemen an sich etslich bilde,
iz si ru zam adir wilde,
also nimpt di schrift an sich
itslich bilde daz sage ich. (953-956, 960-967)

[Scripture/writing is like a married woman who nonetheless sells her body and lies down with many strangers . . . It is also widely taught that Scripture/writing has a waxen nose. The wax is yellow and white, so that the wax may readily take on any form at all. Similarly, I assert that Scripture/writing may take on any image.]

Hagenlocher's major study of this opaque yet provocative set of metaphors leads to significant conclusions about attitudes to writing – notably, that whereas the written word had previously been endowed with a particular authority, reliability and even sanctity as a result of its almost exclusive association with the Church, the spread of literacy meant that by the middle of the thirteenth century, it started to be seen (at least by non-clerics) a mere medium of communication, used by virtually anybody, and for any purpose.[52] Hagenlocher thus seeks to explain the apparent oddness in Brun's handling of the Song of Songs at least partly by reference to his status as a layman: despite

---

/ an koniges Salominis bette geleit (1625-6) [For this reason I placed this stone on King Solomon's bed]; *seht durch daz ich Salomone sende / desen turen stein an sin bette.* (1649-50) [Behold, for this reason I am sending Solomon this precious stone for his bed]). Solomon's litter thus becomes a textual contruct rather than a historical *datum.* Furthermore, as this litter it later said to signify Mary, it follows that the figure of Mary herself is subject to the *arbitrium* of the author. In 2730-2744, Brun's narrator explicitly presents Mary as his creation, stating that the relationship between the historical Mary and his textual construct is analogous to that between thread (the raw material) and cloth (the finished product).

51 In 780-787, Brun uses the term *lugnis* [lie] to describe the metaphors in Cant 2:3 and 2:9. Cf. Volfing 2003b: 138-139.

52 Hagenlocher 1989: 146.

his having acquired considerable Latin learning, his exegetical project is supposedly marred by his propensity to make basic hermeneutic "mistakes".[53] A less negative approach, however, would be to read the work in the context of Brun's status an aristocrat with an established enthusiasm for courtly romance, and particularly for the works of Wolfram von Eschenbach.[54] Given that Brun's primary literary framework would be that of vernacular fiction, it is perhaps not so surprising that his prominent narrator, who comments on his own handling of the material, and who claims ownership of "his" characters and "his" story-line, has more in common with the high-profile narrator in Wolfram von Eschenbach's *Parzival* than with the typical Latin exegete. While the exposition of the Song of Songs is inevitably very different from the composition of an Arthurian romance, Brun's unique attempt to endow a biblical text with all the hallmarks of fictionality is perfectly consistent with the stated views regarding the infinite capacity of *schrift* to accommodate new literary ventures.[55]

Case Study II: Tochter Syon

The texts belonging to the *Tochter Syon* group all constitute varations on a *fabula* or allegorical narrative affirming the validity of bridal mysticism as an approach to the Song of Songs. However, this *fabula* aims to provide a narrative context for a small selection of verses, rather than for the text as a whole: indeed, as will be shown below, the whole story-line may be seen as an exercise in constructing a situation in which the verse *Vulnerasti cor meum, soror mea!* (Cant 4:9), as spoken by the bridegroom, becomes literally true.[56]

The Latin *Filia Syon* is thought to date approximately from the end of the twelfth century and occurs in three main recensions known as V, W, and Z; however, the differences between the three are so relatively minor that W (which in turn constitutes the source for the two German versions to be discussed below) may be taken as representative of the Latin handling of the material.[57] Like other Latin philosophical allegories, this text operates with personifications of abstract concepts: thus the eponymous Daughter of Zion (representing the human soul) interacts with her "companions" Timor, Oratio, Caritas, and Sapientia. The story-line focuses on the plight of the lonely and love-sick Daughter of Syon. Finding nothing the world worthy of her love, the Daughter languishes for some higher object of affection and is on the point of

53 Hagenlocher 1989: 138-139; Green 1994: 200-201.

54 This enthusiasm is also borne out by the *Schöppenchronik*, according to which Brun instituted a Grail festival at Magdeburg. Cf. Wolff 1978: 1056-1057.

55 Cf. Volfing 2003b.

56 This verse is conventionally interpreted by reference to the Incarnation and Passion: Mary's virtue "wounds" God in that it effectively forces him to undertake the Incarnation; or Love personified is said to be responsible specifically for the wound in Christ's side. Cf. Keller 2000: 248-252.

57 Cf. Schmidtke 1995: 951-954.

fading away, when she consults her companions for their advice. To resolve the crisis, two of these companions (Oratio and Caritas) embark on a journey to seek out the bridegroom in heaven. On this journey they carry certain vital implements: a bow and arrow, and a little flask. Oratio faints on the threshold of heaven, but Caritas enters boldly and uses her bow and arrow to shoot the bridegroom in the heart, obtains some vital drops of blood which she puts in the flask, and returns to the Daughter to revive her. Shortly afterwards, the bridegroom himself appears in order to grant the Daughter an experience of full *connubium* and the text ends with a erotically suggestive descent into the wine-cellar (1:3: *cellaria*; Cant 2:4: *cella vinaria*).

In its handling of the archetype of a mortal bride's yearning for her divine bridegroom, this story-line shows certain broad affinities with other philosophical allegories, such as the Cupid and Psyche story (Apuleius) or Martianus Capella's account of the marriage of Mercury and Philology. More specifically, the quest undertaken by Caritas and Oratio appears to follow the model of the celestial journey as set out in Alan of Lille's *Anticlaudianus*, in which Phronesis is aided by various female personification in her quest to reach the throne of God. However, the difference between these two works is profound. In *Anticlaudianus*, the purpose of Phronesis' journey is to appeal to God to create the *homo novus* who will rout the vices from the world and introduce the new golden age. Phronesis thus achieves an outcome which is of objective universal benefit, and which readily lends itself to a "heilsgeschichtliche" interpretation: although indications are that Alan did not intend his own work to be read in this way, later adaptors readily identified the *homo novus* with Christ.[58] In the *Filia Syon*, conversely, the benefits achieved are essentially private and subjective, relating to the personal union between Christ and the individual soul.

Notwithstanding the inherent seriousness of the subject-matter, the Latin *Filia Syon* is characterized by a certain playfulness and lightness of touch. Rather than engaging with experiential mysticism, it has the air of an intellectual or literary exercise. In particular, the anonymous author indulges in elaborate literary games with biblical citations (not only from the Song of Songs) which are either placed in the mouths of allegorical characters or spoken by the narrator.[59] Many of these embedded verses are completely divorced from their original context. For example, when Caritas wounds the heart of the bridegroom, he twice asks a question (*Quis me tetigit?*) which is lifted from Luke 9:45 and/or Mark 5:32, where it is spoken by Christ after he has been surreptitiously touched by the woman suffering from heavy bleeding.

58 Cf. Ochsenbein 1969.

59 There are also oblique reference to the exegetical tradition – for example, Caritas refers to the notion of the various leaps of Christ (into the womb, onto the Cross etc.), which is based on the exegesis of Cant 2:8: *venit saliens in montibus, transiliens colles*. Cf Pfannmüller 1913: 115-116.

Given that the *Filia Syon* uses the same question in a context which is also about the flowing of blood, it is tempting to try to look for a closer connection with the original story; however, it seems more likely that a well-known verse is simply being re-cycled in situation where it might plausibly have been uttered. Such recycling is of well known in the liturgy where biblical phrases are turned into antiphons or responsories with little regard for the original context.[60] The fact that Latin is the common language of the Vulgate and of the narrative means that quotations, allusions and linguistic borrowings merge fairly seamlessly into the narrator's own prose, and that the inventiveness and linguistic virtuousity underlying this mosaic of citations are likely to have been appreciated by a trained clerical or monastic audience. However, these literary effects are less easily recreated in the numerous German versions, which in any case fulfilled a rather different function, given that their primary audience consisted of religious women for whom the experiential possibilities of bridal mysticism held an enormous – and gender-specific – appeal.

The *Tochter Syon* by Lamprecht von Regensburg (ca. 1250) clearly recognizes bridal mysticism not only as an exegetical methodology, but also as a cultural phenomenon which, while laudable in itself, is also faintly threatening in its effective gender exclusivity. Although, on the face of it, the hierarchical paradigm of bridal mysticism appears to underscore the near-universal cultural assumptions about the relative status of men and women (with masculinity being upgraded by association with divinity), bridal mysticism could also be understood as a great leveller between the sexes. As all human beings are potential brides, and hence "women", in relation to Christ, the infinite hierarchical difference between God and creatures relativizes and even obliterates the much smaller one between men and women. Indeed, given that bridal mysticism encourages all Christians to relate to Christ through the assumption of the feminine gender implicit in the bridal role, it would seem that this approach grants women a head start. As Lamprecht's narrator notes with some surprise, women seem to do better than men in the techniques of mysticism:

> diu kunst ist bî unsern tagen
> in Brabant und in Baierlanden
> undern wîben ûf gestanden.
> herre got, waz kunst ist daz,
> daz sich ein alt wîp baz
> verstêt dan witzige man? (2838-2843)

> [This art has arisen in our times amongst the women of Brabant and Bavaria. Good Lord, what kind of art is this, where an old woman has more success than do intelligent men?]

60 Cf. Volfing 2001: 60-97.

The answer supposedly lies in that very imperfection which is inherent in female nature:

mich dunket des, daz sî dâran:
wirt ein wîp ze gote guot,
ir senftez herze, ir ringer muot
in einvaltigen sinnen
si enzundet schierer binnen,
daz ir gerunge begrîfet
die wîsheit diu von himel slîfet,
dan ein herter man tuo,
der ungelenke ist darzuo. (2844-2852)

[The answer seems to me to be as follows: if a woman comes to love God, her soft heart and weak spirit in a simple mind mean that she is ignited with an inner flame, and comes to fathom the wisdom which flows from heaven, more quickly than would a hard man, who is unaccustomed to this.]

This extract clearly illustrates the ambivalence with which male authors approached bridal mysticism. On the one hand, this form of piety constituted a valuable tool for harnessing the religious energies of women – and there was clearly a demand of texts written in this vein. On the other hand, however, Lamprecht manifests a characteristic desire to denigrate an area of spiritual expertise (*kunst*) in which appears biased in favour of women – or at least in favour of stereotypically female qualities – and which could potentially lead to a form of spirituality with no place for the traditional structures and hierarchies of organized religion.

This concern with preserving existing authoritative structures continues into the fifteenth century[61] and is made abundantly clear in a *Tochter Syon* treatise associated with the Dominican convent of Unterlinden in Colmar.[62] This text places a striking local twist on the narrative material by suggesting that the Daughter spends the rest of her life, post spiritual *connubium*, as a nun in Unterlinden. Furthermore, the story of the Daughter and her yearning for *connubium* is embedded within a longer treatise, where it is combined with other standard devotional allegories, as well as with more disparate elements. This treatise may be divided into five individual sections, of which all but section (iv) are in prose.

61 See footnote 28 above.

62 The treatise (edited by Rieder 1900: 80-90) occurs in a single manuscript, Basel, UB, cod. E III 13, 1r-6v. This entire manuscript is concerned with the Dominican reform movement; and the text is unlikely to have been composed/compiled before the reformation of Unterlinden in 1418. Cf. Schmidtke 1995: 958.

(i) A 'Tochter Syon' narrative, of which the beginning is missing.
(ii) A short account of the bridegroom's decision to place the Daughter in the convent of Unterlinden ("Gartenallegorie").[63]
(iii) The bridegroom's specifications for an ideal "inner" convent ("Herzkloster-allegorie").[64]
(iv) A poem, entitled *Nota recapitulacio*, in which a speaker reflects on the self-discipline which will be required of her in Unterlinden.
(v) A celebration of the value of liturgical song, addressed by an authoritative voice to the virgins of Unterlinden.

The treatise thus integrates the connubial allegory into a broader discussion of key elements of religious life, providing a framework within which private mystical experiences are validated, but nonetheless presented as subordinate to the upholding of monastic discipline and to the collective worship in the liturgy.

While section (v) covers the liturgy, and sections (iii)-(iv) focus explicitly on the importance of authority and discipline within a convent, even the *Tochter Syon* narrative in section (i) contains a few vital changes which help to accommodate this overall programme. For example, whereas Latin *Filia Syon* ends with a joyous descent into the wine-cellar, this version of *Tochter Syon* omits the wine-cellar, choosing instead to locate the encounter with the bridegroom in the garden. This change clearly facilitates the transition to the "Gartenallegorie" in section (ii), where the *hortus conclusus* (Cant 4:12) is identified both with the actual garden of the convent of Underlinden, and with the notional garden associated with the idealized "convent of the heart". Furthermore, given that according to the traditional exegesis of the Song of Songs, the garden generally represents communal religious life, while the wine-cellar stands for a greater level of privacy and of withdrawal from the community,[65] the focus on the garden rather than on the wine cellar has is entirely in keeping with the didactic programme of the overall treatise. Similarly, while at the end of the *Filia Syon*, only the Daughter enjoys *connubium*, this treatise extends the privilege of this experience to all her allegorical companions. These figures call out to the bridegroom in unison, using the phrase *veniat dilectus meus in hortum suum* [May my beloved enter into his garden] to invite him collectively into their garden and onto their bed.[66] In this work, therefore, even the moment of *connubium* is not entirely private, or unique to any one bride.[67]

63 For this motif, see Schmidtke 1982.
64 For this motif, see Bauer 1973.
65 Küsters 1985: 275.
66 Rieder 1900: 85. This phrase is a conflation of Cant 6:1 (*Dilectus meus descendit in hortum suum*) and Cant 7:11 (*Veni, dilecte me, egrediamur in agrum*).
67 In this respect, there are certain similarities with Mechthild's text, which (as discussed in Section I above) also operates with a multiplicity of brides. However, the fundamental difference is that while Mechthild's brides interact dialogically (each speaking with an

It might be argued that the treatise ultimately fails as a literary unit because the values which it promotes most strongly (i.e. those of the communal religious life and of the liturgy) stand in fundamental opposition to those of bridal mysticism. As Küsters notes, a certain devaluation of the individual is fundamental to the liturgy,[68] while bridal mysticism "zumindest punktuell ein Verlassen der gemeinschaftlichen Lebensordnung, ein Überschreiten der religiösen Standards, ein Aussetzen der obligaten asketischen Leistungen und nicht zuletzt ein Aussondern aus der liturgischen Öffenlichkeit [bedeutet]."[69] Nonetheless, despite the structural opposition between liturgy and bridal mysticism, the former can accommodate, and even nurture, the latter, offering "einen unbekannten Raum der 'inneren Jenseitigkeit', einer privaten Enklave inmitten der klösterlichen Öffenlichkeit".[70] In a well-balanced religious community (such as the one presented programmatically in section (iii)), bridal mysticism will not be a threat to the liturgy, but rather an avenue to it - it is, after all, the union with the bridegroom which brings about the Daughter's calling. Furthermore, in view of the collective use in section (i) of pre-formed biblical formulations (e.g. when the female figures all call out to the bridegroom), it would seem that this treatise ultimately goes some way towards stressing the elements which are in fact common to bridal mysticism and to liturgical practice. Both are, after all, structured religious experiences rooted in Scripture – and both require a deep level of conformity, whereby prescribed roles, and patterns of emotional response, are assimilated wholesale.

Like Brun von Schönebeck's *Das Hohe Lied*, the *Tochter Syon* narrative testifies to the almost boundless adaptability of the Song of Songs material in the medieval period. The hermeneutic methodology, coupled with the "quest for narrative" which characterized the exegetical stance of many twelfth century theologians, encouraged a highly permissive form of imaginative engagement with the text. Writers did not only respond to the text itself, but also to the exegetical traditions and narrative extrapolations which had grown up around it. Consequently, rather than being inhibited by the sacrosanct status of the word of God, vernacular writers saw the apparent liberties taken by the theologians, and went on to take even greater liberties themselves – be it in terms of historicizing the fantastical (Brun), or of subsuming an already highly diluted Song of Songs narrative into a pastoral treatise on convent life (Unterlinden version of the *Tochter Syon*). Just as the allegorization of the Song of Songs had paved the way for bridal mysticism, and hence for the potentially threatening spiritual empowerment of religious women, so the same

individual voice), the brides in this treatise speak with in unison, with one voice. It is precisely in its emphasis on orderliness and submissiveness within the communal religious life, this treatise diverges sharply from Mechthild's fundamental endorsement of an individualistic and subjective spirituality.

68 Küsters 1985: 214-215.

69 Küsters 1985: 325.

70 Küsters 1985: 284.

hermeneutic approach was highly conducive to the literary empowerment of vernacular authors – even of those whose literary objective was precisely to control and contain the "excesses" of bridal mysticism.

Bibliography

I. Primary Sources:

ALAN OF LILLE, Anticlaudianus. Texte critique avec une introduction et des tables, Textes philosophiques du moyen âge 1, ed. R. Bossuat, Paris 1955.
– De planctu Naturae, ed. N. Häring, Studi Medievali, Ser. 3, 19.2 1978: 797–879.
APULEIUS, Cupid and psyche (Apvlei Metamorphoseon Libri IV 28–VI 24), Cambridge Greek and Latin Classics: Imperial Library, ed. E. Kenney, Cambridge 1990.
AUGUSTINE, In Iohannis Evangelium Tractatus 124, Corpus Christianorum: Series Latina 36, ed. R. Willems, Turnhout 1954.
BERNARDUS SILVESTRIS, Cosmographia, Textus minores 53, Leiden 1978.
BERNHARD OF CLAIRVAUX, S. Bernardi opera, 8 vols., Editiones cistercienses, ed. J. Leclerq, H. Rochais and C. Talbot, Rome 1957-1977.
BIBLIA SACRA IUXTA VULGATAM CLEMENTINAM, Biblioteca de autores cristianos, ed. A. Colunga and L. Turrado, Madrid 1982.
BRUN VON SCHONEBECK, Das Hohe Lied, Bibliothek des Literarischen Vereins in Stuttgart 198, ed. A. Fischer, Tübingen 1893.
[PS.] CICERO, Ad C. Herennium de ratione dicendi (Rhetorica ad Herennium), Loeb Classical Library, ed. and transl. H. Caplan, London/ Cambridge/MA 1954.
DANTE, Le Opere di Dante, ed. M. Barbi et al., Firenze 1960.
HEINRICH VON MÜGELN, Die kleineren Dichtungen Heinrichs von Mügeln, Erste Abteilung, Die Spruchsammlung des Göttinger cod. Philos. 21, Deutsche Texte des Mittelalters 50-52, ed. K. Stackmann, Berlin 1959.
HONORIUS OF AUTUN, Expositio in Cantica canticorum, Patrologia Latina 172, 347-496.
ISIDORE OF SEVILLE, Isidori Etymologiarum Libri XX, ed. W.M. Lindsay, Oxford 1911 [reprinted 1985].
LAMPRECHT VON REGENSBURG, Sanct Francisken Leben und Tochter Syon, ed. K. Weinhold, Paderborn 1880.
MARTIANUS CAPELLA, De nuptiis Philologiae et Mercurii, ed. J. Willis, Leipzig 1983.
MECHTHILD VON MAGDEBURG, Das fließende Licht der Gottheit. Nach der Einsiedler Handschrift in kritischem Vergleich mit der gesamten Überlieferung, 2 vols., Münchener Texte und Untersuchungen zur deutsche Literatur des Mittelalters 100-101, ed. H. Neumann with G. Vollmann-Profe, München 1990-1993.
PHILIP OF HARVENGT, Commentaria in Cantica canticorum, Patrologia Latina 203, 181-490.
PRUDENTIUS, Works, 2 vols., Loeb Classical Library, ed. and transl. H. Thomson, London/Cambridge,MA 1949.
RUPERT OF DEUTZ, Commentaria in Canticum Canticorum de Incarnatione Domini, Corpus Christianorum: Continuatio Mediaevalis 26, ed. R. Haacke, Turnhout 1974.
THOMAS THE CISTERICIAN, Commentaria in Cantica canticorum, Patrologia Latina 206, 17-862.
DAS ST. TRUDPETER HOHELIED: eine Lehre der liebenden Gotteserkenntnis, Bibliothek des Mittelalters 10, ed. F. Ohly with N. Kleine, Frankfurt am Main 1998.
SEUSE, H.: Deutsche Schriften im Auftrag der württembergischen Kommission für Landesgeschichte, ed. by K. Bihlmeyer, Stuttgart 1907.

UNTERLINDEN VERSION OF THE TOCHTER SYON (Mystischer Traktat aus dem Kloster Unterlinden zu Colmar in Elsaß), ed. K. Rieder, Zeitschrift für hochdeutsche Mundarten 1 (1900), 80-90.
WILLIAM OF NEWBURGH, Explanatio sacri epithalamii in matrem sponsi, Spicilegium Friburgense 6, ed. J. Gorman, Fribourg 1960.
WILLIAM OF ST. THIERRY, Expositio super Cantica canticorum, Patrologia Latina 180, 473-546.
WILLIRAM VON EBERSBERG, Exposition in Cantica Canticorum und das Commentarium in Cantica Canticorum Haimas von Auxerre, ed. and translated by H. Lähnemann and M. Rupp, Berlin 2004.

II. Secondary Sources:

ALLEN, J.B. (1971): The Friar as Critic: Literary Attitudes in the Later Middle Ages, Nashville.
ASTELL, A. (1990): The Song of Songs in the Middle Ages, Ithaca.
BAUER, G. (1973): Claustrum animae. Untersuchungen zur Geschichte der Metapher vom Herzen als Kloster. Vol. 1: Entstehungsgeschichte, München.
BELL, D. (1977): The Commentary on the Song of Songs of Thomas the Cistercian and his conception of the Image of God, Cîteaux 28, 5-25.
BRINKMANN, H. (1980): Mittelalterliche Hermeneutik, Tübingen.
CURSCHMANN, M. (1988): 'Imagined Exegesis: Text and Picture in the Exegetical Works of Rupert of Deutz, Honorius Augustodunensis, and Gerhoch of Reichersberg', Traditio 44, 145-169.
COPELAND, R./MELVILLE, S. (1991): Allegory and Allegoresis, Rhetoric and Hermeneutics, Exemplaria 3, 159-187.
DICKE, G. (2003): Aus der Seele gesprochen. Zur Semantik und Pragmatik der Gottesdialoge im 'Fließenden Licht der Gottheit' Mechhilds von Magdeburg, in N. Henkel/M.H. Jones/N. F. Palmer (eds.), Dialoge. Sprachliche Kommunikation in und zwischen Texten im deutschen Mittelalter. Hamburger Colloquium 1999, Tübingen, 267-278.
DRONKE, P. (1975): Eine Theorie über fabula und imago im 12. Jahrhundert, in H. Fromm/W. Harms/U. Ruberg (eds.), Verbum et Signum. Beiträge zur mediävistischen Bedeutungsforschung, 2 vols., München, vol. 2, 161-176.
FLINT, V. (1974): The Commentaries of Honorius Augustodunensis on the Song of Songs, RBen 84, 196-211.
FREYTAG, H. (1982): Die Theorie der allegorischen Schriftdeutung und die Allegorie in deutschen Texten besonders des 11. und 12. Jahrhunderts, Bibliotheca Germanica 24, Bern.
FULTON, R. (1996): Mimetic Devotion, Marian Exegesis and the Historical Sense of the Song of Songs, Viator 27, 85-116.
– (1998): Quae est ista quae ascendit sicut aurora consurgens? The Song of Songs as the historia for the Office of the Assumption, Mediaeval Studies 69, 55-122.
– (2002): From Judgment to Passion. Devotion to Christ and the Virgin Mary, 800-1200, New York.
GÄRTNER, K. (1988): Das Hohelied in Frauenlobs Marienleich, Wolfram-Studien 10, 105-116.
GREEN, D. (1994): Medieval Listening and Reading: The Primary Reception of German Literature 800-1300, Cambridge.
GRÜNKORN, G. (1994): Die Fiktionalität des höfischen Romans um 1200, Philologische Studien und Quellen, Berlin.
HAAS, A. (1975): Die Struktur der mystischen Erfahrung nach Mechthild von Magdeburg, Freiburger Zeitschrift für Philosophie und Theologie 22, 3-34.

HAGENLOCHER, A. (1989): 'Littera Meretrix. Brun von Schönebeck und die Autorität der Schrift im Mittelalter', Zeitschrift für deutsches Altertum und deutsche Literatur 118, 131-163.

HASEBRINK, B. (2000): Spiegel und Spiegelung im 'Fließenden Licht der Gottheit', in: W. Haug/W. Schneider-Lastin (eds.), Deutsche Mystik im abendländischen Zusammenhang. Neu erschlossene Texte, neue methodische Ansätze, neue theoretische Konzepte. Kolloquium Kloster Fischengen 1998, Tübingen, 157-174.

HAUG, W. (1984): Das Gespräch mit dem unvergleichbaren Partner. Der mystische Dialog bei Mechthild von Magdeburg als Paradigma für eine personale Geschprächsstruktur, in: K. Stierle/R. Wanring (eds.), Das Gespräch, Poetik und Hermeneutik 11, München, 251-279.

HÜBNER, A. (1963): Das Hohe Lied des Brun von Schonebeck und seine Quelle, in: W. Simon/W. Bachofer/W. Dittmann (eds.), Festgabe für Ulrich Pretzel, Berlin, 43-54.

JEAUNEAU, E. (1964): Note sur l'École de Chartres, Studi Medievali 3rd ser. 5, 821-865.

KASTEN, I. (1995): Formen des Narrativen in Mechthilds Fließendem Licht der Gottheit, in C. Brinker et al. (eds.), Contemplata aliis tradere. Studien zum Verhältnis von Literatur und Spiritualität, Bern.

KELLER, H. (1993): Wort und Fleisch: Körperallegorien, mystische Spiritualität und Dichtung des St. Trudpeter Hoheliedes im Horizont der Inkarnation. Frankfurt a.M./New York.

– (1995): Von handfestem Gesit und durchsichtigem Fleisch: Impressionen aus der deutschsprachigen Hoheliedauslegung des 12. Jahrhunderts (St. Trudpeter Hohelied), in: P. Michel (ed.), Symbolik des menschlichen Leibes, Bern, 121-137.

– (2000): My Secret is Mine. Studies on Religion and Eros in the German Middle Ages, Leuven.

KNAPP, F.P. (1980): Historische Wahrheit und poetische Lüge. Die Gattungen weltlicher Epik und ihre theoretische Rechtfertigung im Hochmittelalter, Deutsche Vierteljahrsschrift für Literaturwissenschaft und Geistesgeschichte 54, 581-635.

KÖBELE, S. (1993): Bilder der unbegriffenen Wahrheit. Zur struktur mystischer Rede im Spannungsfeld von Latein und Volkssprache, Bibliotheca Germanica 30, Tübingen/Basel.

KÖPF, U. (1987): Hoheliedauslegung als Quelle einer Theologie der Mystik, in: M. Schmidt/D. Bauer (eds.), Grundfragen christlicher Mystik. Wissenschaftliche Studientagung Theologica mystica in Weingarten vom 7-10.11.1985, Mystik in Gegenwart und Geschichte 1.5, Stuttgart/Bad Cannstatt, 50-72.

KREWITT, U. (1971): Metapher und tropische Rede in der Auffassung des Mittelalters, Beihefte zum Mittellateinischen Jahrbuch 7, Ratingen.

KÜSTERS, U. (1985): Der verschlossene Garten. Volkssprachliche Hohelied-Auslegung und monastische Lebensform im 12. Jahrhundert, Düsseldorf.

LANGER, O. (1987): Mystische Erfahrung und spirituelle Theologie. Zu Meister Eckharts Auseinandersetzung mit der Frauenfrömmigkeit seiner Zeit, Münchener Texte und Untersuchungen 91, München.

LAUSBERG, H. (1960): Handbuch der literarischen Rhetorik. Eine Grundlegung der Literaturwissenschaft, 2 vols., München.

MATTER, E.A. (1990): The Voice of my Beloved. The Song of Songs in Western Medieval Christianity, Philadelphia.

MENHARDT, H. (1962): Die Mandragora im Millstätter Physiologus, bei Honorius Augustodunensis und im St. Trudpeter Hohenlied, in W. Schröder (ed.), Festschrift für Ludwig Wolff zum 70. Geburtstag, Neumünster, 173-194.

OCHSENBEIN, P. (1969): Das Compendium Anticlaudiani: Eine neu entdeckte Vorlage Heinrichs von Neustadt, Zeitschrift für deutsches Altertum und deutsche Literatur 98, 81-108.

OHLY, F. (1958): Hohelied-Studien. Grundzüge einer Geschichte der Hoheliedauslegung des Abendlandes bis zum 1200, Schriften der wissenschaftlichen Gesellschaft an der Johann

Wolfgang Goethe-Universität Frankfurt am Main. Geisteswissenschaftliche Reihe 1, Wiesbaden.
– (1958-59): Vom geistigen Sinn des Wortes im Mittelalter, Zeitschrift für deutsches Altertum und deutsche Literatur 89, 1-23.
PFANNMÜLLER, L. (1913): Frauenlobs Marienleich, Quellen und Forschungen zur Sprach- und Kulturgeschichte der germanischen Völker 120, Straßburg.
RIEDLINGER, H. (1958): Die Makellosigkeit der Kirche in den lateinischen Hohelied-kommentaren des Mittelalters, Münster.
RINGLER, S. (1980): Viten- und Offenbarungsliteratur in Frauenklöstern des Mittelalters. Quellen und Studien Münchener Texte und Untersuchungen 72, München.
RUH, K. (1990-99): Geschichte der abendländischen Mystik, 4 vols., München.
SCHIEWER, H.-J. (2000): Uslesen. Das Weiterwirken mystischer Gedankenguts im Kontext dominikanischer Frauengemeinschaften, in: W. Haug/W. Schneider-Lastin (eds.), Deutsche Mystik im abendländischen Zusammenhang. Neu erschlossene Texte, neue methodische Ansätze, neue theoretische Konzepte. Kolloquium Kloster Fischingen 1998, Tübingen, 581-603.
SCHMIDTKE, D. (1982): Studien zur dingallegorischen Erbauungsliteratur des Spätmittelalters. Am Beispiel der Gartenallegorie, Tübingen.
– (1995): Tochter Sion-Traktat, in: K. Ruh et al. (eds.), Verfasserlexikon, 2nd ed., vol. 9, 950-960.
SPITZ, H.-J. (1972): Die Metaphorik des geistigen Schriftsinns. Ein Beitrag zur allegorischen Bibelauslegung des ersten christlichen Jahrtausends, Münstersche Mittelalterschriften 12, München.
– (1986): 'Spiegel der Bräute Gottes'. Das Modell der vita activa und vita contemplativa als strukturierendes Prinzip im St. Tudpeter Hohen Lied, in: K. Ruh (ed.), Abendländische Mystik im Mittelalter. Symposion Kloster Engelberg 1984, Germanistische Symposien. Berichtsbände 7, Stuttgart.
STOLZ, M. (1996): Tum-Studien. Zur dichterischen Gestaltung im Marienpreis Heinrichs von Mügeln, Bibliotheca Germanica 36, Tübingen/Basel.
STÖRMER-CAYSA, U. (1998): Entrückte Welten. Einführung in die mittel-alterliche Mystik, Reclam-Bibliothek 1634, Leipzig.
SUERBAUM, S. (2003): Dialogische Identiätskonzeption bei Mechthild von Magdeburg, in: N. Henkel/M.H. Jones/N.F. Palmer (eds.), Dialoge. Sprachliche Kommunikation in und zwischen Texten im deutschen Mittelalter. Hamburger Colloquium 1999, Tübingen, 239-255.
VOLFING, A. (2001): John the Evangelist and Medieval German Writing: Imitating the Inimitable. Oxford.
– (2003a): Dialog und Brautmystik bei Mechthild von Magdeburg, in: N. Henkel/M.H. Jones/N.F. Palmer (eds.), Dialoge. Sprachliche Kom-munikation in und zwischen Texten im deutschen Mittelalter. Hamburger Colloquium 1999, Tübingen, 257-266.
– (2003b): The Song of Songs as Fiction: Brun von Schönebeck's 'Das Hohe Lied', in: W. Jones/W. Kelly/F. Shaw (eds.), 'Vir ingenio mirandus'. Studies Presented to John L. Flood, Göppingen, 137-154.
WACHINGER, B. (1992): Frauenlobs Cantica canticorum, in: W. Haug/B. Wachinger (eds.), Literatur, Artes und Philosophie, Fortuna Vitrea 7, Tübingen, 23-43.
WELLS, D.A. (1992): Die Allegorie als Interpretationsmittel mittelalterlicher Texte. Möglichkeiten und Grenzen, in W. Harms and K. Speckenbach with H. Vögel (eds.), Bildhafte Rede in Mittelalter und früher Neuzeit. Probleme ihrer Legitimation und ihrer Funktion, Tübingen, 1-24.
WILLIAMS-KRAPP, W. (1990): "Dise ding sint dennoch nit ware zeichen der heiligkeit." Zur Bewertung mystischer Erfahrungen im 15. Jahrhundert, Zeitschrift für Literatur-wissenschaft und Linguistik 80, 61-71.

WISNIEWSKI, R. (1995): Das Frühmittelhochdeutsche Hohe Lied – sog. St. Trudpeter Hohes Lied – Mit dem Text der Klosterneuburger Handschrift, Frankfurt a.M./Berlin.

WOLF, L. (1978): Brun von Schönebeck, in: K. Ruh et al., Verfasserlexikon, 2nd ed., vol. 1, 1056-1061.

ZERFASS, C. (1995): Die Allegorese zwischen Latinität und Volkssprache. Williams von Ebersberg "Expositio in cantica canticorum", Göppinger Arbeiten zur Germanistik 614, Göppingen.

Lieder der Liebe
Herders Hohelied-Interpretation

Ulrich Gaier

Herders kommentierte Übersetzung des *Hohenlieds* charakterisiert RUDOLF SMEND als „die wissenschaftsgeschichtlich bedeutendste Einzelschrift, *Lieder der Liebe*, in der Herder dem bis heute gültigen Verständnis des Hohenliedes die Bahn gebrochen hat" (FHA 5, 1323).[1] Der folgende Beitrag hat deshalb zunächst einen Blick auf das Deutungsproblem und die Deutungsgeschichte des *Hohenliedes* unter dem kritischen Blick Herders zu werfen und seine Befassung mit dem AT vom Sachlichen und von der Intention her zu charakterisieren, wie sie sich aus den Hauptschriften *Aelteste Urkunde, Lieder der Liebe* und *Vom Geist der Ebräischen Poesie* ableiten läßt. Dann ist auf die Übersetzung, vor allem auf Herders Verfahren der „Mentalübersetzung" und auf den vielsinnigen „bequemen" Begriff der Liebe einzugehen, die Herder erlauben, das *Hohelied* als ganzes und in seinen einzelnen Liedern literal zu lesen. Darauf aufbauend wird Herders zugleich historische, philosophische und mythisch-poetische Interpretation des *Hohenliedes*, seine Neubegründung des kanonischen Status für den Text und seine scharfe Unterscheidung von *interpretatio* und *applicatio* im hermeneutischen Prozeß herausgearbeitet, die ihm sozusagen eine „Mentalanwendung" des Textes ermöglicht.

Deutungsgeschichte in Herders Kritik

Das Hohelied wurde in vorchristlicher Zeit zu jüdischen Hochzeitsfeiern gesungen, nachdem es wahrscheinlich erst im 5./4. Jahrhundert v. Chr. gesammelt und mit der (wohl in salomonischer Zeit begonnenen, aber ebenfalls ins 5. Jahrhundert herabreichenden) Weisheitsliteratur dem fiktiven Verfasser Salomo zugeschrieben worden war. Herder läßt die Verfasserschaft bewußt offen; ob Salomo selbst, ob ein unbekannter „Verfasser oder

1 Mit der Sigle FHA ist die Ausgabe Herder 1985-2002 bezeichnet, in deren 3. Band S. 431-521 Herders Übersetzung, Kommentar und Abhandlung über das *Hohelied* abgedruckt ist. Auf meinen Kommentar dieses Textes ebd. S. 1199-1263 beziehe ich mich hier vor allem hinsichtlich der dort nachgewiesenen Sachinformationen.

Sammler" (FHA 3, 496), dem man den im Text genannten Ehrennamen des Bräutigams (Schelomo[2]) in Kontamination mit dem König Salomo gab, oder verschiedene Dichter im salomonischen Geiste – Herder will die Entscheidung über diese Frage nicht übernehmen; wichtig ist ihm allein, daß „dies Buch im größten Verstande *Salomonisch* [ist], ein *Abdruck* nämlich von dem *Geschmack*, von der *Liebe*, von der *Üppigkeit* und *Zier*, wie sie zu Salomons Zeiten, und sonst nimmer im hebräischen Volk lebten" (FHA 3, 492). Schon in der Verfasserfrage ist Herder damit auf der Linie der modernen Forschung.

In den ersten nachchristlichen Jahrhunderten kam die allegorische Deutung von der Liebe Gottes zur Synagoge auf, mit der der Text im Kanon der heiligen Schriften gesichert werden konnte; christliche Deuter schlossen sich an und interpretierten das Liebesverhältnis typologisch als Vorausdeutung auf die Liebe zwischen Christus und seiner Kirche. Der syrische Bischof Theodor von Mopsuestia (um 325-428), der in Kenntnis der orientalischen Hochzeitsbräuche den profanen Charakter der Lieder behauptet hatte, wurde unter anderem deshalb auf dem Konzil von Konstantinopel 553 als Ketzer verdammt. Herder benennt das Problem:

> Da der Wortverstand des Textes so klar ist und dieser doch nicht in die Bibel der genannten Leute [mit Hypothesen über Einheit und Heiligkeit des Textes] zu passen schien; so quälte man sich, so ersann man. Schon *Theodor* von *Mopsvest* ward auf einem Konzil verdammt, weil er einen Wortverstand dieses Buches annahm; unter Juden und Christen ward dieser bald verdrungen und statt dessen Allegorie und Mystik gefädelt (FHA 3, 487).

Grundsatz Herders ist: „Ich lese das Buch und finde in ihm selbst nicht den kleinsten Wink, nicht die mindeste Spur, daß ein *andrer* Sinn *Zweck des Buchs*, erster *Wortverstand* Salomos gewesen wäre" (FHA 3, 512). Dennoch lehnt er Deutungen als „gleichsam moralische oder poetische oder philosophische *Anwendungen*" mit einem „Meinetwegen!" (ebd.) keineswegs ab; „auch manche mystische Auslegungen des Hohenliedes durch Christen [...] enthalten ein Meer von Empfindungen, feinen Gedanken und lieblichen Gespinsten, davon die Seele des Auslegers voll war und sie doch irgendwo ausgießen wollte" (FHA 3, 514). Gemeint ist damit die sogenannte Brautmystik, mit der Bernhard von Clairvaux in den Liebenden des *Hohenliedes* Christus und die minnende Seele allegorisierte; Herder nennt in diesem Zusammenhang „Sarbievius, Jo. Angelus und viele andre, die einzelne Worte des Hohenliedes auf den Gegenstand, den sie in Gedanken hatten, *poetisch* ausgebildet haben" (FHA 3, 514). Sowohl der Jesuit Sarbievski (1595-1640) als auch Angelus Silesius (Johannes Scheffler, 1624-1677) haben Dichtungen über Motive aus dem *Hohenlied* geschrieben, in denen sie sich an die mystisch tropologische Deutungsweise der Brautmystik anschlossen. Als Anwendung läßt Herder all das gelten, hatte sich doch auch Luther trotz seiner Literallesung und

2 Schreiner 1981: 97f.

Ablehnung allegorischer Deutung (FHA 3, 515 A 52) „Trost über die Verwaltung des Regiments“ gesucht (FHA 3, 517), also eine Form der tropologischen Deutung angelegt, wie er auch in der Vorrede seines *Hohelied*-Kommentars rühmt, das Buch enthalte zum Leben nützliche Lehren und spende Trost (zitiert FHA 3, 517).

Läßt Herder alle diese Anwendungen mehr oder weniger gelten, solange sie nicht den Wortsinn verbiegen, hat er für die neueren und zeitgenössischen Deutungen nur Spott:

> In der neuern Zeit endlich, da der Scharfsinn so sehr emporkommt, ists beinah Mode geworden, daß jeder glückliche Ausleger auch eine eigne glückliche Hypothese habe. (FHA 3, 487)

Während er Bossuets Vermutung, es sei „ein Hochzeitslied Salomons in sieben Tagen“, nur referiert (FHA 3, 487), wohl weil ihm einerseits die Festlegung auf „Hochzeitslied“ nicht einleuchtet, weil ihm andererseits die „sieben Tage“ als Strukturprinzip näher lagen, wendet er sich voll Ekel und Spott von der Hypothese des früher so hoch verehrten Johann David Michaelis ab. Dieser hatte in einer kommentierenden Anmerkung zu seiner Ausgabe von Robert Lowths Werk *De sacra poesi Hebraeorum praelectiones academicae* (1753) die im Orient übliche Verkündung und Beglückwünschung zu der in der Hochzeitsnacht vollzogenen Entjungferung im *Hohenlied* vermißt und die Hochzeitslied-These abgelehnt:

> Er dichtete eine glücklichere Hypothese, von einem Eheliede voll orientalischer Liebesränke, intrigues d'amour, Eifersucht, Brunst, Zank, Begier nach einer Nacht, wie sie zwar nicht bei uns, in unsern leider! einpaarigen Ehen, aber desto mehr in jenen morgenländischen Harems stattfinde; und seine Verehrer nannten dies „die deutlichste, wahrscheinlichste Hypothese, die nur dem heutigen, berühmtesten deutschen Ausleger für dies dunkle Buch zu erfinden aufbehalten gewesen: eine Hypothese, die eine so wichtige moralische Absicht entdeckt, die niemand mit Grunde für eines biblischen Buchs unanständig halten könne (FHA 3, 487f.)[3]

Weil er einen Haremsroman in dem Buch sah, betrachtete Michaelis es nicht als kanonisch und schloß es aus seiner *Deutschen Übersetzung des Alten Testaments mit Anmerkungen für Ungelehrte* einfach aus. Einflußreich bis ins 19. Jahrhundert und hochgerühmt von Johann Theophil Lessing, dem Bruder des Dichters und Verfasser einer Hexameter-Übersetzung des *Hohenlieds* samt begleitenden Eklogen, war Johann Friedrich Jacobi mit folgender Roman-Hypothese: Schulammit, eine Schäferin und mit einem Schäfer verlobt, wurde wegen ihrer Schönheit mit Gewalt in den Harem des Königs Salomo entführt; sie wehrte aber die Versuche des lüsternen Königs, sie gefügig zu machen, so erfolgreich

3 Der zitierte Lobredner Michaelis' ist K.H. Runge in v. Pufendorf 1776: Vorrede.

ab, dass er sie endlich freilassen mußte. „Sie ist also ein Muster einer ehlichen Tugend und der Zufriedenheit mit einem niedrigen Stande.“[4]

Hier liegen also die zeitgenössischen Lesungen vor, die aufgrund der historischen Einordnung durch den Orientalisten Michaelis und seine Nachfolger Jacobi, Runge und Lessing einen profanen Charakter des Textes behaupten. Wichtig für die Einschätzung von Herders Leistung ist, daß sie nun mit ihren hinter den Text gestellten Romanen profane allegorische Lesungen vorschlagen, durch die beispielsweise der nur ein einziges Mal vorkommende Name Schulammit auf alle liebenden Mädchen des Textes aufgeprägt wird und sie damit als bestimmte Person mit bestimmtem Charakter zusammenfassend gedeutet werden.

Mit diesen profanen Lesungen geraten die Autoren allerdings in Begründungsschwierigkeiten bezüglich des kanonischen Status des *Hohenlieds*. Michaelis schließt den Text stillschweigend aus, Jacobi verspricht schon im Titel seines Buchs den Beweis, „daß selbiges für die Zeit Salomons und seiner Nachfolger sehr lehrreich und heilsam und eines heiligen Dichters würdig gewesen“; es ist also die tropologische Lesart, die Anwendung auf die persönliche Lebensführung, die wenigstens historisch behauptet werden kann und die Kanonisierung des Textes rechtfertigt; über die Heiligkeit für die Gegenwart ist damit nichts ausgesagt.

Solche „glücklichen Hypothesen“ seien es gewesen, die des stillen Liebhabers Herder Gang an die Öffentlichkeit provoziert hätten (FHA 3, 488). Wie gezeigt, stellt er sich gegen die gesamte allegorische und mystische Deutungstradition, sofern sie behauptet, die Absicht des Textes liege in der angenommenen Deutung; dagegen begrüßt er geistreiche Deutungen als Anwendungen des Grundtextes, dessen Wortlaut allerdings nicht dadurch angetastet werden dürfe. Rundweg lehnt er die zeitgenössischen Roman-Allegorien ab, die den Text in einen erzählbaren Zusammenhang bringen, die redenden Personen zu einheitlichen Charakteren mit bestimmten Schicksalen machen und den Text auf einen konsequenten Erzählakt zurückführen. Nein, für ihn sind es *Lieder der Liebe* im Plural, es ist das *canticum canticorum*, es sind einzelne Lieder mehrerer Autoren oder eines Autors zu verschiedenen Zeiten, gesammelt (FHA 3, 462, 464 u.ö.) unter dem Thema Liebe (FHA 3, 483) im salomonischen Geiste (FHA 3, 491), vielleicht ein „*Ausbund*, eine *Blumenlese*“ (FHA 3, 486) von Salomons eigenen Liedern – jedenfalls ist „das Siegel der *Seele Salomons* [...] *Einheit gnug* auf diesem Buche“ (FHA 3, 495). Auch mit dieser Liederthese hat Herder die Position des heutigen Verständnisses markiert.

4 Jacobi 1771: 14f.

Überblick über Herders Befassung mit dem AT

Wie kam Herder zu seinen selbständigen, die bisher geübte Interpretation des *Hohenlieds* überwindenden Auffassungen? Carl Redlich, Herausgeber von Herders *Liedern der Liebe* in der Suphanschen Werkausgabe, weist darauf hin, daß Herder ja im dritten Teil seiner Veröffentlichung eine Sammlung von Nachdichtungen des *Hohenlieds* aus einer spätmittelalterlichen Historienbibel veröffentlicht hat, wie er sich überhaupt um deutsche Übersetzungen von Willirams *Hohelied*-Paraphrase über Luther bis in seine Gegenwart bemüht hat. Redlich meint nun, Herders These vom Einzelstück-Charakter des Textes sei von diesen spätmittelalterlichen Minneliedern „abhängig“: „Von diesen 44 alten Liedern stehen nämlich 41 (es fehlen 13, 20 und 36) nach der Ordnung des Hohen Liedes gereiht im Text vor den Herderschen Nachbildungen.“[5] Die Annahme ist nicht plausibel, da es sich bei diesen mhd. Liedern um z.T. freie Paraphrasen einzelner Stellen des *Hohenlieds* handelt. Herder dagegen bringt eine fortlaufende Übersetzung, teilt sie jedoch in einzelne Lieder und „Szenen“ (FHA 3, 496) auf, die er mit seinem *commentarius perpetuus* voneinander trennt. Außerdem darf man nicht wie Redlich von „Nachbildungen“ sprechen, sondern von einer philologisch exakten Übersetzung, die oft bis in den Wortlaut hinein mit der heutigen Einheitsübersetzung übereinstimmt.

Es ist vielmehr Herders „anthropologische Archäologie“ in seiner Befassung mit dem AT, die seine Unabhängigkeit von der traditionellen Exegese seiner Zeit bedingt. Ausgangspunkt ist die Erkenntnis seines Lehrers Johann Georg Hamann: „Poesie ist die Muttersprache des menschlichen Geschlechts.“[6] Um diese Muttersprache zu erforschen und in seiner Gegenwart unter veränderten Voraussetzungen zu rekonstruieren, befaßte der junge Herder sich in den ihm zugänglichen Kulturen und Literaturen mit den ältesten greifbaren Zeugnissen, studierte die Ode, die einfachen Formen des Gesangs, sammelte Volkslieder, arbeitete jahrelang an einer „Archäologie des Morgenlandes“. Bei den alttestamentlichen Büchern kam ihm das von Michaelis kommentierte Werk Lowths *De sacra poesi Hebraeorum* entgegen, in dem sowohl der Gesichtspunkt der Poesie wie auch der Aspekt der Geschichtlichkeit und kulturhistorischen Einbettung dieser alten und nach damaligem Begriff ursprungsnahen Texte herausgestellt waren.

In der 2. Sammlung von Fragmenten *Über die neuere deutsche Literatur* (1767) versucht Herder den „Geist einer Nation“, nämlich der deutschen, „durch große Beispiele“ zu ändern (FHA 1, 276), und untersucht bei den „Deutsch-orientalischen Dichtern“, ob sie solche Vorbilder sein können. Klopstock mit seinen von der griechischen Tradition ins Orientalische ausgreifenden Oden und dem christlichen Epos *Messias* kommt am besten weg, weil er orientalische Dichtung gleich gar nicht nachzuahmen sucht:

---

5 Herder 1877-1913: 8, XIV.
6 Hamann 1968: 81.

> Elend nachahmen sollen wir also gar nicht, und ein *Hudemann* ist in seinem *Lucifer* und in seinem *Tode Abels* der Bemerkung und der Ärgernis unwürdig – aber wie können wir uns von solchen *Hudemanns* befreien? Wenn wir uns aufmuntern, morgenländische Gedichte, als Gedichte zu studieren, erklären zu lernen und bekannt zu machen. Unmöglich können wir sie übersetzen, und nachahmen, ehe wir sie verstehen, und die morgenländische Philologie, die in unserm Deutschlande seit einiger Zeit blühet, wird, wenn sie sich mit Geschmack vereinigt, schlechte und dumme Nachahmer zerstreuen (FHA 1, 292).

An Michaelis hält Herder sich mit seiner Argumentation, die orientalische Landschaft könne hier nicht sinnlich vergegenwärtigt werden, die Vaterlandsgeschichte, die Nationalvorurteile, die Mythologie, der Geist der Religion, die ganze poetische Sphäre, die Sprache seien grundverschieden und bedürften zunächst eines Übersetzers, „der zugleich Philosoph, Dichter und Philolog ist: er soll der Morgenstern einer neuen Epoche in unsrer Literatur sein!" (FHA 1, 293) Würde aber ein solcher Triceps[7] gefunden, so würden wir bald auf ein Buch hoffen können, das so hieße:

> Poetische Übersetzung der morgenländischen Gedichte; da diese aus dem Lande, der Geschichte, den Meinungen, der Religion, dem Zustande, den Sitten, und der Sprache ihrer Nation erklärt, und in das Genie unsrer Zeit, Denkart und Sprache verpflanzt werden (FHA 1, 292).

Damit zeichnet Herder sich den Weg seiner orientalischen Studien vor, insbesondere auch seiner Übersetzungen in allen dem AT gewidmeten Werken. Eine solche Übersetzung, fährt er fort, halte er für eine „Originalarbeit, die mehr Einfluß auf unsere Literatur haben kann, als zehn Originalwerke"; sollte sie auch nicht „wirklich neue Genies zu erwecken" das Glück haben, so werde sie durch die Erfahrung fremdkultureller Vollkommenheit den Modernen auf sich selbst zurückweisen:

> Siehe hier deine Natur, und Geschichte, deine Götzen und Welt, deine Denkart und Sprache: nach diesem bilde dich, um der Nachahmer dein selbst zu werden. Und willst du von einer der vorzüglichsten Nationen ihre Schätze nützen: siehe hieher! Ich suche dich mit der Kunst bekannt zu machen, wie sie Geschichte und Religion in Gedichte zu wandeln wußten; raube ihnen nicht das Erfundne, sondern die Kunst zu erfinden, zu erdichten, und einzukleiden! (FHA 1, 292f.)

Herder hat also kein theologisches oder exegetisches, sondern ein poetologisches und durch dieses hindurch anthropologisches Anliegen, mit dem er unmittelbar auf seine Zeit und Nation wirken möchte. Die ursprungsnahen Texte des AT sollen nicht durch ihre äußere Gestalt, ihren Bilderschmuck und ihre Inhalte auf die Gegenwart wirken; sie sollen als poetische Muttersprache des Menschengeschlechts im Modernen die Poiesis wecken, ihn „die Kunst zu erfinden, zu erdichten, und einzukleiden", ihn

7 Vgl. Gaier 1987.

„Geschichte und Religion in Gedichte zu wandeln" lehren und in dieser Rückführung auf die menschlichen Schaffenskräfte überhaupt ihn seine eigene kulturelle Denkart und Sprache poetisch ergreifen lassen.

Herders erste Bemühung galt danach seinem Projekt einer „Archäologie des Morgenlandes" mit einem im Manuskript überlieferten Text *Über die ersten Urkunden des menschlichen Geschlechts. Einige Anmerkungen* noch aus Riga Anfang 1769 (FHA 5, 9-178), in dem Gen 1-11 in großen Teilen übersetzt und vor allem bezüglich der Schöpfungsgeschichte Gen 1,1 bis 2,3 ausführlich besprochen und interpretiert wird. Er wendet sich gegen die „dogmatischen, mystisch-allegorischen, philosophischen, naturkundlichen, historischen und anderen Erklärungen, die allesamt den Sinn dieser ‚Urkunden' verfehlen", und „unternimmt hier zum ersten Mal in größerem Maßstab den Versuch, sich unter Beiseiteschiebung all jener Mißverständnisse in die frühe biblische Zeit zurückzuversetzen und ihre Dokumente unmittelbar, ‚sinnlich', ‚fühlend' zu begreifen. Das gelingt ihm um so besser, je mehr er diese Dokumente menschlich nimmt und sich damit von der orthodoxen Inspirationslehre entfernt."[8] Gen 1,1 bis 2,3 ist ihm „Gesang über die Gewohnheit [...]: 6 Tage sollt du arbeiten etc.".[9] Die Poiesis betrifft also die Strukturierung und Einteilung der Zeit im Gesamtablauf von sechs Werktagen und einem Ruhetag, in der inneren Struktur der sieben Tagwerke von Parallelismen 2/3 und 5/6, 1/4/7; diese Symmetrien und Parallelismen zeigen den von Lowth betonten Parallelismus der orientalischen „heiligen Poesie"; der Wechsel von einzelnstehenden Tagen 1, 4, 7 und einander parallel entgegengesetzten Tagen 2/3 und 5/6 erinnert an die „Zusammenordnung der Pindarischen Strophe, Antistrophe, und Epode" (FHA 5, 45) oder an die „Symbolischen Tänze der Alten Morgenländer", wo der Vortänzer und -sänger, der „Präsul mit dem ersten Stück anfängt, und die Chöre einander antworten: jener wieder einfällt, und diese antworten, bis er endlich beschließet – so siehet man eine Heilige Symbole, wie z. E. in späteren Zeiten Aegyptische Priester in ihrem Tanze die Bewegungen der Gestirne ausdruckten." (FHA 5, 48) Diese poetischen Strukturen inszenieren körperlich Grundformen des Denkens: Einheit und Mannigfaltigkeit, Wiederholung und Entgegensetzung, Analyse und Synthese, Anfang, Mitte und Ende, Ursprung und Ziel, entwickelnde Wiederaufnahme, Fortschreiten und Reflexion. Die Tageseinteilung läßt sich übertragen auf die Gliederung der Lebenszeit, auf die Geschichte der Schöpfung, die Rituale, die Verehrung und Nachahmung Gottes, die Grundordnung des gesellschaftlichen Lebens. Die „Heilige Symbole" kann später zur Darstellung kosmischer Zusammenhänge dienen, sie ist von Anfang an heiliger Schriftzug, Hieroglyphe (obwohl Herder diesbezüglich hier noch seine „Vermutungen" zurück hält), „lebendige Gedächtniskunst" (FHA 5, 48) der geordneten Aufbewahrung komplexer Zusammenhänge mittels

8 Smend in FHA 5, 1332f.

9 Herder 1977-1988: 1, 261.

Schematisierung und „Stäben der Erinnerung" (ebd.). Wie schon in den Fragmenten *Über die neuere deutsche Literatur* (vgl. Gaier in FHA 1, 1010-19) wendet er die Struktur zur Generierung und Gliederung seines eigenen Textes an (Smend in FHA 5, 1332) und belegt damit ihre Leistung als Gedankengenerator und Ordnungsprinzip nach dem göttlichen Vorbild der Schöpfung.

Die „zweite Urkunde" Gen 2,7-23 sieht Herder als spätere „Sammlung einzelner Nachrichten" (FHA 5, 27), die dritte Gen 2,25 bis 3,19 „Von der Schlangenverführung, von Veränderung des Gartenlebens und von dem Ursprunge der Menschlichen Mühseligkeit" (FHA 5, 90) reiche wieder in vormosaische Zeit zurück wie die erste. Wichtig für Herders Auffassung des Christentums ist, daß er gemäß diesem Titel die Vorgänge nicht als Sündenfall betrachtet, der den Menschen erlösungsbedürftig macht, vielmehr als ätiologischen Mythos zur Frage, wie der von Gott privilegiert geschaffene Mensch den Mühseligkeiten des Erdenlebens ausgesetzt wurde; mythisch rousseauistische Antwort: durch Ungehorsam, Vorwitz, „eitle Wissbegierde, durch eine unnatürliche Verfeinerung seiner Seelenkräfte, durch eine Überspannung seiner Einbildungskraft und Begierden – kurz! durch Übertreibung seiner Bedürfnisse und dadurch daß der Mensch aus seiner Natur hinausging – dadurch ward er elend." (FHA 5, 97) Schon im April 1768 hatte Herder gegenüber Hamann den „Baum der Erkenntnis Gutes u. Böses" so erklärt:

> Es ist das Risquo, das der Mensch auf sich nahm, außer seinen Schranken, sich zu erweitern, Erkenntnisse zu sammeln, fremde Früchte zu genießen, andern Geschöpfen nachzuahmen, die Vernunft zu erhöhen, und selbst ein Sammelplatz *aller* Instinkte, *aller* Fähigkeiten, *aller* Genußarten seyn zu wollen, zu seyn wie Gott (nicht mehr ein Thier) u. zu wißen p.[10]

Hier geschieht also nicht der Sündenfall, der den Menschen von Christi Erlösungstat abhängig macht, sondern der Ausgang des Menschen aus der Tierheit ins Menschsein mit dem Risiko aller Selbständigkeit und Verantwortung für sich selbst, das den Menschen vor den Tieren auszeichnet.

Herder arbeitete weiter an der Archäologie des Morgenlandes und veröffentlichte 1774/76 *Aelteste Urkunde des Menschengeschlechts*, wiederum bezogen auf Gen 1-6. Was er in den *Ersten Urkunden* noch zurückgestellt hatte, die Darlegung seiner „Vermutungen" über die Herkunft und Verbreitung der den Schöpfungsprozeß strukturierenden „Heiligen Symbole", wird hier ausgeführt: Die „Schöpfungshieroglyphe" ist in allen Kulturen des Orients grundlegend für Religion, Gesellschaftsordnung, Kunst, Schrift, kurz für die gesamte Kultur, und weist auf einen Ursprung im zentralasiatischen Hochgebirge. Diesem historischen Zugang wird hier die tägliche sinnliche

10 Herder 1977-1988: 1, 98. Das „p." am Zitatende = perge, und so weiter.

Erfahrung des Tagesanbruchs an die Seite gesetzt, dessen poetische Verbildlichung als Siebentagewerk Gen 1 darstellt. Ausgearbeitet wird die Hieroglyphe als „Denkbild“, als Anleitung zur Erfindung, Exploration und Ordnung von Gedanken zu einem gegebenen Thema mittels der schon in den *Ersten Urkunden* besprochenen Denkprozesse. Kant sprach in seiner Analyse von einer *methodus tabellaris*,[11] d.h. einer geregelten Findungs- und Ordnungskunst für Gedanken und Erkenntnisse; Herder strukturierte danach viele seiner Schriften aus dieser Zeit, sah vor allem aber für „*Dichter* und *Künstler* [...] das größte Ideal und Vorbild Eurer Kunst vom Himmel hinunter“ (FHA 5, 299), eine „höhere Dichtungslehre“ der Naturpoesie (FHA 5, 480). Dieser philosophische und poetologische Aspekt der Hieroglyphe, der schon in den *Ersten Urkunden* mit den Symmetrien, Parallelisierungen, Entgegensetzungen der Schöpfungstage beschrieben ist, rechtfertigt keineswegs Christoph Bultmanns Meinung: „die Hieroglyphenthese ist der Interpretation von Gen 1 nur aufgesetzt und hat keine zentrale Funktion für die Deutung von Schöpfung“.[12] In vielen Punkten unhaltbar, von der Altertumswissenschaft widerlegt und schon von Herder oft mit gewaltsamer Rhetorik behauptet sind allerdings die historischen Belege zur Omnipräsenz der Hieroglyphe, obwohl in vielen mediterranen Kulturen des Altertums die dreifach triadisch gegliederte Siebenzahl angewandt wird[13] und über die häufigen alt- und neutestamentlichen Verwendungen sich mit dem Juden- und Christentum verbreitet hat. – Die Sündenfallgeschichte begründet auch hier nicht die Erlösungsbedürftigkeit, sondern die Mühsale des Menschen; Christi Kommen gibt der Menschheit einen Impuls ins geistige Leben:

> Tod Adams, Gesetz und Sünde war also ein neben eingekommener eingemischter Sauerteig, daß durch das Hinzukommen einer neuen höhern Gnade höheres Leben, höheres Gute würde, als je durch Adams Selbststreben hätte werden können. Der Komet sank, bis er sich dicht an der Sonne, Kraft dieser, neu und höher aufschwang. (FHA 5, 610)

Die *Lieder der Liebe*, 1778 veröffentlicht, stellen sich durch historische Einbettung, philosophische (Schöpfungshieroglyphe) und anthropologische Analyse („Liebe“), endlich durch poetische Übersetzung in die Reihe der Arbeiten, die Herder in den *Fragmenten* dem Übersetzer als „Philosoph, Dichter und Philolog“ zur Aufgabe gemacht hatte, um dadurch auf die Denkart und Literatur seiner Zeit zu wirken. Wir gehen im folgenden darauf ein.

Vom Geist der Ebräischen Poesie (1782/83) will eine „Anleitung für die Liebhaber derselben und der ältesten Geschichte des menschlichen Geistes“ sein, wie der Untertitel verspricht. Auch hier geht Herder als Triceps vor, will in der Einleitung „das Poetische im Bau und Reichtum ihrer Sprache“, dann philosophisch „die *Urideen*, die sie von den ältesten Zeiten empfangen hatten“,

---

11 Hamann 1955-1979: 3, 81.

12 Bultmann 1999: 147.

13 Vgl. z.B. Roscher 1904.

„Drittens die *Geschichte ihrer Väter* bis auf ihren Gesetzgeber" beschreiben (FHA 5, 663); wieder geht er auf „dunkle oder mißdeutete Geschichten, des Paradieses, des Falls, des Turmbaus, des Kampfs mit Elohim" ein, um die hebräische Poesie verständlich zu machen. „Zweck meines Buchs" sind jedoch die Übersetzungen: „Sie sind die Sterne dieses sonst öden Raums: sie sind die Frucht und mein Buch nur Schale" (FHA 5, 666f.); hier sind es insbesondere die Psalmen, die er poetisch übersetzt und strukturiert, historisch einbettet und philosophisch analysiert. Die Begriffe *Poesie*, *Ebräisch* und *Geist* im Titel bezeichnen die dreifache Zugangsweise.

Auch in anderen theologischen Schriften geht Herder auf alttestamentliche Texte ein. Wie in den besprochenen Werken ist sein Anliegen gemäß dem zitierten Programm in den *Fragmenten* immer, auf der Basis der verfügbaren Informationen aus der Orientalistik ein Verständnis für die Texte zu erzeugen, das sie ohne allegorische oder mystische Deutungen „menschlich" zu lesen lehrt. Hat er ganz früh die „Einziehung der Philosophie auf Anthropologie" gefordert (FHA 1, 132), so könnte man hier von einer Einziehung der Theologie auf Anthropologie sprechen. Die Übersetzungen, historisch belehrt, philosophisch vielsagend und poetisch schön, dienen als Nachbildungen der poetischen „Muttersprache des menschlichen Geschlechts" zur Förderung einer in ihrem ganzheitlichen Sinne zu erneuernden Gegenwartsliteratur.

Lieder der Liebe: Übersetzung

Ansätze zur Übersetzung des *Hohenlieds* gibt es auf Einzelblättern von 1776 im Nachlaß Herders, ja, schon 1772 hatte er „den Hiob und das Hohelied Salomons" der Braut Caroline Flachsland versprochen, da sie an Volksballaden „in aller ihrer rohen Einfalt" Gefallen gefunden hatte.[14] Aus dem Jahr 1776 gibt es drei Fassungen, die erste und dritte vollständig;[15] die endgültige Fassung erschien in Leipzig 1778 und diente zugleich als Verlobungsgeschenk an Carolines Bruder Sigmund Flachsland. Der Titel *Lieder der Liebe. Die ältesten und schönsten aus dem Morgenlande* weist darauf hin, daß Herder den Text literal und „menschlich" lesen wird, daß er ihn als aus von einander unabhängigen Liedern zusammengestellt betrachtet, die durch ihr Alter und ihre besondere Schönheit ausgezeichnet sind, daß sie aber allgemein aus dem „Morgenlande" stammen und mithin dem König Salomo weder als Verfasser noch als Gegenstand notwendig zuzuschreiben sind. Allerdings überschreibt Herder sein erstes Kapitel „Salomons hohes Lied", was er im zweiten „Über den Inhalt, die Art und den Zweck dieses Buchs in der Bibel" im Sinne des „salomonischen" Geistes relativiert, in dem die Lieder geschrieben seien. Ein drittes Kapitel „Von Übersetzungen desselben,

14 Herder 1977-1988: 2, 154.
15 Dazu vgl. Irmscher 1963.

insonderheit Einer in alten Minneliedern" bespricht Willirams Hohelied-Paraphrase (um 1069), druckt 41 paraphrasierende Lieder über Stellen aus dem *Hohenlied* aus einer spätmittelalterlichen Historienbibel ab und gibt Hinweise auf einige Übersetzungen ins Lateinische und Deutsche, von denen nur Salomon Codomanns *Pervigilium Pacis* (Rothenburg/T. 1626) und Johann Theophil Lessing mit seinen Eklogen Lob erhalten. Unübertroffen ist für Herder immer noch Luthers Übersetzung:

> Man verzeihe also meine Kühnheit, mein Stammeln: es war mir um *Seele, Zweck, Geist des Buchs* zu tun in *jedem einzelnen Bilde und Liede.* Hat man diese gefasset, so gehe man zu Luthers Übersetzung; sie ist uns, trotz einzelner Fehler, noch immer unersetzt und unerreichbar an Süßigkeit und ungezwungener Einfalt, so wie an Stärke und Leben. (FHA 3, 490f.)

Herder legt seine Übersetzung so an, daß er immer, unabhängig von der Kapiteleinteilung, eine Textpassage im Zusammenhang übersetzt, die nach seiner Auffassung ein „Lied" ist, mit Sprecher und Adressat eine bestimmte „Szene" eröffnet, einen eigenen Kommunikationszusammenhang bildet. So ergeben sich vom Textanfang her folgende Einheiten als verschiedene Lieder: Cant 1,2-4; Cant 1,5-8; Cant 1,9-14; Cant 1,15-2,7, und so fort. Ans Ende jeder so konstituierten Liedeinheit schließt sich Herders fortlaufender Kommentar, in dem die „Szene", die Sprechsituation, der Status der Sprecher beschrieben, die Sprechakte verdeutlicht, Unbekanntes und Kulturfremdes in Fußnoten mit morgenländischen Realia erläutert werden. Das alles hat zum Ziel, den modernen Leser in die Sprech- und Kommunikationssituationen der fremden Kultur so weit einzuführen, daß sie ihm plausibel, verständlich und nachvollziehbar erscheinen, ohne jedoch ihre prinzipielle Andersheit zu verlieren:

> Könnet ihr euch einen Monarchen Orients denken, dem in seinem Garten der Liebe lieblicher geschmeichelt werde [als in Cant 1,2-4]. Statt Eifersucht und Neides, statt Zanks und Untreu, ist aller Stimme nur Eine Stimme, aller Gedanke und Herzen nur Ein Herz. (FHA 3, 435)

Eine Fußnote weist auf den Unterschied dieses Liedes aus dem Harem des Königs zu den üblichen „kläglichen" Berichten über den „Zustand der Weiber im Morgenlande" hin. Es geht Herder also darum, in seinem *commentarius perpetuus* durch Information, Rekonstruktion der Sprechakte und -situationen in seinem Leser ein Verstehen zu wecken, das nicht etwa in der für jede und insbesondere interkulturelle Hermeneutik fatalen Gadamerschen Horizontverschmelzung besteht, sondern das seine Fähigkeit zur Konstruktion und Rekonstruktion zwischenmenschlicher und kultureller Situationen überhaupt aktiviert. Er führt den Leser also in die *energeia* der Mitmenschlichkeit zurück, von der die Beziehungsformen der eigenen bzw. der salomonischen Kultur nur jeweilige *erga* sind – auch in der Schrift *Über den*

Ursprung der Sprache hatte er ja den Menschen als „*ein Geschöpf von Besonnenheit und Sprache, Besinnung und Sprachschaffung*" bezeichnet (FHA 1, 750).

Dieser schöpferische Raum von „Besonnenheit und Sprache", den die schaffenden Akte der Besinnung in jeweilige Sprachformen ausbuchstabieren, die auch ganz anders sein können, dieser Raum ist es auch, in den Herder mit dem Zusammenspiel von Übersetzung und laufendem Kommentar führt. In seinen *Alten Volksliedern* von 1774, also aus derselben Zeit, hatte Herder in einem Aufsatz „Wäre Shakespear unübersetzbar?" fingiert, von einem verstorbenen Freund „kleine Zettel – Anfänge, Zeilen, Lieder, Auftritte von einer *Übersetzung Shakespears*" geerbt zu haben:

> Wahrscheinlich sollt ich's nicht Übersetzung nennen: nur *hingeworfne Stellen* und *Zeilen*, die ihm vielleicht seine *Mentalübersetzung* des Dichters (doch immer *die beste*! und sie geschieht immer in *der Muttersprache*!) nur *erleichtern* sollten: vielleicht sonst nur kleine *einzelne Zwecke*, *Anbiegungen* und *Bereicherungen* unsrer Sprache: Versuche eines *Wettlaufs* auf *einige Schritte* mit dem allumfassendsten und alltönendsten Dichter (FHA 3, 26).

Mit dem Begriff der Mentalübersetzung deutet Herder in den vor der Entscheidung für einen bestimmten Wortlaut liegenden Raum, in dem dem Übersetzer viele Möglichkeiten mit ihren Bedeutungsnuancen gleichzeitig bewußt sind, die eigentlich alle gewahrt und nicht in einer Festlegung geopfert werden müßten. Die Mentalübersetzung entscheidet sich nicht, sie ist der Zustand der Sprache überhaupt, der freien schwebenden Besonnenheit, aus deren Besinnung der dann gewählte Sinn, das Gesprochene geschaffen wird. Walter Benjamin hat in seinem Aufsatz *Die Aufgabe des Übersetzers* argumentiert, etwa bei „Brot" und „pain" sei das Gemeinte dasselbe, die „Art des Meinens" widerstrebt sich in beiden Sprachen, jedoch ergänzt sie sich in den beiden Sprachen, denen sie entstammen. Und zwar ergänzt sich in ihnen die Art des Meinens zum Gemeinten. Bei den einzelnen, den unergänzten Sprachen nämlich ist ihr Gemeintes niemals in relativer Selbständigkeit anzutreffen, wie bei den einzelnen Wörtern oder Sätzen, sondern vielmehr in stetem Wandel begriffen, bis es aus der Harmonie all jener Arten des Meinens als die reine Sprache herauszutreten vermag. So lange bleibt es in den Sprachen verborgen. Wenn aber diese derart bis ans messianische Ende ihrer Geschichte wachsen, so ist es die Übersetzung, welche am ewigen Fortleben der Werke und am unendlichen Aufleben der Sprachen sich entzündet, immer von neuem die Probe auf jenes heilige Wachstum der Sprachen zu machen: wie weit ihr Verborgenes von der Offenbarung entfernt sei, wie gegenwärtig es im Wissen um diese Entfernung werden mag.[16]

Herders Mentalübersetzung in der Muttersprache kann als Rückführung einer Sprache in ihren Zustand der „reinen Sprache" gesehen werden, in der sich schon innerhalb der bestimmten Sprache, angeregt durch die

16 Benjamin 1972: 14.

fremdsprachliche Formulierung, alle möglichen Arten des Meinens einander ergänzend sammeln und der messianischen Totalität des Meinens zustreben, von der Benjamin spricht. Solche Mentalübersetzungen erzeugt Herder nun, indem er zwar die philologisch bestmögliche – und oft wörtlich die heutige Einheitsübersetzung vorwegnehmende – Formulierung wählt und in die übersetzten Liedverse setzt, aber in seinem Kommentar oft einen Schwarm anderer Möglichkeiten, ja sogar falsche, in der Geschichte der Übersetzung erwogene, zur Sprache bringt. So bietet der masoretische Text für Cant 1,7 wörtlich übersetzt „eine sich Lausende"; die *Septuaginta* führt ihn auf einen ähnlichen Wortstamm zurück und erhält die Bedeutung „eine sich Verhüllende", was allerdings nach Lessings[17] Bemerkung die Implikation der Hure mit sich führt. Herder wählt in seinem Text „eine Verhüllete" (FHA 3, 436), nimmt aber in seinen Kommentar andere Übersetzungsvarianten auf: „Sie schmachtet ihm nach, unbekannt und schamrot, lange wie eine Verlorene umirren zu müssen, nach ihm in fremden Gezelten zu fragen" (FHA 3, 437). „Schmachten" bringt Herder nach Albert Schultens' *Origines hebraeae* (einem hebr. etymologischen Wörterbuch); diese Lösung ist sprachlich nur bei Änderung des Wortstamms zulässig, aber Herder begleitet sie noch mit einer Anmerkung, die auf den schmachtenden, schwindenden Wortlaut des Originals hinweist. „Umherirren" hatte, die heute akzeptierte Lesung vorwegnehmend, der französische Theologe und Orientalist Samuel Bochart vorgeschlagen; die Schamröte der „Verlorenen" nimmt die Huren-Implikation der *Septuaginta* auf. Dieses Verfahren erzeugt im Leser den Zustand der Potentialität vieler Arten des Meinens, den wir beim Übersetzen vor der Entscheidung für eine Formulierung kennen, erzeugt also eine Mentalübersetzung auf dem Weg zur „reinen Sprache", in die anthropologische Möglichkeit des Meinens und Sprechens überhaupt sowie die Totalität des Meinens des jeweiligen Gegenstandes. Wir werden sehen, daß Herder auch hinsichtlich der Bedeutung des Textes auf eine Form der „Mentalanwendung" hinsteuert.

Schöpfungshieroglyphe im Text und im Begriff der Liebe

Der Text des *Hohenliedes* besteht nach Herders richtungsweisender Lesung aus Einzelliedern; deren Einheit ist zunächst der Geist Salomos und der großen Friedensperiode in der Geschichte des Volks Israel (FHA 33, 495).

> Offenbar aber hat der Verfasser oder Sammler noch einen feinen *Faden der Einheit* durchgewebt, über den ich mich, nicht weil Ich ihn finde, sondern weil er *wahr* und *lehrreich* ist, freue. Er verfolgt nämlich die *Liebe* von ihrem ersten *Keim*, von ihrer *zärtesten Knospe*,

17 Lessing 1777: 31.

durch alle *Stufen* und *Zustände ihres Wachstums*, ihrer *Blüte*, ihres *Gedeihens* bis zur reifen *Frucht* und neuen *Sprosse.* (FHA 3, 496)

Herder analysiert den Text in sieben „Szenen", davon sechs als das „Buch der Liebe" einer Generation (es handelt sich ja um verschiedene Paare) in den Stadien der Liebe vom ersten Kuß bis zur ehelichen Treue und dem „ewigen Bunde alter Freundschaft" (FHA 3, 498); die siebte Szene zeigt die nächste Generation, die dabei ist, wieder von vorn zu beginnen. Dabei weist Herder auf die Oppositionen und Parallelismen hin, die er in der Schöpfungshieroglyphe herausgearbeitet hat: Szene 2 Frühling der Liebe, begleitet von getrennten Arbeitsaufgaben der Liebenden, dagegen Szene 3 Vermählung; Szene 5 Tanz der Schönheit und Wollust, dagegen Szene 6 stille und ruhige Liebe ehelicher Treue. Parallel Szene 1 Unsicherheit und wachsende Gewißheit der Liebe, mit Szene 4 Verschwinden des Geliebten nach der Türsalbung, leidvolle Suche, Gewißheit. Parallel Szene 2 „er ist ihre Beute" mit Szene 5 „kriegerisch". Parallel Szene 3 Vermählung mit Szene 6 dem „ewigen Bunde alter Freundschaft". Parallel Szene 1 mit Szene 7 das Mädchen, das sich zur Beziehung mit einem Mann vorbereitet, gegen Widerstand parallel mit Szene 4.

> Dies wäre der Faden des Buchs, seinem Inhalt nach; doch bitte ich, daß er nicht zum Ankerseil gemacht und eine scholastische Metaphysik der Liebe daran gereihet werde. Die einzelnen Stücke müssen ihr individuelles Leben behalten; dies ist nur Fassung vieler Perlen an Einer Schnur; das *Lied der Lieder* (FHA 3, 499).

Eine begriffliche Schöpfungshieroglyphe baut Herder in seiner Entwicklung des Begriffs „Liebe" auf. „Was sagt das Buch vom Anfang bis zum Ende? Mich dünkt: Liebe, Liebe."

> Es ist fast keine Situation und Wendung, keine Tages- und Jahrszeit, keine Abwechslung und Einkleidung, die nicht in diesem Liede, wenigstens als Knospe und Keim, vorkäme. Die Liebes des Mannes und Weibes, Jünglinges und Mädchens, vom ersten Kuß und Seufzer bis zur reifen ehelichen Treue – alles findet hier Ort und Stelle. [...] Palast und Hütte, Garte und Feld, Gassen der Stadt und Einöde, Armut und Reichtum, Tanz und Kriegszug, alles ist erschöpft, alles gefühlt und genossen (FHA 3, 484).

Dieser erste Begriff der Liebe betrifft die Ausschöpfung der anthropologischen Totalität von Beziehungsformen zwischen Mann und Frau. Herder hat in diesen Jahren seine Sammlung der *Volkslieder* (1778/79) mit Texten aus aller Welt unter demselben Gesichtspunkt angelegt, fundamentale menschliche Situationen und Beziehungsformen in poetischen Gestalten sich aussprechen zu lassen und sie nach der Schöpfungshieroglyphe zu ordnen (FHA 3, 918-925): Thema ist der Mensch, sofern er sich in seinen Verhältnissen gegeben und aufgegeben ist. Was dort jeweils nur angedeutet und durch einige

Beispiele veranschaulicht werden kann, ist hier an dem eingeschränkten Thema „Liebe" erschöpfend dargestellt.

Dieser erste, anthropologisch allgemeine Begriff wird nun auf den historischen eingeschränkt: „Dazu kommt nun, daß nichts so *verschieden ist, als Morgenlands Poesie, Sprache und Liebe gegen die unsre.*" (FHA 3, 489)

> Der Inhalt des Buchs also, Liebe und orientalische Liebe *aus denen Zeiten*, macht alles am schwersten. Wenn sich der Europäer im Punkte der Weiber recht bescheiden dünkt, wird er dem Morgenländer oft unerträglich; und wenn dieser sich über sie mit Manneswürde, und der freien offenen Einfalt ausdruckt, die allein Unschuld ist, so jucken unsre Ohren; unser *Geschmack* ist beleidigt, wir wollen *Zweideutigkeiten* und *Krebillonsche Hüllen* (FHA 3, 490).

Die historische Differenz wird, wie Nationaleigentümlichkeiten überhaupt, drittens da überwunden, wo ein Moment der Humanität gelingt und als ein zwar nationalkulturell entstandenes, aber der ganzen Menschheit als Denkmal ihrer gelösten Aufgabe des Menschseins aufgestelltes Ideal erscheint: die Salomonische Periode. „Seit Vater Adam sein Hohelied der Liebe im Paradiese sang, wenn und wo konnte diese zarte Blume des Friedens und der Ruhe so gedeihen, als in diesem Salomonischen Tale des Friedens?" (FHA 3, 492) Die Differenzen unter den Menschen schwinden in der „Salomonischen Liebe", zunächst in der innerkulturellen Beziehung, wo die Liebenden aus dem/der Geliebten den *„Nachklang* [...] *ihrer eignen Seele*" hören, denn nichts verschwistert, nichts verbindet so sehr, als Liebe. Sie gibt und nimmt, bis sie nichts mehr zu geben oder zu nehmen hat, bis sie Eins ist. Sie ist der Stimmhammer der Herzen zum Einklange: man bildet und wird gebildet, hört und singt nach. (FHA 3, 491)

Salomonische Liebe zieht mit der Königin von Saba Fremdes an und überwindet damit auch kulturelle Differenzen; sie tönt aus den Weisheitsbüchern: Der durch die Schöpfungshieroglyphe gestiftete „Faden der Einheit" (FHA 3, 496) des durch das „Siegel der Seele Salomons" geeinten Buches (FHA 3, 495) führt, wie gezeigt, zum modellhaften Gang durch die Stationen der Liebe und führt damit historisch Individuelles in der Salomonischen Liebe und anthropologisch Allgemeines in dem natürlichen Entwicklungsgang aller Liebesbeziehungen zusammen. Die Begriffe 1-3 sind einander also wie anthropologische Totalität, historische Individualität und ideal-historische Modellhaftigkeit zugeordnet; die Gegensätze verbinden sich durch den von Salomo und seiner Periode geleisteten Moment gelungener Menschheit.

Der vierte Begriff ist Liebe als Grund aller „Menschenglückseligkeit" und göttlicher Segen „fühlender Geschöpfe: er segnete damit Pflanze und Baum, Tier und Menschen"; „Liebe ists, die sich über alles Schöne und Gute freuet, die es zu sich, sich zu ihm stimmet, zur *Harmonie*, dem Kinde des Himmels, dem mannichfaltigen *Einklange in aller Schöpfung.*" (FHA 3, 504f.) Diese Liebe als alldurchwaltendes biologisches Band der Natur ist Heuchlern und Bigotten ein

Ärgernis; das *Hohelied* als Lebensform natürlicher Beziehung könnte „Arznei für unser krankes Jahrhundert" werden (FHA 3, 506). Durch diesen und in diesem Naturbegriff der Liebe sind die Liebesbegriffe der ersten Triade aufgehoben.

Fünfter Begriff: „Liebe ist die größte *Weisheit*, und die größeste Weisheit selbst im ernsten Sinne des Predigerbuchs ist und bleibt *Liebe*." (FHA 3, 508) Auf Liebe gegründet, kann die Herrscherqualität der Weisheit ihr Reich immer weiter über Menschen und Natur ausbreiten.

Sechster Begriff, zunächst negativ: Salomo der weiseste der Weisen „vergaß zuletzt seine Kinderweisheit, die Furcht des Herrn" und suchte „fremde Götter". „Der *weiseste* König, und wird zuletzt der größeste Tor durch Weiber." „Der zu zärtliche König wird durch seine Weiber, der zuletzt aberweise König durch einen unweisen Sohn bestraft." (FHA 3, 509f.) Das Unmaß der natürlichen Liebe und die Überspitzung der weltlichen Herrscherweisheit bringt die „Waage der Wiedervergeltung" (FHA 3, 510), die Nemesis und Adrastea des späteren Herder, rächend ins Spiel, die die Weisheit Gottes als Prinzip des kosmischen Reichs eingesetzt hat. Deshalb heißt es:

> O Liebe, die Christus lehrte und ausgoß, Liebe, die Johannes in seinem Glanz bis in jene Welt hinüber malet, wie anders bist du! Eine nie versiegende Aurora; scheint sie hier unterzugehen, so geht sie mit höhern Farben in einer ewigen Welt auf! (FHA 3, 510)

In den Weltprinzipien der Liebe und der Weisheit erscheinen hier, gereinigt von den törichten irdischen Exzessen, die ewigen Prinzipien des Reiches Gottes; so bildet dieser sechste Begriff wieder eine Synthese aus dem vierten und fünften Begriff der Liebe.

Am Schluß fügt Herder, um nicht den Eindruck zu erwecken, er klebe allein am Wortverstand, eine Rechtfertigung „von dem *kirchlichen Gebrauche* dieses Buchs und seiner gewöhnlichen *Anwendung* so viele Jahrhunderte her" an (FHA 3, 516): Kirche als Braut Christi.

> Überhaupt ist *Kirche, Staat, Ehe*, und die einzelne *Menschheit*, wie sie in allen dreien gepflegt oder gemißhandelt wird, Ein Ding; überall ohne Gott nichts, und überall, aufs zärteste betrachtet, *Braut* Gottes an der Hand Jesu Christi: ein *Siegel auf seinem Arm*, ein *Gepräge auf seinem Herzen*. [...] Die allgemeinen Bande dieser Einrichtungen, die *lebendige Bauart* dieser nur verschieden *genannten* Gebäude ist also Eins; und der Geist derselben ist Ein Geist – Liebe (FHA 3, 518f.).

Dies ist ein siebter Begriff der Liebe, in dem nun die Liebesbegriffe der beiden Triaden synthetisch zusammengeführt werden: Liebe in menschlichen Beziehungen, Liebe als Reichs- und Ewigkeitsprinzip manifestieren sich in menschlichen Einrichtungen und deren „lebendiger Bauart" nach dem Muster des Reiches Gottes, wo nicht nur das Ganze, sondern auch „die einzelne Menschheit [...] gepflegt" wird. Herder hat damit eine Schöpfungshieroglyphe zu dem Begriff Liebe in der Interpretation des *Hohenliedes* entwickelt, die in drei

Triaden von Polarität und Steigerung, Entgegensetzung und Verbindung, Naturgegebenheit und geistig-geistlicher Aufstufung alle Aspekte der Liebe auseinander entwickelt und im Abbild eines Reichs Gottes in menschlichen Einrichtungen sich verwirklichen läßt. Man wirft Herder gern unscharfen Begriffsgebrauch vor; an diesem Beispiel wird sichtbar, warum seine Zentralbegriffe so vielsinnig anwendbar sind und welcher innere Zusammenhang in diesen oberflächlich gleichlautenden Anwendungen herrscht, kurz: welche Begriffsarbeit darin steckt, wenn auch nicht die definitorisch sondernde der Logik, sondern die organisch nach der Schöpfungshieroglyphe entfaltende, steigernde und anreichernde der Systematologie, wie Herder sie nach Johann Heinrich Lamberts Vorgang ausbaut.[18] Darin wendet er die *methodus tabellaris* der Schöpfungshieroglyphe für die Entwicklung „bequemer" (vgl. FHA 4, 714)[19] Begriffe an, erstmals in der Schrift *Über den Ursprung der Sprache*, wo er statt *des* Ursprungs sechs Ursprünge und deren Verwirklichung in der Geschichte entfaltet.[20] Begriffe wie Ursprung, Kraft, Liebe, Humanität nennt Herder deshalb bequem, weil sie mit der inneren Entfaltung ihrer Bedeutungen von der materialen bis in psychische, geistige, geistliche Anwendungen brauchbar sind und Konjekturen über analoge Verhältnisse in den verschiedensten Disziplinen erlauben. Auf diese Weise werden wie hier beim Begriff Liebe von der Biologie, Kulturgeschichte, Anthropologie und Geschichtsphilosophie über Kosmologie, Theologie, Ethik und Soziologie alle Disziplinen berührt und aufeinander bezogen; ein universeller Zusammenhang als großer, *in praxi* zu lebender und zu erprobender Ideenentwurf konzentriert sich in dem Begriff „Liebe".

interpretatio und applicatio

Ein wahrhaft fürstliches Verlobungsgeschenk! Zugleich aber auch Herders moderne Rechtfertigung für den Platz des *Hohenliedes* in der Bibel. Denn wir sahen, daß schon mit der Näherung an die literale Lesung bei Michaelis, Jacobi, Lessing die Frage nach der Kanonizität des Buches aufkam, von Michaelis durch Ausschluß vom Kanon, von Jacobi und Lessing durch einen Roman von der gegen den lüsternen König sieghaft behaupteten Unschuld vom Lande und mithin eine tropologische Lesung beantwortet wurde. Herder fand nichts außer „Wortverstand" im Text: „Ich ging nochmals zum Buche, zu sehen, was da war, und zog die ältesten und neuesten Ausleger zu Rat, nur keiner war mir lieber als der von allen beleidigte klare *Wortverstand*, der Ausleger aller Ausleger." (FHA 3, 489) Es ist und bleibt für Herder eine nach dem besprochenen „Faden der Einheit", dem natürlichen Stufengang der

18 Vgl. Gaier 1998.
19 Zur Auseinandersetzung mit Kant darüber vgl. Gaier 1994.
20 Gaier 1988.

Liebesbeziehung unter Menschen arrangierte Sammlung von Einzelliedern möglicherweise verschiedener Verfasser, die durch „das Siegel der Seele Salomons" (FHA 3, 495), den Friedensgeist der salomonischen Periode in der Geschichte Israels zusammengehalten sind. Deshalb muß er sich der Frage stellen: „Aber warum steht denn das Lied *in der Bibel*? Ich kann nicht anders antworten, als, warum steht *Salomo* in der Bibel und warum war er, der er war?" (FHA 3, 501) Es ist also zunächst die Figur Salomos, die den kanonischen Ort des *Hohelieds* begründet:

> In der Natur spricht Gott nicht vom Holzkatheder zu uns und so wollte er auch nicht in der Schrift zu uns sprechen; sondern durch Geschichte, durch Erfahrung, durch Führung Eines Volks, dem ganzen Menschengeschlecht zum Vorbilde. (FHA 3, 501).

Deshalb müssen die „Hauptpersonen" auf dem Weg des göttlichen Ratschlusses „festgestellt" und „entwickelt" werden:

> Hier stehen sie als Sterne in dem himmlischen Bilderkreise, der die Erde umschlinget und der, wenn hienieden Alles wie Staub und Nebel, Trümmer und Ameisen, aufwallet und hinsinkt, *stehet* und *bleibt*, uns Zenit und Nadir, Zeichen, Zeiten und festen Standpunkt verleihet. In dem Kreise stehet auch Salomon mit seinen *Tugenden* und *Fehlern;* was ihn also *ins Licht setzt, bestimmt*, wie ihn die Bibel bestimmt haben will, das ist *Urkunde seiner, Belag* zu *seinem Leben*, sein *Wort* und *Tat* (FHA 3, 502).

Die Lehrmethode der Bibel ist, an Schicksalen oder wie hier Schriften „historisch und charakteristisch" bestimmter Personen (FHA 3, 503) unverrückbare Maßstäbe und Orientierungen, Anschauungen gesetzmäßiger Schicksalsabläufe im Leben als „Sternbilder" an den Himmel zu setzen – es sind die fundamentalen Mythen der Menschheit; in den *Humanitätsbriefen* werden auch die griechischen Heroen und Götter als „Himmel glänzender Sternbilder", „anschauliche *Kategorien der Menschheit*", „*Ideal der Menschenbildung in ihren reinsten Formen*" gedeutet (FHA 7, 364f.). Im Zusammenhang unter den drei salomonischen Schriften, die einander gegenseitig beleuchten, im Zusammenhang mit Salomos unwürdigem Ende erhält das *Hohelied* eine „lehrreiche Stelle [...] in der Bibel":

> Es ist ein notwendiger *Belag zu seinem Leben*, eine *Beurkundung* des *Segens*, den *ihm Gott versprach*, ein *Schlüssel zu seinen übrigen Schriften*, zusamt *seiner Denkart und dem sonderbaren Schicksal seines Alters und Ausgangs*. Unter den Büchern des alten Testaments ists eine Rosen- und Myrtenlaube im Tale des Frühlings rings umher voll schöner Aussicht auf alle Seiten der Menschheit (FHA 3, 512).

Zu diesem mythisch modellhaften Sternbild, im Rahmen dessen die Lieder als authentische Belege zur Charakterisierung Salomos literal zu lesen sind (vgl. oben den 3. Begriff der „Liebe"), tritt nun zweitens im Text selbst der als Denkbild nach der Schöpfungshieroglyphe gestaltete naturpoetische Gang der Liebesbeziehung unter Menschen, der zugleich den in seiner Universalität heiligen Begriff der Liebe modellhaft veranschaulicht, welchen Herder hier ebenfalls mittels der Schöpfungshieroglyphe entwickelt und strukturiert. Historische Bestimmtheit, philosophische Universalität, vermittelt durch mythisch-poetische Modellhaftigkeit, das sind die drei Zugänge des philologischen Historikers, des Philosophen und des Dichters, die die literale Lesung des *Hohenliedes* rechtfertigen. Diese Kriterien gelten auch für die anderen biblischen Bücher und begründen mithin den Kanon neu, wir haben ihre Anwendung in den anderen alttestamentlichen Schriften erkannt und bis in die Programmatik der *Fragmente* von 1767 zurückverfolgt.

Nun ist zwar Herder der erste, der in aller Strenge die literale Lesung verlangt und mit drei guten Begründungen dennoch die Stelle des *Hohenliedes* im Kanon der alttestamentlichen Bücher behauptet. Aber: „Mich dünkt, man antwortet mir: ‚wohl! aber könnte das Buch nicht *noch mehr* bedeuten? sollte nicht noch ein *andrer Sinn*, ein *tieferer* Verstand *dahinter* sein?' Meinetwegen!" (FHA 3, 512) Wie zitiert, legt er dar, daß er im Text keine Spur von Allegorisierung gefunden hat; in den Angeboten „*neuen* Sinnes" betont er die Subjektivität:

> Er trägt immer die Gestalt seines Vaters, des Erfinders: fühlte der fein, so ist auch die Seide des Märchens fein, die er aus Salomo spinnet; ist er grob, so kommt auch so ein dickhäutiges Schiffseil von Allegorik heraus, daß dem Leser die Nerven zittern. (FHA 3, 513)

Nach der Aufzählung einiger rabbinischer Allegorien sagt er: „Sie sind gleichsam moralische oder poetische oder philosophische *Anwendungen*, wie die jüdische Auslegungskunst liebt und in feinen Gesetzen bestimmt: den natürlichen Wortsinn aber müssen sie weder ersetzen noch verdrängen wollen, sonst sind sie verführend" (FHA 3, 514). Auch christlich mystische Auslegungen sind „abgeleitetes, tausendfach versetztes Wasser, nicht die klare *Quelle* des Ursprungs" (FHA 3, 514). Herder unterscheidet also scharf zwischen ursprünglichem Wortsinn und vielen möglichen Anwendungen:

> Jedermann aber siehet, daß diese unendlichen, so augenblicklichen, so unbestimmbaren *Anwendungen* den Ersten *Wortverstand* nicht aufheben, sondern *voraussetzen, bestätigen* und gleichsam *bewähren*. (FHA 3, 516)

Auch für Herders eigene Anwendung auf Kirche, Staat, Ehe als Braut Christi gilt: „nie vergesse mans, daß es *Anwendung* sei, nicht ursprüngliche Absicht, sonst wird *Eine* Anwendung die andre hassen und verfolgen, da sie doch alle, und unzähliche ihrer, Schwestern untereinander und Töchter *Eines Wortsinnes*, des Textes der Liebe, sein und bleiben." (FHA 3, 519) Was diese Anwendungen möglich macht, ist die mythisch-poetische Modellhaftigkeit des Textes, der sich auf unabsehbare Weise konkretisieren läßt, und die poetische Gestalt der Lieder und der Sammlung:

> Man sieht leicht, daß in einer so zarten Sprache des Herzens, bei den so abwechselnden Gestalten und Szenen aller Menschenschöne, Liebe und Freude, Raum für die Empfindungen einer ganzen Welt ist. (FHA 3, 514)

Hat Herder bei der Übersetzung im Leser die Mentalübersetzung mit einem Schwarm von möglichen Ausdrücken um die gewählte Formulierung herum zu erzeugen gesucht und ist so mit ihm in den Raum der reinen Sprache vorgedrungen, so findet sich dieselbe Struktur bei der Auslegung des Textes: um den einfachen Wortverstand herum eine unabsehbare Schar möglicher Anwendungen, die den Wortsinn „*voraussetzen, bestätigen* und gleichsam *bewähren*". Wenn jede dieser Anwendungen individuell geprägt ist und sich den Text aneignet, wie „jede Speise, die wir genießen wollen, verdaut, in unsern Saft verwandelt werden und also gewisser Maße ihre Natur verlieren *muß*" (FHA 3, 516), wenn Herder sie sich und seinem Leser am Ende vorführt und vergegenwärtigt, befindet er sich, komplementär zur reinen Sprache als dem Ursprung, nun auf dem Weg zur „reinen Bedeutung" des Textes, der gegenüber der „Wortverstand" ebenso, wenn auch privilegiert, als kulturspezifische und individuelle Auslegung erscheinen muß. Es ist also sinnvoll, Herders „Mentalübersetzung" auch eine „Mentalauslegung" zuzuordnen.

Rudolf Smend hat Herders *Lieder der Liebe* in einem Vortrag als „Juwel" unter Herders alttestamentlichen Schriften bezeichnet. Vielleicht ist es gelungen, hier einige Facetten dieses Textes aufblitzen zu lassen, von dem er selbst am 29.12.1778 an Hamann schrieb:

> Das Hohelied ist nicht der Rede wert; nur durch die Heurath meines Schwagers, der aber noch nichts davon weiß und durch das Zureden meiner Frauen, weil es seit 4. Jahren dalag, erpresst, u. weiß übrigens nicht, woher es kommt und wohin es gehet?[21]

Bibliographie

BENJAMIN, W. (1972): Gesammelte Werke, Bd. IV/1, Frankfurt a.M.

BULTMANN, C. (1999): Die Biblische Urgeschichte in der Aufklärung. Johann Gottfried Herders Interpretation der Genesis als Antwort auf die Religionskritik David Humes, BHTh 110, Tübingen.

GAIER, U. (1987): Poesie als Metatheorie. Zeichenbegriffe des frühen Herder, in: G. Sauder (Hg.), Johann Gottfried Herder 1784-1803, Hamburg, 202-224.

– (1988): Herders Sprachphilosophie und Erkenntniskritik, Stuttgart/Bad Cannstatt.

– (1994): Poesie oder Geschichtsphilosophie? Herders erkenntnistheoretische Antwort auf Kant, in: M. Bollacher (Hg.), Johann Gottfried Herder. Geschichte und Kultur, Würzburg, 1-17.

– (1998): Herders Systemtheorie, AZP 23, 3-17.

HAMANN, J.G. (1955-1979): Briefwechsel, hg. v. W. Ziesemer und A. Henkel, Wiesbaden.

– (1968): Sokratische Denkwürdigkeiten. Aesthetica in nuce, hg. v. S.-A. Jørgensen, Stuttgart.

21 Herder 1977-1988: 4,76.

HERDER, J.G. (1877-1913): Sämmtliche Werke, hg. v. B. Suphan, Berlin.
– (1977-1988): Briefe, Gesamtausgabe 1763–1803, bearb. v. W. Dobbek/G. Arnold, 9 Bde, Weimar.
– (1985-2002): Werke in zehn Bänden, hg. v. G. Arnold u.a., Frankfurt a.M.
IRMSCHER, H.D. (1963): Probleme der Herder-Forschung I., Deutsche Vierteljahrsschrift für Literaturwissenschaft und Geistesgeschichte 37, 266-317.
JACOBI, J.F. (1771): Das durch eine leichte und ungekünstelte Erklärung von seinen Vorwürfen gerettete Hohe Lied. Nebst einem Beweise, daß selbiges für die Zeiten Salomons und seiner Nachfolger sehr lehrreich und heilsam und eines heiligen Dichters würdig gewesen, Celle.
LESSING, J.T. (1777): Eclogae Regis Salomonis, Leipzig.
LOWTH, R. (1753/61): De Sacra Poesi Hebraeorum Praelectiones Academicae [...]. Notas et epimetra adjecit Johannes David Michaelis, Göttingen.
MICHAELIS, J.D. (1769-1785): Deutsche Übersetzung des Alten Testaments mit Anmerkungen für Ungelehrte, Göttingen/Gotha.
ROSCHER, W.H. (1904): Die Sieben- und Neunzahl im Kultus und Mythos der Griechen, Leipzig.
SCHREINER, S. (1981): Das Lied der Lieder von Schelomo. Mit 32 illuminierten Seiten aus dem Machsor Lipsiae, Bremen.
VON PUFENDORF, F.E. (1776): Umschreibung und Erklärung des Hohen Liedes oder Die Gemeine mit Christo und den Engeln im Grabe nebst andern Biblischen Erklärungen, hg. v. K.H. Runge, Bremen.

'Do not awaken love until it is ready'
George Seferis' *Asma Asmaton* and the translation of intimacy

Constanze Güthenke

Why, one might ask, would a translation of the Song of Songs by the Greek poet George Seferis (1900-1971), Nobel laureate though he is, be attractive for a collection on new approaches to the Song of Songs? What is in it for the reader not specialized (or even interested) in what is admittedly a small literature?[1] There are several answers to this question. What is at stake is the conception, and conceptualization, of an ancient tradition, when that tradition is desired to be part of a contemporary, national expression. In Seferis' case, in addition, this is the treatment of a biblical text not so much in its Hebrew as in its Greek Septuagint translation. I for one would also be curious to see a contribution on the Song of Songs in later Hebrew and Israeli literature, where some of the issues of national self-understanding, the appeal to a linguistic and literary ancient tradition, and their implications for literary production might bear a certain resemblance to those of Greek writing too. Seferis, certainly, appropriates the Greek Septuagint version of the Song of Songs, as much as its physical environment, as a productive model of his, consciously Greek, writing. What is more, the Song of Songs becomes especially appropriate for a literature that conceives of its practice and its strengths as potentially off-canonical while also as able to rely on that same canon. To identify such patterns might help to shift the focus away from the implicit exceptionalism, that so easily attaches to the so-called small literatures, and on to the interpretive range that the Song of Songs and its particular reception history allow. Seferis choice of this particular biblical text is not accidental either: it allows him to frame the Song of Songs as a flexible and generative text of desire and longing in terms of a relationship of intimacy with that almost personified text and its tradition; in short, in translating a text ostensibly concerned with intimacy, translation itself is explored and valued as

---

I wish to thank David Connolly for talking about Seferis, Anselm C. Hagedorn for asking me to write about Seferis, and the Program in Hellenic Studies at Princeton University for making sure I do it properly.

1 I use the term advisedly and in its literal sense, preferring it here above both 'minor' or 'peripheral'.

an act of productive and difficult intimacy. To abstract from Seferis, this act might comment on the all too often unexamined patterns of thought and imagery with which we, as readers, poets or scholars, continue to claim traditions: in terms of a quasi-personal relationship with it.

Seferis' translation of the Song of Songs as *Άσμα Ασμάτων* (from now *Asma Asmaton* [Song of Songs]), although finished in 1963, was first published in Athens in 1965, in a limited edition accompanied by a series of wood-cuts by the painter and graphic artist Tassos; in 1966 a second edition followed, this time replacing the illustrations with the facing Greek text of the Septuagint. Although the translation has seen nearly ten re-editions, its status as a 'work of love' of the translator and as a beautiful book, based on a beautiful text, seems to have guided interpretation and scholarly reception alike.[2] Grazing past the fate of an illustrated coffee-table item only narrowly, the text would appear the result of an effort undertaken largely for personal delectation and guided by personal choice. That this is neither an exhaustive nor a satisfactory account is the premise of this present study.

From early on in his dual career as a diplomat and writer, Seferis concerned himself with the state of Greek writing and the potential and burden of movement between cultures. Seferis' deliberate approach to translation, as one such form of movement, is apparent from the name given to his translation of the Song of Songs: it is a μεταγραφή (*metagrafe*), literally a transcription as opposed to a translation, a term he gives to all his attempts from ancient Greek writings.[3] Seferis was a lifelong translator of literature, both interlingual (from other languages) and intralingual (from within the Greek language, i.e. from classical and post-classical Greek). Among the former works are those of Valéry, T.S. Eliot or Yeats, among the latter the translations of the Song of Songs and the Apocalypse of John, as well as a selection of classical prose and drama.[4] As it is increasingly acknowledged that translation for Seferis formed "a life-long concern running alongside his poetic theory and practice" (Iatromanolakis 1980: 227), the choice, terminology and

2 Kokolis 2001: 61, n.2 lists the available scholarly commentary on Seferis' biblical translations since their publication.

3 The *Asma* is subtitled *Metagrafe*, and Seferis adds a note on his use of terminology to distinguish interlingual from intralingual translation. He refers his reader to the term as denoting translation already in Thucydides and Lucian (Seferis 1965: 65). In his prologue to the Apocalypse, he further elaborates on the distinct practice indicated by the term (Seferis 1966: 15).

4 Apart from Eliot, whose *The Waste Land* Seferis published separately, Seferis put together a selection mainly of modernist poetry under the title *Αντιγραφές* [Copies] (Seferis 1965); the biblical translations also appear separately, while a collection of other intralingual translations appeared posthumously under the tile *Μεταγραφές* [Transcriptions] (Seferis 1990). Both kinds of translation are scattered throughout Seferis' diaries and correspondence, quite apart from resonating in his own poetry.

method of his practice have come under new and critical scrutiny.[5] What is recognized is the programmatic nature of Seferis' experimental expansion and care of the Greek language with a view to a modern Greek literature, clearly outlined in the prologues to many of his published translations;[6] and yet, too little thought has been spent on the place which the translation of biblical texts in particular occupies in his poetic cosmos. The most recent, and only book-length study on those translations so far (Kokolis 2001), sets out to deconstruct the default attitude of reverence toward Seferis' every literary act, including his translations, and it does so by training the focus on his inaccuracies or unsuitable choices as a translator. To take a critical look at Seferis' skill and reputation as a translator is surely valid; however, Kokolis's approach would appear to rest on insufficiently defined criteria for what are 'good' or 'right' translations, guided largely by personal preference or tacitly assumed standards, rather than awareness for the need to establish a critical framework in which Seferis' selection of texts and their position within his work as a whole can be evaluated.

The larger concern within which my approach to Seferis is formulated is the frequency with which narratives of love and a discourse of love appear in the literature of modern Greece, constantly at pains to evaluate, to define and to create its relation to other literary traditions, including its own. I here follow Luisa Passerini's suggestion that "the two discursive traditions on Europe and on love came together at various times and in various points of view" (Passerini 1999: 1). Passerini's interest is in the inter-war years of the twentieth century and the contemporaneous visions of a shared European-ness. She identifies an overlap of those visionary formulations with a discourse of and on love, at a time, as she point out, when the model of love that is reaffirmed as the most European, and most civilized, is that of the chivalrous Romance (prominently suggested, for example, by de Rougemont 1939): "as if", she says, "a need of the time were the reaffirmation of the centrality of love in European culture as the starting point for a social regeneration" (Passerini 1999: 3), in the hope of transforming a civilization in crisis. Although Seferis may not be so much preoccupied with European-ness (or pan-European visions) *per se*, the discourse of love as a discourse akin to that of social and political community seems worth investigating in his case too. His rendition of the Song of Songs, I suggest, does offer such a commentary, integrated into

5 Iatromanolakis 1980; Vayenas 1989; Connolly 2003, with bibliography.

6 Especially in the prologues to *The Waste Land* and the biblical texts; so, for example, prefacing the Apocalypse: "Και η γλώσσα μας χάνει ολοένα ευκαιρίες για να γίνει μιά γλώσσα εύρωστη, γυμνασμένη και αποτελεσματική. Θα είχε τόσα πολλά να ωφεληθεί αν αποφάσιζε ν' ασκηθεί πάνω σ' αυτά τα κείμενα." (Our language is continually wasting opportunities to become a language that is robust, flexible and effective. It would benefit greatly if it were to test itself against these [religious] texts) (Seferis 1966: 17, transl. Connolly 2002: 34, with further quotations).

the literary patterns and preoccupations of Seferis' own poetic work, while even, for the case of Greece, offering a complementing model or vision of love that stands at an angle to that of the West.

At the same time Seferis' work is a commentary on the selective claims to a biblical heritage or tradition, making questions of appropriateness, canonicity and belonging the bridge to concerns of a national literature. The ostensible particularity and universality of the Song of Songs (and its reception history), paired with its intimation as an off-canonical work, allow for the particular margin in which Seferis situates his own translation.

Seferis' choice of text

Seferis first mentions a translation of the Song of Songs in 1942, when, exiled with the Greek Government first to Crete, on to Egypt and then South Africa, he is *en route* back partly over-land to Cairo. According to his diaries, staying over night on the shores of Lake Victoria, he improvises a sight translation of the Song for his wife Maro, although this is not the myth of origin he later establishes.[7] He takes the project seriously up again around the time when he assumes diplomatic responsibilities for Cyprus at the Greek Foreign Ministry, all this after a stint at the embassy in Beirut and his first encounters with Cyprus, on the way to and from there, in the early to mid-50s. In the Easter week of 1960 he finishes the translation in London where he has by then been posted as ambassador (Seferis 1990: 175ff.).

The intense activity on the text in the Easter week cannot have been without resonance for Seferis; in his semi-autobiographical novel *Έξη Νύχτες στην Ακρόπολη* [Six Nights on the Acropolis], begun in the 1920s after his return from Paris and revised and completed around the same time he begins to think seriously about the translation of the Song of Songs, the main character's erotic epiphany and consummation of a love affair with the elusive, ambivalent and attractive figure Salome occurs, prominently, on Good Friday. The juxtaposition of erotic and religious resurrection moments in the novel is deliberate, and the completion of the *Asma* on such a significant date, whether intended or not, suits Seferis' attention to a text whose textual history is dominated by the friction between erotic value and religious exegesis.

---

7 "Dead tired (…) we fall into our beds and sleep straight after the meal. I open at random a copy of the Old Testament that is left by my bedside table (as in every other room). I chance upon the Song of Songs. While I am translating for Maro I fall asleep" [Σκοτωμένοι από την κούραση (…) πέσαμε και κοιμηθήκαμε αμέσως μετά το δείπνο. Ανοίγω στην τύχη την *Παλαιά Διαθήκη* που είναι αφισμένη πλάι στο προσκέφαλό μου το ίδιο και στα άλλα δωμάτια). Πέφτω στο *Άσμα Ασμάτων*. Με παίρνει ο ύπνος καθώς μεταφράζω της Μαρώς.] (Seferis 1993b: 214).

As just mentioned, Seferis' 'public' account of his choice of the Song of Songs for translation differs from the war-torn improvisation. It seems no less of an intensely personal one, though, when, in the prologue to the *metagrafe*, he quotes the biographical experience of Palestine and Lebanon, where he is posted in the early 1950s, as the point of origin:

> At the time I was a guest in a high mountain village in Lebanon; it was there that I started [the rendition]. The mountains didn't leave me with the same impressions which I had of the landscape reading the Song of Songs; in its weightless and translucent air they were harder, more naked, poorer; maybe an additional incentive to begin this task was my desire (επιθυμία) to find a more familiar way of dialogue with the place.[8] (1965: 7)

Beyond the intense experience of place, which is a staple of Seferis' reflections on poetic choice, the Song of Songs slots into a sequence of non-canonical or, better, off-canonical and marginal texts which Seferis establishes for himself and his art as reference-points: those, for example, of the *Memoirs* of General Makriyannis, a self-educated witness of the Greek War of Independence; of *Erotokritos*, an early seventeenth century Cretan verse romance; or of the *Odes* of Andreas Kalvos, who experiments with ancient meters and modern sentiments in the face of Greek national revival in the 1820s too.[9] Another text, which, around the same time, draws Seferis' attention, is the Apocalypse of St. John (the Book of Revelation), a text, which, at least in the Orthodox tradition, itself has a long and complex history of shifting in and out of the canon. As with the *Asma*, it is the strong sense of place, or of the link to a particular place, which Seferis is at pains to show has provoked his renewed attention to those authors, and more often than not this occurs during Seferis' own peregrinations or forms of exile in times of crisis: the epiphanic memory of *Erotokritos* occurs in 1941 while in flight in Crete; the essay on Makryannis and his indictment of national disunity is conceived in Egypt; while the attention to Kalvos reaches its peak in Great Britain, Kalvos's own place of exile, in 1960.

Even if tinged by marginality, the canonicity of the Song of Songs (and the Apocalypse) is not without effect: Seferis writes to Rex Warner in 1963 that the publication of his two biblical translations is held up by problems with the Greek Church (unpublished correspondence, Beaton 2003: 486). Whatever

---

8 Με φιλοξενούσε τότε ένα αψηλό χωριό του Λιβάνου· εκεί την άρχισα. Το βουνό δε μου έδινε τις ίδιες εντυπώσεις που είχα για το τοπίο διαβάζοντας το Άσμα· μέσα στον αλαφρύ και διάφανον αέρα του ήταν πιο σκληρές, πιο γυμνές, πιο φτωχιές· ίσως ένα πρόσθετο κίνητρο στο ξεκίνημα αυτής της εργασίας να ήταν η επιθυμία μου να βρώ έναν τρόπο οικειότερης συνομιλίας με τον τόπο (Seferis 1965: 7).

9 Seferis's essays are entitled 'A Greek – Makriyannis' (1943), 'Erotokritos' (1946) and 'Kalvos, 1960' (1960), published in Seferis 1974a and Seferis 1974b respectively. All three were writers who, at the time of Seferis' attention to them, were not (or no longer) considered a relevant part of the received canon; their changed status now, in turn, has to a significant extent been catalyzed by Seferis' endorsement of them.

the precise nature of those problems, Seferis is surely aware of the conflicted past of biblical translations in Greece. In the background looms an explosive cultural and political history: it probably reached its high (or low) point in the suspicion of anti-Greek sentiment that two demotic translations of the New Testament had aroused in 1901, and the bloody riots that followed (Carabott 1993).[10] Seferis must also have been aware of the success and hostile reaction alike with which demotic(izing) translations of other ancient texts had met, for example the version of the *Iliad* by Alexandros Pallis (who had approached the epos by way of a folk song traditions and the songs of the *klephts*), or of the riots occasioned by the first demotic translations of Greek tragedy in the same decade (Iatromanolakis 1980: 276). Seferis accordingly argues in his prologue that many have the opinion (to his mind difficult to grasp) that the New Testament in particular could and should only be read in ancient Greek (Seferis 1965: 7).

Interestingly though, but in line with his particular care for the Greek language, Seferis pays little or no attention to the linguistic and especially the literary qualities of the original Hebrew of the Song of Songs, a fact which his ignorance of Hebrew alone can hardly justify. Seferis relies on the Septuagint text alone, treating the *Asma* as a Greek text alongside other works of Greek antiquity, and he consults standard English and French text edition and translations of the time.[11] Although his concern with the Greek language and its transmission is made to hang from a text whose canonical status, in religious and Orthodox terms at least, had a long memory of ambivalence and contention, his choice tallies all the more with Robert Alter's definition of (biblical) canonicity: it "rests in being the literary repository of the language of the culture" (Alter 2000: 48). Seferis translates the notion of such a literary repository to the 'canon' of the Greek Septuagint, or, more precisely, he seems to extend it to include the entire body of literature in Greek.

At the same time, it is its linguistic tradition that renders the Song of Songs so suitable to exercise the Greeks' relation to their language, a theme, as we saw, that runs through Seferis's oeuvre, especially his translations, in many forms. To use Connolly's term, Seferis' translations are the products of a linguistic and poetic workshop (Connolly 2002: 31), where the capacities of the

10 One of the two translations was put forward by a Protestant Bible Society, incurring suspicions of proselytism; the other translation, also by Pallis, was initiated by Olga, the wife of King George I of Greece, whose Russian origins led to charges that her effort was but a thinly-disguised move to promote Pan-Slavist ideas.

11 Seferis makes use of the following translations and editions of the text: Edouard Dhorme's Old Testament (French), Paris 1957; the edition of the Song of Songs by the *Ecole Biblique* in Jerusalem, ed. A. Robert (Paris, 1951); the Song of Songs transl. by Hugh J. Schonfield (London, 1959) and the *Old Testament in Greek, according to the Septuagint*, ed. by Henry Barclay Swete D.D., 2nd ed. Cambridge, 1896 (Seferis 1963: 8).

Greek language are tested to its full. Thus Seferis notes in his diary on the 14th of April 1960:

> Συνέχισα και τελείωσα μετάφραση 'Ασματος ασμάτων. Περίεργη πάλη με την γλώσσα. [Continued and finished translation of Song of Songs. Peculiar wrestling match with the language] (Seferis 1990: 180).

How, then, does Seferis treat the language of the Asma? In line with his desire to stay as closely and flexibly as possible to the Greek original (Seferis 1966: 12), he integrates into a version closely oriented on the Septuagint a variety of registers, or rather register associations: very ornate, high-literary words, often taken directly from the Greek of the Septuagint, such as βόστρυχος [locks] or νάμα [spring, stream; also eccl. and fig.], are combined with sometimes archaizing demotic words (γιορτάνια [earrings]; πλουμίδια [trimmings]; ροδαμίζω [bloom]; γούρνα [trough]; μίσεψε ο χειμώνας [winter has gone]), or antiquated, medieval expressions (αναγάλλιασμα [rejoicing]; συναπάντημα [encounter]; δραγάτες [guards]), next to very common and plain ones, following a simple syntax with even a deliberate touch of the (ostensibly simple) Greek folk song tone (μάνα [mother]; περιβόλι [garden]; παλικάρια [palikars; young men]). Integrating his choice of words into the deliberate web of sensuousness that Seferis spins above his poetic exercise, he invokes the sheer beauty of some of the Septuagint vocabulary as justification: "several times – and there were not a few – as I tried to translate [the ancient Greek], I would stop at a place and think 'Well, this is so beautiful, why should anyone want to change it?'" (1965: 7).[12]

Seferis, I would argue, is in fact engaged in a deliberate 'Hellenizing' of the text, framing the attitude to the material as a relationship of intimacy, of a quasi interpersonal form: for the lay-out of the text he adopts from the French edition of the *Asma* (Ecole Biblique, Robert 1951) the division into a prologue and six scenes, which do not correspond to the division into verses. The apportioning of speech to a male and female speaker and a group of women, which has a long exegetic tradition (going back both to the early Christian (Origen) and Jewish context) but no direct naming or marking of characters in the text, appears in Seferis' *Asma* as a *dramatis personae* of bride (νύφη), husband (άντρας) and chorus (χορός), adding concreteness and corporeality to the shifting narrative voice.[13] Moreover, Seferis intertwines the associations of classical Greek dramatic practice (two protagonists and chorus) with those of the Greek popular tradition, naming the individual scenes as 'songs' (τραγούδια). This tallies with Seferis' (increasingly pronounced) positive vision

12 [ό]σες φορές – και δεν είναι λίγες – δοκιμάζω να τα μεταφράσω, σταματώ πάντα σε κάποιο σημείο με τη σκέψη: "Μα τούτο είναι τόσο ωραίο, γιατί να τ' αλλάξει κανείς;" (Seferis 1965: 7).

13 Ohly 1957: 17-25.

of popular culture. Based on his consultation of some current scholarship, he calls the Song a "wedding song" (1965: 9), embedded in a shepherd society (ποιμενικό λαό) of Palestine. He quotes the scholarly opinion of Dhorme (Paris 1957) that the text is the result of a compilation of the fourth century B.C., inspired by the persistent memory of Solomon and comprising several pieces from Judea, Moab and Syria, while also betraying "palpable" (αισθητές) Hellenistic influences. This dating seems, in recent scholarship, now more or less confirmed, as are the Hellenistic influences and parallels, including especially those of sexually connoted vocabulary with comparable Greek motives.[14] The hybrid character of the Hebrew text, however, is now thought to owe to the highly literary textual culture of classical and Hellenistic Greece (certainly familiar to Seferis, see below) and ancient Palestine, much more than to the Romantic immediacy of popular expression.

For Seferis, the *Asma* originates in the ritual context of a shepherd Aphrodite, where erotic desire and the longing of separation from the beloved are hymned with passion; contrary certainly to received Orthodox interpretation, to him "it remembers in no way the relation between man and God", even if it found its way into the canon by the first century AD at the synod of the Rabbis of Iabnech (1965: 10). He recounts briefly the history of its allegorical Christian interpretation, but concludes that such an approach with its eschatological interpretation is difficult for him to accept: it does not *touch* (συγκινούν) him the way the Cántico of John of the Cross does, for example, who uses the Song of Songs to illustrate the longing of the soul for union with God. Seferis, in his selective summary of Orthodox exegesis, further singles out the fifth century bishop and theologian Theodoros of Mopsuestia, whose cosmic interpretation of the Song of Songs, with little attention to allegory, was overshadowed by the condemnation of his writings by the fifth Ecumenical Council. Yet, Seferis admits, "I hope it is obvious though that I do not want to give the *Asma* an exclusively naturalistic, as they say, interpretation." (1965: 11) Strong sentiments and deeply rooted passions, he continues, such as the longing of the people of Israel (a traditional allegorical interpretation of the Song of Songs), can be nourished even by different additions and can annex alien passions (or, in other words, translate them into their own longing) as long as they touch the human soul, and that includes for him the erotic desire of the *Asma*. All the more, this makes for the particular richness of the graft (μπόλιασμα) (1965: 11). While Seferis insists on not getting entangled in questions of dogma, his reading does not preclude the "longing" (πόθος) of a people as a valid association of the text, compatible with the tradition of exegesis, a point to which I will return below. In other words, he considers the *Asma* a particularly fertile and meaningful ground, with a multifaceted cultural

---

14 See e.g. Dornseiff 1936; Müller 1992; Hagedorn 2003, as well as the contributions by Müller, Hagedorn and Hunter in the present volume.

genesis, with both a universal claim and a 'national' compatibility, yet without adherence to a particular dogma. The present translation of the Song *continues* its history as text and graft;[15] the result is the presentation of a poem abounding in images of the new bloom of spring.

Erotic Imagery and Vocabulary in Seferis

Seferis uses a wealth of different imagery for the act of translation (such as copying, grafting, or the reconstruction of a prehistoric beast from single vertebrae; see summary in Connolly 2002: 30ff.), including that of procreation and family similarity (again in the 1936 prologue to *The Waste Land*), but it has gone unnoticed so far, that in the prologue to the *Asma* he also relies strongly on the vocabulary of love and passion to justify his approach. The erotic passion of the characters becomes conflated with the erotic character of their textuality. The prologue suggests that "it was the *attraction* (έλξη) which the text of the Old Testament in the Septuagint exercises upon me that made me attempt a rendition of the Asma Asmaton into our contemporary language" (7) [my italics].[16] He speaks of his *desire* (επιθυμία) to render the work, and it is the sheer *beauty* of ancient texts that motivates him to ponder whether ancient texts can and should be translated (yes, he adds, they should). He is *touched* (συγκινούν) by later versions of the Song of Songs. His aim is to help Greeks *love* their language: "Yet this modern day Greek kosmos, if it wants to stop one day being spiritually underdeveloped, as they say, must live in familiarity with and must *love* the texts which are its heritage and its tradition; and how should this happen without translations?" (7f.)[17]

On a different level, the formulations of erotic nature in the *Asma* correspond to a long-standing and well-rehearsed use of erotic vocabulary in Seferis's own poetry. The theme of bodily love and the lack resulting from the actual fulfilment of sexual desire appears in Seferis' work early on, not only in the first version of *Six Nights on the Acropolis*, but especially in the rhymed poetry

15 For the organic image of the graft as a figure of Western thought that is active in appropriating Greek antiquity, see recently Gumpert 2001. Gumpert interestingly combines reflection on grafting with attention to the figure of Helen, linking the discourses of erotic desire and of the appropriation and creation of tradition. Although he includes a chapter on Seferis' treatment of the Helen figure, he does not extend his view to the *metagrafes*. For aspects of Helen overlapping with the bride of the Song of Songs in his Cyprus poems, see below.

16 Νομίζω πως είναι η έλξη που ασκεί απάνω μου το κείμενο της Παλαιάς Διαθήκης των Εβδομήκοντα που με παρακίνησε να δοκιμάσω την απόδοση του Άσματος των Ασμάτων στη σύγχρονη γλώσσα μας (Seferis 1965: 7).

17 Όμως τούτος ο σημερινός ελληνικός κόσμος, αν πρόκειται κάποτε να πάψει να είναι πνευματικά υπανάπτυκτος, καθώς λένε, πρέπει να ζήσει με οικειότηατ και ν' αγαπήσει αυτά τα κείμενα που είναι η κληρονομία του κι η παράδοσή του· και τούτο πώς να γίνει χωρίς μεταφράσεις; (Seferis 1965: 7).

(e.g. "Αυτοκίνητο" [Automobile] or "Ερωτικός Λόγος" [Erotikos Logos]), which has, certainly in the English-speaking world and literary criticism, been somewhat, if not entirely, neglected.[18]

While working on *Six Nights on the Acropolis* and the erotic tensions around which the novel is structured, Seferis jots down a haiku (itself a foreign verse form translated into Greek writing) that he keeps in the edited version of his diaries under the title "Ομόνοια 1929" [Omonia 1929] (Seferis 1975: 110):

Ήλιος και Ιούλιος
στα πεζοδρόμια βόσκουν
βυζιά κοπάδια.

Ilios and Ioulios
on the walk ways pasture
herds of breasts.

The bucolic eroticism, grafted onto a foreign poetic form as much as onto a modern cityscape, prefigures the same vocabulary that later belongs to the *metagrafe* of the Song of Songs. Seferis at the time experiments with a historical repertoire of erotic writing, translating passages, for example, from Apuleius's *Golden Ass*, which also returns by way of allusion in the *Six Nights* (Beaton 2003: 76f.). Another recurring set of ancient texts with an erotic component is the *Palatine Anthology*. Seferis includes translations of several erotic poems from the *Palatine Anthology* in his diaries of 1939 (reprinted in Seferis: 1980: 47-49), while including references to the work as well as epigrams in the style of the *Anthology* in his later poetry (Kopidakis 1988: 69f).[19] His persistent familiarity with this particular collection of short poems and epigrams is translated onto paper in his 1939 essay "Μονόλογος πάνω στην ποίηση" [Monologue on Poetry], where he mentions the collection for the first time, while later references occur often in connection with his ruminations on Cavafy's poetry.[20] Not incidentally maybe, the Alexandrian's erotic sensibility was a significant part of Cavafy's authorial *persona* that proved such an intriguing riddle for the writer Seferis (Iatromanolakis 1980: 266ff). The resonance of the *Palatine Anthology* within the horizon of Seferis' *Asma*, moreover, blurs the distinction between a 'European' Greek classical tradition and a clearly Eastern one in his Song of Songs as he understands it to be a hybrid between the Hellenistic and Near Eastern spheres.

---

18 In the, itself quasi-canonical, complete edition of Seferis poetry by Keeley and Sherrard the rhymed poetry (which is not complete) is relegated to the back of the volume, as an appendix to the more 'properly' Seferian poetry in free verse.

19 The three epigrams, which Seferis includes are *Anth. Pal.* VI, 17 (Lukianos); VI, 22 (Zonas) and VI, 62 (Philippos Thessalonikeos).

20 Direct and indirect references to the collection appear frequently in Seferis' essays (Seferis 1974a: 128; 329f; 347; 367; 443-6).

Kopidakis, in a study of Seferis' poem "Αριάδνη" [Ariadne], which, like the Song of Songs, explores the bodily associations of landscapes, draws particularly on its allusions to the erotic vocabulary and tone of the *Palatine Anthology* (Kopidakis 1988). The poem finishes with the lines:

και το καλάμι καρφωμένο στ' οργισμένο δέλτα...
... βαθύ... πουλί... χιμό [sic]... λαβή... τυφλή... λαβώ... λαβ... λα...
... βύρινθος... άλφα... βήτα... γάμα... δέλτα...

and the reed stuck in the raging delta ...
... deep... bird... juice... grip [*lave*]... blind... strik- [*lavo*]... lav... la...
... byrinth... alpha... beta... gamma... delta...

Kopidakis (1988: 61f.), with reference to Seferis' attested enjoyment of wordplay and homonyms, makes a case for the phonetic presence of the word "love" in the syllable "lab-"). Kopidakis also reads λαβή as alluding to the grip of the wrestler, a semantic field that can in turn accommodate the erotic struggle which recurs in Seferis' poetry, so for example in the untitled and explicitly erotic poem from *Τετράδιο Γυμνασμάτων Β'* [Book of Exercises II], starting Παλεύανε τα χείλια [Labouring/wrestling were the lips][21]; it reappears just as much in the image of the beloved of the Song of Songs, wrestled down and wounded by her longing: είμαι λαβωμένη της αγάπης [I am struck down with love] (for Septuagint τετρωμένη αγάπης; Cant 2:5; 5:8). In that light, the περίεργη πάλη με την γλώσσα, the strange wrestling with language, which Seferis overcomes on Easter Day 1960, rounds the logic of passion back into the discourse of translation.

The sexual vocabulary of the *Palatine Anthology* recurs also in other motives of Seferis' own poetry,[22] e.g. in those of the grapes (here the ρόγα of the breast), the hare, the chase and especially the ρόδι (pomegranate). Take for example the haiku no. 9, from *Book of Exercises* (Seferis 1972: 92):

Νέα Μοίρα
Γυμνή γυναίκα
το ρόδι που έσπασε ήταν
γεμάτο αστέρια.

Young Fate
Naked woman
the pomegranate that burst
was full of stars.

On the subject of the pomegranate, incidentally, Kokolis takes issue with Seferis's (allegedly unsuitable and mistaken) translation of ὡς λέπυρον ῥόας

21 The collection *Book of Exercises II*, again not in its entirety part of the standard English translation of Seferis, is incidentally full of variations on the theme of bodily love.

22 Mackridge 1996; Kopidakis 1988

μήλόν σου [Your cheek is like the skin of pomegranate] (Cant 4:3) as σκελίδα του ροδιού το μαγουλό σου [your cheek is like the flesh of a pomegranate]: from the skin Seferis moves to the image of the core – in the light of the above haiku probably not an entirely incomprehensible choice. Equally, Kokolis criticizes him for using in the same verse the phrase κόκκινη κλωστή [red thread] to describe the line or thread of the lover's lips (Cant 4:3 σπαρτίον το κόκκινον χείλη σου [like a red thread are your lips]), chiding him largely for using an uninspired, unflattering image. Κλωστή, however, is used in one of his earliest published poems, the lyric cycle *Erotikos Logos* (which takes as its theme the renunciation of (a) love (affair))[23], a text where many words of the *metagrafe*'s linguistic reservoir already appear.[24] One central image of the *Erotikos Logos* is that of a pair of snakes, intertwined in another passionate struggle (or act of wrestling), and it is with that image that I want to make a transition to the poem "Έγκωμη" [Engomi], from the cycle written on the heels of Seferis's experience of Cyprus: a poem which closes its central vision of a female figure with the appearance of a snake.

Seferis and Cyprus

Peter Mackridge has claimed that Seferis' eroticism develops from an earlier sensual, yet ambivalent eroticism to a violent and more spiritual version, a notion that would tie in well with Seferis' later imagery of an erotic mysticism and his figures of a redeeming, luminous femininity in the Cyprus poems.

The visionary poem *Engomi* was written, if we accept Seferis' testimony, under the impression of a visit to an archaeological site on the plain of Engomi. Watching the excavations, Evangelos Louizos, Seferis' host, remarks on the female figure of a young local digger. The poem moves from that material scene, material bodies excavating on the historical ground, to the vision of a woman, appearing and disappearing, and on to the workings of memory and the threat of the future. Stillness falls over the landscape when

κοίταζα τα κορμιά που πολεμούσαν, κι είχαν μείνει
κι ανάμεσό τους ένα πρόσωπο το φως ν' ανηφορίζει.
Τα μαλλιά μαύρα χύνουνταν στην τραχηλιά, τα φρύδια

23 Beaton (2003: 90ff.) makes a case for the poems being inspired by the eventual renunciation of the love affair, which Seferis had entertained with Jacqueline Pouyollon in Paris until his return to Greece.

24 The word appears in the following context: "you touched the tree with the apples// the hand reached out. The thread points the way and guides you" [τ'άγγιξες το δέντρο με τα μήλα το χέρι απλώθη κι' η κλωστή δείχνει και σε οδηγεί] (Seferis 1972: 28, II,5f.). Given the erotic connotations of Ariadne in the later poem of that name, and the reference to apples in the Song of Songs, allusions to classical mythology and the biblical text can coexist easily. Other echoes of the Song of Songs are found in II, 9; III, 18.

είχανε το φτερούγιασμα της χελιδόνας, τα ρουθούνια
καμαρωτά πάνω απ' τα χείλια, και το σώμα
έβγαινε από το χεροπάλεμα ξεγυμνωμένο
με τ' άγουρα βυζιά της οδηγήτρας,
χορός ακίνητος.

I looked at the bodies laboring, and they were still
and among them a face climbing the light.
The black hair spilled over the collar, the eyebrows
had the motion of a swallow's wings, the nostrils
arched above the lips, and the body
emerged from the struggling arms stripped
with the unripe breasts of the Virgin,
a motionless dance. (trans. Keeley and Sherrard)

It would be difficult not to hear the praise of the beloved's body in the Song of Songs (that of the dancing Shulamite in Cant 7:2ff.); the same parts of her physique are mentioned, with only slight variations,[25] and Seferis uses in the *metagrafe* similar vocabulary (e.g. ρουθούνια for 'nostrils' – another "inelegant, if not comic" choice, at least according to Kokolis (2001: 69)). The world has stopped moving, the next words "And I lowered my eyes to look all around" a direct quotation from the Book of James, or Protevangelion, where the line is spoken by Joseph confronted with Mary's miraculous pregnancy.[26] In *Engomi*, the vision continues:

Και ξανακοίταξα το σώμα εκείνο ν' ανεβαίνει·
είχανε μαζευτεί πολλοί, μερμήγκια,
και τη χτυπούσαν με κοντάρια και δεν τη λαβώναν.
Τώρα η κοιλιά της έλαμπε σαν το φεγγάρι
και πίστευα πως ο ουρανός ήταν η μήτρα
που την εγέννησε και την ξανάπαιρνε, μάνα και βρέφος.
Τα πόδια της μείναν ακόμη μαρμαρένια
και χάθηκαν· μιά ανάληψη.
Ο κόσμος
ξαναγινόταν όπως ήταν, ο δοκός μας
με τον καιρό και με το χώμα.

And I looked again at that body ascending;
people had gathered like ants,
and they struck her with lances but didn't wound her.
Her belly now shone like the moon
and I thought the sky was the womb
that bore her and now took her back, mother and child.

25 The dove, for example, is replaced by a swallow, associating spring and thereby maybe also associating Greek popular traditions of the swallow as a harbinger of spring, e.g. in the *chelidonismos*, the ancient 'Swallow Song' from the nearby island of Rhodes, in line with Seferis's effort to hellenize the *Asma*.

26 The Protevangelion tells the story of the Virgin's life; it was transmitted as part of the Apocrypha, and although is does not enjoy canonical status in the Orthodox Church, it is widely used in its iconography.

Her feet were still visible, adamantine
Then they vanished: an Assumption.
The world
became again as it had been, ours:
the world of time and earth.

The metamorphoses introduced by Seferis' biblical high diction are seamless: while Christ is associated in the piercing with the lance, the verb for 'pierce', λαβώναν, harks back to the verb used for being struck or wrestled down by love. Similarly, the description moves from the Song of Songs to the woman of the Apocalypse ("A great portent appeared in the heaven: a woman clothed with the sun, with the moon under her feet, and on her head a crown of twelve stars", Rev 12:1), while the shining belly allows the sphere of the dancing Shulamite (Cant 7:3) to overlap with that of the childbearing woman of the Apocalypse (Rev 12:2; 12:5). The vision finishes:

Αρώματα από σκίνο
πήραν να ξεκινήσουν στις παλιές πλαγιές της μνήμης
κόρφοι μέσα στα φύλλα, χείλια υγρά·
και όλα στεγνώσαν μονομιάς
στον άδειο τόπο με το λιγοστό χορτάρι και τ' αγκάθια
όπου γλιστρούσε ξέγνοιαστο ένα φίδι,
όπου ξοδεύουνε πολύ καιρό για να πεθάνουν.

Aromas of terebinth
began to stir on the old slopes of memory
breasts among leaves, lips moist;
and all went dry at once (...)
in that empty place with the thin grass and the thorns
where a snake slithered heedless,
where they take a long time to die.

Engomi is probably one of the most prominent of Seferis' poems inspired by his encounter with Cyprus, collectively published under the title *Ημερολόγιο Καταστρώματος Γ'* [Logbook III]. In the developing vision of a *unio mystica*, a redeeming, yet sensual love, Cyprus impressed Seferis by its sensuality and the sensuality it provokes in turn (Seferis 1986: 99; further Beaton 2003: 307ff), manifest in such figures as that of the female vision, where the Panagia, the female figure of the Apocalypse, Helen,[27] the Beloved of the Song of Songs and Aphrodite (whose island, after all, this is) all merge.[28]

27 The Helen of Seferis' poem of the same title is that of Euripides' tragedy: the phantom that has gone to Troy while the real Helen remains in Egypt. She is linked to Cyprus through the figure of Teucer, the narrator of Seferis' poem, himself a native of Cyprus and the only to know the truth about her real whereabouts. Her beauty, too, echoes in the mystical vision of the woman at Engomi, as she is realistic and only intimated alike.

28 Regarding the female vision, Thomaidou-Morou (1983: 14) refers to an encomium to the Virgin from the Greek-Venetian anthology *Ἄνθη Εὐλαβείας* (1708) where the appearance

Engomi, however, and its female figures, is not the only echo of the Song of Songs in *Logbook III*. The short poem "'Όνειρο" [Dream] has the opening line Κοιμούμαι κι η καρδιά μου ξαγρυπνά [I sleep while my soul lies awake], which is a direct quotation from the Song (Ἐγὼ καθεύδω, καὶ ἡ καρδία μου ἀγρυπνεῖ, Cant 5:2) and a literal repetition of Seferis' translation of that verse. What makes Cyprus such an appropriate place to reconsider the Song of Songs? The actual writing and later the publication of the *metagrafe* coincides with his intense engagement with Cyprus, as a political locus and a cultural inspiration alike. Seferis first encountered Cyprus *en route* to his posting in Beirut in 1953, and he returned to visit it again from there a year later, this time moving West. To him it was, tellingly, a revelation (Seferis 1972: 335), in particular for its transformative and challenging character as both originally Greek and differently Greek, in short, as a somewhat more pure and unspoiled version of Greece:

> First impression: from here one experiences Greece as (suddenly) spacious, broader. The sense that there is a world that speaks Greek; that is Greek. Which does not depend on the Greek government; and this last is what contributes to this feeling of spaciousness (Seferis 1986: 98).

In Cyprus Seferis experiences what Beaton aptly terms the sense of an "expanded Hellenism" (Beaton 2003: 307), formulated on the basis (quite literally) of a natural sensuality in a location much closer to the Levantine coastal land than to Greece, and a popular culture that to Seferis seems richer and more attractive than that of Greece at the time; significantly, it is those same aspects that, in his prologue to the *Asma*, he claims also drew him to the Song of Songs.

Europe in Love; the Asma Asmaton *between East and West*

The nature of the relation of the Modern Greek text version to its tradition and to its origins in the biblical text, which in turn is set in a specific culture and territory with a varied history and varied influences – this relation is itself expressed in the language of erotic longing and love for this very text. Regarding Seferis' choice of his particular object of desire, we asked what made its particular attraction. Rather than risking to get caught up in semi-

---

of the Panagia is linked with that of the bride of the Song of Songs: "Among the multitude of angels were many, as we read in the song of songs, who would ask, jubilant and amazed: who is she, who is taken above, clad in light, like dawn into the dazzling light of day, chosen like the sun, more beautiful than the moon?" [Ανάμεσα εις τόσα πλήθη των αγγέλων, δεν λείπουν πολλοί, καθώς διαβάζομεν εις τα άσματα των ασμάτων, να ερωτούσι περιχαρείς τε και έκθαμποι· ποία είναι τούτη, οπού ανάγεται εις τα άνω, φωτοστόλιστος ως η αυγή εις την έκλαμψιν της ημέρας, εκλεκτή ωσάν ο ήλιος, ωραία υπέρ την σελήνην;]" (Karathanasis 1978: 12).

psychological playfulness, I have suggested a perspective beyond the question of biography (without wanting to dismiss biographical factors) from which to view Seferis' inclusion of the Song of Songs within his poetic range and interest. A perspective that takes account of the attention to particular place, to literary and linguistic tradition, to the practice of identity and to the ramifications of erotic language.

Seferis appropriates a canonical model and topos of Western literature, he relocates it to its Eastern setting, but in turn transposes and reexamines it as a Greek text (to the total exclusion of its Hebrew environment) – more *metafora* than *metagrafe*. He is an author who is of course greatly involved in questions of Greekness, of Greek literature and its relative position vis-à-vis European literature (and particularly that of France). His *metagrafe* of the Song of Songs, I suggest, can be read as an alternative love discourse, an alternative model of love, that claims universality, while the foregrounding of its textual and cultural position between Eastern and Western traditions links identity to erotic discourse.

Seferis, in his prologue, would deliberately not exclude the possible appropriation of the theme of longing by a nation and through a national interpretation, as it occurred, he argues, in the case of the people of Israel. What is more, in his footnotes to the *Asma*, Seferis, at this very point, refers to the end of his essay on *Erotokritos*, where he speaks of the reading of *Erotokritos* by the "enslaved people" as an act of transformation of the chivalrous Romance – that model of European civilisation – into a history of the καημών της ρωμιοσύνης, the "longing of Romiosini":[29]

> βλέπω τον *Ερωτόκριτο* να κυκλοφορεί, ανάμεσα στο σκλαβωμένο Γένος, και να περιφέρει τα σύμβολά του, όπως λέγαν άλλοτε τα παιδιά τα κάλαντα ... και να μεταλλάζει το ρομάντσο της ιπποσύνης σε μία ιστορία των καημών της Ρωμιοσύνης (1974:317).

> I see the *Erotokritos* circulate among the enslaved people, carrying around with it its tokens, as the children once would sing the *kalanda* ... and it would transform the chivalrous Romance into a history of the longings of Romiosini.

The longing of the princess Areti and Erotokritos for each other, the pining of the people and the searching for the lover of the Song of Song flow together in the care of the language practiced in the act of translation/*metagrafe*.

29 *Romiosini* is an alternative term for "Greekness", as well as the community of Greeks and the extent of their Greekness (used as the term "Christendom" would be), used within Greece in opposition to *Ellenismos*. It draws on the *romios*, denoting the Greek population during the Byzantine Empire and subsequently (as *rum*) under Ottoman rule. For its ideological charge, especially from the nineteenth century onwards, and the implications of this malleable binary until the present day, see Herzfeld 1982.

Conclusion

I have tried to bring together different strands of Seferis' poetic practice and the factors impacting on it in order to circumscribe the space, which the Asma occupies in his work. Like a red thread (evoking Ariadne and the Bride's lips alike now) the vocabulary and imagery of the Song of Songs weaves through Seferis' work. The *Asma* is compatible with different aspects and interests of his work, and it answers the underlying parallel preoccupations of translation and different modes and models of erotic love that run alongside each other in his poetic work. The geographical "origin" of his interest (a Seferian strategy, if one so wishes, in its own right) in the East answers to the geographical „homecoming" of translating it to the congenial environment of longing as much as sensual expansion, which Seferis linked with the island of Cyprus. An island, incidentally, one of whose most relevant features to Seferis' mind was their own song and troubadour culture going back to the Medieval period (Seferis 1986: 107).

The Song of Songs, written after the Septuagint Greek of a Hebrew text that was probably cast in written form with Hellenistic influences, is a textual place that is both Greek and non-Greek, that is as open and untouched by the territorial Greek present as is, to an extent, the magic of Cyprus on its first encounter. "It is terrific sometimes with what clarity the Greek can see the distance separating him *both* from the East *and* the West", Seferis writes in Beirut in 1953 (1986: 69), in the face of the landscape that he finds much starker and harsher than expected, compared to the Song of Songs, but which inspires him to work on its translation. It is this central and marginal position, a distance extending in two directions that Seferis' work on the *Asma* translates over to Cyprus.

Seferis felt sharply what he considered the political and personal risk of attempting to integrate Cyprus into the Greek world as it stood: "Question:", he asks, "are we worthy to administer Cyprus, without doing harm to this world, improving it without turning it into a Greek provincial place, like Kerkyra or Thessaloniki?" (1986: 98) The new Greek *kosmos* which Seferis discovers on Cyprus bears a family resemblance to the Greek state. Yet there is as much danger to its survival as there is in the uncanny image of procreation, which Seferis uses for the act of translation in the prologue to *The Waste Land*:

> Γιατί εκείνο που έχουμε στις μεταφράσεις των ποιημάτων δεν είναι διόλου μία προσέγγιση προς το έργο όπως γράφτηκε, αλλά ο καρπός της επιμειξίας δυό φυσιογνωμιών, που μοιάζει θλιβερά κάποτε με την οικογένεια του μεταφραστή.
>
> For what we have with the translation of poems is not an approach to the work as it was written, but the offspring of the intercourse of two physiognomies, which sometimes bears a wretched resemblance to the family of the translator. (Seferis 1936:16)

That which is intimately known is familiar, but to Seferis translation amounts to family resemblance, with the accompanying dread of creating a misshapen, bastardized progeny. This is the flipside of intimacy with the body of tradition.

Biblical scholarship of the Song of Songs is still debating (productively or not) the lightness or darkness of the text's character, putting critical weight in turn on its exuberance or its sense of longing and absence. Whichever reading one prefers, of the Song as much as of Seferis' *metagrafe*, it is one phrase, however, recurring three times as a pleading refrain, that must have resounded in Seferis's project most profoundly: μην την ξυπνάτε, μην την ξαγριεύετε την αγάπη, όσο να το θελήσει – "Do not awaken love until it is ready".

Bibliography

ALTER, R. (2000): Canon and Creativity. Modern Writing and the Authority of Scripture, New Haven.

BEATON, R. (2003): George Seferis. Waiting for the Angel. A Biography, New Haven.

CARABOTT, P. (1993): Politics, Orthodoxy and the Language Question in Greece. The Gospel Riots of November 1901, Journal of Mediterranean Studies 3, 117-138.

CONNOLLY, D. (2002): The Least Satisfying Form of Writing: Seferis on Translation, Journal of Modern Greek Studies 20, 29-46.

DORNSEIFF, F. (1936): Ägyptische Liebeslieder, Hoheslied, Sappho, Theokrit, ZDMG 90, 589-601.

GUMPERT, M. (2002): Grafting Helen. The Abduction of the Classical Past, Wisconsin.

HAGEDORN, A.C. (2003): Of Foxes and Vineyards: Greek Perspectives on the Song of Songs, VT 53, 337-352.

HERZFELD, M. (1982): Ours Once More. Folklore, Ideology, and the making of Modern Greece, Austin.

IATROMANOLAKIS, Y. (1980): Epilogue, in: George Seferis, Μεταγραφές, Athens, 227-316.

KARATHANASIS, A. (1978): Άνθη Ευλαβείας, Athens [originally published in 1708].

KOKOLIS, X.A. (2001): Ο Μεταφραστής Σεφέρης, Athens.

KOPIDAKIS, M. (1988): Αριάδνη. Σχόλια στον ερωτικό Σεφέρη, 2nd ed., Athens.

MACKRIDGE, P. (1999): Ο ηδονικός Σεφέρης, in: N. Vayenas (ed.), Εισαγωγή στην Ποίηση του Σεφέρη, Iraklio, 455-462.

MÜLLER, H.-P. (1992): Das Hohelied, in: H.P. Müller/O. Kaiser/J.A. Loader, Das Hohelied-Klagelieder-Das Buch Ester, ATD 16/2, 4th ed., Göttingen, 3-90.

OHLY, F. (1957): Hohelied-Studien. Grundzüge einer Geschichte der Hoheliedauslegung des Abendlandes bis 1200, Schriften der wissenschaftlichen Gesellschaft an der Johann Wolfgang Goethe-Universität Frankfurt am Main. Geisteswissenschaftliche Reihe 1, Wiesbaden.

PASSERINI, L. (1999): Europe in Love, Love in Europe. Imagination and Politics between the Wars, New York.

DE ROUGEMONT, D. (1939): L'Amour et l'Occident, Paris.

SEFERIS, G. (1936): Έρημη Χώρα, Athens [The Waste Land].

– (1965): Άσμα Ασμάτων, Athens [The Song of Songs].

– (1972): Ποιήματα, Athens [Poems].

– (1974a): Δοκιμές (1936-1947), Athens [Essays 1936-1947].

– (1974b): Δοκιμές (1948-1971), Athens [Essays 1948-1971].

– (1975): Μέρες Α' (1925-1931), Athens [Diaries 1, 1925-1931].
– (1986): Μέρες ΣΤ'(1951-1956), Athens [Diaries 6, 1951-1956].
– (1990): Μέρες Ζ' (1956-1960), Athens [Diaries 7, 1956-1960].
– (1993a): Τετράδιο Γυμνασμάτων Β', 2nd ed., Athens [Book of Exercises 2].
– (1993b): Μέρες Δ' (1941-1944), Athens [Diaries 4, 1941-1944].
– (1996): Αντιγραφές, Athens [Copies; originally published in 1965].
– (1998): Έξι Νύχτες στη Ακρόπολη, 6th ed., Athens [Six Nights on the Acropolis].
THOMAIDOU-MOROU, M. (1983): Στοιχεία από τη Βίβλο και την Χριστιανική εικονογραφία σε ποιήματα του Σεφέρη (unpublished doctoral dissertation), Athens.
VAYENAS, N. (1989): Ποίηση και Μετάφραση, Athens.

Index

I. Hebrew Bible

Genesis
1-11 323
1-6 324
1:1-2:3 323
1 325
1:1 46
1:4 46
1:26 280, 283
2:7-23 324
2:25-3:19 324
3:16 31, 262
4:7 31
16:4 46
23:9 38
24:23 212
24:28 212
24:53 34
27:37 41
30:38 59
30:41 59
31:43 41

Exodus
2:16 59
18:16 34
18:23 31
24:6 55
28:27 58
29:5 58
30:22ff 282
31:4 58
38:30 38
39:20 58

Leviticus
16:18 263
19:13 263

Numbers
20:22 99
20:25 99
21:17 248
21:27-30 248
22:18 41
23 36
23:7 34

Deuteronomy
1:31 46
1:41 41
4:5 34
4:10 52
4:36 52
8:9 34
8:13 38
12:30 55
21:7 41
25:9 41
26:5 41
27:14f. 41
28:10 34
30:12 52
32:38 38
32:39 46
33 36
33:13 33, 211
33:14 33
33:15 33f.
33:16 33
33:28 211

Joshua
6:10 52

Judges
5 36
5:14 34
5:15 35
6:17 30
6:22 46
7:12 30
8:26 30
20:40 49

Ruth
1:8 212

1Samuel
9:27 52
18:7 248
18:15 46
19:17 59
26:6 41

2Samuel
4:7 207
6:5 55
7:28 39
22:15 34

1Kings
1:3-4 13
1:33 38
3:1 304
3:14 29
4 9
4:13-14 10
4:32-33 10
4:32 9, 16
5:12 110
5:22 55
6:37 37
7:10 37
9-10 10
10:1-13 304
10:23 10
11:1-3 10, 190
11:4 29
11:36 29
13:6 41
18:39 39
19:11 34
22:28 34

2Kings
3:2 46
4:2 51
4:3 51
4:7 51
6:11 59
6:12 207
6:13 55
8:1 31

1Chronicles
24:19 31
25:7 54
28:9 34, 36
29:2 49

2Chronicles
6:26 38
7:3 48
7:19 38
21:3 34
26:15 58
29:17 31
30:1 31
31:16 31
32:23 34

Ezra
1:6 34
2:68 31
3:6 37

Nehemiah
2:8 65
6:3 59
9:22 34, 36
9:24 34, 36
12:39 57
13:7 31

Esther
1:6 48f.
6:1 208
6:4 31

Job
3:25 31
6:1 41
6:30 47
12:5 58
12:11 47
16:5 38
16:12 57
20:7 36
20:13 47
28:1 47
28:15-19 19
28:16 47
28:17 47
28:19 47
29:10 47
31:24 47
31:30 47
32:2 47
34:3 47
40:22 36

Psalms
4:5 208
7:10 34
8:6 53
19:11 47
21:4 47
30:8 36
34:12 38
36:7 34, 36
45:1 268
45:10 47
45:13-15 12
50:10 34, 36
65:12 53
75:9 57
76:5 34, 36
77:4-5 208
77:18 34, 36
87:1 34, 36
101:2 31
101:8 261
102:8 208
103 40
103:3 51, 209
103:4 51, 53
103:5 51
116:7 51
116:19 51
117 40
118:26 38
119 40
119:27 47
119:103 47
122:5 29
124 40
125 40
133 40
133:3 34, 36, 210
135:9 51
137:6 47, 51
144 40
146:4 58

Proverbs
1:20-21 18
1:20 61
2:1-5 18
2:16-19 20
3:13-16 18
3:13 18
3:18 19

4:6	17
4:8	17
5:3	20, 47
5:15-20	16
5:15-19	17
5:16	61
5:20	20
7:4	19
7:5-27	20
7:10-15	20
7:10	20
7:12	61
7:14-20	20
7:16-17	20
7:18	20
8:1-4	18
8:6-21	19
8:7	47
8:10-11	18
8:17	17-19
8:18-19	18
8:19	47
8:21	17f.
8:22-31	14
8:34	18
8:35-36	18
8:36	19
10:20	18
15:17	15
16:16	18
17:9	210
18:22	18
19:2	209
20:15	18
22:1	18
22:13	61
24:13	47
25:11-12	18
25:12	47
27:21	47
29:13	35f.
31	20
31:10	18

Qoheleth

1:12-2:16	13
1:12-2:12	256
1:17	39
2:3	54
2:5	65
2:13	46
2:17	46
2:23	39
3:13	39
3:18	46
4:8	39
5:4	46
5:5	59
5:18	39
8:17	46
9:7-9	123
10:20	209
12:7	123
12:13-14	15

Canticles

1:1-12	271
1:1-6	98
1:1-2	304
1:1	8
1:2-14	264
1:2-12	264
1:2-4	327
1:2	46, 69, 81, 126, 281, 270
1:3	126, 184, 213, 270f., 282, 307
1:4	11, 80, 249
1:5-8	327
1:5-6	197, 201
1:5	11, 19, 62, 83, 212, 283
1:6-7	98
1:6	30, 33, 38, 46, 57, 62, 184, 193, 250, 275, 281
1:7-8	12, 250

1:7	30f., 55, 59, 61, 80, 209, 329
1:8	155, 283
1:9-14	327
1:9-11	19, 249
1:9	31, 41, 48, 209, 231
1:10	12, 61, 69
1:11	12, 47, 69, 280
1:12-2:3	270
1:12	11, 30, 48, 60, 66, 86, 249, 284
1:12-13	184
1:13	12, 282
1:14	250
1:15-2:7	327
1:15	48, 184, 209, 249, 252
1:16-17	249
1:17	33, 55, 58, 304
2:1-2	19, 82
2:1	84, 156, 282
2:2-8	41
2:2	48, 209, 249
2:3	47, 84, 155, 200, 249, 305
2:4-7	83, 86
2:4	31, 84, 307
2:5	33, 43, 46, 48, 87, 131, 156, 158
2:6	208
2:7	15, 30, 32f., 38, 83, 207, 211
2:8-17	81, 87
2:8-14	126, 250
2:8-9	42, 81, 249
2:8	34, 62, 281, 307
2:9	18, 31, 56, 61, 103, 264, 281, 305
2:10-14	87, 187
2:10	31, 41, 43f, 48, 51, 80, 209
2:11-13	42
2:11	46, 58, 283
2:12-13	270
2:13-14	88, 155
2:13	48, 51, 57, 62, 80, 103, 209
2:14	46, 80, 249, 252f., 275, 279
2:15	57, 98, 156, 201, 213
2:16-17	207
2:16	12, 43, 53, 82, 84, 189, 218, 270
2:17	30f., 34, 80, 156, 188
3:1-6	304
3:1-5	81, 85f., 206-213, 224-225
3:1-4	20, 188, 209f., 212, 221
3:1-2	210
3:1	30, 97, 206-208, 221
3:2-3	184, 186
3:2	30, 60, 209, 263
3:3	30, 187, 236
3:4-5	83
3:4	30f., 46, 84, 191, 212, 270
3:5	15, 30, 32f., 38, 83, 98, 102, 207 , 212f
3:6-11	12, 13, 81, 86, 251
3:6-8	97, 101
3:6	18, 37, 43, 49, 69, 251
3:7-11	9, 190
3:7-8	98, 127, 191
3:7	11, 30, 39, 59f., 69, 97
3:8	37, 53f., 98
3:9-11	249
3:9	11, 67, 69f., 98, 102, 251, 264, 304
3:10	48, 122, 212
3:11	10f., 30, 33, 52f., 98, 117

3:15 32
4:1-7 89, 91, 231, 249
4:1-6 100
4:1-5 81, 87, 89, 184
4:1-3 101
4:1 30, 48, 69, 99, 101, 184, 209, 252, 261
4:2-3 102
4:2 30, 32, 97
4:3 33, 48, 69, 92, 97f., 101f., 349
4:4-7 97, 101f.
4:4 29, 62, 69, 101
4:5 90, 97, 101f., 156
4:6-8 101
4:6 30f., 99
4:7 48, 92, 97, 99f., 102, 209, 253
4:8-12 11
4:8 34, 69, 88, 99f., 102, 209, 251
4:9-12 159
4:9-11 249
4:9 54, 87-89, 99, 191, 209, 306
4:10-5:1 91, 103
4:10 19, 99, 131, 191, 209
4:11-14 85
4:11 32f., 126, 209, 251, 270
4:12-5:1 82, 250f.
4:12-15 81, 249
4:12 20, 84, 99, 155, 191, 209, 310
4:13-15 130
4:13 33, 65f.
4:14 20, 66, 69, 184
4:15 52, 84, 251
4:16 33, 85, 186, 208, 250
5:1-2 159
5:1 11, 20, 41, 83, 85, 97, 99, 184, 102f., 191, 209
5:2-6:3 81, 86
5:2-8 206-213, 221, 224f.
5:2-7 87
5:2-6 56, 196
5:2 30, 43, 46, 48, 62, 80, 82, 87, 187, 206, 208f., 253, 352
5:3 56, 82
5:4-6 158
5:4 210
5:5 20, 44, 82, 270
5:6-6:3 87
5:6-7 184, 186, 188
5:6 20, 44, 82, 209f.
5:7 82, 187, 193, 210, 237
5:8 30-33, 38, 43, 82f., 87f., 131, 158, 185, 212
5:9 30
5:10-16 89, 91, 184, 231, 249
5:10-11 131
5:11 18, 47f., 62, 69
5:12 184, 252
5:13 33
5:14-15 18, 131
5:14 37, 58, 69
5:15 37, 49, 251
5:16 47, 92, 212
6:1-3 83
6:1 210, 310
6:2-3 12, 82, 85
6:2 31, 44, 155, 250
6:3 43, 84, 189
6:4-10 81, 87, 231
6:4-7 89f., 249
6:4 48, 69, 72, 87f., 209
6:5-7 101
6:5 30, 32, 46, 62, 87f.

6:6 30, 32
6:7 48, 69, 102, 261
6:8-9 10, 190
6:8 39
6:9 32f., 39f., 191, 253, 267
6:10-11 101
6:10 83, 99f., 249, 251
6:11-12 100
6:11 31, 44, 60, 65, 97, 99-101, 250
6:12 209
7:1-8 81
7:1-7 110, 249f.
7:1-3 100
7:1 12, 33, 99
7:2-10 87
7:2-7 90f.
7:2-6 89
7:2 61
7:3 55, 57, 351
7:4 101, 156
7:5 11, 83, 97, 101, 251f.
7:6 58, 87, 158, 249
7:7-8 19, 202, 232
7:8-10 249
7:8-9 128, 156, 200
7:8 31
7:9 62, 262f., 267
7:10 31, 43, 46f., 189
7:11-13 20
7:11 31, 84, 262, 310
7:12-13 129
7:12 200, 250
7:13 31, 57, 186, 250, 303
7:14 31, 33, 155, 250
8:1-2 191f.
8:1 20, 263
8:2 31, 48
8:3-4 83
8:4 15, 30, 32f., 38, 83, 207, 212
8:5 43, 62, 155, 191
8:6-7 13-15, 19, 78, 81
8:6 46, 62, 69, 212f., 271
8:7 19, 44f.
8:8-9 193
8:8 30, 209
8:10 19
8:11-13 84
8:11-12 11, 190
8:11 31, 42, 57, 250
8:12 13, 30f., 38, 57
8:13-14 250
8:13 18, 52, 80, 86
8:14 31, 34, 188

Isaiah
5:1-7 123
5:1-2 42
10:1 34
13:12 47
13:17 47
14:10 41
15:3 60
18:6 58
22:13 248
23:16 248
29:13 37
35:4 38
38:11 38
40:19 47
46:6 47
47:2 48
49:26 48
51:2 38
51:20 37
56:12 248
57:8 208
59:20 31
60:17 47
66:13 38

Jeremiah
2:33 210
5:1 60
6:4 35f.
9:16 16
9:20 60
11:15 51
13:3 36
29:32 46
31:18 37
32:2 57

Lamentations
1:1 55
3:12 57
4:1 47
4:2 37, 47
4:4 47

Ezekiel
3:26 47
4:12 35f.
4:15 35f.
5:16 34
7:19 47
23:17 208
23:41 48
33:31-32 123
34:23 29
40:17-18 48
41:8 37
42:3 48
43:6 98

Daniel
1:10 59
5:5 56
6:19 208
8:13 54
10:5 47

Hosea
2 284
2:7 247
3:5 29
4:13-14 11
7:11 11
8:1 47
10:11 37
11:11 11
14:6 11
14:9 55

Joel
1:5 48
3:3 49
4:18 48

Amos
3:9 34
5:16 60
6:4 48
6:5 29
7:14 41
9:11 29
9:13 48

Jonah
1:6 58

Nahum
2:5 60

Habakkuk
3 36
3:6 34

Haggai
2:6 54
2:18 37

Zechariah
8:9 37
12:7f 29
12:10 29
12:12 29

13:1 29

II. QUMRAN

1QH
5.31 47
1QIsa[a] 31, 34, 51
1QM
5.12 33
13.12 31
15.10 31
17.4 31
1QS
2.3 42
11.22 31
4QCant[a] 28, 96ff.
4QCant[b] 69, 72, 96ff.
4QCant[c] 96ff.
4QHa
13.31 47
4QSam[b] 28
4Q22 31
4Q163
f8 10.3 55
4Q416
f2 iv.3 31
4Q429
f3.4 47
4Q522
f9ii.6 55
6QCant 96ff.
6Q4 31
6Q18
f2.4 31
11Q5 31

III. ARAMAIC

CIS
ii 43.2-3 53

KAI
202
B.5 53
214
28 53
216
18 58
222
A.38 35
B.5 35
B.8 34
B30 54
B.32 53
C.4-5 53
223
B.5 34
C.5 53
224
2 35
10 35, 54
11 53
15f. 34
225
10 35
12 57
266
8 57

TAD
A2.5.9 35
A3.8.8 35
A4.2.9 35
A4.2.13 35
A4.7.10 35
A4.7.11 35
A4.7.15 35
A4.7.29 35
B2.6.16 35
B3.10.13 35
B3.11.3 35
B4.1.2 35
C1.1 44
C1.1.36 59

C1.1.126 59
C1.1.132 33
C1.1.163 47
C3.7 35, 70
D7.57.7 35
D7.47.8 70

IV. New Testament

Matthew
9:15 298
22:1-14 298
24:32 270
25:1-13 298
25:5 281

Mark
5:32 307

Luke
9:45 307

John
3:29 298

Acts
19:1-8 298

Romans
2:5 286
3:1-8 284
9-11 274, 281, 284f.
11 284f.
11:13ff. 284

1 *Corinthians*
15:28 284
2 *Corinthians*
3:13-15 286

Galatians
4 283
4:21-31 296
4:24 282

Ephesians
5:25-32 298

Revelation
12:1 351
12:2 351
12:5 351

V. Egypt

O DM
1038,2 157
1078,3 153
1406,3 157

O Nash
12 158

pAnastasi
I 25,2-6 117
IV 11,8-12,5 143f.

pChester Beatty
I 1,2-4 131
I 2 5-6 128
I 3,4-6 127
I 3,6-9 118
I 4,6-8 131
I 16,9 122
I 17,2 158
I 17,3 158
I 17,4-5 155
I vso.
C1,1-2 146
C1,8 158
C2,9-C3,4 141f.
C3,4-9 146

C4,8-9 158
G1, 5-7 153
G2,1-2 156

pHarris 500
1,8 153
1,11-12 128
1,11-2,1 127
2,2 157
2,2-3 131
2,5-6 127
2,5-9 126
2,9-11 127
2,11 158
3,1-8 126
3,8-9 155
3,12-4,1 129
4,5-7 129
4,6-7 155
7,3-4 127
7,7-8 155
7,8-9 155

pTurin 1966
1,11 129
1,13-15 129
2,5-6 156

T(heban)T(ombs)
60 119
82 121
181 118

Wenamum
2-68-69 109

VI. ANCIENT NEAR EAST

Gilgameš (Ninive Rezension)
VI,6ff. 164
VI,9 164

Hymnenkatalog aus Assur
I,6 170
I,20-22 170
I,42 170
II,8 171
VII,7-24 171
VII,11 171
VII,13 171
VII,18 171
VIII,3 170

Nabû und Tašmētum
1-5 175

Nanāja und Muati
1 173
5-6 174
7-14 174
9 174
14 174

Nergal and Ereškigal
82 164

Rīm-Sîn
8-13 171
14-19 172
20-25 172

Šulgi
X, 30 165, 168

VII. ANCIENT GREECE

Aeschylus
Choephori
660 221

Alcaeus
fr. 10 (L-P) 235
fr. 374 (L-P) 216

Anacreon
fr. 385 (PMG) 217
PMG 432 236

Anacreonta
fr. 33 211

Anthologia Palatina
5.150 221
5.153 196
5.164 196, 216f.
5.165 217, 221
5.170 198
5.189 211
5.209 198
5.210 196, 197
6.119 199
9.332 199
9.313 199
11.196 222
12.71.3 185
12.125 208
12.153 198
12.161 198

Apollonius of Rhodes
Argonautica
3.287-98 193
3.443-47 194
3.761-65 194
3.956-61 231
3.961-65 194
3.1022-24 194
4.43-49 195
4.167-70 195

Archilochos
fr. 193 (West) 236
fr. 196A 232,233
fr. 196A 1-8 234
fr. 196A 42-53 234

Aristophanes
Acharnes
526 220
Birds
13-142 186
Clouds
516 222
Ecclesiazusae
721-4 219
911-14 237
952-75 237f.
Frogs
751 222
Knights
517 223
Lysistrata
592 222
Peace
763 186, 223
Wasps
1025 223

Athenaeus
14.639a 239
14.621d 217
15.697c 239

Bacchylides
fr. 5.172-5 218
fr. 20b.6-9 219

Collectanea Alexandrina
184 239

Euripides
Bacchae
773-4 219
Hippolytus
32 221
131-134 185
Ion
891 235

Orestes
175 221
Trachiniae
676 218
Troades
645ff. 208

Fragmentum Grenfellianum
1ff. 214-224
11 217
11-13 221
12 217
25 223
28 223
29-30 221

Herodas
Mime
1 185
2.34-37 210
4.60-62 193

Herodotus
Histories
1.206 218
1.105 218
1.131 218

Hesiod
Works and Days
586 231
fr. 305f (West) 248

Homer
Iliad
3.437-47 232
4.452-5 250
7.333 221
11.398 220
14.312-28 232
15.25 220
17.227-8 229
18.276 218
18.525-9 229
18.536 250
18.555-9 250
18.569ff. 258
20.371-2 229
21.49-125 228
22.25-32 231
22.122-30 228
22.393f. 248
23.641-2 229
Odyssey
1.242 220
8.363 218
6.1-40 233
6.15-9 233
6.154-9 231
6.160-8 232
6.180-5 233
6.244-5 233
9.440 220
21.297-8 221

Homeric Hymn to Aphrodite
45-6 232
77 232
132 233
151 233
155 233,235
155-67 233

ICr IV 72
IX.34-7 220

Lucian
Amores
13 220
De dea Syria
54 219

Lyrica Adespota
8c 221
Mimnermus
fr. 1.1-5 219

Pindar
fr. 128c.6 248
Plutarch
Table Talk
696c6 222

Poetae Melici Graeci
853 239

Ps-Phocylides
215-6 207

Sappho
fr. 2,1 (D) 250
fr. 5,3-13 (D) 251
fr. 16.17 231
fr. 31 (L-P) 185, 223
fr. 60,3 (D) 246
fr.70-1 237
fr. 96 231
fr. 96,25-30 251
fr. 98,1-6 (D) 247
fr. 98,5-11 (D) 251
fr. 105a 200
fr. 121 236
fr. 123,5 (D) 250
fr. 130 (L-P) 222
fr. 132b (D) 250
fr. 168B (Voigt) 222, 236, 237

Sophocles
Trachiniae
959 220
975 220
986 220

Theocritus
1.45-49 201
2.1-63 185
2.8-9 186
2.55-56 185
2.64-166 185
2.82-83 185
2.82-90 185
2.85 185
2.98-90 185
2.90-91 186
2.96-98 186
2.100-101 186
2.106-10 185, 186
2.114-116 186
2.114-138 187
2.115 187
2.124-125 186
2.138-43 235
2.140 222
5.112-113 201
6.2-6 242
6.49-66 243
7.132-134 200
8.25-7 241
8.28-32 241
8.33-60 241
8.71 241
8.82-7 241
8.88-93 241
9.1-6 241
9.7-13 241
9.22-7 242
9.28-36 242
10.26-29 197, 201
10.31 222
11.25-29 191
14.3 185
14.43 189
15.52-54 187, 190
15.69-70 187
15.70-75 187
15.84-86 188
15.89-95 187
15.97-88 188
15.128 189
17.93-94 190
17.128-130 192
18.27 221
18.30-1 231

27.67-71b 243
27.72-3 243
30.1-2 185

Theognis
257-60 235
579-82 235

Theophrastus
Characters
27.9 210

Thuycidides
8.17 220

Xenophon
Cyropaedeia
7.5.32 220
Symposium
1.15 220

VIII. OTHERS

Ben Sira
42:11 207

Eusebius
De Martyribus Palaestinae
X.3 289
Historia ecclesiastica
VI.18.1-2 288
VII.12 289

J.G. Herder
FHA
1,132 326
1,276 321
1,292 322
1,293 322
1,750 328
1,1010-19 324
3,26 328
3,435 327
3,436 329
3,437 329
3,462 320
3,483 320
3,484 330
3,486 320
3,487 318, 319
3,488 320
3,489 331
3,490 327, 331
3,491 320, 331
3,492 318, 331
3,495 320, 329, 331, 334
3,496 318, 321, 329, 331
3,498 330
3,499 330
3,501 334
3,502 334
5,503 334
3,504 331
3,506 332
3,508 332
3,509 332
3,510 332
3,512 318, 334, 335
3,513 335
3,514 318, 319, 335, 336
3,516 332, 335, 336
3,517 319
3,518 332
3,519 335
3,918-925 330
4,714 333
4,489 333
5,9-178 323
5,27 324
5,45 323
5,48 323
5,90 324

5,97 324
5,299 325
5,480 325
5,610 325
5,663 326
5,666 326
5,1323 317
5,1332 323, 324
7,364f. 334

Hippolytus
In Canticum Canticorum
1.3 278
26-27 278

Jerome
Apologia contra Rufinum
I.13 287
II.19 288
Ep.
33.4 278,279
37.1 280
57.5 279

Macrobius
Saturnalia
5.14.6 229

Origen
Comm. in Cant.
Prolog. 1 277,279
Prolog. 2 280
Prolog. 3 277,280
Prolog. 4 282
I.1 280,281,282
I.2 281
I.2a 281
I.2b 281
I.3 280,282
I.5 280
II.1 283
II.2 280,283
II.3 281,283
II.5 283
II.8 280,281,282, 284
II.10 282
III.4 282
III.11 281,282
III.12 280
III.13 282
III.15 279,283
Comm. in Rom.
II.10-III.1 284
III.2 285
VII.11-VIII.12 284
VIII.6-12 284
VIII.8 284
VIII.10 285
VIII.12 285
Contra Celsum
I.45 287
I.55 287
II.31 287
III.12 289
V.54 289
De principiis
I.3.4 287
IV.2.4 276
IV.2.5 276
IV.3.14 287
Ep. ad Africanum
6 287
Hom. in Cant.
1.1 279,280
1.6 280,283
2.3 282
3.15 279
Hom. in Ex.
3.2 289
10.2-4 290
11.2 290
22.1-4 290
Hom. in Gen.
2.2 289
2.2-5 290

3.5 290
6.1-3 290
11.1-2 290
Hom. in Jerem.
12.5 289
12.13 287
Hom. in Jesu Nave
10.2 289
11.6 289
12.3 289
Hom in Lev.
1.4 275
4.7 290
8.9 289
10.1 290
10.2 287
13.4 290
16.2 290
Hom. in Matt.
12.23 289
14.3 289
Hom. in Num.
7.1 289
7.1-2 290
9.1 289,290
9.4 290
12.1-2 290
12.2 289,290
26.3 290
27.1 289
Sel. in Ezech
9.2 287

Ovid
Amores
1.5.19-22 231

Rufinus
Apology against Jerome
II.41 285

Virgil
Eclogues
4.58-9 229
7.1-8 242